Coffee

Coffee

A Comprehensive Guide to the Bean, the Beverage, and the Industry

Edited by
Robert W. Thurston
Jonathan Morris
and
Shawn Steiman

ROWMAN & LITTLEFIELD
Lanham • Boulder • New York • Toronto • Plymouth, UK

Published by Rowman & Littlefield
4501 Forbes Boulevard, Suite 200, Lanham, Maryland 20706
www.rowman.com

10 Thornbury Road, Plymouth PL6 7PP, United Kingdom

British Library Cataloguing in Publication Information Available

Library of Congress Cataloging-in-Publication Data
Coffee : a comprehensive guide to the bean, the beverage, and the industry / edited by Robert W. Thurston, Jonathan Morris, and Shawn Steiman.
   p. cm.
Includes bibliographical references and index.
ISBN 978-1-4422-1440-8 (cloth : alk. paper) — ISBN 978-1-4422-1442-2 (electronic)
1. Coffee industry. 2. Coffee. I. Thurston, Robert W. II. Morris, Jonathan, 1961– III. Steiman, Shawn.
  HD9199.A2C59 2013
  338.4'766393—dc23
                                                          2013014865

Contents

Preface

Putting this book together has been a great deal of work, but also a lot of fun, not to mention a terrific learning experience for the three editors. We have certainly learned a lot from each other. Just when you think you know something about coffee, you become aware of how much else you might explore. That is partly because the industry is changing so fast, from the way coffee trees are mulched to how to make a pour-over cup. But even if the industry stood still today, the amount of information available on any given aspect of coffee would be huge, and unknowable in its entirety for any one individual. That is why we have called on so many experts on one area or another of agriculture, processing, retailing, cup preparation, and consumption, to name a few fields.

We are deeply grateful to our contributors. Their generosity with their time and knowledge raises a basic question about the coffee industry: Why are coffee people so nice? Why, when academic historians like Robert Thurston and Jonathan Morris wander in, and at first don't know the difference between pulped naturals and pulp fiction, are coffee people so helpful? (The two of us consider Shawn Steiman a coffee person to the core.)

So while all three editors are proud of this book, we have also been humbled by making it. We hope that the articles will appeal not only to people in the industry and the millions of coffee fanatics (geeks, they sometimes style themselves) around the world but also to many others. This guide presents a wealth of information about a basic agricultural product that has played a major role in history, affects the economic and social life of many millions today, and is relentlessly studied and modified by scientists, roasters, baristas, and home consumers.

Although we have tried to produce a non-ideological work, the editors' and contributors' preferences—not always in agreement—will become clear. Above all, we've aspired to provide a source of coffee knowledge for all who seek it and all who can benefit from it. We want the best for those involved with coffee, beginning with the farmers. We are dedicated not to charity or condescension but to the empowerment of industry members.

Finally, we hope this volume will be a pleasure to read.

Introduction

Robert W. Thurston

In this volume, the editors and the contributors have tried to provide a useful guide to coffee from the ground up. The articles we have assembled cover a great range of topics, from soil to roaster, barista, and home use. We are well aware that people's tastes vary widely. Some prefer coffee in a grocery store can, already ground, or even instant coffee that requires almost no effort to prepare. Others pay considerably more money for select whole beans, which they grind before making each cup. They weigh the coffee and the water, then keep one eye on the temperature of the water and the other on the clock, as they count the seconds in the various steps of making the beverage. Still other folks want coffee only at cutting-edge cafés—or, to use an upscale term, coffee bars—made by an experienced, skilled barista.

Whatever your particular pleasure in a cup, we believe that all aspects of the coffee industry should interest anyone who cares about the earth, farmers, globalization, or even basic economics. In these pages, a wealth of material applies first to coffee but also to wider issues; a good example is "organic." Many coffee terms are explained in the glossary in the back of the book. If a term is in the glossary, it will appear in **boldface** the first time it is used in a chapter that discusses the term at length or in a context in which its meaning may not be clear. Since this is a handbook, readers may want to consult the index to find where the topics that most interest them are discussed. But of course all are invited to start with the first page and read straight through.

Everyone connected to the coffee industry has a story about *the* cup of coffee, the one that opened eyes, nose, and palate to the realization that coffee could be an excellent beverage. In the 1950s and 1960s, my mother made coffee in a steel drip pot, using ground, canned Maxwell House. I remember vividly that the results smelled and tasted like bitter, burnt metal. But there was that one intriguing puff of marvelous fragrance when she opened a new can. Years later, I happened upon a special deal for a kit with a carafe, a plastic filter cone, paper filters, and a can of ground coffee. All of a sudden, I had much better coffee than I had ever tasted before.

The cup, whatever it was for the initiated, opened the way for a journey deeper and deeper into the complexities and pleasures, along with disappointments, of coffee. If we can hook anyone into that journey with this book, we will be happy indeed. But this is not just a volume for snobs.

1

That's partly because coffee begins with dirt. Agriculture is one of the most fickle businesses; growing and selling coffee is one of agriculture's most volatile sectors. From planting a seedling until a tree bears usable coffee fruit—called berries or cherry, usually in the singular—can take four years. The weather, war, emergence of a new producer (like Vietnam in the late 1990s), and changing tastes can wreak havoc on production and the price farmers can get for their beans, which are in fact the seeds of the coffee fruit.

Boom-and-bust cycles have affected coffee from the 1880s on. In the 1930s, the bottom fell out of the market; Brazilians, the largest producers for decades, responded by dumping coffee into the ocean or burning it, producing steady smoke and an acrid odor over Rio. The price of coffee alternately soared and dove in the following decades, until it hit the miserably low figure of about 40 cents a pound in New York in the fall of 2004, at a time when it cost farmers at least 70 cents a pound to produce a crop, or more like $1 in many parts of the world. But in June of 2011, bad weather in several major producing countries, combined with increased demand for coffee, pushed the New York **C price** above $3 before it began to subside a little.

When I visited Kenya in 2004, several people told me "coffee is an old man's crop." No one wanted to enter the business. But at current prices, growing coffee has become attractive again. Still, farmers, especially ones raising coffee on a small scale, maybe on a hectare (about 2.5 acres) or two of land, capture little of the money that consumers in the Western world spend on beans or the brew. Among the subjects this book covers is why that difference exists, what is being done about it, and what the future for coffee producers might look like.

Consumers' tastes and desires for coffee have followed their own twisted paths. In an illustration entitled "US coffee consumption—a nation goes soft," the **NGO** Oxfam finds that in 1970, Americans drank 36 gallons of coffee per person per year. In 2000 the figure was 17 gallons, while soft drink guzzling went from 23 gallons per capita to 53 gallons.[1] These figures tally, unfortunately, with increased obesity in the U.S.

On the other hand, anyone not living in a cave for the past thirty years knows that coffee has surged to the forefront of public culture in many parts of the world. New coffee shops have

Figure I.1.   Where coffee grows. Map by Lara Thurston.

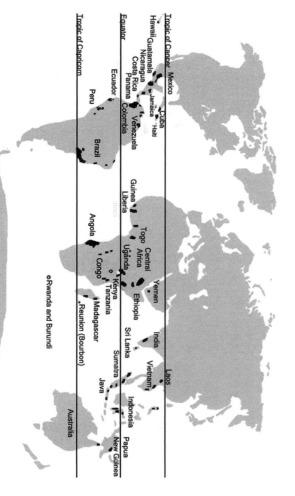

changed the face of not only American cities, but also British, German, Colombian, Kenyan, and Indonesian towns, to name a few others. The U.S. counted about 2,000 local or small chain shops in the early 1980s; by the end of 2008, America could boast 27,715 **specialty coffee** outlets, of which 11,100 or 47 percent were Starbucks.[2] Having opened its 100th outlet in Indonesia, Starbucks plans to launch another 15 there this year. But the champion of recent expansion is probably Costa Coffee, owned by Britain's Whitbread Corporation. Two Italian brothers, immigrants to the UK, founded Costa in 1971. Absorbed by Whitbread in 1995, Costa now has 1,871 coffee bars and plans to reach 3,500 in the next five years.[3] The firm also operates vending machines, self-service bars, and coffee kiosks. Like Starbucks, Costa Coffee is already an international presence, with stores in Eastern Europe, the Middle East, China, Russia, and India.

Despite this **third wave** of coffee conquests, most people around the world drink what snobs in the business—in fact they happily refer to themselves as coffee geeks—would call mediocre or outright bad coffee. First of all, about 40 percent of the coffee sold globally, as we shall see below, is **robusta**. Properly called *Coffea canephora*, robusta is a tougher plant than its relative *Coffea arabica*. Accordingly, robusta's taste is rougher, bitter, and lacking in subtlety. Robusta goes into instant coffee, grocery store cans, and many espresso mixtures, especially in Europe, where it helps produce the brown foam called **crema** and to provide an extra kick of **caffeine**. Americans still buy most of their coffee in cans, either metal or plastic: 57 percent of purchases for home brewing were for such containers, a 2011 survey found, while 31 percent went for bagged coffee (whole bean or ground), and 8 percent for **capsule** or **pod** products.[4]

Like wine, coffee is marked by extremes and everything in between. You can buy a bottomless cup fairly cheaply across the United States. In Europe you have to buy mediocre coffee one cup at a time, although Britain, Germany, and the Scandinavian countries prepare some excellent drinks. Recently a drugstore near my home ran an ad for Folgers coffee in a plastic tub, already ground, decaf or regular, for $1.43 a pound. At that price, the results, no matter how you brew, will disgust any coffee geek. Moreover, the farmers who grow the coffee beans used for such a grim product earn virtually nothing.

For most Americans, and many people in other lands, everyday coffee remains the stuff of jokes: "Drink Coffee: Do Stupid Things Faster with More Energy," reads a popular refrigerator magnet, the ultimate cultural signpost of our times. If the coffee at Dunkin' Donuts might deliver that extra energy, and might also be deemed barely drinkable by people in the high end or specialty coffee business, Dunkin' smiles broadly on the way to the bank. It leads the pack of retailers in America, with about 6,800 stores across the country, and another 3,000 abroad. Dunkin' sells some 1.5 billion cups of coffee worldwide each year, to help wash down 900 million doughnuts consumed in the U.S. alone.[5]

Dunkin' can provide a close encounter with a doughnut, while other coffees have taken me to a near-spiritual plane, for example Ethiopian Yirgacheffe in certain years, or fabulous beans from the Kona Coast of Hawaii. Such coffee can cost $35, $40, $60, $100 a pound. But after an initial investment in equipment for home brewing, anyone can have a cup in the kitchen for 35 or 40 cents. The most expensive coffee in the world, **kopi luwak**, at some $300 a pound, continues to elude me; the people I know who have tasted it say it's terrible.

Whatever kind you drink, or even if you don't touch coffee, it calls for attention and respect. Consider the impact of the crop and the beverage over the past four centuries, longer in the Middle East and parts of Africa:

- Coffee was the first commodity truly traded around the whole world, making globalization more than 350 years old.

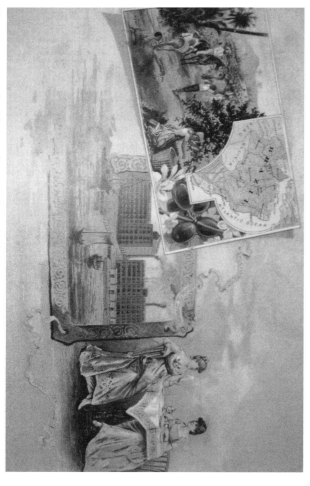

Figure 1.2. An Arbuckle's "trade card" from the late 1880s, one of a series of "countries of the world." One of a few illustrations of the day that connected consumption, in this case by elegant American women, with coffee farming. Slavery had been abolished in Brazil in 1888; perhaps that's why the woman picking coffee below the map is smiling. Courtesy of Special Collections, Miami University

- Coffee and slavery, or some other form of forced, unfree labor, were inseparable for nearly 300 years, into the 1880s.

- Coffee has profoundly affected the environment, particularly in the destruction of forests in Latin America and the Caribbean. On the other hand, coffee farmers and buyers today are often leaders in efforts to redeem the land and to practice **sustainable** agriculture. "**Social responsibility**," to both the land and the people who work it, has become a catch phrase for everyone working in coffee, from the smallest farmers to the biggest multinational corporations. Sometimes they even follow through on that idea.

- Coffee has been both a mirror of social life in the consuming (as opposed to the producing) countries and a powerful factor in changing social standards and interaction. To mention a few examples, coffee helped introduce major changes in the gender roles and images of women in Britain as coffeehouse culture developed in the 1600s. Coffee provided the dominant social lubricant in American social life from the late 1800s until the early 1970s. And just try to think of Italy from 1900 on without coffee.

- More than a few writers depended on coffee or coffeehouses to keep putting words on paper. Here is a selection of outstanding names: Samuel Richardson, who penned the first books in English recognized as novels, beginning with *Pamela* in 1740; the great French *philosophe* Voltaire, who wrote a play translated into English in 1760 as *The Coffee House, or Fair Fugitive*; the German philosopher Immanuel Kant (1724–1804); the French realist novelist Honoré de Balzac (1799–1850); T. S. Eliot, American-born but an emigrant to England, who wrote with longing "I have measured out my life in coffee spoons," in the poem "The Love Song of J. Alfred Prufrock" in 1915; and the cosmopolitan American Ernest Hemingway sitting with a pencil and paper in Paris cafés in the 1920s. Paul Erdos, 1913–96, a Hungarian scholar, often worked around the clock. He once said, "A mathematician is a machine for turning coffee into theorems."[6]

- TV shows like *Friends* and *Frasier* chose a neighborhood coffeehouse as a meeting point and social ground. Coffee has had a bit or a major part in countless movies, and it flows through popular music in a way that no other substance does. "Black Coffee," "Coffee in Bed," "Coffee and Reefer" resonate widely in Western countries; substituting tea, lemonade, or even any alcoholic beverage would produce strange results. Coffee is a perfectly acceptable, even favorite drink in Muslim countries, while of course alcohol is forbidden. Only Westerners who avoid coffee for religious reasons do not interact directly with the brew's great cultural and social influence. Yet everyone feels the presence of coffee.

- Caffeine, above all in coffee (but also in tea, chocolate, soft drinks, energy drinks, and as a booster in various headache tablets, among other sources) is the world's most widely consumed drug—in the sense of a substance ingested that alters body chemistry or mental state. Is it good or bad for your health? We investigate the latest findings on that issue.

- Coffee grows in some 70 countries around the world. Figures on how many people work with coffee are not exact, but the **International Coffee Organization**, based in London, estimates that 26 million people are occupied with coffee in 52 producing countries.[7] Millions more are employed in importing, roasting, investigating, and making coffee in the developed world.

- According to the United Nations, at the peak of coffee imports in 2009, consuming countries were spending about $27.1 billion a year to purchase coffee.[8] But, considering the cost of roasting, storage, transportation, labor, and other factors in the actual making of a cup of coffee, the coffee business may amount now to some $100 billion annually.[9]

- Alas, contrary to claims made in many books and articles, coffee is *not* the second most valuable commodity (after oil) sold internationally. Aluminum and copper fetch more money, while among agricultural products, wheat, flour, sugar, and soybeans all outstrip coffee.[10] Coffee probably held first place for a time, as the spice trade declined in the 1500s and 1600s and before sugar became an everyday item, beginning in Britain. In recent decades, coffee exports have also dropped as a portion of foreign earnings for most producing countries. Yet in looking for ways to bolster the economy from Nicaragua to Tanzania, or how to create more secure, decent jobs, coffee continues to be especially important.

Meanwhile, the global consumption of coffee, especially of high-end or specialty coffee—which we define and discuss in depth—is rising steadily. This progression owes much to Starbucks and the march of its outlets throughout America since the 1980s. Starbucks had to close some stores in the Great Recession that began in 2007 but has recently regained ground. As for the independents, they too declined for a while, but their number has and will certainly continue to increase. Whether a wonderful or an evil company, Starbucks has been the tide that since the 1980s has generally lifted all boats. As a coffee shop owner from Long Beach, California, once told me, "There is a Starbucks going up across the street from my shop. If they would let me, I'd volunteer to go over and hang drywall, just to get them going sooner." He figured that people would come to Starbucks and then get curious about the store across the street; maybe it had better coffee.

Coffee has a long, highly checkered political history. Coffeehouses did not create English political parties and thus serve as midwife to democracy, but the atmosphere over a steaming (and probably horrible tasting) cup did facilitate trading ideas about politics. English conservatives feared this "bourgeois public sphere" so much that in 1676, Charles II banned coffeehouses. His edict was never widely enforced, while his repeated meetings with coffee businessmen in succeeding years, although marred by occasional arrests for "sedition" and some local closings of houses, signified a gradual lessening of royal control of business in general.[11] Political power was shifting from scepter to cup. Revolution in France may not really have gestated in the coffeehouses of Paris, but again the cafés served as discussion centers and meeting points for people seeking change. Latin America has been the biggest site of disputes over labor and land—in short, over the region's most vital issues—and the scene of repeated revolutionary activity that grew in key respects from the coffee business.

This book aims to provide, in one usable volume, a guide to all aspects of the coffee business. The entries and personal stories woven around them start from the ground up; where and how is coffee grown? Then the narrative moves through the stages of processing, exporting, importing, roasting, and making the beans into beverages. On paper or your screen is a guide, a handbook, a reference tool, one intended to inform and to please. But we also ask blunt questions about what practices improve the land and help coffee people and what techniques or habits are harmful. A huge issue is where the money goes and why. *If*—and this is a very big if—it costs $3 for a cup of coffee in a large American or European city, but a farmer gets only $3 a day, the contributors discuss why that might be so. Greed alone plays a small part in this equation, to the extent that it expresses the truth at all.

No product available anywhere in the world is more laden with the baggage of guilt, desire, and promise than coffee. The guilt comes from the $3 cup/$3 a day formula: Western consumers should do the right thing and fix that situation. But while many coffee farmers, let alone the day laborers they often hire to pick the ripe coffee fruit, remain poor, it may be that much of the guilt surrounding the beverage is misplaced. We look carefully at the idea of fair trade, among other schemes intended to help producers, but equally hard at basic factors that contribute to the cup/farm difference.

Longing and coffee have mixed for centuries. "Passion" is a word often associated with coffee. In the past few years, ad campaigns have turned to the bizarre or the extreme. Lavazza Coffee promotions, for instance, show that sex and coffee are strongly linked, especially in the Italian mind. But here, too, this book reveals a long tradition of blending coffee with the pursuit of romance, the exotic, or simply escape from daily life. This was true by the last decades of the nineteenth century, if not well before. Today relaxation and "me time," in which an individual, almost always a woman, achieves isolation from everyone and everything else, are among coffee's promiscuous promises. A Taster's Choice ad of a few years ago announces, for example, "Serenity. Tranquility. Balance. It's all right here—made fresh in your cup."[12]

Like wine, coffee offers a path to sophistication. The *New York Times Magazine* published a special advertising section in February 1999 that proclaimed, "Coffee requires that we treat it as a prized commodity, storing and brewing it with loving care. . . . Each coffee bean acquires a distinctive taste, depending on how it is roasted."[13] Borrowing consciously from the vocabulary of wine, and simultaneously attempting to draw on Americans' notion (or anxiety) that sophistication comes only from Europe, **terroir** has emerged as a fashionable term to suggest the great care that individual farmers put into growing coffee.[14]

Such appeals to good taste, offered even by makers of instant coffee, are hardly new in the history of coffee advertising. Since the 1880s, coffee sellers have tried, and are still trying, everything from teaching easy steps to better housewifery to serving the beverage as a social lubricant to transporting the consumer through the cup to exotic locales to, inevitably, associating the drink with sex.

What is new in the atmosphere surrounding the brown liquid is the designation since the 1980s of coffee as an ethical compass. "Can Coffee Drinkers Save the Rainforest?" asks one journalist, while another wants to know "Can Great Coffee Save the Jungle?"[15] Forest or jungle, the task would be a big responsibility, and quite distant from saving oneself through a cup of instant tranquility. The Green Mountain Coffee Company proclaims on its bags that, "Great coffee changes everything." Of course, these lines imply that drinking bad coffee will further degrade the environment in producing areas.

The biggest transnational coffee sellers, Kraft (U.S.), Nestle (Swiss), Sara Lee (U.S.), Folgers (also U.S., recently sold by Procter and Gamble to the Smucker Corporation), and in some counts Tschibo (German), together continue to sell more than 50 percent of the world's coffee annually. Because their presence in coffee is so large, they are under steady assault by green activists, coffee connoisseurs, and labor advocates. Perhaps everyone who touches or tastes coffee, from the farmers to the stressed urbanites of the UK and the U.S., is being "mugged in your cup."[16] Yet there are positive trends as well, even among the coffee giants.

Starbucks prides itself on its initiative "to foster a better future for farmers and a more stable climate for the planet," as well as on "economic transparency" through evidence of payments along the supply chain that demonstrate "how much of the price that we pay for green coffee gets to the farmer." The company is "collaborating with innovative nonprofit organizations to support their neighborhood revitalization efforts and improve community education, employment, health, housing and safety."[17]

That all sounds wonderful. But perhaps even Starbucks—to some, Starbucks above all—is the devil in the brew? A search on the web for anti-Starbucks images turns up a sea of them. "Corporate Coffee Sucks" is fairly mild, "Friends Don't Let Friends Drink Starbucks" a bit harsher. "Starsucks" kicks the language up a notch, while the famous mermaid surrounded by "StarFuck Off" challenges conventional good taste.[18] Is the company really so bad, or is it just so well known that it has become a convenient target for consumer discontent? After all, at least one business group has recently given Starbucks a "corporate responsibility award" for its practices.[19] The controversy over good Bucks, bad Bucks, will certainly continue.

And where might coffee fit into the debate over slow food vs. fast food, artisanal food vs. industrial food?[20] Coffee and indeed the entire food business are experiencing profound changes everywhere. The drink can be a slow consumable, prepared with care in a nearly ritualistic fashion; it can be a fast beverage or, of course, an instant one. McDonald's is now hard at work trying to square the circle by selling slow coffee inside its fast food restaurants. Customers are apparently willing to take an extra second or two before they cross from the hamburger side of a McDonald's into a plusher McCafé.

Coffee drinkers in most countries cannot be strict locavores, who consume only food products transported to them from less than 150 miles away. No transoceanic trade, no coffee in the major consuming countries, outside of small amounts produced in the Hawaiian Islands, Puerto Rico, and Australia. Is the long-distance trade itself a problem? Surely most observers of the business and most coffee drinkers would say no; the issue is rather how to improve the global flow of coffee and money. Income needs to rise in the producing countries, making long-haul trade essential. Already, promising trends in coffee consumption, and with it upscale cafés and higher-paying jobs, have appeared in some producing countries. When the middle class, its tastes, and its consumption grow in the developing world, less high-quality coffee will go out onto the global market. A smaller supply for export will help to keep prices up. If this hopeful cycle is not destroyed by global warming, it will improve life for coffee farmers.

Part of the difficulty in talking about coffee in recent years has been that writers and conferences tend to focus on **arabica**, the good beans that are turned into "specialty," "differentiated," or "gourmet coffee." Robusta, typically the target of sneers from people engaged with specialty coffee, accounts for a great deal of the world's production and for much of the money that coffee fetches. This volume pays attention to robusta and to what the specialty industry calls "**commodity coffee**," essentially anything sold in a grocery store can or plastic tub.

The models of how to grow, select, and sell coffee offered in these pages are partly about how to extract more money from consumers—because good coffee is on a par with good wine in many respects and ought to command as high a price as fermented grape juice does—how to lower costs for the producer, or how to eliminate some of the middlemen who handle coffee on its way (generally) north to the consuming centers, all with the goal of keeping more money in the pockets of growers and roasters.

The book as a whole endorses no particular formula for growing and marketing coffee; large farmers may make money and provide excellent facilities for migratory pickers, for example. Co-ops may work well or may be plagued by internal problems that hamper their effectiveness and hurt profits. This volume's motto might be "whatever works."

The coffee plant itself is the subject of constant efforts to improve yields and hardiness. Researchers in the producing countries are at work daily grafting, pruning, testing biosprays made from naturally occurring ingredients, trapping bugs in homemade goo, or adding insects to control diseases on the plants. Non-organic pesticides and insecticides have never been cheap, but from 2007 to 2008 they doubled in price in many parts of the world.

Finally, coffee farmers, like their compatriots in any other field of agriculture, are always looking for more ways to earn money. They grow other crops alongside or between the coffee trees. Got birds? Bring on the ecotourists. Got beautiful land? That almost goes without saying where coffee is grown, so build a lodge and invite visitors from the northern hemisphere. All you need is capital and a low level of violence across your country; yet those are two things not easy to come by in many parts of the coffee world, as several of our writers show.

Surely the best way to make coffee good for the earth, for the people who grow, pick, process, and sell it, as well as for consumers, is to educate the last group. Coffee drinkers, especially in the consuming countries of the north, need to become more aware of what goes into the dark brew. Several entries emphasize this thread.

If conditions in producing countries are really to improve, more money must make its way down the commodity chain and into the farmers' hands. The alternative, especially when the world price of coffee dips below the cost of local production, as it did in 1999–2004, is dire poverty, movement from the countryside to the fetid slums of a city like Managua, Nicaragua, and then north through Mexico to the United States. In some cases people could not move; they stayed in the villages and starved.[21]

How to produce good coffee, whether to promote organic agriculture or not, and whether co-ops are the best organizations for the crop, are among the major issues explored here. How to get more money to the farmers, through lowering their costs, through fair trade, direct trade, certification labels, or by honing consumers' tastes, are other crucial questions. The editors and contributors hope to educate more people about coffee, making them yearn for good coffee, as they define it for themselves, in the cup, for the planet, and for farmers.

NOTES

1. Charis Gresser and Sophia Tickell, *Mugged: Poverty in Your Coffee Cup*, Oxfam Research Report, September 10, 2002, http://www.oxfamamerica.org/publications/mugged-poverty-in-your-coffee-cup, p. 9. The "source" for the figure is given as "US Department of agriculture/Davenport & Company."

2. Dan Bolton, "Recession reconfigures coffee retail," *Specialty Coffee Retailer* 16, no. 8 (August 2009): 12.

3. Zoe Wood and Simon Bowers, "Costa Coffee chain to double in size," *Guardian.co.uk*, April 28, 2011.

4. The National Coffee Association USA (NCA USA), *National Coffee Drinking Trends Study* (New York: NCA USA, 2011), 41; a sample across the country of 2,663 people aged 18 years and older.

5. http://news.dunkindonuts.com/press-kit, June 11, 2011.

6. T. R. Reid, "Caffeine," *National Geographic*, January 2005, 16.

7. International Coffee Organization, "World Coffee Trade 2012," http://www.ico.org/trade_e .asp?section=About_Coffee ICO, accessed April 10, 2012. Slightly different figures are given in Daniele Giovannucci and Jason Potts with B. Killian, C. Wunderlich, G. Soto, S. Schuller, F. Pinard, K. Schroeder, and I. Vagneron, *Seeking Sustainability: COSA Preliminary Assessment of Sustainability Initiatives in the Coffee Sector*, Committee on Sustainable Assessment. September 2008, Winnipeg, Canada, 3. COSA is affiliated with government agencies in the U.S., Europe, and Latin America.

8. United Nations International Merchandise Trade Statistics, *Yearbook 2009*, Commodity Pages, 071, Coffee and Coffee Substitutes, http://comtrade.un.org/pb/CommodityPagesNew.aspx?y=2009, accessed June 11, 2011.

9. This is the estimate made by Ric Rhinehart, Executive Director of the Specialty Coffee Association of America, in October of 2011. Ric Rhinehart, "The new market reality," *Specialty Coffee Chronicle* 3 (2011): 6.

10. Mark Pendergrast, "Coffee second only to oil? Is coffee really the second largest commodity?" *Tea & Coffee Trade Journal*, April 1, 2009. Thus Pendergrast has revised the conventional claim about coffee's second place in world trade made in, for example, his own *Uncommon Grounds: The History of Coffee and How It Transformed Our World* (New York: Basic Books, 1999), xv.

11. Brian Cowan, *The Social Life of Coffee: The Emergence of the British Coffeehouse* (New Haven, CT: Yale University Press, 2005). The classic discussion of the bourgeois public sphere is Jürgen Habermas, *The Structural Transformation of the Public Sphere: An Inquiry into a Category of Bourgeois Society*, trans. Thomas Burger and Frederick Lawrence (Cambridge, MA: MIT Press, 1989). The original, German version was published in 1962.

12. *Smithsonian*, May 2002. The picture is of a cup of coffee by itself against the background of a Japanese sand garden. Or see the ad "Welcome to Starbucks. Seating capacity: one." *The New Yorker*, May 6, 2002. The photo is of a French café chair with a cup of coffee sitting on the seat—no people in sight—in a charming cottage or apartment courtyard. In fact, ads that tout escape to tranquility are aimed particularly at women, whose magazines in America today constantly urge females to live at a frantic pace, then to find "stress-busting tricks," as "My Health Secret" put it in *Health Magazine*, December 2008, 160.

13. "The Art of Coffee" [advertisement], *New York Times Magazine*, February 7, 1999, 36, 38.

14. George Howell's Terroir Coffee Company is perhaps the best example of this approach; see http:// www.terroircoffee.com. Howell aims to educate consumers about excellent coffee, with the expectation that their pleasure and his profits will increase.

15. Jennifer Bingham Hull, "Can Coffee Drinkers Save the Rainforest?" *Atlantic Monthly*, August 1999; Katherine Ellison, "Can Great Coffee Save the Jungle?" *Smithsonian*, June 2004.

16. Gresser and Tickell, "Mugged," 10.

17. http://www.starbucks.com/responsibility/sourcing/coffee; http://www.starbucks.com/responsi bility/community/community-stores; both accessed June 9, 2013.

18. My search for "anti-Starbucks" through Google produced "about 216,000" results, June 11, 2009, while Google Images turned up 4,140 results. However, many may be duplicates.

19. One award is from the Corporate Responsibility Office Association. The judges for the prize are two professors from business schools, the director of Institutional and SRI Marketing, Calvert Company, and the chief investment officer, Domini Social Investments. http://www.thecro.com/?q=node/167, June 11, 2009. Starbucks is also, once again, on the list of *Forbes Magazine's* 100 Best Companies to Work For. An assessment that appears to be more or less balanced can be found in *Human Resources*, June 3, 2008: surveys of Starbucks' employees conducted randomly around the globe every two years found, in the last round, that 86 percent were satisfied or very satisfied with working conditions, pay, and benefits. On the other hand, Starbucks has recently been involved in a number of unfair labor practice suits in the U.S. See http://stopstarbucks.com.

20. See, among other recent works, Alexander Nützenadel and Frank Trentmann, eds., *Food and Globalization: Consumption, Markets and Politics in the Modern World* (New York: Berg, 2008); Richard Wilk, ed., *Fast Food/Slow Food: The Cultural Economy of the Global Food System* (Lanham, MD: AltaMira, 2006); and Kate Soper, Martin Ryle, and Lyn Thomas, eds., *The Politics and Pleasures of Consuming Differently* (Basingstoke, UK: Palgrave Macmillan, 2009).

21. Gresser and Tickell, "Mugged," 10. I traveled in the Matagalpa region of Nicaragua in October 2004. Villagers reported starvation among neighbors who could no longer make money from coffee.

Part I
THE COFFEE BUSINESS

1

Strategies for Improving Coffee Quality

Price Peterson

Editor's note (RT) on the Peterson farm operation: Price Peterson heads a family team, with his wife Susan, his daughter Rachel, and his son Daniel, that produces some of the world's finest coffee. Their farm, La Esmeralda, is high on the side of Mount Baru in western Panama. Early in this century, Daniel discovered some Gesha (or Geisha) plants growing wild on their land. Gesha would seem to be an unlikely candidate for the best coffee ever: it is a spindly tree whose branches tend to curl up instead of the usual down; it isn't especially productive; and it is more than ordinarily susceptible to leaf rust, the bane of Latin American growers. Nevertheless, the Petersons felt that the Gesha, originally brought to the New World from Ethiopia in the 1950s, had extraordinary potential. They were right. Within a few years the variety was winning Best of Panama competitions; from 2005 through 2007, it was chosen best coffee by the Roasters Guild of America, an unprecedented run.

Price, who holds a PhD in neurochemistry from the University of Pennsylvania, is a meticulous farmer and craftsman. Some thirty years ago, he gave up a tenured position at Penn and moved with Susan to Panama. Working closely with American importers like George Howell, the Petersons have developed special practices to make sure that their coffee does not lose quality on its way to the consumer. For example, they dry pulped beans to 12 percent humidity, then pack the coffee into plastic bags for weeks, while they monitor it for changes in taste. When the results are satisfactory by their exacting standards, they repack the coffee in vacuum-sealed bags and ship it immediately. Now sold directly through an online auction each May, the best of Price's Gesha has sold for as much as $130 a pound green. That means importers must bring it to the U.S. and roast it here; the final price for the best of the La Esmeralda Gesha can then be over $200 a pound. Often rated at 95 points or more, this is coffee to die for.

Finally, the Petersons have done a remarkable job providing facilities for their pickers. They encourage indigenous families to return each year, and they do. For the Petersons, sustainability refers to people as well as to the land. Thus the growers have set up a daycare center for harvesters' children, a nutrition program for them, and weekly visits by a physician and a dentist. Like the gorgeous farm itself, the degree of trust on all sides is a wonderful thing to see.

*A further note on the terms in Price Peterson's article: We chose to put this piece first, partly because Price mentions so many important factors, up to the level of export from a producing country, in achieving good to great coffee. Many specific words he uses, like **Q-grader cuppers** or **mucilage**, are explained in the glossary.*

13

Figure 1.1. Price Peterson on his farm, 2008. Photo courtesy of Hacienda La Esmeralda, Boquete, Panama.

Thirty years ago, I bought a new Ford pickup truck for twenty-six bags of coffee. Today, a new Ford pickup costs 151 bags of coffee. To stay in business, the coffee farmer must either produce more coffee with fewer resources on cheaper land or separate himself from "**commodity coffee**" by producing a high-quality crop. Quality—always determined by buyers' perceptions—can be either taste or a social, environmental, or health advantage.

If farmers opt for quality, they should choose the tangible or the intangible, either taste or a perceived benefit to the earth and society. The advantage of producing coffee with excellent taste is that it can be universally and permanently recognized by the educated consumer who values his palate. But high-quality coffee, as rated on a scale discussed below, will probably also be more costly to produce.

Farmers who opt for intangible quality usually do so because they must. Issues of climate, the varieties available for cultivation in a given area, or culture preclude the achievement of good taste. In such cases, farmers need to invest in a socially perceived value such as **organic**, **green**, **bird-friendly**, or **certification**, for example by **Fair Trade USA**, that satisfies some buyers' need to feel that their coffee delivers moral benefits. These values are neither universal nor permanent, but they may allow producers to survive for a period.

How can high-quality coffee, marked by exceptionally good taste, be produced? It should be said at the outset that universally accepted standards for evaluating taste in coffee now exist. Internationally, there are now certified **Q-grader cuppers** from fifty-four countries who cup and evaluate coffee by the same standards. The Q system allows for remarkably objective scoring and evaluation of coffee's quality. Just as there is a 100-point tasting system for appraising wine, there is a similar one for evaluating coffee, developed by Ted Lingle and the **Specialty Coffee Association of America (SCAA)**. In general, coffees scoring over 80 points are said to qualify as **specialty coffee**. Beans in this range are considered out of the commodity category and worthy of serious consideration as fine coffees.

Like fine wines, quality coffees are rarely the product of large corporate efforts. They generally come from small farms in privileged climes where a compulsive artisan is at work.

THE PLACE

There is an old saying that a good farm is the product of "the man, not the land." To a degree that remains true. I have seen good coffee grown on a parched and sun-drenched sandy hillside in Southern California by a young graduate of the California Polytechnic State University. I have also seen good coffee grown in a valley in Panama where it rained 360 days of the year, and people talked not about soil but about the quality of mud. In both cases, the producers were exceptional farmers.

The perfect coffee farm would lie within 12 degrees of the equator, so that it would have fairly even sun- and day-length; it would be gently sloped to facilitate drainage and harvesting; it would receive about 2 meters of rain with a marked, but short, dry season; and the wind would blow at no more than 7 kilometers per hour year round. For great coffee it would have daytime temperatures in the low 20s Centigrade with nighttime temperatures around 12 degrees. Finally, it would be nice if it had no insect or fungal enemies. To my way of thinking, the only thing on this wish list absolutely necessary to grow specialty coffee, as opposed to commodity, is the nighttime temperature. Frequently, that cold (but never freezing) night is described in producing countries as altitude, leading to a general belief that quality coffee requires the highest altitude.

That too is generally true. Still, above a certain altitude, depending on latitude, coffee trees will grow, albeit slowly, but the fruit production will drop to unreasonable levels.

Infrastructure is an often underappreciated requirement. Decent roads are required to get the harvest rapidly and reliably to a processing station. Water must be available for spraying for pest control. At harvest, communication between processor, transport trucks, and pickers is essential, not to mention an adequate number of pickers, attracted by desirable and accessible housing and sanitary facilities for the whole family.

THE COFFEE TREE

In discussing **arabica** coffee, it should be kept in mind that nearly all the coffee in the New World is descended from just a few beans and two varieties—'Typica' and 'Bourbon.' This extremely narrow genetic base has been hybridized within itself and with a very few other varieties. Almost no additions have come from the hundreds, perhaps thousands, of varieties existing in coffee's original home, Ethiopia. Since New World coffee has been more or less the same for the past 200 years, the only factors affecting quality have been cultural and climatic—not much else was possible. In turn, this led to very subtle differences in taste and to the appearance of very fine-tuned cuppers. By analogy, any idiot can taste (or see) the difference between a red and white wine; few can tell the difference between a Jamaican Blue and a Kona coffee.

The discovery of a new taste in coffee—a Pacamara or a Gesha—has been a rare and remarkable event. We are now finding that there are varietal taste differences in coffee that are as striking as the difference between a chardonnay and a Burgundy. This awareness of the great range of coffee tastes marks a whole new epoch. Why didn't this understanding occur earlier with Ethiopian coffees, which range so widely in characteristics within one country? Probably the answer is very poor processing, in turn due to a lack of infrastructure, a lack of skills essential in preparing the beans for export, a dearth of compulsive artisans, and few market opportunities.

A giant step toward better quality occurred in the 1950s with the development of dwarf coffee varieties. These trees facilitate coffee culture greatly, especially for cultivation of commodity coffee. To my knowledge, there are no dwarf "land race" varieties that would improve matters for the quality coffee producer. It would be highly desirable to have coffee trees resistant to insects (especially the **coffee berry borer,** called *broca* in Latin America) and fungal disease. Probably such plants will arrive in the form of genetically altered coffees with highly desirable taste characteristics. Technically, this sort of tree is within our grasp—we lack only mature and knowledgeable consumers whose increasing demand would push the process of developing new varieties forward.

HARVEST

It is commonly and truthfully said that the mature **coffee bean** is "perfect" at harvest; processing cannot improve on that condition—processing can only reveal, damage, or destroy it. The coffee fruit, or **cherry,** must be harvested at perfect, all-red maturity. It will tolerate a few days before or a few days after it peaks, but not more. Harvesting too early makes the cup grassy and raw; too late and **fermentation** has begun, resulting in an unstable winey-

ness. Stripping tree branches of all their fruit at once, ripe and unripe berries together, or any practice other than a careful ripe-fruit-by-ripe-fruit removal has no place in the eyes of the compulsive artisan. Unfortunately, stripping by hand or machine is the common practice in commodity production. Hand picking can only be done properly by workers prideful of their craft, who are being rewarded at a level commensurate with their dedication. This is *not* the place to cut costs.

It is essential that once plucked from the umbilical connection to the tree, the fruit be depulped, cleaned, and dried rapidly but at low temperature. Harvested fruit left in bags overnight, or even in the sun for too many hours, leads to unpleasant-tasting coffee. Precisely why this happens is unknown. Independent of heat from the sun, piles or bags of fruit generate heat from the activity of microorganisms in the fruit as well as cellular processes of the still-alive fruits and seeds. It is possible that this heat creates changes within the seed that translate to tastes we don't like. Alternatively, the low oxygen levels in those piles and bags may cause metabolic reactions within the seeds that produce the unwanted results. Potentially, even the rotting fruit itself may somehow be responsible for the diffusion of undesirable flavors-to-be.

Thus processing must begin within a few hours of harvest and continue uninterrupted. Again, the need for adequate infrastructure here cannot be overemphasized. Any decoupling between harvest and processing is probably where most coffee in the world is destroyed—certainly potentially high-quality coffee often suffers from this problem. In country after country, one sees great high-grown coffee harvested and then destroyed between various delays, among them efforts to haul the crop to roads on shoulder or mule back over a period of days. Coffee handled this way is steadily rotting, until it finally arrives, still damp, in the warehouse of a "coyote" or middleman and waits until a truckload can be accumulated and sent to a large central mill for final processing. At best, beans tortured in this fashion now call for a rescue operation to salvage a portion of the harvest as commodity coffee. I remember a large processor in La Paz, Bolivia, where a modest amount of space and machinery was required to finally dry and mill such coffee, but where vast resources were dedicated to density selection, electronic color selectors, and finally dozens of hand selections in order to separate out a drinkable beverage.

DEPULPING

There are several types of machines available to remove the skin and pulp from the cherry and then separate the pit or beans from the rest, a process called **depulping**. It is not rocket science and the only requirement is that this equipment not scrape or damage the bean. The bean comes from this process with a thick covering of a very viscous long-chain sugar that is essentially an agar. Since this slimy mucus-like sugar coating is separated from the bean by the parchment (or hull), it has little effect on the cup quality of the coffee. However, it makes drying, especially on a concrete surface, a hazardous experience. Traditionally mucus was removed **(demucilation)** by leaving the beans, wet, to sit for up to 36 hours or until the amylase enzymes in the fruit pulp could break down the slime. The coffee was then washed and dried. Within the past several years, so-called demuciladors (*desmucilinigadores*) have been developed. These machines rub the beans against each other as they emerge from depulpers and literally rub the agar coating off, which oozes away as a thick syrup. The beans can then be dried immediately in a continuous process without suffering the delays of the previous batch process.

DRYING

Great tomes have been written on the art, perhaps science, of **drying** coffee. I once met a young PhD student in physics doing his doctoral thesis on the drying of coffee. All this is not without justification. By cutting through a moist coffee bean with a sharp knife, one can begin to appreciate the complex life of a water molecule, subject to the banging around of Brownian motion, trapped inside and trying to get out by sliding down a moisture gradient through the barriers of cell walls, increasingly concentrated dissolved solids, and woody cellulose layers. It is not a simple matter. And, all the while, the cells of the bean are metabolizing, destroying some molecules and creating others, many of which will ultimately determine just how your cup will taste.

To complicate the issue, the coffee bean is a mixture of certain proportions of sugars, proteins, nuclei acids, fats, and cellulose, plus a few minerals. We also know that after all this is semi-incinerated by the roaster, few of these original compounds exist, while a veritable zoo of new organic molecules has been created. In the raw bean, there is little or no taste. In a water extract of the burnt and ground bean, there is a world of highly flavored compounds—*and we have no idea how those compounds are related to drying and roasting.* Attempting to relate the outcome to the processes through sophisticated chemical analysis was the life work of Ernesto Illy, of the Italian Illy coffee family and company. But success was partial and fleeting. Thus we come back to how best to dry coffee.

The simple prescription would seem to be to dry the coffee as promptly as possible, without letting the bean temperature rise to the level where chemical reactions, other than normal metabolic ones, would occur. This approach has the limited virtue of doing minimal damage. In other words, since you don't know how to help it, don't make it worse.

One of the few major achievements of the past century in coffee processing was the introduction of the rotary warm air drier as an alternative to sun drying on an outdoor patio. In tests that monitor the temperature of well-raked beans drying on a patio, I've seen variations from ambient, around 21°C, to 50°C. This is not a process—this is shooting craps! The rotary warm air drier (*guardiola*) allows almost perfect control of both temperature and **moisture** (humidity). Initially, when beans are at 30 percent humidity (having had surface water removed in a pre-drying process), evaporative cooling permits the use of very hot air input (80–90°C) without significantly heating the beans themselves. As humidity drops into the high teens, air temperature can be reduced to 60–70°, while the bean temperature remains less than 40°. Finally, as 12 percent humidity is approached, air temperature can be further lowered, so that bean temperature never gets much higher than body temperature. This level of control and consistency is unobtainable with patio drying, although approachable with careful African-style drying on elevated screens.

By the time the coffee, in parchment, is dried to 11 or 12 percent, nearly all of the artisan's efforts at preserving the virtue of the ripe fruit are exhausted. The critical period has passed and the coffee will be all it can be. From here on out it is *carpintería*, carpentry, as the Spanish say.

DRY PROCESSING

After drying, quality coffee is stored or aged for four to eight weeks, a step called **dry processing**. Although no one knows why, during this period the cup changes from a grassy or **green**

taste toward its mature optimal cup. The coffee is stored away from the elements with the hull or *pergamino* (**parchment**) intact.

Shortly before shipping, the next step begins. This involves first milling off the hull and, to a lesser degree, the underlying "onion" or **silverskin**, a thin translucent layer adhering tightly to the green bean. The coffee is then selected and sorted for size, density, color, and mechanical **defects**. After this it is packaged and shipped to the roaster.

For centuries the package of choice at this stage has been the jute bag. In fact, the standard international measure of coffee is the **bag**—a jute sac containing 60 kilograms, or 134 pounds, of coffee beans.

Throughout the period of "aging," quality coffee, like wine, is constantly cupped and evaluated. Drying necessitates batch rather than continuous process. Thus, although the coffee may be coming from the same variety on the same farm, subtle differences creep into batches (depending on the microclimate, whether the fruit was picked at the beginning, middle, or end of harvest, etc.) that make one batch cup out slightly differently from another. It is these differences that may lead cuppers to give one batch a score of 92 and another a 94. Although seemingly slight, these few points will make coffee cognoscenti value one coffee at $5 a pound and another at $100. It is that last distinction, between excellent and superb, for which the **third wave** coffee buyer lives!

NOW, THE CRYSTAL BALL

A few years ago Bob Fulmer, the coffee guru of Emeryville, California, commented that five or ten years down the road, the customer would enter the coffee shop and first say that he would like, for instance, a Pacamara. After a while, he would say, "a Honduran Pacamara." And, finally, he would add, make it a triple shot with fat-free milk, cinnamon, and whipped cream. This is similar to the follower of Bacchus who would first order a bottle of merlot, then "make it a Chilean merlot." Either drinker might ultimately prefer a beverage that originated on a certain farm, from a certain altitude.

That increasing refinement of taste is exactly what we in the specialty coffee sector wish to promote. We want to provide more opportunity for customers to express their individuality through their purchases. We await the day when, in addition to the current options of 'Typica' or 'Bourbon' from a dozen different origins, consumers can have their choice of a dozen varietals from twenty origins.

Following on the improvements mentioned earlier in packaging coffee, efforts are under way to develop "perfect" storage systems that allow whole or partial coffee harvests to be kept in inventory for several years while maintaining perfect quality. Like fine wines, this would enable harvests of exceptional years to be identified and marketed at enhanced prices. Then the coffee drinker might enter his favorite coffee shop and order a Pacamara, from Honduras, from the 2004 harvest, triple shot with fat-free milk, cinnamon, and whipped cream. Now you have a dozen varietals from twenty origins and from seven different harvests. I believe that leaves the buyer with 1,680 different ways to express himself!

2

The Coffee Plant and How It Is Handled

Shawn Steiman

Coffee is a handsome tree with dark, shiny leaves that grow in pairs along branches. The white flowers, when open, offer a heady and refreshing scent. The fruits, usually red when ripe (though yellow, pink, and orange colors exist on some varieties), are juicy and inviting. Coffee is a tropical plant, so it survives in a fairly narrow temperature range (not too hot, not too cold).

Aside from the temperature requirements, it isn't too picky. It grows on a range of soil types, preferring slightly acidic soils that drain well enough so the plant won't drown after heavy rains. It doesn't much matter what the elevation is, either, so long as the air temperature is comfortable. Like any other living organism, it needs food and water to survive, but it will likely live through extreme stress, *not* including frost, which kills the trees overnight. After survivable stress, however, a plant won't produce many, if any, fruits for humans to harvest. It can take physical abuse, almost relishing in it; regular pruning is well tolerated and even

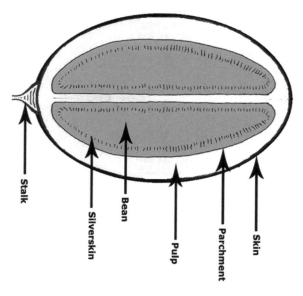

Figure 2.1.   Parts of the coffee fruit. Drawing by Lara Thurston.

Stalk

Silverskin

Bean

Pulp

Parchment

Skin

The Coffee Plant and How It Is Handled

Figure 2.2. African drying racks, as they are known throughout the coffee world, in use in Ethiopia, home of coffee. Photo by Robert Thurston.

necessary to maintain a productive tree. The exception is strong wind. Too much wind and the leaves are injured or blown off, along with flowers.

Humans love this plant not so much for its ornamental properties, of course, but for the taste of the beverage it can produce. It is a long journey from the tree to the cup, though.

The part people care about, the **seed**, is hidden inside the fruits The first step, then, is removing the **coffee fruit** from the trees. This can be done using human hands or machines that shake the trees, forcing them to drop the fruit. Before the seed can be roasted and consumed, it must be extracted from the fruit and dried down to a low level of moisture content. Between the seed and the outside of the fruit, however, are several layers of plant material that also must be removed: **silverskin, parchment,** and **mucilage.**

If the whole fruit and seed are dried down together, in **dry processing,** then all the outer layers can be removed simultaneously, using a machine designed for the purpose. If the seed is extracted from the fruit first, in **wet processing,** then the mucilage and parchment still need removal. Typically, the mucilage is eliminated right away either with a machine or by coaxing microorganisms into eating it. Then, the seed, still covered by the silverskin and parchment, is dried in the sun or in a forced-air dryer. Sometimes, though, the mucilage is not removed and the seeds are dried straight away.

Once dry, the parchment is milled off. Often, some degree of the silverskin remains; it will separate as flakes during the roasting process. Remaining, now, is a collection of hard greenish-bluish seeds of varying sizes. As this collection tends to contain some broken pieces, malformed seeds, or insect- or diseased-damaged seeds, the pile of seeds is sorted by humans or machines. The odd bits are removed and the seeds sometimes separated by size, density, and color.

From there, they are bagged and transported to a port, where they'll eventually be shipped to a warehouse or roaster who will be roasting it before too long. Once roasted, the beans can be ground, brewed, and drunk!

3

Digging Deeper: Cultivation and Yields

H. C. "Skip" Bittenbender

Coffee as purchased by the consumer is a two-species crop from the botanical family Rubiaceae. *Coffea arabica*, known as **arabica** coffee, is considered to have higher cup quality than *Coffea canephora*, known as **robusta** coffee. The majority of coffee produced is arabica whose origins are in the highlands of Ethiopia. Robusta originated in Côte d'Ivoire and Central African Republics, for example, which are warmer and wetter.

As with most crop species that people have moved from their origins to other parts of the world, the genetic variability is quite restricted. At first, Europeans did not realize that Ethiopia, not Yemen, was the origin. Therefore, movement of arabica out of Yemen in the seventeenth century was limited to essentially the varieties 'Typica' and 'Bourbon' that were growing in Yemen at the time. Old commercial arabica varieties grown today are the results of hybridizing these two varieties and natural mutations. Today, coffee breeders are just beginning to explore the great genetic diversity of arabica after numerous coffee collecting trips in Ethiopia that date back to the 1960s. Plant and seed collections exist in Ethiopia, Brazil, Colombia, and Costa Rica, to name only the largest. These collections no doubt hold important traits like caffeine-free, drought and wind tolerance, unique cup quality features, and pest and disease resistance that will be incorporated in commercial varieties in the twenty-first century.

Genetic improvement of *Coffea canephora* (robusta) started much later than arabica. Other diploid *Coffea* species can be crossed with *canephora*,[1] but collections of these species are not as well developed or classified as the arabica or robusta collections.

Most coffee is sold by origin and species, not by variety. This practice resulted from the traditional disconnect between the regions where coffee was grown and the regions where coffee is roasted and consumed. The fact that most growing regions typically produced only a few varieties contributed to the idea that coffees from a specific region had a specific cup quality profile. However, farmers are now testing varieties recently developed by coffee breeding programs with cup quality in mind that will likely become commercial varieties. While it is known that climate, crop management, and processing have a major impact on taste in the cup, the appearance of these new varieties will surprise coffee roasters in the future, as these beans will have characteristics that are not traditionally associated with a particular growing region.

CLIMATE

Coffee, an evergreen tropical crop, evolved under a forest canopy. Traditionally, it is grown in areas typified by calm breezes, not strong winds. Non-equatorial areas have a single rainy season while equatorial regions frequently have a bimodal rain pattern. Fifty inches of annual rainfall is the minimum requirement for coffee cultivation. Irrigation makes it possible to produce in areas where rainfall is inadequate or the length of the dry season is too long for adequate yields on a regular basis. In the ideal climate, the dry season stresses dormant flower buds, so that flowering coincides with the rainy season and the fruit grows and matures into the cooler, dryer season.[2]

Arabica grows best with low temperatures of 59°F (15°C) and high temperatures of 77°F (25°C). Robusta grows better in warmer temperatures, 75 to 86°F (24–30°C). That said, arabica is grown commercially in some areas where the high day temperatures during fruit growth reach 90°F (32°C). Finding the best temperatures for production on the planet means farming at high elevations near the equator and near sea level at latitudes nearer to 23° north or south. High elevation or mountain grown coffee is not about low air pressure, it's about temperature, particularly high day temperature. There is a theoretical relationship between elevation and latitude in determining the suitability of any area for arabica and robusta cultivation. The higher the latitude—within the tropics, so that trees are not threatened by frost—the lower the elevation for arabica can be. For example, in Hawaii, at 19–21° north, excellent coffee is grown from sea level to 2000 feet (about 610 meters) due to the trade winds and mid-ocean environment.

LIGHT

Sunshine is essential for coffee production, even for wild coffee growing in its natural, dry forest **understory** habitat. But unlike many fruit crops—avocado, banana, macadamia, mango, pineapple—coffee tolerates shade well. Today, coffee is grown in areas that are cloudy, like the mountains in Kenya, Colombia, and Hawaii. At lower elevations that are warmer and sunnier, coffee has been frequently grown under shade trees, known as **shade-grown** coffee. Research on coffee photosynthesis (the capture of light energy and carbon dioxide for growth) reveals that coffee leaves need only 20–25 percent of the available tropical sunlight to function at top performance. The additional light energy is not used by the top leaves but does penetrate to the lower leaves. This extra light results in the coffee tree producing more flowers per bud, and thus more coffee fruit growing on the tree. This sounds like a good situation for the farmer, providing more coffee to harvest per tree per acre, but sometimes it's not.

NUTRIENTS

In addition to light and carbon dioxide, coffee requires elemental nutrients from the soil, particularly nitrogen (N), phosphorus (P), potassium (K), and at least ten others to grow and produce a crop. A deficiency in any nutrient can reduce coffee yield and quality. N, P, and K are the nutrients required in the largest quantities by plants; **fertilizers** are labeled by numbers indicating the percentages by weight of these elements. For example, an ordinary synthetic (non-organic) garden fertilizer bag may read 5-7-4 or 5:7:4. The ratio means that of the total weight of 100 pounds (45.4 kilograms), 5 pounds are a nitrate containing nitrogen; 7 pounds are phosphate, which holds phosphorus; and 5 are potash, which provides potassium. The remaining weight is filler.

When coffee is harvested, elemental nutrients are removed. Every ton of green bean removes 90 pounds of N, 5 pounds of P, and 80 pounds of K. If pulp and parchment from harvested cherry is not returned to the orchard, a total of 130 pounds of nitrogen, 8 pounds of phosphorus, and 130 pounds of potassium are removed from the orchard.

These nutrients must be replaced if the farmer wants to maintain healthy trees and continue harvesting the same yield year after year. Nutrients can be applied as synthetic or organic fertilizer; the tree does not care as long as the nutrients are in an absorbable form. See **organic** below. For example, the nutrients lost in the cherry representing 1 ton of green bean equal 5,000 pounds (2,267 kilograms) of organic fertilizer, such as a thermo-compost from yard and tree trimmings that contains, under the best conditions, 2.5 percent N, 2.0 percent P, and 1.5 percent K. The same amount of nutrients for N is found in 650 pounds of 20:5:20 NPK fertilizer. A much larger quantity of organic fertilizer (compost) is necessary to supply the equivalent nutrients of the synthetic fertilizer. These requirements ONLY address the nutrients lost in 1,000 pounds of green bean. More nutrients and therefore more fertilizer are needed to grow leaves, roots, wood, and the cherry pulp.

GROWTH AND YIELD

The arabica coffee tree is generally grown from seed. The seedling initially produces a stem (vertical) and leaves; as it grows, branches (laterals) emerge from the vertical stem. Flowers that become the **cherries** (fruit) are produced on the lateral branches, not the vertical stems. Flowers are produced once on a section of lateral branches where the leaves are one year old. Beyond this section of one-year-old leaves is the youngest part of the lateral branch; this is the section where new leaves are produced in the current year and the flowers and cherry will be produced the next year.

Coffee yield is normally expressed as mass per area, for example, pounds of **green bean** per acre. For farmers who sell their cherry, yield is counted as pounds of cherry per acre. 10,000 pounds of cherry per acre is a good yield; depending on the variety, that's about 2,000 pounds (4,400 kilograms) of green bean per acre. What determines yield? The number of trees per acre, number of verticals per tree, number of laterals with cherry per vertical, number of fruit clusters per lateral, number of fruits per cluster, number of seeds (green beans) per cherry (usually two), and the average weight of each bean.

Several conditions reduce yield:

- **Peaberries**, a condition mostly under genetic control, because only one mature seed exists within each cherry; this can occur in any varietal
- Internode length, the branch material between leaf nodes, because resources are used to create more wood between the clusters instead of additional fruits
- Low light level received by new leaves, whether due to a cloudy climate, mountain shade, or tree shade, because it causes a lower production of flowers and, consequently, of green beans
- Drought and nutrient imbalance

The coffee tree generally does not drop its young cherries when too many are set. Other trees like apple or mango will set excess fruits but drop them before maturity, somehow "knowing" they can't support them with the limited available nutrients and water. In the northern U.S. this is called June drop. But on coffee trees, the cherry has the highest priority for nutrients absorbed by the roots. Thus, no matter how much light, water, and nutrients are available, the tree attempts to grow the cherries. If insufficient nutrients are absorbed to grow cherries, new leaves, and branches, then only the cherries will grow. If this occurs—that is, no new lateral branches and leaves grow—then the next year there will be no flowers and no cherries. This situation is called alternate bearing; one year there will be a big crop but short growth of the laterals and the next year there will be a small crop but long growth of laterals, and the cycle will repeat. If the condition of insufficient nutrients occurs early in the season, then the cherries will demand and receive stored nutrients from leaves, laterals, verticals, and roots. This will result in the loss of all the leaves on laterals with cherries. Then those laterals begin dying, starting at the tip and moving towards the vertical stem. In this die-back, not only is next year's crop destroyed, but this year's crop may be lost as well.

Much research on the management of fertilizer, water, pests, pruning, and light has been done to help farmers have similar cherry (and green bean) yields from year to year. High yield of green beans every year from trees grown in full sun conditions was not possible until synthetic fertilizer was available to farmers. Traditionally, coffee farmers in sunny and hot areas grew coffee in the shade. The tree cover held down yields but also nutrient requirements, which meant that farmers did not have to use as much fertilizer or mulch. Once synthetic fertilizer became available, many farmers, often at the urging of agronomists and governments, began cutting down shade trees and using synthetics to get much higher yields. That practice frequently required less cost and labor compared to using the nutrient-equivalent amounts of organic fertilizer and leaves of shade trees as the source of nutrients. But synthetic fertilizer had to be purchased from outside the farm, leaving growers at the mercy of a separate, volatile, and often fiercely expensive market.

In the late 1980s and early 1990s, an activist program favoring shade-grown coffee began. Initially shade was promoted more to maintain migratory bird populations in the U.S. than to improve coffee quality or limit synthetic fertilizer and other agrochemical use in the environment. In the face of lower yields, the farmers hoped to get a price premium through certification schemes. As we shall see in articles below, that idea has often not worked out well.

Yield is one of the most complex issues in agriculture. Humans invented agriculture for their own well-being, not the plants'. The yield we seek is sometimes flowers, for example orchids; bark, such as cinnamon; fruit pulp like banana; roots, like carrot; stems, for instance pine; and seed, which includes coffee. Yield is determined by genetics, climate, management, light, nutrients, pests, and disease. In short, a great deal goes into the complexity of yield in coffee. In thinking about yield, coffee farmers must consider many factors, including the cost of gathering more cherry from the trees in terms of what must be put back into the soil.

NOTES

1. All species in the genus *Coffea* have two sets of chromosomes. The only exception is *Coffea arabica*, which has four sets of chromosomes. Typically, species must have the same number of chromosomes to breed successfully.

2. After coffee flower buds develop, they become dormant and require a dry period before opening. A sufficient water event can break the dormancy.

4

Coffee as a Global System

Peter S. Baker

Coffee prices have been going up and down a lot recently; this volatility especially worries coffee companies. When things get extreme (high or low), meetings are convened and reasons are looked for. A culprit is duly discovered—currently it seems to be "speculators" (banks are a good target after all)—then a conclusion is reached: "something must be done about it." But subsequently nothing much changes because it is very difficult to know what to do and because the system eventually self-corrects itself anyway.

WHAT IS A SYSTEM?

A system is a collection of components joined up in such a way that it produces its own pattern of behavior over time. A good and familiar example is ourselves; we are a marvel of a fully automated, gently oscillating but mostly resilient and self-correcting system. Coffee production is a system, and fluctuations are a characteristic of a system—in fact within limits, oscillations are a healthy sign—a very regular human heartbeat, for instance, is less healthy than one that fluctuates somewhat. Oscillations are therefore an indicator of a system, one of whose principal properties is self-regulation. But it is surely in everyone's interests to ensure that the oscillations are not too extreme, because another feature of a system is that increasing oscillations can eventually damage the system beyond repair or flip it into a different state, with its own characteristics.

So we have an oscillating coffee production system. Anything to worry about? Worry itself is a good thing in moderation: it's the job of any system to worry. Just as the wonderfully intricate human immune system worries at the slightest sign of an attack from a foreign body, and occasionally gets it wrong when it attacks itself, so the coffee industry needs its own vigilant immune response (sub)system looking for signs of trouble. I see this scanning as my job and believe that it is a key role of academics and support institutes, in general, to do some worrying: negative but constructive feedback, it could be called.

MISSING CONTROLS AND FEEDBACKS

A principal worry is that recent political and economic history has tended to strip away controls that safeguard a range of systems, including coffee. Free-market ideology has been all-conquering, with the single, simple concept that the more things are free and unhindered, the better they work; that is, the price signal in the free-market system is the one signal that really matters.

From the recent history of our troubled global financial system, however, we can see that a free-market approach can be dangerously simplistic. After the 2008 crash, Alan Greenspan professed himself to be in a state of "shocked disbelief", because "the whole intellectual edifice" had collapsed. He famously said, "[I] found a flaw in the model that I perceived is the critical functioning structure that defines how the world works, so to speak."[1] In other words, his understanding of the global financial system was flawed. Some observers, for example Nouriel Roubini and Stephen Mihm[2] and Nassim Taleb,[3] were the worriers who saw exactly what the problems were, that the financial system was so lacking in controls and feedbacks that it was a disaster waiting to happen.

Back to coffee: the principal point here is that coffee production is a very complex system that works at a range of scales from microscale to global, a system composed of many subsystems that we don't really understand well. There are millions of people earning their living from this system, but they make little attempt to see the whole picture and where it might be headed. A useful analogy is the old Sufi tale of the three blind men introduced to an elephant—they all feel a different part, its trunk, legs, and ear, and come to very different conclusions about the elephant-system.

THE COFFEE-CARBON SYSTEM

How can a systems approach help us? Let's take a topical example. Currently there are strenuous efforts by some actors to reduce coffee's carbon footprint. A suggested way to do this is to store more carbon in the form of trees on the farm. Schemes are afoot to encourage farmers to do this; with luck and sufficient financial incentives, farmers might be able to store an extra ton of carbon per hectare per year. With great luck and substantial investment, large numbers of farmers might be able to do this, just as they have enrolled in sustainable schemes.

But if we start to quantify this picture, some doubts creep in. At a global level, growth of certified sustainable coffee has been positive: possibly now one million farmers are part of such programs, though achieving this figure has taken more than a decade. So even if we are optimistic, it is unlikely that we would be able to store stored carbon on more than, say, 100,000 hectares of coffee lands per year. That's a gain of 100,000 tons of carbon, which seems like a lot; but it is equivalent to no more than 500 hectares of forest. We suspect (but don't know because the coffee-system information feedback systems are so poor) that dozens of times more than this area of forest is destroyed each year to plant new coffee. What we do know, but still can't quantify, is that thousands of hectares of coffee are being pulled up each year and replaced by crops that store less carbon, such as pasture.

If we could study the global coffee-carbon system, therefore, and attempt to quantify the stocks and flows that are the characteristic of all systems, we might be able to identify the greatest flows of carbon leaving the system and then decide how to limit them. Available funds could be spent with optimal efficiency. Thus, it might well be more effective to try to optimize production on existing farms so that the pressure on virgin land is reduced.

In the end, it comes down to a question of economics, which is the study of the allocation of scarce resources to competing ends. Therefore a crucial question is, with a limited amount of funds every year to reduce coffee's carbon footprint, how should it best be spent? This question can only be answered effectively by considering the global coffee-carbon system. Once we understand it, we can devise a logical way to tackle a global problem through a global plan. The global coffee mitigation problem cannot be solved by local voluntary schemes—the reward is not there and even with great good will, time is against us.

THE GLOBAL COFFEE ECONOMIC SYSTEM

It is clear that the coffee economy has been run badly in many countries, with very little investment in new capital and very little to improve efficiency, as we can see from chronically low yield figures. Up to now, this has not mattered to the coffee industry as a global system because there has always been new land to exploit. But today land is in short supply, and with the problem of carbon mitigation, destroying forest and savannah to grow coffee should no longer be acceptable. This means that the primary aim of the coffee industry should be to increase efficiency; currently, it is not doing enough in this respect.

The coffee business is a system just like any other; it has a stock of physical capital (farms, machines, and factories). The greater the stock of physical capital in the coffee economy and the greater the efficiency (output per unit of capital), the more output that can be achieved each year. If the fraction of income reinvested in capital stock and the efficiency of that capital (its ability to produce output) are not regulated through feedback from a monitoring system, the capital stock may decline, depending on the lifetime of the capital. Over recent decades, coffee production, like world capital, has been growing exponentially in some countries. Whether this keeps going depends on whether growth can continue faster than depreciation, which in turn depends on several factors:

- The investment fraction—how much income the industry invests rather than takes as profit (the problem of shareholder value, or greed)
- The efficiency of capital—how much capital it takes to produce a given amount of output (low efficiency examples include depleted soils in Africa and diseases not being dealt with)
- The average capital lifetime—how long equipment lasts and what the life of coffee lands is

If the capital stock has a long lifetime, then a smaller fraction of capital must be retired each year. But here is the rub: with climate change, the basic capital stock of coffee (that is, land) is wearing out more quickly. How quickly? We don't know—the feedback about the state of the industry is weak and subject to long delays—but it is probably accelerating. If we don't know what the turnover of land is and how it is changing, then we don't understand our system, the one that supports us and pays our wages. The problem will eventually become evident through the price signal: so long as it is properly interpreted, things may improve. But it is a pious hope that things will always work out for the best, and that is surely no way to run a $100 billion a year business.

A SUSTAINABLE COFFEE SYSTEM?

Despite all the good intentions of the sustainability movement, coffee is not in good shape; arabica especially is in short supply, as effectively its stock has not grown over recent years. We are not looking at sustainable coffee sufficiently as a global system and are not confronting the raft of problems coming our way. Sustainable coffee certifications for example, concentrate almost exclusively at the farm level, so that broader scale issues are not dealt with.

The case of coffee wilt disease (CWD) is an example of this problem.[4] It appeared in just one small locality in the Congo in the 1970s and subsequently spread through Uganda and parts of Tanzania. We reckon it has caused losses to African farmers since then of at least $1 billion. But it could have been quite easily contained and eradicated if it had been tackled early. This did not happen because a very weak and delayed information feedback system existed, and there was no agency (a subsystem) that had the funds and power to respond in a timely fashion.

CWD now poses a principal material threat to coffee sustainability in those coffee countries still free of the disease. But the industry is doing virtually nothing to stop its spread, and sustainable programs do not include advice on what to do nor do they attempt audits to check if transborder phytosanitary checks are working. This is because no one is looking at the coffee industry as a global system; everyone is just working on their own piece of the puzzle.

Alan Greenspan was correct: there is a flaw in the model of how our present neoliberal system works. Somehow everyone working separately for their own self interests is supposed to produce a system that works with optimal efficiency. Too much faith is placed in this "invisible hand," about which Nobel Prize winner Joe Stiglitz once said: "The reason the invisible hand was invisible, is that it wasn't."[5]

The reality then is that, just as our financial system was so poorly understood and regulated, so is our coffee industry. We must do better if we are to protect the long-term interests of the millions who depend on it for their livelihoods.

NOTES

1. Jon Ward, October 24, 2008, http://www.washingtontimes.com/weblogs/potus-notes/2008/Oct/24/he-found-flaw.

2. Nouriel Roubini and Stephen Mihm, *Crisis Economics: A Crash Course in the Future of Finance* (New York: Penguin, 2010).

3. Nassim Taleb, *The Black Swan: The Impact of the Highly Improbable* (New York: Random House, 2007).

4. Noah Phiri and Peter S. Baker, *Coffee Wilt Disease in Africa* (Egham-UK: CAB International, 2009), http://www.cabi.org/uploads/projectsdb/documents/3387/Coffee%20wilt%20Final%20Technical%20 Report.pdf.

5. Joseph Stiglitz, February 22, 2010, Commonwealth Club of California, San Francisco, http://www.youtube.com/watch?v=9qjvwQrZmpk.

5

What Does "Organic" Mean?

Robert W. Thurston

Chemicals available in nature, without human manipulation in a lab or factory, are organic; chemicals produced by laboratory or manufacturing processes are in- or non-organic. The chemical composition of inorganic and organic compounds may be the same; for instance, nitrates may be found in nature and mined or can be manufactured. The U.S. Department of Agriculture defines "organic" and lists government standards for organic farming at http://www.nal.usda.gov/afsic/pubs/ofp/ofp.shtml. "**Organic**" is often linked to "**sustainable**," a word discussed in various places in this book. Bear in mind that sustainable agriculture can also involve non-organic methods and chemicals.

"Organic" food is usually contrasted to "conventional," "commercial," or even "industrial" food. All farming used to be organic. Every substance put on crops to enhance their growth was organic, that is, found in nature, until 1913, when German chemists opened the first factory to produce ammonia. Fritz Haber and Carl Bosch developed the method—hence the name Haber-Bosch process.[1] The term "organic" was not widely applied to farming until the American J. I. Rodale popularized it in the 1940s.

The Haber-Bosch process opened the way to industrial production of ammonia and to its use as fertilizer, which has enabled farmers around the world to greatly increase their yields. Synthetic ammonia, incidentally, also quickly led to the development of cheaper explosives.

Probably everyone could name some substances not allowed in organic farming, for example DDT and malathion. Sewage sludge, antibiotics, growth hormones, and "most conventional pesticides" cannot be used in organic production, says the USDA. Rotenone, derived from legumes, is okay, even though it kills fish and is somewhat toxic to humans. Sulfur occurs naturally and hence is allowed for organics, but I wouldn't put it on cereal. Copper sulfate, which used to be dumped from airplanes onto banana plants and the workers who picked the crop, tending to turn the humans blue,[2] is still permitted—in small amounts and in certain conditions.

Plants don't generally differentiate between nitrogen put around them in manure or in synthetic ammonium products, although the rate of breakdown and usage in the soil can be different. Organic farmers may also use flaming devices to burn off weeds, which takes a lot of fossil fuel and adds to our carbon footprint. Consumers especially dedicated to improving the environment should pay attention to exactly how their organic food is produced. Some coffee farms I have visited that were not completely organic were nonetheless teeming with birds and frogs; judicious use of some synthetic compounds to kill weeds is not always harmful to the earth, as certain inorganic chemicals break down quickly into their constituent elements. Going organic may also increase costs considerably; for instance, spraying some Roundup to deal with weeds may be much less expensive than hiring workers to chop the intruders by hand. Given a choice between organic and non-organic coffee, it would be useful to know how the pickers are treated, how much money is getting back to the farmers, and whether the agriculture is sustainable.

In any event, organic food, with its claim to higher morality and better health, is steadily winning more hearts and dollars in the U.S. The Organic Trade Association (OTA) reports that U.S. sales of organic products, both food and non-food, for example cotton cloth, reached about $28.6 billion in 2010. The organic food market accounted for most of this figure, at $26.708 billion, up steeply from $6.1 billion in the year 2000. Although the growth of organic food sales has slipped in the past several years, from 21.1 percent in 2006 to 7 percent in 2010, the second figure is more than respectable when considered against the paltry general increase in American spending on food in 2010, at 0.6 percent.[3]

The value of organic coffee imported into North America also increased rapidly, at the rate of 29 percent a year between 2000 and 2008, to more than $1.4 billion annually. *The North American Organic Coffee Industry Survey 2010*, by Danielle Giovannucci,[4] details this trend. More than 93 million pounds of organic coffee were imported into the United States and Canada in 2009, a 4.1 percent rise from the previous year. Average annual growth over the past five years has been 21 percent, a trajectory that dwarfs the 1.5 percent annual growth calculated for the conventional coffee industry.

With the green revolution, which peaked in the 1970s, scientists unfortunately persuaded coffee farmers that they would get much better yields if they cut down the **shade** trees that traditionally protected the smaller coffee plants from direct sun. Growers were also urged to dump a lot of manufactured pesticides and fertilizers on the fields. Meanwhile, research stations developed "technified" or **sun-grown**" coffee, which was much more tolerant of direct sunlight.

Yields did increase, but quality suffered, and farmers caught it in the neck when the price of synthetic chemicals soared—up 100% from 2006 to 2008, on average. All the producers I've spoken to want to use less inorganic fertilizer and pesticide on coffee trees, if only to reduce their costs. Now, as I have seen recently in several Latin American countries, many coffee growers are returning to the ways of their grandfathers, by planting more shade trees and other crops between the rows of coffee trees.

In principle, then, everyone is for organic coffee. We all want a cleaner world, and who dislikes seeing gorgeous tropical birds or those fantastic bright little frogs? Ecotourism is expanding steadily on coffee farms, especially in Latin America. Success depends on having clean and beautiful scenery and the wild creatures to go with it.

The labels on bags of organic coffee promise a bright future. As one roaster, Caffe Ibis, puts it, "Organically grown and processed means that both people and planet are protected from harmful herbicides, pesticides and artificial fertilizers." Green Mountain bags claim that "organic farming produces exceptional coffee without chemicals." Ah, no, everything and everybody is made of chemicals—*what kind* and *how the chemicals are produced and used* are the key questions for farmers and consumers.

Certain problems persist in organic agriculture, among them corruption in **certification**. I have heard about this issue directly from farmers in Costa Rica and Ohio, and it popped up again recently in the *New York Times*.[5] Organic does mean, of course, fewer synthetic

Figure 5.1. Depulping coffee on a mechanized farm, Sertaozinho in Sao Paolo State, Brazil. Few small coffee farmers possess this type of protective clothing. Photo by Robert Thurston.

chemicals in our food. Various tests, for instance by the Consumers Union in 2002, have found considerably fewer residues from inorganic compounds in food certified as organically grown than in conventional produce. Yet, as recent deaths in Germany caused by *E. coli* bacteria on organically grown sprouts demonstrated,[6] organic may not always be the safer choice. In any event, all unroasted coffee usually has little inorganic chemical residue. A major study completed in 1993 tested 60 green coffee samples from 21 countries; only 7 percent of the beans had any detectable pesticide residue.[7]

All coffee imported into the U.S. has to meet stringent standards. For instance, there is zero tolerance for DDT residue in beans brought to this country. Although some toxins have been found even in roasted and instant coffee, they have been introduced into the beans by the **coffee berry borer** (*broca*), an insect whose larvae drill into the seeds, not by the application of inorganic chemicals. Since coffee roasting usually takes the beans to 400°F or higher, any non-organic residues in the beans are likely to be burned off.

Given all this testing and processing, the major benefit of organic coffee is not that people ingest fewer harmful chemicals with it. Nor is better taste necessarily the result of growing and processing organically, although fine organic coffees are available. Instead, those who pay a little more to buy certified organic coffee are, above all, helping the farmers and the earth in the areas where the trees grow. When coffee beans are decaffeinated by the "organic" Swiss water process, no "chemicals" (wrong again!) are used, according to the website of the Swiss Water Decaffeinated Coffee Company—only water.

Buying organic is still a useful way of trying to protect farmers and the earth. However, other certification programs may be every bit as valuable in that respect.

Over the last few years, I have interviewed many people involved in the coffee industry, from growers to processors to retailers and consumers. In the excerpts below, some of these interviewees discuss the issue of organic coffee.

Interview with Ernie Carman and Linda Moyher, coffee farmers, Paraiso, Costa Rica, May 20, 2008:

LM: To get organic certification for three or four hectares costs $700 a year. Is that sinful or what?

EC: You know how many people she could pay with that $700? We don't certify ours because our quota is $3,000. And this is the local certifier, not someone flying in from San Francisco. They have to certify the farm and they have to certify the mill.

RT: And that takes years, right?

EC: Well, we've been certified before, and I think that we could get certified again. We just don't do it for philosophical reasons. There are too many people that sell organic coffee that's not organic coffee.

LM: Actually if you're an inspector and you show up at a big farm where they're paying a lot of money to get their certification and you go back and tell your boss, "Oh, I can certify that farm" . . . I mean how do you turn down that kind of money? And that's not even a bribe, that's just the income that they pay.

Interview with Arnoldo Leiva, president of the Asociación de Cafés Finos de Costa Rica [Specialty Coffee Association of Costa Rica], San Jose, Costa Rica, May 27, 2008:

AL: I don't think the organic trend is for Costa Rica. I've seen very very little success, I mean, rare isolated examples, but when it comes to price, in order to compensate for the lack of yield and problems that organic agriculture brings, the differentials and premiums that you have to pay . . . it's too high, which makes it completely inefficient basically. And from the roaster's perspective, I've found that the roasters need to carry [only] one or two organic coffees.

Interview with Eugene and Lucy Goodman, farmers, Butler County, Ohio, October 16, 2008:

RT: Now, so, when you came here [from another farm] were you determined to go totally organic and were you determined to become certified organic farmers here?

LG: No, we are not determined to become certified organic farmers here. We don't want to deal with the USDA's certification program.

RT: So would you call yourselves organic farmers in fact, but not in law?

LG: YES!

EG: YES!

LG: The [USDA] inspector said I'm here one day a year and what you do the rest of the time . . . because they DO NOT tissue test or soil test to get certification.

EG: Right, there is none of that.

RT: Wow.

LG: Unless there's been a specific complaint about a farm, then they will come in and start the chemical testing.

LG: [We use] neem [an oil pressed from evergreens grown on the Indian subcontinent] . . . a little bit of neem oil. Cause what we are trying to do is get the beneficial insect population up to where it's controlling the bad insect population, and it's working . . . but it does take, we've been here three years and when we got here there were no bugs.

RI: Really?

LG: It was a cattle farm and I really don't know what they [did]. I know they used Roundup cause we found bottles of used Roundup all over the place, but we figured they were just hitting the fence lines with that.

RI: Right, so the insects have come back. I assume the birds have come back as well?

EG: Unh huh. And other wildlife like snakes. We had an amazing amount of toads in the pond the first year we were here.

LG: This pond's five years old; it's a really new pond. So it's changed the ecosystem on this land.

LG: It's true when you go into transition [to organic] and you are gonna go for maybe three to fifteen years of low yields and bad disease problems and bad bug pressures when you are taking a farm that's been chemically farmed for fifty years . . . it takes a long time for the soil to recover. Once the soil recovers, everything falls into place, basically. But it takes a long time for the earthworms to come back. The various nematodes, funguses, bacteria. In healthy soil, they say there should be about a billion little critters in about a tablespoon of soil.

EG: And if those are all there, they can do the correct natural interaction. Even if we don't understand it, I think that's the sense. I think with organic, you have everything present, which creates the balance. It does improve the quality of the crop. It does make the plants healthier. A healthier plant produces healthier fruit, a better quality fruit, that lasts longer, we've noticed.

Finally, the organization Organic Monitor sent out an e-mail in March of 2012 that mentioned "growing incidents of food fraud involving organic and sustainable products." This problem was the central focus of attention at the Sustainable Foods Summit in Amsterdam in June 2012.[8]

NOTES

1. David R. Montgomery, *Dirt: The Erosion of Civilizations* (Berkeley: University of California Press, 2007).

2. Dan Koeppel, *Banana: The Fate of the Fruit That Changed the World* (New York: Hudson Street Press, 2008).

3. http://www.ota.com/pics/documents/2011OrganicIndustrySurvey.pdf.

4. The full report may be purchased at https://o.ta.com/bookstore.html. A summary is at http://www.organicnewsroom.com/2010/06/_organic_coffee_market_tops_14_1.html.

5. Kim Severson and Andrew Martin, "It's Organic, but Does That Mean It's Safer?" *New York Times*, March 3, 2009.

6. *Europolitics*, June 16, 2011, at http://www.lexisnexis.com.proxy.lib.muohio.edu/hottopics/lnacademic/?, accessed June 20, 2011.

7. Richard M. Jacobs and Norma J. Yess, "Survey of imported green coffee beans for pesticide residues," *Food Additives & Contaminants: Part A: Chemistry, Analysis, Control, Exposure & Risk Assessment* X, no. 5 (1993), 575.

8. "Amsterdam Summit Tackles Food Authenticity and Sustainable Commodities," announcement from Organic Monitor (industrywatch@organicmonitor.com), e-mail sent March 27, 2012.

6

Coffee under Threat

The Growing Problem of the Coffee Berry Borer

Juliana Jaramillo

Climate change represents an immediate and unprecedented threat to agriculture: the Inter-governmental Panel on Climate Change (IPCC) predicts a 10–20 percent decline in overall global crop yields by 2050.[1] The effects of **climate change** go well beyond the relationship between temperature and a single species, because alterations in climate influence people's most basic decisions, with profound consequences for their social, economic, political, and personal situations.[2] The IPCC has assessed the impact of present and future climate change and projects an increase in the mean global temperature of 1.4° to 5.8°C (2.5° to 10.4°F) by the end of the twenty-first century, as well as a higher prevalence of extreme weather events and changes in precipitation patterns in many areas of the world.[3]

Investigators generally anticipate that the impact of climate change will be greater in the tropical regions of the world, and developing countries are predicted to be more at risk because of their lower capacity to adapt, owing to various socioeconomic, demographic, and policy trends.[4] Thus, since the vast majority of the two most important coffee species, *Coffea arabica* and *C. canephora*, are grown in the tropics, they are especially vulnerable to global climate change.[5]

Small-scale farmers produce about 70 percent of the world's coffee, and more than 100 million people depend on its production for their subsistence. Studies from Brazil, Mexico, and Uganda show that even minimal increases in the mean temperature due to climate change will have disastrous consequences for coffee production, in some cases reducing the area presently suitable for coffee production by up to 95 percent.[6]

Furthermore, the **International Coffee Organization** (ICO) predicts that under various climate change scenarios, coffee production will decrease by up to 10 percent compared with the reference case without climate change.[7]

According to the ICO, the highest yield reductions are expected in Africa and South America, which will result in pushing up coffee prices worldwide. Yet ICO's forecasts consider only abiotic stress (for example, rising temperatures and changes in rainfall patterns) and do not take into consideration that climate-induced stress may also render plants more vulnerable to biotic stresses such as opportunistic herbivores,[8] in particular *Hypothenemus hampei*, the **coffee berry borer** (*broca* in Spanish), the key pest of coffee around the globe.[9]

In natural ecosystems, the dynamic interaction between plants, pests, and their natural enemies is influenced by the biological characteristics of **trophic** levels (the various positions in the food chain), the nature of the surrounding ecosystem, and climatic factors. Global climate change is likely to directly influence the population dynamics of all trophic levels and further disrupt the multitrophic interactions among different biotic communities,[10] modifying the limits of where a species can live and leading to an expansion or contraction of their typical habitat.[11] Until very recently, studies on the effects of climate change on ecosystems focused only on one trophic level (for example, on plants). But, in reality, climate change has significant effects on a multitude of interactions between species, and seemingly minor changes to individual interactions can combine to exert important effects on the structure of entire communities.[12]

Climate change may influence the interactions between species more than it impacts a single species because those interactions are regulated by **phenology** (the cyclical events of an organism's life that are influenced by climate), behavior, physiology, and relative abundance of multiple species. Thus climate change will not just influence a plant species but disrupt the population dynamics and the status of, for instance, its insect pests or pathogens (diseases).[13] This is true because temperature has a strong and direct influence on the pests' and pathogens' ecology, reproduction, and survival,[14] on the number of pest generations per year,[15] on their phenology,[16] and on their distribution range.[17] Indirect effects may include changing host-parasite interactions or alterations in the ways that insects respond to climate-induced changes on the host plant.[18]

Over the past thirty or so years, changing climate, in particular global warming, has already produced numerous shifts in the distribution and abundance of species.[19] As a result, climate change and the spread of invasive species are two of the most important ecological issues facing the world today.[20] These developments are particularly important for coffee, which serves as the economic foundation for many countries in the tropics, and on which so many people depend for their subsistence.

The coffee berry borer attacks fruit on the trees, causing losses exceeding $500 million annually and, worldwide, affects many of the millions of rural households involved in coffee production. Under low pest pressure, the conversion factor (the ratio of freshly picked coffee berries to the amount of processed, parchment coffee) is 5:1; however, a serious coffee berry borer infestation can push this ratio up to more than 17:1, with devastating economic consequences for farmers.[21]

Currently, *H. hampei* is present in all coffee producing areas of the world, except China and Nepal, with the most recent introductions in Puerto Rico in 2007 and Hawaii in 2010. Predictions of the effects of climate change on coffee and the coffee berry borer indicate that even a small increase in temperature (1–2°C or 1.8–3.6°F) would have serious consequences for coffee production. Particularly dire outcomes are predicted for areas where high-quality arabica is presently produced.[22] These authors suggest that a 1°C (1.8°F) increase would lead to a considerably higher number of coffee berry borer generations per coffee fruiting season. The model further predicts that higher temperature increases (more than 2°C [3.6°F]) would result in shifts in the range of latitude and altitude affected by the coffee berry borer. It seems that this worst case scenario is already happening, as changes in the altitudinal range of the coffee berry borer have recently been observed in Indonesia and Uganda; moreover, on the slopes of Mt. Kilimanjaro in Tanzania, the pest is now found at elevations 300 meters higher than its upper range only ten years ago.[23]

A major but largely unexplored impact of climate change is how it will affect the interspecific interactions between parasitoids (parasitic organisms that live and feed on their host, ultimately killing it), other natural enemies, and their hosts.[24] It is predicted that higher trophic levels are often disproportionately affected by drivers like climate change and habitat modification, with specialist natural enemies (parasitoids) more impacted than generalists (predators).[25] Differential influence of climate change on crops, crop pests, and their natural enemies is likely to result in asynchrony (absence of alignment in time of life cycles and processes) and ultimately will have a profound influence on any ecosystem.[26] Native and introduced exotic natural enemies of insect pests appear unable to track climate-driven geographic expansion of their hosts.[27] The natural balance created by both indigenous natural enemies and their hosts and the introduced exotic natural enemies of key insect pests in coffee growing regions like Central and South America and Asia will likely be disrupted. For example, the decoupling of the coffee berry borer and its natural enemies could result in higher pest numbers or more serious outbreaks. Presently, virtually nothing is known about the effects of a warming climate on the natural enemies of *H. hampei* and other coffee pests. Yet it is crucial to also figure estimates of future distributions of natural enemies/competitors of coffee pests and diseases into existing and future models of climate change, which would enable better planning by growers and the coffee industry.

Climate change and its forecasted impact on coffee production will ultimately have huge implications for livelihoods and poverty levels throughout the tropics. To mention a few probable outcomes, the complex agro-ecosystem of coffee production will be disrupted, as climate change directly disturbs the coffee plant and its potential production or by reducing or shifting the land suitable for coffee production. At the second trophic level, alterations in climate will possibly disturb the dynamics of coffee's pests and diseases causing more serious and frequent outbreaks, as climate change will not only have an effect on the life history parameters of the pest itself but also disturb its trophic relationship with natural enemies or antagonists. Finally, climate change will most likely affect the quantity and quality of the coffee produced. Poor, small-scale farmers will not be able to afford expensive adaptation strategies and will therefore often end coffee production altogether. Large-scale farmers will most probably have to rely heavily on applications of synthetic pesticides to cope with the problem, which will reduce the safety of the product. Hence, as climate changes, there is an urgent need to develop efficient and affordable adaptation strategies for coffee cultivation that include management of insect pests like the coffee berry borer and other pests and diseases.

Possibly the best way to counter a rise of temperatures in coffee plantations is the introduction of **shade** trees, which create a diversified and more resilient coffee agro-ecosystem that will perform better under climate change.[28] Positive effects of shade trees in coffee systems have been extensively demonstrated during the last years.[29] Shade trees mitigate microclimatic extremes and can buffer coffee plants from microclimatic variability,[30] leading to a decrease in the temperature around the coffee berries by up to 4°C (7.2°F).[31] A reduction of this magnitude would imply a drop of 34 percent in the intrinsic rate of increase of the coffee berry borer,[32] therefore allowing coffee to grow in areas that will most likely experience increases in temperature, making them otherwise unsuitable for coffee production due to increased pest pressure. For example, a study from Costa Rica indicated that shade levels of 40–60 percent, provided by trees, helped to maintain air and leaf temperatures below or close to 25°C (77°F).[33]

Shade trees also play a role in soil and water conservation and management,[34] which will be critical issues, particularly in Central America and East Africa. Furthermore, Teodoro and his colleagues have demonstrated that coffee berry borer densities were significantly lower in shaded versus unshaded coffee plantations,[35] possibly because shade coffee agro-ecosystems can serve as a refuge for beneficial arthropods (native and introduced), leading to higher levels of biological control.[36] Moreover, in a two-year study in shade-grown and sun-grown coffee in the Kiambu area of central Kenya, borer infestation levels in the shaded plantation were always lower than in sun-grown coffee and remained below the 5 percent economically tolerable threshold level, an effect most likely due to the lower temperatures in the shaded coffee. Lower pest numbers were accompanied by considerably higher yields in shade compared to sun-grown coffee, possibly because of improved soil, nutrition, and water conditions in the former.[37]

Little research has been done in coffee production areas regarding the impact of climate change on functional agro-biodiversity (including work on insect pests) and their interaction/impact on crop production. The problem of inadequate capacity for adaptation to climate change in these areas is critical and in need of immediate attention. More research and action in this regard will begin to fill some of the climate change knowledge gaps in the coffee-production sector and to assist in the development of adaptation strategy packages for climate change on coffee production. Small-scale coffee farmers have little capital to invest in potentially costly adaptation strategies, thus lowering their resilience to changing conditions. Yet the use of shade trees in the framework of more diversified coffee plantations (for instance, by introducing food crops to the system) to suppress coffee pests like the coffee berry borer is rational, affordable, and relatively easy for coffee farmers and other stakeholders to implement. This approach is an important strategy to improve the resilience of agricultural systems, especially in the tropics, in a changing climate. While the introduction of shade trees seems to be the best currently available strategy to combat the coffee berry borer, new tools and solutions need to be discovered to best cope with the inevitable change in climate.

NOTES

1. Intergovernmental Panel on Climate Change (IPCC), "Summary for Policymakers," in *Climate Change 2007* (Cambridge: Cambridge University Press, 2007), 2–18.

2. United Nations Framework on Climate Change (UNFCCC), "Climate change: impacts, vulnerabilities and adaptation," *Manual*, 2007.

3. IPCC, "Summary for Policymakers"; J. T. Houghton, Y. Ding, D. J. Griggs, M. Noguer, et al., *Climate Change 2001: The Scientific Basis* (Cambridge: Cambridge University Press, 2001).

4. K. R. Hope, "Climate change and poverty in Africa," *International Journal of Sustainable Development and World Ecology* 16 (2009): 451–61.

5. A. Addo-Bediako, S. L. Chown, and K. J. Gaston, "Thermal tolerance, climatic variability and latitude," *Proceedings of the Royal Society London Series B Biology* 267 (2000): 735–45.

6. E. D. Assad, H. S. Pinto, J. Zullo, and A. M. Helminsk, "Climatic changes impact in agroclimatic zoning of coffee in Brazil," *Pesquiza Agropecuaria Brasileira* 39 (2004): 1057–64. C. Gay, F. Estrada, C. Conde, H. Eakin, and L. Villers, "Potential impacts of climate change on agriculture: A case of study of coffee production in Veracruz, Mexico," *Climatic Change* 79 (2006): 259–88; Global Resource Information Database (GRID), "Vital Climate Graphics Africa: Global Resource Information Database, Arendal," 2002, http://www.grida.no/climate/vitalafrica/english/23.htm, accessed March 20, 2012.

7. International Coffee Organization (ICO), "Climate change and coffee," report presented to the International Coffee Council, 103rd Session, September 23–25, 2009, London.

8. R. J. C. Cannon, "The implications of predicted climate change for insect pests in the UK, with emphasis on non-indigenous species," *Global Change Biology* 4 (1998): 785–96.

9. A. Damon, "A review of the biology and control of the coffee berry borer *Hypothenemus hampei* (Coleoptera: Scolytidae)," *Bulletin of Entomological Research* 90 (2000): 453–65; J. Jaramillo, C. Borgemeister, and P. S. Baker, "Coffee berry borer *Hypothenemus hampei* (Coleoptera: Curculionidae): Searching for sustainable control strategies," *Bulletin of Entomological Research* 96 (2006): 223–33.

10. C. Parmesan and G. Yohe, "A globally coherent fingerprint of climate change impacts across natural systems," *Nature* 421 (2003): 37–42; W. H. van der Putten, P. C. de Ruiterb, T. M. Bezemera, J. A. Harvey, M. Wassen, and V. Wolters, "Trophic interactions in a changing world," *Basic and Applied Ecology* 5 (2004): 487–94; and M. Tuda, T. Matsumoto, T. Itioka, N. Ishida, M. W. Takanashi-Ashihara, M. Kohyama, and M. Takagi, "Climate and intertrophic effects detected in ten-year population dynamics of biological control of the arrowhead scale by two parasitoids in southwestern Japan," *Population Ecology* 48 (2006): 59–70.

11. J. M. Tylianakis, R. K. Didham, J. Bascompte, and D. A. Wardle, "Global change and species interactions in terrestrial ecosystems," *Ecology Letters* 11 (2008): 1351–63.

12. Tylianakis et al., "Global change"; W. van der Putten, M. Macel, and M. E. Visser, "Predicting species distribution and abundance responses to climate change: Why it is essential to include biotic interactions across trophic levels," *Philosophical Transactions of the Royal Society B* 365 (2010): 2025–34.

13. J. H. Porter, M. L. Parry, and T. R. Carter, "The potential effects of climate change on agricultural insect pests," *Agricultural and Forest Meteorology* 57 (1991): 221–40. M. Cammell and J. Knight, "Effects of climate change on the population dynamics of crop pests," *Advanced Ecological Research* 22 (1997): 117–60; J. Bale, G. J. Masters, I. D. Hodkinson, C. Awmack, et al., "Herbivory in global climate change research: Direct effects of rising temperature on insect herbivores," *Global Change Biology* 8 (2002): 1–16.

14. Bale et al., "Herbivory in global climate change research"; P. J. Gregory, S. N. Johnson, A. C. Newton, and J. S. I. Ingram, "Integrating pests and pathogens into the climate change/food security debate," *Journal of Experimental Botany* 60 (2009): 2827–38.

15. T. Gomi, M. Nagasaka, T. Fukuda, and H. Higahara, "Shifting of the life cycle and life history traits of the fall webworm in relation to climate change," *Entomologia Experimentalis et Applicata* 125 (2007): 179–84.

16. N. J. Dingemanse and V. J. Kalkman, "Changing temperature regimes have advanced the phenology of Odonata in the Netherlands," *Ecological Entomology* 33 (2008): 394–402.

17. R. Karban and S. Y. Strauss, "Physiological tolerance, climate change and a northward range shift in the spittlebug *Philaenus spumaris*," *Ecological Entomology* 29 (2004): 251–54.

18. R. Menendez, A. Gonzalez-Megias, O. T. Lewis, M. R. Shaw, and C. D. Thomas, "Escape from natural enemies during climate-driven range expansion: A case study," *Ecological Entomology* 33 (2008): 413–21; R. E. Forkner, R. J. Marquis, J. T. Lill, and J. Corff, "Timing is everything? Phenological synchrony and population variability in leaf-chewing herbivores of *Quercus*," *Ecological Entomology* 33 (2008): 276–85.

19. Parmesan and Yohe, "A globally coherent fingerprint"; T. L. Root, et al., "Fingerprints of global warming on wild animals and plants," *Nature* 412 (2003): 57–60.

20. N. L. Ward and G. J. Masters, "Linking climate change and species invasion: An illustration using insect herbivores," *Global Change Biology* 13 (2007): 1605–15; S. A. Mainka and G. W. Howard, "Climate change and invasive species: Double jeopardy," *Integrative Zoology* 5 (2010): 102–11.

21. P. S. Baker, J. A. F. Jackson, and S. T. Murphy, "Natural Enemies, Natural Allies." Project Completion Report of the Integrated Management of Coffee Berry Borer Project, CFC/ICO/02 (1998–2002), 2002.

22. J. Jaramillo, A. Chabi-Olaye, C. Kamonjo, A. Jaramillo, et al., "Thermal tolerance of the coffee berry borer *Hypothenemus hampei*: Predictions of climate change impact on a tropical insect pest," *PLoS ONE* 4(8) (2009): e6487.

23. F. L. Mangina, R. H. Makundi, A. P. Maerere, G. P. Maro, and J. M. Teri, "Temporal variations in the abundance of three important insect pests of coffee in Kilimanjaro region, Tanzania," in *23rd International Conference on Coffee Science*, Bali, Indonesia, October 3–8, 2010 (Paris: ASIC, 2010).

24. L. J. Beaumont, A. J. Pitman, M. Poulsen, and L. Hughes, "Where will species go? Incorporating new advances in climate modeling into projections of species distributions," *Global Change Biology* 13 (2007): 1368–85.

25. Tylianakis et al., "Global change and species interactions."

26. Bale et al., "Herbivory in global climate change research."

27. J. K. Hoover and J. A. Newman, "Tritrophic interactions in the context of climate change: A model of grasses, cereal aphids and their parasitoids," *Global Change Biology* 10 (2004): 1197–1208; and Menendez et al., "Escape from natural enemies."

28. P. A. Matson, W. J. Parton, A. G. Power, and M. J. Swift, "Agricultural intensification and ecosystem properties," *Science* 277 (1997): 504–9. M. A. Altieri, "The ecological role of biodiversity in agroecosystems," *Agriculture Ecosystems and Environment* 74 (1999): 19–31; and B. B. Lin, "Resilience in agriculture through crop diversification: Adaptive management for environmental change," *Bioscience* 61 (2011): 183–93.

29. For example, in coffee and cacao plantations, *Agroforestry Systems* 38 (1998): 139–64; R. G. Muschler, "Shade improves coffee quality in a suboptimal coffee zone of Costa Rica," *Agroforestry Systems* 85 (2001): 131–39; C. Gordon, R. Manson, J. Sundberg, and A. Cruz-Angon, "Biodiversity, profitability and vegetation structure in a Mexican coffee agroecosystem," *Agriculture Ecosystems and Environment* 118 (2007): 256–66. See also Rice in this volume.

30. Beer et al., "Shade management."

31. A. Jaramillo, "Solar radiation and rainfall distribution within coffee plantations (*Coffea arabica* L.), *Revista Academia Colombiana de Ciencias Exactas Físicas y Naturales* (Colombia) 29 (2005): 371–38.

32. Jaramillo et al., "Thermal tolerance of the coffee berry borer."

33. Muschler, "Shade improves coffee quality."

34. Beer et al., "Shade management."

35. A. Teodoro, A. M. Klein, P. R. Reis, and T. Tscharntke, "Agroforestry management affects coffee pests contingent on season and developmental stage," *Agricultural and Forest Entomology* 11 (2009): 295–300.

36. I. Perfecto, R. A. Rice, R. Greenberg, and M. E. van der Voort, "Shade coffee: A disappearing refuge for biodiversity," *BioScience* 46 (1996): 598–608; J. M. Tylianakis, A. M. Klein, and T. Tscharntke, "Spatio-temporal variation in the effects of a tropical habitat gradient on Hymenoptera diversity," *Ecology* 86 (2005): 3296–3302.

37. J. Jaramillo et al., unpublished data.

7

Culture, Agriculture, and Nature

Shade Coffee Farms and Biodiversity

Robert Rice

For more than a decade, ecologists, ornithologists, geographers, and others have cast the coffee **agroforestry system**—an agricultural system involving the production of coffee beneath a species-diverse canopy of **shade** trees—as a land use with great conservation potential. Whether a large estate farm or a small **peasant**-operated tract, a shade coffee farm can possess different characteristics that place it beyond a mere site of commodity production. Perhaps the most well known of these dimensions rests with these systems' attraction of and ability to support a highly diverse bird community, an agriculture known as **bird-friendly**.[1] Yet several other ecological benefits have recently been added to shade coffee's ledger,[2] while its socioeconomic rewards are becoming better known.[3]

This chapter focuses on recent findings that support the notion of shade coffee's ecological and agronomic benefits. A central axis of the chapter concerns the role of birds within the coffee agroforestry system. But it will also become clear that regional vegetation biodiversity, establishment of native species, pollination from bees and subsequent fruit set, as well as the role of bats as insectivores within the system, can also be linked to shade coffee sites. Prior to examining the differences between an intensely managed, high-input system and a more traditional low-input, diversely shaded one that satisfies the "coffee-as-habitat," it is worth addressing some basic concepts and terms associated with shade coffee, as well as the recent land management history of some coffee regions.

THE ISSUE OF SHADE

The coffee plant we know and love (*Coffea arabica*) developed as an **understory** shrub in what now is the mid-elevational belt of Ethiopia and the Sudan.[4] As a forest species, it does well in shade and has undoubtedly evolved a short-term tolerance for open sun—a situation the native plant has to confront when treefalls or landslides create light gaps in the natural forest. Within this natural setting, we can imagine millennia in which coffee plants existed in a spectrum of shade conditions, ranging from the densely closed forest cover to the open-sun light gap setting. Arabica's most common natural conditions, however, would tend to be a relatively undisturbed forest setting with a fairly heavily shaded understory.

41

Parallel examples of this shade gradient exist throughout the coffee landscapes of the world. Peasant producers, normally with a relatively small holding or two as their only real estate assets, opt for a more diversely managed "coffee" farm compared with large (or even medium) producers. Because peasant farmers must "thread the needle" each year, as J. Berger puts it,[5] striving to do as well as they can with the little they have, they face a daunting array of challenges. Few such farmers are inclined to devote the entire area of arable land to a single cash crop like coffee. Price fluctuations, diseases, natural disasters, and the general need for other items preclude that strategy. As a result, the "coffee" farm ends up being a farm from which the bean is harvested each year, accompanied by a constellation of other foodstuffs and useful materials like fruits, firewood, lumber, and, sometimes, traditional medicines derived from plants.[6] This diverse agroforestry system supplies the land manager with an array of products that can be consumed by the household, given to workers who help with harvesting or other cultural practices associated with the coffee, or sold on local/regional markets for cash.

Medium and (especially) large farmers are not nearly so dependent upon coffee. Either they have other agricultural lands and crops (**catch crops**) or they have other interests that can protect them against the vagaries of nature that could devastate a single-crop small producer. Moreover, a larger coffee farm demands a larger workforce. Where little to no shade is used, less tending of the shade trees means that more time can be spent directly on the coffee bushes' production—**pruning, fertilizing,** and general cultivation. Where shade trees are involved, a one- or two-species shade cover allows for easier maintenance of the canopy, as workers learn the specifics of how the trees grow and respond to pruning. A uniformity of shade maintenance is more easily attained and maintained.

The result of these two approaches to coffee management creates not only the two extremes on the shade continuum—that is, a very diverse, forest-like setting and a less diverse open-sun or nearly shadeless condition—but also the muddied middle ground of slightly shaded, semi-diverse systems found between these endpoints. It is this managed shade cover, essentially a biodiversity *managed* by the farmer, that in turn allows promotion and presence of an *associated* biodiversity.

Coffee areas in various countries display landscapes attesting to the broad array of management styles in production. In general, where government ministries or research institutes have advocated more modern practices in order to increase yields, for instance in Costa Rica, Colombia, or Kenya, management practices tend toward the less shaded or open-sun end of the continuum. In the 1970s, Central American countries saw a tremendous push to intensify coffee production, a process that included the reduction or elimination of shade trees and the introduction of agrochemical inputs. The campaign hinged on the control of **coffee leaf rust** (*Hemileia vastatrix*), a fungal disease considered coffee's worst pest.[7] Countries such as Costa Rica, Colombia, and Kenya had earlier transformed their coffee areas, greatly reducing the complexity of the traditionally managed systems. Such transformations to the agricultural landscape jibe with the general tendency of agricultural intensification, where a more simplified, less diverse system—ideally, a monoculture—can be used, whose main purpose is to increase yields.[8] By contrast, where less technical assistance has prevailed, either due to a lack of national efforts or because the coffee lies in remote regions where producers have escaped the "benefits" of official development efforts, growers seem more inclined to retain and make use of a shade cover. Rice and Ward present data on the extent of traditional versus **technified** coffee area in northern Latin America, estimating that the region's coffee area had been 41 percent modernized or technified, usually involving the reduction or removal of shade trees—in turn usually an integral part of the intensification of production in coffee.[9] The

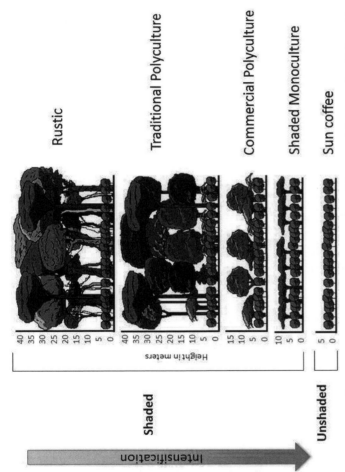

Figure 7.1. Coffee management systems. Source: adapted from Patricia Moguel and Victor M. Toledo, "Biodiversity Conservation in Traditional Coffee Systems of Mexico," *Conservation Biology*, 13, no. 1 (February 1999). Reprinted with permission from Wiley/Blackwell.

coffee landscape of the region, however, presents a mosaic of shade conditions, shaped by the institutional forces mentioned above and the personal choices of the growers themselves. Less is known about other coffee regions, although anecdotal evidence points to similarly varied management styles throughout the coffee-producing world, with intensification of production being promoted or adopted to varying degrees. A consequence of the intensification process is that total biodiversity tends to decline.[10]

What results do these different management styles generate upon the landscape, and how might they affect the farmers involved and the ecology of the systems? Esthetically, a mountainside planted in the curvilinear contours of evenly spaced coffee bushes with no shade trees evokes a certain orderliness. Like hedgerow upon hedgerow, the coffee's regular pattern upon the landscape speaks of constant care and devotion by the grower. But such systems often rank as biological deserts.

Alternatively, a coffee landscape managed with a diverse shade cover presents a hillside nearly indistinguishable from a forested slope. It may be more likely to have early morning mists caressing its flanks and will certainly be home and refuge to an array of bird life (and other wildlife) that its open-sun sibling will never see.

Shaded coffee agroforestry systems contain a species diversity supported by the trees, and the structural diversity, the "architecture" of these systems, mimics that of natural forest. As an agricultural land, however, it cannot and should not be equated to natural forest in its offerings to wildlife and the resultant refuge to biodiversity. Shade coffee cannot be a substitute for natural habitat. But it can be a refuge for biodiversity, providing fairly good quality, supplemental habitat for a number of species.

WHAT WE KNOW ABOUT SHADED SYSTEMS

Certain biological dynamics within agricultural systems are well understood. Entomologists and plant pathologists have studied the life cycle of many insects and pests for decades. But researchers have barely begun to investigate the role that agricultural lands play in providing habitat for organisms that are not pests, thereby enhancing biodiversity protection. How to treat managed lands as potential reservoirs of biodiversity, research on ecological connections, conservation biology, and the potential environmental value of managed lands are all new territory for agroscience.

Shaded agricultural systems like coffee or cacao in an agroforestry setting have been evaluated from the standpoint of agronomic and general ecological aspects provided by shade.[11] Coffee and cacao systems currently attract researchers focusing on the habitat dimensions of the crop management characteristics (there are others, such as rice fields' value for water birds), and although much remains unknown about the ecological potential of such lands, some basic knowledge has emerged. For instance, in a shade coffee farm, the greater the managed biodiversity—the tree species used by the farmer—the greater the diversity of birds found within that system. Local or native tree species tend to harbor greater diversity of birds (and probably insects), most likely due to the co-evolutionary history of these associated creatures. The structural diversity of the shade (its "architecture") also adds to the diversity of bird species found there and can be more critical than the actual number of plant species present.[12]

Shade coffee provides a range of ecological services as well. These are the natural and dynamic processes in natural habitats that "keep the systems going," so to speak. Pollination and subsequent fruit set of the coffee is enhanced in shaded systems, especially where natural forest is nearby. Moreover, there is a degree of biological control within shaded coffee farms compared with less shaded ones.[13] And in terms of native forest tree species recruitment and establishment across the local landscape, shade coffee systems can act as reservoirs for genetic material.[14]

Given the forest-like conditions of these agroforestry systems, it is easy to imagine an array of other ecological services associated with shade coffee. Soil enrichment from continued leaf litter deposits, as well as soil protection from the natural mulch and root networks formed by the trees, provide but two benefits in these forest-like settings. The canopy created by the shade trees obviously acts to intercept the impact of heavy rains upon the soil and channels nutrients via stem and trunk flow into the surrounding soil. As shade tends to suppress weeds that would otherwise flourish in more open-sun conditions, the need for labor or chemical means to control weeds decreases. Not only does the shaded system allow fewer weeds to exist, but more sunlit systems tend to engender a more aggressive weed community.[15] Less well understood, but intriguing from numerous sources anecdotally, is the degree to which shade coffee conditions help mitigate the effects of regional long-term drying trends and landslide hazard related to increased hurricane intensity, itself a product of climate change. Some recent research efforts, as well as personal observations from growers and this author, point to the benefits of shaded systems with respect to such concerns.[16]

SHADE, QUALITY AND YIELD:
BALANCING ENVIRONMENT AND ENTERPRISE

While shaded agroforestry systems may provide a host of benefits, we should not lose sight of the fact that these holdings are managed for the livelihood and/or subsistence of the local land managers. The crescendo in some marketing tactics and trade journals that sometimes equates shaded coffee systems with rainforest or unquestioningly embraces the notion that more shade is better must be placed in context: these holdings are farms on which people must produce a crop to make a living. To avoid the possibility that farmers' survival strategies get sidelined, a cautionary note should be sounded when touting shade's environmental benefits.

Coffee lands, even when ideally managed in terms of mimicking a forest setting and providing the maximum benefits of a habitat, are agricultural lands. They are not natural forest, and we should not portray them as such. They can be managed in such a way so as to enhance their role as a refuge for biodiversity, but the regular disturbance that goes on from the various cultural practices associated with cultivation, as well as their less-than-natural makeup in terms of plant species diversity, precludes their achieving the habitat quality of natural systems.

For that reason, natural forested areas need to be protected for the numerous ecological and esthetic benefits they offer. Shade coffee holdings provide supplemental habitat and ecological services that complement those of natural forests, and, in certain cases, take the pressure off natural resource use within natural areas.[17] The fetching aspects of these shaded systems derive precisely from this dualism.[18] Within the shade coffee systems, there exists a theoretically optimal balance point in shade cover that allows for maximum habitat qualities, while simultaneously not depressing yields.

Some studies reveal the relationship between coffee yields and shade levels. In Chiapas, Mexico, Soto-Pinto and colleagues measured yield in terms of dry weight of coffee fruits per plant.[19] They found that with increased shade levels, yields tend to decline, with the decrease beginning around 50 percent shade cover. Another Mexico-based study in the eastern state of Veracruz found that farms with more diverse shade ($n = 2$) averaged 5,322 kg of fresh coffee cherries per hectare, compared to 3,958 kg/ha for farms where a single species of shade tree dominated ($n = 8$).[20] Another study from that region found no yield differences between rustic and single-species shade coffee systems, even though the two showed significantly distinct foliage cover, shade tree density, shade tree diversity and number of strata within the shade component. Taken together, these studies suggest that there exists an optimal shade cover that simultaneously allows for adequate production and biodiversity protection.[21]

THE SHADED SYSTEM AS HABITAT

Recent investigations have added to our knowledge of shade's role in providing viable habitat, enhancing biodiversity, harboring biological control agents like birds and bats, and creating conditions for pollination of the coffee itself. This growing body of research points to agroforestry system management as an intriguing and potentially important tool for conservation.

Structurally, coffee plantations mimic natural systems quite well. From work conducted in Chiapas, Mexico's coffee sector, coffee plantations (both rustic and planted shimbillo, *Inga spp.*) were compared with a number of different habitat types. In general, both are more similar to natural forest habitats than to secondary (naturally recovering) habitats. Moreover, considering foliage frequency per stratum of plant life, these shade coffee plantations' vegetational structure was most similar to natural to forest categories such as lower montane forest, low-elevation pine-oak woodland, and gallery forest habitats.[22]

For birds, the canopy cover of shade trees can serve as habitat seasonally or throughout the year, depending upon local climate conditions. Where a marked dry season figures into the equation, the shade cover can be crucial. Researchers have found that in Ecuador, the percentage of cover in the upper canopy seems to affect not only occupancy in general but also the tendency of birds to emigrate (leave the system) during the dry season. This "threshold response," as they called it, occurred in the 21–40 percent shade cover range. Upon approaching 40 percent shade cover, not only does the probability that forest birds species (at least the eighteen they evaluated) will make use of the system increase to 1.0 but that, as the dry season progresses, the probability that these species will leave dives to zero. In other words, at around 40 percent shade cover, birds will definitely use an agroforestry system; the same type of cover allows them to remain in place during difficult months characterized by marked dryness.[23] The take-home message from this study confirms that not all shade is equal and that at least 40 percent cover is needed for a number of avian species.

The role of epiphytes within the shade coffee setting has also been examined. Epiphytes are plants living on other plants, such as certain orchid species and most bromeliads. Depending upon the region, the presence of epiphytic bromeliads within the shade tree stratum leads some coffee farmers to remove them from the tree limbs on a regular basis. In the state of Veracruz, Mexico, where growers perceive the bromeliads to be detrimental to the shade trees, epiphyte removal is a common practice. Given that a number of bird species make use of epiphytes in several ways—nesting material, foraging substrates, next sites—bird communities might be expected to change with whatever cultural practices and attitudes related to epiphytes exist on a farm. Epiphyte removal might also be expected to change the microclimate of the setting.

Researchers arranged with a grower in Veracruz to remove epiphytes from some plots as usual but leave them intact in others, in order to compare bird communities.[24] As expected, plots without epiphytes tended to harbor a less diverse bird community, and plots with epiphytes showed a significant difference in average bird abundance throughout the year. Not surprisingly, resident bird species known to use epiphytes as nesting substrates were significantly more abundant in plots where the epiphytic plants were left on the trees.

By capturing, marking, and recapturing birds within the coffee setting, this first-ever experimental design showed that habitat selection by certain bird species can be linked to a single variable—the presence or absence of epiphytic vegetation. The common bush-tanager, a bird that nests and forages in epiphytes in the Veracruz region, moved from plots without epiphytes to those where epiphytes were present. Another bird species that does not make obvious use of the epiphytic component, the golden-crowned warbler, displayed no difference in the probability of movement between the two treatments.[25] Thus, while shade trees can act to provide habitat for birds in general, the nuances associated with certain management practices by growers can lead to a greater understanding of the conservation value of shade coffee systems overall and how best to manage them.

INDIRECT BENEFITS OF SHADE COFFEE AS HABITAT

What emerges from the habitat characteristics of the shaded system reveals some intriguing ecological connections. The presence of birds and other organisms in the shade coffee setting establishes the types of linkages and services not normally associated or recognized with agricultural lands. These connections range from the socioeconomic to more strictly ecological phenomena like the spread and recruitment of tree species within the surrounding landscape.

In Chiapas, a recent study examining the gene flow of a native understory tree (*Miconia affinis*) of the family Melastomataceae revealed strong connections between shade coffee farms and nearby forest fragments. Not only can the farms help cement genetic connectivity with contiguous habitats, but they can actually serve as sources for forest regeneration. Given that both resident and migratory birds disperse the seed of *M. affinis* and that native bees are necessary for pollination, the maintenance of intact, traditionally managed coffee farms (i.e., shaded coffee farms) that can serve as viable habitat for these organisms becomes even more important. The authors concluded that "it is imperative to highlight the ecological function of shade coffee farms, not only in providing refuge for native fauna, but also in preserving habitat connectivity and gene-flow processes essential for reforestation by native tree species."[26]

The value of bees to coffee productivity came into sharp focus when a researcher at the Smithsonian Tropical Research Institute in Panama examined global statistics and the arrival time of the (accidentally) imported African honeybee, which has hybridized with long-established European honeybee populations in the Americas. He concluded that the bees were partly responsible for the increased yields (more than 50 percent) seen during the last two decades of last century in the Americas' coffee regions.[27] The lesson here, too, is that management of coffee that creates or maintains viable habitat for a number of organisms, in this case pollinators, can have positive economic results. These findings coincide with research on coffee and pollinators in other studies and coffee regions,[28] where native bee populations were found also to contribute to pollination services for coffee, and forest remnants as well as shade-diverse farms were seen as quality habitat for bees.

It is worth pointing out that not all bee species that pollinate coffee flowers react similarly to the conditions of the coffee habitat or to the surrounding landscape. In Indonesia, Klein et al. examined fruit set in coffee by looking at the types of bees responsible for pollination.[29] Rare solitary bees showed greater success in inducing fruit set compared with more common social bees and were also more prevalent where light intensity was greater. Social bees, however, showed greater species diversity nearer forests. With the forest-like setting of shade coffee systems, greater social bee diversity would be expected. Given bees' positive role in overall fruit set,[30] shade trees in the coffee agroforestry system may well tend to enhance overall bearing of fruit.

BIRDS, BATS, AND BIOLOGICAL CONTROL

Assuming that the coffee agroforestry system may serve as bona fide habitat, this agricultural setting obviously displays some of the same dynamics found within natural habitats. Organisms interact in innumerable ways, the most basic of which is that of food web relations. From studies of birds as predators within the shade coffee system, we know that traditionally shaded coffee farms indeed provide evidence of such interactions.[31]

A group of researchers familiar with shade coffee and shade cacao from a variety of perspectives and settings conducted a meta-analysis of data found in forty-eight studies. All studies used netted exclosures to exclude birds from the crop itself or from the canopy, and such treatments were paired with open (non-netted) treatments. This meta-analysis sought to address whether the magnitude of bird predation on arthropods (insects, spiders, etc.) (1) differs between the shrub layer and the canopy layer, (2) can be related to the presence of migratory birds, and (3) is associated with bird diversity and abundance.[32]

Combining data from Guatemala and Mexico conducted in coffee agroforestry systems, the authors found that arthropod abundance fell by 46 percent and 4.5 percent in the canopy and coffee layers, respectively. Though scant in terms of number of studies, these subsets of data show a consistent pattern in which birds produce greater impact on arthropods in the canopy.

When seasonality was addressed by examining the contribution to arthropod reduction by migratory birds, the results showed no significant difference for total arthropod reduction. However, for large arthropods (more than 5 mm in length), migrant bird presence did lead to a significant difference in arthropod reduction. Decreases averaged 36 percent when migrants were present versus 24 percent when absent.[33] As for resident birds, a field experiment in Chiapas showed that a diverse shade component associated with coffee creates conditions in which bird predation ranks higher than in less shaded, more vegetationally simple systems.[34] Finally, the data from the meta-analysis study support the notion that bird diversity trumps abundance and density of birds in reduction of arthropods.[35]

An intriguing dimension to the role of birds as consumers of arthropods (i.e., predators and therefore potential biological control agents) emerges from a study in Jamaica's Blue Mountain and Kew Park areas. Researchers excluded birds from coffee plants to examine the degree to which they might be predators of the **coffee berry borer** (*Hypothenemus hampeii*), the *broca* of Latin America, one of coffee's most worrisome insect pests. Birds did have access to another set of coffee plants, the "control" portion of the field experiment. The plants from which birds were excluded had significantly higher levels of borer infestation, more borer broods, and greater damage to the coffee berries. The conclusion was that birds were controlling the insects. Some seventeen species of birds were identified in the study as predators of the borer, with nearly three-quarters being neotropical migrants overwintering on the island. Of these, three warbler species in particular emerged as the primary predators: black-throated blue warbler (*Dendroica caerulescens*), American redstart (*Setophaga ruticilla*), and prairie warbler (*D. discolor*). Average abundance and diversity of birds showed a positive relationship with the amount of shade tree cover as well, and the pest control benefit was determined to average $75/hectare. This is the first study to examine the extent to which birds provide an ecological service by acting as biological control agents against an economically important insect pest. It links the ecological and economic services to conservation via the shade component of the coffee agroforestry system.[36]

Bats also consume insects. Most studies of changes in insect numbers due to natural predators have assumed that, where netting is used to exclude birds from coffee or shade trees, only birds' presence or absence matters. But a clever experiment in Mexico sought to tease out the role of bats as insect predators by placing exclosure netting on individual coffee plants only in the day to exclude birds, only at night to exclude bats, and day and night to exclude both birds and bats, while leaving a control set without exclosures. While both birds and bats play important roles in controlling insects in the coffee system—this was a shaded organic farm with more than 120 species of birds and more than 45 species of bats—the bats figured into the overall insect control throughout the year, adding to the birds' role. Arthropod densities on plants where both birds and bats were kept away averaged 46 percent higher than on the control plants. Most interesting, however, is that bats had a greater impact on insects in the wet season, when their absence from the exclosures allowed for an 84 percent increase in arthropod densities.[37]

Differentiating between diurnal and nocturnal predators with such studies reveals the complexities related to the ecological services of these agricultural systems. With bats' well-known role as insect predators, coupled with the fact that their numbers are dwindling globally, the crucial need to maintain viable habitat for them becomes evident.

Another meta-analysis, conducted using twenty-seven data sets that addressed shade coffee's role as a refuge for biodiversity, assessed the system's ability to harbor species richness of birds, ants, and trees.[38] The focus of the study was land management intensification and its effects upon the diversity of these three taxa. The data allowed the authors to establish a management index based on the degree to which coffee sites in all the studies had been intensified. The intensification gradient follows the shade gradient in figure 7.1 for the most part, with a number of vegetation characteristics used to define the levels of intensification, and the management index being proportional to management intensity.

Not unexpectedly, tree diversity declines as the management index increases. Birds and ants also show species loss with intensification, with ants being more sensitive to management practices. All coffee management categories showed a loss of ant richness, which was mirrored by losses in bird richness—except for rustic and shade monoculture systems.[39] Dwindling forest bird species correlate significantly with the management index, indicating that losses are greater as the management practices become more intense.

One insight gleaned from this study relates to resident birds versus migrants. As management intensifies, resident bird richness tends to fall off. In contrast, migrant birds showed no discernible loss in richness as the management index increased. However, their species richness did decline in most of the coffee systems when compared to forest.[40]

CONCLUSIONS FOR POLICY MAKERS AND CONSUMERS

Many of the studies of shade coffee and its ability to provide a viable habitat for a range of animals support the notion that there can be a positive correlation between conservation and the marketplace. That is, certain management practices can result in varying degrees of habitat protection and provision. For agricultural planners and policy makers in **producing countries**, the shade coffee option offers a double benefit. It can serve as a land management strategy to provide supplemental habitat to natural landscapes (protected forests, forest remnants, riverine or gallery forests, etc.), as well as provide a livelihood to the thousands of families that depend upon coffee directly or indirectly. For countries concerned about preservation of biodiversity and rural poverty, shade coffee provides a nexus for the attention that governments need to give to both. For consumers, the shade coffee issue—in particular those coffees that have a shade certification like Bird Friendly® or Rainforest Alliance Certified™—offers a chance to make purchases that support growers involved in good land stewardship. For both policy makers and coffee consumers, these management strategies allow for the linkage of conservation to the market place.

NOTES

1. R. Greenberg, P. Bichier, and J. Sterling, "Bird populations in rustic and planted shade coffee plantations of eastern Chiapas, Mexico," *Biotropica*, 29, no. 4 (1997): 501–14; J. Wunderle and S. Latta, "Avian resource use in Dominican shade coffee plantations," *The Wilson Bulletin* 110, no. 2 (1998): 271–81; C. Tejeda-Cruz and W. Sutherland, "Bird responses to shade coffee production," *Animal Conservation* 7 (2004): 169–79.

2. T. Ricketts, "Tropical forest fragments enhance pollinator activity in nearby coffee crops," *Conservation Biology* 18, no. 5 (2004): 1262–71; S. Jha and C. W. Dick, "Shade coffee farms promote genetic diversity of native trees," *Current Biology* 18, no. 4 (2008): R1126–R1128; K. Williams-Guillén, I. Perfecto, and J. Vandermeer, "Bats limit insects in neotropical agroforestry system," *Science* 320 (2008): 70; A. M. López-Gómez, G. Williams-Linera, and R. Manson, "Tree species diversity and vegetation structure in shade coffee farms in Veracruz, Mexico," *Agriculture, Ecosystems and Environment* 124 (2008):

160–72; A.-M. Klein, I. Steffan-Dewenter, and T. Tscharntke, "Fruit set of highland coffee increases with the diversity of pollinating bees," *Proceedings of the Royal Society, London, B* 270 (2003): 955–61; A.-M. Klein, I. Steffan-Dewenter, and T. Tscharntke, "Bee pollination and fruit set of *Coffea arabica* and *C. canephora,*" *American Journal of Botany* 90, no. 1 (2003): 153–57.

3. Robert Rice, "Agricultural intensification within agroforestry: The case of coffee and wood products," *Agriculture, Ecosystems, and the Environment* 128 (2008): 212–18; R. Rice, "Fruits from shade trees in coffee: How important are they?" *Agroforestry Systems* 83, no. 1 (2011): 41–49; P. Moguel and V. Toledo, "Conserver produciendo: Biodiversidad, café orgánico y jardines productivos," *Biodiversitas* 55 (2004): 1–7.

4. Another species, *C. canephora,* suited to lower elevations, is the other economically important type of coffee globally.

5. J. Berger, *Pig Earth* (New York: Pantheon, 1979).

6. Rice, "Agricultural intensification." Small producers throughout Latin America relate how a number of plants left to grow within their coffee growing areas are used in making home remedies for various maladies.

7. R. Rice, "A place unbecoming: The coffee agroecosystem in Latin America," *Geographical Review* 89, no. 4 (1999): 554–79.

8. T. Tscharntke, A. Klein, A. Druess, I. Steffan-Dewenter, and C. Thies, "Landscape perspective on agricultural intensification and biodiversity-ecosystem service management," *Ecology Letters* 8 (2005): 857–74; P. A. Matson, W. J. Parton, A. G. Power, and M. J. Swift, "Agricultural intensification and ecosystem properties," *Science* 277, no. 5325 (1997): 504–9.

9. R. Rice and J. Ward, *Coffee, Conservation, and Commerce in the Western Hemisphere,* 1996, Smithsonian Migratory Bird Center, White Paper #2.

10. J. Vandermeer, M. van Noordwijk, J. Anderson, C. Ong, and I. Perfecto, "Global change and multi-species agroecosystems: concepts and issues," *Agriculture, Ecosystems & Environment* 67 (1998): 1–22.

11. J. R. Muschler Beer, D. Kass, and E. Somarriba, "Shade management in coffee and cacao plantations," *Agroforestry Systems* 38 (1998): 139–64.

12. J. M. Vandermeer, et al., "Global change"; R. MacArthur and J. MacArthur, "On bird species diversity," *Ecology* 42 (1961): 594–98.

13. J. Kellermann, M. Johnson, A. Stercho, and S. Hackett, "Ecological and economic services provided by birds on Jamaican Blue Mountain coffee farms," *Conservation Biology* 22, no. 5 (2008): 1177–85.

14. Jha and Dick, "Shade coffee farms."

15. C. Staver, F. Guharay, D. Monterroso, and R. Muschler, "Designing pest-suppressive multistrata perennial crop systems: Shade-grown coffee in Central America," *Agroforestry Systems* 53 (2001): 151–70.

16. S. Philpott, B. Linb, S. Jha, and S. Brines, "A multi-scale assessment of hurricane impacts on agricultural landscapes based on land use and topographic features," *Agriculture, Ecosystems and Environment* 128, nos. 1–2 (2008): 12–20.

17. Rice, "Agricultural intensification."

18. But see I. Perfecto, J. Vandermeer, A. Mas, and L. Soto-Pinto, "Biodiversity, yield and shade coffee certification," *Ecological Economics* 54 (2005): 435–46; C. Gordon, J. Sundberg Manson, and A. Cruz-Angon, "Biodiversity, profitability, and vegetation structure in a Mexican coffee agroecosystem," *Agriculture, Ecosystems and Environment* 118 (2007): 256–66.

19. Lorena Soto-Pinto, Ivette Perfecto, Juan Castillo-Hernandez, and Javier Caballero-Nieto, "Shade effect on coffee production at the northern Tzeltal zone of the state of Chiapas, Mexico," *Agriculture, Ecosystems and Environment* 80 (2000): 61–69.

20. S. Philpott, W. Arendt, I. Armbrecht, P. Bichier, T. Diestsch, C. Gordon, R. Greenberg, I. Perfecto, R. Reynoso-Santos, L. Soto-Pinto, C. Tejeda-Cruz, G. Williams-Linera, J. Valenzuela, and J. Zolotoff, "Biodiversity loss in Latin American coffee landscapes: Review of the evidence on ants, birds, and trees," *Conservation Biology* 22, no. 5 (2008): 1093–1108. No data on actual percent shade cover

were measured in this study, but diverse shade normally corresponds with higher percent cover than single-species or less diverse shade systems (personal observation).

21. Y. Romero-Alvarado, L. Soto-Pinto, L. García-Barrios, and J. F. Barrera-Gaytán, "Coffee yields and soil nutrients under the shades of *Inga* sp. vs. multiple species in Chiapas, Mexico," *Agroforestry Systems* 54 (2002): 215–24. Open-sun coffee systems obviously produce more coffee—and demand higher inputs like agrochemicals—but offer little in terms of habitat or soil protection.

22. Greenberg, Bichier, and Sterling, "Bird populations."

23. R. Mordecai, "A threshold response to habitat disturbance by forest birds in the Chocó-Andean Corridor, northwest Ecuador," talk presented at a panel, "The Value of Shade Coffee," Partners in Flight Meeting, McAllen, Texas, February 2008.

24. A. Cruz-Angón and R. Greenberg, "Are epiphytes important for birds in coffee plantations? An experimental assessment," *Journal of Applied Ecology* 42 (2005): 150–59.

25. A. Cruz-Angón, T. S. Sillett, and R. Greenberg, "An experimental study of habitat selection by birds in a coffee plantation," *Ecology* 89, no. 4 (2008): 921–27.

26. Jha and Dick, "Shade coffee farms."

27. D. Roubik, "Tropical agriculture: The value of bees to the coffee harvest," *Nature* 417 (2002): 708.

28. T. Ricketts, G. Daily, P. Ehrlich, and C. Michener, "Economic value of tropical forest to coffee production," *PNAS* 101, no. 34 (2004): 12579–82; T. Ricketts, "Tropical forest fragments enhance pollinator activity in nearby coffee crops," *Conservation Biology* 18, no. 5 (2004): 1262–71.

29. A.-M. Klein, I. Steffan-Dewenter, and T. Tschartke, "Fruit set of highland coffee increases with the diversity of pollinating bees," *Proceedings of the Royal Society, London, B* 270 (2003): 955–61.

30. A.-M. Klein, I. Steffan-Dewenter, and T. Tschartke, "Bee pollination and fruit set of *Coffea arabica* and *C. canephora*," *American Journal of Botany* 90, no. 1 (2003): 153–57.

31. J. Vannini, "Nearctic avian migrants in coffee plantations and forest fragments of south-western Guatemala," *Bird Conservation International* 4 (1994): 209–32; Greenberg, Bichier, and Sterling, "Bird populations"; J. Wunderle and S. Latta, "Avian resource use in Dominican shade coffee plantations," *The Wilson Bulletin* 110, no. 2 (1998): 271–81.

32. S. Van Bael, S. Philpott, R. Greenberg, P. Bichier, N. Barber, K. Mooney, and D. Gruner, "Birds as predators in tropical agroforestry systems," *Ecology* 89, no. 4 (2008): 928–34.

33. Van Bael et al., "Birds as predators."

34. I. Perfecto, J. Vandermeer, G. López Bautista, G. Ibarra Nuñez, R. Greenberg, P. Bichier, and S. Langridges, "Greater predation in shaded coffee farms: The role of resident neotropical birds," *Ecology* 85, no. 10 (2004): 2677–81.

35. Van Bael et al., "Birds as predators."

36. Kellermann et al., "Ecological and economic services."

37. Williams-Guillén et al., "Bats limit insects."

38. Philpott et al., "Biodiversity loss."

39. Not showing a loss of bird richness in the shade monoculture seems counterintuitive, but it is explained by the authors as being caused by two of the three studies in Veracruz, Mexico, having extremely high richness levels. The *Inga spp.* shade cover in these shade monocultures was tall and dense, creating an ambience more similar to a commercial polyculture; Philpott et al., "Biodiversity loss."

40. Philpott et al., "Biodiversity loss."

8

A Guatemalan Coffee Farmer's Story

A Challenging Life in a Beautiful, Harsh Land

Carlos Saenz

I am a small coffee farmer from Guatemala. I live in Genova Costa Cuca, Quezaltenango, about 50 kilometers south of the Mexican border. Coffee plantations cover about 2.5 percent of Guatemalan territory; there are roughly 90,000 producers, with 45 hectares as the average farm size. Today we are confronting a new crisis whose roots go back well into the twentieth century. My family had to muster a great deal of courage to overcome the many obstacles of the last few decades; their determination has given me the chance to continue cultivating coffee. Finca Las Brisas—The Breezes—is the name of the farm that my family has worked throughout four generations, me being the fourth.

I grew up learning day to day from my grandfather, who taught me simple things about the harvest. For example, when I was a little boy I watched the women taking their baskets to collect coffee, and I wanted to participate, so I took my own basket and did the job myself. Or when the tractor passed by the main house taking coffee seedlings to the fields, I ran up to the farm cart to take it with the workers. Little by little I started to really like the crop. I have learned so many things living on the farm in good years as well as bad. For me, cultivating and processing coffee is not a job; it is a way of living, of doing what I really like. I enjoyed it so much that when I graduated from high school I decided to study agriculture at Universidad Rafael Landivar in Guatemala City, about four hours from the farm. However my grandfather was the one who taught me how to be a farmer and to manage things from real life, beyond what we learned in college.

Today, I'm proud to say that I sell roasted coffee (ground or whole bean) locally and to institutional businesses (hotels, restaurants, hospitals, etc.) and work daily to improve my quality standards.

THE CIVIL WAR IN GUATEMALA

Guatemala lived through a long period of political insecurity, in which violence, distrust of government and law, and a culture of fear dominated the country. That culture continues to this day. Producers suffered from kidnappings, murders, invasions, arson of plantations or complete farms, and heavy "war taxes," levied by rebel fighters. The amount of money that had to be paid to them varied depending on the size of each farm; the bigger the farm the higher the war tax. One year the levy might have been the whole crop and the next year it could have been the money intended for payments to the workers. The guerrillas' purpose was to keep the landowners in fear so that most of them didn't return to their farms. The guerrillas always said that if we didn't pay them they were going to take the lands.

The guerillas visited our farm many times. This group split off from the army of Guatemala because one group of soldiers didn't agree with the ones in charge. They adopted the flag of the people most in need in the country, the really poor ones. The rebels wanted to take the lands, especially coffee farms, and give them to all these people. Actually today some of the ex-guerrillas form part of our government. They would ask us to give them "war taxes" in the form of food, money, or simply time. We were sometimes obligated to listen for hours to horror stories about the government and the army, while the guerrillas tried to convince us that what they were doing was correct. We could only listen and give them something to drink or eat and obey their commands. We had to give them what they wanted or else they would burn the farm or kill us. They would appear from anywhere, from streets or highways, or from any direction in the mountains. From the government side, soldiers were killing entire villages that they assumed had connections with guerrillas. There were problems from both sides. People around our finca lived day by day with fear because we really didn't know what could happen; there were killings in the region.

Peace agreements between the government and the rebels, finally signed in 1996, were meant to bring an end to the longest war in our history, one that had lasted 36 years. The problems of the war years had a terrible impact on the entire national economy. Still today, every week, I fear something terrible may happen. This insecurity is something we live with constantly all around the country. It is hard to imagine a possible solution to the security problem since we don't have a government that provides security or law enforcement. In Guatemala you cannot even trust people who are in charge of our security.

Poverty, hunger, unequal land distribution, and racism continue. The indigenous people suffered specially because of lack of opportunities and education. But the profound, continuing impact of the civil war is not the only problem we face; there are other important challenges for Guatemalan coffee farmers. The government has never provided any policy or support for coffee farmers who want to invest or succeed.

PRICE DROP

In 2001 the price of coffee fell from over $1 a pound on the world market to less than $0.50. This collapse was largely due to the increase in supply from Vietnam, which became a major coffee producer by the late 1990s, and because of the increases in Brazilian production. The price drop has been a total disaster for us. One of our main difficulties is paying off the farm debts. It's hard to obtain loans at a low interest rate, for there has been a general lack of confidence in the coffee business during this period. For this reason, over the past seven years, we have paid a high rate of interest for loans, 20 percent annually, and have to pay a large amount of money every month to the banks. Since we wanted so much to keep the farm, our only option was to go deeper into debt. Some other farmers had to sell their lands and move to other regions of the country.

During this crisis, many big farms that produced prime coffee and extra prime had disappeared because they were not paid well compared with prices for the hard and **strictly hard bean** (SHB) coffee. And more small farmers in the high altitude mountains started cultivating coffee, producing strictly hard beans. The future for those farmers is bright because of the quality beans they can produce at high altitudes. The main difference between strictly hard beans and primes or extra primes is the acidity that is more accentuated in the SHB beans as well as a more intense aroma and body.

Mine was one of the prime coffee farms that were about to disappear. In addition, it is widely said that the average coffee farmer receives about 1 percent of the price of a cup of coffee bought in a café. This is why I decided to add value to the **green coffee** I produced. I invested in a coffee **roaster**, purchased with a loan at 18 percent, so that I could take production from the seed to whole bean or ground, bagged coffee. Taking control of more steps in processing coffee provided me with extra income, helping to preserve my family's tradition. Some of the farms in the area are beginning to offer ecotourism, which is attractive to people who like the coffee environment.

The government started to promote agricultural diversification in the late 1990s, so that farmers didn't have to depend on just one crop, and if there was a decrease in price it wouldn't cause a national crisis. The government finally did something positive for coffee farmers. I already had the roaster at this time, but not enough customers to consume the amount I used to produce. My only way out of the problem was to eliminate more than half of the coffee plantation. Huge swaths of land that formerly held coffee with beautiful stands of shade trees lay smoldering or blackened, being readied for planting pastures for fattening cattle. My grandmother told me once, "You are the only one in this family who has the guts to throw the coffee plantation away." I also have one part of the farm planted in rubber trees, which helps the farm to stay stable. Working hard, twelve hours daily, six days a week, I have been able to expand my coffee production again and increase my sales of roasted coffee, so I've been able to replant. The *finca* has 110 hectares total, of which 45 are now planted with coffee. The rest has been planted with rubber trees.

MAIN CHALLENGES

In continuing to produce high-quality coffees, our main challenges are labor scarcity, high oil prices, global warming, and competition from big farmers and large agrobusinesses. Our coffee-growing costs, including fuel and other inputs, constantly increase. However, the biggest expense is hand labor, especially in picking coffee. We rely on hand labor because the topography means we cannot mechanize; most of our slopes are too steep to run machinery over them.

My pickers are families that live near the farm. But that's not the case for all farms, most of which have to transport pickers from long distances because of a lack of workers in their regions. The conditions in which pickers live vary from farm to farm. On my *finca* they live in concrete houses with running water and electricity generated on the farm. We also provide a piece of land to each family so that they can cultivate corn for themselves. Of course there are problems with roads, bridges, and infrastructure everywhere, so it can be very difficult to move from one place to another.

SUCCESS

For coffee farmers, success is producing **specialty coffee** that commands a high price. If certain other conditions, particularly the problems of labor and interest rates are solved, farmers can do this in Guatemala: our coffee is cultivated in the best volcanic soils of the globe, under natural shelter and with an adequate combination of **altitude** and specific microclimates of each region. For this reason Guatemala's coffee is positioned as a high-quality product. In Central America, Guatemala is the largest exporter, followed by Honduras and Costa Rica, respectively.

The use of large trees for shading coffee is a Guatemalan coffee-growing custom and is said to have been initiated here. Coffee grown under the proper level of **shade** takes longer to mature, which favors the development of rich and complex flavors. Shade-grown coffee is an agroforestry crop that combines the goals of **sustainable** agriculture with environmental protection. Many species of birds, reptiles, and insects live in these trees and are admired by people who visit us, especially friends and family. I don't offer ecotourism at the farm, but it is something we want to do in the future. Since our coffee is shade grown, we form part of Guatemala's coffee forests, which bring environmental benefits, like protecting soils, biodiversity, and water resources, and help in diminishing the harming effects of global warming.

The biggest support for coffee farmers is provided by ANACAFE, the Guatemalan National Coffee Association. It operates local offices that give small farmers like me access to technical seminars and workshops, regional coffee fairs, and other services. ANACAFE offers services like **cupping** seminars, lab analysis, market information, and service centers. ANACAFE's main goal is to promote internal quality coffee consumption. We are seeing that the market inside Guatemala is growing. More and more people, especially young ones, are starting to drink coffee. The country's **Cup of Excellence** competition is highly beneficial because it results in people constantly demanding more quality coffee. Producers are working harder to obtain the quality the market is asking for.

Providing employment and education is another big success of coffee. About 9 percent of the country's working population is employed in the coffee sector. To help everyone in the business, the Coffee Foundation for Rural Development, FUNCAFE, works to achieve human development in rural coffee communities. The foundation runs educational programs and health centers and promotes food security. The last program teaches people how to produce and prepare nutritive food made from all sorts of esculent plants produced in a garden, for example, small bunches of carrots and beet-root leaves, beverages, ice creams, marmalades, and many other types of food preparations. I believe that all the efforts the foundation carries out are giving positive results, especially with all the families that have been suffering because of the natural tragedies of the last several years.

At Finca Las Brisas we have renewable energy because we have a hydroelectric facility. My grandfather set it up sixty years ago, and we are operating it with the same equipment he installed back then. With it we can do **wet processing** of harvested coffee and provide reliable electric energy for the main house and the homes of the workers, which have two bedrooms, a kitchen-dining room, and a bathroom.

OPPORTUNITIES AND POSSIBLE SOLUTIONS

We intend to look for markets in Asia and Europe to obtain better prices for our coffee, which will reflect the high quality of our product. Today the U.S. absorbs about 40 percent of Guatemalan coffee exports. As a strategy we have to go beyond the **C price** contract; we aim to move coffees toward the premium-price markets like certified coffees, specialty grades, and in-country auctions of excellent coffees. About 10 percent of my coffee is now sold as **C coffee**; the rest we sell locally, already roasted and ground. My expectation for the future is to sell my coffee already roasted directly to the U.S.

We also intend to produce coffees that command an even higher price, for example **organic.** Right now we don't have any type of **certification**, but we are working on that. Corruption is everywhere here in Guatemala and certifying coffee is no exception.

Finally I can say that despite the problems we have faced we are thankful for having the opportunity to produce one of the best coffees of the world.

9

Pickers

Robert W. Thurston

At the bottom of the coffee **commodity chain** in terms of income are hired agricultural laborers, especially pickers. These are not necessarily unskilled people; anyone who has picked coffee will say that the job is not easy and that to do it right takes at a minimum some experience. Unless the technique is crude **strip harvesting**, the **cherry** should be twisted slightly as they are pulled from the tree's branches. Forcefully pulling ripe fruit straight out from a tree can damage a branch and harm the next year's crop.

Pickers also have to be able to work on slopes that are steep, slick with moisture and often mud, and located at altitudes where the air is thin. Sometimes the hillsides are so hard to work on that the pickers tie themselves to larger trees. One false step and hours of work can be spilled down the mountain. Stinging insects may also visit the trees and the humans.

Pickers must work fast, for two reasons. First, they are typically paid by the weight of the cherry they bring in, with deductions for too many defective fruits, branches, or other excess material. It is not unknown for some temporary hands, especially if they are not regulars on a farm, to add to the weight of what they deliver to a collection point by loading a few stones into a basket. Second, when the coffee is ripe, it needs to be picked quickly, lest the cherries overripen on the branches and start to ferment, turning them into **raisins.**

Picking is hard physical labor. While not exclusively a man's job, male pickers predominate in the fields. Often pickers have to be able not only to fill basket after basket tied around the waist and then empty each full one into a large sack but also to lift the sacks onto a truck and from there into a collecting basin. It's a humbling sight to witness an endless loop of workers picking up sacks of wet coffee cherries; when a 125-pound person lifts his or her own weight onto a shoulder repeatedly during a day, then day after day, the wear and tear on the body is severe. Nevertheless, I have met pickers who have done this kind of work for four decades.

Family members, of course, are often pickers as soon as they can reach even the lower branches of the trees. Kids may start to harvest coffee at the age of seven or eight. The temptation or the necessity to keep children out of school in order to help on the farm is often powerful, so that many young pickers never get the education that would be necessary to lift them out of manual labor into better jobs. In Hawaii into the 1950s, the school year in some areas was arranged to allow children time off to participate in the harvest.[1]

Figure 9.1. A member of the La Pita, Nicaragua, coffee co-op picking in 2004. Photo by Wayne Gilman.

Figure 9.2. Three pickers relax after a long day on La Combia Farm, Colombia, 2008. Behind them is a building with showers and lockers. Photo by Robert Thurston.

Besides the physical difficulties of picking coffee, it is always seasonal work. The job may continue for several weeks, since the cherries do not all ripen simultaneously, and pickers may have to make four or more passes through the orchards to collect all the mature fruit. Workers may start at lower altitudes and over the course of several weeks go higher and higher, including going to different farms situated at different levels above the sea. Pickers may migrate from one region of a **producing country** to another, or across a border, as Nicaraguans often do to work in Costa Rica or other countries. But, usually sooner than later, the annual harvest is over. Somehow the hired hands, or the family members, must make a living until the next harvest. As Price Peterson noted earlier, they don't always survive.

Arnoldo Leiva, head of the Costa Rican Specialty Coffee Association, told me that Nicaraguans who come to pick in his country never seem to earn enough money to buy their own land back home. "What I've found is that they're at least able to save money and send it back to their relatives in Nicaragua. But I doubt they're making enough money. Actually, when they finish the harvest season in coffee they move to oranges, melons, sugar cane, and some of them try to stay in construction as well. But in the case of Nicaragua this is a matter of basically surviving for them because there's no jobs in Nicaragua."[2]

How much do pickers get paid? This brings the story back to the vexed question of the cost of a cup of coffee in the consuming world compared to the money farmers or workers (**peasants**) receive for coffee beans. In my various travels and readings, I have heard many figures on how much pickers have earned. Here is a short list:

- Brazil and Cuba into the 1880s: zero. Pickers were slaves.
- Kona, Hawaii, 1928: $1–1.25 per "bag," 110–120 pounds of cherry. A good picker could fill ten a day. Then in the Depression, pay fell to 40 cents a bag.[3]
- Coopedota, a co-op in Santa Maria, Costa Rica (CR), 2008: $20–40 a day.
- Café Cristina, a private farm in Paraiso, CR, 2008: $30–40/day (though a really good picker on a good farm in the region can earn twice that amount).
- Colombia, a general report from 2008: "800,000 people are employed each year during the coffee harvest season; most of these workers migrate from one region to another searching for farms where the harvest is still in progress. The most skillful pickers are able to collect up to 550 pounds of ripe berries per day making around $30 US dollars."[4]
- Finca La Esmeralda, Boquete, Panama, 2008: As Price Peterson noted, Indians who come down from the high mountains to pick his coffee can make several hundred dollars each in a few weeks. Peterson has provided housing with separate rooms, showers, and toilets. A nurse, a dentist, and a doctor if necessary visit the pickers every week while they are on the farm.[5]
- Seraozinho farm, Sao Paulo state, Brazil 2010: Pickers can make $1,200 a month, working for 24–26 days. But this figure refers to men driving mechanical harvesters.
- Guatemala: "Conditions for coffee workers on large plantations vary widely, but most are paid the equivalent to sweatshop wages and toil under abysmal working conditions. . . . coffee pickers have to pick a 100-pound quota in order to get the minimum wage of less than $3/day. A recent study of plantations in Guatemala showed that over half of all coffee pickers don't receive the minimum wage, in violation of Guatemalan labor laws. Workers interviewed in the study were also subject to forced overtime without compensation, and most often did not receive their legally-mandated employee benefits. The total average income reported was Quetzales 1006 ($127.37/month)."[6]

Pickers, that is, those who harvest coffee fruit with their hands, will certainly continue to be of great importance on the farms that put most emphasis on quality. However, just as in the U.S. tomatoes, grapes, and a host of other crops are not picked by American citizens but by poorly paid immigrants who work by the season, it will become increasingly difficult in producing countries to find reliable pickers.

As the educational and living standards rise in any country, picking coffee becomes less desirable work. Costa Rica and Hawaii are perhaps the best examples of this trend; in both, it is difficult to find local people to do hard, dirty jobs. The success of a coffee-producing country can therefore be measured in a crude way by how hard it is to find people on the spot to pick the fruit. Questions of where to get labor, how much people must be paid to pick, and whether small mechanical devices can be developed to work on steep hills are pressing issues in many areas.

NOTES

1. Gerard Y. Kinro, *A Cup of Aloha: The Kona Coffee Epic* (Honolulu: University of Hawai'i Press, 2003), 62.

2. Interview with Arnoldo Leiva, San Jose, Costa Rica, May 27, 2008.

3. Kinro, *Cup of Aloha*, 32. The bag size is taken from a personal communication from Kinro to Shawn Steiman, May 1, 2012.

4. A post by Andres Castro on Barista Exchange, November 24, 2008, http://www.baristaexchange .com/group/farmersproducers/forum/topics/do-you-want-to-know-more-about.

5. For more on pickers in Panama, see Emily Haworth, "Coffee Pickers: Why Should We Care?" post on coffeegeek.com, May 8, 2012.

6. A post by the Organic Consumers Association, no date, but probably 2000. Unfortunately, the study mentioned for Guatemala is not cited. At http://www.organicconsumers.org/starbucks/coffeelabor.htm, accessed April 29, 2012.

10

Coffee Processing
An Artisan's Perspective

Joan Obra

If you only think of coffee as a beverage, you're missing most of the experience. For those of us lucky enough to work with coffee from harvest to roast, taste is just one part of the adventure. We begin at the tree, tugging ripe coffee cherries from branches. We continue with fingers in untoasted coffee, pulling out broken bits. And we end with long, airy sips of coffee, critically evaluating the flavors in the cup.

Along the way, we ask questions. Do we want the delicate, clean feel of a washed coffee? Or the more assertive, fruity aroma of a naturally dried coffee?

All of the steps in processing transform the seed of the coffee fruit into green beans ready to be roasted. I hate the term **processing.** It's too vague and inelegant for the art of coaxing flavor from coffee. It doesn't hint at the complexity of crafting artisan beans. "Processing" fails to emphasize the importance of our jobs as coffee producers; simply put, if we deliver defective beans, no skill in roasting or brewing can make that coffee exceptional.

What actually happens during processing? After harvest, the goal is to dry the coffee seed while preserving its taste potential. Most times, we remove multiple layers of the coffee **cherry** and expose the **seed** as it dries. Sometimes, we dry the seed inside the whole coffee cherries.

Every drying method runs risks of ruining the final cup. Mold is a big threat, as is **fermentation:** too much of either and unwanted flavors can appear. With all of this in mind, let's take a closer look at coffee processing by Rusty's Hawaiian, my family's company. Our laboratory is a twelve-acre coffee farm and micromill in the Ka'u District, a vast, rural area on the southern side of the Big Island of Hawaii.

Perched on the Mauna Loa volcano with a view of the ocean, this old sugarcane field seduced my parents. After seeing it in the late 1990s, Rusty and Lorie Obra took a chance on an early retirement, sold their house in New Jersey, and moved to Hawaii. Rusty dreamed of creating high-quality coffee in Ka'u. But he died in 2006, leaving Lorie to fulfill his vision. Since then, her **green beans** have won several domestic and international awards.

How did Lorie meet my father's expectations? Here's our theory: she approaches coffee processing with the sensibility of a chef. Instead of building flavors in, say, a beef stock, she builds flavors in coffee beans before they're roasted. With the mentorship of R. Miguel Meza, the former roastmaster of Paradise Roasters in Ramsey, Minnesota, Lorie learned the **flavors** desired by the **specialty coffee** industry.

She and Miguel study the different characteristics of our farm's coffee **varieties,** such as 'Red Bourbon,' 'Typica,' 'Yellow Caturra,' and 'Red Caturra.' Lorie processes them in different ways, with the goal of highlighting certain flavors in each one. "I'm always trying to figure out how each coffee wants to express itself," she says.

Lorie can spend years tweaking a processing method before she is satisfied. Taking this approach isn't easy, especially with the limited equipment and resources of a tiny family operation. But we feel the investment in research and development is necessary. In the United States, where labor costs are high compared with other coffee-producing countries, we must compete with excellence, not low prices.

The payoff can be big. After two years of experiments, Lorie and Miguel developed a processing method that heightens the acidity and sweetness of the 'Red Bourbon' variety. Called Kenya-style Red Bourbon, this coffee won the 2011 Hawaii Coffee Association's statewide cupping competition.

Our price of $25 per 3.5 roasted ounces, or more than $114 a pound, reflects the distinction and rarity of the Kenya-style Red Bourbon. We have only about 120 trees of this variety. Last year, we quickly sold out of the crop.

Other producers have taken a similar strategy of focusing on quality and have also fetched high prices for green beans. For example, Finca El Injerto has won the prestigious **Cup of Excellence** Competition in Guatemala multiple times. Earlier this year, El Injerto auctioned off a rare lot of its coffee for $210.50 per pound. It consisted of the rare 'Mocca' variety, treated with **washed processing.** That figure is astronomically higher than the average cost of $2–$3 per pound of specialty-grade green coffee.

Now that the reasons for a quality-driven approach are clear, it can be examined in practice. First, there are many ways to process coffee. Producers adjust their methods depending on scale, equipment, resources, and location. Our experience is just one example, and it is by no means definitive.

Much of the action at our little mill begins in the late afternoon, with the arrival of up to hundreds of pounds of coffee cherries. We examine them anxiously. Most of the time, the harvest shows varying degrees of ripeness.

Lorie pours the cherries into buckets filled with water. Using small colanders, we scoop up any floating cherries and set them aside. These so-called floaters contain low-density beans that won't roast properly. We dump the rest of the cherries onto wire racks and begin to sort them by color. Depending on the quality of the harvest, we may sort coffee by hand until after midnight.

Greenish, underripe cherries are removed, because they'll make coffee taste astringent and grassy. Brown, overripe fruit also is discarded, because they lend a fermentation flavor to coffee. Beyond these choices, there's a range of ripeness that we must evaluate, cherry by cherry. Our ideal: a ripe coffee cherry with full color, which will lend sweetness to the cup.

After this step, it's time to consider other factors. For the next few days, for example, the weather forecast may indicate lots of sun and wind. The beans will dry quickly, so it's a perfect time to make honey coffee. Also known as **pulped natural** coffee, honey coffee is one of our most labor-intensive products. But there's a payoff: If done correctly, its sweetness is terrific in espresso blends.

We pour the 'Typica' cherries into the pulper. The pale coffee seeds, wet with **mucilage,** spill out and pile into a plastic bin. We lug the coffee beans to wire racks, spread them out, and shut down for the night.

Joan Obra

Early the next morning, I'm back at the wire racks with a wooden rake. My task: rake the beans periodically until they're no longer sticky. If I'm lucky, the coffee will dry to the touch by early afternoon. But if it rains, or if there is no wind, I'm stuck at the racks for the better part of a day. Otherwise, the beans may clump together like caramel popcorn and run the risk of turning moldy. Throughout the day, Lorie checks on my progress and looks at the coffee.

Soon, she's picking out anything broken, misshapen, or discolored.

By the end of the day, her pile of rejects has grown. She'll continue removing defective beans during the next few days, until the coffee has sufficiently dried for long-term storage. At this stage, the beans are covered in a papery covering known as **parchment**. Afterwards, it's a waiting game. We let the coffee beans rest for a few months to let their flavor mature.

When we think it's time, we pull out a sample. The parchment is tinted a light golden color from the dried fruit. Lorie pours the beans into the huller, which strips them of their papery skins. "You smell that?" she says. Now missing their parchment covering, the green beans have a light scent of sweet berries.

After roasting them, it's time for a taste test. Miguel hands me a white ceramic cup with the ground coffee. It smells like honey. When we taste it, Miguel points out the berry flavors, fuller body, and sugar-like sweetness in the cup. "It has more intense aromas than a washed 'Typica,'" he says. There's only one thing left to do: remove any **defects** in the green beans. Depending on the amount we need, we'll pull out the defects by hand or machine.

This is just one example of a processing method. Equally challenging are natural 'Red Caturra' and natural 'Yellow Caturra.' For natural-process coffees, we don't remove the cherry

Figure 10.1. A fabulous bunch of 'Typica' cherries, Musula, Honduras. Photo by Martha Casteneda.

skins. Instead, we place the coffee cherries from these varieties directly on separate wire screens, then rake them frequently to prevent mold and to dry them quickly. The results are sweet grape flavors in the 'Red Caturra' and tropical fruit in the 'Yellow Caturra.'

A less labor-intensive coffee is washed 'Typica.' We use the pulper to strip the skins off coffee cherries. Then we cover the beans with water and allow them to ferment overnight. This is the most important part of the washed process. Lorie discovered that small differences in the amount of liquid and the length of fermentation have a drastic impact on flavor. Her goal: soak the beans in water long enough to bring out bright flavors and floral, berry, and citrus tones.

The following day, we scoop the beans out of the water and spread them in thin layers on wire screens. Fermentation has removed the mucilage clinging to the beans, making them easier and quicker to dry; without the sugary mucilage, molds are less attracted to the seeds. We rake the beans occasionally to speed the drying process.

Of course, Lorie continues to tinker with these methods and others. Like roasting and brewing, coffee processing is a delightful mix of science and art—and a heck of a lot of work.

So when you drink your next cup of, say, washed 'Caturra' from Finca Villa Loyola in Colombia, think about the processing method. Imagine that coffee producer soaking pulped coffee beans in water or sniffing a handful of green beans. Think of the producer's satisfaction in producing artisanal coffee, as well as the intimate connection to the experience. Better yet, visit our farms and mills. Chew on a coffee cherry. Peel parchment off of green beans. We guarantee that coffee will never again be just a drink.

11

Women in Coffee in Colombia

Olga Cuellar

In Colombia, gender inequalities have permeated all aspects of agriculture, including coffee, through production, harvesting, postharvesting, distribution, and marketing. But women's presence in coffee farming has increased significantly over the last several decades, and women now seek further advancement through the global market.

Profound economic and social changes in the past few decades have helped promote these trends. The introduction in Colombia of free trade in coffee during the 1990s as the **International Coffee Agreement** ended, guerrilla activity, violent displacement of communities, male migration to towns, and the lack of rural job opportunities have all contributed to change.[1] In the last twenty years, Colombian conflicts between guerrillas, paramilitaries, and militaries have cost the lives of at least 70,000 people. More than 3 million people have been internally displaced and many have "disappeared," in the classic Latin American sense, killed by one side or another. War and violence were not considered a perversion of politics but efficient mechanisms to achieve political goals.[2]

These factors present new challenges and opportunities for the Colombian coffee industry. The situation has fostered the rise of market interest in coffee produced by women, the creation of female associations that increase the visibility of women's needs, and the attention of national and international organizations that improve access to financial support.

Since the mid-1980s, new concerns within the coffee industry, and in some cases national and international programs arranged by international firms with producers, have led to an increasing commitment to provide equal opportunities for men and women, thus creating more balanced socioeconomic opportunities for producers without discrimination based on gender, race, class, or ethnicity.

Migration patterns, new methods of coffee production, a growing global market, and a decline in income due to the absence of male producers have all led to an increasing number of women actively involved as coffee producers in order to provide daily sustenance for their families. As Deere and León de Leal indicate, in the 1960s, women's presence in agricultural labor was related to the lack of alternative employment opportunities and male migration to urban settings.[3] Although women did contribute to agricultural production, men were still considered the primary farmers. The same authors suggest that agricultural decisions were part of the male domain.[4]

Today, the demands of capitalism and local circumstances have transformed labor divisions and perceptions of appropriate work for women. In regions where men migrate from the countryside in search of work, changes in gender-related labor division have affected local attitudes that designate men as the primary agriculturalists and breadwinners. Women and young children frequently remain in rural areas, while husbands and teenage sons and daughters migrate, leading to what has been called the "feminization of agriculture."[5]

In the last decade, policy makers, researchers, and agricultural development organizations have begun to acknowledge an increase in female participation and have sought to engage women in development and sustainability projects. Before the early 1990s, little attention was paid to how the transformation of the coffee industry affected women's everyday activities. Now development projects regularly incorporate a gender perspective. Moreover, some development agencies, including the World Bank, the United States Agency for International Development (USAID), the International Co-operative Alliance (ICA), the Food and Agriculture Organization of the United Nations (FAO), and the United Nations as a whole, have resolved that by 2015, besides eradication of hunger and poverty, gender equality and the empowerment of women's lives, especially in rural areas, must be achieved.[6] Several programs within the coffee industry also reflect interest in helping women obtain leadership positions and enhance marketing. Organizations such as the **Coffee Quality Institute** (CQI) and the **International Women's Coffee Alliance** (IWCA) are in the process of evaluating how programs can better address women's needs. This article considers the voices of those not usually heard at the national and international level regarding their experiences in the coffee value chain, from farm production to marketing.

My research focuses on one organization, the Asociación de Mujeres Caficultoras del Cauca (Association of Women Coffee Growers of Cauca, AMUCC), in the state of Cauca, Colombia. Cauca is well known to coffee buyers for having the appropriate altitude, climate, and soil to produce exceptional coffee.[7] Yet owing to the sociopolitical context, the state of Cauca has struggled to stay informed of new advances in coffee production and to improve market opportunities.

This case study focused on the formation of a women's association and the adoption of new coffee quality standards in order to participate in the international market. AMUCC fits into to what Goodman calls the "moral economy,"[8] as the organization was formed due to an appeal from a medium-sized Spanish coffee roaster, SUPRACAFÉ.[9] The roaster established a **direct trade** relationship with AMUCC to sell their coffee in Spain. In this arrangement, quality and ethical values will translate into premium prices, economic benefits such as assistance to build infrastructure, and organizational aid to female members of AMUCC.[10]

In the summer of 2007, I conducted in-depth interviews with nine leaders of AMUCC, as well as with other informants. Twenty-one other women filled out surveys. I wanted to explore how women perceive themselves and their level of participation when they form part of a mixed gender association and how they perceive themselves as coffee growers and members of strictly female associations, as well as their roles in AMUCC's decision-making process. I also spoke with husbands, sons, and other male relatives.

CAUCA

AMUCC is located in Popayán, the capital of the state of Cauca, in the southwestern corner of Colombia, facing the Pacific Ocean to the west. Cauca has approximately 1,250,000 inhabitants[11]; AMUCC has members in twelve of Cauca's forty-one total municipalities. The regional economy is mainly based on agricultural production, including coffee, sugar cane, fique (a natural fiber), and other cash crops.[12] Cauca forms part of one of the seven coffee production regions in Colombia.

Cauca has been populated by indigenous peoples, their Afro-Colombian descendants, and **peasants** (*mestizos*). Historically, land distribution and ownership have created conflict among these diverse populations. As a result of the resistance of the large haciendas' owners to the redistribution of land, struggles have occurred in the past. In the early 1970s the Páez and the Guambianos (indigenous communities) as well as some peasants who occupied private land invaded more than twenty haciendas in the state of Cauca.[13] Agricultural laborers in coffee have also demanded a regulated wage and welfare and social security benefits. Workers have claimed abuse by landowners.[14] The 1959–60 Agricultural Censuses showed that almost 50,000 Colombian farmers did not have titles to the lands they occupied and that farm managers operated over one-third of Colombia's agricultural land.[15]

A principal objective of Colombia's 1994 Agrarian Reform Law was to eliminate the inequitable concentration of rural property. Most of the land struggles during the late 1960s and early 1970s accompanied the emergence of agrarian capitalism, that is, production for the market.[16] After the land reform, small-scale producers represent 64 percent of all coffee growers in Colombia. They own an average of one hectare per producer: 28 percent own 1–3 hectares, 5 percent own 3–5 hectares, 4 percent own 5–20 hectares, and just 0.56 percent own more than 20 hectares.[17]

Most of the economic struggles of Caucan peasants still revolve around lack of access to land, inequality of land distribution, difficulties in agricultural production, and competition with products imported from Ecuador, which have been subsidized by the Ecuadorian government. The combination of these economic and social struggles has led some peasants to begin cultivation of illicit crops, especially coca.[18] Cultivation of illegal crops has some benefits, such as a secure market, ease of transport, and greater profit than other agriculture products. Controlling production of illicit crops was and continues to be a complex challenge for the government and local agencies. One woman coffee producer told me, "It is the reality. Money from coca is easy; you have to work less and you get more. But at the same time it brings more violence to the community."[19]

The Land Reform of 1994 reassigned around 12 million hectares for redistribution to 65,000 rural families by 1998.[20] Although generally successful, the reform produced several new problems. More than a few peasant and indigenous communities had to resettle and migrate to other areas. Many poor peasants were excluded because they lacked the documents necessary to acquire credit, they had unpaid debts, or the land was overpriced.[21] Moreover, some distributions were based on political favors and gave preferences to certain local elites. This unequal distribution only created more conflict among various groups. The new legal codes promoted the movement of peasants from one state to another, resulting in overpopulation in some regions. According to Grusczynski and Rojas,[22] in 2003 more than two-thirds of the land distributed in 1994 presented high levels of desertion, indebtedness, and, in many cases, abandonment of lands. Yet agrarian reform in Colombia in the early 1990s included among potential beneficiaries poor peasant women or female heads-of-household who previously did not own property. Thus land redistribution increased the number of independent women farmers.

Knowledge about agricultural quality is not easily disseminated in Cauca. This is due partly to a dearth of technical assistants who help all coffee producers in the state. According to conversations with some coffee technicians in Cauca in 2007 (based on information from the 1997 Coffee Census by the Federación Nacional de Cafeteros de Colombia [FNCC]), there were only 800 of them for more than 85,000 coffee producers. Nonetheless, coffee production in Cauca has become more specialized, producing documented origin and differentiated coffees, which have special qualities that add market value. At the same time, rural problems have led women to become more involved in coffee production and to actively participate in all stages of the coffee **value chain**. These changes helped prompt local initiatives to organize women's groups or organizations, among them AMUCC.

A PORTRAIT OF AMUCC

AMUCC was formed in 2002 at the request of SUPRACAFÉ. This company, another Spanish foundation,[23] and the local cooperative CAFICAUCA[24] were interested in developing a line of coffee produced by women. The first attempt took the form of a program for women that later turned into an association, AMACA (Asociación de Mujeres Agropecuarias del Departamento del Cauca). Three hundred women from a single municipality formed this group. After just one year, a misunderstanding took place among AMACA, SUPRACAFÉ, and the cooperative, leaving AMACA to sever ties with the cooperative and the Spanish company.

The two sponsoring organizations did not give up. They formed a new association that included women from across different municipalities in Cauca. This was the birth of AMUCC. Today, this association has 390 members—all women—who are producing coffee.

Each side in this arrangement has a specific role. The Spanish coffee company is the buyer and evaluator of the coffee's quality. The Spanish foundation provides financial backing to the association. The role of the cooperative is to store, hull, pack, and export the coffee to Spain. AMUCC's goals, as well as those of the Spanish coffee buyer, include coffee production that focuses on social and environmental **sustainability**, in addition to improving living standards for coffee producers and their communities. Negotiation with the Spanish buyer generates more opportunities for women members to sell their coffee at better prices and establishes networks that create more options in the international market. In addition, producers are becoming familiar with **marketing** processes. They are learning how to deal with coffee buyers, while becoming aware of the quality of the coffee they have produced in order to obtain better prices. The women conduct production cost and revenues analysis, interpret coffee price fluctuations, and learn how to adjust to them, among other practices that facilitate their access to the international market.

AMUCC's wide coverage in Cauca makes its membership highly heterogeneous. Within the association there are substantial differences in socioeconomic status, determined largely by home municipality. For example, municipalities close to Popayán are more developed. Women from these communities have better access to infrastructure, land, and economic assets. On the other hand, women who live in southern Cauca, far away from Popayán, have less access to such facilities and possibilities. This situation makes a considerable difference in production costs and in the challenges women face in growing, transporting, and marketing coffee.

On average, members of AMUCC have from one to three hectares of land per producer. In the state of Cauca, this plot size is considered small-scale production. Medium-scale producers have from five to eight hectares, and large producers have more than ten hectares. In 2007, AMUCC produced 2,500 bags of coffee, the equivalent of 10 exportable containers. From these, the Spanish buyer purchased 40 percent, with the rest sold to local buyers.

To become a member of AMUCC, a woman had to own at least one hectare of land (with a legal title), on which she had to produce high-quality coffee. As they considered joining

AMUCC, women had more leverage to demand legal title to land from a husband, family, or the government. Once in the organization, women had much better access to the coffee market, recognition as coffee producers, credit and cash income, training, and other services. In some cases, these factors transformed the way women, families, and community members perceived gender roles and women's participation as producers in the coffee sector. Moreover, when women have the opportunity to become active participants in commercial production, they often increase their decision-making power within the household and the community.[25]

THE EMERGENCE OF WOMEN PRODUCERS IN CAUCA

The state of Cauca has been characterized as a colonial region in which class, gender, and ethnicity have played profound roles in the construction of social and political relationships. Cauca was populated by Spaniards, and a Catholic heritage has influenced Caucanos' patterns of behavior, activities, and labor division. In Cauca, additionally, there was a big difference in the sense of gender roles and family traditions between rural and urban dwellers. Women in rural areas were expected to do household chores and participate in communal responsibilities that did not require a long commute from home. As a result, Caucanos assumed that there was a natural gendered labor division, excluding women from active participation in public spheres such as the market and other political and economic institutions. Nevertheless, in reality women and men share the same spaces and they divide their responsibilities according to their necessities.

Cultural patterns stereotyped "women's roles" and "men's roles," a dynamic reinforced by political and religious organizations. For example, the FNCC and other coffee organizations excluded women. The country's customs have been strongly patriarchal. Into the mid-1960s, women could not take part in forming coffee associations, which hampered their role in communities' decision-making processes.[26] Nevertheless, local and external circumstances caused women to get close to the public sphere.

AMUCC has experienced the problems and challenges of creating a women's organization. At the same time, the association's story illustrates interactions among the diverse participants in the coffee industry (coffee producers, associations, cooperatives, FNCC, NGOs, buyers, roasters, and consumers) and how complex it is to establish direct trade, which includes traceability and a more secure market for women. Women in AMUCC have demonstrated their capacity to improve quality practices in coffee production and to strengthen their organization. By sharpening these skills, women have been able to target a promising international market. As this has happened, women have gone from being virtually unnoticed participants in coffee to high visibility in the market and as primary coffee growers.

Members of AMUCC began to address topics such as access to land, technical knowledge and assistance, inputs (agrochemicals, infrastructure, and transportation), credit and capital, and the implementation of high-quality standards and sustainability. In order to meet the demands of European roasters interested in women-produced coffee, the cooperative CAFI-CAUCA developed the program Mujer Caficultora (Woman Coffee Grower) in 2000.

AMUCC TODAY

AMUCC is an association of 390 women. The membership is heterogeneous, composed of married women (77 percent), single women (10 percent), and single heads of household (13 percent). Additionally, some members are from the indigenous communities of Guambianos (2 percent). The average age of AMUCC women is forty years old; there are few young members. Most women have children, an average of four per family. The educational level of women in the sample was typically middle school, while eight from the twenty-four finished only first or second grade. Among the participants there is just one professional, an agronomist.

In order to join AMUCC, women must demonstrate that they own the land where they grow coffee. According to a survey conducted by CAFICAUCA in 2005 among all of its members, on average women own two hectares of land per producer, a statistic confirmed by my survey. Women gained legal rights to land in two different ways. About 20 percent of the twenty-four AMUCC members whom I interviewed have title to the property. Another 60 percent possessed a notarized paper stating that the owner—the woman's family or her husband—gave total right and control of a piece of land to the woman. The other 20 percent had no legal claim but were in the process of obtaining a valid document; to join AMUCC, these women must have at least a provisional document.

IMPACT OF AMUCC IN WOMEN'S LIVES, HOUSEHOLDS, AND COMMUNITIES

More than a housewife, now I am also a coffee producer.

—Yolima, member of AMUCC, July 2007

Today I am not just a housewife, I am also a coffee grower. . . . maybe I always was, but I did not identify myself like this.

—AMUCC participant[27]

When asked why they decided to become coffee growers, many women answered that they were raised in the coffee industry and had never considered an alternative. For them, growing coffee was a way to survive in the future from a women's associa-tion? Women's responses about the formation of a female group were all related to the new opportunity of being considered as coffee growers and marketers. One woman said "Before, we [women] did not know which coffee our husband took to sell to the local town, we did not know how much he earned, how much he spent, nothing. We were outside the business."[28] Another AMUCC member, Ana, recalled that "we [women] did not have any rights. . . . men always have been privileged by the FNCC and other organizations." Camila commented, "we were also workers but were not recognized for it." Finally, Amelia noted that "women always depended economically on their husbands, they were in charge of selling the coffee. . . . Now women can do it also."[29] In general, AMUCC members were pleased to have the opportunity to organize, unite, and experience a positive change in the coffee industry.

I asked AMUCC members why they thought the association was only for women. What benefits do they receive now, and what do they expect in the future from a women's associa-tion? Women's responses about the formation of a female group were all related to the new opportunity of being considered as coffee growers and marketers. Other women chose to grow coffee because it was then easier for them to work at home, where they could take care of their children and household chores. Still other women started to grow coffee ten years earlier because they thought it was a viable economic option. Just one converted from growing illicit crops to coffee, because she and her husband realized that coca brought violence and more social conflict to the region.

Women mentioned several tangible and intangible benefits that AMUCC provided: access to the specialty coffee market by establishing a direct trade relationship with the Spanish buyer, acquiring materials to build solar dryers, and gaining more knowledge about coffee, prices, new markets, and buyers' demands. Ana noted, "before we produced coffee and did not acknowledge quality standards, prices, certification and better trade for our coffee."[30] Several coffee buyers I spoke to felt that women add a special and unique touch to the coffee industry, their ability to translate theory into practice, to produce quality, also their community focus and their capability to establish priorities in order to benefit their families and their communities, create a better scenario in coffee trade.[31] Income, naturally, is a central concern for women: Yolima said, "what motivates me to participate is to have another standard of living, that's what we want to have . . . our pesitos [money]."[32] Another respondent said, "Now I do not have to ask for money, also if I want I can provide education and supply the need of my children. This is a great feeling. Before my economic contribution was less. Now I could be become a role model for my own children and community."[33]

Participants in the association noted that among their own gender, they felt more confidence, received support, and had the opportunity to network with women from other municipalities with whom they could share experiences. Association members also mentioned that being in a group of just women could allow them to receive external support from the market and from organizations interested in working with female coffee growers. In sum, women's associations allow women to feel comfortable and to create an environment in which they can talk, give their opinions, and learn how valuable their contributions to coffee production are. These feelings were also shared by women members of other coffee associations in Cauca: "I was afraid to talk, but since I have been participating in the association I am not shy anymore. Now I am not afraid to talk with important people, such as international buyers. If I have to talk, I do. I see how other women are afraid to express themselves and talk in front of multitudes. . . . I understand . . . but this is a process where you will lose that fear when you start to speak up."[34]

The women in the study were affected on a personal level. Women mentioned several times that one of the most memorable days as part of AMUCC was when they got the chance to travel to Popayán to participate in a meeting. They see membership in AMUCC as an opportunity to escape from their daily activities as housewives and function as businesswomen. They have become more economically independent of their husbands and have the feeling of contributing to their household expenses. Women members from other associations have described similar transformations in their lives. A female member of ASOMUCA (Asociación de Mujeres de Cajibio) said, "Since we [women] are members of a group of only women, we learn to speak up, we learn to negotiate with our husbands. . . . this is a great benefit, we have won a space in our homes."[35]

However, women also indicate an increase in their work. As Meertens mentioned, a work day for rural women consists not just of tasks in coffee production but also household chores.[36] On average women work sixteen hours a day and men fourteen hours in rural areas in Colombia. In extreme cases women work four or five hours longer than men.[37] An activity especially burdensome for women has been cooking for wage laborers, an average of ten per day, during the coffee harvest. Preparing food is an activity exclusively carried out by the women. Even when these women had to attend the meeting in Popayán, sell coffee to cooperatives, or attend a training day, they still had to get up early to prepare food.

But husbands and younger members of the family have begun to help women more. For example, in the case of cooking for laborers, husbands began to take food to the fields and to wash the dishes, chores that only women used to do.[38] When husbands were asked what they think about their wives' new roles, most men first expressed acceptance. However, when the conversation continued, they complained about women's new carelessness in some aspects of household tasks. Some men protested that women were spending more time outside of the home. Despite such complaints, most husbands support their wives' efforts because the household benefits economically. Natalia's husband said, "I think her participation has been beneficial for us, now we have solar dryers because of that . . . that helps improve quality in our coffee."[39]

A member of AMACA called membership "a process of awakening," in which women strengthened their capabilities.[40] She also thinks women have gained more ownership over the association because they have had to become more involved in all the processes, as well as learning about all the market. Another member, Alicia, said, "Now we are not anymore in a paternalistic relationship, we were and we did not want that this partnership ended like that. . . . We learned a lot, we think and act by ourselves. . . . Now we know where and how to go. . . . We have today a better business vision and we learned about accountability, administrative and management process. For me, we are on the right path.[41]

Other women were pleased about what they had learned but also expressed a need for even better information: "Before we just knew a few things about coffee, now we are aware of cost of production, profits, and international prices in the market. But we need to learn more. . . . There is a long way that we [women] have not crossed yet." Another woman in a focus group said, "We in this process have been able to improve coffee quality through accessing information about quality standards, but in order to continue improving we need more consistent technical and training assistance."[42]

Finally, being part of AMUCC has brought some changes in women's communal life. In a municipality with eighty members of AMUCC, the association seems to have had a great impact. The leader of this community mentioned that the group has helped unify neighbors and families. This community has suffered from violence and a high presence of guerrillas and paramilitaries. According to this respondent, AMUCC is the first formal organization in the municipality. Florina stated that "one of the consequences of violence is the loss of trust in the community, people tend to isolate themselves, they are afraid and there is no cooperation. . . . Nevertheless, since we have been part of AMUCC there is more collaboration, integration and we are starting to re-create community bonds."[43]

Additionally, women mentioned that when other women from the municipality observe improvements, this instills hope. Therefore, as Yolima noted, "a lot of people are seeing women working and getting something back, thus people [women] get motivated and even if they are currently not a member of any association, they get motivated to work in the field."[44]

In sum, the significance of the AMUCC association for women is a source of "development, peace, growth, a new space for women, a place in which we can share with other women, friends and coffee growers all the difficulties, struggles, as well as the successes we have been through, a context from which we learned a lot, and a significant space in which we come out ahead and we have been able to speak up as women."[45]

LAND, POWER, AND MONEY

Another gain has been the women's access to land. In Cauca, access to land was not limited for women, but it was expected that women were part of a family farm and that the owner of the land was the head of the household, usually a man. In many regions, moreover, women are not recognized as the primary agriculturalist within a family. This translates into their inability to access or inherit land. In some regions in Latin America, even if a woman can inherit land, it is expected that she will renounce, share, pass on, or sell it to a male relative.[46]

Women inherit land when they are the only daughter or when there are no male members left in the family. Also, if the mother is a widow or her husband abandons her, this makes it easier for the daughters to inherit the land. A female producer in Costa Rica mentioned that, "I am glad that I never met my father. I can imagine if he was there I could not be here, I could not have land, and my life would be totally different. With my mother as the head of household, I was able to have land and be here today as a coffee grower with my own land."[47]

Members of AMUCC also identify as owners of land with the ability to gain other assets, training, technical assistance, and key information for the production of high-quality coffee. As Amelia pointed out in the interview, "Today I can say this lot of land, this farm is mine."[48] As another woman said, "We now can access our own piece of land; I manage it, and I know how much I invest on it and how much I can earn. That makes a huge difference."[49] Women's income represents financial independence for them, which contributes to their sense of having more authority and decision-making power in the household and community.

In sum, women members of AMUCC are today more than coffee growers and marketers: they are also owners of land, economic contributors to their families, role models for their children, leaders in their communities, and representatives of a new sociopolitical position in Cauca. Women's visibility in both production and marketing of coffee is thus increasing.

As the International Research Workshop on Gender and Collective Action[50] pointed out, access to information is a power resource that changes attitudes about family and economic alternatives.[51] As a result, although some of the relationships the women of AMUCC are involved in are still highly unequal, they now coexist with greater opportunities for independent action by the producers.

Moreover, women can share knowledge of practices and strategies with other women inside or outside of AMUCC. They are learning how to access information, lead, organize, and maintain the association. Their experiences with the market are giving women the tools to create better opportunities in this same market, and this translates into women having power to decide and negotiate.

As a result of women's increased access to land and their improved profits, women can now also obtain loans and credit. The majority of AMUCC members do not have credit today, but they are planning to apply for credit in the future in order to invest in their farm or to buy land. Also, being a member of AMUCC facilitates the application and approval of bank loans.[52] As is demonstrated in an FAO study, in Colombia women who have achieved property rights have better access to credit.[53]

Global restructuring of the coffee industry, together with changes in local forms of patriarchy in coffee areas, continually reshape women coffee growers' lives. Today, no one engaged in coffee production can escape the demands of the international coffee market. Coffee growers in many countries are now forced to seek alternative sources of income, such as producing specialty coffee, in response to these new pressures and demands.

Over many years, women in Colombia have participated in the work of the farm as well as of the house. Now the National Federation of Coffee Growers, as well as other NGOs and local institutions, have recognized that AMUCC is a collective group of women who work effectively in coffee and who operate projects targeted to meet the specific needs of women.

As a result of international gender equity policies and the creation of new organizations that include women, today governmental and nongovernmental programs are highly interested in working and creating partnerships with AMUCC, since they see the association as an exemplary role model for other women's organization in Colombia. For instance, the president of AMUCC was invited to participate in the Specialty Coffee Association of America (SCAA) Exhibition and Conference in May of 2008.

Nothing in this study is meant to imply that women's continuing roles as housewives and mothers have become unimportant. On the contrary, women can combine their tasks and develop their roles as mothers and wives as well as producers and marketers. This will undoubtedly increase their work at home and on the farm in certain respects, but it is an economic opportunity for them and a way to meet household needs.

There is no "fairy tale" where women will rise one day as coffee growers, produce their coffee, and sell it with consistent success on the international market. Nor is there any easy solution to basic problems of poverty. Sometimes pessimism creeps in: Florina said, "the cost of production is more and more expensive every day and what we get from coffee is to pay what we already owe and after we pay that, our hands are empty again. . . . We cannot save. . . . Sometimes I see there is no future for us."[54] As women coffee producers begin to access the international market, no linear process of growth and development occurs. Rather, a cycle of growth and stagnation occurs, affected by many factors. This is not a simple commodity transaction of production and consumption. It is also a life cycle that involves human, economic, and social capital, as well as external factors such as price fluctuations, environmental conditions, and definitions of quality set by the buyers and coffee industry in relation to terms negotiations and marketing strategies.

Coffee is a commodity and a business; in order to be commercially viable, it has to attract consumers. Women's participation in the specialty coffee industry is not neutral. The bigger companies use coffee produced by women as a marketing strategy, without assuming a real social (in addition to economic) relationship with the female producers, one that would go beyond paying a better price and would recognize coffee producers' work while taking local circumstances into account.

Even with all of the advances that this group has achieved, it must be emphasized that variables such as increasing industrialization of coffee production, the use of new technologies, fluctuations of prices, and political violence in Colombia influence coffee production and shape women's decisions. Women located in insecure areas sometimes have to pay insurgent groups a percent of the money that they bring back to the municipality. They may have to ask for permission to become members of the association, and they are aware that this permission and other agreements could change, depending on the person in charge of a guerilla-paramilitary group.[55]

In the more secure areas, many women have a higher socioeconomic status, have more access to land, sometimes own cars and trucks, and have a better socioeconomic class position. Also, children are able to attend private schools and some of them were even attending colleges in Popayán. Young populations that belong to these higher socioeconomic groups have greater economic and academic opportunities.

Even though in this research women acquired access to land and other infrastructure assets, as well as membership in a legally constituted coffee association, economic independence and the ability to make their own decisions for their land was often limited where men were still considered the primary coffee growers. Women continued to be immersed in the family system and supported by their husbands. Women and men in Cauca considered the fact that women were getting more accessibility and recognition important; however, husbands were concerned about the idea that these new patterns will change established relationships in the family.

Much writing about agriculture links women to subsistence farming and men to commercial production. But Caucan women are not merely "helpers"; they are full coffee producers for the national and international market.[56] The division of labor in coffee production remains important, but no simple gender-based division exists. Interviews with producers indicated that members of the household divided their tasks according to individual abilities, skills, and preferences. In some families, men recognized that women have been developing better strategies to produce high-quality coffee, and these men decided to apply those same methods to their own production. In one of the families that I visited, a husband said, "My wife goes to those workshops and she learns how to improve our production, when she gets here she teaches me and we put in practice that knowledge in our farm."[57] Moreover, women declared that men also contributed to their improvement and often the sexes complemented each other, helping and establishing a collaborative and efficient system in which each one took turns assuming the same task in the coffee production, depending on the circumstances.

In summary, the objective of the household is to carry out activities that maintain its members, following culturally defined "normal" standards of living.[58] Therefore, a new program or policy should not interrupt processes that have already been arranged within the family. Future projects need to understand coffee farmers' family patterns and dynamics, as well as their mode of work as a family system. The focus on individuals and women as coffee growers and marketers is a recent phenomenon. Hence, the issues over the division of labor and the struggles for greater independence for women are new experiences for the entire family.

AMUCC opened new alternatives for household maintenance and enhanced women's visibility. However, members are immersed in family, community, and a specific region. Coffee production occurs in a family context, set in turn in broader social and cultural institutions. As Jelin points out, "family was never, nor will be, detached or isolated from wider social, political, and economical determinations."[59]

True change must be the result of a long-term process shaped by attitudes about family and gender. Considering the family as the basic unit of production allows project organizers and business managers to understand how local people construct their own reality. This approach is fundamental to success, since it enables program directors to comprehend points of view of various members of a specific community. Always the multiple forces shaping a community, including history, physical and natural environment, and local customs, must be taken into account.

NOTES

1. Edelmira Pérez Correa and Luis Llambí Insua, "Nuevas ruralidades y viejos campesinismos: Agenda para una nueva sociología rural latinoamericana," *Cuadernos de Desarrollo Rural* 59, no. 4 (2007): 51.

2. G. Sánchez, "Guerra y política en la sociedad colombiana," *Análisis Político*, no. 11 (1990), 9–11.

3. Carmen Diana Deere and Magdalena León de Leal, "Rural women and the development of capitalism in Colombia agriculture," *Women in Latin America* 5, no. 1 (1979): 64.

4. Deere and León de Leal, "Rural women," 65.

5. "Confronting the Crisis in Latin America: Women Organizing for Change," Isis International and Development Alternative with Women for a New Era (DAWN), 1988; Farah and Perez, *Mujeres rurales*;

Jane S. Jaquette and Gale Summerfield, eds., *Women and Gender Equity in Development Theory and Practice* (Durham NC: Duke University Press, 2006), 143.

6. UN Web Services Section, 2005, State of Public Information, United Nations, http://www.un.org/millenniumgoals/, accessed March 11, 2012.

7. Olga L. Cuellar interviews, Fieldwork in Cauca and Bogotá, Colombia, August 2007.

8. David Goodman writes in "The International Coffee Crisis: A Review of the Issues," that, "Using labels and other discursive devices, intensely 'local' narratives of coffee-growing communities and their farming practices are transported to distant global markets, building a relational 'moral economy' between producers and consumers." In Christopher Bacon, V. Ernesto Mendez, Stephen R. Gliessman, David Goodman, and Jonathan A. Fox, eds., *Confronting the Coffee Crisis: Fair Trade, Sustainable Livelihoods, and Ecosystems in Mexico and Central America* (Cambridge, MA: MIT Press, 2008), 9.

9. Since 1990 Supracafé S.A. has specialized in the import and buying of exclusive high-quality coffees. They exclusively sell high-quality, naturally roasted 100% pure arabica coffees with gourmet classification, among other products such as specialty teas, sugars, and chocolates and a range of coffees (http://www.supracafe.com/ingles/empresa.htm).

10. AMUCC receives a premium for its coffee, above the market price, from the Spanish Roasting Company.

11. Luis Solis-Gómez, *Los pueblos del Cauca*, 2nd ed. (Popayán, Colombia: Libros de Colombia, 2000).

12. Misión Rural, "Una perspectiva regional," *Informe final*, 9 (Bogotá, Colombia: IICA con TM Editores, 1998), 60.

13. Leon Zamosc, *The Agrarian Question and the Peasant Movement in Colombia: Struggle of the National Peasant Association, 1967–1981* (Cambridge: Cambridge University Press, 1986), 82.

14. Zamosc, *Agrarian Question*, 144.

15. Dale Adams, "Colombia's land tenure system: Antecedents and problems," *Land Economics 42*, no. 1 (February 1966): 45.

16. Zamosc, *Agrarian Question*, 74.

17. Encuesta Nacional Cafetera, Gerencia Técnica, Oficina de Estudios y Proyectos Básicos Cafeteros, Sistema de Información Cafetera SICA, Bogotá, 1997.

18. Misión Rural, "Una perspectiva regional," 60.

19. Cuellar interviews, June 2007.

20. Saturnino M. Borras, "Questioning market-led agrarian reform: Experiences from Brazil, Colombia and South Africa," *Journal of Agrarian Change* 3, no. 3 (July 2003): 377.

21. Roberto Forero, "Evaluación de Proyectos Piloto de Reforma Agraria en Colombia: Informe Preliminar, Junio 15 de 1999," unpublished World Bank document.

22. Diana Gruszynski and Manuela Rojas, "Notas sobre una reforma agraria distributiva y consideraciones sobre el sistema de seguimiento de la política," *Planeación & Desarrollo XXXIV*, no. 2 (2003).

23. Café Mundi was founded in 2004 by diverse small and medium-sized coffee roasters and has the objective of developing some programs in coffee producer countries. Its mission is to develop programs with a social responsible perspective, and its main goal is to improve coffee growers conditions. http://www.cafemundi.org/quienessomos.htm.

24. *Revista CAFICAUCA: Comercialización con sentido social*. Popayán: CAFICAUCA, 2005.

25. Ana Spring, ed., *Women Farmers and Commercial Ventures: Increasing Food Security in Developing Countries* (Boulder, CO: Lynne Rienner Publishers, 2000), 1.

26. Cuellar interviews, June–July 2007.

27. Cuellar interviews, June 2007.

28. Cuellar interviews, May–June 2007.

29. Cuellar interviews, June 2007.

30. Cuellar interviews, June 2007.

31. Diverse independent coffee buyers, May–June 2007.

32. Cuellar interviews, May 2007.

33. Cuellar interviews, July 2007.

34. Woman member of AMUCC, Cuellar interviews, July 2007.

35. Cuellar interviews, June 2007.

36. Donny Meertens, "Women's Roles in Colonisation: A Colombian Case Study," in *Different Places, Different Voices: Gender and Development in Africa, Asia, and Latin America*, ed. Janet Monsen and Vivian Kinnaird (New York: Routledge, 1993), 264.

37. Meertens, "Women's Roles," 266.

38. Cuellar interviews, June–July 2007.

39. Cuellar interviews, July 2007.

40. Cuellar interviews, July 2007.

41. Cuellar interviews, July 2007.

42. Cuellar interviews, June–July 2007.

43. Cuellar interviews, June 2007.

44. Cuellar interviews, June 2007.

45. Cuellar interviews, June 2007.

46. Carmen Diana Deere and Magdalena León de Leal, "The Importance of Gender and Property," in *Empowering Women: Land and Property Rights in Latin America* (Pittsburgh: University of Pittsburgh Press, 2001), 7.

47. Cuellar interviews, October 2007.

48. Cuellar interviews, July 2007.

49. Cuellar interviews, July 2007.

50. As reported in Lauren Pandolfelli, Ruth Meinzen-Dick, and Stephan Dohrn, "Gender and collective action: Motivations, effectiveness," *Journal of International Development* 20 (2008): 1–11.

51. And see Lourdes Beneria and Saviti Bisnath, ed., *Labor Standards, Women's Rights, Basic Needs: Challenges to Collective Action in a Globalizing World* (New York: Routledge, 2004).

52. Cuellar interviews, July 2007.

53. FAO (Food and Agriculture Organization), "La Situación de la Mujer Rural en Colombia," 2006, 96.

54. Cuellar interviews, June 2007.

55. Cuellar interviews, June–July 2007.

56. Spring, *Women Farmers*, 295.

57. Cuellar interviews, June 2007.

58. Elizabeth Jelin, "Family and Household Outside World and Private Life," in *Family, Household and Gender Relations in Latin America*, ed. Elizabeth Jelin (New York: Routledge, Chapman & Hall, 1991), 29.

59. Jelin, "Family and Household," 37.

12

How a Country Girl from Arkansas Became an Importer Leading Other Women in Coffee

Phyllis Johnson

I love the smells of fall. The ripening crops, the leaves, and the cooler temperatures were exciting times for me growing up in rural Arkansas. I was taught at an early age to work hard, believe in myself, and stay true to my beliefs. Most of our family activities involved working on the farm. In the summertime we chopped cotton. Most people who aren't familiar with chopping cotton will say, "Oh, that's like weeding your garden, right?" Not really. From the time I can remember until I was sixteen years old, chopping cotton meant waking up at 5:00 a.m. during the summer months, getting dressed in long-sleeved, lightweight cotton shirts, long pants, and a wide-brim straw hat. We were on our feet for twelve hours a day, five days a week. My mom would pack our lunch and we would have a picnic every day underneath a shade tree. I often wonder why chopping cotton had such a profound effect on my life. I think because it was one of the most difficult things I've had to do both physically and mentally. At the end of the summer the kids could spend a little money on school clothes and supplies, but most of our earnings went to repair our home or for something the family needed. Growing up in rural Arkansas as the youngest of eight children with only one parent on the scene taught me the value of hard work and perseverance.

Chopping cotton for sixty hours a week in the hot sun prepared me to stick to completing my college degree in microbiology, excelling as an employee in various jobs, and having the faith to start and operate BD Imports while raising a family along with my husband. My company grew out of the desire to express myself through my life work, while discovering my capabilities. After graduating from college, I worked as a researcher, buyer, marketing manager, and regional sales representative for various scientific companies. I had great jobs that paid well and allowed flexibility and creativity. But I felt there had to be something more. My talents, my skills, my opportunities should not just be for my own benefit. I had to find a way to give back to others. As an African American growing up in the South, I was constantly reminded of the sacrifices made by others so that I could have the privileges that I enjoyed. I felt the need to take advantage of every opportunity afforded me by my older siblings and my mom.

I had no idea the biggest way to give back would be coffee on an international level.

In my work after college, I traveled a lot around the U.S. I'd developed an appreciation for African handmade crafts. On business trips I looked for retailers that sold rare and unique pieces. In Minneapolis, I routinely visited a small shop in the downtown area, and eventually I became good friends with the Kenyan owner. He would tell me long stories about his people and the meaning behind each craft. For me, the meaning behind the craft was what made each piece special and unique. I felt that my purchases made a difference in the lives of the crafters. In 1999 I was visiting the shop when I noticed a 132-pound bag of green coffee the owner had brought back along with his crafts. I asked him about the large strange-looking bag lying on the floor. He said, "That's coffee, we grow coffee in Kenya, the very best in the world, known as Kenya AA." Before he could say anything more I said to him, "That's it! I'm going to import coffee from Kenya to the U.S."

Back at my hotel, I started the process of forming my company. In my early childhood my older siblings nicknamed me blood dog; I liked to fight and bite my siblings, who always enjoyed taunting me, but always in fun. As I grew older they called me BD for short. So I thought, BD Imports, it'll take the tenacity of a blood dog to make this company work. I remember calling my husband Patrick that night and telling him the story and the name of the company. He and I had discussed our desire to own a business on several occasions. He was excited and supported the idea from the very start.

I never thought about having to tell potential customers the meaning behind the name until sheer embarrassment came upon my face when I was first asked by the owner of a small coffee roasting plant in Madison, Wisconsin. Looking back over the past twelve years, it has taken the tenacity of a blood dog to survive. I kept my day job as a regional sales representative and studied coffee on the side. My husband continued his employment for a major technology company while we both spent after hours working to build BD Imports. For four years I would carry two briefcases in my car, one filled with scientific literature and wares and the other with coffee samples. It was an exciting time for me. I enjoyed the visits to coffee roasters more than talking to scientists. Still, I felt like a fake, not able to totally commit to what I really wanted to do for fear that I would not be successful. After years of trying to manage two jobs I decided that I had to follow my heart, give up my scientific career, and engage fully in coffee. I can truthfully say that in twelve years I've never regretted the decision or looked back.

The coffee community was and remains today extremely welcoming and exciting. BD Imports was built on the idea of importing great coffees from Kenya, telling the beautiful stories about the people to buyers, and making them feel the same way I did in that Kenyan craft store. Needless to say coffee is quite different than handicrafts. I embraced the idea of learning as much as I could about coffee, so I applied myself and did what it took to learn about the industry. Whenever I would feel intimidated I would always say to myself, "You chopped cotton and passed organic chemistry; how hard can it be to learn about coffee?" Looking back, I now realize there were so many things working in my favor, things I can't explain. I was fortunate when one of the largest exporters of Kenyan coffee decided to respond to a letter he received from me looking for an exporter. Mr. Amu Malde was just about to retire from a thirty-year career in the Kenyan coffee industry when he received my letter. He was so patient and walked me through the process of how the Kenyan coffee industry worked. He helped to give me a competitive advantage with his knowledge and cupping expertise. He devoted 100 percent of his time to BD Imports. My samples of Kenyan coffee stood out head and shoulders above the rest on cupping tables. There were times when I would meet with skeptical and reluctant buyers to drop off samples and talk about my company and later receive a phone call from a very excited and polite buyer saying they'd not seen Kenyan coffee like mine in years.

My company has gone through many changes through the years. I've lived life through BD Imports. The real fabric of who I am has been revealed through my efforts in running the company. A few years ago, we decided to stop doing business with one of our largest customers. I felt that BD was being misrepresented by the customer. We were showcased as a leading minority supplier in their corporate publications, when we only sold about 25,000 pounds of their 10 million pound total. A great deal of my time was devoted to educating this customer about coffee and to assisting in assembling promotional materials about our relationships with farmers. It became obvious to me that we were not going to grow our business with this customer. This customer was interested in using BD Imports primarily as a way of advertising their efforts towards supplier diversity without offering us a real chance at expanding the relationship. It was difficult to walk away from a relationship that I'd poured five years into building. Being promoted as a key supplier without being able to realize a greater value for my company made me think that this must be how coffee farmers feel. Since I ran the company and had the final say, I could determine who to do business with.

Soon after we discontinued this relationship, the downturn of the global economy began. Customers who'd relied on BD Imports as their primary supplier of African coffees looked to alternate and cheaper suppliers. Despite never having missed a monthly payment in seven years on our line of credit, our bank decided to end the relationship with BD Imports. The bank had featured our company as part of a major advertising campaign in print and on radio. Although I worried, I knew there was something more meant for us and the company. I just didn't know what it was.

In 2002 my husband and I made our first trip to Kenya. We decided to visit two cooperatives out of the twenty or so that we'd purchased coffee from since starting BD Imports. The Kaburu-ini cooperative in Nyeri was expecting us and prepared a wonderful event in which coffee farmers, local politicians, and cooperative officials came to greet us. The women sat patiently on the damp ground outside of the tent while the men sat in chairs underneath it. My husband and I along with other special guests sat at a head table. When it came time for me to speak all the women got up from the ground and flooded the tent. There was a special connection that I felt towards the women, and obviously they felt the same. Unknown to me and my husband, BD Imports had purchased a small lot of about fifty bags at the highest price the cooperative had ever received. The farmers were excited to meet the buyer of their special coffee. They were thrilled that it was an African American woman from the U.S. One local politician mentioned that they had expected a European male to show up. The farmers gave me a Kikuyu name, Nyawire, meaning hard-working woman. I along with the local politician planted a coffee tree on the land. While visiting the cooperative an elderly man pulled me to the side and said that I should focus on helping the women in the cooperative. He told me that they do all the work. Since 2002, BD Imports has purchased coffee from Kaburu-ini many times.

Throughout the history of BD Imports, we've shown a commitment to women in coffee. In 2003 we purchased the first small lot of coffee produced by Buf Café in Rwanda. Epiphanie Mukashyaka is an exceptional leader who was among the first women in Rwanda to own a coffee washing station. She serves as a great role model for the many women who've entered the industry in recent years. In 2004 she was featured on a PBS special highlighting the success of Rwandan women after the genocide. I sat on my sofa filled with great pride watching her. Later in the year I was invited by USAID, the United States Agency for International Development, to speak in Washington about my experience in working with Buf Café. Meanwhile, Epiphanie has gone on to great success. She competes in the Rwandan Cup of Excellence and her brand is well known around the world.

In Kenya, BD Imports helped to establish one of the first indigenous Kenyan woman-owned export companies, DEMAC Trading, and in Ethiopia the company purchased the first lot of coffee offered for sale by Amaro Gayo, a coffee processing station owned by Ms. Asnakech Thomas. Ms. Thomas was one of the first women to own a coffee processing station in Ethiopia. She has also gone on to build a strong brand for her coffee internationally. I'm very proud that BD Imports offered opportunities to these women and many more.

I'd poured all that I had into building BD Imports while trying to help women in coffee. In 2009 I made the decision that even though business had become extremely difficult, I would stay committed to my passion. With more time on my hands, I decided to volunteer with some good friends who devoted time to the **International Women's Coffee Alliance** (IWCA). They'd always looked to me to start the IWCA chapter expansion into Africa. Several obstacles hampered that effort, namely that I'd been extremely busy trying to grow my company and that I lived in the Chicago area, not in Africa. However, I was determined to make something happen in Africa while I had time to devote to volunteering. Looking back, I realized that I'd already tried through BD Imports to help advance women in coffee. I'd visited African coffee-producing countries and seen the vital role that women played in production and harvest, but I also noticed the lack of women involved in decision making roles. The IWCA offered an opportunity to help advance women in a different way, through development efforts that were supposed to lead to trade relationships. I wasn't sure how this was going to work, but I was more than willing to try.

We decided that we would hold a workshop in East Africa inviting women leaders in coffee from various countries to discuss IWCA's work in Central America. When seeking support for the workshop, I was advised to contact the International Trade Center (ITC) in Geneva, Switzerland, an affiliate of the United Nations and World Trade Organization. ITC senior advisor Morren Scholer, who had been engaged in similar projects for years, agreed to help sponsor our efforts. The ITC and **Coffee Quality Institute** (CQI) supported our first workshop in Africa. Concentrating on the workshop in Africa pulled me away from my company for eight months. But I got an opportunity to lead work that I'm passionate about. I felt extremely blessed to be in Uganda with a fantastic team of volunteers from IWCA along with ITC representatives to speak to women from nine African countries. We talked about working together as part of a global network to help advance women in coffee.

Although it made me feel great to give in such a way, it didn't do very much toward getting BD Imports back on its feet. On the third and final day of the workshop in Uganda, I was sitting with other IWCA volunteers recapping the event and the excitement that we all felt from the African women. That night my husband called to say that BD Imports had been awarded a coffee contract to supply in-room coffee for a major international hotel chain. What great news at a great time! Again, staying committed to our beliefs had paid off. The relationship between BD Imports and the hotel company had begun three years earlier. The company's strategic sourcing manager said their decision was due to our integrity, passion, and the way that we conducted ourselves, along with the quality of the product that allowed BD Imports to compete with some of the giants in coffee.

Today, I continue to manage BD Imports while leading the ITC/IWCA Women in Coffee Program. The company is growing, and the Women in Coffee Program is entering its third year in 2012. We've established IWCA chapters in Burundi, Kenya, and Rwanda and are working toward bringing on Uganda, Tanzania, and Ethiopia. This work has helped ignite the interest of partners around the world. The IWCA chapter network has grown from five countries in Central and South America to nine countries on several continents, with interest from Brazil, India, Peru, Honduras, Indonesia, and many others. We anticipate that twenty countries will join our network over the next three years.

The struggles women in coffee face have become even more real to me in recent years. During 2010 I accepted with great humility the opportunity to speak about the ITC/IWCA Women in Coffee Program at conferences in the U.S., Tanzania, Nicaragua, El Salvador, the World Trade Organization's celebration on International Women's Day in Geneva, Switzerland, and the ITC Women Vendor's Forum and Exhibition in Chongqing, China. Due to the many speaking engagements I was absent when awarded by my local community the YWCA Leader Luncheon award for empowering women.

Once I heard a story about someone given a choice to stay in what appeared to be a safe situation on a boat docked in shallow water versus going out into the risky deep blue sea. The storyteller carefully built a mental picture of what life was like in both situations. Obviously it was more comfortable to stay in the shallow waters closer to the land. However, the shallow waters were murky, had little plant and sea life, but lots of rocks and even broken glass. The deep blue water was beautiful and clear, brilliantly colored with plant and sea life. Gaining access to the many resources coffee has offered me has provided the opportunity to learn and grow far beyond my beginnings in rural Arkansas. When I think of my experiences as a coffee importer, I liken my story to the person who chose to take the boat to the deep blue sea, experiencing all the brilliance of what life has to offer. Yes, I've run into some real dangers in deeper waters, but I'm very happy that I chose new challenges.

13

The Role of Nonprofits in Coffee

August Burns

Doña Cielo walks up the steep path deep in the heart of coffee country to the village of El Cua in the northern highlands of Nicaragua. She thinks about Elena, the woman she will visit today. Cielo works as a community health promoter, encouraging women from these remote communities to travel to a rural clinic where local doctors can screen them for cervical cancer using a fast, effective, and affordable method. She knows that cervical cancer is a community issue, killing women in the prime of their lives while they are still raising children and are relied upon by their families as major breadwinners. Doña Cielo's first priority is women like Doña Elena, the woman at the end of the dirt path. The cervical cancer screening is being sponsored by the local coffee cooperative and is saving women's lives.

Doña Cielo is one of hundreds of community health promoters who have been trained over the past fifteen years by Grounds for Health in basic information, outreach, and health communication skills to get women in remote communities the screening services they need. Grounds for Health is a nonprofit organization based in Waterbury, Vermont, that works in coffee-growing communities to address alarmingly high rates of cervical cancer. They have found the coffee industry to be a key ingredient to success in addressing one of the major killers of women across the globe.

From its founding, Grounds for Health has been steeped in the world of coffee. But it all began rather by accident. Its founder, Dan Cox, a coffee business owner, was on a buying trip to Oaxaca, Mexico, accompanied by a close friend, retired ob/gyn Dr. Francis Fote, who was just along for the ride. While Dan spent the day buying coffee, Dr. Fote—or "Doc Fote" as Dan calls him—traveled to a few clinics to get the lay of the land. At the end of the day, Dan returned to the hotel to an excited and agitated Dr. Fote. "What's gotten into you?" Dan asked. Doc Fote explained he had visited a hospital that looked immaculate on the outside, but was falling apart behind the front doors. He had spoken with a doctor who told him that women were dying from cervical cancer at dangerously high rates—four to five times higher than in the U.S. This was all despite the fact that cervical cancer is nearly 100 percent treatable. The reason? Women did not have access to simple, early screening or treatment. "We have to do something," exclaimed Dr. Fote. "Who is *we* and what is *something*?" replied Dan. But he already knew the answer. Thanks to his business connections, the "we" became the coffee industry, and the "something" was clear enough—to prevent unnecessary deaths from cervical cancer. A few phone calls to friends produced enough funding to get started in that small Mexican community. The coffee industry has provided financial support for Grounds for Health ever since.

From those first phone calls, Grounds for Health has grown to become a leader in the global fight against cervical cancer, and it is the organization's relationship to coffee that has made it all possible. The success of Grounds for Health is a story of what can happen when individuals have the vision and willingness to make a difference—to do something about a problem rather than turn away and leave it for someone else to take care of. It is also a story of the power of a private industry that contributes to the well-being of others and strives to make the world a better place.

Worldwide cervical cancer claims more women's lives than any other form of cancer, and 88 percent of these deaths occur in developing countries.[1] This is despite the fact that cervical cancer is nearly entirely treatable when detected early and treated right away. The reason for these abysmal statistics is a lack of health care infrastructure for simple screening and treatment.

Most coffee-farming communities are located in developing nations, in rural mountainous areas where a lack of roads, transportation, health facilities, and health care providers severely limits access to health services. Women in these remote areas are often the most challenging to reach with services of any kind. They suffer from a lack of information, difficult access, obstacles to returning for follow-up, and the burden of other pressing demands on their time and resources. When aid does come to developing countries, these rural women are often the last to receive services, if at all. But for Grounds for Health and for the coffee industry, these women—the ones at the end of the dirt path—come first.

Since 1996, Grounds for Health has provided direct services to thousands of women and has trained hundreds of in-country doctors and nurses in up-to-date, high-quality medical practices so they can continue screening for and treating cervical cancer on their own. By partnering with coffee companies, medical professionals, and local coffee cooperatives, Grounds for Health works to create locally managed, sustainable, and effective cervical cancer prevention and treatment programs in coffee-producing regions.

A PRACTICAL AND SUSTAINABLE MODEL FOR DEVELOPING COUNTRIES

The Grounds for Health model is an excellent example of best practice in a people-public-private collaboration. It leverages three key partnerships: the community-based coffee cooperative, the local and national ministries of health, and coffee-industry funders.

Grounds for Health establishes programs in coffee-growing communities only upon invitation from the coffee cooperatives. The co-op leadership must demonstrate commitment to the program through community support and investment. Through the co-op, the community mobilizes to ensure that members get the information they need and that women at risk are identified and motivated to seek screening services. Because the co-op is a local organization, it has the community's trust. Thus the co-op can use its trucks to transport women to the screening campaigns and guarantee support for follow-up care for the women who need it.

Grounds for Health provides the technical assistance, including capacity building and management training for the cooperative, training of doctors and nurses in medical skills, and donations of essential equipment to get the services up and running. Together with leaders in the coffee co-ops, Grounds for Health partners with health authorities from the local ministry of health to identify the medical personnel, facilities to be used, and to ensure ongoing support and maintenance of services. These partnerships and local buy-in to the programs are vital to ensuring sustainability.

This is all made possible through financial contributions from the coffee industry, Grounds for Health programs are supported by donations from over 250 coffee-related companies from the U.S., Canada, Australia, Taiwan, the United Kingdom, and more. Coffee industry supporters contribute through direct donations, coffeehouse promotions, premiums on coffee sales, and contributions of green coffee and merchandise to an annual online coffee auction. Most coffee companies that buy beans from Grounds for Health's coffee cooperative partners have a direct interest in the health and well-being of the people who produce the product they sell. Yet even companies that do not work with partner co-ops recognize the importance of supporting the programs. The economic and social burden of cervical cancer is significant and impacts many families and coffee farms, making it an important issue for all players in the coffee supply chain.

The impact of Grounds for Health's relationship to its funders cannot be overstated. Many nonprofits devote much of their time researching, writing, and reporting to funders. The unique collaborative model developed in our case not only links women to life-saving services, but it also provides Grounds for Health with a steady source of income to stay focused on its mission. Because of the philanthropic efforts of the coffee industry, Grounds for Health's funding is direct and immediate, without cumbersome strings attached. This gives Grounds for Health the much-needed flexibility to discover and implement what works in each of the individual communities it serves.

For example, over the past decade the World Health Organization and the Gates Foundation have invested in developing alternative methods for the early detection and treatment of cervical cancer in low-resource settings. One such method, called single visit screen and treat or the single visit approach, meets their requirements for "low-resource appropriate" technologies. Using simple vinegar, cotton balls, and a good light, the single visit approach has been shown to be as effective as the Pap smear in detecting early cell changes,[2] but requires few resources, demands no special equipment, and only costs 25 cents per woman in materials.

Research has concluded that the single visit screen and treat method is safe, acceptable, and cost-effective. This simple method relies on visual changes on a woman's cervix that indicate early disease presence when simple household vinegar is applied. When pre-cancers are identified, this test is then followed by immediate treatment with cryotherapy. If every woman had access to even one screening in a lifetime (and timely treatment of any pre-cancer), it could reduce the rate of cervical cancer by 30 percent. With three screenings in a lifetime, it could be possible to realize a 64 percent reduction. This is a goal worth striving for.[3]

However, and perhaps most importantly to this reduction of the rate of cervical cancer, the single visit approach provides immediate results—the key to getting women to same-day treatment and stopping the disease. Instead of sending a woman away to wait for results and then asking her to return to the clinic for follow-up care, she gets her results on the spot, and any treatment necessary can be performed at the same time. She only has to make the long, difficult trek once, which is essential since the hardships of travel have proven to discourage women from returning for follow-up care.[4]

Thanks to flexible funding from the coffee industry, Grounds for Health was able to become one of the first organizations in the world to integrate this innovative approach into its programs. By being early adopters, Grounds for Health has learned how to best implement the single visit approach and has transformed the organization into an internationally recognized resource for preventing cervical cancer in low-resource settings.

Grounds for Health has been able to capture and share its lessons learned with the global network of organizations focused on cervical cancer prevention. Without the work of the coffee industry to improve women's health, these lessons might have remained undiscovered by other groups.

KEYS TO SUCCESS

Grounds for Health has found several keys to success in its operations:

- Community support and ownership of a program are keys to sustainability. People invested in their own progress and well-being will work to ensure that health services continue long after outside help is gone.
- The single visit approach is feasible in low-resource settings.
- The single visit approach is effective; it saves women's lives.
- Minimally trained health care personnel can attain excellent competency through highly focused, hands-on interactive training.
- Providing cervical cancer prevention services creates a gateway for poor women in rural areas to access other reproductive health services.
- By providing women's health services, the co-op gains credibility as a positive community resource, which can help the co-op attract new members and strengthen its negotiating power, thereby having an economic impact as well.
- Funders who buy coffee from Grounds for Health co-op partners benefit from a healthy, strong coffee community, which ensures long-term supply.
- All funders can share Grounds for Health's story with their customers, which helps cause-related marketing campaigns and can increase brand loyalty.
- The community benefits from better health services for years to come.

Grounds for Health is distinctive in its targeted approach and proven results. The organization is dedicated to cultivating lasting partnerships and sustainable programs that focus on saving women's lives and provide positive change for everyone involved. The generosity of the specialty coffee industry has led to a major public health breakthrough with results that will long be felt in the communities it touches—in all developing nations, not just coffee-growing ones. It is a model of socially responsible giving that other industries should be inspired to follow, and it shows that the coffee industry has the power to transform lives.

NOTES

1. http://globocan.iarc.fr/factsheets/cancers/cervix.asp.

2. C. Sauvaget et al., "Accuracy of visual inspection with acetic acid for cervical cancer screening," *International Journal of Gynecology & Obstetrics* (2011): doi:10.1016/j.ijgo.2010.10.012.

3. S. J. Goldie, L. Gaffikin, J. D. Goldhaber-Fiebert, et al. "Cost-effectiveness of cervical-cancer screening in five developing countries," *New England Journal of Medicine* 353, no. 20 (2005): 2158–68.

4. S. Luciani and J. Winkler, *Cervical Cancer Prevention in Peru: Lessons Learned from the TATI Demonstration Project* (Washington, DC: Pan American Health Organization, 2006).

14

Hunger in the Coffee Lands

Rick Peyser

Editor's (RT's) note: The film Men with Guns (dir. John Sayles, U.S., 1997), features disturbing images of "coffee people" starving in a fictitious, composite Central American country. In October 2004, I traveled in Nicaragua and visited the umbrella co-op CECOCAFEN that Rick Peyser mentions below. Further into the mountains, I heard stories of extreme food deprivation, even of starvation, in the months following the coffee harvest.

Nicaragua remains the second poorest country in the Western Hemisphere, above only Haiti. Per capita income in 2011 was estimated at $3,000, putting Nicaragua in 167th place around the world. One-third of all adults are illiterate, while water-borne infections diseases weaken or kill many people (The World Factbook, https://www.cia.gov/library/publications/the-world-factbook/geos/nu.html). Given these points about Nicaragua in general, coffee farming is not the only culprit in food insecurity. However, the monoculture of coffee, like old-style cotton production in the American South, can be an important factor in leading to hunger.

For a recent review of the efforts by wealthier countries to improve food security in poor lands, see "Feeding the World in the 21st Century: Exploring Connections Between Food Production, Health, Environmental Resources, and International Security," published by the Program on Food Security and the Environment, The International Initiative, Stanford University, 2009.

HUNGER AMONG COFFEE FARMERS: NICARAGUA AS A CASE STUDY

In August of 2007 I flew with Don Seville of the Sustainable Food Lab, based in Hartland, Vermont, from our cool home state to steamy Managua, Nicaragua. There we connected with representatives from CIAT (the International Center for Tropical Agriculture), an agricultural research organization based in Cali, Colombia, that works all over the world.

We gathered in Managua to prepare for a week of one-on-one interviews with small-scale coffee farmers. Shortly after completing my twentieth year at Green Mountain Coffee Roasters (GMCR), I took on a new role in the company: director of social advocacy and coffee community outreach. I wanted to know more about the specific challenges and opportunities that small-scale coffee farming families were facing.

The questions we would ask were partly to collect basic information on families (e.g., number of children, education levels, literacy), as well as on coffee production (including the amount of land owned, the family's earnings from coffee last year, its costs of production, and certifications). Were the farmers happy with the prices they received? From there, we discussed more personal issues. Were there any other sources of income? Did farmers receive remittances from family members abroad? Had they ever thought of doing something other than growing coffee? Had they ever thought of migrating, to a city or another country? Did the family have any health problems last year, and if so, what did they do about them? And finally, did the family have any periods of extreme food scarcity last year, and if so how did they cope with the problem?

We were only going to interview the farmer. If the farmer's spouse was on hand, we could interview him or her separately, not together. CIAT made it clear that interviewing them together could influence the answers that either or both of them gave.

The next morning, we left Managua; about two hours later, we arrived at the offices of CECOCAFEN, where we met with Santiago Dolmus, manager of this **fair trade** umbrella cooperative's social programs. Santiago had helped to arrange interviewees and meeting places for us in communities that supplied CECOCAFEN with coffee. After sharing with him the interview questions and procedures we would follow, we headed north to El Coyolar and the La Esperanza cooperative—a primary-level community-based cooperative within CECOCAFEN.

For ninety minutes we rattled on through potholes of varying sizes and depths. At La Esperanza, my first interview was with Norma Velasquez. We sat down in a large, dimly lit room, on two of the white rigid plastic lawn chairs that are ubiquitous in Nicaragua.

After a few minutes of introductory chit-chat, I explained to Norma that I would be asking her a series of questions and that I wanted to write down her answers. I told her that the information she shared with me would be kept confidential (Norma is not her real name). She asked what we were going to do with the information and told me that a number of people had already come through El Coyolar conducting surveys, collecting information, but they have never seen them again. I explained to Norma that we weren't sure what we were going to do with the information, since we didn't know what the information was yet, but that one thing we would do—and I promised here—was come back and share it with those we interviewed. The cooperative's management wanted to know the results as well, and we felt that it was important and right to share the results with those we interviewed.

Norma and I moved through the questions smoothly, without any interruptions or difficulties. Everything was in Spanish, and I was keeping up well. Finally we arrived at the last question: "Did your family have any periods of extreme scarcity of food last year, and if so what did you do about it?" When I asked this question, Norma put her head down and stared at the table for what seemed like an eternity. Soon she reached into a small pocket in the simple skirt she was wearing and retrieved a piece of clumped up tissue paper that she carefully unfolded and used to soak up the tears that had started running down her cheeks. I didn't know what to think. Had I said something wrong? I waited for Norma to compose herself. After about a minute she began to answer; she and her family had three to four months every year of extreme food scarcity. I asked her which months. She answered, "Usually the end of May through October." "What caused these months of scarcity?" I asked. Norma explained that the coffee harvest usually began the end of October or beginning of November and usually ended by late February. She said that most of her family's earnings from coffee were largely depleted by the end of May, which also marked the beginning of the rainy season and the time each year when basic food staples (corn and beans) increase in price before they are harvested in late autumn. This left her family with three to four months when they had very little income or savings to purchase food. As if this wasn't enough, they had to contend with the moving target of rising food prices.

I probed further: how did Norma and her family deal with this challenge? She said that there were three ways they approached this problem. The first was to eat exactly the same diet but to consume fewer calories. The second way was to eat less expensive foods that they were not accustomed to eating most of the year. And the third tactic was to borrow from friends, neighbors, relatives, or the local cooperative. Norma explained that this debt had to be repaid by the end of the next harvest—thus creating a cycle of debt.

This was my very first interview, so I thought (hoped) that Norma and her family were not the norm, that their experience was exceptional. These interviews were taking place with members of CECOCAFEN, whose farmers were advantaged in the sense that they received all of the benefits of **fair trade certification**—transparency, a social premium, and a guaranteed minimum floor price, among others. I was serving on the FLO (Fair Trade Labeling Organizations International) board of directors at the time, so Norma's story was very disturbing to hear.

What was even more disturbing during the week of interviews was that I received the exact same answer to the question on food security from each respondent. At the end of the first day, I shared my experience with the team members. They had each received the same answers from their interviewees.

In the following days, we continued to interview families, in different communities separated by over an hour on rough roads. After talking to farmers at their cooperative offices, in their homes, or right in the field, I finally arrived by pickup at a small, modest home to conduct my last interview of the week. The driver dropped me off on the outskirts of a small hamlet. I walked down a small hill to a 20 foot by 20 foot wooden plank home with a tin roof. I approached the house to knock, but there was no door, so I knocked on the doorframe. A few seconds later Eduardo, a farmer, appeared and invited me into his home. The house had a cement floor and looked sturdy; I commented on the structure, and he said that the house was sixty years old and had served his family well. He didn't know how much longer it would last, though, as it was infested with termites.

The home had a wooden wall separating its two rooms. After about five minutes of interviewing, Eduardo's wife, Esmeralda, came around the partition, and started helping her husband answer my questions. I knew that this wasn't what CIAT had wanted, but I couldn't ask her to leave her own home! Soon their four children, all between five and sixteen years old, came around the corner.

I thanked them for taking the time to speak with me. When I had walked about halfway up to the road I turned around and looked back. There was the family, all huddled in their doorway, watching me walking back up to the road. We waved at each other. All of a sudden, I felt the great weight of all the stories I had heard that week. This was a moment that changed me as a person, as much or more than my first trip to **origin**. Tears welled up in my eyes as I realized that this family could be my family; it could be your family; it could be anyone's family. It was simply the luck of the draw that my family lived in Vermont and had plenty of everything we needed. Hearing one family after another share their struggle to put food on their family table months of every year was painful to hear. It just wasn't right.

The next morning, as I waited for my plane to take off, I couldn't stop thinking about the families who had so openly shared their lives with me, both their dreams and this awful annual period of food scarcity. I wasn't sure I wanted to continue to work in the industry that I had grown to love. How could I not have known about this challenge? I had spent months volunteering in coffee communities, spending many weeks in the homes of coffee farmers. No one had ever spoken of this period, yet it was so common in Nicaraguan coffee communities that it has its own name: "los meses flacos" (the thin months) or "la vaca flaca" (the thin cow).

I felt stupid and almost betrayed. After I arrived home I took a week of planned vacation. During this week I called Dan Cox, a friend and former colleague. Dan, who founded Coffee Enterprises, had been in the coffee business for twenty-six years and had traveled to coffee lands many times over the years. He asked me to come visit him in his new offices on the edge of Lake Champlain. As he showed me around the beautiful rooms, he asked me, "So what have you been up to?" I told him about the interviews and what I had learned about food insecurity. He said, "You're shitting me." I said, "No, I wish I was." I continued to reach out to others I knew in the industry, who had also been in the industry for years and who had spent plenty of time in coffee growing communities. All of them were surprised by what I had heard from families.

Two months later, CIAT came to Vermont to share the results of their interviews, not just in Nicaragua but in two departments of Guatemala and two states of Mexico. In total, 179 hour-long interviews had been conducted in all three countries. About 67 percent of those interviewed said that they had experienced between three and eight months of extreme scarcity of food last year, and all but 16 percent had experienced some scarcity of food last year. As the meeting came to a close, Sam Fujisaka, part of the CIAT team that came to share the results, turned to me and said, "So Rick, what are you going to do with this information? Are you going to put it in a nice binder and put it on your office bookshelf and do nothing with it like most companies, or are you going to do something with it?" Sam's question hit a nerve and I immediately replied, "Of course I'm going to do something with this," not having a clue what that "something" was going to be.

I realized that the new role I had started with GMCR provided me with the opportunity to perhaps make a small difference for at least some families in our supply chain. In the spring of 2008, after sharing the interview results with the interviewees and CECOCAFEN's management team, Green Mountain sponsored a meeting where members of the co-op, with the participation of some local NGOs, developed two primary strategies to overcome these months of food insecurity: (1) diversify the family's coffee parcel to grow coffee and food for the family's own consumption and to sell in the local market, and (2) grow and store basic grains.

When this "strategic summit" ended, CECOCAFEN developed a proposal to GMCR to launch a food security project based on these two strategies. In the early summer of 2008, GMCR agreed to support this project, with the goal of benefitting approximately 300 families (or 1,800 people) who live in CECOCAFEN communities.

I saw that this challenge of food insecurity had to be fought on two fronts. First we had to work with other communities, too, and second, we had to generate awareness within the specialty coffee industry. How could this phenomenon, so common in coffee communities, be unknown or not spoken about in the halls of the industry? This challenge was too big for GMCR to take on by itself.

In 2010, I shared the CIAT results with the industry at the annual **SCAA** Symposium and Conference. In 2011 the film *After the Harvest: Fighting Hunger in the Coffeelands* premiered at this gathering. This unbranded twenty-minute film, narrated by Susan Sarandon, brought the images and voices of coffee farmers in the midst of this challenge, as well as their solutions, to many members of the industry. People were moved, and we are still working to build collaborative efforts that will help families develop sustainable answers to this annual period of food insecurity.

For me, I was finally able to see this challenge as a new beginning of my career in coffee. Today, the food security projects that GMCR supports are helping 47,000 families (or 227,000 individuals) become more food secure.

Food, of course, is fundamental; it is the basis of good health, the ability to learn, and the ability to work. Without adequate nutrition, children under the age of three may experience stunting that can have an irreversible impact on their physical and mental capacities for their entire lives.

The families who grow specialty coffee have something in common with many people in other rural areas around the world. Their children are leaving. They are migrating to urban centers where they perceive greater opportunities for a better life. For the first time on our planet, there are more people living in urban centers than in rural areas. Given the challenges presented by food insecurity, limited health care services, impure water, and lack of access to a secondary education in coffee communities, why should they stay? Would you? This begs the billion dollar question: Who is going to grow the next generation of specialty coffee, if we don't provide families with the tools they need to improve the quality of life so young people want to stay and continue to grow high-quality coffee?

Editor's postscript (RT): A recent study of Nicaraguan coffee farmers identifies severe problems among those who raise certified coffee.[1] The authors surveyed 327 co-op members living in the departments of Madriz and Nueva Segovia. All farmers were growing arabica. But "certified pro-

Figure 14.1.   La Pita kids. Photo by Robert Thurston.

ducers are more often found below the absolute poverty line than conventional producers. Over a period of ten years, our analysis shows that organic and organic-fairtrade farmers have become poorer relative to conventional producers."[2] In the regions studied, one-third of all coffee farmers have incomes below the extreme poverty line of $1/day/person ($246.80/year/person); among organic and organic/fair trade (FT) certified, the figure is 45 percent.

The additional production costs of **organic**, which may include hiring labor outside the family, not to mention the cost of becoming and remaining certified, are often greater than the premium farmers receive for organic beans. These costs are even higher for farmers who are certified both as organic and as FT. Organic producers also tend to have less land, but more family members, than non-organic farmers do. Moreover, organic yields, because of the extra labor involved, can be lower than for conventional coffee, which also depresses the amount the family earns for certified coffee.

Fair trade **farm gate prices**, money actually paid to farmers themselves, rather than to a co-op, can actually be lower than for non-FT farmers at the same level of bean quality, for instance if a co-op has to pay off debts. Conventional farmers may also earn more overall income than FT co-op members, by selling animals and raising other crops.

The study's authors are cautious in their conclusions, as their respondents had to have occupied the same farm for at least ten years, and the selection of farmers may not have been absolutely random. Yet the investigators conclude that "coffee yields, profitability and efficiency need to be increased, as prices for certified coffee cannot compensate for low productivity, land or labor constraints."[3]

Excerpted from an interview with Price Peterson, La Esmeralda Farm, May 24, 2008:

Peterson: The Nogöbé Indians [who live at higher altitudes and come down to pick coffee for us] are very poor. Generally they'll come to harvest here, families of two three four, and leave here with $300 or $400 in their pocket, after three or four months. But they've spent money while here buying some things. And literally they need to live on that the rest of the year. So we're talking about people well below the extreme poverty level; this is much less than a dollar a day per person. They go back into the mountains about March. In April, May they'll plant a little bit of corn, a little bit of this and the other. And by July they've usually run out of money . . . if they haven't just run out there's been a family emergency, they've had to spend $200 to get someone to a hospital.

Numerous times, you'll have maybe a sixteen-year-old woman with a seventeen-year-old husband, and they've got two kids and a baby. And they finish one year and come back the next year and there's only two kids, where's the baby, ay, . . . the milk dried up in July, the baby died. I remember, this happened several years ago, when a returning family came in and I said, you know, how are things going, oh they're not very good, and I said what do you mean, and he said well you know we're down to one meal. Well, one big meal a day, you can get by on that. And he said, Mr. Price, you don't understand, one meal a week.

NOTES

1. Tina D. Beuchelt and Manfred Zeller, "Profits and Poverty: Certification's Troubled Link for Nicaragua's Organic and Fair Trade Coffee Producers," *Ecological Economics* 70 (2011).

2. Beuchelt and Zeller, "Profits and Poverty," 1316.

3. Beuchelt and Zeller, "Profits and Poverty," 1323.

15

The "Price" of Coffee

How the Coffee Commodity Market Works

Robert W. Thurston

For some 130 years, most green coffee has been sold through urban commodity exchanges that can seem utterly chaotic: a bunch of men in the pit, also called the ring, wave bits of paper, yell in a language all their own, use several telephones simultaneously, and apparently parasitically absorb much of someone else's money day by day.

It would be good for anyone who cares about coffee, or any aspect of transnational business, to step back from such images for a few moments. First, commodity transactions are steadily moving out of "pits" to quiet cubicles and computers. Much more important is to understand how commodities markets work, what the coffee industry and the media call the **price of coffee**, and why that figure is important at any time. The main issues will be listed first, then will be explored in more depth.

1. A commodity is anything that can be bought, sold, or traded, including labor and services. Coffee is designated a "soft commodity," along with other nondurable, agricultural products like cocoa, sugar, and frozen concentrated orange juice. Coffee as a soft commodity, referring to all coffee, should not be confused with **commodity coffee**, which refers to any beans below **specialty coffee.**
2. There is a "spot" or cash market for coffee acquired and paid for today.
3. There is a long-term or "futures" market that allows purchasers to contract for a certain amount of coffee, of a certain quality, to be delivered in New York or another port on a specified date.
4. When articles or films about coffee talk about its "price," the word usually refers to the dollar figure that **arabica** coffee currently sells for on the New York commodities exchange, which handles both spot and futures trades. The exchange used to be called the New York Board of Trade, NYBOT for short; in 2007 IntercontinentalExchange acquired NYBOT, so now the exchange is ICE.[1] On the exchange, several grades of coffee are sold; the most common one is called Coffee "C"®. Anyone who wants to get a rough idea of how the arabica coffee business is going needs to look at the **C price** and how it is changing over time. The "benchmark contract for Arabica coffee" and "the world's leading coffee contract," Coffee C is the figure that the industry and the media look at to price arabica.[2] The C price is also the mark that **Fair Trade** and other buyers

92

use to write contracts. **Robusta** is traded largely on a London exchange; this chapter won't discuss that side of the industry, but the outlines of robusta trade are virtually the same as for arabica.

5. Big producers, importers and roasters, and speculators all buy and sell on ICE. In addition to simply trading in actual coffee, anyone with deep pockets and a willingness to take large risks can purchase or sell coffee futures or options on them.

This commerce is big: on ICE, coffee futures and options trade the "equivalent of 7 times the world's coffee production annually."[3] That is, contracts may be bought and sold so often that their dollar value, added up, is seven times greater than the actual value of the coffee.

Why go to all this trouble and expense in dealing with coffee? Wouldn't it be a great deal simpler, and probably cheaper, just to send someone down to a coffee farm, buy the coffee there, and ship it to a roaster? The answer to the first question has to do with history, the answer to the second with the logistics and financing of large volumes of coffee. On the other hand, Fair Trade and **direct trade** do not go through the ICE, while a select group of farmers, among them Price Peterson (in "Strategies for Improving Coffee Quality"), has been able to sell through annual Internet auctions. This article explores why most arabica is bought and sold on ICE.

THE HISTORY OF COFFEE TRADING

Although coffee beans and the beverage were for sale on the streets of some Italian cities by the 1620s, the first market in the beans as a commodity developed in Amsterdam in the 1640s. *The Coffee Trader*, a novel by David Liss, re-creates the excitement and risks of the bourse, as dealers shout offers to buy or sell in Latin, Dutch, and Portuguese. The traders are Danish, French, German, Dutch, and Jews exiled from Spain and Portugal.[4] Everyone tries to find out what is happening on the markets in London, Hamburg, and cities farther afield. From a very early date, the business of buying and selling coffee was truly international.

As the novel shows, a trade in coffee **futures** also dates back to the seventeenth century. In these arrangements, dealers agree with a commission merchant to buy a specified amount of coffee, usually of a stated quality, to be physically delivered on a later date. Producers or, more likely at this early point in the business, middlemen who had purchased coffee from Arabs in the Middle East could sell futures in Amsterdam through commission merchants. We will return to what these possibilities still mean for the business.

Despite the early appearance of futures, purchasing coffee long remained overwhelmingly a matter of using the spot market. This was largely because not only was the crop highly unpredictable but transporting goods over long distances in sailing vessels was as well. A ship would arrive in New York or another port, news of the cargo would spread among dealers, and bidding would begin. In early 1871, for example, dealers in New York bought 1,375 bags (200 pounds each) of Brazilian coffee brought into port by the ship *Contest*, and another 967 bags from the *Freya*.[5]

But spot trading proved to be chaotic and ruinous for many businessmen: "uncontrolled cash market speculation brought about a calamitous market collapse in 1880."[6] Two years later, a group of coffee buyers formed the Coffee Exchange of the City of New York so that, following the lead of a cotton exchange founded in 1870, coffee futures contracts could be bought and sold.

Another basic part of the story has to do with transportation. During the 1870s, railroad building boomed in numerous countries, and regular transoceanic steamship lines began to handle whatever the rails brought to the ports. These developments hardly reached into all parts of coffee country then or for decades to come; into the 1950s or beyond, much coffee came down from the mountains on the backs of donkeys or people. To this day, roads in Africa or Mexico, for example, are often so bad that moving coffee is slow and expensive.

Yet by the time the New York Coffee Exchange opened in 1882, shipping had become cheaper and more reliable. In 1886, a telegraph cable connected Brazil with the U.S.,[7] so that information about supply in the biggest producing country reached American traders almost instantaneously. The business settled into the framework that continues to the present. Within a few years the telephone, then later computers and the Internet, sped up trading coffee but did not change its essential contours.

THE CREATION OF THE COFFEE "C" PRICE

In theory, any product might be sold using a system of futures, contracts to pay something now and the full agreed-upon sum when the product is delivered. But few people would sign a contract to purchase, for example, a car six months from now, knowing that cars will be available for sale at that time. The price of the car you want will probably be about the same in six months, barring swings in the price of gasoline that would favor either sippers or guzzlers. Buying futures is a way to take some of the risk out of purchasing any item that can change rapidly in quantity and availability, a problem that applies above all to agricultural commodities. Signing a contract for the delivery of a specified amount and quality of coffee smoothes, or tries to, the peaks and troughs of the business that in the past brought down so many companies. Doing business through futures makes life more predictable; by purchasing futures, a candy manufacturer, for example, can know in March what he will pay for sugar in September and can plan around that cost. The candy maker can "discover" the price of sugar, as the commodities people put it.

This desire for predictability eventually led to the creation of the C price. It is determined on a given day or hour by hour as trading goes on, by averaging the "nearby" futures contracts for delivery of mild, washed (wet processed) arabica coffee from nineteen different countries. Brazil, in an important new move that recognizes improvements in quality there, will soon be added to the list. "Nearby" means on the next possible arrival date.

Beans sold through C contracts might be called fairly good coffee, but certainly not great according to the best palates in the industry. Some countries' coffee commands a premium over the average C price, while coffee from other lands is discounted below the C level. In early 2001, Colombian coffee, for example, traded at a premium of four cents. Mexican coffees at a discount of seven cents a pound. But by July 2011, Mexicans had reached par, while Colombians commanded a 2 cent premium (or 200 "basis points"); Ecuadorans were minus 4 cents. Effective with delivery for March of 2013, Rwandans will rise from a 3 cent to a 1 cent discount, while Brazilians will be discounted 9 cents a pound,[8] which means that dealers think their quality still has much room to improve.

FUTURES TRADING IN COFFEE

How do futures work? To buy futures in a logical way, the users of a commodity have to know their costs of production, including, of course, for the commodity itself. So if an importer figures that a profit can be made on a certain kind of coffee when it can be bought for $2 a pound, he will buy it at that price. But the spot price keeps jumping around; it has always been dangerous to buy coffee only on the spot market, since the price may suddenly go well above the amount an importer can pay and still make a profit. On the spot market, as noted, little if anything is predictable about the cost of coffee. The solution, at least in theory, is to keep track of the futures market and, when the price for delivery in the future goes down, in our example to $2 or less, sign a futures contract. Any number of firms and individuals are at their computers, watching weather reports and other information from **producing countries.** The opinions of respected prognosticators on how much coffee Colombia will produce in a given year, for instance, have great influence on the futures market.

Contracts for futures are economically useful in another way: they keep capital in the hands of the importer, since only a small fee must be paid to the broker, plus a "margin" of good faith money deposited somewhere. This amount is like escrow for a house purchase, to make sure the contract is fulfilled. In recent years even the brokers have sometimes been eliminated, as people can buy futures on their computers.

Large importers, for example Folgers, buy arabica through ICE. More specialized companies may test many different beans from, for instance, one branch of the Andes mountains of Colombia. Then, having selected the best coffees of the hundreds available from that region, an importer can offer a list of ten or twelve to a roaster. That firm will receive small amounts of these coffees, several ounces or a pound at a time, and prepare them in a sample roaster. On the basis of the sample batches, the roasting company will decide which beans it wants to order in bulk. The importer does the leg, mouth, and paper work on the ground so that the roaster can concentrate on the business of getting the coffee ready for customers. Only the biggest or best-known roasters can afford to send their own people over seas and miles of bad roads to individual farms or co-ops. Even then, as the Folgers example shows, the largest firms may simply buy through the exchange. "Great" coffees—another highly imprecise term!—are discovered in producing countries by intrepid souls willing to endure difficult travel and months away from home.[9]

To flesh out our hypothetical C purchase, imagine that an importer, who follows the weather and the political situation in the producing countries closely, decides in March to buy coffee for delivery in September. Since the coffee will arrive several months from the date of the agreement, the importer signs a futures contract with a broker or makes a deal directly on the Internet, and the importer deposits the margin. Let's say the price set in the contract is $2 per pound for Colombian coffee of a certain quality delivered to New Orleans on July 12. C contracts start at a minimum of 37,500 pounds of coffee; an agreement to buy may stipulate multiple C contracts, meaning multiples of the minimum quantity.[10] This kind of trading is not for the faint of heart or those with shallow pockets.

If in the meantime our importer can make money by buying or selling futures contracts, so much the better. Of course, speculators are in the game just to deal in such contracts, without even thinking about physically acquiring coffee, much less roasting it. And, in the ultimate complication, an importer might hedge his risk by buying another futures contract for a little protection: if the first contract was in effect a bet that the spot price would go down, the second contract may be a bet that it will go up. The point is to prevent a catastrophic loss if the price goes against the original plan.[11] (To hedge on a commodity purchase should not be confused with "hedge fund," the ultimate form of gambling, in which wealthy people take great risks in buying stock, real estate, and so forth.)

Anyone purchasing coffee who senses that the C price will change can also purchase options. If you foresee an increase in price, for instance because a frost in Brazil will hurt supply, you can buy a "call" option. This gives you the right, but not the obligation, to purchase coffee at a guaranteed figure. Then, when the coffee arrives, you can sell it for the higher spot market price, which produces a profit on the contract itself. Given the same trend, you could also sell a "put" option. In this case, you reserve the right to sell your coffee at a designated price; of course, someone has to buy the put option. Then, when the spot price rises, you sell the contracted amount at the agreed-on price, and you buy replacement coffee at the lower spot figure. Once more, you have made money on the contract alone, without roasting beans, and often without ever taking delivery of coffee or even seeing it.

Suppose you believe that the spot price will fall. Then you act in the opposite direction; you will sell call options and/or buy put options. Anyone who has bought a call from you must pay the agreed-on price, while you purchase coffee on the spot market at a lower figure. Anyone who has sold a put to you has to honor that price, that is, pay the stipulated amount per pound, while you buy at a lower figure on the spot. Or so you hope.

These are the bare bones of trading large amounts of coffee, one of the key factors that affects its price. There are many other aspects of the C market—for example, "strike increment"—that are not discussed here. But these are the basics.

RECENT TRENDS IN TRADING

Someone will always need to buy coffee on the spot market. Suppose that an importer isn't interested in betting on futures but has a large inventory of green coffee on hand. If the spot price goes up, she can sell the warehoused coffee for more than the agreed-upon futures price; when the shipment comes in, she can renew her inventory at lower cost. Thus it pays to be a big player with inventory and plenty of cash or credit on hand.

Again, all of this is supposed to take a lot of the risk out of dealing in coffee. But futures hardly cure everything. To take just a few recent examples of price swings, between the spring of 1994 and August 1995, Coffee C first shot up more than four times in value, then plunged down even lower than its starting point fourteen months earlier.[12] Here is the way the C price changed from March to June 1997, admittedly an especially wild period in the business:[13]

- February 14: 180. Prices rose to this level after a story that South American countries would not loosen export quotas.
- February 27: 172.85. Prices had obviously fallen since the previous story, but on this date the *New York Times* noted that Coffee C had *risen* 59 percent since January 1. The increase for February 27 was because heavy rains threatened Colombia's harvest.
- March 13: 205. No explanation available.[14]
- March 14: 182.25. Prices fell on a report that Brazil and Colombia were increasing exports.
- March 26: 179.3. Having continued to fall for a few days, the price now jumped on the expectation that supplies would tighten.
- April 10: 189.7. A Colombian official indicated that crops in his country and Brazil would be disappointing.
- April 17: 208. Prices surged after a report that inventories were lower than expected and because Brazilian dock workers in the main port, Santos, staged a job protest.
- April 30: 226. Folgers, the biggest American roaster, raised its retail prices, "heightening worries about this year's supply."
- May 14: 241. A report of "dryness" in Brazil sent prices up.

- May 20: 253.1.[15] Expecting a small Brazilian crop, Folgers again raised retail prices.
- May 30: 318 was the day's peak; C closed at 314.8. The jolt resulted from news of a possible frost in Brazil and of small harvests in Nicaragua and other producers.
- June 3: 254. Futures fell 22.45; fears of a Brazilian frost had ended.
- June 18: 208.7. Prices had continued to fall due to the improved Brazilian picture; now they rose because U.S. inventories might be "tight" before the South American harvest.
- June 24: 175.5. A crop forecaster predicted a bumper crop in Brazil.

Such oscillations have continued, although not in such abrupt succession, to the present, and probably will go on for a very long time to come. Reports like those of 1997 reappear, are confirmed, denied, or countered, all with a profound effect on the C price. Maybe a prediction is wrong, only a rumor, or an outright lie; brokers can't always be sure. Certainly no one trading coffee in 1997 foresaw the great rise a few years later of production in Vietnam, which contributed mightily to pushing the C price down by the early 2000s.

On the ICE market, or indeed for the price of **green coffee** anywhere, changes in the supply of any kind of coffee, including robusta, can have a major impact on how much roasters must pay. When huge amounts of robusta began to emerge from Vietnam in the late 1990s, the price of both robusta and arabica tumbled. The reason for a fall in robusta's price is obvious, but why did arabica also drop? That happened because big corporations used robusta in their canned blends, and some Italian and French roasters in particular used, and still use, robusta in espresso blends. In addition, the biggest players began to find ways of taking some of the harshness out of robusta by forcing water through the beans after roasting. Then more robusta could be added to the blends. As a result, demand for arabica dropped, taking the price down with it.

When the C price rises, as it did steeply from June 2010 to April 2011, it tends to pull the price of better coffee up with it. Tom Owen, a widely respected buyer and coffee expert for Sweet Maria's Coffee, remarks that "prices we pay importers, and what importers pay farmers, are generally tied to the C market, with a contract written for 'C market + $0.40 + import costs' or 'C market + $0.40.' So when the market goes up the contract is worth more." In late 2010, Sweet Maria's contracts for purchasing coffee directly from farmers averaged "something . . . like $2.79/pound."[16] But since those contracts were tied to the C price, the cost to Sweet Maria's and other importers of buying coffee also had to rise. Eventually, if the C figure goes up, importers will increase the price of the coffee they sell to roasters.

Even with all these complications, the C price is the best way of following the market price for arabica. At any time, the C figure is used to judge the state of the coffee business. When the price slid to just above 40 cents in late 2001, that amount was generally well below the cost of production for Latin American and other farmers. In short, it was not worthwhile to grow coffee, and many producers left the business. Coffee in the middle range, between robusta and the best arabica grades, was in deep trouble. But by October of 2010, Coffee C had climbed above $2.00, due to increasing demand around the world and a poor harvest, the third in a row, in Colombia. In late April of 2011, the price reached $3.10, the highest it had been since 1997. As noted, all of this applies to pretty good coffee. The best beans do not go through ICE.

IMPLICATIONS FOR FARMERS

When the C price is high, every segment of the coffee industry reacts; all players must pay more for their beans because overall demand rises. Growers can get more for their crops, particularly for medium-quality coffee (the demand for superior coffee, cupped at 80 points and above, is much less elastic). When farmers can get more money, considerable difficulties can arise for co-ops, as members may break ranks and sell coffee to middlemen instead of honoring a previously signed common contract. It can be extremely difficult to refuse to sell to someone who shows up at a farm and offers cash on the spot for a crop. The local buyers, often called *coyotes*, hardly a term of endearment, may offer low prices in bad times; but whether prices are high or low, ready cash is often a farmer's dream, or desperate need.

Collecting from a co-op after it finally delivers coffee and receives payment may mean that a family waits a long time for income. Once a co-op is broken in periods of good prices, it can be extremely hard to reconstruct it.

None of these ways of buying and selling coffee, whether on the ICE or otherwise, guarantees a profit. If someone bets via contracts that the price will rise, but instead it falls, he loses. Hedging protects traders only to a certain extent.

Are the brokers and the speculators parasites? They don't grow coffee, often don't care about it—it's just another commodity—and they may never see it. They may operate by using other people's money. But they do enable capital to flow from place to place and into productive enterprises, and they earn money, if things go right, for someone. That's the way of the world, and whatever is in your cup, the C market marches on.

NOTES

1. ICE Futures U.S., Coffee C® Futures, https://www.theice.com/publicdocs/ICE_Coffee_Brochure.pdf, accessed July 9, 2011.

2. ICE Futures U.S., Coffee C® Options, July 9, 2011, https://www.theice.com/productguide/ProductDetails.shtml?specId=14.

3. ICE Futures U.S., Coffee C®, Brochure, July 9, 2011.

4. David Liss, *The Coffee Trader* (New York: Random House, 2003), especially 126–27. The scene on the floor of the Amsterdam exchange is on 346–51.

5. "Commercial Affairs," *New York Times*, February 13, 1871.

6. *Coffee Futures and Options* (New York: New York Board of Trade, 2004), 6. See also Mark Pendergrast, *Uncommon Grounds: The History of Coffee and How It Transformed Our World* (New York: Basic Books, 2010), 63–66.

7. Victor M. Berthold, *History of the Telephone and Telegraph in Brazil, 1851–1921* (New York: 1922), 14.

8. ICE Futures U.S., Coffee C®, Brochure, 4, except for the 2013 figure for Rwandans and Brazilians, in ICE Futures U.S., Coffee C® Futures.

9. See tales of such journeys in Michaele Weissman, *God in a Cup: The Obsessive Quest for the Perfect Coffee* (Hoboken, NJ: Wiley, 2008).

10. New York Board of Trade, "Coffee Mini 'C,'" New York: NYBOT, n.d.

11. New York Board of Trade, *Understanding Futures and Options* (New York: NYBOT, 2004), 9; Joe Parcell and Vern Pierce, "Commodity Futures Terminology," http://agebb.missouri.edu/mgt/risk/terms.htm, accessed December 8, 2008.

12. Parcell and Pierce, "Commodity Futures Terminology," 7.

13. Unless otherwise noted, each date is from the *New York Times*, referring to the previous day's trading.

14. New York Board of Trade, *Coffee Mini 'C'* (New York: NYBOT, n.d.) 2.

15. *New York Times*, May 22, 1997.

16. "What Happens When Coffee Prices Go through the Roof?" http://www.sweetmarias.com/library/content/oct-nov-2010-what-happens-when-coffee-prices-go-through-roof, accessed August 22, 2013.

16

Appreciating Quality

The Route to Upward Mobility of Coffee Farmers

George Howell

All too often in the coffee industry, mediocre quality has been the norm. Until very recently with the rise of a new generation of coffee **roasters**, growers whose coffees are on difficult mountainous terrain (where most coffees with the great potential are raised) were not incentivized to produce great quality; their goal was simply "acceptability." As time goes on, however, this model has become more and more economically unsustainable. Commodity prices for run-of-the-mill coffee have hovered below and just above the cost of production. With profits at a bare minimum, producers could not sink money into the kind of artisan production that would result in high-quality coffee.

The distribution of marketplace prices for coffee still reflects the old ways of a market geared almost exclusively towards quantity and the immaturity of a genuine quality market, such as exists in tea and wine. The price of the vast bulk of coffee today is well under $10 a pound, retail. Only a minute percentage of coffees rise above $10. Then, like detached stars high above, appear small island coffees; these are Hawaiian kona, Puerto Rico, Jamaica, and Saint Helena, made famous by Napoleon's imprisonment there. Thus Saint Helena's coffee can sell for over $50 a pound. All islands, all nearly unobtainable, all story and myth. While Jamaica's Blue Mountains have great potential and Hawaii does produce some very good quality, these coffees are not multiples better, let alone better at all, than the great Central Americans and the exquisite Kenyans, by any stretch of the imagination. **Capsule** coffee may sell for well over $20 a pound, but the consumer is paying for the convenience of having an individualized stale cup, not for quality.

The most expensive coffee in the world is **kopi luwak**—$300 and more for one pound. Frankly, this is coffee from assholes. These are the "noble" beverages, developed over millennia by cultures that valued ever greater efforts to produce higher qualities. Prices vary over a huge range of qualities and prices while offering great solid values for customers. Where is there anything remotely like that in coffee? Prices for the highest quality coffees must begin to challenge the $10 to $15 price limits before **specialty coffee** farmers are really going to benefit by being incentivized to produce ever better qualities. La Esmeralda in Panama and El Injerto in Guatemala have achieved this kind of commodity independence. Many more should follow.

At $10 a pound for coffee, you are paying less for a twelve-ounce cup of coffee than for a twelve-ounce can of Coke. From a $10 bottle of wine, generally considered not very expensive, the cost is $4.73 for a twelve-ounce serving, versus $0.53 for a twelve-ounce serving of coffee at the same price. At $4.73 for a twelve-ounce serving of coffee you would pay $85.00 per pound. Quite a leap!

Coffee is in its infancy. It first appeared as a brewed beverage a mere six hundred years ago, when tea and wine were already established. The methods used to bring out this coffee were exceedingly primitive. Only recently has coffee developed the technology to really produce a perfect cup. Harvesting, processing, shipping, storage, and roasting have dramatically improved in recent times as well, thanks to modern technology. Drip and espresso brewing are only now being perfected and really becoming able to bring out coffee's great potential. It's our time's choice to make coffee a noble beverage alongside tea and wine, or not. The flip side is that if farmers in difficult regions are not incentivized, they will give way to industrialized coffees without great distinction, grown in flat lands at lower altitudes. Heirloom varieties that release great flavor notes will be gone.

The wine market has seen the results of its emphasis on high quality. Even when the price of average-quality wine has decreased, the fine wine market has remained strong: "It seems counterintuitive, what with France, Italy, Spain, and Australia suffering wine gluts over the past few years, and the E.U. contemplating yanking out vines, even California's central valley has seen one hundred thousand acres culled in the past five years, but the premium end of that market, wines costing twenty five dollars a bottle and up, is on a tear, with sales growth averaging more than thirty percent over the past three years."[1] *Wine Spectator* noted the same great disparity between average and the highest-quality wine: "The highest priced wines usually come from places where at least one winery gets twice the price of anybody else making the same kind of wine."[2]

This is where specialty coffee should aim; it needs heroes, it needs great estates. We are beginning to see this happen in places like Huehuetenango, Guatemala, where El Injerto has become a legend. Until now all the well-known coffee companies of specialty have mainly sold blends, blends that keep the coffee farmer anonymous and therefore chained to a buyer's market. The newest wave of coffee shops is beginning to emphasize the farm or the smallest unit cooperative that is producing the coffee, the variety, the region, and the country. Coffee has begun to enter the age of branding.

If we imagine a quality pyramid, specialty coffee sits atop a giant trapezoid of mass market coffee and forms somewhere around 20 percent of coffee sales. This specialty piece is not divided into horizontally layered qualities but rather vertical slices—dark roast, light roast, fair trade, organic—not one better quality than another, just different kinds side by side. And then, on top of the pyramid, constituting far less than 1 percent, sit the estate coffees, whether from small farms, cooperatives, or large farms.

Yet that highest if terribly small segment of coffees can have a huge effect. That's what the **Cup of Excellence** was all about in 1999 when it was first launched in Brazil. Suddenly people in specialty found an enthusiasm that they had been completely missing. People from around the world came and drilled down from "acceptable" coffees to masterpieces over several intensive days. Each day they drilled down further, re-**cupping** coffees that had come from the earlier batches, culling each time, and then arriving to the ten finest.

These ten winners went on to an Internet auction, where roasters competed against each other, and still do, yearly, in eight different countries, on the Internet to buy these fine, very small lots of coffee. Last year, one particular farm in Guatemala sold its coffee for over $80 per pound, **green**. Panama's La Esmeralda sold for over $100 in one of these competitions several years ago. Luxury markets are marked by excess. Excess reflects a product's status. It affects the price chain far down that product's quality ladder. Coffee's future will be one of more segmented qualities and prices. Wine has shown us the way.

To appreciate truly fine single-estate coffees, it is best to drip-brew using a paper filter. Extraction and control are maximized and the resultant beverage is clear, allowing the flavor of the brew to be highlighted—as opposed to cloudier preparations that obscure the nuanced complexity of a finer bean, much like a cloudy wine. The purpose of brewing roasted coffee is to extract a fairly precise amount of the bean's soluble solids (a sugar cube is a soluble solid).

Up to 30 percent of a coffee bean can be extracted, but 18 to 22 percent is the ideal, the range where black coffee is sweetest. Extracting more will result in bitter, harsh, tobacco-like flavors. This simple rule is often unrecognized by fine restaurants and even in cafés. Extraction using the drip method involves correct temperature, ideally right around 200°F; it requires mild turbulence in the filter to make sure all the grounds are evenly extracted and, equally important, calibration between time and grind: the coarser the grind, the longer the ground coffee should be in contact with hot water; the finer the grind, the shorter the time. Espresso takes seconds and thus requires extra fine grind; Chemex, having an extra-thick filter, coarse grind—all to extract that 20 percent from the coffee. In the realm of drip grind, finer grinds will result in a greater proportion of dust—which releases everything (therefore over-extracts) immediately.

It is better to aim for coarser grinds, thereby reducing the percentage of dust and extra fines, and to lengthen the time—up to six minutes for a full pot of coffee. Finally, the quality of the water (having correct mineral content), quality of the coffee, and quality of the filter are critical. A paper filter needs to be rinsed with hot water before brewing to eliminate all the off-flavors paper will otherwise transfer to the drink.

Espresso is made to be consumed immediately after being brewed. It is like a brandy and should be served immediately; but for a drip, it is not a matter of tasting the first sip when it is piping hot and judging it then and there. Fine, lighter-roasted, drip coffee is to be savored, experienced over twenty to thirty minutes as the coffee cools and gradually reveals itself. Really hot coffee will sting and close your taste buds. At the initial temperature, the most one can get is the first aromatic glimpse of what is coming.

As the cup cools to an ideal 135°F, look for sweetness and clean cup, sweetness from the ripeness of the coffee, clean cup from the processing. A coffee that is not perfectly clean is murky, muddled, often confused with "rich." Only after the coffee begins to cool should one look for the aromatics in the drink itself and begin to perceive layered notes of chocolate, nuts, honey, fruit, and flowers in changing combinations as the temperature changes. Great coffees come in a rainbow of their own natural flavors—as long as they are truly fine and not overly roasted with caramel and bitter "saucy" notes.

Along with **flavor** come **acidity**, **body**, **mouthfeel**, and finally **aftertaste**, which ideally should begin to sweetly disappear. The great diversity of coffee's flavor profiles has only begun to be explored by the industry, let alone the consumer. But mistakes in properly producing a quality coffee, from farming to processing to shipping to roasting to storing to, finally to brewing, can dull flavor profiles until all colors smear into brown and everything tastes the same. That's if the coffee doesn't taste awful!

NOTES

1. Janet Morrisey, "Fruit of the Vine," *Time International* (Atlantic Edition), November 12, 2007.
2. Matt Kramer, "QPR," *Wine Spectator*, May 31, 2001.

17

What Is Specialty Coffee?

Shawn Steiman

At the SCAA meetings and trade show in 2011, *The Morning Cup*, published daily while the show was going on, asked coffee professionals "What does specialty coffee mean to you?"

Here are four answers:

Hannah Eatough, Harrogate, UK: "It means fantastic quality and coffee that is ethically sourced. It's fantastic coffee you want to drink again and again."

Chris Demarse, Muncie, Indiana: "There are a few characteristics basic to specialty coffee: transparency, sustainability, equity, and quality."

Mary Metallo-Tellie, Scranton, Pennsylvania: "It means great taste, made with great passion, great quality . . . lots of fabulous things."

Jean Mare Irakabaho, Kigali, Rwanda: "High-quality coffee that is correctly processed. It's a coffee that makes consumers happy, boosting the income and livelihood of farmers."[1]

WHAT IS SPECIALTY COFFEE?

The world has a lot of coffee waiting to be drunk. It can be bought in bags, cans, tins, jars, and bricks. It can be whole bean or ground, waiting to be brewed, instant, or pre-made and ready-to-drink. It can be drunk at home or away, prepared by person or machine. All these possibilities, and many others, will produce a different experience for the drinker who eventually tries the coffee; to put it mildly, not all cups of coffee are the same. People, with their inherent and economic needs to categorize and differentiate objects, strive to group and understand all those different cups of coffee—how they taste and how they came to taste that way—by indicating a sense of quality in the liquor.

According to Don Holly, administrative director of the **Specialty Coffee Association of America** (SCAA), writing in 1999, Erna Knutsen coined the term **specialty coffee** in 1978. She was describing coffees that came from specific geographic microclimates and had unique flavor profiles. She observed that not all coffees tasted the same, and the ones that were clearly differentiated by taste, in a good way, were special. Holly's exploration of defining specialty coffee, which works its way through the process of producing coffee, highlights a point that is likely shared by many in the industry: "It is not only that the coffee doesn't taste bad; to be considered specialty it must be notably good." He ends his piece with an acute summation: "Specialty coffee is, in the end, defined in the cup."[2]

A decade after Holly wrote his definition, Ric Rhinehart, executive director of the SCAA, ventured a more detailed explanation. Writing from the vantage point of a more developed industry, Rhinehart's discussion not only covers the process of coffee, from seed to cup, and the ultimate result of that process, but includes the actors of that process. Rhinehart writes, "In the final analysis specialty coffee will be defined by the quality of the product, whether green bean, roasted bean or prepared beverage and by the quality of life that coffee can deliver to all of those involved in its cultivation, preparation and degustation."[3]

Unfortunately, neither Holly nor Rhinehart quantified how a specialty coffee tastes different from a nonspecialty coffee, known as **commercial coffee**; rather, their definitions were philosophical propositions that explained what must happen in order for a special cup to exist and who must benefit from it. Any person foolish enough to attempt a definition, including this author, recognizes that the task is impossible before it even begins.

IN THE BEGINNING

Perhaps, at one time, the world of coffee was dichromatic. There was mass-produced, somewhat generic, caffeine-laden coffee, and then there was *other*, coffee that could no longer be considered just coffee. This coffee, newly (re)discovered, excited a handful of artisans who cherished it, sought it out, and celebrated it to the point where their efforts and ideals created a new industry: the specialty coffee industry.

Through its rapid growth and expansion, specialty coffee continued to define itself as *other*, a significantly amorphous construct that allowed specialty coffee to be an umbrella term for anything that was different. The lack of a more stringent definition permitted the flourishing of coffees and beverages that rightfully can be called specialty. Now, this *other* is full of many *others*, and the leaders of the industry are left to philosophize about what they want specialty coffee to be, not necessarily what it is.

Certainly, the SCAA, the original and largest, most influential trade group and voice of the specialty coffee industry, has a place in defining the term that is their name and mission. They can and should categorize the amorphous world of specialty coffee. To some extent, they and other influential organizations have. The groundwork has been laid.

SCAA STANDARDS

In 2009, the SCAA published revised quality standards for **green coffee**.[4] It established physical criteria necessary to be deemed "specialty," but it also states that the coffee must meet a minimum **cupping** score of 80, based on its cupping protocol and assessment scheme.[5] The cupping protocol establishes a 100-point scoring system by which all coffees can be assessed. Exactly what the 80-point demarcation delineates for the cup quality is not absolute, as the point count from the various categories that make up the scoring system can vary for individual coffees. In general, though, as long as the coffee doesn't have any detectable **defects** like moldy or sour, it is likely to reach the 80 mark.

While the users of the system all agree that this is a reasonable demarcation, few, if any of them, would be excited to drink an 80-point coffee. The demarcation, while practical, hardly

SPECIALTY COFFEE: THE GRAY AREA

It is one thing to acquire a carefully sourced, carefully roasted, carefully brewed coffee, rate it, and identify it as specialty. It is quite another to go out into the active marketplace, pick a product off the shelf, and celebrate or decry it as specialty. Arguably, this is where the specialty coffee industry, in its amorphous glory, struggles the most with its identity.

Hardcore specialty coffee fanatics tend to think that only plain, black coffee, sourced and prepared with great intention and care, can ever really be specialty coffee. Yet the specialty marketplace is full of options that are nothing like that but, by most definitions, are, in fact, specialty. In any given U.S. supermarket, one can find roasted and bagged coffee, ready-to-drink beverages, and individually packaged coffee **pods** and cups, that are grouped separately from what is universally accepted as commercial coffee (industrial/canned coffees produced by gigantic companies whose coffee component is often only a small part of their business model). These coffees often have a provenance and history that fits the specialty definition. While they may not be quite as fresh as they could be and they may not get brewed to the exacting standards of the industry, many of the coffees themselves will garner an 80-point score. Yet not all members of the specialty industry agree that they are specialty.

The lines become blurred when one flavors coffee after roasting or, in the café, flavor is added to the final beverage. The addition of a sweetener, a time-honored practice, certainly changes the flavor of coffee, arguably putting it underneath the 80-point score. The murkiest place is at the juncture of black coffee and milk. A coffee, acquired from a specific farm and carefully crafted into a beverage, may not be specialty when milk is added. Yet brew that same coffee as an espresso and mix it with textured milk, and the resulting cappuccino is a hallmark of specialty coffee.

At the core of the gray area is a lack of agreement about what specialty coffee can be and when it is allowed to be specialty. The 100-point SCAA scale is meant to evaluate green coffee, and the protocol defines what coffees are likely to ascend to the 80-point mark. It isn't able to cope with the life of the coffee after that moment. If chocolate macadamia nut flavoring is added to a 95-point coffee, is it still specialty coffee?

This highlights the challenge of defining specialty coffee. Is it measured by what is actually in the cup or by the beans that, at one point in time, were able to make the grade? This question alludes to the problem of specialty coffee being composed of *others* and no single person or entity having authority or justification to delineate membership for a global phenomenon.

Holly and Rhinehart understood this problem. This is why they never discussed what specialty coffee tasted like. They understood that specialty coffee isn't something that is drunk or experienced; it is an idea to be embraced. There never can be a definitive, quantitative description of specialty coffee. Coffee quality and specialty coffee are moving targets that shift with culture, the times, and the drinkers defining them.[6] Thus, the definition of the specialty coffee beverage must constantly be revisited and reworked as needed. Specialty coffee is defined not by what the coffee itself tastes like but by the people who interact with it.

represents desirable or sometimes even acceptable coffees; "not bad" is not exactly "special." Nonetheless, this numeric turning point of specialty-or-not is necessary, as it establishes minimum qualifications and a benchmark to which everything can be compared. Unfortunately, making the specialty grade says little about what the coffee actually tastes like.

Specialty coffee is the idea that some coffees, both directly and indirectly, make a difference in the lives of all those who come into contact with them. To farmers, it may give them greater income or personal pride. To consumers, it may give them a taste that lingers in their memory, not just their mouth. As Rhinehart wrote, it is about the quality of life.

Taken one step further, it is coffee that changes our perception of the world. Specialty coffee is coffee that makes us think. It makes us think about what we taste, what we feel, and how that coffee influences the world around it.

NOTES

1. "SCAA asks: What does specialty coffee mean to you?" *The Morning Cup*, April 30, 2011, 2.

2. Don Holly, "Coffee FAQs: What is the definition of specialty coffee?," *SCAA Chronicle* (December 1999).

3. Ric Rhinehart, "What Is Specialty Coffee?," June 2009, http://scaa.org/?page=RicArtp1, accessed February 28, 2012.

4. SCAA, *SCAA Standard | Green Coffee Quality*, revised November 21, 2009.

5. SCAA, *SCAA Standard | Cupping Specialty Coffee*, revised November 21, 2009.

6. For a more thorough discussion of coffee quality, see "Coffee Quality and Assessment" in this volume.

18

Where Does the Money Go in the Coffee Supply Chain?

Robert W. Thurston

We've all handed over cash to a coffee seller, but have you ever wondered what that cash pays for? The trail from the coffee tree to your street is long, and the SCAA offered a snapshot, adapted here, of all the stops along that trail.

Let's say that you own a coffee bar. To stay in business and to live, you need to make a profit. That means money in the bank after all your expenses have been paid. Just what are your costs? This example covers expenses at each of the stages from export to a cup sold in your shop, using certified **Fair Trade, organic** coffee. Your part comes in toward the end. The journey starts with milled **green coffee**—that is, coffee beans that have only the **silverskin** as a remaining cover—sold in a producing country to a U.S. importer at $1.50 a pound. The importer must then pay additional fees and costs (all figures are per pound):

- .095 for shipping and customs entry
- .05 for warehouse and logistics
- .095 for finance and storage
- .15 for importer margin

Thus to this point, the importer has added .39 to the cost of a pound of coffee, making the total of inputs so far $1.89 per pound.

The coffee is then shipped to a roaster. Costs mount up this way:

- .12 for shipping
- .44 shrinkage loss at 18% of weight (such loss is typical in the roasting process, since some of the weight of the green beans is in water that will escape as steam)

Now the total cost is $2.45/pound. The next costs are these:

- .39 for packaging
- .55 direct labor
- .10 Fair Trade USA fee for maintaining certification

This brings the coffee's cost to $3.49.

But the **roaster**/wholesaler has other expenses:

- .94 for wages, excluding direct labor
- 1.68 sales, general, and administrative
- .38 interest, depreciation, amortization, lease

Now the total invested in the pound of coffee is $6.49.

Assuming that the roaster sells the coffee to a café at $7.25, the pre-tax profit is .76. On this amount, state and federal taxes are .27, leaving the roaster's net profit per pound at .49, about 6.7 percent of the sale price.

You, the retailer, now make coffee as a beverage in your shop.

One pound of coffee yields 7.5 liters (about 253.5 ounces by volume) of coffee beverage, using 60 grams (22.12 ounces by weight) of ground coffee per liter (33.8 ounces by volume) of water. The costs of serving this coffee are as follows:

- a cup of coffee, for this illustration, is 475 milliliters (let's say 16 ounces by volume)
- therefore 16 cups of coffee per pound brings the shop $28.00
- Hold on: you need to pay out, besides the 7.25 you already spent on the beans,
- 2.00 for cups
- .46 for lids
- .16 for stir sticks
- .56 for condiments (milk, sugar, cream, artificial sweeteners, and so on)

Still, so far you have made a gross profit per pound of $17.57. Sounds pretty sweet. But there are some other matters to take care of:

- 5.60 for labor!

Labor in the coffee bar is the biggest single expense of all, more than 3.7 times what the green beans sold for as they were exported from the producing country. So the *value added* to the product is overwhelmingly in the consuming countries. We are closer to understanding why the farmers do not receive a huge portion of the cost of a cup of coffee in an American or European shop.

But of course there are further costs in your shop. Sticking with the U.S. example, they are:

- 1.96 for the lease
- .70 for utilities
- .84 for marketing
- .56 for repairs and maintenance
- 4.20 for general and administrative expenses (e.g., telephone, wireless, bookkeeping)

All this drops your net profit to $3.71/pound. And we're still not done! You will have to buy new equipment at some point to keep going, and unless you have big bags of your own money lying around, you will have to borrow funds. Therefore you must spend:

- 1.12 for depreciation, amortization, interest
- .91 for state and federal taxes. Did you think the tax men would forget you?

Your net profit now stands at $1.68, or 6 percent of the sales income.

Let's review the retail segment. You paid for the coffee, labor, condiments, heat, light, rent, and so on, a total of $20.72 per pound of coffee. Subtracting the $7.25 paid for the roasted coffee beans leaves $13.47. In other words, you, the coffee bar owner, paid 1.8 times as much for everything else as for the coffee. Buying the beans amounted to about 35 percent of your total expenses. We are now much closer to understanding why the farmer gets only a small portion of what it costs for a cup of coffee in a café.

Here ends the SCAA's tale of where the money goes. Of course, expenses vary hugely across the U.S., not to mention Europe and Japan. In some locations, rent and labor are much higher than suggested here. Moreover, the example is of certified Fair Trade organic coffee. Other coffees of similar quality may cost significantly less, while the most desirable ones, rated at 90 points and above, would cost more. And, to state the obvious, the price of green coffee rises and falls with the weather, production around the world, political unrest, and other factors. When the price rises, you may find it difficult to pass the additional cost on to your customers. The squeeze is on.

My own interviews with coffee bar owners suggest amendments to the outline above. Retailers say their expenses to buy beans are usually less than 20 percent of all costs. Everywhere labor is the greatest expense. Skilled **baristas**, who need at least six months of on-the-job training before they can serve customers independently—amid orders from impatient people for lattes, double espressos, macchiatos, cappuccinos with skim milk, small, large, and ultra-grande, all to be made and served *now*—command much more pay than those who merely push a few buttons and wait for a machine to pour the brew.

Every shop owner will be asked for donations or to sponsor many events. There should be trips to origin, to coffee shows and conventions, perhaps for more training.

When the numbers are crunched hard, the injustice of the infamous $3 a day for farmers, $3 for a cup of coffee in the U.S. becomes a highly slippery matter. To be sure, the average barista or coffee bar owner, if she stays in business, lives a good deal better than the average, say, Kenyan farmer. But the two countries are really different. If Kenya had the infrastructure and especially the labor costs of the U.S., the farm/cup comparison would be much more valid. As things are, it is not a particularly useful exercise to think about how much a peasant earns per day in terms of how much it costs an urban westerner to buy a cup of coffee, especially one laced with milk in some fashion.

The simple fact of the coffee chain is that value is overwhelmingly added in the consuming areas. That remains true if the example concerns a café in a producing country. The cost of making a cup of coffee in Sao Paulo or Nairobi is high, partly because transportation and energy expenses are serious there. Labor is cheaper outside of Western Europe, Japan, and the U.S., but it is hardly free. In any event, consumers everywhere do need to think carefully about how the farmers can receive more money for their crop; the future supply of coffee depends on this issue.

As for the moral question of who lives better, consider the plight of peasants who *don't* have coffee or a similar desirable commodity to sell. Manual labor, whether in a field in Nicaragua or a McDonald's in Los Angeles, does not add very much to the final cost of a processed item. Everyone who drinks coffee should look squarely at the way expenses mount up along the chain; we cannot ignore the reality of business expenses, which does not help solve farmers' problems.

NOTE

This chapter is adapted by Robert W. Thurston from a project of the Specialty Coffee Association of America, 2010, with permission.

Part II

THE STATE OF THE TRADE

19

The Global Trade in Coffee

An Overview

Robert W. Thurston

From the trickle of coffee that went from the Middle East to Western Europe in the early seventeenth century, the global trade in coffee has grown to huge proportions. Contrary to popular belief, coffee is not the second most valuable commodity traded legally around the world. Instead, coffee is "the world's most widely traded tropical agricultural commodity, accounting for exports worth an estimated $15.4 billion in 2009/10, when some 93.4 million bags were shipped."[1] But at a total value, in some reports, of $100 billion annually, the entire business of coffee, from tree to coffeehouse and your house, is doing well. That is not to say that farmers in many lands are prospering.

Several articles in this book discuss the growth of coffee agriculture and trade into the twentieth century. Any number of attempts to stabilize if not control the price of coffee rested on the efforts of individual countries, especially Brazil, in the early twentieth century. The first of these was the "valorization" scheme of 1905–08, in which the Brazilian government bought up large amounts of coffee and stored it, while tax policy aimed at driving production down—and prices up—by imposing new levies on coffee hectarage.[2] In the 1930s, Brazil burned copious quantities of coffee and dumped tons more into the sea. Residents of Rio de Janeiro and Sao Paulo reported that there was a permanent cloud of coffee smoke above each city. In 1937, the country destroyed 17.2 million **bags**, at a time when global consumption was 26.4 million bags.[3] But the Depression drove prices down so far, to less than 7 U.S. cents a pound, that these programs did little to improve the situation.

In 1940, when World War II was already under way in Europe, the U.S. government feared that the low price of coffee coming from Latin America, and the resulting poor incomes for farmers there, would push many of them into sympathy with either fascism or communism. The American side therefore proposed the Inter-American Coffee Agreement (IACA); it stipulated that the U.S. would import no more than 15.9 million bags a year, while Latin American governments would control production. This agreement succeeded in doubling the price of coffee by the end of 1941.

By the mid-1950s, equilibrium between supply and demand developed, and all international agreements lapsed. But fluctuations in price and new fears in the U.S. of communism in Latin America after the Cuban Revolution of 1959 spurred the regions' governments to try once more to control supply, and hence prices. The year 1962 saw the first **International**

111

Coffee Agreement (ICA), which set export quotas for most of the world's producing nations. When the price fell below $1.20 a pound, quotas would be tightened, reducing the amount of coffee on the world market and pushing the price up. At a price of more than $1.40, quotas were loosened—in what was called the corset system—allowing countries to export more and sending the price down.[4] When weather conditions caused a steep rise in prices, as in 1975–77, the quota system was abandoned entirely. This first ICA went through three revisions before the whole arrangement collapsed in 1989. By that time, American fears of radicalism in Latin America had subsided, while some producing governments felt that the quota system restricted them unfairly.

Although a new ICA finally emerged among producers in 1994, and was revised in 2001 and 2007, the agreement did not set quotas or other mechanisms to control production and export. Other attempts to regulate the market have foundered. When controls disappeared in 1989, the **International Coffee Organization**, created in 1963 to oversee the first ICA, became a body dedicated to gathering information and running programs designed to enhance quality and production.[5] In this new guise, the ICO, which now has thirty exporting members and five importing ones (U.S., the European Union, Tunisia, Norway, and Switzerland) has proven to be a rich source of data and knowledge about coffee.

ICO figures for the period from 1999/2000 to 2009/2010 show that the total production of coffee around the world has not surged upward. However, the price **free on board** (written as FOB, meaning that all charges, taxes, duties, and other costs in the producing country have been paid, and the coffee is on board a ship ready to head out to sea) has fluctuated a great deal, and the value of exported coffee has risen dramatically since 2004/05. Here are samples from the data:[6]

Table 19.1. Quantity and Value of Global Exported Coffee, Selected Years

Year	Value of Exports in US$ (billions)	Million Bags	US Cents per Pound FOB
1999–2000	8.7	89.4	74
2000–2001	5.8	90.4	49
2001–2	4.9	86.7	43
2004–5	8.0	89.0	76
2007–8	15.0	96.1	118
2009–10	15.4	93.4	125

While consumption increased rapidly in Japan after 1980, making the country the third largest importer in the world, behind the U.S. and Germany, Japanese demand has leveled off in the past decade. Western European consumption overall is down slightly from the numbers of the early 2000s; this drop appears to be due to the aging of the population and the attraction of energy drinks among young people. On the other hand, coffee is steadily gaining popularity in Eastern Europe, especially Russia, whose imports are now roughly on a level with the UK's. The chapters on individual consuming countries in this section provide more information on specific nations.

Robusta continues to amount to about 30–40 percent of all coffee exported, **arabica** 60–70 percent. **Soluble** (instant) coffee, made largely from robusta, continues to dominate in Eastern Europe and in much home consumption, for example in the UK. Robusta production is likely to rise as global warming makes more land suitable for the hardier variety and unfavorable for arabica.

Brazil continues as the uncontested king of production of both basic species, and output is likely to increase there, barring extensive frosts. Mechanization, particularly in harvesting, is already well developed in Brazil, making its productivity much higher than in countries where picking is by hand. Colombia, which used to be the world's second largest producer, has suffered in recent years from the coffee berry borer, climate change, and some diversion of agriculture into coca. Colombia's difficulties are among the factors that have driven the price of arabica much higher since 2009. For the first time, Ethiopia's production surpassed Colombia's in 2012.[7]

Although dependence on coffee for foreign export earnings has fallen as a percentage of virtually all producing countries' income,[8] coffee continues to be extremely important in the economy of many lands. Burundi leads this group, with 59 percent of its foreign earnings coming from coffee. Ethiopia is next at 33 percent in 2010–11, followed by Rwanda at 27 percent and Honduras at 20 percent. For Brazil and Vietnam, the figure is only 2 percent.[9]

A major, continuing concern throughout the coffee industry is that only a small portion of the aggregate wealth generated stays in the **producing countries.** An Oxfam report of 2002, admittedly near the nadir of coffee prices in recent decades, found that ten years earlier, exports captured one-third of all value of the coffee market. At the time of the report, that figure had fallen to less than 10 percent.[10] Of a total market value estimated at $70 billion in 2006, exporting countries reportedly earned only $5 billion.[11]

However, the increase in the total "value" of coffee has come from many sources, of which most are incurred in consuming countries. Advertising, wages, rents, insurance, utilities, transportation, and other costs all figure into the ultimate value of coffee. In producing countries, prices of fertilizers, pesticides, and fuel for transportation rose considerably from the early 1990s to 2006; only in the current recession has the cost of some of these items fallen. More precisely, their cost has fluctuated considerably. See "Where Does the Money Go in the Coffee Supply Chain?" for more information on why coffee in consuming countries costs as much as it does. Whatever the causes of the falling share of producing nations in the total value of the coffee market, the global industry has tried and is trying many ways of raising farmers' income.

What the future may hold is always uncertain, more so for agriculture, and still more so for coffee. Plant a tree, wait two to four years for it to bear usable fruit, and hope; a great deal can change in a short period. Nonetheless, a few guesses seem safe. The ICO predicted in early 2009 that consumption would exceed production by a large amount during that year, which proved to be the case. Colombia's problems combined with increased demand for coffee within Latin America, Europe, and Japan caused the overall picture to tip in favor of demand over supply.[12] As of late 2011, the deficit of coffee relative to demand was some 2.9 million bags, mostly arabica.[13] It seems safe to predict that at least in the short term, many farmers will try to increase arabica production, even as climate change works against it.

In October 2010, a "wildly diverse group of coffee professionals from around the world" met in Texas "to decide whether and how the coffee industry should support a global research and development program to increase supply and quality of arabica coffees." After three days of discussion, the group unanimously agreed that was an important, global goal. In early 2012, attendees at the original meeting and other individuals and organizations, including leading companies in the specialty coffee industry, decided to establish World Coffee Research, an organization that will provide information and assistance to arabica growers everywhere.[14] To ask whether this and other efforts to boost the quantity of arabica will send the world into yet another cycle of over-production and falling prices is sheer speculation. We can only hope that the intricate mix of factors affecting the supply of arabica will align well enough with demand to maintain and raise farmers' income.

Figure 19.1. Coffee still grows wild in Ethiopia, but it will be a battle to preserve wild genetic stock in view of increasing population pressure and deforestation in the country. Photo by Robert Thurston.

NOTES

1. "World Coffee Trade," International Coffee Organization, http://www.ico.org/trade_e.asp?section=About_Coffee, accessed February 23, 2012.

2. William H. Ukers, *All About Coffee*, 2nd ed. (New York: The Tea & Coffee Trade Journal Company, 1935), 458–61.

3. Bryan Lewin, Daniele Giovannucci, and Panayotis Varangis, *Coffee Markets: New Paradigms in Global Supply and Demand. Agriculture and Rural Development*, World Bank, Discussion Paper no. 3 (Washington, DC: Agriculture and Rural Development Department, World Bank, 2004), 24.

4. Aashish Mehta and Jean-Paul Chavas, "Responding to the Coffee Crisis: What Can We Learn from Price Dynamics," Staff Paper No. 472, University of Wisconsin-Madison, Department of Agriculture and Applied Economics, March 2004, 4: http://www.aae.wisc.edu/pubs/sps/pdf/stpap472.pdf, accessed February 23, 2012.

5. International Coffee Organization, History; http://www.ico.org/history.asp, accessed February 23, 2012.

6. "World Coffee Trade," ICO.

7. International Coffee Organization, "Exporting countries: total production, 2007–2012" http://www.ico.org/prices/po.htm, accessed May 29, 2013.

8. Charis Gresser and Sophia Tickell, *Mugged. Poverty in Your Coffee Cup* (Oxford: Oxfam, 2002), 8. Figures at that time for coffee as a proportion of export earnings were, for example, Burundi 79 percent, Ethiopia 54 percent, and Honduras 24 percent.

9. "World Coffee Trade," ICO.

10. Gresser and Tickell, *Mugged*, 2.

11. http://tutor2u.net/economics/revision-notes/as-markets-coffee.html, accessed February 25, 2012. For an estimate that producing countries captured 20 percent of "total income" in coffee in the 1980s, but 13 percent in the mid-1990s, see David Goodman, "The International Coffee Crisis: A Review of the Issues," in *Confronting the Coffee Crisis*, ed. Christopher Bacon (Cambridge, MA: MIT Press, 2008), 6.

12. Bloomberg News, "Global Coffee Deficit May Hit 8 Million Bags, ICO's Osorio Says," February 12, 2009, http://www.bloomberg.com/apps/news?pid=newsarchive&sid=apdey3NI.1FI, accessed February 25, 2012. Osorio is Nestor Osorio, executive director of ICO.

13. This is according to a report by Maquarie Research, as reported in C&C, *Coffee and Cocoa International* 38, no. 5 (November 2011): 4.

14. "WCR Ready to Launch Research," *World Coffee Research News*, March 1, 2012.

20

Coffee Certification Programs

Robert W. Thurston

For coffee, **certification** means that an external agency, either governmental, a private firm, or an **NGO** (non-governmental organization), has determined that particular coffees, farms, or co-ops have met certain standards. These may relate to the price paid for the coffee, agricultural practices, environmental conditions, presence of shade trees and wildlife on a farm, or conditions for farmers and hired workers. As of 2009, 16 percent of all U.S. coffee imports had at least one certification. In the Netherlands, this figure reached 30 percent. The global figure, however, is about 8 percent.[1]

The certifying agency typically arranges educational and monitoring programs for coffee growers. If non-governmental, these programs are funded by donations and by encouraging or requiring importers to pay more for certified coffee than the current market price for similar, non-certified beans. A major goal of most certifying bodies is to ensure that coffee is traceable; that is, the consumer will know where the coffee came from, as opposed to purchasing coffee in a can that may, at best, be marked simply "arabica."

The major certifying groups, with their criteria and method of operation, are discussed in the following sections.

USDA

The United States Department of Agriculture certifies products sold in the U.S. as **organic.** Various agencies of individual states, for example California, impose additional requirements for organic certification within their borders. Many other countries, from Canada across Western and Central Europe to Japan, administer their own certification programs. USDA works through the National Organic Program and provides guidelines (such as the "National List of Approved and Prohibited Substances") for organic agriculture production. New substances may be added on either side, or existing ones shifted, as new scientific information becomes available or as the public petitions for changes. The USDA list is important for certification of any product sold as organic in the U.S., whether produced here or abroad, as well as for foreign certifying programs.

FAIR TRADE USA

Fair Trade USA (formerly TransFair USA) signs export contracts with associations of producers, usually co-ops. Fair Trade (FT) agreements are made with producers for coffee **FOB** (free on board, meaning that the coffee is loaded onto an export vessel and has had all of its costs paid, including taxes, duties, and loading charges, and is therefore ready for export). FT contracts provide a minimum price for coffee, which can rise if the **C price** goes higher than the minimum, but can never fall below that figure. As of April 2011, the FT minimum for **natural processing** arabica became $1.35, for **washed processing** beans $1.40, and for organic $1.70. FT contracts also require that purchasers pay a "social premium" of an additional 20 cents a pound. Money gathered by co-ops from this charge is to be spent on projects to improve the quality of life for farmers, for instance schools or a clean water supply.

UTZ KAPEH GOOD INSIDE

Utz Kapeh Good Inside is largely concerned with conditions for farm workers. "Utz Kapeh" is a phrase from a Mayan language meaning "good coffee." The organization's website proclaims that its seal "is the guarantee that your coffee is responsibly grown."

Utz does not entirely oppose the use of synthetic **pesticides** and **fertilizers**; however, it urges farmers to keep their application to a minimum and "requires certified producers to train its employees on health and safety procedures and the correct use of pesticides."[2] All children living on certified farms must have access to education, and workers and their families must be provided with "decent housing, clean drinking water and healthcare services." Utz-certified farms must work to reduce water usage and erosion, in part by using native trees to hold the soil and provide shade. More widely known in Europe than in the U.S., Utz is now steadily adding businesses that use its coffee on both sides of the Atlantic.

Unlike Fair Trade, Utz does not play a role in negotiating prices for farmers, but importers are expected to pay a premium above the going market price for the coffee.

RAINFOREST ALLIANCE

Some two decades old, Rainforest aims to halt and reverse deforestation, promote the use of **shade** trees on coffee farms, and support **sustainable** agriculture, not only in coffee but for other crops and even livestock. Like Utz Kapeh, the Alliance is not totally committed to organic farming. Here is Rainforest's statement on its website regarding agrochemicals:

Sustainable Agriculture Network (SAN) standards are based on an internationally recognized integrated pest management model, which allows for some limited, strictly controlled use of [synthetic, non-organic] agrochemicals. SAN standards emphasize two important goals: wildlife conservation and worker welfare. Farmers certified by the Rainforest Alliance do not use agrochemicals prohibited by the United States Environmental Protection Agency and the European Union, nor do they use chemicals listed on the Dirty Dozen list of the Pesticide Action Network North America. Managers of certified farms are required to use biological or mechanical alternatives to pesticides whenever possible. When farmers determine that agrochemicals are necessary to protect the crop, they must choose the safest products available and use every available safeguard to protect human health and the environment.

Like Utz Kapeh, Rainforest is not involved in writing contracts for coffee or other products. But the group notes that "most farmers are able to receive a price premium because their farms are certified." In early 2010, Rainforest Alliance made a "significant change to its fee structure. Previously, it had charged farmers $7.50 per **hectare** (about 2.5 acres) for certification. Now, like most certification organizations, the Alliance imposes its fee on coffee importers, charging 1.5 cents per pound."[3]

SMITHSONIAN BIRD FRIENDLY

The Smithsonian Migratory Bird Center (SMBC) encourages the production of shade-grown coffee and the conservation of migratory birds through its "Bird Friendly®" seal of approval. This designation is given to shade-grown coffee produced on organic farms, which must meet USDA standards. Farmers seeking to join the Smithsonian program must work with an approved private or public coffee certifying agency; these are located in several Latin American and European countries, Indonesia, and the U.S. All of the agencies on the Smithsonian list are also allowed to confer organic certification as well as the Bird Friendly seal. Becoming Bird Friendly requires at least three years of visits by an approved agency, which, on behalf of Smithsonian, checks the amount and type of shade on the farm.

The SMBC maintains, although other specialty coffee experts detect no difference, that shade-grown coffee is better tasting, because "beans ripen more slowly in shade, resulting in a richer flavor." There are also important advantages in improving the health of farmers; number and variety of birds on the land, which can boost ecotourism; amount of organic matter added to the soil as trees die and rot and from annual leaf litter; wood and fruit products from the shade trees; and "potential for a premium price in excess of the organic premium." In this program, farmers bear the costs of certification, although importers are expected to pay above market for the coffee.

4C

The 4C Association, inspired by the United Nations Millennium goals of 2003, which are designed to eliminate poverty and hunger across the globe, was organized in 2006. 4C "aims at increasing coffee producers' net income through quality improvements, improved **marketing** conditions, cost reductions, increasing efficiency and optimization of supply chain functions." Any farmer or business in the coffee chain may join the organization. The fee for a small-scale producer is a one-time only charge of €7.50 (about $9.52 in the fall of 2012), "making the 4C Association accessible to a huge number of coffee growers worldwide, whereas trade and industry members pay up to €160,000 [about $203,200] annually." **Roaster** members commit to buying increasing amounts of certified coffee over time. 4C's guidelines relate to improving sustainability in growing, processing, and marketing coffee. "Through its global network, 4C provides support services including training and access to tools and information."[4]

C.A.F.E.

Starbucks's own certification program, C.A.F.E, stands for Coffee and Farmer Equity Practices. Through this label and through Fair Trade, Starbucks imported about 155 million pounds of certified coffee into the U.S. in 2006,[5] the last year for which data are available. The guidelines for C.A.F.E. have to do with wages, prohibitions against child labor, worker safety and training, environmental practices, and workers' access to decent housing, medical care, and education.[6] Workers must be paid the regional or national minimum wage. Farms and processing facilities must score above a certain number of points altogether and in each category to qualify for the program. Starbucks then pays a premium for beans certified under C.A.F.E.

Certification itself has become a contentious issue; the numerous studies on whether certification delivers more money to the farmer are inconclusive. Some research shows higher income when farmers sell certified beans, while other research does not. A problem for small producers in many regions, and perhaps in entire countries such as Nicaragua, is that the costs of certification and of producing organic coffee may not be offset by higher prices received for the beans. "Certified coffee producing families, especially organic-fair trade certified ones, face labor constraints and thus need to hire additional labor."[7]

A study of 327 randomly selected farms in Nicaragua found that organic producers have the highest level of **productivity**, followed by conventional farmers, while organic–fair trade farmers ranked lowest. The last category receives the highest **farm gate price** for coffee. Yet these producers have a lower level of profitability than organic (non-fair trade) producers. This can be due to various factors, among them yield per hectare, labor costs, and family labor constraints. Finally, the same survey finds that the increased labor costs of organic farmers put their average income below the national poverty line, while the other two groups are somewhat above it. The authors of the study conclude that productivity and efficiency of the farms must increase, as "prices for certified coffee cannot compensate for low productivity, land or labor constraints."[8]

The issues surrounding certification become especially acute when coffee prices are high. Of course, prices have lurched up and down as long as anyone has kept track of them; however, as we suggest elsewhere in this book, a number of factors now in place seem likely to keep the price of good arabica beans, at least, high for years to come.

Coffee writer Rivers Janssen points out that when the C price was low, as in 2000–05, "For coffee farmers earning well below the cost of production, a potential premium of several cents per pound was at least a lifeline, and many were willing to take on the additional labor, cost and risk of certifications in hopes of making a better living." But today, "some roasters are wondering whether certifications hold the same relevance they did just a few years ago."[9] Paul Rice, head of Fair Trade USA, was moved in a recent report to remark that, "In today's high 'C' market, it's only natural to ask if Fair Trade is still relevant." Rice asserts that it is, because FT works for sustainable agriculture and for development projects that benefit farmers.[10]

But when prices are high, co-op members may break ranks and, instead of delivering coffee as promised to the co-op, sell to "coyotes," independent buyers who visit farms. Coyotes with cash in hand can be tempting to farmers in any circumstance, because they pay immediately—farmers don't have to wait for the co-op to complete its contract and distribute money, which often occurs only once a year. Janssen also notes that farmers and co-ops alike may pursue certification and then not find buyers for their more expensive beans.[11] Certification costs can be expensive, the process of gaining it lengthy, and the paperwork daunting for producers. When the price of all coffee is high, there is less incentive to separate excellent beans from run-of-the mill ones, which obviously takes time, labor, and special care.

Rainforest Alliance appears to have less of a problem in this scenario than other certification systems because most of its approved farms are estates that do not need to sell to coyotes.

I have seen this principle at work on the extremely large farms of Ipanema Coffee in Brazil's Sao Paulo and Minas Gerais states. 4C, with its minimal cost to small farmers, may also do well in keeping them in the system.

Even as the current economic downturn and the sharp rise in the C price began, roughly in September 2008, the report "Seeking Sustainability" found that, "A majority (60 percent) of certified farms [surveyed in five countries] reported an improved overall economic situation due to certification and generally superior net incomes as compared with conventional farms, and this despite the fact that a majority (62 percent) of certified farms reported reduced yields."[12] In other articles in this book, authors report *increased* yields with the use of shade trees or organic methods. Yet the problem remains that if yields on certified farms are not significantly higher than in conventional agriculture, and all the difficulties of becoming certified remain in place, farmers may sell outside of certification schemes if the price is right.

After all, as John Gaberino of Topeca Coffee puts it, "The farmer wants a better quality of life. Period."[13]

NOTES

1. Daniele Giovannucci and Jason Potts with B. Killian, C. Wunderlich, G. Soto, S. Schuller, F. Pinard, K. Schroeder, and I. Vagneron, "Seeking Sustainability: COSA Preliminary Analysis of Sustainability Initiatives in the Coffee Sector," September 2008, 2, Committee on Sustainable Assessment, Winnipeg, Canada. COSA is affiliated with the United Nations, the International Coffee Organization, and government agencies in the U.S., Europe, and Latin America.

2. All citations, unless otherwise noted, are from the website of the organization being discussed.

3. Pan Demetrekakis, "Sustaining interest: What's the true value of 'sustainable' coffee?" *Specialty Coffee Retailer* (July 2011): 18.

4. http://www.4c-coffeeassociation.org/en/4c-in-a-nutshell.php.

5. Giovannucci and Potts, "Seeking Sustainability," 4.

6. http://www.scscertified.com/retail/docs/CAFE_GUI_EvaluationGuidelines_V2.0_093009.pdf, accessed September 5, 2011.

7. Tina D. Beuchelt and Manfred Zeller, "Profits and poverty: Certification's troubled link for Nicaragua's organic and fairtrade coffee producers," *Ecological Economics* 70 (2011): 1317.

8. Beuchelt and Zeller, "Profits and poverty," 1321, 1323.

9. Rivers Janssen, "The Certification Conundrum: Are Certifications Still Important?" *Roast Magazine*, May–June 2011, 26.

10. Fair Trade Certified, in *Coffee Review 2010–2011*, 4, available at http://www.fairtradeusa.org/sites/default/files/Impact%20Report%202010-11%20COFFEE-LowRes.pdf, accessed September 3, 2011.

11. Janssen, "Certification Conundrum," 27.

12. Giovannucci and Potts, "Seeking Sustainability," ix.

13. Janssen, "Certification Conundrum," 26.

21

Direct Trade in Coffee

Geoff Watts

Most innovations come about in response to a specific need or as the result of an effort to solve a specific problem. Sometimes they take form in a very deliberate way, step-by-step, the product of organized research and careful planning. In other cases they develop more spontaneously, sparked by a simple idea or inspiration or even somewhat accidentally. What successful innovations typically have in common is that they somehow make things better. The concept of **direct trade** (DT) as it exists in coffee came to life in response to a tangible need, for a reliable supply of high-quality coffee. But DT has also been an attempt to solve a host of other dilemmas common to the coffee trade. In the coffee industry, business and politics, agriculture and communities, national economies, and commodity markets all intersect. Many parts must move in tandem.

DT was born out of frustration with the options available to progressive coffee companies that wanted to buy and sell a caliber of coffee that was limited in production and difficult to consistently access and whose vision for their business included a strong desire to address **sustainability** issues that are inextricably tied to coffee production. DT evolved as a means of surmounting the many obstacles that confront **roasters** frustrated by an inability to impact the conditions in which the coffees they sell were produced or to obtain a level of quality that would give them a competitive advantage in an increasingly taste-driven marketplace.

The lack of availability of what we will call "exceptional quality"—coffees that can legitimately qualify as culinary delights by virtue of their intrinsic sensory traits, and which are in every meaningful way artisanal products rather than commodities—was dramatic at the time the term "direct trade" was coined. There were many reasons for this, but the most fundamental was a grave lack of transparency and traceability in the way coffee was typically handled. A chasm existed between coffee roasters and coffee farmers, arguably the two most important actors in the coffee supply chain in regard to quality. They were separated by geographic distance, language barriers, and an opaque chain of custody progression in the coffee supply chain. Roasters often felt that buying coffees was much the same as shopping for clothing at a retail outlet store—buyers were essentially getting coffees "off the rack" and were limited to choosing from the available stock on hand. Extremely high quality was scarce and finding it was akin to hunting for buried treasure. There wasn't much opportunity to participate in its

Figure 21.1. An ox-drawn cart (*carreta*) still in regular use on coffee farms in Honduras as of 2012. Photo by Martha Casteneda.

development or creation. It was extremely difficult to know exactly who produced the coffee, under what conditions it was cultivated, and how the grower was compensated.

Following the clothing analogy, there was a need to work closely with a tailor to create something specific that would possess all of the traits of exceptional coffee. This is a more costly way to go about acquiring goods, but as long as the goods are of especially high quality there is plenty of tangible value to justify the increased expense.

To better understand why DT has become so important in coffee, it is useful to consider some of the basic motivations that led roasters to seek alternatives to the traditional approach to sourcing coffees. One key is differentiation; for **specialty coffee** to succeed in attracting consumers away from mainstream **commodity coffee**, it must offer something qualitatively different. If consumers are asked to pay more for their coffee than they have in the past, it is critical that they be able to easily grasp the value proposition; the coffee must taste significantly better than the baseline established by average commodity coffees they are accustomed to. The story matters, too, and it surely makes it easier for coffee drinkers to get excited about a beautiful coffee if they have some assurance that the farmers responsible for its creation are materially benefiting from its sale. Telling compelling stories about coffee and the benefits to farmers that are tied directly to boutique coffee, and providing detail about where the coffees come from, can create connections that allow consumers to feel good about their purchases and feel attached to them in a way that doesn't happen when coffees are sold in an anonymous manner. The knowledge that there are ethical reasons to support high-quality coffee can help enhance its perceived value.

But ultimately the coffee must be able to tell its own story by way of taste. Once consumers have made the decision to upgrade the quality of the coffee they drink and begin to pay more attention to taste details, their expectations rise further, and at that point differentiation becomes even more crucial. The decision about what coffees to drink doesn't always get permanently locked in as a binary proposition of quality or lack of quality; instead it often becomes increasingly nuanced, where ever-higher levels of quality are sought. The farther away from the baseline a coffee can get the more chance it has to succeed. And as the presence of high-quality coffees in the marketplace grows, more options become available to consumers, at which point differentiation takes another leap forward.

Once consumers embrace the idea that coffee should taste good, their next step is to begin trying to identify their preferences within a spectrum of coffees where all have some degree of "goodness." For this reason the pursuit of better quality is and will always be one of the primary motivations for most roasters that engage in direct trade with coffee growers. They want to roast and sell something that their competition does not have, and they acknowledge the need to become more active participants in the supply chain if they expect to gain access to great coffees. They can phrase the effort to acquire coffees that will give them a competitive advantage as a problem-solving endeavor, where the aim is to overcome some of the common obstacles that face companies seeking separation from the mainstream coffee industry. These companies are setting themselves up to succeed within the specialty sector. What follows is a list of obstacles to this quest and a brief explanation of how a direct trade approach can provide the solutions to overcome them.

PROBLEM ONE: FINDING EXCEPTIONAL QUALITY COFFEE

This is the most fundamental underlying problem in coffee: the huge majority—somewhere far north of 90 percent—of the coffee produced in this world is patently low in quality. The biggest reason for this is economic: prices paid to farmers for raw coffee are generally not high enough to cover the added costs involved in improving quality. Growers have little incentive to spend more on cultivation, harvesting, and processing when there is no reliable mechanism for recovering those costs and profiting from the increase in quality. Unless there is clear reward for higher quality coffees, reality dictates that farmers will choose to produce as much coffee as possible each year at minimum cost.

This is one obstacle to quality that can be effectively resolved through a DT approach. If a roaster desires an exceptional level of quality, the most straightforward way to obtain it is to find a farmer (or group of farmers) capable of producing it and create agreements that give them a compelling reason to do so. The alternative is to engage in a perpetual needle-in-a-haystack search that leads to inconsistency in product quality and excessive costs due to scarcity in the marketplace.

PROBLEM TWO: INVESTMENT REQUIREMENTS

Of course it isn't as simple as making an agreement and waiting for the results to appear. There are many other obstacles to achieving quality goals that need to be explicitly addressed in order to raise the probability of success. Farmers need access to the financial resources needed for investments that result in better quality. Most of the costs involved with producing great coffees accrue well before the eventual sale of the coffee, and many farmers don't have adequate capital or access to credit to finance the crop from start to finish. Those who do are often borrowing from local institutions at prohibitive interest rates that can outweigh the profit earned from the increased quality, making the whole proposition break-even at best. Thus the roasters/importers must often invest resources in helping kick-start the process by identifying expected increases in production costs and finding pre-financing solutions, either themselves or through third-parry microfinance organizations.

PROBLEM THREE: THE DIFFICULTY OF CREATING EXCEPTIONAL QUALITY

Creating neutral, inoffensive coffees is a relatively formulaic endeavor, but producing extraordinary ones is still an elusive pursuit. There is no single blueprint or simple recipe. The fact that few farmers evaluate their own coffees in a systematic way from a taste or sensory perspective complicates matters further. There are many growers who, even if quality is their goal, are disconnected from the end result in a way that makes the whole idea of quality somewhat elusive. Managing all the variables that lead to great tasting coffees is a daunting task in any circumstance, but becomes especially challenging absent the ability to measure results and determine what is working and what is not. Sensory analysis is a world unto itself, and detailed coffee quality evaluation conducted by way of tasting is a skill that requires some level of practice, especially if the goal is to identify cause-and-effect relationships between things that happened in the field and tastes manifested in the prepared coffees.

Therein lies a conundrum: although a general formula of sorts can be followed that should increase the likelihood of a quality outcome, agriculture is tricky and methods need to be adjusted based on a large number of environmental variables specific to each farm and each growing season. Significant research that correlates small details in cultivation and processing with quality-related nuance in top-tier coffees is practically nonexistent, so those pursuing it are for the most part left to their own devices to create those correlations. That means lots of experimentation and trials, which are necessarily a slow and long-term process given the fact that coffee harvests occur just once annually.

The challenge is compounded when the very definition of quality is itself variable—although there is some basic agreement across the industry about what a good coffee ought to taste like, there are many different ideas about what makes a coffee *great*. The buyer is ultimately the one who qualifies the coffee and pays the premium, so that farmers trying to create quality without having specific knowledge about who will buy it and how they are assessing value are in effect chasing a moving target when making decisions during harvest that impact the eventual taste of the coffees.

DT can help to solve this dilemma, since roaster and farmer become partners who can create a relatively specific quality target and calibrate with one another to ensure that they are applying the same lenses and metrics when evaluating the coffees post harvest. With a feedback loop in place, farmers and roasters can work towards ever-increasing quality in a deliberate way. Quality-related experimentation can be done with reduced risk since both parties are participants and can agree to share responsibility for the outcome. Successes can be more easily quantified and replicated when the farmer and the buyer are keeping score as a team.

PROBLEM FOUR: FARMERS' CONSERVATIVE APPROACH TO PRODUCTION COSTS AND THE FLUCTUATING MARKET

Since the value of coffees has long been tied tightly to the commodity market (the **C price**), farmers without specific buyers who choose to increase their production costs in an effort to achieve higher quality are always at risk that their investment will fail to yield a return and that any loss could well be compounded if the market sinks when it comes time to harvest and sell. There are plenty of farmers who know they could produce better coffees but simply do not choose to because they feel the risk that the extra expenses will be wasted is just too high. By partnering with a roaster willing to make price commitments well in advance of harvest, much of the risk of investing in improved quality is alleviated.

In these agreements, roasters take on a degree of risk, given that they are locking themselves into a price level that could end up being significantly above market once harvest time comes. Moreover, there is really no guarantee that the coffees themselves will meet every degree of expectation with regard to quality. But those risks are somewhat mitigated by other factors. If the farmers have the necessary resources, the right motivations, and a true commitment to doing the best work possible, there is a high probability that the coffees will be excellent. And for every year that the market tanks, it will probably surge another time, so there is only a small potential downside to long-term commitment. If roaster and farmer can find a valuation arrangement in which both stand to benefit each year, then market fluctuations and volatility become far less relevant than they would be otherwise and each side can proceed to invest in growth with a relative degree of confidence.

Mitigating volatility in the market is something that both parties crave, and establishing direct relationships based on real production costs can be a powerful advantage for each. Developing a consistent supply chain is a paramount concern to those companies looking to stay competitive.

PROBLEM FIVE: THE NEED FOR TRACEABILITY AND TRANSPARENCY IN THE SUPPLY CHAINS

As mentioned earlier, traceability has been difficult to establish in the coffee industry due to the way the crop is brought to market. Most farmers have no idea where their coffees end up once they leave the farm, and most roasters cannot trace the coffees they are selling all the way back to **origin** (the farm where it was grown). Coffee often changes hands three to six times before it reaches the roaster, and intermediaries in the supply chain do not like to disclose their costs or sources. Most coffees are anonymous by the time they reach the consuming markets. That presents a myriad of additional problems for the roaster. How can coffees be marketed when little is known about their source? How can any sustainability be assured without direct knowledge of how and where the coffees were produced? How can anyone tell what percentage of the final price of the **green coffee** went to the actual farmer—that is, what is the **farm gate price**?

Frequently the primary producers (the farmers) receive far lower a share of the price paid for the exported coffee than is warranted based on their role in the coffee's production. This difference is due to inefficiencies in the chain or their distance from the final buyer. All this obscures and dilutes the connection between a coffee's intrinsic quality and its value to the farmers responsible for its existence. Without a clear, tangible, and consistent link between the quality of a coffee and its worth as measured by actual return of profit to the farm gate, there is little to no incentive for a farmer to increase quality beyond a certain acceptable level. By working directly together, roasters and producers can better define the role of any necessary intermediaries, quantify the costs of their participation in the chain, and protect an agreed-upon farm gate price. By negotiating directly and defining the value of the coffees on their own terms, the roaster and farmer effectively change the way in which the coffee is traded, relegating intermediaries to a role that is more easily replaceable and where they can be compensated at competitive rates for the services they provide.

A large degree of control over the exchange is moved out of the hands of the traders or service providers and into the hands of the primary producer and roaster. Transparency and traceability concerns are mostly alleviated in a single stroke. Equally important, this means that premiums paid for quality are far more likely to be invested in improving quality, since the financial benefits are more easily measured by the farmer. A very useful mechanism in many DT models is a tiered pricing structure, where a baseline quality is established and incremental premiums are agreed upon for coffees that beat the mark. In this way, quality and price move together in tandem, in effect validating the idea of a perpetual quest to push quality upwards.

PROBLEM SIX: ENVIRONMENTAL ABUSES IN SOME FARMING SYSTEMS

As with most agricultural products, there are many different ways to produce coffee. Some approaches to growing coffee are ecologically sound, others not so much. One of the most important environmental issues in coffee production systems surrounds the use of water in coffee processing. The two biggest concerns are the unnecessary waste of vital water resources and the disposal of contaminated water from fermentation tanks. By working directly with farmers, roasters can influence the way coffees are being produced and verify that good practices are being followed at the farms. In most cases coffee growers are not looking to be intentionally wasteful or to contaminate the environment around their farms, but many are unaware of the impact that they are having or unfamiliar with new methodologies that can address water issues. The idea of water conservation in many traditional growing areas is relatively new—not too long ago, water seemed to be endlessly abundant—and many farmers simply don't realize that there are ways they can dramatically reduce usage without compromising quality. When it comes to wastewater management, various low-cost solutions can be implemented, some of which actually create useful byproducts. DT provides roasters with the opportunity to either choose to work with farmers who are already practicing sustainable production techniques or to assist farmers to reduce impact on the environment.

HOW DIRECT TRADE MAKES THINGS BETTER

DT is not a passing trend. It is a proven, effective model founded upon a powerful idea: that coffee roasters and coffee farmers, through close collaboration, can solve many of the challenges they each face, even though their respective challenges differ. As coffee consumption becomes more differentiated, strategies for success in the industry change profoundly. Creating better-quality coffees has become a legitimate way for coffee farmers to separate themselves from the unforgiving commodity market and achieve a level of stability that was elusive in the past. Roasters understand that they need exceptional and consistent quality in order to avoid the race to the bottom that characterizes the traditional coffee marketplace, in which the aim is to maximize efficiency and offer coffees for a slightly lower price than the competition. The traditional model places the goals of farmers and those of roasters in perpetual opposition, a condition that leads to ever-deteriorating quality and has yielded few real benefits to anyone other than perhaps savvy traders who can make money in the margins.

Direct trade is actually an ancient practice; producers and sellers of all sorts of goods have found ways to work closely together for centuries to solve various problems. The idea is becoming more attractive to farmers and roasters today, largely owing to the fact that the coffee landscape has fundamentally changed over the last couple decades. Unprecedented volatility in the commodity market, changes in climate conditions, and significantly increased production costs have led farmers to seek alternatives to the traditional trade channels.

Further benefits follow. As direct trade relationships grow and scale up in quantity, roasters can become hubs for new networks that connect like-minded farmers from many different countries who would otherwise not be in contact with each other. Those networks facilitate the transfer of knowledge between farmers and provide a platform for the sharing of valuable, hard-won experience related to quality improvement. Innovative methodologies for process control, plague prevention, soil management, and other critical farming practices can be exchanged between places as distant from one another as Kenya and Honduras. This type of exchange was rare prior to the advent of a DT approach to coffee sourcing, but it has become exceptionally useful.

Another characteristic of DT that makes it so effective is its inherent flexibility; it can be adjusted to afford maximum benefits to both farmers and roasters (and by extension to consumers) in each context where it is applied. It is a form of trade that has many of the same characteristics of human relationships, where the needs of each participant can be expressly addressed in response to changing conditions. One of the most challenging aspects of buying coffee is that the rules change from country to country and place to place. There are some common threads, but working with coffee farmers in Rwanda is a qualitatively different experience than working with growers in Costa Rica or Guatemala. The same goes for Indonesia, Peru, Ethiopia, Kenya, Bolivia, and so on. Substantial differences exist in the way coffee is produced and the chain of custody it undergoes (often governed by local law, sometimes as a result of historical circumstance or tradition) that a truly effective model needs to be tailored and custom-fit to each particular place.

When roasters engage with growers and ask them to help find the best possible methods of working together, the results can be truly inspiring. Really it is that one idea, farmer and roaster working together in solidarity for mutual benefit, that defines direct trade more than anything else. The fact is that roasters need farmers to be committed to doing the best possible work and elevating the quality of their coffees up towards their topmost potential, and farmers need roasters to help fund that work, create markets for their coffee, and teach consumers to recognize that quality and sustainability are both inextricably tied to prices. The coffee industry has been eating itself from the bottom up for many decades, creating a dysfunctional economy that actually discourages quality production, suppresses upward mobility for the farmer, and puts roasters in a position where they are marketing style rather than substance. DT was designed as a solution to that tragic reality, and it is becoming more effective with every passing year. It is a perpetual work-in-progress rather than a static system, which is especially important given how quickly the world is changing, and offers a compelling alternative to traditional approaches to working with coffee.

22

Fair Trade

Still a Big Plus for Farmers and Workers around the World

Paul Rice

In a high **C market**, it's only natural to ask if **fair trade** is still relevant. It is, of course, because fair trade is about so much more than price. Fair trade is a comprehensive approach to sustainable development that supports farmers with quality improvement, environmental stewardship, business capacity training, access to credit, and community development funds to help improve lives. Moreover, consumers are increasingly looking for the credibility of third-party **certification** to provide assurance that their coffee was ethically and sustainably sourced.

This chapter looks at some of the most important missions of **Fair Trade USA**, the premier certifying organization in the United States.

MARKET ACCESS

Market access and supply chain stability are core objectives of Fair Trade USA. We constantly recruit, train, and certify new producer groups, expanding benefits to more farming communities each year. Since 2005, the number of Fair Trade coffee producer groups has more than doubled. In addition to farm-level certification, importers and roasters frequently enlist our support to help them identify and partner with high-quality Fair Trade farmers in specific origins. We also partner with global financial institutions, industry partners, **NGOs**, leading social entrepreneurs, and in-country service providers to help maximize the benefits of Fair Trade for producers and businesses. These partnerships enable targeted projects that help farmers improve quality, increase productivity, improve access to capital, and become stronger business partners.

One big success is a Brazilian program in partnership with the U.S. Agency for International Development and an NGO called SEBRAE-MG. Together we have invested over $2 million in infrastructure, training, and technical assistance for nearly 6,000 farmers from Sao Paulo, Minas Gerais, and Espirito Santo.

ENVIRONMENTAL STEWARDSHIP

In a high-price market, farmers may be tempted to cut corners to maximize yields and income. Fair Trade encourages farmers to take a long-term approach to agriculture, embracing **sustain-**

able practices that conserve natural resources. Our rigorous environmental standards protect water resources and adjacent forests, restrict the use of hazardous **pesticides**, agrochemicals, and GMOs, promote **organic** farming, and help reduce carbon emissions. Farmers must comply with these core standards to get certified and then implement progress requirements every year in order to get recertified.

ACCESS TO CREDIT

Improving access to affordable credit is another fundamental objective of Fair Trade. Without inexpensive credit, farmers are more vulnerable to middlemen and cooperatives are unable to compete effectively with larger traders. Several multinational lenders are working with Fair Trade cooperatives in Kenya, Sumatra, Guatemala, Colombia, and Nicaragua to provide credit so that farmers can upgrade equipment and invest in the processes that promote quality production.

COMMUNITY DEVELOPMENT

Another core benefit of Fair Trade is the community development premium that buyers are required to pay to certified farmers. This premium, currently set at 20 cents per pound (**green**), goes directly back to growing communities to invest in things like education, health care, clean water, job training, organic conversion, and microloans. Over time, these premiums have had an enormous impact on the quality of life for farmers. Since 1998, Fair Trade certification has helped the U.S. coffee industry deliver more than $93 million in premiums back to coffee farmers, $32 million in 2012 alone.

A CASE STUDY OF FAIR TRADE IMPACT: RWANDA

More than a decade after the genocide, Rwandan farmers still struggle to earn a decent living. In 2007, Fair Trade USA joined with the Stichting Het Groene Woudt, a leading Dutch foundation, to empower seven cooperatives that support more than 100,000 people. The three-year program helped cooperative members improve their organizational capacity, strengthen internal transparency and democratic governance, and raise management skills. These cooperatives then invested in improving their coffee quality by building new **cupping** labs and learning how to cup from international experts. One of the participating groups, COOPAC, won the 2010 Rwanda **Cup of Excellence.**

In Rwanda, Fair Trade certification has translated into schools, clean water wells, and long-term economic security. According to Christine Condo, executive director of the Rwanda Economic Development Initiative, "In Africa, it's very difficult for villagers to attend school, but since these cooperatives became Fair Trade, the majority of members, over 90 percent, can send their children to school."

Fair Trade remains committed to consumer education and awareness building, not just about coffee but for a whole range of products. It is just one of many organizations working to bring fair trade benefits to the coffee industry. We hope, through our work, to help people understand the positive difference their small, everyday purchases can make.

PRODUCER COUNTRY PROFILES

23

Hawaii

Shawn Steiman

For most people, coffee from Hawaii—the only commercial coffee producer in the United States—is associated with Kona, a region on the Big Island (also called Hawaii Island) comprising two political districts: North Kona and South Kona. People rarely know that coffee is grown on five islands in ten geographic regions across the state. While Kona was the only region producing coffee for nearly a century, that changed in the early 1990s. Kona's long dominance is a bit surprising, considering that when coffee first arrived to Hawaii, it came to a different island.

Coffee most likely reached Hawaii in 1825, via Brazil.[1] While there is no certainty about what variety those first plants were, they were all **arabica.** Coffee was first planted in Mānoa valley on the island of Oahu but soon moved to other islands. By the end of the century, coffee grew commercially in various regions across the islands, and Kona had won a reputation for high quality. In 1892, the variety 'Typica' arrived via Guatemala and found favor among farmers. Then a crash in world coffee prices in 1899 pushed coffee out of most regions in Hawaii, where it was replaced with sugarcane. Only in Kona, where the land was unsuitable for the new sugarcane machines and sugarcane production infrastructure was not in place, did coffee remain.[2]

For the better part of the twentieth century, commercial coffee agriculture existed in the islands only in Kona. Without competition from other growing regions, Kona became synonymous with Hawaiian coffee. Coffee spread around the state again, ironically, because of sugarcane. Hawaii could no longer compete with other sugarcane growers around the world, so sugar-growing corporations began diversifying into other crops, with coffee the most successful. By the 1990s, four large, mechanically harvested coffee farms were producing coffee on other islands. The emergence of **specialty coffee** and the Internet helped spur on small farms in other regions of the islands; the two new developments created demand for single-estate coffee and also offered a way to market coffee to people living outside of Hawaii.

The state of Hawaii classifies growing regions according to the political district in which farms are located. Thus there are eight coffee regions in Hawaii: Oʻahu, Molokaʻi, Kauaʻi, Maui, Kona, Hamakua, Puna, and Kaʻū. The last four are all on Hawaii Island. Coffee grows at elevations from 100 to 1,000 meters (350–3,200 feet) at latitudes of 19–21° north. These relatively high latitudes result in lower temperatures at low elevations, permitting high-quality production at what is considered low elevations in most other producing countries.

In 2010, the 830 coffee farms of Hawaii, planted across 3,237 hectares (8,000 acres) of land produced 3.2 million kilograms (7 million pounds) of green coffee. That was less than .04 percent of total world production![13]

As in most producing origins, Hawaiian farms are typically small, less than 2 hectares (5 acres). Some twenty to thirty farms range in size from 2 to 60 hectares (5–150 acres). The four largest farms, all mechanically harvested, range from 60 to 1,215 hectares (150–3,000 acres).

Figure 23.1. Japanese-American families were able to acquire good coffee land in Hawaii beginning in the 1920s. Often the whole family, children included—but only after school—worked on the farm. Here are typical Japanese coffee farm tools, preserved at the Kona Coffee Living History Farm, Captain Cook, Hawaii. Photo by Robert Thurston.

Aside from a few corporate operations, farms in Hawaii are family owned. In Kona, where many farms have been in the family for several generations, owners tend to be descendants of the Asian immigrants who came to work on coffee and sugar farms. Today, they usually harvest **cherry** and sell it to a mill. The mills then sell most of the coffee as **green bean** and a smaller part as roasted coffee. The rest of the farms in Kona and around the state have been more recently acquired. These are usually estate farms that sell their coffee as green bean or roasted product, although some do occasionally sell cherry.

Until recently, Hawaii coffee was not plagued with any particularly bothersome pests or diseases. Hawaii's remoteness and the state-enforced quarantine of incoming coffee material managed to keep them all at bay. In 2010, however, the **coffee berry borer** was discovered in Kona. Currently contained in Kona and Ka'ū, it is only a matter of time before other regions of the state will confront this pest.

Few farmers in Hawaii grow their coffee organically, and the ones that do often raise it for philosophical reasons, not a price premium. Yet with so little pressure from pests and diseases, the use of synthetic treatments on any farm has been minimal.

Of the **certifications** common to the coffee industry, only **organic** is present in Hawaii. As farmers in the U.S., Hawaiian producers are subject to many social, political, economic, labor, and environmental laws. These laws assign rights and obligations that most certifications have designed for coffee farmers elsewhere. Consequently, the notion of fair trade Hawaii coffee, for example, doesn't make much sense. Coffee in Hawaii will always be traded fairly and likely even more "fairly" than certified coffees from elsewhere. Environmental certifications, which sometimes demand stronger rules than U.S. laws, do not fit the uniqueness that is Hawaii; the islands have never been a stopping ground for migrating birds, while the diversity of native, **overstory** tree species is much lower than in most other coffee origins. So, while there could be a place for certifications, the regulations need modification to make sense for Hawaii.

As a producer **origin**, Hawaii is unusual. Farmers tend to be wealthier than farmers elsewhere, so they have access to considerable information and agricultural resources, particularly from the local scientific community, which has been making relevant contributions since the 1950s. Transportation within Hawaii is sophisticated: nearly all roads are paved, and shipping coffee locally or abroad, either green bean or roasted, is simple. As part of a highly developed country, Hawaii has a readily available and accessible local market not just locally but across the United States.

Hawaii coffee is often considered to be overpriced. At their lowest, green beans tend to fetch around $8 per pound but can cost $20 or more, independent of any quality rating. These levels are well above the **C price** and often higher than **Cup of Excellence** prices. Yet, no competitions have set Hawaiian prices; the market determines them.

The simplest explanation for such prices is that consumers are willing to pay them. The demand for Hawaii grown coffee is fairly high and supply is fairly small. Still, other origins have similar conditions but lower prices. What else contributes to this anomaly? Beyond the supply-and-demand situation, there are four pieces to this puzzle.

First, Hawaii has some of, if not the, most expensive coffee production costs in the world. Hawaii is remote; the U.S. mainland is over 3,700 kilometers (2,300 miles) away. No resources such as farm equipment, fertilizers, building materials, and packaging are produced within the state; everything must be shipped across the ocean. Labor costs, too, are high, as farmers must comply with U.S. labor laws.

Second, obeying environmental, safety, and business laws also adds to the cost of farming. The U.S. is an expensive place to do business, hence the export of jobs to other countries.

Third, Hawaii is a costly place to live, and farmers want to live like comfortable Americans. Farmers want the luxuries any U.S. resident wants: cars, mobile phones, TVs, a decent home, and disposable income. To maintain a reasonably high American standard of living, farmers must charge more for their coffee. One can argue that Hawaiian coffee is not expensive, but that all other coffees are undervalued.

Fourth, Hawaii is paradise. At least, that is how it is marketed to tourists and nonresidents (though most residents readily appreciate their good fortune). Hawaii really is an archipelago of beauty and wonder. This image is used to market many Hawaiian products, including coffee. While this alone doesn't increase the price of coffee, it does help maintain a high price, as many consumers of Hawaiian coffee want to capture a vicarious experience or relive one they've already had in the islands.

Hawaii coffee is relatively expensive and is likely only to become more so. Transportation and production costs are linked to petroleum prices. The coffee berry borer has been devastating to marketable yields, and efforts to control it have created additional production costs. How consumers will respond to higher prices in the long run is unknown.

The maturation of the specialty coffee industry has influenced Hawaii farms. Some farmers are beginning to explore methods and varieties that will produce interesting and diverse brews. For example, some farmers are experimenting with **pulped natural** and natural cherry **processing** methods. Others are planting recently released, not-yet-named varieties from a local breeding program. These coffees are marketed to savvy consumers who are willing to pay higher prices for these complex beans. Other farmers, whose classic markets may dry up with higher prices, will likely begin catering to the high end specialty market, helping to bolster an industry suffering from ever-growing production costs.

Hawaii will remain a paradise, and the islands' producers will be able to supply people not just with morning coffee, but with a cup that evokes the sun and beaches of Hawaii, even for those who only know the islands through movies and legends.[4]

NOTES

1. Andrew Bloxam, *Diary of Andrew Bloxam, naturalist of the "Blonde" on her trip from England to the Hawaiian islands, 1824–25* (Honolulu: Bernice P. Bishop Museum Special Publication 10, 1925), appendix.

2. Gerald Kinro, *A Cup of Aloha: The Kona Coffee Epic* (Honolulu: University of Hawaii Press, 2003), 16.

3. USDA, NASS, Hawaii Field Office, "Hawaii Farm Facts," August 2011, 4.

4. For more information about the Hawaii coffee industry, we recommend Shawn Steiman, *The Hawai'i Coffee Book: A Gourmet's Guide from Kona to Kaua'i* (Honolulu: Watermark, 2008), 134.

24

India

Sundrini Menon

The history and romance of coffee in India dates back to the seventeenth century, when a Muslim pilgrim saint, Bababudan, brought seeds to the country from Mecca. He is said to have planted the seeds around his hut in Chikmagalur, the region where Indian coffee cultivation began.

The British began to establish coffee farms in India systematically in 1792. Today, coffee is grown mainly in the southern part of the country through the untiring efforts of the farmers, who cultivate coffee against all odds of nature—pests, diseases, climate, and environment.

India is a department store for coffee, growing both **arabica** and **robusta**, under filtered shade, at altitudes of about 1,500 feet (457 m) to about 4,500 feet (1370 m). The shade comprises evergreen leguminous trees, with nearly fifty different species being found on the plantations. A diversified pattern of **intercropping** is the hallmark of Indian coffee plantations, with pepper, cardamom, cloves, vanilla, areca (betel) nut, as well as fruits such as jackfruit, oranges, and bananas growing alongside coffee.

Globally, India ranks sixth in coffee production. However, the top coffee-growing country, Brazil, produces around nine times as much as India does. Total production in the 2010–11 season was 302,000 metric tonnes of green beans, with arabica accounting for approximately 35 percent of the total. About 65 percent of the coffee is exported; India's share in global production and exports is 4 percent.[1]

As of 2010–11, the total area under coffee cultivation in India was 404,645 hectares. Some 99 percent of the farmers are smallholders with less than 10 hectares of land. The productivity of arabica was approximately 513 pound/acre (575 kg/ha), and robusta was 942 pound/acre (1,056 kg/ha).

The traditional coffee growing areas are the three southern states of Karnataka (Coorg, Chikmagalur, Bababudan, and Biligiri districts), Kerala (Wayanad, Travancore, Nelliampathy, and Kannan Devan districts), and Tamilnadu (Nilgiris, Shevaroys, Pulneys, and Anamalais).

The nontraditional areas where coffee is grown are in Andhra Pradesh and Orissa in south India and in Arunachal Pradesh, Nagaland, Assam, and other northeastern states.

Until 1996, Indian coffee was marketed through the Coffee Board of India, the nodal organization of the government of India devoted to the development of coffee, located in Bangalore. In January 1996, the market was liberalized, with all sections of the coffee farming community

137

then allowed to market 100 percent of their coffee on their own. In the new scenario, many small farmers sell their coffee directly from their farms in the form of dry **cherry** or **parchment** to traders and exporters. The large farmers sell coffee in the clean and graded form, either directly to exporters or through private auctions. Liberalized marketing has helped overseas buyers purchase Indian coffee either at auction or through farm gate purchases, brokers, registered exporters, and, above all, directly from the farmers. Finally, the crowning improvement is that the Indian coffee farmer can now function not only as a grower but also as a dry miller, a trader, an exporter, and a roaster.

As a result of these changes, quality has taken the front seat. The producer ensures strict on-farm monitoring of quality. With this emphasis, pride, and tradition in processing coffee, the Indian farmer has ventured into estate branding of his produce and also into direct marketing relationships with overseas buyers. The era of **relationship coffee** has commenced in India.

The processing and quality standards for coffee continue to follow the Coffee Board of India's specifications, which are mandatory for the coffee farmer. The Board has developed logos that provide identity for coffees by region, an important innovation considering that many of the regional beans have distinct flavor notes in the cup.

While the Coffee Board is no longer concerned with **marketing**, it maintains departments for research and development, extension, promotion, and quality control. In general, the Board aims to increase the **productivity** of coffee without increasing the area under cultivation, to undertake measures to reduce production costs, to encourage coffee farmers to prepare special, estate branded and specialty coffees, to standardize and ensure the quality of Indian coffee, to conduct training programs for quality awareness, and to educate consumers on how to prepare a good cup of coffee. A good example of awareness work is the popular "Kaapi Shastra" program, conducted in cities and towns to educate coffee entrepreneurs and consumers on the art and science of coffee brewing.

Of the almost twelve arabica **cultivars** that have been released to the field, through the tireless efforts of the Central Coffee Research Station (CCRS) of the Coffee Board of India, many are found to possess special intrinsic quality traits, enabling India to prepare special and specialty coffees. The important arabica plant cultivars are 'Kent,' 'S. 795,' 'Sln. 9,' and 'Chandragiri.' To give two examples of successful hybridization, 'Sln. 9' developed with an Abyssinian connection and maintains fruit flavor notes of its Ethiopian parent. 'Chandragiri' is a cultivar not just resistant to various pests and diseases, particularly the leaf rust, but of good yield and cup quality.

Research on plant material involves robustas as well as arabicas. Wide tracts of robusta coffee-growing regions in India have been planted with 'S. 274,' which has been well received around the world. 'S. 274' is an offspring of the Old Robusta/Peradeniya cultivar, which initially came into the country from Sri Lanka. A more recent robusta selection is an offspring of 'Congensis,' as one would expect from Congo. It produces large beans with very fine **cupping** nuances, resembling those of an arabica.

Considering labor for the plantations is now in short supply, a disciplined, organized, and efficient manner of **sorting** has been developed on the farms. Only ripe cherries are moved to **washed processing** or **natural processing** (sun **drying**). In India, natural **fermentation** is being followed by many farms for removal of **mucilage** during the preparation of washed coffees, be they arabica or robusta, enabling the latent intrinsic flavor notes in the coffee beans to emerge. However, at present farmers do not follow a standard model for processing, but rather experiment with the beans and seek to develop techniques that highlight their intrinsic flavor notes.

Sun drying is the main method of drying coffee, considering that, in India, it is the best and most cost effective, usually on raised tables. Today, given climate change and the labor shortages of recent years, trials with mechanical dryers are under way to examine whether drying can be efficient and not adversely affect quality.

The environment too is preserved by treating the effluents from the pulp house naturally, utilizing anaerobic and aerobic methods of lagooning, which help bring the BOD (biochemical oxygen demand) levels down to acceptable limits.

Well-equipped dry milling factories carry out the hulling, grading, and sorting of the coffee beans into carefully defined grades. The coffee beans are finally bulked and packed in special jute "IJIRA bags," which are manufactured with vegetable oil. These **bags** are not only eco-friendly but they also preserve the quality of the coffee. The markings on the bags are most often applied with vegetable dyes, an innovation encouraged by the Coffee Board.

Specialty coffees such as Monsooned coffees, Mysore Nuggets EB, and Robusta Kaapi Royale are offered to coffee connoisseurs around the globe. The Monsooned Malabar and Monsooned Basanally coffees were launched by the Coffee Board of India as early as 1972 and have found acceptance by discerning drinkers. These coffees are specially prepared from quality arabica cherries on the west coast of India. During the monsoon rains, between June and September of a year, the beans are allowed to absorb moisture and undergo distinct visual and **organoleptic** changes during the preparation.

Some 99 percent of exports comprise good quality grades without foreign or extraneous matter. The export houses, many of which have been in business for many years, have earned the reputation of being reliable, quality oriented, and honest. There are also a number of experienced clearing and forwarding agents, who ensure safe delivery of coffee consignments.

Domestic consumption of coffee in cafés began to increase sharply in 1996, when the first coffee bar opened its doors. This café was started by a coffee farmer at a time when computers were making headlines in the Indian market. A cup of coffee with an hour of surfing on the net was introduced by what became the first indigenous café chain from India, Café Coffee Day. Today, a large number of domestic and international chains have set up cafés all over India, so that "café culture" has helped to increase domestic consumption of coffee, from a stagnant figure of 55,000 metric tonnes in 1995 to more than 110,000 tonnes in 2011.[2]

Today, the Indian coffee industry is undertaking a number of measures to upgrade quality. Breeding programs are being reviewed and new cultivar development, for both arabica and robusta, is in progress. The Coffee Board of India is also examining mechanization, including for **harvesting**. The Board has been carrying out trials with the equipment available in the market. Measures are also being implemented to increase production efficiency and research is under way on mitigating the effect of climate change on the quantity and quality of coffee. The extension services of the Indian Coffee Board are being strengthened, in addition to self-help groups being organized amongst small farmers. Value addition to coffee is encouraged, with the government of India also providing a subsidy for coffee roasting and grinding equipment.

"Cupping culture" is blossoming and a postgraduate diploma course on coffee quality has been introduced by the Coffee Board of India; young graduates are trained on all aspects of quality, at every stage of production, enabling them to help in upgrading the quality of Indian coffee. The "Kaapi Shastra" program has already been mentioned.

As competitions tend to spur quality improvement and benefit famers, "The Flavour of India" cupping competition was introduced in 2002. Every year, the competition is conducted for both arabica and robusta coffees.

Coffees of distinct plant varieties and unique processing techniques, marketed as "estate brands," have been gaining ground recently. Balehonnur Corona, Merthi Mountains, Balanoor Bean, Harley Classic, Veer Attikan, Sethuraman Sitara, and Buttercup Bold are some of the estate-branded coffees that have been well received by the international market.

Since 2002, the coffee industry has conducted the India International Coffee Festival biannually. It provides a platform where sellers and buyers can interact, where Indian coffees can be showcased, and where information can be exchanged on the latest developments in the coffee world.

Prospects for Indian coffee are encouraging, in spite of the difficulties farmers face. Indian coffee, until recently considered a "filler" product, has risen from mundanity to a quality stand-alone product, with microlots finding their way into coffee cups around the globe. Indian coffee is an excellent base for **espresso** blends. The future of coffee in our country is bright and getting brighter. The Indian coffee industry is determined, diligent, and innovative. It will continue to improve the quality of the product, the livelihood of the farmers, and the sustainability of the environment.

NOTES

1. *Database on Coffee*, Publication of the Coffee Board of India, June 2011, 4–5.
2. *Database on Coffee*, 75.

25

Indonesia

Jati Misnawi

Coffee is not original to Indonesia, but over time, coffee has spread to almost all corners of the country. Coffee entered Indonesia because of the ambition of Dutch colonial entrepreneurs, the Dutch having conquered the region from earlier invaders, the Portuguese, in 1596. Cultivation of coffee became the backbone of the colonial economy and has been internalized by various cultural communities.

Nicolaas Witsen, a mayor and governor of the Vereenigde Amsterdam Oost-Indische Compagnie (United East India Company, VOC) initiated coffee cultivation in Nusantara, the original name of the island group in Old Java. Witsen recommended that coffee plants be imported into the areas of Dutch colonial rule that had appropriate soil fertility and climate. Above all, that meant Java Island. In 1696, the head of the Dutch colonial administration in Malabar, India, Andrian van Ommen, sent coffee seeds to Java.

Given the Dutch desire to develop a commercial crop in their colony, coffee plants spread across Nusantara under the auspices of the VOC. Cultivation began in Priangan land, in West Java, Java island. The people were soon required to grow coffee in massive quantities. Villagers had to sell all of their production to the VOC and, after the Company went bankrupt in 1798, to the Dutch government, at very low prices.[1] Despite the great difficulties imposed on people by the Dutch colonial system, farmers came to understand both the cultivation of coffee and its commercial value.

THE DEVELOPMENT OF INDONESIAN COFFEE

Centuries later, coffee became an important commercial commodity of Indonesia. It still provides significant economic benefits to the country. Of course, the government has received huge profits through foreign exchange earnings from coffee exports. Coffee still figures among the top ten largest sources of foreign exchange outside of oil. Approximately 67 percent of Indonesia's coffee production is exported. In the upstream sector, coffee has provided an opportunity to the people to demonstrate their expertise and ability to become competent investors. More than 95 percent of the country's coffee plantations are managed by smallholders, whose land is one **hectare** or less. When big companies, both private and government owned, showed reluctance to develop coffee plantations, millions of smallholders increased their production. Smallholder coffee has spread to almost all the islands of Indonesia, resulting in world famous coffees such as Toraja, Mandheling, Lampung, Java, Bali, and Flores.

Until the late nineteenth century, the Dutch government, colonists, and entrepreneurs reaped the benefits of coffee from Nusantara. But in 1885 the golden age of coffee for the Dutch colony began to fade. Direct government involvement in the industrial coffee business started to decline. At the same time, the number of private estates and individuals involved in coffee production soared. Then beginning in 1891, many large planters in Sumatra replaced coffee with crops that were currently more profitable, in particular rubber, whose price was then increasing rapidly. In 1918, the Dutch colonial authorities ended all involvement in coffee regulation. From then on, most of the Java and Sumatra coffee business was held by private companies.

After government involvement ended, the study of coffee cultivation grew rapidly. Several new coffee varieties were imported, while improved breeding and processing techniques were developed. One of the leading pioneers was Teun Ottolander, founder of the Netherlandsche-Indische Landbouw Syndicaat (Dutch East Indies Agricultural Syndicate). It was his idea to start a research institute in Besoeki. This institute, now known as the Indonesian Coffee and Cocoa Research Institute (ICCRI), has since relocated to Jember.

Into the twentieth century, all coffee exported from the Dutch East Indies was known as Java Coffee, although the beans came from all of Nusantara, including areas outside of Java such as Sumatra, Timor, and Sulawesi. But that labeling practice ended in 1921, when the U.S. Department of Agriculture required the brand "Java Coffee" to be applied only to arabica coffee from Java itself (more particularly, East Java). This step was taken even though, according to William Ukers's *All About Coffee* (1932), the best arabica coffee at that time actually came from Mandheling and Ankola of Sumatra Island.

World War II considerably damaged the coffee industry in the islands. Planters turned to food crops such as rice, maize, and cassava. Consequently, the coffee harvest in 1950 was only one-eighth of the pre-war peak.

Indonesia declared its independence in August 1945, but had to fight a bloody war against the Dutch before gaining full sovereignty in 1949. The coffee industry entered a new era when the Indonesian government began nationalizing Dutch companies. Dutch and other foreign companies were nationalized into Perusahaan Perkebunan Negara, or PPN (Government Owned Plantations) in 1958, which then became the pioneer of PT Perkebunan Nusantara (PTPN) (Government Owned Estate Companies Limited). The government divided the plantations it acquired into fourteen companies, based on their location and main crops, in order to decentralize and improve management. PTPN XII, located in East Java, is the main government owned company that produces coffee beans. One of its famous coffees is labeled Java.

However, starting in the 1970s, private farmers began to enter the coffee business, aided by government agencies. Private farmers spread their operations out from North Sumatra, Aceh, Lampung, Jawa, Bali, Sulawesi, Timor, Flores, and Papua. Data from 2010 show that today most Indonesia coffee farms are owned by smallholders, who control 95.5 percent of the total 1.3 million hectares planted in coffee. The remaining land is owned by PTPN (1.7 percent) and private groups (2.8 percent). Small farmers, not the government or private companies, became the real investors and producers in the industry.

THE SITUATION AND PROBLEMS OF SMALL FARMERS

Coffee grows on almost all the islands of Indonesia. Sumatra Island dominates with 74.2 percent of all production, with the largest crops in Bengkulu, Lampung, and South Sumatra areas. The rest of the crop is distributed among Sulawesi (9.0 percent), Java (8.3 percent), Nusa Tenggara (5.8 percent), Kalimantan (2.0 percent), and Maluku and Papua (0.6 percent). More than half of the national production comes from five provinces, South Sumatra (21.4 percent), Lampung (12.6 percent), Nanggroe Aceh Darussalam (8.7 percent), Bengkulu (7.4 percent), and East Java (7.2 percent).

Not only the long history of coffee in Indonesia but also the economic value of the crop makes many farmers rely on its cultivation. Currently, coffee farmers in Indonesia number about 1.97 million, with an average of 0.6 hectares of land ownership. Assuming an average of four family members, at least 7.9 million people depend on coffee and are subject to its wide price fluctuations.

The contribution of coffee in the national economy is quite significant. Coffee is one of Indonesia's main agricultural commodities. The volume of exports in 2009 amounted to 433,000 tons or 7.6 percent of total world exports. The value of exports reached $849.9 million (about IDR 8 trillion). Coffee by value is 0.71 percent of Indonesia's exports, while coffee is 0.16 percent of total GDP. Throughout the last three decades, average annual coffee exports reached 327,000 tons worth $489 million.

Small coffee producers are still plagued by the low price for their crop. Since the 1970s, the prices have overall tended to fall. Farmers gain around 19–22 percent of the total price of a cup of coffee sold in consuming countries. Even the recovery of green coffee prices since 2004 has not made a great difference in this percentage. The **farm gate price** in Indonesia, as elsewhere, is inversely proportional to the value added to coffee in consuming countries. As yet, the small farmers of Indonesia have little bargaining power in the industry.

COFFEE SPECIFICITY

Lying entirely within the tropics, Indonesia is well situated to produce various types of coffee with unique flavor and character. The same coffee variety can produce beans of different characters in different parts of the islands. Arabica coffee grown in Sumatra can be quite different from the same cultivar produced in Java or Sulawesi. In general, the taste of coffee reflects the region of origin. Two major factors in producing different characters in the cup are variations in soil nutrients and climatic conditions. Many Indonesian coffees have become well known as **specialty coffee**, such as Java, Mandheling, Gayo, Flores, Lintong, Kintamani, and Toraja.

In Sumatra, coffee grows well from the tip of Aceh to Lampung. The Gayo Aceh region also produces coffee. Varieties of arabica coffee produced from plantations that stretch along the Gayo highlands at an altitude of 1,200 meters above sea level (masl), in Central Aceh and Bener Meriah province, are generally prepared by **wet processing** methods. Gayo coffee has a strong **aroma** and balanced **body**.

Besides Gayo coffee, the Aceh region also produces a popular robusta coffee, 'Ulee Kareng.' This coffee is produced from the area of Lamno Geumpang Pidie and Aceh Jaya. Ulee Kareng shows gentle character, but it seems bitter with a salty-astringent taste on the tongue at first. Specialty coffee can also be found in North Sumatra, namely Mandheling, Lintong, and Sidikalang coffee. Everything from these regions is arabica.

Mandheling coffee comes from fields in South Tapanuli, North Tapanuli, Simalungun, and Deli Serdang. The term *Mandheling* derives from the local name of the Batak tribe, Mandailing. Mandheling coffee has complex body, low **acidity**, little bitterness, and a spicy, slightly earthy, and small fruit-like flavor.

Lintong coffee, with clean character and good body, comes from Lintong Nihuta of Humbang Hasundutan district in North Sumatra. Sidikalang coffee is produced from the area

Sidikalang Sumbul/Sidikalang of Dairi district at an elevation of 1,500 masl. Sidikalang is known as an arabica coffee with a strong and sharp flavor, high acidity, and balanced body with a slight sensation of grassy and **green** flavors.

Sumatra also produces robustas. One is the widely recognized brand Lampung Robusta. There are four robusta coffee-producing regions on Sumatra: Bandar Lampung, Lampung Barat, Tanggamus, and the Way Kanan. Interestingly, although these coffees come from one province, their characteristics differ significantly.

Since Java Island was the first part of Nusantara where coffee was grown, its coffee is justly famous. One variety is called simply Java Coffee; it is produced from arabica plantations in East Java under the management of PTPN XII. Java arabica coffee's character is medium body, chocolaty, flowery, and **balanced**. Java arabica grows well around Mount Ijen, at its peak between 900 and 1,400 masl. Java arabica is wet processed, fermenting for 24–36 hours, then sun dried. After the Dutch departed, Java coffee spread to five other areas.

Although popular only since the 1990s, Bali is also known for producing special coffee, Kintamani–Bali Coffee. Coffee is widely cultivated in the mountains of Batur at an altitude of 900–1,500 masl. Coffee is **intercropped** there with older orange trees. Bali has particular soil and climatic conditions thought to determine the cup profile, fruity taste with mild acidity. Most lovers of this coffee are from Japan, the United States, the Netherlands, and France. Kintamani coffee is the first agricultural product in Indonesia to obtain a certificate of Geographical Indication recorded by the Indonesian government.

Other parts of Indonesia, Sulawesi and Nusa Tenggara, are the source of Toraja and Flores Bajawa coffee, the flagship specialty coffee. Popular Toraja Arabica coffee actually comes from two areas of South Sulawesi; therefore there are two popular brands, "Toraja" and "Kalosi." Toraja coffee has a highly complex character with the sensation of chocolate, sweetness, and spicy herb notes.

Bajawa Flores coffee is grown on the island of Flores. There the mountainous landscape, dotted with active volcanoes, is marked by andosols: dark, highly porous soils derived from volcanic material that have a high aluminum content. This soil is ideal for arabica coffee. Flores coffee grows at altitudes between 1,200 and 1,800 masl. The cup characters are chocolaty, sweet, fruity, and a slightly citrus **aftertaste**.

KOPI LUWAK (CIVET COFFEE)

Indonesia has yet another generic brand that is also globally famous. This is **kopi luwak** (or just luwak) coffee. This coffee has the quasi-mythological reputation of being the most expensive coffee in the world. Civet coffee beans are actually removed by hand from droppings of the civet cat, an animal of the weasel family. Civets eat the best ripe coffee fruits, both arabica and robusta. The cats have, one might say, done a good bit of processing of the beans as they pass through the animals' digestive tracts. Not surprisingly, kopi luwak is amazingly expensive. In the world market, coffee prices have reached $150 per kilogram. Civet coffee has become so desirable around the world partly because the price is so expensive. Civet coffee stocks are rare. Naturally, it has a unique and special flavor. In the cup the coffee has balanced body, high acidity, and some bitterness, although the characteristics depend on the coffee's nature and handling. Kopi luwak's aroma is intense with sweetness and sometimes a fruity flavor.

HOPE FOR THE FUTURE

Benefits from coffee production have a great impact on small farmers' lives. They hope for stability of coffee prices and achievement of fair price distribution among farmers, processors, retailers, and traders. The Indonesia Coffee and Cocoa Research Institute (ICCRI), with government support, contributes to finding good planting material, developing best agricultural and good handling practices, developing sustainable coffee, promoting the coffee sector at the national and the global level, and determining the need and suitability for increased coffee farming across the country. Specialty coffee is one of the main components in reaching overall coffee sustainability in Indonesia.

NOTE

1. Editor's note (RT): The Dutch system of extracting products from the Indonesian people for little or no payment, resulting in great misery for **peasants**, is described in the novel ***Max Havelaar: Or the Coffee Auctions of the Dutch Trading Company***, by Multatuli (Eduard Douwes Dekker). First published in 1860 in Dutch, the book appeared in English in 1868.

26

Colombia

Luis Alberto Cuéllar

Coffee has been cultivated in Colombia since 1723. The Jesuits are credited with having introduced coffee production, at the junction of the Meta and Orinoco rivers. Production on a large scale began in Colombia around 1830 in Salazar de Las Palmas, a municipality in the Norte de Santander department. The village pastor, Father Francisco Romero, played an important part in spreading this crop, as it was his custom to impose as a penance to his parishioners the planting of coffee trees.

Three branches or *cordilleras* of the Andes, which constitute the heart of the country, traverse Colombia from south to north. The landscape of high peaks and deep valleys is the most densely populated zone and the most important coffee-growing region. Here are the departments of Antioquia, Caldas, Cundinamarca, Risaralda, Tolima, Quindío, Valle del Cauca, Cauca, Nariño, and Huila. To the northeast and in the slopes of the Eastern Range, coffee is grown in the departments of Norte de Santander, Santander, and Boyacá. On the northern coast, it is grown on the slopes of the Sierra Nevada of Santa Marta, in the departments of Magdalena and Cesar, and on the slopes of the Guajira Mountains in the department of Guajira.

COFFEE AS AN EXPORT

Colombia began to export coffee in the decade 1830–1840. Initially, 75,000 70-kilogram bags were exported per year. Between 1880 and 1890, coffee exports reached 240,000 70-kilogram bags annually. During the last decade of the nineteenth century, coffee became a key item among Colombian exports and began to represent a fundamental part of the country's trade balance.

By 1905, exports rose to 500,000 70-kilogram bags annually. The one million 70-kilogram bag milestone was reached in 1913 and the two million figure during the 1920s. This decade featured the departments of Caldas and Antioquia as the largest producers, above Santander. Until 1923, Colombian exports were financed and managed mostly through international brokerage firms with representatives in Colombia. Trade and exports were channeled down the Magdalena River through important ports such as Girardot, Honda, Puerto Salgar, and Puerto Berrío.

CREATION OF THE NATIONAL FEDERATION
OF COFFEE GROWERS OF COLOMBIA

In 1927, the most dynamic sector of the Colombian economy decided to assemble coffee growers to promote the crop and to combat chronic social ills: alcoholism, lack of education, poor communications infrastructure, and deficient public health services. Since the end of the nineteenth century, coffee had been the main export product and the economy's growth engine. The Federación Nacional de Cafeteros de Colombia was founded in 1927 by the Second National Coffee Growers Congress and was composed of all coffee growers. Its members received agricultural extension services, including technical assistance for coffee cultivation and diversification of crops native to the coffee zones. Law 72 of 1927 created the coffee tax, a levy on each bag of coffee leaving the country. Revenue from this tax became the Federación's principal source of income.

The organization conducted health, nutrition, and educational campaigns and built infrastructure such as rural roads, aqueducts, and electrification in the coffee regions. The Federación also organized farmer groups at the village level, helped organize **cooperatives,** and created mechanisms and credit lines and other services that benefited coffee growers and their families.

Another focus area of the Federación has been coffee research. The National Coffee Research Center, Cenicafé, began operations in 1939 in the central coffee region, the department of Caldas, with several research stations spread across the country. The Center has carried out research work in the areas of phyto-improvement of coffee and associated crops, agroclimatology, entomology and physiology of the coffee tree, industrial uses of coffee, the nature and quality of coffee-growing soils, and development of new varieties resistant to insects and diseases.

COFFEE IN THE 1930s

The First International Coffee Congress took place in Sao Paulo, Brazil, on May 15, 1931. It was attended by the world's leading producers, especially the Latin American countries. The Congress resolved to create the International Coffee Bureau as the basis for cooperation among producing countries.

The coffee industry sank into a deep crisis by 1935 as a result of overproduction, strong competition from coffee substitutes, and high import duties imposed by European countries. In this difficult situation, the Federación invited governments and private agencies of the world's coffee-producing countries to a meeting in Bogota in October of 1936. The American Coffee Conference, as the sessions were titled, discussed price stabilization, which would provide adequate compensation to farmers.

Overproduction also led to an agreement between Brazil and Colombia, at that time the second largest producer of coffee. In 1933, Brazil presented a formal proposal for cooperation at the London Monetary and Economic Conference. The most important agreement reached at this meeting was the creation of the Pan-American Coffee Bureau, charged with standardizing the coffee policies of Latin American countries.

As these programs went forward, the Federación created the National Coffee Fund (FNC) in 1940. Its purpose was to regulate internal commercialization and manage inventories to facilitate the fulfillment of the Inter-American Agreement export quotas, agreed upon in Washington in the same year.

COFFEE IN THE 1950s

Between 1954 and 1956, prices reached record levels of an average of US$0.80 per pound, partly due to a frost in Brazil. Revenue from foreign currency increased considerably due to higher volumes exported as well as higher prices. By this time, there was no doubt about the huge economic impact that macroeconomic policy had on coffee. In fact, in order to offset the impact of the coffee-price bonanza on the economy, authorities advocated expanding the liberalization of imports that had started in 1951. They also introduced currency exchange controls. Consequently, a few months later, coffee prices began to fall and thus the exchange control was applied. Between 1956 and 1968, international coffee prices fell to US$0.40 per pound. The impact of this crisis was severe, given that coffee then represented 80 percent of Colombia's exports. As a result, the balance of payments went into deficit, the economy began to decelerate, and inflation spiked. During this time, the country had to stop paying its external debt and to halt import liberalization.

COFFEE IN THE 1960s AND THE INTERNATIONAL COFFEE AGREEMENT (ICA)

With the support of the United Nations, a conference was held in New York in July 1962 to discuss a proposed agreement between **producing** and **consuming countries.** The conference adopted a plan that went into effect at the end of 1963, once certain requirements had been met. Forty-two exporting countries and twenty-five importing countries, representing 99.8 percent of exports and 96.2 percent of imports, signed the agreement.
The main objectives of the 1962 agreement were to do the following:

- Reach a reasonable balance between coffee supply and demand, on foundations that ensured adequate coffee deliveries to consumers and markets, at equitable prices for producers
- Mitigate the difficulties caused by onerous surpluses and excessive fluctuations in coffee prices, which harmed both producers and consumers
- Contribute to the development of productive resources and to the promotion and maintenance of employment and income levels in member countries to help achieve fair wages, a higher standard of living, and better working conditions
- Increase the buying power of coffee-exporting countries by maintaining prices at fair levels and increasing consumption
- Promote coffee consumption by all means possible
- Stimulate international collaboration to address global coffee problems, acknowledging the relationship between the coffee trade and the economic stability of industrial product markets.

COFFEE IN THE 1970s

This decade started with the ICA as an exchange manager between producing and consuming countries through the use of export quotas, in Colombia with the Federación in charge of oversight.

In addition, the ICA established supply contracts with the most important international roasters. Colombia implemented supply agreements with domestic roasters, to which green coffee supply quotas were assigned.

Given that the annual quota assignment for producing countries was linked to production and inventory accumulation, the Federación and the government decided to increase the **productivity** of planted areas and, as a result, promoted a change in the crop profile. A monocrop technology was vigorously developed with the 'Caturra' variety, which involved eradicating **shade** on the coffee plantations. Between 1975 and 1980, production doubled, from six to twelve million bags. In taking this direction, the environment and social sustainability were not taken into account.

COFFEE IN THE 1980s

The 1980s marked the consolidation of the controlled coffee economy in Colombia. Monocrops escalated aggressively, exports doubled, and revenue from exports tripled. The promotion of monocrops was carried out by directing credit only to those who decided to eliminate shade and establish the freely exposed 'Caturra' variety, with densities over 5,000 coffee trees per hectare. Then in 1989 the quota system under the ICA ended.

The U.S. State Department had asserted in 1986 that the quota system had transferred resources from developed countries to developing ones, thus hindering the market's ability to set prices. In addition, the State Department argued that the goal of achieving higher prices was untenable in the medium term, given the cycle of an increase in production resulting from higher prices, then a large supply that would drive prices down. Finally, coffee sales to non-ICA member countries increased in volume and evoked strong objections from ICA countries, as coffee was sold at a lower price to the outsiders.

Under pressure from the U.S. and given the objections about prices, the ICA was then continued without export limits. ICO members agreed to keep the organization going as a discussion and statistical forum.

COFFEE IN THE 1990s

In 1991–92, Colombia recorded its highest harvest ever, close to 16 million bags. This bumper crop resulted from an extensive program involving the renewal and planting of improved varieties promoted by the Federación at the end of the 1980s. These two good harvests temporarily improved coffee revenues despite low market prices. Yet the breakup of plantations in land reform, the serious infestation of the **coffee berry borer** in 1995–1998, and renovations of an important coffee area combined to significantly reduce the national harvest in the following years.

The National Coffee Fund responded by paying growers a bonus for adopting new crops in place of coffee, at approximately US$1,250 per hectare. Production then fell from 17 million bags in 1992 to 11 million in 2000. Still, Colombian coffee exports for the coffee year 1999–2000 rose to 9.0 million bags and in 2000–01 to 9.5 million bags. The value of those exports was US$1.245 billion and US$878 million **FOB**, respectively. Despite the slight increase in exports during the last coffee year, revenues were 30 percent lower. Although Colombia's exports held a 10 percent share by volume of the global coffee trade in 2000, the share of total exported value was 14 percent, an acknowledgment of the high quality of the country's beans.

Figure 26.1. For certain demanding customers, coffee goes through a final hand-sorting in Colombia. The beans move down the lighted conveyor while the workers, mostly women, pick out defective or even slightly questionable beans. In other countries where labor is even cheaper, for example Ethiopia, nearly all sorting is done by hand. Photo by Robert Thurston.

By 2000–01, Vietnam became the world's second largest producer, displacing Colombia, whose production was then 10.5 million 60-kilogram bags. The value of the coffee harvest for that year was US$876 million, about 40 percent less than the figure reached in the early 1990s.

Meanwhile, coffee lost its economic importance among Colombia's exports. Coffee's share of total GDP fell from 10 percent in the 1950s to 2 percent in 2000. Coffee's portion of exports declined from 80 percent in the 1950s to 6 percent in 2000. During this same period, which coincided with the free market era, the National Coffee Fund's revenue stabilization efforts were highly limited, given its financial restrictions. In general terms, Colombia's coffee policy sought to defend producers' income, while providing greater transparency regarding foreign purchase prices and internal sales prices, as the **C price** and coffee harvest volumes both declined. These trends undermined the collection of the coffee export levy and accentuated the deterioration of the Fund's finances.

THE PRESENT AND FUTURE OF COLOMBIAN COFFEE GROWING: SOME CHALLENGES AND PERSPECTIVES

Colombian coffee-exporting activity is divided among private traders and the National Coffee Fund in proportions that have been changing for several decades; currently they are 79 percent and 21 percent, respectively. The United States has displaced Germany as the principal buyer of Colombian coffee. Factors such as the change of preferences in the German market toward cheaper coffees like Brazilian naturals and robusta have influenced the German market share. The third most important destination of Colombian exports is Japan, which in recent years has acquired close to 1.2 million bags annually.

The most powerful and important instrument of national coffee policy has been the FNC. It operates as a public treasury account administered by the Federación. The financial resources of the FNC are provided by the country's coffee producers through the coffee contribution (export levy).

Since the liberalization of the international coffee market in 1989, allocations of the FNC's funds have been constantly debated, as many coffee growers have pressed for greater expenditures on restructuring Colombian coffee agriculture. Nonetheless, significant resources have gone to a number of initiatives:

- To guarantee purchases of national harvests and stabilization of coffee revenues
- To finance agricultural research and extension
- To make national investments in companies that support the sector and regional investments in areas such as aqueducts, schools, and roads
- To restructure debt
- To promote internal and international consumption of Colombian coffee

Since World War II, the Fund has also invested in a series of companies that support the productive sector and in fulfillment of agreements involving the sorting of Colombia's coffee supply. Among companies created in this way are banks and an insurance company; Almacafé, which monitors coffee inventories; Cenicafé, responsible for research and transfer of technologies; and regional structures of departmental coffee grower committees and cooperatives, which oversee policies for purchasing harvests and quality control.

These companies performed important services during the term of the international coffee agreements and represented a substantial financial effort by the National Coffee Fund. The crisis in the international coffee market during the 1990s, as well as the new global tendencies towards liberalization and greater competition of markets in general, generated significant financial difficulties in many of these companies, which drained FNC's equity.

The national debate regarding the role that the National Coffee Fund should play in the future has been very extensive. What is clear is that resources are very limited to continue leveraging diverse investments in regional infrastructure or in national corporations supporting the sector. The fund's function of stabilizing prices and, even more challengingly, coffee revenues is not widely considered to be viable. Negotiations held with the national government have been geared toward complementing FNC's resources with funds from the national budget to maintain purchases of harvests and to sustain rural extension services in coffee-growing departments. Nonetheless, there are not sufficient resources to cover all of the estimated 500,000 coffee growers in the country.

The coffee model established between the National Federation of Coffee Growers and the central government responded effectively when export-quota agreements were in effect, but it encountered problems when facing the free market. In general, the traditional institutional arrangement has sought to protect the direct producer from market events and trends. Regulation and legal norms that govern the Colombian coffee sector and centralized decision-making and planning have already begun to give way to the flexibility required of private initiative in search of new business management alternatives.

Several proposals to end the crisis have emerged, such as supporting the promotion of regional, specialty, and sustainable coffees with high quality standards. This step would be an acknowledgment of Colombia's existing competitive advantages in the international coffee trade, so that producers and their organizations could establish direct relations with purchasers in a sustainable manner.

Another serious problem facing Colombian coffee involves recovering its production level, down from an average of 11 million bags in 2008 to 7.5–8.0 million bags, a reduction of over 30 percent. This decline has been due to intense rains, climate change, an increase in coffee berry borer infestation, new attacks of **coffee leaf rust**, and loss of production as some areas are renewed with resistant and specialty coffee varieties. The replanting is an institutional program directed by the Federación congruent with its strategy to increase competitiveness. Given the current relatively high price of coffee and what appears to be growing demand for superior arabica beans, Colombian growers can be cautiously optimistic.

27

Ethiopia

Willem Boot

Coffee aficionados should consider themselves very lucky. Just imagine how our beloved beverage would fare without Ethiopia's legendary status as its linchpin. Despite Ethiopia's unique heritage as the birthplace of the arabica bean, the motherland of coffee has only partially defined the evolution of the international coffee trade and only marginally contributed to the proliferation of the beverage itself. Why then have so many coffee professionals and enthusiasts developed an unconditional devotion to Ethiopia?

THE EVOLVING COFFEE LANDSCAPE

For thousands of years, Ethiopia has harbored a boundless diversity of coffee species and genotypes. Wild coffee trees can still be found by the millions in the country's diminishing forests in the south and west; these plants are the remnants of a vast coffee ecosystem without equal on Earth. Ethiopia's special place in coffee expresses itself most profoundly through the great array of flavor attributes in the liquor. Professional cuppers, who generally don't shy away from using unconventional superlatives, often find their traditional jargon of taste attributes too limited to describe the mesmerizing range of coffee flavors from Ethiopia. For many aficionados, the intensity and spectrum of Ethiopian flavors elicits a need to understand what is in the cup, and at the same time evokes a quest for the essence of Ethiopian coffee. It appears that the country enjoys a special set of historical, botanical, and sociological conditions that together formed an ideal set of circumstances for the creation of a large international family of Ethiopian coffee zealots. In addition, we should factor in the unlimited kindness of its people, the embedded culture of coffee consumption in daily life, and the ingrained dependency of Ethiopia's economy on coffee.

Ethiopia is a large, landlocked country in the eastern Horn of Africa. It is about three times the size of California in area, or approximately the same size as France, Germany, and the United Kingdom combined. Ethiopia is also the second most populous country in Africa, with an estimated population of 85 million. The famous Great Rift Valley cuts through the heart of Ethiopia, and indeed many of the world's most famous coffees grow along the valleys and mountainsides that make up this feature.

ETHIOPIAN LEGENDS AND COFFEE'S HISTORY

Various studies assert that the term "coffee" originates from Kaffa, a region in the southwest of Ethiopia. Coffee is "bun" or "bunna" in most Ethiopian languages, it is called "tukke" in the Sidama language, "kahwah" in Arabic, and "kahveh" in Turkish. A French cultural anthropologist and botanist, Jacques Mercier,[1] described how three men, Abol, Atona, and Baraka, went on a retreat in search of god. They hoped to receive manna (food) from the sky, but nothing came down, and they almost starved to death. Finally, god appeared to them and described the miraculous impact of two different remarkable plants, "kat" and "coffee." His advice was to chew the leaves of the first plant and to make a special preparation of the second. This could be done by roasting the berries, then boiling them to make an infusion. Miraculously, their hunger disappeared, and they were able to continue their journey. According to the story, each of the men prepared three consecutive infusions. The first infusion is called "abol" (from the Semitic word for "awal" or first), the second one is "atona" or "tona" (from the Semitic "itnin" or second), and the final infusion is "Baraka," meaning blessing, indicating a rite that takes place at the end of the coffee session.

A different legend, which goes back to 1451 CE, concerns an Abyssinian goat herder named Kaldi, who tried the coffee berry himself after observing how his charges became surprisingly wild and jumpy after eating the fruit of the coffee bushes. Kaldi also tried the fruit, which made him mildly intoxicated and invigorated. The monks of a nearby monastery noticed his condition, and soon all the monks chewed the berries before their nightly prayer.

Yet another story has been reported by the French ethnologist Marcel Griaule.[2] While on a visit to Zege, a peninsula at the northern Ethiopian lake Tana, he documented a myth about the origin of coffee telling the story about a local saint Batra Maryam, who lived in the seventeenth century. During one of his prayer sessions, he drove his "mekuamia" (measuring stick) into the ground. Miraculously, the stick developed roots and a coffee tree started growing that produced berries. And this is how coffee was first planted in Zege.

ETHIOPIA VS. YEMEN

In Yemen various stories circulate about the history of coffee. Unsurprisingly, many Yemeni claim the origin of coffee as their country's national pride. One of the Yemenite legends mentions Abu Bakribn Abdallah Al Aydarus as the discoverer of the use of coffee. In the story, Abu Bakr visited the Muslim order of the Qadiriyya in Harar, Ethiopia, in the early sixteenth century. During one of his travels to the region, he accidentally tasted the sweet, juicy berries of a coffee tree while resting beneath it. He immediately noticed the invigorating effects that the fruit had on him.

According to Yemenite legend, three key persons introduced Ethiopian coffee into Yemen: Said Al Dabani, Abu-l-Hasan Ali Ibn Umar Al Sadili (a Sufi who spent time in Yifat, Ethiopia during the fifteenth century during the reign of Emperor Yishak), and Abu Bakr. In any event, it appears that coffee trees were first transplanted from the Ethiopian highlands to the bare Yemeni mountains during the fifteenth century.

PROLIFERATION OF COFFEE TREES IN ETHIOPIA

Many nineteenth-century travelers to Ethiopia reported the widespread presence of coffee trees in the highlands of Abyssinia. For example, Theophile Lefèbre conducted a three-year exploration of Ethiopia between 1839 and 1843 for the French navy; he identified Ethiopia as the homeland of coffee.[3] *Coffea arabica* was found growing wild throughout the entire Changalla region (southwest Ethiopia) and under cultivation around the town of Jimma and the area of Kaffa.

Opinions differ about the actual birthplace of the coffee tree within Ethiopia. Some reports mention Kaffa (western Ethiopia) as the birthplace while other reports suggest that the eastern Harar province was the true birthplace. Major W. C. Harris conducted a survey for the English army in the 1840s on the abundance of coffee in Ethiopia. His book *The Highlands of Aethiopia*, 1844, notes that "coffee grows wild in every wood to the height of eight to ten feet and bends under the load of fruit in Limmu Enarya."[4] He also observed that coffee was dispersed by the civet cat over the mountains of the Itoo and Arsi, where it has flourished for as long as anyone can remember in Ethiopia.

The Ethiopian civet cat, of the same family as the Asian *Paradoxurus hermaphroditis*, is a mammal, whose name is derived from the Arabic "qat al-zabad." This animal has been utilized in Ethiopia for the production of "civet," a secretion produced by the anal glands. In captivity, the substance is harvested by scraping the secretion from the anal glands; it is then used as an aromatic base for perfume. Charles Jacques Poncet, a French physician who visited Ethiopia in the year 1700, reported that merchants kept as many as 300 civet cats, feeding them wheat and milk and harvesting the civet from their glands every week.[5] We can assume that the civet cat has been important for the proliferation of coffee throughout Ethiopia, for its natural behavior is to eat the ripe berries of the coffee tree and to spread the seeds in its excrement around the forests. Many wild coffee trees in Ethiopia are found along river banks and mountainous areas, in the same places where civet cats and other mammals and birds roam in their search for food.[6]

COFFEE AS A FOOD ITEM

The Ethiopian historian Tekettel Haile-Mariam conducted interviews with elderly persons in Kaffa in 1972 and recorded their stories about the traditional use of coffee in the region. Coffee was originally consumed with other food grains; it was particularly important as a sort of energy victual for warriors. As recently as the mid-nineteenth century, coffee cherries would be mixed with butter, red pepper, and other spices, providing a snack for the guests of honor of the family. According to Tekettel's sources, trade in coffee cherries spread throughout Kaffa province for their nutritional value.[7] Only the fresh cherry was in demand, and because of its perishable nature, it had to be transported fast and in a limited radius from the source of cultivation. This aspect of berry freshness must have motivated officials and landlords to plant their own coffee trees in their own administrative zones.

James Bruce, who travelled to Ethiopia between 1768 and 1772, reported on the consumption of roasted coffee beans. "The Gallas (Oromos) ate the roasted bean which they pulverized and mixed with butter to form hard balls about the size of those used in billiards, which kept them in strength and spirits during a day's fatigue better than a loaf of bread or a meal of meat."[8]

Overall, it appears that Ethiopians have embraced many practices to use the integral coffee tree and its fruit to the maximum extent. One example is the coffee drink "chemo," which is still quite popular in the westernmost regions of Ethiopia. Chemo is made by toasting or drying coffee leaves, then crushing and boiling them, while adding various spices and herbs from the forest, for example ginger, pepper, onions, garlic, salt, and tena adam (fringed rue). The drink is preferably served slightly chilled. It has an engaging bouquet of flavors: spicy, refreshing, mildly grassy, and a salt/sweet aftertaste with a noticeable boost due to the extracted caffeine.

ON THE COMPLEX POLITICAL HISTORY OF COFFEE'S HOMELAND

The political history of Ethiopia doesn't lend itself easily to a brief description. From the establishment of the Axumite Kingdom in the first century CE until the abdication of Emperor Haile Selassie in 1974, Ethiopia enjoyed more than nineteen hundred years of successive dynasties involving kings, emperors, and other regional and local feudal rulers. Except for the brief Italian invasion from 1936 to 1941, the country has never been colonized or annexed by a foreign country. Ethiopia's position on the crossroads between the Arabs and western Africa has produced for centuries a rich dynamic between Muslim, Christian, Judaic, and indigenous religions. The year 1974 witnessed both the discovery of the legendary fossil humanoid Lucy in the Rift Valley and the birth of the Derg regime, a Marxist-Leninist state. Agricultural reform policies were implemented. All private landholdings were nationalized. Suspected enemies of the Derg regime were tortured or killed. A period of political and economic havoc followed, intensified by droughts and famine.

In 1991 another revolution followed, instigated by the EPRDF (Ethiopian Peoples' Revolutionary Democratic Front), which has since maintained political control of the country. From 1995 on, a process of gradual reform and modernization has taken place under the leadership of long-term president Meles Zenawi.

The Ethiopian coffee industry has been evolving gradually but slowly. Around the start of the twenty-first century, new policies were adopted to alter the coffee sector from a partially government controlled monopoly to a more diverse industry involving private exporters and cooperative unions.

Around 2005, the maturing international **specialty coffee** industry resulted in a surge of demand for high grade Ethiopian coffee beans. Despite rising coffee export numbers, farmers were still losing out in their quest to build a sustainable livelihood from arabica production. Higher demand and increasing exports did not work well in the prevailing internal coffee marketing system, which involved too many middlemen (akrabies and sabsabis) and an ineffective national coffee auction platform. The government responded with new policies that greatly upset the international specialty coffee community.

In 2009, the Ethiopian Commodity Exchange (ECX) was established; it introduced a high-tech coffee trading platform involving many quality differentiated classes and categories. Unlike the previous auction system, the ECX does not allow any collusion between buyers (exporters) and sellers (producers), in the attempt to guarantee a fair price discovery system that ultimately can create major financial benefits for the coffee farmers.

Specialty coffee buyers were initially appalled by the new commodity exchange, which in its original context did not permit any significant form of traceability of the traded coffee lots. To further exacerbate the grief of coffee aficionados, the ECX de facto mandated the blending of potentially precious coffee lots with potentially mediocre beans.

What has the impact of the ECX been? One can argue that the plight of Ethiopian coffee farmers was alleviated significantly with or *despite* the introduction of the new system. Coffee industry specialists conclude that the architects of the new model were simply lucky, because of the concurrent major rise in international coffee commodity prices. Time will tell. In any case, with the evolution of the Ethiopian coffee industry, a new category of specialty coffee exporters is emerging: the private estate holders. Projections are that by the year 2025 the combined production of these new "coffee barons" will exceed 25 percent of Ethiopia's coffee exports.

ORIGIN OF ORIGINS

As the "**origin**" of all origins," Ethiopia has countless unique features, especially the thousands of heirloom varietals that grow in the hundreds of thousands of small coffee plots around the country. In many cases, farmers grow their own unique heirloom varietals. In most regions, from eastern Harar to southern Sidama and to the western highlands of Lekempti, smallholder farms pool their coffees at local milling stations, each farmer contributing his or her privately crafted coffee. The result is a complex mélange of unique flavors, the truest expression of local **terroir** to be found anywhere on the planet. The rich complexity in a cup of Yirgacheffe, for example, is largely a product of these special circumstances that occur nowhere else in the world. It is impossible to make generalizations about the flavor and essence of Ethiopian coffee, which is as varied as it is rich.[9]

NOTES

1. Jacques Mercier, *Art That Heals: The Image as Medicine in Ethiopia* (New York: Museum for African Art, 1997), esp. 63.

2. Marcel Griaule: *Abyssinian Journey* (London: Miles, 1935).

3. Theophile Lefebre et al., *Voyage en Abyssinie exécuté pendant les années 1839, 1840, 1841, 1842, 1843, 1845–51.*

4. William Cornwallis Harris, *The Highlands of Aethiopia* (London: Longman,1844).

5. Charles Jacques Poncet, in William Foster, ed., *The Red Sea and Adjacent Countries at the Close of the Seventeenth Century*, series 2, no. 100 (London: Hakluyt Society, 1949), 136–37, quoted in Karl H. Dannenfeldt, *Journal of the History of Biology* 18, no. 3 (Autumn 1985): 422. See also Ronald S. Love, "A French Physician at the Court of Gondar: Poncet's Ethiopia in the 1690s," *Proceedings of the Western Society for French History* 31 (2003).

6. Christine B. Schmitt, *Montane Rainforest with Wild Coffea Arabica in the Bonga Region (SW Ethiopia): plant diversity, wild coffee management and implications for conservation* (Göttingen: Cuvillier, 2006), 31, 39, and 62.

7. Tekettel Haile-Mariam, "The Production, Marketing and Economic Impact of Coffee in Ethiopia," PhD dissertation, Stanford University, 1973.

8. James Bruce, *Travels to Discover the Source of the Nile: in the years 1768, 1769, 1770, 1771, 1772, and 1773*, vol. II (Edinburgh: Ruthven, 1790–91), 469.

9. For more on Ethiopian coffee, see Yared and Lemma Getachew, "History of Harar Medhane-Alem Secondary H.S.," Basha Mawi, Speech at the Roundtable Conference, Harar, Ethiopia, 2008; and Daniel Humphries and Willem Boot, *Ethiopian Coffee Buying Manual* (Washington, DC: USAID, 2011).

28

Vietnam

Robert W. Thurston

The big story in Vietnamese coffee, and in fact in global output, is the huge increase in production that began there in the early 1990s. As late as 1980, the country produced only a negligible quantity of beans, and exports were almost unheard of. In the postcolonial, post-Vietnam war era, coffee was first exported in 1981, with 68,700 tons leaving the country. By 1987, about 100,000 **hectares** were devoted to coffee. By 1997–98, Vietnam produced 5.8 million **bags**, or about 348 million kilos, putting it into fourth place globally, behind Brazil at 22.5 million bags, Colombia at 10.5, and Indonesia at 6.7.[1] By 2000, Vietnam had moved into second place.

Various figures have been offered for the size of the 2011–12 Vietnamese harvest, from 18.5 million to 21.67 million bags,[2] while Brazilian production for the harvest year 2012–13 is projected at 50.6 million bags.[3] The Vietnamese may well have permanently outstripped Colombia, at 8.5 million bags in 2011–12.[4] Today in Vietnam about 500,000 hectares are planted in coffee, a figure the government wishes to stabilize.

Robusta makes up 97 percent of Vietnamese production by foreign estimates, just under 93 percent by government figures.[5] Although the country is trying to switch gradually to arabica, the Ministry of Agriculture does not anticipate any change in robusta's share of the crop for at least five years. The country ranks first in the world in robusta production, at around 4.3 million bags in 2008–9. While Vietnam has found, or created, a great niche for itself in robusta, that does not mean that the country's income from coffee has made farmers wealthy. Robusta is always considerably cheaper than arabica on the import markets; in late January 2012, robusta was selling for 111.08 delivered in New York, while arabica fetched 220.08 (or $1.11/pound versus $2.20/pound).

Coffee was first planted in Vietnam in 1857, by French landowners or, in some accounts, missionaries. The plant grew on only a few thousand hectares into the 1970s. Then several developments spurred the country's meteoric rise. The **International Coffee Agreement** collapsed in 1989 after the United States withdrew from it, complaining that free market principles were undermined by the accord, which set quotas for each country's production, and that the price of coffee was too high. Then in 1994 and again in 1997, bad weather in Brazil caused world prices to soar; this trend lured both the Vietnamese government and many

158

farmers further into coffee production. Moreover, after 1991, state-owned import companies brought in fertilizer at prices considerably below world market figures.[6]

When the price of coffee beans slumped terribly once again, beginning in early 1998 and reaching an abysmally low point in 2002–04, many blamed the situation on the flood of beans from Vietnam.[7] Certainly the increase in Vietnamese production contributed significantly to the slide in prices, for two reasons. First, although the coffee exported was overwhelmingly robusta, so much coffee was available globally, and so many drinkers stuck with instant coffee or cheap grocery-store blends containing robusta, that the price of all coffee fell. Second, the largest importers found they could remove some of the bitterness inherent in robusta by forcing steam through batches of beans. But, as numerous parts of this book show, the demand for coffee overall and for specialty coffee in particular has driven the price of all beans up once more.

Did the World Bank encourage Vietnamese farmers to plant coffee at the expense of farmers elsewhere? Did the Bank want to push down the cost of coffee so that Western consumers would pay less or Western companies would make more money? The Bank has vehemently denied such charges, for example in a "Frequently Asked Question" and response released in September 2004:

Q: Did the World Bank encourage Vietnamese farmers to plant coffee to the detriment of farmers in other coffee producing countries?

A: Vietnamese coffee expansion began well before 1994. The Bank only began lending again in the rural sector in Vietnam after 1996. The Bank has supported Vietnam's very successful drive to grow its economy and reduce poverty, but none of its investments has been designed to promote coffee production.[8]

Thus the World Bank denied playing a major role in Vietnamese coffee expansion. Of course, loans for any purpose would have freed some capital inside the country for investment in coffee production. In any event, since 2004, rising production in Vietnam has mirrored the general increase in the price of coffee, not lowered it.

The World Bank's policies are designed to promote capitalism and privatization, but those goals appear to have fit well with the Vietnamese government's own plans after the late 1980s. State agencies maintained price controls on basic foodstuffs while supporting the expansion of coffee production by several means. These included providing farmers with subsidized land and preferential loans and in some cases seedlings, fertilizer, irrigation, and agronomic support.[9] Loans to farmers by state banks were at rates as low as 1 percent interest. Into the late 1980s, most land was government-owned; then came a switch to cultivation by private farmers, mostly operating with long-term leases. By 2003, only 5 percent of coffee acreage was still government-owned and operated. These policies were in line with a general set of projects that allowed more entrepreneurial activity.

To summarize Vietnam's rise to second place in global production, the country has had some of the world's lowest production costs and highest robusta **productivity**. A large pool of labor was available and willing to work cheaply, sometimes for a dollar a day. The coffee industry now employs about 600,000 workers, 800,000 at the peak of the harvest season.[10] Cheap land, government policies and subsidies, the increased demand for robusta around the globe, and the collapse of the ICA all played a role. The World Bank's contribution should be placed fairly far down on any list of reasons for Vietnam's success.

For a country desperately trying to recover from decades of war and to raise a low general standard of living, coffee represented a way to enter world markets, earn hard currency, and put people to work. A secondary benefit from the government's point of view was the opportunity to move more people—especially ethnic Vietnamese—onto the land. This trend has come at the expense, for example, of ethnic Cambodians who once lived in the central and western highlands, the main area of Vietnamese production.

Serious challenges confront Vietnam as it tries to lower costs and improve coffee quality. "Vietnamese production is . . . heavily dependent on intensive irrigation and a massive use of inputs and **fertilizers**."[11] The cost of farming this way, in terms of inputs and damage to the land, cannot be sustained. Water for irrigation is becoming a precious and expensive resource. According to the Vietnamese Coffee & Cocoa Association (Vicofa), some 137,000 hectares of old and low-quality coffee trees need to be replaced, accounting for more than 25 percent of the total area in coffee.[12]

Most of the country's coffee is grown in the western highlands, at an elevation of 500–700 meters. The relatively low altitude will hamper efforts to switch to arabica. Few fields have shade trees, and farmers are reluctant to take land out of coffee production to plant them. Climate change is a problem here as elsewhere; severe droughts have occurred within the normal dry season, while rainfall as the plants flower has become more erratic. About 70 percent of the arable land in coffee is planted from seeds; 30 percent is planted from clonal stock. This agricultural structure may leave Vietnam particularly open to plant diseases and pests, already a serious problem in the country. Low quality remains a challenge, as, for example, ripe and unripe berries are often mixed together in the harvest. More coordination among farmers is needed, while capital for expanding the use of dryers and patios, among other improvements, is in short supply.[13]

On the bright side, Dang Le Nguyen Vu opened the first Vietnam-owned gourmet coffee shop in Ho Chi Minh City in 1998. By 2004, his franchise network employed more than 6,000 people, and his company had opened export branches in Tokyo, Singapore, Taipei, New York, Toronto, Paris, and other European Union cities.[14] As in China, Vietnamese entrepreneurs direct their coffee marketing efforts at home to a young clientele. The international chain Gloria Jean's ran six coffeehouses in Vietnam by the end of 2011 and planned to open twenty more in the next five years.[15] Starbucks plans to enter the country in 2013.[16] Such expansion is taking place in a context of rapid economic growth: Vietnamese per capita income rose from $220 in 1994 to $1,168 in 2010.[17] With due allowance for the economic setbacks suffered around the world beginning in 2007, Vietnam seems likely to continue on this general upward trajectory. Internal consumption will likely rise along with exports. The country has proven itself amazingly resilient in the past, and it has a good chance of overcoming its current problems in coffee production and quality.

NOTES

1. http://www.nationalgeographic.com/coffee/map.html.

2. The first estimate is from International Coffee Association [ICA], "Monthly Coffee Market Report," December 2011, 5. The second estimate is from http://www.topcommodities.net/2011/09/vietnamese-coffee-production-forecast.html.

3. ICA, "Monthly Coffee Market Report," 5.

4. ICA, "Monthly Coffee Market Report," 6.

5. Bui Ba Bong, [of the] Ministry of Agriculture and Rural Development [Vietnam], "Vietnam: Sustainable Coffee Development," presentation at the World Coffee Conference, Guatemala, February 26–28, 2010, 10.

6. Daniele Giovannucci, Bryan Lewin, Rob Swinkels, and Panos Varangis, *2004 Vietnam Coffee Sector Report* (Washington, DC: World Bank, 2004), 21. 50 percent drop in prices in VN.

7. See, for example, Charis Gresser and Sophia Tickell, *Mugged: Poverty in Your Coffee Cup* (Oxford: Oxfam, 2002), 18. Available at www.maketradefair.com/assets/english/mugged.pdf. While this report only briefly mentioned Vietnam's increased production as a major factor in the then-crisis in coffee, Anthony Wild in *The Independent*, April 3, 2004, saw a darker purpose in the World Bank's role in Vietnam. Perhaps that was an appropriate stance for the author of *Coffee: A Dark History* (New York: Norton, 2005), published soon after.

8. http://web.worldbank.org/WBSITE/EXTERNAL/EXTSITETOOLS/0,,contentMDK:2026394 1~menuPK:534295~pagePK:98400~piPK:98424~theSitePK:95474,00.html.

9. Giovannucci et al., *2004 Vietnam Coffee Sector Report*, 21 (p. 3 of Background section).

10. Giovannucci et al., *2004 Vietnam Coffee Sector Report*, 20.

11. ICA, "Monthly Coffee Market Report," 6.

12. As noted in United States Department of Agriculture, Foreign Agricultural Service GAIN Report, May 15, 2011, 2.

13. This description of problems is largely based on Bui Ba Bong's presentation in Guatemala.

14. *The Vietnam Investment Review*, December 15, 2004.

15. *The Australian*, November 14, 2011.

16. *The Belfast Telegraph*, July 9, 2011.

17. United States Department of State, Bureau of East Asian and Pacific Affairs, "Diplomacy in Action Background Note, Vietnam," January 5, 2012.

29

Brazil

Carlos H. J. Brando

A silent revolution has swept across the Brazilian coffee business in the last two decades. New approaches, recent technologies, and a modern view of the market have helped Brazil to reshape the business, from seed to cup.

Improvements in efficiency and quality have made Brazilian coffees more competitive and, at the same time, changed the image of the country from a producer of volume to a producer of quantity *and* quality. From the choice of **varieties** to be planted to cultivation, harvesting, and postharvesting processing, an emphasis on quality started to influence many activities. Brazil is not only producing some very fine coffees but it is also tightening quality controls at all levels of the business and orienting its marketing to focus on coffee quality.

Coffee plantations migrated to the north, away from frost prone areas, in the direction of the flatter, more easily mechanizable areas of the *Cerrado*, the Brazilian savannah. Drier regions started to use irrigation increasingly to counter the negative effects of periodic droughts. Brazil already irrigates more than 10 percent of its coffee plantations: about 40 percent of the conilon (the Brazilian robusta) areas of Espírito Santo and South Bahia, and almost 25 percent of the arabica plantations in western and eastern *Cerrado*, in Minas Gerais, are currently irrigated.

Coffee yields that used to be only ten to twelve 60-kilogram **bags** per hectare have already reached twenty bags per hectare and are about to go even higher, a national average that few countries have achieved. New, high-density planting techniques, coupled with advanced soil fertilization and disease-resistant varieties, have enabled whole regions to produce average yields in excess of thirty bags per hectare. Certain areas, like the *Cerrado* of Bahia, reach fifty bags per hectare.

The matrix of production changed, along with the portfolio of products offered to the market. Today Brazil produces almost all types of coffee that the market demands, in volumes and qualities that please operations from the microroaster to big multinationals. The production share of conilon, which used to vary between 15 and 20 percent of the national output, may reach 25 percent over the next years. The crop estimate for 2012 indicates that Brazil may produce between 48 and 52 million bags of coffee, of which around 12 million were conilons.

The logistics and cost of processing and transporting the crop have improved greatly with bulk handling and the privatization of highways. Vitoria harbor has gained in export share

Figure 29.1. A good example of large-scale "technified" Brazilian production. Rio Verde farm, Sao Paulo state, Brazil. Photo by Robert Thurston.

compared to Santos, as conilon production increased more than 50 percent in recent years. The sophisticated exporting sector demonstrates that it can deliver large crops without bottlenecks. In 2012, Brazil exported 33.4 million bags of coffee, a new record for the sector, with revenues of about US $9 billion.

Domestic coffee consumption is an especially bright spot; it doubled from 6.5 to 13 million bags between 1992 and 2002. More recently, the consumption of coffee has been growing at 5 percent per year in Brazil, while world consumption has been increasing at just 2 percent per year. In 2011, national coffee consumption surpassed 19 million bags, and the industry expects that it will soon reach 21 million bags. Brazil is now the second largest **consuming country** in the world, after the United States. Local consumption represents a captive market for 30 to 40 percent of Brazilian coffee production, an unquestioned competitive advantage.

The quantitative and qualitative advantages of the Brazilian coffee business have been heavily supported by the research and development model implemented by the Coffee Research Consortium, managed by Embrapa (the Brazilian Agricultural Research Company). The consortium is unique in the coffee world. It brings together the most traditional and prestigious research institutes in the country with younger centers exploring new technologies or located in new producing areas in a model that is decentralized and pluralistic, monitored by all involved in the sector. All research work is oriented to the needs of the clients, be they coffee growers, the industry, or the consumer. This intensive research effort created the basis of the revolution in the Brazilian coffee business that is still going on; there is much more to come in future years.

THE FUTURE OF COFFEE PRODUCTION IN BRAZIL

Although the future of the Brazilian coffee sector seems bright, some doubts remain. The strong Brazilian currency and increasing production costs, especially labor, have caused the country's formerly low production costs to reach levels comparable to those prevailing today in Colombia and in the most costly Central American producers. The challenge now is how to benefit from the temporary "price bonanza" on the global market to increase competitiveness through both lower costs and higher added value. If that is not done, it is highly unlikely that Brazil will be able to retain the high market share achieved in recent years.

ARABICA

Brazilian growers of arabica coffee need to address three critical areas to retain their leadership: irrigation to increase yields, mechanization to lower costs, and quality enhancement to improve price differentials.

Average Brazilian yields grew from 10–12 bags/hectare to 18–20 bags/hectare mostly due to higher coffee tree densities. The next round of increases in arabica average yields, perhaps to 30 bags/hectare, is likely to come from irrigation. Less than 20 percent of the area under arabica is irrigated today, which causes the country to lose as much as one full arabica crop every six to seven years due to droughts that affect different growing areas. Not only is a wide array of irrigation technologies available today, but prices of equipment have fallen substantially in recent years. Demand for irrigation equipment is soaring.

Harvesting will be the central focus of mechanization efforts. Only 20 percent of the arabica crop is mechanically harvested today. Manual strip harvesting will be progressively replaced by mechanical stripping, using handheld harvesters that are compatible with coffee planted on mountain sides, no matter how steep. This change can increase a picker's efficiency four- or fivefold; it is no surprise that pickers themselves are buying such machines for as low as US $500 per unit. Large coffee harvesters, with their own wheels and engines, are the preferred choice for areas that are flat or have moderate slopes; in this case each machine replaces up to a hundred pickers.

The technology to bring about this new revolution is already available because the Brazilian Coffee Research Consortium has done a great job itself and in cooperation with the private sector, especially the fertilizer, agrochemical, and equipment manufacturers. The great obstacle is how to make this technology reach the largest number of arabica growers quickly and at a reasonable cost. What may be required is the creation of management and technology "packages" adapted to the main arabica producing regions, including financial support for reconversion and renovation and also efforts to expand technical assistance and rural extension services, especially for smallholders.

Competitiveness can be greatly enhanced by climbing the "quality ladder." Whereas husbandry can help improve quality substantially (for example, in the choice of varieties and nutrition practices), the largest potential gains lie in postharvest processing, especially in the use of the **pulped natural processing** system that produces coffees known in Brazil as CD ("Cereja Descascado"). Pulped naturals command a higher price because they have the typical sweetness and body of high-quality naturals, yet are free from the astringency that can occur in Brazilian naturals when climate is adverse. CD production has gone beyond the specialty coffee niche and has already surpassed seven million bags in some years. Washed Brazils will become deliverable at ICE Futures New York in 2013.

In spite of the safety net of domestic consumption, which absorbs about 30 percent of the average arabica production, Brazilian growers of arabica will have to gain competitiveness in order to retain their current share of world exports. This task is difficult but not impossible, as there are still large traditional areas to be **technified**. Irrigation may lower production costs by ensuring production in dry years, and there are new frontiers to be explored, especially technological, but also geographical. However, these are mid- to long-term solutions. In the short run, improved farm management, better use of existing financial instruments, and value addition have a better chance to enhance the competitiveness of Brazilian arabicas.

CONILON

The future of conilon growing in Brazil looks positive from either perspective, domestic consumption or exports. Total demand for conilon in 2012 is estimated at approximately 14 million bags, against production of 12 million. Some 9 or 10 million bags went to domestic roasters and 3 to 4 million bags went to the soluble industry (about 80 percent of which will be exported as soluble coffee), leaving a million or so bags for export. Conilon definitely has room to expand.

Conilon production may increase in three different ways: greater yields in current areas, new plantings in traditional conilon areas, and the opening of new areas. Technology developed on some farms in the leading producer state of Espírito Santo has steadily improved yields to first 6, then 10 and now a record breaking 12 tons/hectare, whereas the average yield for the state is 25.5 bags/hectare (1.5 tons/hectare) to be compared with the average national yield of 22 bags/hectare (1.3 tons/hectare).[1] There is much room for growth in existing areas, particularly considering that the high yields reported above have not been obtained in test plots but in actual plantations and refer to four-year sliding averages. Since high-yielding conilon is mostly planted in low altitude areas that are not very far from the ocean and that benefit from lower labor costs, existing technology will have to be tested and most probably adapted as conilon moves into higher areas that are considering this alternative to arabica production.

Another area gaining attention is quality improvement, with increasing interest in the production of **washed** conilons for the high end of the domestic market and exports.

FINAL REMARKS

High coffee prices pose a unique opportunity for Brazil to continue its production revolution in order to ensure its competitiveness when coffee prices fall back closer to historical levels.

Sustainability may be the basis of the new coffee revolution in Brazil, which is today the world's largest supplier of sustainable beans. The potential to increase volumes of this type of coffee is still huge. Brazil's high yields bless the country's growers with the unique ability to invest in order to become socially and environmentally responsible, as well as to produce coffees that are truly sustainable.

The challenges are huge, the tools are readily available, and good coffee prices create the conditions for their use. The big question is whether recent and future profits, before coffee prices fall down again, will be enough to offset the decapitalization (and even losses) that affected most Brazilian coffee growers this decade and whether the coffee sector and government will together devise and implement policies to support the turnaround. If not, we will have only the survival of the fittest, which are not few, and Brazil will no longer increase its market participation and will certainly lose market share in arabica.

At the same time, the Brazilian coffee sector as a whole should be looking for ways to add value to the share of its coffee production that is today exported as **green coffee.** Considering that Brazilian coffees are key components of most blends around the world, Brazil should open its frontiers to imports from other origins to enable the country to become an export platform for finished products—roast and ground as well as soluble—to be made by the private sector (i.e., existing or new national and multinational companies). This export platform might eventually create for arabicas the same price protection shield that today exists for conilons.

NOTE

1. Editor's (RT) note: The figures for average production in the state and in Brazil as a whole are taken from *P&A Coffee Newsletter* 5, no. 51, October 7, 2011, http://www.peamarketing.com.br/coffidential/coffidential-051.pdf, accessed April 10, 2012.

30

Supporting Coffee Farmers' Response to Market Changes

Jeremy Haggar

The decade 2000–2010 witnessed dramatic changes in the world price of coffee, starting with a global oversupply of coffee and prices of less than $0.50 per pound (New York **C price**) and ending with unsatisfied demand and prices rising to $3.00 per pound in 2011. During the period of the extremely low coffee prices between 2000 and 2003, export earnings from coffee halved and accumulated losses in Central America amounted to $800 million.[1] This led to half a million workers losing their jobs and poverty levels in coffee regions rising significantly. Similar effects were seen on the 20 million families worldwide that depend on coffee production.

At the same time, consumers have demanded better quality, and the markets for certified socially and environmentally responsible coffee have grown considerably. During this period, considerable engagement has taken place between the producer sector, the coffee industry, and international development agencies, which are looking to manage and support producers in responding to this dynamic environment. This article will examine some of the results of this dynamic in Central America.

THE RESPONSE TO MARKET CRASH IN COFFEE PRICES

In response to social and economic impacts of the fall in coffee prices between 1999 and 2003, the major donors in Central America—The World Bank, Inter-American Development Bank, and USAID—called a meeting in April 2002 in Guatemala of all interested parties in the coffee sector and presented and discussed a strategy for response.[2] In essence, the donors indicated they were not willing to refinance the sector to continue as before, but were willing to invest in changes to increase the competitiveness of the coffee sector, essentially focusing on improving quality for **specialty coffee** markets and diversification for areas that were not competitive. Among other initiatives stemming from this event were three regional projects: one funded by USAID, implemented by Chemonics; a second funded by IADB, implemented by Technoserve; and a third funded by the World Bank, implemented by the Tropical Agricultural Research and Higher Education Centre (CATIE). Similar initiatives were undertaken in other parts of the world such as by ACDI-VOCA in Colombia and Technoserve in Tanzania. These projects had similar objectives overall: to improve the quality of coffee produced,

167

increase the business capacity of the producer organizations, and strengthen ties to the buyers of quality coffee. Between 2004 and 2007, the CATIE project "Linking Farmers to Coffee Markets" was implemented in alliance with the National Coffee Association of Guatemala (ANACAFE), the Honduran Coffee Institute (IHCAFE), and the Association of Small Coffee Producer Cooperatives of Nicaragua (CAFENICA). The rest of this article will use this project to illustrate the process of building capacity in forty-nine producer **cooperatives** across Guatemala, Honduras, and Nicaragua, with a combined membership of about 3,500 families. These co-ops, in turn, were members of ten **marketing** co-ops.

SUPPORT AND TRAINING FOR FARMERS

Although the productive part of the strategy of Linking Farmers to Coffee Markets focused on coffee quality, it was also evident that productivity was very low, and this also affected the economic viability of coffee farming. Therefore, training was provided on recuperating the productivity of existing coffee plantations, primarily through improved agronomic practices such as **pruning** to recover plant productivity, shade regulation, soil fertility management, and management of pests and diseases. This was provided as a year-long series of training sessions covering the main topics of coffee management at the time of year that corresponds to that management. During harvest and processing, the project prioritized aspects of quality control during harvest. The project provided training of between twenty and thirty extension agents and farmer promoters in each country who in turn trained some 2,000 farmers across all countries.

The business aspect of the program was designed following a diagnostic of the entrepreneurial capacity of the producer and marketing cooperatives—which revealed considerable differences in capacity. To cope with these, a series of formal training sessions in strategic planning, financial management, and commercial management were given but with individual follow-up with each cooperative to adequately apply these principles to their needs and capability. Both farmers and cooperatives were supported in developing capacity to manage **certification** processes, where this was an objective of the cooperative. Also, marketing cooperatives received training in improving their quality control and traceability systems, in collaboration with the Technoserve/IADB Central American Coffee Project. Furthermore, equipment was provided to establish **cupping** laboratories in each country. In the area of marketing support, promotional leaflets, videos, and web pages were developed for the different organizations, and participation in the **Specialty Coffee Association of America**'s annual symposium and expo was supported with experienced facilitators organizing and mediating meetings with coffee buyers.

TRAINING OUTCOMES

Coffee farmers made modest improvements in their management of coffee with a 10–20 percent increase in the number of farmers pruning bushes, fertilizing, and regulating shade. Slightly better improvements were achieved in implementation of practices to ensure coffee quality with a 20–50 percent increase in the number of farmers only picking red cherries, correctly fermenting the coffee, and **grading** the washed coffee. Likewise, almost twice as many farmers (the majority) improved their record keeping of farm management, contributing to compliance with certification standards.

In the area of business management, the majority of cooperatives developed strategic plans, revised or developed financial management procedures, analyzed their cost structures, and reviewed their strategies of marketing alliances. Seventeen of the cooperatives achieved new certifications, mostly with Rainforest Alliance, Utz Certified-Good Inside, and C.A.F.E. Practices (about half of the co-ops were already certified organic prior to the project). Probably most significantly, as a result of the analysis of marketing alliances, in Honduras, six cooperatives that previously had no affiliation to a marketing cooperative decided to form a new marketing cooperative, CORECAFE. Although this initiative took time to establish and CORECAFE was only legally formed in the last months of the project, four years later, the organization managed to export eleven containers of coffee, four of them certified Rainforest Alliance. Overall, the prices received by uncertified coffee farmers improved from $0.77/ pound to $0.87/pound, also halving the negative differential against the New York C price (the negative differential being a function of the perceived quality of coffee from these country origins). The price for organic coffee, however, remained stable at $1.02/pound. No sales of other certified coffees were made during the period of the project.

The combined effects of improved production, quality, business capacity, and marketing came together in Honduras, where the producers increased their participation in the annual **Cup of Excellence** program, achieving three winners in the 2007 competition. One of these, from a small organic cooperative, attracted attention from a specialty coffee buyer, Atlas Coffee, which has subsequently bought the coffee from this cooperative every year. Another winner was Dona Maria Irma Gutierrez, who attributed her success to the training provided by the project.

OUTCOMES IN THE LIVES OF COFFEE PRODUCERS

The changes in coffee production and income were different among the three countries. In Nicaragua and Honduras between 2004–05 and 2006–07, coffee **productivity** among participants increased by 10–25 percent, while net income almost doubled (from $724 to $1,591 per family in Nicaragua and $2,192 to $4,040 per family in Honduras). In Guatemala, productivity declined by 11–13 percent, although net income of organic farmers stayed the same ($880 per family) and it decreased for conventional farmers (from $2,887 to $2,146 per family). The main reason for this difference is that, during this period, the daily wage rate increased by 30–50 percent in Guatemala, limiting the capacity of Guatemalan farmers to invest in improvements while increasing their costs. Nevertheless, averaged across Central America, the income of 2,000 farming families increased by $800 per family. The volume of coffee sold by the cooperatives increased by 24 percent to over 95,000 100-pound sacks while the value of sales increased from $6,695,000 to $9,094,000, an increase in value of over $2 million.

It can never be certain to what degree the project contributed to these changes, but we do know that improvements occurred through increased efficiency of production and improved market differentials, areas in which the project worked, and not through a simple increase in world price, which was fairly stable during this period. Nevertheless, we obtain a clear picture of how coffee producers were able to respond to changing market conditions. Prior to the project—during the coffee crisis of historically low prices (2001–2003)—small-scale farmers were making $200–300 per year net income from coffee production. During the recovery period covered by these projects, this situation generally improved, with farmers able to moderately increase investment in production, although still without sufficient income to completely renovate the coffee plantations as would be required to substantially improve yields. However, farmers did increase net income to between $1,000 and $4,000 per year (for coffee farms of an average 1–3 hectares [2.5–7.5 acres]). Subsequent collaboration with these same farmers in Nicaragua and Honduras has shown that although they have increased gross income from coffee production by 20–70 percent, this gain has been consumed by ever increasing daily wage rates and prices of inputs such that in 2009–10, their net incomes were largely unchanged. Price increases during 2010 and 2011 may once again affect the scenario, possibly enabling farmers to finally invest in renovating coffee plantations to increase productivity. As ever, the hope is that this doesn't then sow the seeds of overproduction and another coffee price crash. Planning the economic and agronomic management of a crop whose productive lifespan is over twenty years and during which prices may fluctuate sixfold is a perpetual challenge for both producers and the industry.

NOTES

1. F. Castro, E. Montes, and M. Raine, "Centroamerica La Crisis Cafetalera: Efectos y Estrategias para Hacerle Frente," Sustainable Development Working Paper No. 23, 2004, The World Bank, Washington.

2. IADB/WB/USAID. "Managing the Competitive Transition of the Coffee Sector in Central America," Discussion Document, presented Antigua, Guatemala, April 2002.

CONSUMER COUNTRY PROFILES

31

Introduction to Consumer Countries

Jonathan Morris

Between the eighteenth and twentieth centuries, coffee was essentially grown in three areas—Asia, Africa, and Latin America—in order to be consumed in two others—Europe and North America.[1] **Producing countries** rarely consumed their own coffee: locals preferred other beverages, for instance *mate* in Latin America, while several producing countries, which were dependent on the crop for valuable external revenues, prevented their peoples from sampling the final product. Kenya, for example, refused to allow coffee to be roasted in the country until 2002. The only major exceptions to these continental divisions were Ethiopia, where it is estimated that around half of the crop is consumed by domestic drinkers, and Japan, which became one of the leading **consuming countries** after 1945.

The situation today looks rather different. Between 2000 and 2010, the share of world production consumed in the traditional markets fell from 60 percent to around 52 percent, while the amount of coffee remaining in producer countries rose from 25 percent to 31 percent. Meanwhile the emerging nontraditional markets have continued to increase their share of world consumption, from 15 percent to 17 percent. In terms of absolute volume, world consumption increased by 27.4 percent between 2000 and 2010, but while in the traditional markets this figure only grew by 11.6 percent, in the producing countries it rose by 56.7 percent and in the emerging markets by 41.9 percent.[2]

The **ICO**'s figures for 2010 show that Brazil is now in second place, behind the U.S., in terms of the total volume of coffee consumed, and catching up fast with an annual growth rate of 4.1 percent to America's 1.6 percent. In seventh place is the Russian Federation, whose 16.9 percent increase in imports between 2009 and 2010 saw it overtake such traditional markets as Canada, Spain, and the United Kingdom. Yet the Russian Federation, although the largest of the emerging markets, is far from the fastest growing. That title goes to its neighbor Ukraine, where the total volume of coffee consumed during the first decade of the twenty-first century rose at an annual rate of 23.6 percent.

The expansion of consumption in Russia and Ukraine is symptomatic of a phenomenon that Slavenka Drakulic, a Croatian writer, pointed out in her 1996 book *Café Europa*,[3] that a Western-style café, often called "Europa," sprang up quickly in every major European city east of the Elbe River following the collapse of the Soviet Union in 1991. These shops became a key symbol of aspirations for a new life and a longing, especially among young people, to be more "European." Coffeeheaven, a leading coffee shop chain in Poland, Latvia, Bulgaria, and Slovakia, now operated by Costa Coffee, used to claim that its coffeehouses "feel as familiar and relaxed as a café in London, Paris or Rome. . . . the Coffeeheaven concept combines the best of two converging worlds: Western experience with 'new' Europe's aspirations, talent and youth."[4]

In emerging markets outside Europe, however, the reference point is nearly always America, with coffeehouses appearing to offer access to the Western style of life. Starbucks, along with McDonald's and KFC, have built their appeal in China partly on the appeal of experiencing something American while eating and drinking.

In the traditional markets too, change is afoot. European countries such as France, Germany, and the United Kingdom have developed very different consumption patterns and industry structures over time, but the impact of the specialty, or perhaps more precisely **espresso**, revolution that swept out of home markets at the end of the twentieth century, has impacted them as much as the U.S. and Italy. The rise of single-portion **(capsule)** systems promising to bring the experience of the coffee shop into the kitchen threatens to overturn these even further. Meanwhile consumers are increasingly influenced by ethical factors in their coffee choices, as our detailed discussion of Denmark demonstrates.

If this book is updated ten years into the future, we may well be discussing different consumer giants—perhaps China, which is already showing great interest in the bean among its elite, or Turkey, which is rapidly increasing its consumption after over a century of tea as the dominant beverage in the country that first brought coffee to Europe. For now these profiles give a flavor of the evolution and current nature of coffee culture in some of the world's leading consumer markets.

NOTES

1. See "Coffee: A Condensed History" in this volume. Australasia, with relatively low absolute volumes of both production and consumption in world terms, remains classified among the emerging markets by the ICO.

2. Robério Oliveria Silva, ICO, "International Coffee Outlook," presentation to India International Coffee Festival, New Dehli, 2012.

3. Slavenka Drakulic, *Café Europa: Life after Communism* (New York: Norton, 1997).

4. http://www.coffeeheaven.eu.com, accessed May 25, 2006.

32

Denmark

Camilla C. Valeur

Examining Danish consumers' interest in **sustainability** and **certification** is a useful case study of current trends in the market for certified coffee.[1] The Danish domestic market is in the top tier in regard to coffee consumption per capita and market share of sustainable coffees. Danes are the second thirstiest consumers in Europe at 9.7 kilograms per person annually.[2] According to the Danish Coffee Association, imports of green (not decaffeinated) coffee into Denmark from all sources amounted to 35,592 tons (593,200 **bags**) in 2010, compared with 30.889 tons (514,817 bags) in 2009. This is an increase of 4,703 tons (78,383 bags) or 15 percent.

Four companies dominate the Danish market: Sara Lee, Kraft Foods, BKI, and Peter Larsen. These four are responsible for about 90 percent of the retail and the home/restaurant/café (known as "horeca") market, while fifteen to twenty microroasters make up the rest.[3] Most importers and roasters offer **sustainable** coffees, in particular **organic** and **Fairtrade International** certified. Some microroasters present their entire product line as sustainable and as integral to their business philosophy (see, for example, Just Coffee.dk). In supermarkets, the four bigger companies dominate, while microroasters are found in the specialty shops and in the out-of-home market.

Danish consumers are in the top tier as well in demand for sustainable products in general and in particular regarding coffee. About 40 percent of consumers are regular buyers of fair trade–certified products, and sales of Fairtrade coffee have been growing over the last five years, although 2011 witnessed a small decline. The main reason for the decrease from 2010 to 2011 was the significant price increases of raw materials; the value of imports has risen while the amount of coffee has declined. The financial crisis has affected price elasticity among consumers, and higher prices for coffee have created a downscaling effect in which a number of consumers have started to buy cheaper products. But for consumers of certified coffees, this trend has been weaker; those who buy certified coffees tend to be more loyal and less price sensitive.

Danish consumers are also in the top rank around the world in spending on organic products. Per capita annual outlay on organic products in 2009 was the highest in the world, and the market share of organic food sales was 7.2 percent.[4] In comparison, organic food and beverage sales represented approximately 4 percent of overall food and beverage sales in 2010 in the U.S.[5] The market share of sustainable coffees in the U.S. was 11 percent in volume and 14.5 percent in value in 2010, 10.7 percent in volume and 14.2 percent in value in 2011.[6]

TRENDS IN CONSUMPTION AND THE ISSUE OF SUSTAINABILITY IN DANISH COFFEE

A key reason that Danish consumers buy certified coffee is concern for the farmers who produced it. Another factor is health concerns (consumers of organic food products in particular cite health as an important reason for choosing organic products over conventional). Consumers claim that they are willing to pay around 10 percent more for Fairtrade-certified products if they feel certain that the extra cost is benefiting farmers. According to a study from 2008, the principal reason Danish consumers cite for their purchase of Fairtrade products is that they want to feel that they make a difference in the world and to help farmers and workers.[7]

It is therefore crucial that consumers have faith in certification. According to a survey carried out by Capacent Epinion for the Danish Chamber of Commerce, nearly a third of the respondents (31 percent) replied that the main reason for increasing their consumption of Fairtrade products is their growing trust in the Fairtrade label as a guarantee of distinct benefits for the farmer.[8]

This response implies that consumers do not buy anything that claims to do good unless they feel sure that a product delivers on this promise. Sociologist and consumer analyst Eva Steensig maintains that a paradigm shift is under way: consumers increasingly abandon the "because it feels good" economy and demand documentation for sustainability, health or environmental benefits, or indeed whatever a product or company may claim.[9] Anthony Aconis has recently argued that one of the eight emerging global trends in consumerism is "Clean-Real," a megatrend that refers to consumers demanding clean products from clean companies. That means no hidden chemical ingredients, no unsustainable production methods, and most of all no misleading or unreliable communication. "Consumers want proof that farmers are actually benefiting from Fairtrade or any other sustainability claim on the product."[10] This trend is confirmed in a report from 2011 on "Trends in the Food Sector" from the Aarhus School of Business,[11] in which the authors explain that consumers want to buy products grown or developed with respect for social and environmental issues.

WHO TO TRUST?

We don't trust companies,[12] but Danish consumers have a high level of trust in the European organic label and the Fairtrade label. A survey undertaken by Capacent Epinion notes that 75 percent of respondents agree that labels like Fairtrade are guarantees of sustainability in agriculture.[13]

A threat to consumers' trust in the labels is reports that the labels are not upholding their claims. So when cases emerge that show some farmers selling organic products are not upholding organic principles or that farmers are not benefiting from the Fairtrade premium, consumers' trust in the labels can weaken.[14] At the same time, it seems that a majority of consumers are not changing buying habits due to negative stories. Purchasers seem to know that the fairtrade issue is a complex process in which results and impact are not always easily measurable. Simultaneously, consumers believe that most organic farmers are meeting the standards for that designation.

Since the value of the labels depends on consumers' trust, and since thorough checks of results are the key to maintaining confidence, many labels are strengthening their internal monitoring and evaluation. Further, to be able to document impact is crucial, and the International Social and Environmental Accreditation and Labeling (ISEAL) Alliance has launched a multistakeholder process to help their members—including the governing bodies of Fairtrade, Organic, Rainforest Alliance, Utz Certified, 4C, and many other systems—to improve their understanding and implementation of credible forms of impact assessment. Many of the leading **sustainability** labeling organizations have independently begun working with IISD's (International Institute for Sustainable Development) Committee on Sustainability Assessment (COSA) to better understand the effects of their work at the field level. These and other efforts indicate the complexity of impact measurement and the importance given to this issue by the certifiers and by their stakeholders. A newly published Fairtrade report documents the number of farmers involved in Fairtrade and also the benefits for farmers related to the Fairtrade Bonus.[15] The Fairtrade organization in Denmark, Fair Trade Danmark, has announced that it will greatly increase its documentation of impact in order to show more clearly how Fairtrade makes a difference.

HOW SHOULD THE DOCUMENTATION BE COMMUNICATED TO CONSUMERS?

With growing demand from consumers, there are now efforts to provide evaluations or portals for more transparent and credible information. This goes beyond basic corporate sustainability reporting guidelines such as those promoted by the Global Reporting Initiative. New organizations such as Global Impact Investing Network, Big Room Inc., and People4Earth .org are all interested in consumer-accessible platforms that more explicitly examine sustainability efforts. Some groups are developing ratings that reward companies and products that contribute to sustainability and expose those that disregard sustainability values or even use unsavory or fraudulent practices. According to various sources in the Danish coffee industry and in the retail market, the growing interest in **traceability** systems is another indication for the expanding need to document sustainability.

Utz Certified, like organic systems before it, stands out as an early mover in the implementation of traceability systems for sustainable coffees and has used its online traceability system as a parameter for differentiation in the market since 2002. A pilot project currently being tested in a large supermarket chain with Utz coffee allows consumers to use smartphones to scan the coffee packaging on a screen located close to the coffee shelves and to see precisely the farmers or cooperatives that have produced and delivered the coffee and to learn about their stories. The pilot project is the result of close collaboration among figures throughout the **value chain**: the producer cooperatives, the importer and roaster, and a certifier with a traceability system.[16]

According to a large Danish retailer, traceability systems will play an important role in the future and will be used to trace more and more variables, like carbon footprint and product freshness, and will communicate this information to consumers by using a mixture of different technologies.[17]

The big challenges here are determining what information to offer to consumers and where and when to make it available. The example just given dates from 2009; it showed that over time consumers ceased to scan the product in the supermarket, whereas a mobile solution that came later was much more preferred. The mobile solution meant that consumers with smartphones could scan the product in their home at any time, which implied a greater likelihood of finding the right moment to do so.

Requirements for information about sustainability may be different in the business-to-business (B2B) market. According to a Danish trader, importers increasingly expect more from their suppliers in communicating and documenting the effects of their sustainability initiatives, not only through certifications but also other documented sources.[18] In business-to-consumer (B2C) markets this can take place by describing specific corporate social responsibility (CSR) projects and initiatives on the web page or through other channels of communication. In B2B markets **roasters** and importers can invite their customers to visit selected suppliers in coffee-producing countries to "document" the effect of their initiatives.[19]

THE IMPACT OF CLIMATE CHANGE AND CO$_2$ DOCUMENTATION

The Danish National Consumer Agency has noted that climate is currently very much the focus of many CSR efforts and is ranked number three of the issues that most preoccupy Danish consumers.[20] Their 2008 report indicates that Danish consumers are very interested in a carbon footprint label; three out of four consumers agree that a climate label would facilitate their shopping for more climate friendly products.

According to a survey undertaken by Aspecto for AgroTech, an authorized technological service institute, consumers do want more clear and accurate information, but they don't necessarily want more labels.[21] They feel they are already drowning in an information swamp. One solution could be to integrate the carbon footprint aspect into existing labeling systems.

Still, there is increasing interest in information on climate and sustainability, as evidenced by the common use of Ecological Footprint, the Global Footprint Network measures,[22] and the emergence of basic standards platforms such as People4Earth. At the field level, COSA has integrated carbon sequestration into its metrics for all production systems and intends to measure the differences between conventional approaches and the various sustainability initiatives. The goal is to determine whether there is a significant difference in their ability to manage carbon and thereby mitigate negative climate effects. According to certification organizations like Utz and Rainforest Alliance, it is almost certain that carbon control will be a part of future sustainability labeling systems even if it is unclear how or when such systems will be marketable.

In 2009, the Danish Coffee Network hosted a Coffee Climate Conference in Copenhagen intended to motivate further communication and research on how the coffee value chain is affecting global climate and vice versa.[23] The network has also worked with roasters and coffee bars in Copenhagen to reduce their companies' CO$_2$ emissions and to create value out of their waste. The latter initiative, which has been implemented together with the municipality of Copenhagen's engineers, gives companies the right to use a Climate+ logo as a way to communicate their efforts to consumers.

THE WAY FORWARD

Danish and other organizations dedicated to fairly traded commodities and sustainability now need to do two important things:

- Provide credible and transparent information in the right amount (what), at the right time and place (where and when)
- Increase collaboration between certification schemes and researchers as well as between companies and researchers (especially within private labeling)

Danish consumers have significantly increased their consumption of sustainable coffee since 2005 and are willing to pay a higher price as long as they feel confident that their purchases affect farmers and the environment positively. Consumers increasingly request documentation on sustainability, which has put greater pressure on the entire supply chain, including roasters and certification organizations, to credibly document impact. Many coffee companies depend on certification to communicate sustainability impacts effectively, without overburdening consumers with information or requiring too much effort. One of the more immediate challenges is to develop a trustworthy system to measure the CO_2 footprint of products and to integrate the data into existing sustainability labels.

Expectations that companies will take responsibility for the sustainability of their products and the demand for documentation are likely to increase the use of traceability systems in some form. At a minimum, these will be systems that can trace improvements and violations of ethical standards. Some of the challenges in this effort stem from the fact that many coffee farmers are living in distant rural areas, with no access to the Internet. Some are illiterate. Simultaneously, since these systems will have to be both reliable and relatively low-cost, it is likely they will need to be integrated into proven field metrologies, for example radio frequency identification (RFID), to make the necessary information available to end-consumers. In some cases, such as B2B markets where direct verification is possible, this trend may not need to rely on technology alone but can also involve dialogue and field visits (which in any event are important elements in the direct trade concept).

In the last several years, consumer price elasticity has shrunk as the price of coffee has risen. These trends make the market for sustainable coffees more difficult to operate in. Yet basic questions related to sustainable coffee and how to communicate its social and environmental value to consumers remain valid.

NOTES

1. Sustainable approaches in coffee refer to organic, Fair Trade, Organic, UTZ CERTIFIED, Rainforest Alliance, and other certifications, including private standards, with a stated objective to improve the social, environmental, and economic conditions of small farmers, their land, families, and so on.

2. According to the European Coffee Report (2010/2011), European Coffee Federation, www.ecf-coffee.org. However, some sources place Norway's consumption ahead of Denmark's.

3. Association of Danish Coffee and Tea Importers.

4. Research Institute of Organic Agriculture.

5. Organic Trade Association's 2011 Organic Industry Survey.

6. Source: AC Nielsen. It is important to note that between 65 and 75 percent of fair trade–certified coffees also are organic certified and may thus be represented twice in the data extractions.

7. Analyse Danmark 2008.

8. Capacent Epinion 2008.

9. Eva Steensig, "Fairtrade out and robots in," interview on Danish Radio (DR), December 3, 2008, http://www.dr.dk/P1/Krause/Udsendelser/.

10. Anthony Aconis, *Storegasm: Eight Global Trends That Define Our Shopping Today and Tomorrow* (Copenhagen: Where2go, 2008), 80–93.

11. Athanasios Krystallis Krontalis, Joachim Scholderer, Karen Brunsø, Klaus Grunert, Lars Esbjerg, Lisa Lähteenmäki, and Tino Bech-Larsen, "Trends i fødevaresektoren 2010–2015," Lecture, Aarhus School of Business, MAPP Centre, 2010.

12. According to a survey by the Danish National Consumer Agency (2008), 50 percent of consumers believe that companies have the primary responsibility for the sustainability of products that are produced in Denmark, including raw materials. However, consumers do not trust firms to accurately measure or report their own sustainability and their actions toward it.

13. Capacent Epinion.

14. In Denmark a documentary made in 2008 by Tom Heinemann claimed that Fairtrade made no difference to workers on tea estates. He had visited tea estates in Asia and Kenya and found that "fairtrade workers were working under miserable conditions just as the workers at conventional estates." In 2009 some Danish organically certified milk farmers were caught not upholding the standards for medicinal use.

15. *Monitoring the Scope and Benefits of Fair Trade*, 3rd ed., 2011.

16. Anita Aerni, Key Account Manager Europe, Utz Certified.

17. Brian Sønderby Sundstrup, Social Responsibility Developer, CSR FDB.

18. Lis Correa Rasmussen, Trader, NAF Trading.

19. Kurt Dalsgaard, Director Kontra Coffee.

20. Danish National Consumer Agency (2008).

21. AgroTech 2009.

22. http://www.fooprintnetwork.org.

23. The Danish Coffee Network was created in 2005 with financial support from the Danish Development Assistance (Danida) with the objective to improve the Danish coffee culture and promote sustainability in the coffee value chain. Members of the network are micro roasters, larger industrial roasters, traders, importers, retailers, cafés, certification organizations, and private consumers.

33

France

Jonathan Wesley Bell

If Italy and Germany can be said to lead European industry and markets through innovation, engineering, design, and economic persuasion, then it falls to France to lead in fashion and discernment. Appreciating fine coffee in France, more than anywhere else, is a matter of class. Two French classes have set the coffee standard in fashion and appreciation for centuries and continue to do so: the elite and the intelligentsia.

During the centuries that France governed European cultures in language, philosophy, art, and literature, the café became a signature of this imperialism. The coffee consumed in the nation's vast landscape of cafés was mainly colonial in origin, largely **robusta** from the empire's various coffee-producing areas. But not all French cafés served rough coffee. Excellent coffees from many different origins were and are a remarkable aspect of this corner of the French market.

Above the café realm, coffee became "French" first in court at Versailles. Louis XV not only had coffee grown in the botanical gardens there, he also roasted it himself. The power in fashion of the French king and his court throughout Europe is of considerable importance in understanding the continuing authority of French consuming trends. This explains why France is a market that coffee powers covet and where new concepts in coffee are often zealously promoted.

It is not surprising that a quarter of Nespresso pod global sales, at the time of this writing, are in France. Nor that it is the French who first gave Senseo a bonanza in sales.

Twenty-five years ago France still lingered in its imperial days and the masses largely drank robusta; **arabica** coffees were for the intelligentsia and the elite. Except for the United Kingdom, no country in Europe has witnessed greater coffee change in the past quarter century than France. It has gone topsy-turvy.

The national cup by **green coffee** contents is now 80 percent arabica. Coffee for home consumption has become a near monopoly of the super-hyper markets. This is roast and ground; whole beans have almost disappeared from these stores, although their sales by coffee boutiques and such are increasing. The brand array in big stores is now staggering; a "hyper" market in France may shelve more than sixty coffee references.

In the process of radical change in its coffee market, France lost control of its own once grand coffee industry. The great French green coffee trading houses are almost gone. The country's ports formerly bustling with colonial coffees have turned to other commodities. Antwerp and Hamburg handle most of the coffee that eventually reaches France.

The nation's coffee roasting has been subsumed as well by international interests. The bulk of the market is shared by **Kraft, Sara Lee,** and **Nestle,** with much of the rest taken by store-brands plus the Italian companies Lavazza, Segafredo, and Illy. Even Malongo, a vigorous roastery located in Nice and known for its staunch promotion of the finer origins and of so-called ethically traded coffees, is owned by the Belgium company Rombouts.

Horeca (hotel-restaurant-café) sectors continue to be the lifeblood of smaller local **roasters,** who provide most of the coffee going to cafés. Yet change is sweeping even this fabled French market segment. The number of cafés has declined by about 20 percent in past years. Some of the decline in regard to coffee is due to competition from new concepts in home consumption—the **pod** and **capsule.** Other competition arises from dedicated espresso bar and coffee shop chains. These include McCafé, Columbus, **Starbucks,** and other companies—all in expansion.

What coffee trends are in fashion and demand? Most certainly Italian-style **espresso.** Single-estate or single-**origin** coffee (as opposed to arabica blends). Bio and "ethical" coffees are also seeing rapid growth.

France is a wealthy nation, and its coffee market is worth billions of euros. The market also benefits from population growth, unlike most other European coffee-drinking nations. This growth partly explains the steady if modest expansion of consumption. The nation drinks beverages made from something more than 300,000 tons of coffee per annum.

Setting France aside as a mass coffee market is its zest for fashion, in good taste of course. Also setting it apart is the enduring passion for coffee among its elite and the intelligentsia. It is these classes that now profile the best French cup as a single-origin coffee of distinction, lightly roasted, served in porcelain. The famed French "nose" remains the ultimate arbiter. Even the **Specialty Coffee Association of America**'s aroma kit is called "Le Nez du Café."

Figure 33.1. Even in coffee-producing countries, instant coffee counts for a lot. This roadside ad is from rural Kenya, 2004. Photo by Robert Thurston.

The nation's cultural prowess in thought, art, and literature in combination with the French genius for nuances in taste and aroma are what make its coffee market unique to this day.

Any commentary on coffee in France should honor the work of Philippe Jobin. He represents the small class of French experts/enthusiasts for coffee study class at its most distinguished. His astonishing book *The Coffees Produced throughout the World* remains both classic and alive.

To summarize the current French market:

- France is the second largest coffee market in Europe.
- About 80 percent of consumption in roast and ground coffee is of arabica. The national cup is characterized by a large percentage of Brazilians, followed by Vietnamese, Colombians, and other milds.
- Ground/roasted coffee (R&G) dominates the store sector. The sector is controlled by labels belonging to KJS (Maison de Café), Sara Lee (Douwe Egberts), and Nestle. Almost 80 percent of sales are of 100 percent arabica blends.
- By format, store sales show a flattening of R&G coffees to about 70 percent. Single-portion sales have gained to nearly 30 percent of the sector and are the most dynamic. More than 10 percent of shelf sales are of single-origin coffees. Bio/ethical coffees have risen to 5 percent of sales.
- Something more than 20 percent of French consumption is in **soluble**. Another 5.5 percent is in decaffeinated coffee.
- Out-of-home coffee drinking comes to 25 percent of France's total consumption, of which 17 percent is through horeca.
- Of total coffee, 26 percent is now brewed from **pods**, **capsules**, or sachets. This makes the brewer accessory market of great and expanding added value importance.
- At-home drinking is a strong growth sector for espresso pods and capsules, where Nespresso leads, as well as coffee-in-bag formats such as Senseo.
- In all, 72 percent of the French people drink coffee every day, and more than 90 percent of French home kitchens have a coffee maker of some kind.

Generally, either at home—with traditional roast and ground, or now increasingly in single-service products—as well as in the out-of-home sector, the profile is clear: the French are electing to move upwards in coffee quality and are willing to spend money to enjoy a different, better kind of cup.

34

Italy

Vincenzo Sandalj

Italy, the fourth biggest coffee-importing country, is the birthplace of **espresso** and the cradle of one of the most popular coffee cultures in the world. The country boasts a lively coffee industry, which has become one of the biggest exporters of roasted coffee and its related equipment.

While coffee consumption developed relatively late compared to other more affluent Western countries, it took off strongly during the second half of the twentieth century. Per capita consumption grew from an average of 3.5 kilograms in the 1970s to 5.7 kilograms in the first decade of the new millennium. Recently, it appears to be leveling off at this high figure.

Home consumption accounts for about two-thirds of the total quantity and about half of the value of coffee consumed, while the remainder is out-of-home consumption (hotel-restaurant-café, or **horeca** market), supported by a noteworthy 150,000 coffee bars. If we also add the restaurants that serve espresso, the total number is well in excess of 200,000 units. Decaffeinated coffee accounts for 7 percent of the market, while **soluble** coffee hovers just above 1 percent. Certified, organic, and ethical coffees are slowly becoming more popular but consumption is still far below the levels reached in the northern European countries.

Until the 1950s, Italians used to prepare coffee at home with the *napoletana*, a **"flip over" drip brewing system**. This device was later widely replaced with the *moka*—a stovetop brewer utilizing steam pressure—which remains the most popular coffeemaker in Italian households. A much bigger revolution occurred in the out-of-home market. During the first half of the twentieth century, **espresso machines** were first patented and then produced commercially, while mass consumption of espresso and **cappuccino** developed in the 1950s and 1960s.

The proportion of domestic consumption among all coffee drunk has remained relatively stable in recent years. Bigger changes can be observed in the horeca market, where a steady decline in bar consumption has been counterbalanced by an increase in vending and in **single-serving** coffee machines; these already account for 10 percent of total coffee imports and a much higher proportion of the value. This segment features a very high growth rate, close to 20 percent per year. In the single-portion market, paper **pods** account for 25 percent of the value, while plastic **capsules** account for about 50 percent. Aluminum capsules, the remaining 25 percent of the market, show the highest rate of growth. These capsules are mainly closed systems that can be used only with dedicated machines.

Figure 34.1. Italy's cities and towns are still graced by gorgeous settings in which to have coffee, read a newspaper (but not to web surf), or listen to music. Caffè Pedrocchi, Padua, is a center for art and especially classical music in the city. Photo by Robert Thurston.

Italy imported 7,684,913 60-kilogram green coffee **bags** in 2010 and re-exported the equivalent of 2,460,015 bags, almost exclusively roasted coffee. The continuous rise in total imports is supported by a steady increase in roasted coffee exports, which grew 9.6 percent in 2010. The main suppliers of green coffee are Brazil, Vietnam, India, Indonesia, and Uganda, while the market share of the different groups is the following: Colombian milds 4.59 percent, other milds 19.25 percent, Brazilian naturals 37.33 percent, and robustas 37.76 percent.

Italy had no coffee-producing colonies, except Ethiopia for a very few years, so importing patterns do not reflect any particular historical tie. The development of taste preferences was mainly due to economic reasons, but the strong Italian emigrant community in Brazil may have played a role in promoting commercial cooperation. In 1959, an important warehouse was established by the Instituto Brasileiro do Café in Trieste, in order to sell its stocks of old coffees at discounted prices, and remained active for more than a decade. In those years, the percentage of Brazilian coffee in Italian blends rose significantly.

The main ports of importation are Trieste, Savona, and Genoa. There are over 900 **roasters** catering for a widely differentiated market. Italians have very strong and historically rooted regional culinary traditions, and coffee is no exception. Since in Italy a coffee blend is the starting point of a true espresso cup, there is a very specific Italian approach both in choosing the appropriate components and in blending them into the right product. There are several thousand blends available to the final customer, but most of them conform to the regional preferences in the various market areas.

In northern Italy there is a preference for arabica-based blends, with variable or no robusta component, while in southern Italy robusta coffees are the main or sole ingredient of the mix chosen by the roasters. In central Italy, a golden 50/50 rule is customary. The roast degree also changes accordingly, with northerners preferring a lighter one and the southerners a darker one. Furthermore, the **extraction** in the cup will be longer in the north, while in the south only a true *ristretto* will be accepted, with sugar floating on the thick *crema*. Even *cappuccinos* are a northerly preference and nearly absent from Rome downwards. This substantial variety often puzzles foreigners, who tend to wonder what the "real" Italian espresso is. The answer is, there are many.

Among the key players, Lavazza is by far the biggest roaster and accounts for nearly half of the domestic consumption. Segafredo Zanetti, the leader in out of home consumption, has a smaller overall market share but, if the international operations of the group are taken into consideration, it is notably bigger than Lavazza. Kraft Foods owns the brand Caffè Splendid, which is second in home market share. Nestlé, including its soluble coffee, is very active in vending and especially in the single-serve capsules market with the worldwide brand Nespresso. Illycaffè is the leader in the out-of-home, high-quality market segment, with a growing single-serve market share and other important ventures. Café do Brasil, with the brand Kimbo, is the market leader in southern Italy. There are another twenty medium-sized to large regional companies and a galaxy of small to medium roasters scattered all over the country. Altogether they have sales of nearly 3 billion euros (about $3.95 billion at the exchange rate of mid-April 2012), of which 1 billion are outside Italy.

In spite of the large number of bars, which are mostly individual- and family-managed operations, Italy has not developed significant coffee bar chains. The only notable exception is Autogrill with its brand Acafé, located on highways, stations, and airports, and the newborn Enicafé, found in gas stations. The remaining coffee bar chains are relatively small, and there is no indication that they might change the established market patterns because of the extreme fragmentation and low profitability of the sector. The price of an espresso cup, at around 1 euro, is one of the lowest in Europe. The retailer can survive only by selling other beverages, spirits, and food and by exploiting the elasticity of family labor. These low margins, combined with the culture of quickly consuming coffee while standing at the bar (that is, without table service) would make it very difficult for a chain such as Starbucks to function in Italy, as consumers would be unlikely to accept the high prices it charges to cover its costs.

The biggest Italian roasters purchase their green coffee directly from international traders, usually through brokers and agents, while the smaller companies buy predominantly from local importers, based in the main ports and cities. The world leader in coffee logistics is the Trieste-based Pacorini group, with operations in many countries around the world. Another important part of the Italian coffee sector is the mechanical industry, which includes producers of espresso machines, roasting and packaging equipment, vending machines, and related services. Among the most well-known brands are Faema-Cimbali, Astoria-CMA, Brasilia, and Rancilio. Italy is the world leader in some of these sectors, which rely heavily on foreign markets for their double digit growth of recent decades.

The big number of coffee players in the Italian market has given rise to several trade associations. Assocaf Genova and Associazione Caffè Trieste, established in 1891, are the historical trade associations that pay special attention to their respective ports and related trade. The most important roasters' associations are AIIPA and Associazione Italiana Torrefattori, while the Federazione Caffè Verde groups green coffee importers. The main coffee associations are represented in the national Comitato Italiano Caffè, but there are several other regional trade associations, like Altoga and Gruppo Triveneto Torrefattori. The Trieste Coffee Cluster is the only officially recognized industrial coffee cluster in the world.

There are two main coffee events in Italy, which alternate each year. The biggest is the HOST/SIC which takes place at the Milan fair, probably the single biggest coffee show in the world, while TRIESTESPRESSO EXPO is held in the Adriatic city. Among the numerous **trade magazines** that are focused on the world of coffee, we can mention *Bargiornale*, *Coffeecolours*, *Coffee Trend Magazine*, *L'Assaggio*, *Mixer*, and *Notiziario Torrefattori* among many others. The Milan based e-journal *Comunicaffè* is dispatched daily to 25,000 subscribers.

The dissemination of Italian coffee culture is the main task of several schools, training centers, and institutes, such as Università del Caffè, Istituto Nazionale Espresso Italiano, and Accademia del Caffè, to mention just a few. Many roasters and individuals have small collections of historical machines and coffee makers, but the most complete private collection of espresso machines is the one owned by Enrico Maltoni and featured regularly in exhibitions around the world.

Italy can pride itself on an extremely vigorous coffee culture and industry that has spawned offspring on all continents. In spite of stagnating domestic consumption due to the aging population, the local market is a lively laboratory of new coffee styles and products. Italian coffee and equipment manufacturers export an ever growing proportion of their output. This development is likely to continue in the foreseeable future, supported by the unstoppable craze for espresso and cappuccino in emerging markets.[1]

NOTE

1. For more on the Italian coffee market, see *Coffitalia, 2011–12 Directory* (Milan: Beverfood, 2012); *Caffè* (Rome: Comitato Italiano Caffè); *Coffee Market Reports*, International Coffee Organization, London; and Jonathan Morris, "Making Italian espresso, making espresso Italian," *Food and History* 8, no. 2 (2010): 155–84.

35

United Kingdom

Clare Benfield

The British are traditionally a nation of tea and instant coffee drinkers at home, but out of home it's a different story. The UK (population 62.4 million) is becoming a nation of **specialty coffee** drinkers, most of whom, unlike their continental counterparts, favor longer, milky drinks rather than straight **espresso.**

So widespread has the uptake of café culture been in the UK since its initial growth spurt in the 1990s—in cafés, restaurants, motorway service stations, offices, leisure centers, and so on—that it is now a successful sector indeed. The UK currently leads in Europe in the growth of consumption and number of outlets, defying a recession that for many around the world is the toughest since the 1930s.

The branded coffee shop market in the UK totaled 4,871 outlets in 2011, marked by more than 8 percent growth from the previous year. Turnover in 2011 was some £2.1 billion, more than twice the 2005 figure. When independents and nonspecialist coffee-serving operators are added, this total rises to over 15,000. Allegra Strategies, which has compiled these numbers, predicts a grand total of 18,000 coffee retailing outlets here and a £7 billion turnover by 2015.[1]

Among the branded, coffee-focused chains are 1,342 Costa outlets in the UK, almost twice the number of Starbucks and well ahead of Caffè Nero, AMT Coffee, Caffè Ritazza, Café Thorntons, and Esquires. Other major, coffee-serving brands in the out-of-home (hotel-restaurant-café, or **horeca**) sector with a national UK presence, but who are food-focused, include Prêt à Manger and EAT. Smaller, regional, coffee-dedicated mini-chains such as SOHO Coffee Company and Coffee #1 in the South West are on the rise. Independents, too, who have tremendous scope to create a strong consumer draw by specializing in premium, artisanal coffees, are making their presence felt, providing leading-edge inspiration for the bigger players.

The UK's more traditional venue for drinking, eating, and socializing, the local pub, has faded away in many places or undergone a more female-friendly makeover in order to survive. Until quite recently, many local authorities actively encouraged the arrival of café culture in their areas to counteract fears of a binge-drinking culture after the UK relaxed licensing laws in 2003. Lately, as residents and consumers see high streets that all look the same, the artisan retailer is increasingly courted, but then challenged by high rents.

In both rural regions and the cosmopolitan cities (not least London, where the City in particular provides an affluent, high-foot-traffic testing ground for new foods and beverages), UK consumers have embraced **espresso-based drinks** and allied products, for example healthy smoothies and indulgent cakes.

Overseas travel has led to greater product knowledge and, coupled with education—encouraged by many of the sector's main players, the majority of whom are responsive to the public's concerns about sustainability and ethical sourcing—means that more and more UK consumers recognize, if not expect, high-quality **specialty coffee** beverages wherever they are. Brands such as Whitbread-owned Coffee Nation, which became Costa Express, have also brought premium coffee to the nation's vending machines.

Thus, despite economic uncertainty, UK consumers are refusing to give up what, for many, has become part of their lifestyle. One in ten UK adults now visits a coffee shop daily, according to Allegra, even though in 2011 consumers spent slightly less per visit than before.

Frequently taken away, coffee is also savored in relaxed, lounge-type venues that can be anything from a trendy extension of home to a hotel, pub, community hub, bistro-style farm shop or garden center, or a Wi Fi-enabled meeting place that's a comfortable alternative to the office.

IN AND OUT OF FAVOR

Coffee drinking in the UK began, most writers maintain, in the 1650s. For more on the drink's history in Britain, see "Coffee: A Condensed History." In the eighteenth century, assisted by the rise of the British empire and its many tea-producing lands, cheaper tea took over and coffee took a back seat. The ceremony of afternoon tea at home gravitated from the aristocracy to all classes. This trend has experienced a certain a resurgence today as hotels look to optimize their sumptuous backdrops, and tea shop entrepreneurs attempt to take on the perceived might of the coffee shops by reminding us of our traditional national drink. For the moment, though, it seems that when it comes to coffee's main UK beverage rival, we are only truly happy with our tea if we can make it in our own way, at home. Conversely, with coffee, we have increasingly come to appreciate and value the art, skill, and convivial input of **baristas** and their **espresso machines**.

The close of the nineteenth century saw the start of the iconic Lyons Corner Houses. In effect, these were cafés selling tea and coffee, as well as food such as cakes and sandwiches. They served all classes and became places where women could meet and socialize on a "respectable," unaccompanied basis. However, rationing during and after World War II curtailed their success, as ingredients became scarce or too expensive.

The availability of vacuum-packed, freeze-dried instant coffee during the war meant that consumers no longer needed to visit cafés to have a coffee. But what did begin to change after the end of rationing in the 1950s was the gradual rise in quality, even if the coffee-serving outlets themselves alternated between becoming places for the young, then the not-so-young.

Less than efficient coffee-making machines which, in many cases, only succeeded in producing boiled and frothy, coffee-flavored water were replaced by espresso machines that formed the heart of many a coffee bar in cities across the land (such as Bar Italia's iconic Gaggia machine in London's Frith Street). These enterprises became places for the young to socialize, leaving the pubs to the older generation until the late 1960s, when coffee venues started to decline in popularity, while the alcohol-serving public houses lured the nation's youth to an edgier venue.

It wasn't until the 1980s, after the launch of Costa's first railway-focused coffee retailing kiosks, that trends really started to favor coffee again. With a range of issues at play from a greater demand for more portable food items "to go" for an increasingly time-poor consumer, as well as an interest in all things European—not least the fashion and style of Italy, and its espresso tradition—the stage was set for a revolution, still under way today.

THE MARKET

For 2009, the **International Coffee Organization** (ICO), by combining its own consumption statistics with Euromonitor market research data, calculated the UK's breakdown of coffee imports at over 2.1 million 60-kilogram **bags of green coffee** (of which 57,420 were re-exported), 861,628 60-kilogram bags GBE (green bean equivalent) of roasted coffee (184,851 were re-exported), and over 1.1 million 60-kilogram bags GBE of **soluble** coffee (649,991 were re-exported), totaling 4,131 million 60-kilogram bags. This equated to a total consumption of over 3.2 million 60-kilogram bags, a per capita consumption of 3.14 kilograms per year in 2009 (the ICO reported a figure of 2.6 kilogram GBE at its 107th session in 2011).

In 2010, the total UK consumption figure reportedly fell slightly to just over 3.1 million 60-kilogram bags (the 2010 breakdown of green, roasted, and soluble imports had not been published at the time of writing), while the total import figure rose to 4.292 million bags.[2] Of particular note, the ICO believed, was the share of fresh versus soluble consumption, with fresh outperforming soluble in the U.S., Germany, France, Japan, Italy, and Spain but not in the UK or the Russian Federation, although in all of these countries more coffee was consumed at home than away.

Between 1997 and 2010, the majority of the UK's imported coffee came from Vietnam (14 percent), Brazil (11.7 percent), Colombia (9.4 percent), and Indonesia (6.1 percent), totaling 41.2 percent, and 32.1 percent was composed of re-exports from Germany (13.6 percent), Netherlands (7.6 percent), Spain (4.1 percent), Ireland (2.4 percent), France (2.3 percent), and Italy (2.1 percent), according to ICO figures. Thus re-exports accounted for nearly a third of the UK's coffee.

Soluble coffee still predominates in the UK, accounting for 79.8 percent of the UK's national coffee consumption (most of which is at home), but the consumption of roasted coffee has grown from 15.8 percent in 1997 to 24.9 percent in 2010. According to the market analysts Mintel, the in-home UK coffee market is worth £55.3 million in volume sales and £831 million in value sales.[3] Currently, when adults reach the 65-plus age bracket, their instant coffee consumption falls from an average of 13.4 cups a week to 11.9, leading industry analysts to suggest that more could be done to promote the energy and health-enhancing properties of the beverage.

Influenced by the rise of the coffee shop and specialty coffees, consumers are increasingly buying more premium roast and ground coffees, and indeed coffee beans, together with investing in the associated brewing techniques. Most homes at least have a **French press**, if not some form of **filter**, stove top, or **pod** machine. However, some of the latest pod devices are far more premium than others, so some consumers view them as too expensive. Espresso machines of both modern and bygone eras are popular, as fashionable kitchen accessories for some—not least the rising number of "coffee geeks," even if they lack the necessary skill to use them!

INDUSTRY PLAYERS

The UK coffee sector can be divided into two halves: one comprises the big, consumer retail brands (Nescafé, Kenco, Douwe Egberts, etc.) drunk at home and outside of it too, as many of these companies also serve caterers—Nestlé's Milano, for example. The second sector consists of the out-of-home café and coffee shop brands and supplier network.

Company-owned and franchised, or licensed, outlets (often within other retail concepts, such as department stores or service stations, for example)—namely Costa, Starbucks, Caffè Nero, Café Thorntons, AMT Coffee Ltd, BB's Coffee & Muffins, Coffee Republic, Puccino's, and Krispy Kreme—typify the way the branded coffee shop chains operate in the UK, resulting in a uniform product offering, style of outlet, and use of suppliers. For independents, there is greater freedom to source rarer coffees and use bespoke machines and coffee-making processes. As is often the case on the Continent and elsewhere, it is not always usual in the UK for a business's equipment to be supplied free on loan. This may be because coffee is not drunk in as high, regular volumes as it is in other countries.

Coffee is bought and sold by roasters, investors, and price speculators as a commodity, and the number of coffee roasters is on the rise. Many small, up-and-coming roasters are on the scene, together with long-established and highly respected names like Matthew Algie. On-site roasting by small outlets remains rare but is likely to take off.

Most of the coffee-making equipment and associated technology used in the UK comes from mainland Europe, with the majority of coffee machine companies having an agent or their own UK presence (Cimbali UK, for example). The UK has one homegrown espresso machine maker—Birmingham-based Fracino, which is a successful exporter, too. As barista skills are still lacking, bean-to-cup machines are popular, although most of the big-name chains operate semi-automatic espresso machines.

TRADE ORGANIZATIONS, MEDIA, AND EVENTS

Trade associations include the **Speciality Coffee Association of Europe (SCAE)**, which has a UK chapter dedicated to promoting high standards in coffee making and to helping adjudicate and organize the yearly Barista Championships.

Other groups active in promoting high-quality beverage-making include the Beverage Standards Association and the Café Society. The Coffee Trade Federation is an amalgamation of other organizations that represented roasters, merchants, and brokers, having joined forces with the British Coffee Association in 2008. The London-based ICO promotes coffee consumption via programs designed to increase consumption as well as aid the coffee producer, and the London-based Fairtrade Foundation is heavily involved in coffee.

UK **trade magazines** with a specific coffee focus include *Café Culture, Fresh Cup, Coffee Trend, Food and Drink Network UK, Café Business*, and *Vending International*.

The Caffè Culture exhibition is a yearly coffee trade show. The "lunch!" show also has strong coffee sector appeal. Increasingly, the big, alternating Hotelympia and IFE hospitality shows feature a coffee emphasis. Other events of note include UK Coffee Week, the London Coffee Festival, and the Bath Coffee Festival.

London was also home to the world's first dedicated tea and coffee museum, the Bramah Tea and Coffee Museum (founded by Edward Bramah, who died in 2008). The museum has closed, aiming to re-open after refurbishment, but no definite plans or location has been announced to date.

HERE TO STAY

Many people in the UK food business, and for that matter unrelated business sectors, look at the recession-defying coffee sector with envy in these challenging economic times.

UK chain and independent restaurants, as well as quick service restaurants like McDonald's, look set to continue upping the quality of their coffee offering as they seek a "me, too" stake in what's proving to be a highly profitable and persistent coffee shop phenomenon. No ambitious UK food business can afford to ignore this area in times of so-called austerity.

Allegra predicts that the UK's branded coffee chain market will drive the overall market. They expect it to grow at 6 percent compound annual growth and exceed 6,000 outlets by 2015, with sales to grow by 10.7 percent annually, to £3.2 billion by 2015.

At the same time, the presence of UK brands abroad will likely increase. Costa may still be viewed by Britons as a UK-bound entity, but become an expanding global force, with more European outlets (1,444) than its U.S.-based rival, Starbucks (in third place with 1,253 after McCafe with 1,326).[4]

An increasingly older, but better-informed and more coffee-aware, connoisseur-level consumer seeking to balance quality with value for money, health, and sustainability considerations, is likely to characterize the future of the UK's coffee sector.

Barista training will be in greater demand. A more scientific approach, notably at independents, to preparing and serving, say, more **single-origin**, shop-roasted coffees will ensure that these artisans continue to engage customers. In turn, this will influence the nature and product quality in the chains. They will be increasingly debranded yet will attempt to further foster a local community feel by valuing their human resources and partnerships (business and charitable) as a critical component of success at home and worldwide.

NOTES

1. Allegra Strategies, *Project Café 11 Europe* (London: Allegra Strategies, 2011).
2. ICO, "Drinking Patterns in Selected Importing Countries," Report, 107th Session of the ICO, London, September 26–30, 2011.
3. Mintel, "Coffee—UK," Report, April 2011.
4. Allegra Strategies, *Project Café 11 Europe.*

36

Russia

Robert W. Thurston

From the late seventeenth century on, Russia became a tea-drinking country. Good coffee, by the standards of the day, became available in the largest cities of the Russian empire only toward the end of the nineteenth century. After the revolution of 1917, coffee became a rarity. When I first lived in the USSR in 1978–79, "coffee drink" (*kofeinyi napitok*, which could also be translated as caffeine drink) was the only product resembling coffee that was regularly available. It tasted harsh, thin, and burnt. Then, during the last decades of the Soviet period, some Cuban and then Vietnamese coffee, in cans, appeared in food stores. These products represented a big step up in quality, to something like American grocery store brands.

On more recent visits, I have tried coffee shops in the major cities of Russia and Ukraine. Quality varies immensely but can be quite good. A store in Khar'kov, a large city now in independent Ukraine, sold a nice array of home espresso machines as early as 2002. Latte appeared, too. With the rise of the "new Russians" (a misnomer, as people from various ethnicities are in the group) who have solid middle or upper class incomes, luxury items of all sorts have become widely available.

As Andrew Hetzel recently put it, "Russia is still a sort of Wild West capitalist gold rush, meaning that huge opportunities are everywhere—particularly in the segment of specialty goods and services that includes coffee." Hetzel reports that one Russian company with which he has worked, Soyuz Coffee Roasting, has developed "three brands of specialty with quality standards set on par with the better micro-roasters of North America, only at three to five times their size."[1] Sarah Allen of *Barista Magazine*, commenting on a military band/horse show now held each summer on Red Square, says "This is Moscow, Russia. It's not go big or go home, as much as go big, bigger, biggest, or you might as well leave the country." The show, called the Spasskaya Tower Military Music Festival, featured coffee booths for the first time last summer. Seven of the top baristas in the world, including several world champions, made coffee nonstop for five nights.[2] But I would add that the capital and St. Petersburg are far wealthier and up to date than the rest of the country.

Russians actually consume very little coffee in their "coffee" shops. These stores typically make less than 5 percent of their revenue from coffee sales. The rest comes from long food menus, alcohol, and cigarettes.[3] Yet coffee is a hip drink for young people.

The International Coffee Organization, which has kept data on Russia for only a few years, reports that in 2010 the country imported 1.445 million **bags** of **green coffee.** But this figure was far outstripped by imported **soluble** coffee, at 2.302 million bags. Consumption per capita was 1.57 kilos,[4] far below American figures, let alone Scandinavian thirst. But Soyuz Coffee, and undoubtedly a host of competitors that will soon follow, will work hard to wean Russians from instant to good, better, and finally as-good-as-it-gets coffee. While revenue from oil exports holds out, the country will surely continue to raise its coffee standards.

NOTES

1. Andrew Hetzel, "Russia," part of a longer essay entitled "The New Frontier: Specialty Coffee's Emergence in China, India, the Middle East and Russia," *Roast Magazine,* January–February 2012, 32.

2. Sarah Allen, "Field Report: Russia," *Barista Magazine,* October/November 2011, 24.

3. Hetzel, "Russia," 32–34.

4. International Coffee Organization Statistics, Country Data Sheets, 2010, Russian Federation, http://www.ico.org/countries/russia/pdf, accessed May 5, 2012.

37

Ukraine

Sergii Reminny with Jonathan Morris

Ukraine, with 49 million people, was once the second largest republic in the Soviet Union. But after gaining its independence in 1991, the country is now following its own path, in economics, politics, and coffee. Ukraine has recorded by far the most dynamic growth in coffee consumption within the emerging markets during the past decade, with an average annual increase of 23.6 percent between 2000 and 2010. By comparison, its nearest competitors—the Russian Federation, Turkey, and Israel—experienced annual growth rates of around 7 percent in the same period.[1]

Since the dawn of the new millennium, Ukrainian coffee consumption per capita has risen nearly tenfold, from 0.2 kilograms in 2000 to 1.96 kilograms in 2010. What explains this dramatic growth? The answer is simple: Ukraine's geographical position, and in particular its western extension into the heartlands of Central Europe. We can distinguish four main areas of the country, each with distinctive drinking patterns.

- **The West:** The western area includes the major cities of Lviv and Uzhgorod. The *vitiesi* ("westerners") are by far the biggest coffee consumers in the country, drinking three to four times the Ukrainian average. These so-called "pro-European regions," are still influenced by their historical connection to Austrian or Hungarian coffee culture.
- **The Center:** The central area's major city is Kiev. The Ukrainian capital has always accounted for 20–25 percent of the national turnover, and its central position and administrative importance explain why modern coffee development in the Ukraine began here, with the first private restaurants, fast-food chains, and supermarkets chains reaching into the provinces from the capital in the 1990s.
- **The East:** The major cities in the east are Donetsk and Kharkov. The east, where the Ukrainian language often yields to spoken Russian, has traditionally been influenced by that country's culture. The relatively affluent industrial cities in the east have experienced the highest rate of economic development over the last decade and have quickly begun to adopt the consumption of **specialty coffee,** starting with **espresso.**
- **The South:** The principal cities in the south are Odessa, Simferopol, and Yalta. Also predominately Russian-speaking, it includes subtropical Crimea and is an attractive tourist region. The atmosphere is more relaxed in the south, befitting the beauty and

climate of the region, and coffee has quickly become popular under the independent state. The season for tourism and coffee in the south is really summer; winters are quiet and uncrowded.

As Slavenka Drakulic, a Croatian writer, pointed out in her 1996 book *Café Europa*,[2] a Western-style café, often called "Europa," sprang up quickly in every major European city east of the Elbe River—a zone that includes Ukraine—following the collapse of the Soviet Union in 1991. These shops became a key symbol of a new life and of a longing to join "Europe." Ukraine, or major parts of it, has adopted this same object of desire.

After more than a century of alternating rapid industrial growth, war, and stagnation, Ukraine may be poised for significant economic improvement, although that also depends on the purchasing power of Western Europe and of Russia. Whether Ukraine can exploit these tentative opportunities to improve standards of living and to drink more coffee remains to be seen.

NOTES

1. Robério Oliveria Silva, ICO, "International Coffee Outlook," presentation to India International Coffee Festival, New Dehli, 2012. Annual growth rates over 2000–2010 in the Russian Federation were 7.0 percent, Turkey 7.7 percent, Israel 6.8 percent.

2. Slavenka Drakulic, *Café Europa: Life after Communism* (New York: Norton, 1997).

38

Japan

Tatsushi Ueshima

Coffee was introduced to Japan by Dutch merchants at the Dejima Trading Post in Nagasaki in the 1690s, during the Edo era, a period of national isolation. It was not until the Meiji era (1888) that the first coffee shops appeared in towns across Japan. Coffee in those days was still a luxury item imported from abroad, like wine, and it barely reached the general public. It was only when trade resumed after the Second World War that coffee began to spread in Japan.

In 1950, a mere forty tons of green coffee were brought into the country, but the amount rose after the complete liberalization of imports in April 1960 and again after Japan joined the **ICO** in 1964. Japan currently imports over 410,000 tons of coffee per year, a result of the postwar westernization of lifestyles and rapid economic growth. Japan ranks as the third largest coffee-importing country in the world.

Besides the increase in population and the improvement in living standards after about 1950, major factors in the growth of Japanese coffee consumption have been efforts by the industry to create a unique domestic coffee culture, to encourage competition based on a national understanding of fair rules, and to build consumer awareness.

A UNIQUE COFFEE CULTURE IN JAPAN

Coffee shops started to reappear across Japan in the mid-1960s. These shops, somewhat different than their U.S. counterparts, all had wait staff looking after their customers. The coffee shop business was seen as an appealing business. "I could run something like a teahouse" and "My only option is a coffee shop," were common attitudes. No experience was necessary, there was no limit on age or gender, and a relatively small amount of capital was required to be independent. The image of coffee shops was not bad compared with the bar business; it was neat and clean, enjoyed respectability, and provided a site where owners could exercise their creativity. Consequently, the number of shops increased by 3.2 times in twelve years, from 50,000 shops in 1970 to 160,000 shops in 1982. People with no experience whatsoever danced to their own business tune.

Shops made coffee in ways different than home users, using flannel cloth filters and coffee siphons. They also developed new-to-Japan menu items such as iced coffee, which helped create a uniquely Japanese coffee culture. In addition, ways to provide coffee outside coffee shops were explored and developed to satisfy the new Japanese drinker, who lacked the long history of café and in-home coffee-drinking culture that the Europeans and Americans enjoyed. Coffee specialist shops for over-the-counter coffee sales to customers began to sell **single-origin** coffees such as Mocha and Kilimanjaro by weight. Furthermore, a wide variety of coffee products was developed, such as **single-serving** options, to address the increasing number of single-person households and single-serving meals.

Coffee has become an essential beverage for various aspects of life in Japan, with a variety of ways available for buying and consuming coffee, such as regular coffee, instant coffee, ready-to-drink coffee beverages, and office coffee. Among the different options, the greatest impact came from the development of canned coffee. Canned coffee was developed for the first time anywhere in the world in 1969 by the founder of Ueshima Coffee Company, Tadao Ueshima. This pioneering invention, which provides hot or cold coffee in a can, transformed the nature of coffee into a readily available casual beverage, creating new coffee-drinking occasions and needs. Canned coffee quickly became widespread in Japan. This trend also paved the way for a new sales channel, vending machines, which could operate without particular problems in the relatively crime- and vandalism-free Japanese environment. The vending machines dramatically expanded sales opportunities.

As a result, the market for coffee for industrial use, defined as on-the-spot beverages such as canned coffee, grew to account for 40 percent of the overall non-instant coffee market in the four decades since canned coffee was invented. This growth shows the extent of the impact that canned coffee invention had on the development of the coffee industry in Japan.

COMPETITION BASED ON FAIR RULES

As the coffee market in Japan grew and developed, a spate of new companies entered the market and competition intensified. Fair competition, Japanese style, was seen as a prerequisite for the healthy growth of an industry. Therefore in 1977, the Fair Competition Code for Coffee Beverages was adopted, which required labeling detailing the amount of coffee contained in the ready-to-drink product. To regulate labeling for both regular and instant coffee, the All Japan Coffee Fair Trade Council was formed in 1991. The Council established a self-imposed code, regarded as the strictest in the global coffee industry, which stipulated that products had to display the name of the producing country of the main coffee beans contained (measured by percentage of weight) and to require a minimum content of 30 percent of those coffee beans when indicating the coffee-producing region and variety. These rules helped to boost consumer confidence in coffee and to raise the position of coffee in the Japanese culinary world. Here was a major turning point in the transition of Japan's coffee market from "expansion of volume" to "pursuit of quality."

CONSUMER AWARENESS CAMPAIGN

An industrywide awareness-building campaign was essential to the development of the coffee market in Japan. When the All Japan Coffee Association was launched in 1980, a comprehensive effort to raise awareness about coffee began across the industry, with the goal of advertising and promoting the taste, joy, and health benefits of the beverage.

The campaign evolved with the times, and new scientific information on the effects of coffee in the human body was published in Japan during the 1990s. This publicity was needed to dispel the deep-seated, negative image that coffee was bad for health. In 1995, the Association for Science and Information on Coffee (ASIC) held its biennial conference in Kyoto on the theme of "coffee and health" in an effort to improve the image of coffee.

As coffee drinking at home became more established, the Association of Regular Coffee Industry for Household Use was established in 1990 to promote the trend. After the specialty coffee boom arrived in Japan, the Specialty Coffee Association of Japan was formed in 2003. The Association sends Japan's top baristas to world competitions to showcase their high-level skills, and it promotes sustainable coffees, such as organic and certified coffees, in the pursuit of true specialy coffee from seed to cup.

Industry participants have exerted themselves to reach each aspect of everyday life and to raise the value of coffee for the Japanese people in each trend of the times, and this effort has contributed to the increase of coffee consumption and the growth of the coffee industry.

THE DECLINE OF THE COFFEE SHOP

As these trends continued, the coffee industry in Japan continued to explore ways to meet new demands while responding to shifting social structures and consumer tastes, with the goal of ensuring continued growth and development. The years since 1980 have been an exciting time for the coffee industry, which owes its success to the passionate industry players and the eagerness of consumers. Many long-time industry members are grateful to all those who have contributed to its success. However, the country's economic growth is slowing against the backdrop of an aging society and a low birthrate, which together result in population decrease. The coffee market has entered a period of stability or little growth; the number of coffee shops has declined by almost 50 percent since its peak in 1982.

Another cause of this decrease has been the overlapping governmental structures that regulate the coffee industry. The Ministry of Agriculture supervises green coffee trading; the Ministry of Economy, Trade, and Industry monitors retail businesses; and the Ministry of Health, Labor, and Welfare watches over retail food services. At times the policies followed by these agencies contradict each other, and it can be very difficult to get the ministries to cooperate in approving a change that affects all of the coffee industry. As a result, cross-sectional efforts for the overall market became sluggish and development across sections was insufficient.

Yet another factor contributing to the decrease in the number of Japanese coffee shops was the introduction of fashionable self-service cafés, where, like cafés or fast-food service establishments in the U.S., customers ordered and received their coffee across a counter. Some of these self-service cafés sold a cup of coffee for a mere 150 yen, half the average price charged by coffee shops at the time. The main target market of the self-service cafés was the baby-boom generation. Following the end of the war in 1945, a total of 8.06 million people were born between 1947 and 1949. According to some estimates, the self-service café's ability to pull in customers was three to four times higher (or 400 to 500 people per day) than coffee shops could attract. Self-service cafés won overwhelming support from the baby-boom generation of salaried workers, whose wallets were under pressure from mortgages and the costs of educating their children.

COFFEE SHOP REVIVAL

The number of coffee shops perhaps declined too far for the current, quickly changing demographic structure. The baby-boomers have retired, have disposable income, and have time on their hands, but relaxing places are scarce. These people find the tall stools in self-service cafés uncomfortable and the menus complicated and difficult. Efficient management, not comfort, is the current business model for self-service cafés, which mainly follow the culture of the West. For these reasons, coffee shops with tables and wait staff have been undergoing a revival of late. Lifestyles change in a thirty-year cycle, as do generations. The ability to respond swiftly to new lifestyles determines the growth or decline of an industry.

The coffee industry in Japan has absorbed Western business models while responding to domestic taste and demands for high quality and has managed to develop and expand the market, overcoming numerous challenges. The twenty-first century is said to belong to Asia, and the Japanese coffee industry will focus its efforts on increasing the number of consumers by renewing its ability to address, improve, and revolutionize any issue important in a market of three billion people.

39

Germany

Britta Zietemann

Germany is the second most important coffee-importing country in the world, following the United States. Only the U.S. and Brazil consume more coffee than the Germans. Moreover, Germany is an important manufacturer of decaffeinated and **soluble** coffee, and the harbor cities Hamburg and Bremen are major hubs for the import and re-export of green and processed coffee.

HISTORY

Coffee was a luxury product when it was first introduced to Germany. In 1673, the first German **coffeehouse**, "Schütting," opened in Bremen; it is still there. Coffeehouses opened in other German cities in the seventeenth century, for example Hamburg, Leipzig, and Munich. With this development, the coffee market began to flourish, although at this point only the wealthy could afford coffee. As Germany (or rather Prussia at that time) had no colonies where coffee grew, the country had to buy **green coffee** from neighboring nations. To prevent the public from buying green coffee and hence sending German money abroad, Frederick the Great implemented a roasting duty that in effect prohibited private roasting. The coffee market remained in royal hands until Frederick died in 1786.

After the abolition of the state monopoly, and with the beginnings of industrialization, coffee increasingly became a beverage for all citizens. Poorer people used coffee to stay awake when working long hours in the factories and as a substitute for beer or food. The phenomenon of the *Kaffeeklatsch*, groups of women who met for afternoon coffee, cake, and chat, spread throughout the classes as coffee became democratized. At the same time, important inventions for the coffee industry were made in Germany. A German chemist, Friedlieb Ferdinand Runge, isolated the caffeine molecule in 1819, having been encouraged to study coffee by the poet Johann Wolfgang von Goethe. In 1905, the German Ludwig Roselius succeeded in decaffeinating coffee, and Melitta Bentz, a German housewife from Dresden, invented the paper coffee filter system that bears her name.

By the start of the twentieth century, coffee was an internationally traded good with Hamburg supplanting Le Havre as the principal European trading port. Then two world wars led to phases of overproduction, declines in consumption, and the implementation of international trade agreements.

After World War II, Germany was split into two states that formed the frontline of the Cold War: the Federal Republic of Germany (FRG), a member of NATO usually known as West Germany, and the socialist German Democratic Republic (GDR or East Germany), part of the Soviet bloc. In the 1950s coffee was seen as a symbol of economic success and reconstruction, as well as of social status. During that decade, almost all West Germans could afford to drink coffee, whereas in the GDR, coffee was out of ordinary people's reach. In East Germany coffee was also mostly mixed with cheaper surrogates such as peas, **chicory**, or roasted cereals, leading to consumer protests in the 1970s. In order to improve the quality of coffee, the GDR sought an ideologically friendly country to supply it with reasonably priced coffee and signed a contract with Vietnam to promote coffee plantations there. This arrangement helped spark the expansion of production in Vietnam, which accelerated after the fall of the Berlin Wall, resulting in the country becoming the second biggest supplier of green coffee, largely robusta, in the world (see "Vietnam" in this volume).

In the 1970s, many small and medium **roasters**, as well as hundreds of importers and agents, were based in Hamburg. During the last decades of the twentieth century, the number declined, and coffee was seen as a bit old-fashioned. Recently, however, these sectors have begun to grow again. Currently, around 300 roasters and about 10 importers and agents serve the German market.

Over the last decade, the image of coffee has changed. Coffee is now seen as a modern beverage that symbolizes the dynamic, mostly urban, society. It fits well into the healthy and modern lifestyle of the twenty-first century and is the most consumed beverage in Germany.

MARKET PROFILE

Imports and Exports

Germany is an important trading and manufacturing hub for coffee. In 2010, imports of green coffee into Germany reached a volume of 18.2 million 60-kilogram **bags** (1.1 million tons), an increase of 3.7 percent compared with the figures from 2010. Some 580,092 tons were re-exported in 2010, either processed or unprocessed.

In 2010, Brazil remained Germany's largest supplier (more than 6.2 million bags) and Vietnam the second biggest (3.3 million bags). Colombia, the third most important supplier until 2008, has dropped significantly, to eleventh place in 2010, due to lower production. In 2011, Peru (1.4 million bags) and Honduras (1.2 million bags) were the third and fourth largest sources of imports into Germany. In fifth place was Ethiopia with 909,503 bags.

Most of the re-exported nonprocessed green coffee goes to Poland, followed by Austria, Denmark, Hungary, and the UK. Decaffeinated coffee is primarily exported to the U.S., then Spain, Italy, the Netherlands, and Belgium. Coffee extracts, soluble or liquid, are exported to the UK, France, Ukraine, Poland, and the Netherlands.

Domestic Consumption

Coffee is the most consumed beverage in Germany with an average of 149 liters per capita, equivalent to 6.4 kilos of green coffee per person. In comparison, Germans drink 135 liters of water and 107 liters of beer each year.

Altogether, the country's consumption in 2010 amounted to 406,500 tons of roasted coffee (377,500 nondecaffeinated roasted coffee and 29,000 decaffeinated coffee) and 16,600 tons of soluble coffee. Included in the total of roasted coffee are 59,000 tons of coffee for use as **espresso** and 37,650 tons of **single-portion pods** and **capsules.** Around 76 percent of the market for roasted coffee is dominated by roasted and ground (filter) coffee. Nevertheless, the consumption of **espresso** and *caffè crema* increased by 10 percent in 2010 compared with the year before. German use of espresso has increased especially rapidly within the last few years. Single-portions (pods and capsules) are on the rise in Germany. Compared with the year before, the capsule segment grew by 30.4 percent in 2011. The consumption of pods increased by 1,000 tons and amounted to 31,000 tons in 2011. Use of single portions has increased by five times since 2005. The consumption of soluble coffee has remained steady for many years, with a slight increase of 1.2 percent in 2011 compared with 2010.

The demand for certified coffee is growing. In 2011, the market share of certified coffee was 3 percent. A rise is expected from this point forward, as many industrial roasters and manufacturers of soluble coffee have signed agreements to shift the entire or a high percentage of their coffee to sustainably produced products within a few years.

Out-of-Home Consumption

The out-of-home market amounts to 25 percent of the total coffee market and includes consumption at gastronomic venues such as cafés, coffee shops, coffee bars, hotels and restaurants (hotel-restaurant-cafés, or **horeca**) as well as in offices and other workplaces. Most of the coffee consumed out of home is drunk in bakeries (31.5 percent) and cafés (13.5 percent).

Figure 39.1.   Caffe Moro, Heidelberg, Germany. This shop, which sells a great deal of coffee and has a loyal clientele, benefits from its location on the longest pedestrian-only street in Europe. It is indeed a kind of "third place." Photo by Robert Thurston.

Some 9.9 percent is bought at vending machines, 10.2 percent when travelling and at petrol stations, and 7.9 percent in coffee shops or coffee bars. Other venues where coffee is consumed out of home are bars or pubs (4.8 percent), fast food restaurants (5.3 percent), and restaurants (5.5 percent).

A total of 2,147 coffee shops existed in Germany in 2011. They have contributed to the growing popularity of **espresso-based drinks**. About 47.2 percent of the beverages consumed out of home are coffee specialties, with **cappuccino** being the most popular (16.6 percent) followed by **latte/macchiato** (16.3 percent) and **caffè latte** (13.9 percent). The largest percentage (52.8 percent) is still traditional coffee, while 0.4 percent is pure espresso.

STRUCTURE OF THE INDUSTRY
AND THE GERMAN COFFEE ASSOCIATION

The coffee industry in Germany is divided into coffee importers, agents, warehouse keepers, roasters, decaffeinators, manufacturers of soluble coffee, manufacturers of roasting equipment, gastronomical venues, and **sustainability** organizations. The German Coffee Association, based in Hamburg, represents the entire industry throughout the **value chain**, as many market players in all segments are members. The Association's duties are principally active lobbying, maintaining positive legal and political conditions, providing an expert information service for members, and promotion of a positive image of coffee in Germany.

The German Coffee Association is the most important group for the country's coffee industry. Among the 130 members are almost all the big market players and many smaller industry members. The Association has an extensive network of contacts with other institutions and organizations. Nationally, the German Coffee Association has close partnerships with the Federation of German Wholesale, Foreign Trade and Services (BGA) and the German Federation for Food Law and Food Science—Food Matters (BLL). Moreover, the German Coffee Association is a member of the German Institute for Standardization (DIN) and the Research Association of the German Food Industry (FEI). On an international level, the German Coffee Association is an active member in the European Coffee Federation (ECF), the Association for Science and Information about Coffee (ASIC), and the **Speciality Coffee Association of Europe (SCAE)**. The Federal Republic of Germany is a member of the **International Coffee Organization (ICO)**. All memberships and cooperating partnerships ensure close collaboration on national and international issues. The network also enables the German industry to gather and spread information and create positive conditions for the coffee industry.

Most of the importers, agents, warehouses, decaffeinators, and bigger roasters are based in or around Hamburg and Bremen. Some other major roasters and manufacturers of soluble coffee process their coffee in Munich, Frankfurt, and Berlin; smaller roasters are spread nationwide.

In Germany, there are several trade fairs that include coffee, but they mainly deal with hotel and catering services (Internorga) or vending machines (EUvend). There is one distinctive trade fair that focuses on coffee, COTECA (trade show for coffee, tea, and cacao), held in Hamburg every two years. It is concerned with the coffee industry from bean to cup.

CURRENT TRENDS AND FUTURE PROSPECTS

The German coffee market has changed significantly during the last few years. Consumer habits have shifted toward a greater focus on quality, convenience, and lifestyle but also on the fresh preparation and instant consumption of the product. The growth of espresso and espresso-based beverages, as well as the increased use of single portions, underline this development. Nevertheless, a majority of German coffee drinkers still consume roasted, ground coffee.

Projections are that total consumption will remain around the level of 149 liters per capita but that the proportions of beverage types used within the coffee market will fluctuate and may change profoundly. Conveniently brewed and consumed coffee as well as quality and sustainable production and preparation are the big issues for the future.

40

United States

Robert W. Thurston

Steven Topik and Michelle McDonald in "Why Americans Drink Coffee" discuss the growth of demand here in the nineteenth and early twentieth centuries. This article's goal is to describe trends in consumption over the past several decades and to suggest some directions that American coffee drinkers will take in the future.

USDA figures show that Americans' highest per capita consumption of coffee occurred in 1946, at 16.5 pounds, and 1949, at 19.1 pounds. The figure has varied since, but moved more or less steadily downward after the late 1940s, so that in 1960 the rate was 15.9 pounds per person and by 1970 only 13.6. The nation reached the nadir of consumption to date at an even 6 pounds in 1995. From there a modest rise began, so that Americans drank 7 pounds in 2009, the last year for which data are available. That level meant we drank less per person than in 1910 (the first year USDA kept track), when the nation consumed 7.7 pounds per man, woman, and child.[1]

The numbers from 1946 to 1960 or so raise questions about the usual arguments on the undoubted decline of coffee drinking in the U.S.: that soft drinks began to eclipse coffee, that heavy admixtures of robusta beans in blends made the brew taste so bad that consumers forsook coffee, or that a collapse in sociability caused people not to gather around the coffee pot. While those factors surely contributed to coffee's declining popularity, they did not figure on a large scale until consumption of the dark brew had already begun to fall. Maybe soft drinks were a greater villain in coffee's story than our figures indicate—the USDA started to keep statistics on soft drinks only in 1947—since Coca-Cola in particular became ever more popular after the turn of the twentieth century.[2] But as that happened, intake of coffee also rose, from the 1910 figure to almost double that in 1940, at 13 pounds, and still upward until the late 1940s.

The curve of milk consumption per capita in America closely parallels the movement of coffee intake in the twentieth century and to the present:

- 1909: 294.1 pounds
- 1945: 384.2 pounds
- 1960: 291.6 pounds
- 2009: 177.6 pounds[3]

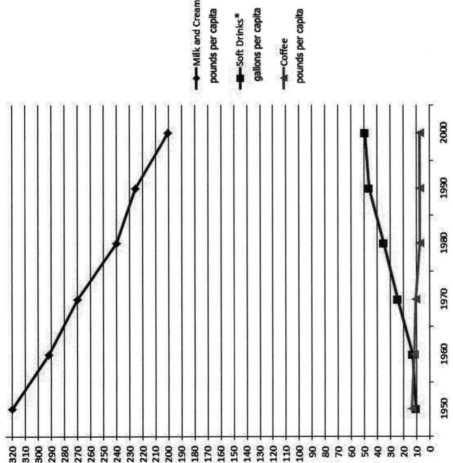

Figure 40.1. Consumption of beverages in the United States, 1950–2000. Source: United States Department of Agriculture. Economic Research Service. Food Availability: Spreadsheets. Updated July 13, 2011. http://www.ers.usda.gov/data/foodconsumption/FoodAvailSpreadsheets .htm#dyfluid. Chart by Lara Thurston. *Note that data on soft drinks have been kept only since 1947.

Today Americans drink only 60 percent as much milk as we consumed in 1909 and 46 percent as much as in 1946.

A big part of the wartime high for coffee and milk can be explained by the great numbers of men and women in uniform; many were eating and drinking better than they had for a long time, as the U.S. did not fully recover from the Depression until we joined the war in earnest in 1942. People at home had more money in their pockets, while those in the armed forces received a fairly decent flow of comestibles every day.

But after the war, even in the boom years of the 1950s and 1960s, consumption of coffee and milk both declined more or less steadily. Was booze to blame? Probably not: American guzzling per person, according to the National Institutes of Health, was slightly higher in 1860 than in 1970, 2.53 gallons to 2.52 gallons, but there was no steep rise in alcohol usage along the lines of coffee and milk from the early twentieth century to the end of the war. Data for 1896–1900 are given as an average, 2.06 gallons; to that we can compare

- 1946: 2.3 gallons
- 1960: 2.07 gallons
- 2007: 2.31 gallons (this is the last year for which we have information)[4]

Americans may be heavy drinkers, but their alcohol intake per person has not risen much for 150 years.

Considering all this, the primary cause of coffee's decline per capita in the U.S. after World War II would seem to be that young people started drinking other beverages; they thought of coffee as their parents' drink, not theirs. But the appeal of soft drinks received a great new boost after the war. Car culture boomed, encouraging young people, who now had more spendable income than the cohorts who grew up in the 1940s, let alone in the 1930s, to cruise the streets in search of fast food. The "walking city" declined for the middle class as more and more families moved to the suburbs. There they knew their neighbors less well than in the city, or not at all, and community did begin to slip. For more on this point, see "Part III: The History of Coffee and Its Social Life."

The U.S. has led the world for many years in total imports of coffee. In 2010, 24,378,000 **bags**, at 60 kilograms each, entered the country. In second place was Germany, at 20,603,000 bags—but much of that quantity was destined for re-export.[5] While we import a lot of coffee, American consumption per capita lags well behind that of other countries. We downed coffee **liquor** at the rate of 4.1 kilograms (9.02 pounds) per person in 2009; the Finns remained the champions at 12.1 kilograms, followed by Denmark at 9.5 and Norway at 9.2.[6] Scandinavia is well caffeinated, as anyone who has attended any sort of meeting there can attest. Coffee breaks are occasionally interrupted by speeches and other presentations. Adult Finns may drink 10–12 cups a day, while the heaviest users among Americans who drink coffee, those aged 40 to 59, average about 4 cups per day. Consumers of coffee aged 18 to 24 are the lightest imbibers, at 2.5 cups.[7] Thus the American coffee industry still faces the challenge that has confronted it since the end of World War II: how to attract more consumers to drink more coffee, and especially how to get young adults to use it.

Nor do Americans on the whole drink especially good coffee, by the standards of this book and of the specialty sector. About 60 percent of all coffee drunk in the U.S. in 2010 was **commercial coffee** (not gourmet or **specialty coffee**).[8] The "can package format" dominates how coffee is purchased, at about 57 percent; that is, most American coffee drinkers buy the product already ground at grocery stores. Of those who used brewed coffee in 2010, 18 percent drank a flavored liquid. Among the drinkers of instant coffee, about 10 percent used a flavored type. **Espresso-based drinks** have lately shown significant gains: in 2010, 8 percent of people had consumed them on the "past day," and in 2011 the figure rose to 14 percent.[9] **Capsules** or **pods** are on the rise and are now used by some 8 percent of consumers.[10] On the other hand, the **Specialty Coffee Association of America** reports that the percentage of residents who drank specialty coffee outside the home was 2.7 percent in 1995 and 14 percent in 2009. The last figure represents a slight drop from the high point of 17 percent in 2008,[11] presumably due to the recession.

As we would expect from the data on the form in which coffee is purchased, most coffee is drunk at home. Some 85 percent of those surveyed consumed coffee there, while 27 percent had coffee out of the house—and some people used coffee both in and out, making the figures add to more than 100 percent.[12]

That canned, ground coffee leads the market points to another basic feature of American consumption: large corporations dominate sales. But this scene is changing steadily, following a sixty-year trend. Independent brands that arose after the Civil War were slowly swallowed by ever-larger companies; Maxwell House, for example, became part of the Sara Lee family. **Folgers** began as a small California company in the 1850s, grew to be an American giant, and remained independent until Procter and Gamble (P&G) absorbed the brand in 1963. In 2008 Folgers moved to a company previously best known for jams and syrups, the J. M. Smucker Corporation.

The **Big Four** of the late 1990s and early 2000s, Kraft (an American company), Nestlé (Swiss), P&G, and Sara Lee (American), or Big Five counting Tchibo (German), controlled some 69 percent of the global market in 1998.[13] But this group has shifted and shrunk. Recently Sara Lee announced plans to sell "a majority of its North American food-service coffee and tea operations" to Smucker. The two companies have "also entered into a licensing agreement to cooperatively develop liquid coffee technologies to drive long-term growth."[14] At a minimum, this cooperation means further consolidation in mass market coffee, not just in the U.S. but around the world. Sara Lee is now busy selling off its various parts, and the company may disappear as a coffee player or dissolve completely.

The USDA, citing a report by the Hoover Corporation, found that from 2000 to 2004, Folgers (then with P&G) had a market share of ground coffee sold in the U.S. of 38 percent by volume. Maxwell House (Kraft) had a market share of 33 percent, and the Sara Lee brands Hills Brothers, Chock Full O' Nuts, MJB, and Chase & Sanborn, which were all once independent labels, together held 10 percent of the market. Private-label brands had a market share of about 8 percent, by volume, in ground coffee. Folgers' market share rose from 37 percent in 2000 to 42 percent in 2004; the Sara Lee brands dropped from 11 percent to 7 percent.[15] Estimating the total market share of all coffee sold in the U.S. by the Big Four or Five companies is a game, but probably a safe guess is somewhere around 60 percent. This does not mean that these corporations have been able to corner the market. A report commissioned by the Dutch government found in 2002 that, "at the supply chain down to the countries of origin, there is no evidence of cartel behavior of the roasting industry."[16]

The recent story in American coffee that has caught everyone's attention has of course been the rise of **Starbucks**. The company started small in Seattle in the 1970s; Howard Schultz, who worked for the original owners, bought them out in 1987. Under his leadership, the company grew by 2012 to run 17,244 stores in 54 countries. Plans are under way to bring the brand to India and Vietnam and to grow Starbucks' own coffee in China. The company's total revenue for the last quarter of 2011 was $3.44 billion,[17] up 16 percent from the previous quarter. Schultz remarked in his second memoir, published in 2011, that Starbucks annually sold about $10 billion worth of coffee and milk around the world.[18] But at the rate of the year's last quarter, the company would take in more like $12–15 billion per annum.

Starbucks has *not* crushed independent coffeehouses in America. In 1991 an estimated 1,650 stores sold specialty coffee in the U.S. By 2008, 27,715 were in business. Of those, chain operations, including Starbucks, amounted to 47 percent, or some 13,000 shops.[19] At that point, Starbucks ran some 11,000 stores. The number two company in America in non-franchised coffee stores is Caribou, which has more than 400 stores in 15 states in the East and Midwest. In conversations with people working in the specialty coffee business as independents, I have heard repeatedly that Starbucks has been a godsend to the coffee industry in general. Feelings from the independents toward the mermaid are often a mixture of envy, a sense of awe at what Schultz has built and at his wealth, criticism of the quality of the coffee for the reliance on dark roasts, or "Starbucks is in the milk drink business," and worse. Yet there is also the feeling that Starbucks introduced Americans to the idea that coffee could be much better than the swill they were used to. Throughout the specialty coffee industry, independents find that customers often move on from Starbucks in search of even better coffee, which the small fry are sure they can deliver. As a report from the Specialty Coffee Association of America puts it, "Overall, we believe that specialty coffee (such as Starbucks) has benefitted from being viewed as an affordable luxury by value/price conscious [sic] consumers that are looking for inexpensive ways to treat themselves."[20]

In any event, the largest seller of out-of-home coffee in America is not Starbucks but Dunkin' Donuts, at nearly 1.5 billion cups of brewed coffee each year. For all that Starbucks has grabbed the public's imagination, people still go to Dunkin' much more often. And now McDonald's is moving into direct competition with Starbucks, as McCafés sprout across the land. The Golden Arches are now upgrading the look of their American stores, at a cost of more than $1 billion.[21] The company's coffee sales rose 38 percent from the beginning of 2010 through April of that year, on top of 25 percent growth in 2009.[22] Is there no limit to the number of places where Americans will drink coffee?

And yet, as the figures on overall consumption in the U.S. show, the growth in the number of all stores selling coffee away from home, together with the best efforts of the giant corporations, have not induced the populace to drink more coffee. Despite the 27,000 shops and the placement of Starbucks on opposite corners in a number of cities, overall consumption has remained pretty flat in recent years. As Americans have taken to drinking better coffee, they have drunk less of it. They moved away from the office coffee pot and three or four coffee breaks at work each day, while picking up 36 or even 72 ounces of soft drinks at a time, and they turned less often to coffee.

On the good side for the whole industry, Americans in the age group 18–39 have begun to drink somewhat more coffee in the past year or two, itself a sign of recovery from the recession. In a National Coffee Association survey, 40 percent of those 18–24 reported that they drink coffee daily, up from 31 percent in 2010, and marking a return to the recent high level of 2009. Some 54 percent of those 25–39 said that they drink coffee each day, a jump up from 44 percent in 2010 and about even with the 53 percent reported in 2009. Overall, more than three-quarters of Americans say they drank coffee within the past year.[23]

What kind of coffee do we drink? The best available information covers the U.S. and Canada; see "What Does 'Organic' Mean?" Certainly consumption of coffee labeled **organic** is increasing in North America; from 2004 through 2009, growth was 21 percent, far higher than the 1.5 percent annual growth in the conventional coffee industry.[24] As for certified coffees of all kinds, see "Coffee Certification Programs." In 2009, 16 percent of all coffee imported into the U.S. was certified by at least one organization."[25] Attention to **certification** has spread to all of the large companies; Caribou, for instance, promises that by the end of 2012 all of its coffee will be certified by Rainforest Alliance. Starbucks states that it "bought 269 million pounds of coffee in fiscal 2010. Some 84% of that—226 million pounds worth—[was] from C.A.F.E. Practices-approved suppliers. We paid an average price of $1.56 per pound for our premium green (unroasted) coffee in 2010, up from our $1.47 per pound in 2009."[26] Note that Starbucks' average price of coffee bought in 2010 was well below the coffee **C price** in New York; see "The 'Price' of Coffee."

All of McDonald's European stores, as well as those in Australia and New Zealand, now serve only Rainforest Alliance certified coffee; U.S. operations are moving toward "greater transparency into how . . . coffee is sourced." For this country, McDonald's "has begun a dialogue with coffee industry organizations to assess their ability to partner with our suppliers to deliver certified sustainable coffee that meets our U.S. specifications."[27]

As for how the coffee is prepared, in Starbucks, and increasingly in McDonald's and even Dunkin' Donuts, espresso-based drinks rule. Cutting-edge coffee bars and home suppliers have made great strides in the quality of **espresso** in recent years, and American aficionados have widely adopted **pour-over** devices to make a **single portion** or carafe of coffee. The variety, and price, of **espresso machines** for the home available through upscale catalogs is mind-numbing.

With a little effort, U.S. consumers can find coffee out of the home, or make coffee themselves with the right equipment, that is as good as any beverage around the world. The best and the worst coexist here. If as a nation we consume less coffee than our grandparents did, we often drink better-tasting and more socially responsible beverages than they had.

NOTES

1. United States Department of Agriculture, Economic Research Service, Food Availability: Spreadsheets, updated July 13, 2011, http://www.ers.usda.gov/data/foodconsumption/FoodAvailSpreadsheets .htm#dyfluid, accessed February 5, 2012.

2. See Mark Pendergrast, *For God, Country, and Coca-Cola: The Definitive History of the Great American Soft Drink and the Company That Makes It*, 2nd ed. (New York: Basic Books, 2000).

3. USDA Dairy (fluid milk and cream).

4. "Apparent per capita ethanol consumption for the United States, 1850–2007 (gallons of ethanol, based on population age 15 and older prior to 1970 and on population age 14 and other thereafter)," National Institute on Alcohol Abuse and Alcoholism, National Institutes of Health, updated October 2009, http://www.niaaa.nih.gov/Resources/DatabaseResources/QuickFacts/AlcoholSales/consum01.ht, accessed February 7, 2012.

5. International Coffee Organization (ICO), Statistics: Importing Countries, Imports of all Forms of Coffee from All Sources, Calendar Years 2010 to 2011, http://www.ico.org/historical/2010-19/PDF/IMPORTSIMCALYR.pdf, accessed December 9, 2012.

6. International Trade Centre, *The Coffee Exporter's Guide*, 3rd ed. (Geneva: ITC, 2011), 21–24. Available at http://www.intracen.org/The-Coffee-Exporters-Guide—Third-Edition/.

7. The National Coffee Association USA [NCA USA], "National Coffee Drinking Trends Study," Report (New York: NCA USA, 2011), 30; uses a sample across the country of 2,663 people aged 18 years and older.

8. NCA USA, "National Coffee Drinking Trends Study," 31.

9. NCA USA, "National Coffee Drinking Trends Study," 13. "Past day" refers to consumption on the day before a respondent filled out the survey.

10. NCA USA, "National Coffee Drinking Trends Study," 33, 41.

11. SCAA, Specialty Coffee in the USA 2008–2009 (chart).

12. NCA USA, "National Coffee Drinking Trends Study," 42.

13. S. Ponte, "The 'latte revolution'? Regulation, markets and consumption in the global coffee chain," *World Development* 30, no. 7 (2002): 1108.

14. *BusinessWire News*, October 24, 2011.http://www.businesswire.com/news/home/20111024005743/en/Sara-Lee-Corp.-Announces-Sale-Majority-North, accessed February 14, 2012.

15. "The Coffee Value Chain," USDA, no date, but probably 2005, http://www.ers.usda.gov/publications/err38/err38b.pdf, accessed February 14, 2012.

16. Quoted in Brian Lewin, Daniele Giovannucci, and Panos Varangis, "New Paradigms in Global Supply and Demand," *World Bank Agriculture and Rural Development Discussion Paper No. 3*, March 2004, 8.

17. *The New York Times Business Day*, February 15, 2012.

18. Howard Schultz and Joanne Gordon, *Onward: How Starbucks Fought for Its Life without Losing Its Soul* (New York: Rodale/Macmillan, 2011), 238.

19. SCAA, "Specialty Coffee in the USA 2008–2009" (chart).

20. SCAA, "Themes and Trends within the Specialty Coffeehouse Industry," Sector Report, January 2011, 19.

21. *USA Today*, May 9, 2011.

22. Chicago Breaking Business, "McDonald's to Hold Prices; Coffee Sales up 38 Percent," June 3, 2010, http://archive.chicagobreakingbusiness.com/2010/06/mcdonalds-to-hold-prices-coffee-sales-up-38.html, accessed February 15, 2012.

23. NCA USA, "National Coffee Drinking Trends Study," 2.

24. "The North American Organic Coffee Industry Survey 2010," by Daniele Giovannucci, with support from the Specialty Coffee Association of America. The full report may be purchased at https://ota.com/bookstore.html. A summary of its main points is at http://www.organicnewsroom.com/2010/06/_organic_coffee_market_tops_14_1.html.

25. Daniele Giovannucci and Jason Potts with B. Killian, C. Wunderlich, G. Soto, S. Schuller, F. Pinard, K. Schroeder, and I. Vagneron, "Seeking Sustainability: COSA Preliminary Analysis of Sustainability Initiatives in the Coffee Sector," September 2008, 2. Committee on Sustainable Assessment, Winnipeg, Canada. COSA is affiliated with the United Nations, the International Coffee Organization, and government agencies in the U.S., Europe, and Latin America.

26. http://www.starbucks.com/responsibility/sourcing/coffee, accessed February 15, 2012.

27. http://www.aboutmcdonalds.com/mcd/sustainability/library/policies_programs/sustainable_supply_chain/coffee.html, accessed February 15, 2012.

Part III

THE HISTORY OF COFFEE AND ITS SOCIAL LIFE

41

Coffee, a Condensed History

Jonathan Morris with material from Robert W. Thurston

Studying the history of coffee is a lot like barista training; the more you learn, the more you realize you don't know. Coffee involves so many fields and subdisciplines—agricultural, business, consumption, cultural, diplomatic, development, economic, environmental, food, gender, geographical, political, religious, rural, social, technology, trade, just to mention those discussed in the chapters of this section—that any attempt to provide an overall guide to the subject must be highly selective. The chapters that follow offer a selection of just how diverse the approaches to coffee history can be.

Coffee has always been a transnational, indeed transcontinental, industry, but the focus of both production and consumption of the bean, naturally intimately linked, have shifted significantly over the centuries. One of the more surprising features of the history of coffee is how often the ties between producers and suppliers have been recast. Here we provide a brief history of the bean's progress from its first known appearance in the Red Sea region to today's global trade

THE WINE OF ISLAM

Ethiopia is commonly considered the birthplace of coffee. Here *Coffea arabica* still grows wild in highland forests. As Willem Boot's contribution notes, many myths have arisen about how humans discovered the possibilities of coffee as a beverage. What does seem clear is that the Oromo people, a Muslim tribe from the regions of Sidamo, Kaffa, and Jimmah, began simmering the desiccated **cherry** husks from the coffee plant in boiling water for around fifteen minutes, producing a hot infusion known as *buno* in the local language and *qishr* in Arabic. Coffee was not initially farmed for this purpose; the husks were simply scavenged from the wild. Across the Red Sea on the Arabian peninsula, the Sufi movement, a mystical Muslim sect, was winning more followers, particularly in what is now Yemen. The Sufis held all-night vigils known as *dhikers*, during which they would consume a concoction called *qahwa* as part of their devotions. It seems that their drink of choice originally took the form of *kaffa*, an infusion prepared from the leaves of the hallucinogenic plant known as *khat* (*kat, qat*) but that at some point during the fifteenth century, this was superseded by *qishr*. Several accounts record

215

that this change occurred on the suggestion of a mufti known as Muhammad al-Dhabani (died 1470) who had travelled in Ethiopia and noted that *qishr* helped overcome feelings of fatigue (a problem for Sufi worshippers who had to return to their jobs during the day). He recommended that, during any shortage of *khat*, *qishr* could be substituted in *qahwa*.[1]

The Sufis spread knowledge of this new form of *qahwa* up the Arabian peninsula to the holy cities of Mecca, Jeddah, and Medina and eventually to Cairo, the center of the Mameluk empire, where it was recorded being used by Yemeni students at the Al-Azhar Islamic university during the 1500s.

A key turning point occurred in 1511 when the governor of Mecca, having dispersed a nighttime gathering of men on the grounds of the mosque drinking *qahwa* (presumably Sufis at prayer), subsequently coerced the city's religious leaders into ruling that consuming *qahwa* was un-Islamic because it promoted intoxication. The judgment was referred to the authorities in Cairo but was overruled, effectively giving the green light to coffee consumption.[2]

It is likely that the real intention of Mecca's governor had been to indirectly attack the taverns that served alcohol to non-Muslims but claimed to provide coffee for the devout. Instead the **coffeehouse** was legitimized as a secular meeting place for Muslims, where men could meet as equals and be entertained by storytellers and musicians, including veiled female singers.

Following the Ottoman conquest of the Mameluk Sultanate in 1517, *qahwa* spread around the eastern regions of the Mediterranean, known as the Levant, with the first coffeehouse opening in Istanbul, the Ottoman capital in 1554. During this process coffee acquired the Turkish name *kahve*.

The preparation process also appears to have changed during this journey. While the original *qishr* involved using the whole of the husk, only beans were used by the time the drink reached northern Arabia and Egypt. Beans would be lightly toasted in a pan before being cooled, crushed, and mixed with spices, notably cardamom, and then cooked with water for some time in a closed pot with a long spout (*jamana*), before being served as a semi-translucent light brown liquor. By the time kahve reached Turkey, however, the beans were being blackened over a fire, then ground into a fine powder using a mill. The results were placed in an *ibrik*, a wide-bottomed open pot with a narrowing neck and broader rim, to which water was added and the liquid boiled and re-boiled several times. This produced the beverage that a Turkish poet described as "the negro enemy of sleep and love." The differences between Arabian and Turkish (or Mediterranean) coffee can be observed side by side in contemporary Lebanon, where the Muslim population still drink the former, the Christian the latter.[3]

The demand for coffee was originally met from shipments from the port of Zeila, now on the border of Somalia and Djibouti. It was added to cargoes of spices from India and offloaded at ports on the Red Sea where the beverage had been adopted—the first recorded shipment being to the Sinai peninsula in 1497. This trade came under the control of the Banyans, a Gujarati merchant caste that dominated shipping throughout the Indian Ocean.[4]

The Banyans also operated credit networks, and it seems likely that they funded the planting of coffee by Yemeni peasants among the subsistence crops that they grew on terraces surrounding the mountain villages of the interior. Established in the 1540s, these remained the sole source of cultivated coffee for the next 150 years. The beans eventually arrived at Bayt-al-Faqih on the coastal plain, where they were warehoused prior to dispatch to the ports of Mocha and Hudaydah in Yemen for shipping. Although it was actually Hudaydah that supplied the internal needs of the Ottoman empire, Mocha became known as the principal port for coffee, as it supplied the needs of the rest of the Muslim world, especially the settlements surrounding the Persian Gulf, Arabian Sea, and Indian Ocean.

Mocha's position at the center of the spice trade also made it the logical place for European traders returning from the East Indies to try to acquire coffee directly, beginning in the early eighteenth century. However, the volumes available remained low, and it could take months to purchase sufficient stock to fill a ship's hold. As consumption in the European continent increased, it was almost inevitable that alternative sources of supply were established, leaving Mocha to decline, at the same time that much of the Muslim world shifted its preference from coffee to tea. Yemeni coffee remains a rarity today with output constrained by both geography and politics. Ethiopia, however, began cultivating coffee in the late nineteenth century and remains one of the most popular African origins.

THE EXTRA-EUROPEAN COFFEE CULTURE

Coffee was first noted in non-Ottoman Europe in 1575 when an inquiry into the murder of a Turkish merchant in Venice recorded the presence of coffee apparatus among his possessions. Although émigrés from the Ottoman empire, frequently Greek or Armenian Christians, spread coffee to other lands, and it appears to have been prescribed by apothecaries for certain ailments, no real takeoff in foreign consumption occurred until the 1650s. It was then that the first coffeehouses began to appear in England.

Coffee arrived in Europe together with two other hot beverages, tea and chocolate, at roughly the same time. They all had stimulating, not stultifying, characteristics. But each beverage acquired certain cultural connotations that strongly affected its diffusion.[5] Chocolate entered Spain in 1585, a result of the Spanish conquest of the Mayan peoples of southern Mexico. It became popular as a breakfast beverage among the Spanish aristocracy and later spread to Austria and France. It was seen as a medicinal, nourishing beverage due to its high fat content, one particularly beneficial to women.[6] Tea was likewise regarded as more feminine, particularly in those societies such as England where coffee had become closely associated with the male environs of the coffeehouse.[7] Tea's triumph within the British Isles was complete when it was adopted as the beverage of the working classes from the second half of the eighteenth century; as the anthropologist Sidney Mintz has argued, it was the combination of tea with sugar that fuelled the industrial revolution by delivering energy boosts to the workforce without interrupting production.[8]

Yet coffee gradually conquered the continent, coming to be seen as a signifier of respectability among the bourgeois households that adopted it. Breakfast changed from a meal based around a grain porridge washed down with beer or wine to one centered on a sugared hot drink plus bread. J. S. Bach's *Coffee Cantata* (1732–34) may have been intended to poke fun at the fad for the drink, but its libretto featured three generations of women falling for the charms of coffee, which they held to be "lovelier than a thousand kisses, sweeter far than muscatel wine." These phrases clearly echoed common sentiments. Leading authors meanwhile made extensive use of coffee to spur on their creativity; Voltaire reputedly consumed some forty cups a day in the Parisian cafés that doubled as artistic salons. By the end of the eighteenth century, during which Europe's population grew by around 50 percent, coffee consumption is estimated to have risen from 2 million to 120 million pounds, significantly faster than tea (1 to 40 million pounds) and eclipsing chocolate (2 to 13 million pounds).[9]

The first signs that coffee drinking was acquiring an audience beyond the elite classes came in the Netherlands, where the proportion of the sales of the Dutch East India Company (VOC, from its name in Dutch) derived from tea and coffee rose from just over 4 percent at the end of the seventeenth century to just under 25 percent at the end of the 1730s. In terms of revenue generated this amounted to a 1,312-fold increase, a figure that does not capture the full extent in the increase of tea and coffee imported via Amsterdam, given that unit prices fell significantly over this period. Extensive research into probate records confirms that the habit of coffee drinking spread deep into Dutch society; many poor households possessed coffee paraphernalia. A commentator remarked in 1726 that coffee "had broken through so generally in our land that maids and seamstresses now had to have their coffee in the morning or they could not put their thread through the eye of their needle."[10]

Demand was both met and stimulated by the establishment of commercial coffee cultivation in Java (see "Indonesia"). Coffee was probably previously planted in the Malabar region of India, then brought by the Dutch to Java. That island became the first **origin** to compete against Mocha in the world market. Once shipments to Amsterdam became regular following the bumper harvest of 1711, it did not take long for production to surpass Yemen's. Whereas in 1721 90 percent of the coffee sold in Amsterdam came from Mocha, by 1726 Java supplied 90 percent of the beans.[11]

The quality of Javanese coffee was generally held to be lower than Mocha, but then so was the price the Dutch paid for it. The VOC operated by obliging the lord of a community to provide the company with a fixed amount of coffee, for which it paid a predetermined price. The lord in turn required his subjects to produce coffee as part of the tribute they paid to him. This system provided little incentive to invest in growing better coffee at any point in the chain, and the trees were often cultivated poorly on land ill-suited for the purpose. The lower quality of the Java helps explain the appearance of the world's first coffee blend, Mocha Java, in which the acidity of the Mocha added flavor to the body of the Java. The cheaper Java also helped to keep down the price of the blend.

Java's dominance of world trade did not last long, however. The VOC also planted coffee in the Dutch Latin American colony of Guiana (today Suriname) in 1712 and started shipping it back to Amsterdam in 1718. Meanwhile the French East India company introduced coffee to the island of Bourbon (now Réunion) in 1715. Profits made from coffee were such that the company granted the French state a monopoly of all production in 1723 and declared that it would repossess all the concessions it had granted on which coffee was not grown. In both Guiana and, especially, Bourbon, cultivation was carried out on large plantations that used African **slave labor.**[12]

The French also transplanted coffee plants to their Caribbean territories, notably St. Domingue (now Haiti) in 1715 and Martinique in 1723. Coffee growing took second place to sugar production, however, and in St. Domingue was principally cultivated on the remoter hillsides by people of color, with the island's settler elite forming the major market for the beans.[13] However, in the latter part of the century, coffee farming became more intensive and export-oriented, shifting to a slave-based plantation system. In 1767 coffee revenues in St. Domingue were only a quarter of those of sugar, yet between 1787 and 1789 they were of roughly equal value, making St. Domingue easily the largest coffee-exporting origin in the world, with the French colonies as a whole generating over two-thirds of the world supply.

This growth in exports was closely linked to the expansion of domestic consumption in France. The combination of coffee with warm milk in the form of *café au lait* created a beverage sufficiently close to chocolate in its sweetness and calorific value to become the new breakfast favorite.[14] Recipes using coffee frequently appeared in French cookbooks after the 1730s. By the late eighteenth century, even the lowest classes were drinking a version of *café au lait*, doubtless adulterated, to start their day. Indeed, the *sans culottes*, the urban radicals of 1789–94, included demands for more access to coffee in their manifestos at the start of the revolution.[15]

Inspired by events in France, St. Domingue's slaves staged their own revolution in 1791, leading to a civil war that lasted until 1804, when the black-led Haitian Republic was declared. Coffee production was dramatically disrupted during the conflict, and the new state failed to recapture the markets it had lost. The plantations were mostly broken up and coffee was either cultivated on small mountainous plots or simply scavenged from the surviving trees.

The demise of St. Domingue's coffee created opportunities for other producers. Asian production revived in Java and also Ceylon (today Sri Lanka), where the Dutch had introduced coffee as a garden crop to be grown by the Sinhalese people. When the British gained control of the entire island after 1815, they moved to intensify coffee production on the lines of the plantation system operating in West Indian sugarcane fields. Although some local entrepreneurs acquired plantations, ownership remained largely among European settlers, frequently colonial officials themselves. By the 1860s, Ceylon had become the largest coffee exporter in the world.[16]

In 1869, however, **coffee leaf rust** fungus, *Hemelia vastatrix*, hit the Ceylon plantations. Over the next forty years it spread to points as far apart as Samoa in the Pacific and Cameroon in West Africa. Coffee cultivation in the colonial economies of Africa and Asia was devastated, with their overall share of world output dropping from 33 percent at the time of the outbreak to just 5 percent in 1914. In Ceylon during the 1870s, planters abandoned coffee cultivation and switched to tea. Experiments with alternative species of coffee led other producing regions, notably those in West Africa and contemporary Indonesia, to replant with the hardier **robusta** species. For more detail on this upheaval, see "The Ecology of Taste."

For Europe too, its time at the center of the coffee economy was over. Consumption continued to rise, not least in regions such as Germany, which had come late to coffee, having been held back by several factors: the desire of rulers such as Frederick the Great of Prussia to protect homegrown products (in this instance beer) and the value to the treasury of state monopolies on both the importing and later roasting of coffee, policed by agents known as "coffee sniffers" during the later eighteenth century (see "Germany").[17] However, just as the Latin American nations were to usurp the position of the colonial producers within the world markets, North America overtook Europe as the principal importer of coffee, as it developed into a mass consumer society, embraced by European immigrants in search of a better lifestyle that might, among many other things, offer them the chance to drink more coffee.

A NEW WORLD OF COFFEE

The old notion that America became a nation of coffee drinkers in the wake of the Boston Tea Party of 1773 is effectively laid to rest in the chapter "Why Americans Drink Coffee." Britain's colonies were not just the major source of American tea but also, through British possessions in the Caribbean, the primary origin of American imports of coffee. As Topik and McDonald explain, the thirteen American colonies adopted an embargo on British tea and coffee from the Caribbean in 1774. The Revolutionary War further disrupted supply from British holdings. The new United States turned for coffee to St. Domingue, then Cuba, and finally Brazil in the mid-nineteenth century.

Yet imports did not solely assuage some great American thirst for caffeine. Instead, coffee had become a key part in America's re-export trade with Europe, the final destination of well over half the coffee that entered the U.S. in the 1800s. The Great Atlantic and Pacific Tea Company (note that the word coffee is not in the name), founded in New York in 1859, became the first truly national grocery store chain by the late nineteenth century, yet carried little coffee. Even in the early 1880s, the number of cups of coffee brewed in the U.S. was probably roughly equivalent to those of tea. It was only as increasing numbers of immigrants arrived from Europe, bringing not so much a taste for coffee as the cultural aspiration to be able to afford it, that consumption really took off (see "United States").

The vast bulk of the new supply of coffee to the U.S. came from Brazil, as "Why Americans Drink Coffee" shows. Other Latin American states also expanded their output to fill the gap left by the ravages of coffee rust in Africa and Asia, but they were unable to compete with Brazil's commodity approach based on volume of outputs; they instead relied on quality to differentiate their offering—none more so than Colombia, whose high-grown **Colombian milds** were prized for blending with the Brazilian **naturals** to add flavor. By acting collectively to control the stocks in world circulation, Latin American states were able to promote price stability, enabling them to plan investments more rationally while providing an assured return to farmers. This approach started with the Brazilian "valorisation" of 1906 and culminated in the establishment of the **International Coffee Organization** (ICO) in 1962, which assigned export quotas to its members.

America meanwhile had evolved into the first mass market for coffee. During the Civil War, branding and packaging began to develop together, so that American housewives no longer simply bought **green coffee**, often from an open barrel in a general store, perhaps placed next to fragrant fish or pickles. The big American coffee companies, Arbuckles, **Folgers**, and Hills Brothers, began as small operations, often in the western states and territories. As the railroads spread to every town in the land, as printing techniques evolved to permit first color drawings and then photographs, and as the mass market magazines emerged, Americans purchased more and more packaged coffee, either green or roasted. Advertising in popular magazines reinforced the notion that the way that American housewives prepared and served coffee was an important marker of their status and value in and outside the home.[18]

To all this there was a dark side, sometimes a vicious one. For some three or four decades, beginning in the early 1930s, coffee advertisements fairly regularly featured violence by males against women. Such ads were supposed to be funny, but a hot cup of coffee thrown in the face no longer seems amusing.

Even if ads did not directly promote violence against inept wives, inferior coffee in the home was depicted as threatening many a postwar marriage, while correct preparation could guarantee domestic peace or even land a man in the first place. Mrs. Olson came to the rescue of clueless—but always white and gorgeous—homemakers in these ads, which ran for twenty-one years beginning in the early 1960s.[19] It's easy to make good coffee, she would tell distressed young women. Just use Folgers—"It's mountain grown!"—as though other coffee grew in swamps.

Aside from what these ads tell us about gender roles during the first six or seven decades of the twentieth century, they also point to coffee's centrality in American life in that period, when sales of coffee in the U.S. frequently accounted for over 50 percent of world trade, with per capita consumption reaching record levels immediately on either side of the Second World War. The ads also reveal an increasing concentration of coffee into the hands of a few large roasters, able to contest the mass market within the most popular channels

Figure 41.1. A Chase and Sanborn comic strip ad, *Good Housekeeping*, November 1934. By finally buying good coffee, Mrs. Goof saves the marriage, for what it might be worth.

of communication. By the 1950s the five largest roasters in the U.S. roasted over one-third of all coffee and controlled 78 percent of all stocks, supplying the remainder as green to grocery chains to roast for their own store blends.[20]

THE GLOBAL BEVERAGE

Starting in the 1930s, the American grocery sector changed from shelves accessible only to clerks, who handed packages and cans to patrons, into self-service supermarkets. The new alignment came to dominate the distribution channel for coffee and led in turn to a transformation of the structures of the coffee industry: the major food conglomerates who supplied the new outlets purchased the leading coffee brands (and associated companies). As this retail revolution was exported to the rest of the globe, an elite group of multinational giants came to dominate the world market, buying up the major brands in each region.[21] By 1998, the **Big Five**—Phillip Morris (now part of Kraft), Nestle, Sara Lee, Proctor and Gamble (which has since sold its coffee business to Smucker's), and Tchibo—accounted for 69 percent of global coffee sales.[22]

Their common business formula was based on a combination of high volume and low pricing, designed to attract customers confronted with a wide choice of products. Although some brands were positioned as premium, they made little reference to origins, not least because in order to maintain the volumes of output, it was necessary to constantly adjust the blends to fit with available coffee. As more robusta became available at lower prices, it inevitably found its way into these blends, with roasters relying on a combination of consumer ignorance and thrift to shift their products.

A series of innovations in the first half of the twentieth century combined to dramatically extend product ranges. Ludwig Roselius of Hamburg first perfected a **decaffeination** process in 1903. He created the Kaffee Hag brand in 1906 (marketed in France and the United States under the name Sanka, from the French *sans caféine*), before the label was sold to General Foods in the 1920s and subsequently to Kraft. Melitta Bentz, a housewife from Dresden, patented the filter paper system in 1908 that still bears her name. This technique prevented any coffee grounds from ending up in the cup, in contrast to a typical outcome when using linen bag filters in the coffee pot, the principal method of domestic brewing over the previous two centuries. Not only did this improve the appearance of the coffee and give a sense that it had been "cleaned" of impurities, it also reduced preparation time.

Such time saving was taken to a new level with the launch of the first **soluble** (or "instant") coffee, Nescafé, produced by the Swiss giant Nestle in 1938. Soluble sales took off in the 1950s and were further boosted once the original spray-dried techniques were superseded by freeze-drying as utilized in the premium "Gold Blend" brand launched in the late 1960s, known as "Taster's Choice" in the U.S. The costs of production equipment for both decaffeinated and instant coffee are such that producing it is only undertaken in large-scale specialist plants. Instant coffee was particularly successful in the UK, where it was adopted as an easier beverage to brew than tea during the advertising breaks on the newly launched commercial television network. Even today soluble in the UK still constitutes an estimated 80 percent of the at-home market, while soluble accounts for around 40 percent of total world coffee consumption.[23]

The decline in per capita coffee consumption in the U.S. from the 1950s onward has often been blamed on the "mass marketers." Trish Rothgeb dubbed these figures the "first wavers," who had "made bad coffee commonplace . . . who created low quality instant solubles . . . who blended away all the nuance . . . who forced prices to an all-time low!"[24] As Kenneth Davids shows in "The Competing Languages of Coffee," this was in many ways typical of an early discourse within the **specialty coffee** movement, which aimed to educate consumers about coffee and raise their perception of quality, at least to the point that they understood coffee came from a tree, not a can!

In order to introduce customers to specialty coffee, dedicated entrepreneurs turned to another innovation intended to speed up the brewing process, albeit in bars, the **espresso machine.** As Jonathan Morris recounts in "The Espresso Menu," the first pressure brewing machine to enter into production was the 1905 Ideale. However, the espresso rules were effectively rewritten by Achille Gaggia in 1948, who developed a machine with a spring-loaded piston that delivered shots under high pressures, topped with **crema.**

Espresso-based drinks, such as **cappuccino** and **caffè latte,** albeit often prepared to very different recipes than in Italy, were used by the U.S. specialty coffee movement to tempt people into their shops. From this start was born the format that spawned Starbucks and its host of imitators (see "Coffeehouse Formats through the Centuries"). When the **Specialty Coffee Association of America** was formed in 1982, only forty people attended its first meeting. By 1998, the SCAA estimates, there were "10,000 operating units" serving specialty coffee in America. In 2005, the estimate was 20,000, a figure that includes Starbucks and other chains selling better-than-grocery-store coffee.[25]

In 1994, Starbucks began to take its formula abroad, starting with Japan, and now has some 15,000 stores in over 50 countries. In Europe another version of the speciality (note the additional "i") coffee movement emerged in Scandinavia, giving birth to what became the **World Barista Championship.** The commercial element of these trends was the reproduction of the coffee shop format; the UK market, for example, has grown from 371 branded coffeehouses serving premium (that is, espresso-based) beverages in 1997 to 4,907 in 2011.[26]

This highly visible expression of consumer culture coincided with a crisis in producer countries, as prices on the world coffee market reached new lows at the turn of the millennium. The average price of exported coffee in U.S. cents per pound fell from 74 in 1999–2000 to 43 in 2001–2. Within the industry this was widely blamed on the demise of the **International Coffee Agreement** (ICA) in 1989, a result of political pressures for market liberalization from the U.S. in particular. The end of the ICA and its export quotas assisted in creating a glut of robusta from nontraditional origins such as Vietnam. The oversupply forced the price of all coffee down to the point that producers claimed it was impossible for them to cover their costs (see "Vietnam"). Starbucks in particular found itself the target of denunciations of exploitation and unfair practices in the coffee trade, both by demonstrators during the riots that accompanied the meeting of the World Trade Organisation in Seattle in 1999 and in films such as *Black Gold* (2007), whose director freely admitted that he focused upon the chain because "the average person on the street can't see Nestle or Kraft—they're not in your face."[27] The crisis also spurred interest in ethical **certification** programs like **Fair Trade USA, Fairtrade International,** and Rainforest Alliance.

In recent years, however, coffee export prices have again started to rise, reaching 125 cents per pound in 2009–10 and going above 300 in April 2011, a reversal usually ascribed to rising demand from new markets in which the coffee shop format has taken hold. The potential for growth in traditional tea-drinking regions such as Russia and China, where the economic elite have already switched to coffee as a status beverage, may be game-changing within the industry. However, the trend is most powerful in producer countries that formerly displayed little interest in the final product. In India, for example, the locally owned company Café

Coffee Day, which first opened in 1996, expanded to some 1,270 outlets by 2012 and, significantly, became part of a vertically integrated holding company that also operates its own coffee estates.[28] Brazil, meanwhile, is no longer merely the world's biggest coffee producer but has suddenly become the second largest consumer nation in the world, behind only the U.S., with growth predicted to continue at an average of 3–5 percent per annum for the coming years, significantly higher than either Europe or North America.[29] The U.S. has virtually stagnated in consumption, even while the number of coffee shops continues to grow. Does this portend yet another profound shift in the nature of the world coffee trade? The next few years will tell.

NOTES

1. Ralph S. Hattox, *Coffee and Coffee Houses: The Origins of a Social Beverage in the Medieval Near East* (Seattle: University of Washington Press,1985), 11–29.

2. Hattox, *Coffee and Coffee Houses*, 29–45.

3. Vittorio Castellani aka Chef Kumalé, *Coffee Roots* (Turin: Lavazza, 2006), gives a good account of coffee in the Middle East today.

4. Michel Tuchscherer, "Coffee in the Red Sea Area from the Sixteenth to the Nineteenth Century," in *The Global Coffee Economy in Africa, Asia, and Latin America, 1500–1989*, ed. William Gervase Clarence-Smith and Steven Topik (Cambridge: Cambridge University Press, 2003), 50–66, provides the best account of the organization of the trade.

5. Wolfgang Schivelbusch, *Tastes of Paradise: A Social History of Spices, Stimulants and Intoxicants*, trans. David Jacobson (New York: Vintage, 1993), 15–96.

6. Sarah Moss and Alexander Badenoch, *Chocolate: A Global History* (London: Reaktion Books, 2009).

7. Helen Saberi, *Tea: A Global History* (London: Reaktion, 2010).

8. Sidney Mintz, *Sweetness and Power: The Place of Sugar in Modern History* (New York: Viking, 1985), 214.

9. Jordan Goodman, "Excitantia: Or How Enlightenment Europe Took to Soft Drugs" in *Consuming Habits: Drugs in History and Anthropology*, ed. Jordan Goodman, Paul E. Lovejoy, and Andrew Sherratt (London: Routledge, 1995), 126.

10. Anne E. C. McCants, "Poor consumers as global consumers: The diffusion of tea and coffee drinking in the eighteenth century," *Economic History Review* 61 (2008): 177.

11. Steven Topik, "The Integration of the World Coffee Market" in Clarence-Smith and Topik, *Global Coffee Economy*, 28.

12. Gwyn Campbell, "The Origins and Development of Coffee Production in Réunion and Madagascar, 1711–1972" in Clarence-Smith and Topik, *Global Coffee Economy*, 67–71.

13. Steven Topik, "The World Coffee Market in the Eighteenth and Nineteenth Centuries from Colonial to National Regimes," LSE eprint Working Paper 04/04, London, 2004, 16. Available at http://eprints.lse.ac.uk/22489.

14. Julia Landweber, "Domesticating the 'queen of beans': How old regime France learned to love coffee," *World History Bulletin* 26, no. 1 (Spring 2010): 10–12.

15. Colin Jones and Rebecca Spang, "Sans Culottes, sans Café, sans Tabac: Shifting Realms of Necessity and Luxury in Eighteenth Century France," in *Consumers and Luxury: Consumer Culture in Europe 1650–1850*, ed. Maxine Berg and Helen Clifford (Manchester: Manchester University Press,1999), 37–62.

16. Rachel Kurian, "Labour, Race and Gender on the Coffee Plantations in Ceylon (Sri Lanka), 1834–1880," in Clarence-Smith and Topik, *Global Coffee Economy*, 173–90.

17. Alan Weinberg and Bonnie K. Bealer, *The World of Caffeine: The Science and Culture of the World's Most Popular Drug* (New York: Routledge, 2001), 86–87.

18. Jackson Lears, *Fables of Abundance: A Cultural History of Advertising in America* (New York: Basic Books, 1994); Leigh Summers, *Bound to Please: A History of the Victorian Corset* (New York: Berg, 2001); and Lori Anne Loeb, *Consuming Angels: Advertising and Victorian Women* (New York: Oxford University Press, 1994).

19. *Los Angeles Times*, July 25, 1996, http://articles.latimes.com/1996-07-25/news/mn-27699_1_virginia-christine, accessed July 1, 2011.

20. Topik, "The Integration of the World Coffee Market," 46.

21. On this process see Victoria de Grazia, *Irresistible Empire. America's Advance Through 20th-Century Europe* (Cambridge, MA: Belknap Press of Harvard University Press, 2005).

22. Benoit Daviron and Stefano Ponte, *The Coffee Paradox. Global Markets, Commodity Trade and the Elusive Promise of Development* (London: Zed Books, 2005), 92.

23. See Benfield, "United Kingdom," this volume, and Howard Schultz, *Onward: How Starbucks Fought for Its Life without Losing Its Soul* (New York: Rodale, 2011), 252.

24. Trish R. Skeie (Rothgeb), "Norway and Coffee," *The Flamekeeper, Newsletter of the Roasters Guild,* Spring 2003.

25. https://www.scaa.org/?page=history, accessed May 20, 2012.

26. Allegra Strategies, *Project Cafe11 UK* (London: Allegra Strategies, 2011).

27. J. Dawson, "Wake Up and Smell the Coffee," *The Sunday Times* (London), June 3, 2007, Culture Section, 1.0.

28. http://cafecoffeeday.com, accessed 24 May 2012.

29. "Brazil: Sara Lee sees consumption growing by 3–5% annually," *Comunicaffè* (ejournal), Milan, May 25, 2012.

42

Coffeehouse Formats through the Centuries

Third Places or Public Spaces?

Jonathan Morris

What is a **coffeehouse**? The question is more complicated than it seems at first. Many places that sell coffee would never be described as coffeehouses. A more nuanced definition is that a coffeehouse is a business whose principal source of income derives from coffee beverage sales; yet this notion eliminates many of the places where people have congregated to drink coffee over the centuries.

Coffeehouses sell beverages and intangible goods. The sociologist Roy Oldenburg makes the point in his now famous formula: coffeehouses are examples of **third places** that "host the regular, voluntary, informal, and happily anticipated gatherings of individuals beyond the realms of home and work."[1] Typically, coffeehouses have indeed acted as third places, but they have frequently been surrogates for both the home and the workplace.

Coffeehouses, then, sell not just coffee but also time and space. The trick is to identify customers with time who need space and to rent a spot to them in the price charged for coffee, as the various elaborations of the coffeehouse format recorded over the centuries demonstrate.

The first coffeehouses spread up the Arabian peninsula and around the Levant under the jurisdiction of the Ottoman empire during the sixteenth century.[2] Their appeal lay in providing the first public spaces, apart from the mosque, in which Muslim men could socialize with each other in the absence of alcohol, which was, of course, forbidden by their religion. Inviting a companion to one's home would have necessitated negotiating a myriad of conventions connected to social rank, while meeting at a coffeehouse where patrons were seated and served at long benches according to the order in which they arrived, reinforced the sense of interacting with others on an equal footing. Coffeehouses were both the source and beneficiary of a new attitude within the empire, particularly appreciated by middle-level bureaucrats. Several sultans sought to suppress coffeehouses as sites of sedition, but their orders appear to have been "overlooked" by many local officials.

The first European coffeehouses were established in England in the 1650s, some two decades before they appeared in France and modern-day Germany and over thirty years prior to the opening of coffeehouses in Austria and Italy. This might seem surprising given the relative proximity of the latter countries to the Ottoman empire's Balkan territories, but it is probably best explained by the relative weakness of the monarchy and the guilds in England compared with the continent. It was easier in England to start a new business than it was elsewhere in Europe.

When Pasqua Rosee opened the first coffeehouse in London in 1652, the country had just concluded a period of nine years of civil war, during which the king had been executed and a commonwealth proclaimed.[3] In a period of intense uncertainty, coffeehouses provided a public space where individuals of various political persuasions could meet to plan and debate.

It is no accident that London, the stronghold of the parliamentarians, contests the claim for the earliest coffeehouse in England with Oxford, the royalist city par excellence, in which an establishment was certainly operating by 1653 but may have been preceded by an operation founded in 1650.[4] After his restoration to the throne in 1660, Charles II twice started to suppress coffeehouses as centers of opposition, but each time was dissuaded by his ministers, who pointed out the use his own supporters made of them. By 1663, there were 82 coffeehouses reported in the City of London—the autonomously governed square mile at the heart of the capital's commercial activities—while in 1739, Henry Maitland recorded 144 in the City and 551 within the entirety of the metropolis—around 1 per 1,000 head of population.[5] What were the reasons for their success?

The first, though for very different reasons than in the Muslim world, was the absence of alcohol in coffeehouses. "Pure" water was too dangerous to drink, so until this point all beverages had been some form of fermented alcohol, usually the weak ale known as "small beer." Coffee, along with tea and chocolate, both of which also made their way onto coffeehouse menus by the 1660s, offered a fundamentally new form of refreshment. Coffee in particular was attractive in that it replaced the gradual diminution of brain function associated with the use of alcohol with an apparent increase in activity caused by the stimulation from caffeine. Furthermore, as long as they were not trading in alcohol, coffeehouses could not be said to infringe upon the licenses of the inns and taverns, and consequently their numbers were not subject to regulation.

Coffeehouses then provided public venues where businessmen might meet and conclude deals not only in the absence of the distractions caused by the presence of other drinkers in the taverns but also with a sense that their faculties were heightened as they traded. Rosee's premises were located in St Michael's Alley, right beside the Royal Exchange, while Edward Lloyd's coffeehouse, founded in 1688, became a center for maritime insurance; Jonathan's and Garraways were used for trading stocks, pre-dating, and subsequently running in parallel to, the more official exchanges until the end of the eighteenth century. Far from being third places away from work, these coffeehouses were essentially workplaces in themselves.

Meanwhile, coffeehouses continued to offer an environment in which well-bred gentlemen of varying ranks could meet without regard to the minutiae of status and engage with each other in conversation and debate. Such discussions might indeed focus on overtly political issues, nurtured in part by periodicals such as *The Tatler* (1709–11) and *The Spectator* (1711–12 and 1714), both written and read principally in the coffeehouse itself. This led Jurgen Habermas to identify the eighteenth-century coffeehouse as one of the first institutions in which bourgeois "public opinion" was shaped and articulated, independent of the state.[6]

Equally, however, the coffeehouse provided a rendezvous for a new social grouping of so-called **virtuosi**, whose inquiring mindset sought stimulation through exposure to exotic novelties and curiosities, irrespective of whether these were the products of the arts and humanities. Scientific research also benefited, including the early work of Isaac Newton; he founded what remains Britain's premier scientific association, the Royal Society, in a London coffeehouse.[7]

Figure 42.1. An engraving by H. O. Neal, 1763, caricaturing coffeehouse regulars as wastrels and swindlers. Satan looks on happily from a perch at upper right, while Britannia swoons helplessly at the left. Library of Congress.

One new element added to the coffeehouse formula was the assertion of authenticity as a form of **marketing**. Rosee, a Greek Orthodox citizen of the Ottoman-controlled port city of Smyrna, used his own image to symbolize this, trading under a sign depicting a caricature of himself known as the Turk's Head. Later, he and his partner, Christopher Bowman, would distribute handbills extolling the virtues of coffee, claiming that, "It is observed in Turkey, where this is generally drunk, that they are not troubled with the Stone, Gout, Dropsie or Scurvey, and their Skins are exceedingly cleer and white."[8] Bowman appears to have made these advertisements available to other coffeehouse owners to promote the beverage, conferring authority upon claims that few were in a position to challenge.

Despite this early flourishing, by 1815 only twelve establishments in the whole of London described themselves as coffeehouses. What went wrong? First, the social inclusiveness of such establishments was strictly limited. For women, the coffeehouse remained principally a workplace, whether as proprietors (many were run by widows), members of the serving staff, or offering other services, such as prostitution in the all-night coffeehouses that doubled as bordellos. Relatively few women patronized coffeehouses in this early period for social purposes, preferring to utilize the tea gardens whose open-air settings made them more acceptable places in which to be seen.

Second, the advent of more specialist workplaces and work tools saw businessmen and traders move out of coffeehouses into offices designed to accommodate the new practices.

Meanwhile as the political upheavals of the seventeenth century subsided, to be replaced by a renewed emphasis on social distinction, social interaction reverted to a more exclusive basis, with many coffeehouses converting to private clubs.

Finally, but most important, coffee never held much appeal for the common people, or "plebs" as they were known at the time. The 551 coffeehouses in the London of 1739 pale in significance besides the more than 8,000 establishments that served alcohol, most famously gin, to the masses. By the mid-eighteenth century, it was common for "coffeehouses" to serve mainly alcohol, with coffee as merely a side offering.[9]

Early American coffeehouses followed much the same trajectory. In 1670 Dorothy Jones was licensed in Boston to sell "coffee and cuchaletto"—that is, chocolate. The first known coffeehouses in what became the United States opened in Boston in the late 1680s or early 1690s. Early American coffeehouses, especially the Green Dragon in Boston, were described as centers of political discussion and even the birthplaces of revolution. But the American colonists, too, preferred alcoholic beverages. Colonial and early republic records are filled with laws and court judgments against drunkards and those who served them. The frequency with which such laws were adopted by colonial and state governments and the multitudinous known violations of these statutes suggest that alcohol intake in early America was not much tempered by the use of coffee.[10]

Attempts by the nineteenth-century temperance movement in Britain and the U.S. to combat alcoholism through the creation of "coffee taverns," frequently located next to taverns or pubs, indicated how difficult it was to adapt the coffeehouse format to suit an industrial age. Although there were over 1,000 coffee taverns in Britain during the 1880s, these were again dwarfed by the more than 100,000 licensed premises.[11] Commercially, these enjoyed little success, not least because the ambiance was far from relaxed, with the zeal of the proprietors to promote abstinence less than conducive to an evening of leisure. Ultimately one of the most significant factors behind the early takeoff of the coffeehouse in England, the absence of alcohol, also proved to be one of the biggest constraints on the format's continued success.

Elsewhere in Europe, different formats evolved for coffee service. In France, a wave of "Turkomania" arose during the sojourn of an emissary from the Ottoman sultan to the French Sun King, who spent the year the king forced him to wait for an appointment by entertaining the French aristocracy in a mocked up coffeehouse.[12] However, attempts by various Armenian traders to build on this event in the manner of Pasqua Rosee in London failed, not least because of battles between the various guilds over who could sell the new beverage, a dispute resolved only in 1676 when this right was given to a combined guild of distillers, brandy merchants, and eau de vie sellers.[13] An Italian immigrant, Francesco Procopio, established a temporary set of coffee rooms at the annual St. Germain fair, serving both coffee and alcohol of various kinds, appealing to a high-class clientele. Ten years later, in 1686, he opened the Café Procope, which still trades on the same site today, proclaiming itself to be "world's oldest restaurant."

It was this **café** format, in which sales of brewed coffee are combined with those of meals and alcohol, which dominated the continent for over three centuries. At first, following the Procope model, such cafés consciously targeted an elite market. These grand venues, with their splendidly furnished rooms, pristine tablecloths, and immaculately attired waiters, spread around Europe, providing suitable refreshment and relaxation to those travelers engaged in the Grand tour. In Italy, for example, Caffè Florian opened on St Mark's Square in Venice in 1720 and the Caffè Greco in Rome in 1760. There was little sense of these being, even in theory, open or democratic establishments, although their respectability ensured they were patronized by women as well as men.

At the other end of the scale were the working men's cafés, whose numbers increased dramatically in France after the revolution of 1789, when a fusion between the eighteenth-century wine merchants and the upper-class café produced a nineteenth-century proletarian version of the latter.[14] Here, customers were not greeted, seated, and served by waiters but interacted informally with the owner and his family. Between the 1860s and the 1880s, almost a quarter of Parisian couples who were married in civil ceremonies chose a café owner as their witness, and it seems that they saw the café as an extension of, rather than separate from, their home. A frequent defense if one partner was accused of beating another in a café was that they believed they were in a domestic setting, so that violence between them was a private affair. Of course, much of that violence was facilitated by alcohol, leading again to the paradox that the café was the primary location in which coffee was taken outside the home, but coffee was rarely the principal source of the café's income.

Similar patterns can be observed across most of Europe, albeit with some local variations. Vienna was twice at the center of a coffeehouse culture—the first time in the 1680s, when Franz Georg Kolschitsky, whose ethnic origins appear as opaque as the stories that he assiduously promoted concerning his role in the relief of the Siege of Vienna, opened the Blue Bottle (*Blaue Flasche*) Coffeehouse.[15] Kolschitsky blended authenticity and adaptability to suit the desires of his customers. On the one hand, he and his staff dressed in Turkish-style clothing, clearly intended to communicate their authority in coffee matters, along the lines of many of his stories. On the other hand, the introduction of milk and cream into the coffee transformed the entire nature of the beverage, making it much more palatable to Austrian tastes.

Vienna's second coffeehouse moment came towards the end of the nineteenth century, when it briefly assumed the mantle of Europe's cultural capital. Many of the leading protagonists in this phenomenon were denizens of Vienna's coffeehouses, where they supposedly whiled away the hours reading newspapers, playing games, and either writing or discussing each other's work. Peter Altenberg (1859–1919), the writer who epitomized this trend, even had his mail delivered to his favorite haunt, the Café Central, whose customers also included the Russian revolutionary Leon Trotsky.

These institutions did sell coffee, time, and space, although in most other respects they were modeled upon the European grand cafés. Some of their patrons, for instance Altenberg, may have been indigent, but they were usually subsidized by their companions; the cafés were used as much for work, or touting for work, as they were for simple socializing. The same could be said of the so-called *flaneurs*, who penned literary works in the sidewalk cafés of nineteenth-century Paris, or the impoverished J. K. Rowling, writing her first Harry Potter book in the warmth of an Edinburgh café.

A further variation worth noting is the *Konditorei*, popular in both Austria and Germany. These are essentially pastry shops that also provide for consumption on the premises, usually accompanied by a hot beverage. They are the out-of-home setting for gatherings of housewives known as the *Kaffeeklatsch*, usually held in mid-afternoon when their husbands are still at work. Again the absence of alcohol was important in making these socially acceptable venues for women. Even today, the leading purveyors of coffee outside the home in Germany are bakery store chains, with over 12,500 outlets in the country.[16]

The evolution of the **espresso** bar over the first half of the twentieth century was as much about a revolution in service as it was about the beverage itself. The advent of what were known as American bars in Europe, in which drinks were simply passed over the counter without the need for a waiter, was complemented in Italy by the development of coffee machines that could prepare an individual cup on demand.[17] Customers downed their beverages standing up. The format fitted the apparent acceleration in the pace of life and proved particularly popular in transport termini and in bars serving the urban bourgeoisie.

It was only during the postwar economic transformation of Italy from an agrarian to an industrial society that this became a mass phenomenon. Small-scale bars opened up to provide migrants with an alternative venue for socializing to the confines of the home or for watching television. Coffee formed an important part of the offer, despite the concurrent presence of alcohol. As one of the cheapest beverages on offer, it constituted the lowest possible price to pay to enjoy the environment of the bar. The lack of a service component kept the prices down, while the spread of high-pressure brewing machines meant that the coffee offered a different sensory experience than the drink made at home did.

Not all of these features survived their transfer abroad. The *Eiscafés* that became an established feature of German high streets in the 1950s combined a coffee offer with an ice-cream one, attracting a predominantly younger clientele who might have gained some experience of espresso coffee culture on their family holidays to Italy.[18] Similarly, the 1950s coffee bars in Britain proved particularly popular with teenagers who felt excluded from pubs but could listen to their music on the café jukebox after the end of the school day. Coffee, though at the heart of the menu, formed relatively little part of the attraction of the English espresso bar, and subsequent generations were seduced by the advent of colorfully furnished quick service chain restaurants and the switch to sweeter lager-style beers at the pub.[19]

American coffeehouses began a slow revival in the twentieth century, originally under the guidance of Italian Americans who opened espresso bars in neighborhoods like San Francisco's North Beach or New York's Greenwich Village. Some of these sites became famous for poetry readings by Beat writers like Allen Ginsberg and for musical performances by artists like Joan Baez and Bob Dylan. Again the coffeehouses suffered once television began to offer stay-at-home entertainment, and diners became the principal purveyors of the cheap, bottomless cup of coffee.

The 1980s college coffeehouse program in the U.S. targeting students who had plenty of time on their hands but who were under the legal drinking age is often cited as having nurtured the **coffee shop** customers of today.[20] However it was the realignment of the service format to fit the rhythms of the working day that accounted for much of the specialty industry's early success in America. The coffee carts that started to appear in Seattle beside queues for the ferries and on the street outside stores such as Nordstrom essentially catered to commuters on their way to work or those who were prepared to pay for a good cup of coffee, as opposed to that provided free in the office itself. Offering a takeaway service was therefore a vital component of the formula.

Subsequently, the transformation in the nature of work itself has favored the continued growth of the coffee shop, not so much as a separate third place but as an extension of the workplace. The decline of manufacturing and the rise of mobile technology mean that the main components of most office jobs—working on the computer screen, communicating on the telephone or via the Internet, and holding face-to-face meetings—can be easily conducted within the coffee shop. The value of these contemporary coffeehouses lies as much as in enhancing, as escaping, productive labor.

Regarding the social roles of coffeehouses, several continuities with previous formats can be observed. The absence of alcohol in most incarnations has turned them into public spaces that feel safe and welcoming to those social groups who, whether by law or convention, have been excluded from drinking establishments. Socializing at the coffee shop avoids the modern-day versions of status anxieties that can operate around issues such as the tidiness of one's home.

Meanwhile for travelers, a coffee shop, and in particular a branded coffee shop, offers the chance for an experience of home away from home: a place where one knows not just how to order one's latte but also how it will taste and where one can be confident that certain facilities, notably bathrooms, will be provided to an acceptable standard. This is the "no surprises" model of American business, as one motel chain used to put it.

So can contemporary coffee shops live up to the requirements of the third place as advocated by Oldenburg or provide the platform for shaping public opinion identified by Habermas? Most contemporary observers suggest not. Bryant Simon, who conducted exhaustive ethnographic research sitting in branches of Starbucks, found that few conversations between strangers arose at the coffee shop.[21] A project analyzing the behavior of Scottish coffee shop customers determined that, as one tabloid newspaper scathingly put it, the reason people go to cafés is to drink coffee.[22]

Yet, having discovered that coffee shops were not hotbeds of political discourse, the Glasgow researchers also suggested that social theorists had underplayed the importance of enjoyment in literally being members of the public.[23] While there was little evidence of intentional conversation between strangers, they identified how moments of haphazard contact—requests to share tables or borrow the newspaper—could lead to conversation if warmly received, while some customers assisted mothers with children in cleaning up spills, making space, and entertaining their children for short periods. Being present during acts of kindness between strangers might, in itself, be much of the point of visiting a coffee shop.

Coffeehouse formats have varied significantly in terms of who is served, but ultimately they have been successful by paying attention to the needs of their clientele in relation to time and space as much as to coffee.[24] That is not to ignore the centrality of coffee in many (though not all) formats where it is presented in a way that justifies pricing appropriate to the experience that accompanies it: low in the case of an Italian espresso bar where it is consumed fast with minimal service, high in a coffee shop where the customer might be planning on working at a table for a few hours.

Expecting coffeehouses to serve as third places may be loading too much expectation onto their powers of social integration, yet at the same time misses the point that they can serve as extensions of, and even substitutes for, the home and the workplace. Ultimately, patronizing a coffeehouse is about sharing a human experience: as Asaf Bar-Tura has recently put it, people come to coffee shops "to be around other people, without actually having anything to do with them."[25] This may not match up to Oldenburg's ideal, but it constitutes an extremely powerful business opportunity.

NOTES

1. Roy Oldenburg, *The Great Good Place* (New York: Marlowe, 1997), 16.
2. Ralph S. Hattox, *Coffee and Coffeehouses: The Origins of a Social Beverage in the Medieval Near East* (Seattle: University of Washington Press, 1985).
3. The two best studies of the English coffeehouse are Markman Ellis, *The Coffeehouse: A Cultural History* (London: Weidenfeld & Nicolson, 2004), and Brian Cowan, *The Social Life of Coffee: The Emergence of the British Coffeehouse* (New Haven, CT: Yale University Press, 2005).
4. The only evidence to support this claim comes from a memoir written nearly twenty years later; see Ellis, *Coffeehouse*, 30.
5. Ellis, *Coffeehouse*, 172–73.

6. Jurgen Habermas, *The Structural Transformation of the Public Sphere*, trans. Thomas Burger (Cambridge, MA: MIT Press, 1989).

7. Cowan, *Social Life of Coffee*, 10–13, sets out his conception of the virtuoso mindset.

8. Anon., *The Vertue of the Coffee Drink*. 1656? The original is in the British Library: available from *Early English Books Online* at http://gateway.proquest.com.

9. Antony Clayton, *London's Coffeehouses* (London: Historical Publications, 2003), 103–7.

10. See Sharon V. Salinger, *Taverns and Drinking in Early America* (Baltimore: Johns Hopkins University Press, 2002).

11. Clayton, *London's Coffeehouses*, 131.

12. Julia Anne Landweber, "Turkish Delight: The Eighteenth Century Market in Turqueries and the Commercialization of Identity in France," in *Proceedings of the Annual Meeting of the Western Society for French History* 30 (2004): 202–11.

13. Ellis, *Coffeehouse*, 80–83.

14. See W. Scott Haine, *The World of the Paris Café* (Baltimore: Johns Hopkins University Press, 1996).

15. On both the first and second Viennese coffee moments, see Harold B Segel, *The Vienna Coffeehouse Wits 1890–1938*, trans. Harold B. Segel (West Lafayette, IN: Purdue University Press, 1993).

16. Allegra Study Tour, European Coffee Symposium, Berlin, 2011.

17. Jonathan Morris, "Making Italian espresso, making espresso Italian," *Food and History* 8, no. 2 (2010).

18. Patrick Bernhard, "La Pizza sul Reno: Per una storia della cucina e della gastronomia italiane in Germania nel XX secolo." *Memoria e Ricerca* 23 (2006): 66.

19. Clayton, *London's Coffeehouses*, 145–67, provides an account of this era.

20. Telephone interview with Ted Lingle, then executive director of the SCAA, December 20, 2004.

21. Bryant Simon, *Everything but the Coffee: Learning about America from Starbucks* (Berkeley: University of California Press, 2009), 94–118.

22. Tony Bonnici, "£140k on Why We Go to Café," *The Sun*, November 19, 2005.

23. Eric Laurier and Chris Philo, "The Cappuccino Community: Cafés and Civic Life in the Contemporary City," Final Report: ESRC Research Project, R000239797, 2005, 17. Download from http://web2.ges.gla.ac.uk/~elaurier/cafesite/texts/final_cappuccino.pdf.

24. See Robert W. Thurston, "Reflections on Coffee's Social Life: New and Old Ideas on Coffee Bars, Social Interaction and the 'Third Place,'" *Roast Magazine*, May/June 2012.

25. Asaf Bar-Tura, "The Coffeehouse as a Public Sphere: Brewing Social Change," in *Coffee: Philosophy for Everyone: Grounds for Debate*, ed. Scott F. Parker and Michael W. Austin (Chichester, UK: Wiley Blackwell, 2011), 96.

43

Why Americans Drink Coffee

The Boston Tea Party or Brazilian Slavery?

Steven Topik and Michelle Craig McDonald

On the evening of December 16, 1773, a group of longshoremen, smugglers, and other Sons of Liberty poorly disguised as Narragansett Indians marched down Griffin's Wharf in Boston Harbor. There they smashed open 342 casks on the British ships *Dartmouth, Beaver,* and *Eleanour* and dumped 45 tons of tea into the bay. Remembered as the Boston Tea Party, this act was a catalyst of the American independence movement. It is also remembered in a somewhat less heroic light as the event that converted North Americans from tea sippers to coffee drinkers.

Coffee has played an important role in the creation of American national identity, symbolizing independence from British authority and culture. But as with many stories key to national identity, myth making is also involved.[1] After Boston, the narrative continues, democratic pioneers spread the habit westward as the new nation stretched to meet its destiny. In the nineteenth century, coffee was viewed as quintessentially American, just as tea was British or Chinese, beer German, and wine French. The United States became the world's largest consumer of coffee by the middle of the nineteenth century and went on to master and reshape the industry.[2] So runs the triumphalist version.

This chapter argues that the real story is not so pretty or inspiring. Coffee's success in the United States derived more from slavery and the end of European colonialism in the Caribbean and in Brazil than it did from patriotic fervor or a sense of new nationhood. In other words, coffee, the symbol of democratic culture, bourgeois sociability, and capitalist energy in the U.S., succeeded because of faraway events: the Haitian Revolution and, more important, the unprecedented expansion of Brazil's slave-driven agriculture.

The United States certainly played a crucial role in the transformation of coffee from luxury beverage in the seventeenth century to mass consumer drink by the mid-nineteenth century. This metamorphosis reinforced coffee's egalitarian and democratic symbolic significance to eighteenth- and nineteenth-century pamphleteers and chroniclers such as Thomas Paine, Domingo Faustino Sarmiento, Alexis de Tocqueville, and other purveyors of the North American story of equality.[3] But political tracts and travelers' accounts are only one way to gauge coffee's increasing importance in American life. Merchant account books also document coffee sales to mariners, brewers, laborers, and widows by the 1760s, though this trade was not especially large before independence. Afterward, however, elite Boston and Philadelphia women like

Abigail Adams and Elizabeth Drinker described its popularity among the well-to-do in the 1780s and 1790s, and even slaves received coffee as payment for overwork in Virginia iron works.[4] So common did it become to find coffee pots and cups on American tables that within years of independence, European visitors considered the commodity an indelible part of the new nation's identity. "Our supper was rather scanty," wrote François Jean Chastellux, a French traveler to Virginia in 1787, "but our breakfast the next morning was better . . . we are perfectly reconciled to this American custom of drinking coffee."[5]

By the mid-nineteenth century, the United States led global coffee importation, although the commodity's overseas pedigree was usually erased. Domestic coffee roasters chose American landscapes or the familiar face of Uncle Sam over exotic or foreign imagery for their trade cards once **branding** began after the Civil War.[6] On the rare occasions advertisements divulged provenance or **origin**, they mentioned Java or Mocha as sites of export, which held historical appeal and were more highly prized in the global market. Indeed, on the western frontier, coffee was known as "jamoca," a combination of "java" (Indonesia) and "mocha" (Yemen), although nearly all of it in fact came from Latin America.[7] Overall, however, coffee became divorced from its origins in the nineteenth-century U.S.—geographically sanitized—in the campaign to supplant tea and cider as the all-American drinks.

War also boosted coffee's assimilation into American daily life. During the Civil War, Union troops considered coffee necessary for victory. General William Sherman called it "the essential element of the ration," ordering that coffee and sugar "be carried along, even at the expense of bread, for which there are many substitutes."[8] By the early twentieth century, coffee was renamed "cup of Joe." Why exactly is disputed, but the likely reason was to honor coffee's close identification with "G.I. Joe" in World Wars I and II and in recognition of its contributions to America's overseas efforts. The nickname also underscores coffee's common touch, since "Joe" in the U.S. often signifies the ordinary fellow.[9] Coffee became an American custom, for civilians and the military, elite and proletarian, male and female alike. Today, people around the globe drink coffee partly as a sign of Americanism and modernism. Yet coffee drinking was hardly predestined in the British North American colonies, and its unexpected, centuries-long path to dominance says much about both U.S. national identity and Brazil's key part in the story.

COFFEE AND THE BOSTON TEA PARTY

America's interest in coffee began almost as early as colonization itself. John Smith, one of England's earliest settlers in Virginia, was among the first people to describe "coffa" or "coava" in English. He wrote of it in his travel accounts from Turkey fourteen years before he helped found Jamestown in 1607 and almost twenty years before England's first **coffeehouse** opened.[10] But it is doubtful that Smith brought coffee across the Atlantic. Whenever it arrived, interest grew slowly, and at the end of the seventeenth century coffeehouses still clustered in port cities, limiting opportunities of rural Americans to participate in public consumption, and the high cost curbed its incursion into private homes. William Penn complained in 1683 that British taxing and transport policies had raised the price of coffee to a stunning 18 shillings and 9 pence per pound, well beyond the means of most colonial families. Although the price of coffee dropped over the next several decades, coffee consumption remained low, at about one-eighteenth of a pound per capita by 1783. That was just enough to brew a few cups of coffee per person annually.[11]

Both popular and scholarly histories point to the Boston Tea Party as the watershed event that forever changed America's relationship to coffee. "It is sufficient here to refer to the climax of agitation against the fateful tea tax," observed William Ukers, longtime editor of *The Tea and Coffee Journal*, "because it is undoubtedly responsible for our becoming a nation of coffee drinkers instead of tea drinkers, like the English." The Boston Tea Party of 1773, he argued, left Americans "with a prenatal disinclination for tea" and "caused coffee to be crowned 'king of the American breakfast table" and the sovereign drink of the American people."[12] Recent popular coffee studies agree.[13] One account even proposes that "European colonialism seemed to dictate where coffee was cultivated and drunk," but, "in the case of the United States, it was the end of colonialism, *dramatically reflected in the Boston Tea Party* [italics added by authors], that marked its rise to prominence."[14] Finally, gender historians link coffee drinking to grassroots tea boycotts to demonstrate women's participation in both consumer culture and in U.S. politics; these women created "Republican Motherhood" in the 1780s, an ideology that saw women as pivotal vehicles for the transmission of social norms and democratic ideas to the next generation of American citizens.[15]

Other sources seem at first to support these interpretations. Certainly revolutionary leaders such as Paul Revere, Samuel Adams, and John Adams and patriotic groups like the Sons of Liberty used the Green Dragon coffeehouse (also called a tavern) in Boston and New York's Merchants' Coffee House to protest the Stamp and Townsend Acts.[16] And coffee's patriotic potential was not limited to cities. During the summer of 1774, John Adams wrote that when he asked an innkeeper, "Is it lawful . . . for a weary Traveller to refresh himself with a Dish of Tea, providing it has been honestly smuggled, or paid no Duties?" the proprietress replied, "No sir . . . we have renounced all Tea in this Place. I can't make tea . . . but [can] make you Coffee."[17] Adams' recollection demonstrates that some Americans, in this case a rural innkeeper and a representative of the Continental Congress, identified coffee with national ideas of freedom.

But the association was short-lived. The 1765 and 1769 embargoes of British goods shipped to America focused on England, America's source of tea, and Ireland. But a third intercolonial boycott in 1774, beginning just months after Adams's Massachusetts excursion, included the British Caribbean, America's chief coffee supplier. Coffee, in other words, became as politically charged as tea. Some colonial representatives pleaded that banning West Indian trade "must produce a national Bankruptcy," but their arguments received short shrift from those who considered Caribbean commodities like coffee "intoxicating poisons and needless luxuries" that should be sunk at sea "rather than [brought] ashore."[18] By 1777, even Adams changed his mind about coffee, writing to his wife, Abigail: "I hope the females will leave off their attachment to coffee. I assure you, the best families in this place have left off in a great measure the use of West India goods. We must bring ourselves to live upon the produce of our own country."[19] Coffee, in other words, was still considered an international drink that competed with beverages made from domestically grown trees, for example apple cider. So how did coffee again become nativized?

COFFEE AS THE DRINK OF DIPLOMATS

Before the 1774 boycott, most North Americans' coffee came from Britain's colonies in Jamaica, Grenada, Saint Vincent, and Dominica. But in 1783 Parliament banned shipments of British colonial produce in U.S. vessels, precisely when North American interest in the commodity was booming.[20] Prerevolutionary coffee imports peaked at just over $1 million in

1774, but British West Indian coffee alone entering the U.S. was worth $1,480,000 per annum 1802–04, while coffee imports from the rest of the world topped $8 million.[21]

It turns out that those imports were not just to slake North American thirst. Over half of America's coffee imports left shortly after they arrived. Commerce had moved between Britain's mainland American colonies during the colonial period, but America's re-export trade by 1800 was international. Initially, much of these re-exports went to Amsterdam, Paris, and London, but after 1790 U.S. traders made new inroads into Germany, Italy, and even Russia, beginning the association of America and coffee in the minds of some European consumers. Because tropical goods generally, and coffee especially, were important to American interests, U.S. access to the West Indies was a serious concern.

Merchants and farmers bitterly debated the pros and cons of tariffs for goods that competed with American manufactures, but more often they agreed on trade concessions for commodities America did not produce. Tea and coffee figured prominently in these discussions since congressional delegates recognized that both "enter largely into the consumption of the country, and have become articles of necessity to all classes."[22] In 1774 they created a three-man European Commission—John Jay, John Adams, and Benjamin Franklin—to oversee negotiations and authorize treaties with several European nations and the Barbary Coast.[23] The "plan of treaties" would have been ambitious for any nation. With only a small army and no formal navy, the U.S. could not achieve its objectives militarily. Instead, Congress equipped its European commissioners with the strongest weapon at its disposal, American purchasing power, and declared that nations refusing trade treaties with the United States would face discriminatory tariffs and market restrictions. During the commission's first two years, however, only Prussia agreed to a treaty based on the model of free trade.[24]

Frustrated as 1785 drew to a close, America's European commissioners found themselves haggling with countries like Austria that offered no prospects of tropical goods profits. This situation prompted Jefferson and his colleagues to promote a preferential treaty with France early in 1786, a move that aligned the United States with the only military force able to challenge Britain.[25] "It will be a strong link of connection," Jefferson wrote, "the more [so] with the only nation on earth on whom we can solidly rely for assistance till we stand on our own legs."[26] Moreover, it gave U.S. importers access to the French Caribbean colonies, especially Saint Domingue (later Haiti), the leading producer of sugars and coffee in the Caribbean since the early eighteenth century.

American merchants rallied behind Jefferson's plan. In October 1786, the French agreed to a series of trade concessions, including use of American ships and lowered tariffs in both France and the French Antilles.[27] The shift to French coffee suppliers was obvious, providing more than three-quarters of North America's coffee by 1791.[28] The realignment of trade partners was reinforced because Britain continued to officially exclude American ships from its Caribbean colonies. But the British discovered that intentions alone were insufficient: war in Europe undermined the Royal Navy's ability to patrol the region.[29] U.S. ships thereby gained much greater freedom of movement. American neutrality was more than a diplomatic objective; it had been essential to the nation's future commercial prosperity ever since the first overtures of the European Commission.[30] The newfound maritime opportunity led to greater investment in specific commodities: "The consumption of coffee, sugar, and other West India productions increases fast in the north of Europe," far-sighted Silas Deane correctly told Congress in August 1776.[31]

But without trade agreements, Americans could not continue or expand their budding business with the lucrative Caribbean colonies; and without neutral shipping they would be unable to bring tropical produce to their consumers—at a time when war between Britain and France provided prime opportunities for Americans to enter European markets for goods whose prices were skyrocketing.[32] With neutrality and the trade agreements, on the other hand, the former thirteen colonies' future was much rosier. As one savvy trader noted in a precocious definition of what came to be known as neocolonialism, America would accrue "all of the benefits of colonization without the administration and expense."[33] So while the nascent nation expanded its continental territory westward, it also extended its commercial influence southward. The re-export trade, with coffee as its flagship product, became essential to the national economy. Political advocates of free trade portrayed re-export merchants as "patriots" whose trade was "a necessary link in the chain of our society and of our place in the world."[34] Re-exportation of foreign-grown coffee, like coffee drinking in the 1770s, became a patriotic act that inspired national and international attention.

COFFEE AND SLAVERY

Patriotic Americans tended to conflate independence and freedom just as they confused commercial and civil liberties. **Slavery**, however, posed the biggest challenge to coffee's association with American freedom. Throughout the eighteenth and nineteenth centuries, Caribbean and Latin American slaves produced most of the coffee Americans drank. Even East Indian coffee laborers, while not technically enslaved, could hardly be called free.[35] At times, the relationship was even more direct—some coffee importers traded in slaves as well and some coffeehouses doubled as slave markets. Both British and American emancipationists recognized the powerful cultural connections between commodities and the labor that produced them in their boycotts of slave-produced sugar; but coffee, like tobacco and cotton, faced far less resistance.[36] By 1800, the cost of a coffee embargo would have been too high for America. The new nation made more from the re-export of coffee overseas than from re-exports of tea, sugar, and molasses combined; coffee represented 10 percent of all U.S. trade income and 25 percent of its re-export income, high figures for a commodity that North America did not produce itself.[37]

Were everyday North Americans aware of how their coffee was produced? Travel narratives, a popular eighteenth- and early nineteenth-century literary genre, included several accounts of coffee plantation slavery. This literature suggests that Americans knew where and how their coffee was produced, but little public backlash occurred.[38] A few writers noted with irony the duplicity of abolitionists' boycotts of slave-produced sugar while consumption of other slave products continued apace. "Oh, they say, do not use the polluted thing; beware of sweetening your coffee with slave-grown sugar," wrote Reverend Robert Burns, a member of Glasgow Young Man's Free Trade Association. But how could "slave-grown tobacco, cotton, and coffee" be acceptable, he reasoned, "while slave-grown sugar must be productive of moral disease?"[39] Most writers, however, remained silent. In fact, public reaction to the incongruity of coffee's connotations of freedom and its origins in slavery remained largely unexplored in public debate before 1848, when protests came not from socially conscientious American consumers but from disgruntled British planters. These men, forced to use nonslave labor after Britain abolished slavery in 1838, protested the prospect of competing for the American market with slave-produced coffee from Brazil.[40] American reactions, however, remained tepid; an 1859 *New York Times* article noted only that coffee, along with some other tropical goods, were "necessaries of life" for the "northern latitudes which embrace the largest civilized portions of the human race"; its unfree origins, however, were a necessity of the trade.[41]

In reality, French, rather than British, Caribbean colonies had supplied most of America's coffee needs for decades by the 1860s. In French Saint Domingue, the principal exporter of coffee to the U.S. until 1803, "gens de couleur" (free people of color) played a large role in the colony's coffee industry, owning one-third of the plantation property and one-quarter of the slaves in Saint Domingue in 1789.[42] Saint Domingue's place in American commerce dramatically declined, however, after Toussaint l'Ouverture, himself a former slave and a failed coffee grove owner, led revolutionary forces against French colonial troops.[43] St. Domingue, renamed Haiti, became the second European colony in the Americas to gain independence and the first to abolish slavery. Rather than applaud this double freedom, the United States government refused to recognize Haiti's independence or to send an ambassador to the new nation until 1862.[44] America's domestic north-south sectional conflict shaped its international commercial and diplomatic policy toward the former colony, leading the federal government to encourage coffee importation from slave-rich Brazil rather than from emancipated and free Haiti.

Brazil did not win its preferred position easily. The most obvious substitute for Haiti was Cuba. Hundreds of French planters fled Haiti for Cuba, bringing with them their slaves and coffee-planting knowledge. Spanish colonial masters loosened their control of foreign trade and slave imports as coffee prices shot up in response to Haiti's conflagration. Indeed, in the first decades of the nineteenth century coffee was a more attractive investment than sugar, and Cuba's coffee exports went primarily to the United States rather than to the distant Spanish motherland.[45] Americans, who coveted the rich, fertile Cuban soil, even began investing in coffee plantations on the island. However, nature, in the form of violent hurricanes in 1842, 1844, and 1846, destructive civil wars in 1868, 1878, and 1880, and the astounding success of sugar in the burgeoning U.S. market reduced Cuban coffee to such a minor role that by the end of the century the island was importing coffee from Puerto Rico.[46] In Cuba, land and slaves formerly used for coffee cultivation were turned to sugar.[47] In Brazil the opposite occurred as sugar lands, capital, and slaves were channeled into coffee production. With assistance from nature and war, the swelling U.S. market for coffee and sugar had opposite consequences for Brazil and Cuba.

COFFEE BECOMES AMERICANIZED

Eighteenth-century tea boycotts whet North Americans' appetite for coffee, but did not guarantee that the U.S. would become known as a nation of coffee drinkers. Although colonists briefly abandoned tea drinking, they soon returned to importing it from China. In 1859, the U.S. imported more than 29 million pounds of tea; by 1870 the figure was 47 million pounds and by 1881 more than 81 million pounds. That was more than a pound per capita. True, Americans imported 455 million pounds of coffee in 1881, but tea imports had been growing, not shrinking. Moreover, some traders estimated that four times as much ground coffee as tea leaves was needed to produce the same amount of beverage.[48] Since the volume of coffee imports was 5.5 times that of tea imports, actual consumption of coffee and of tea was probably quite similar in 1881. Independent Americans drank far more tea than colonial Americans had. Indeed, most coffee roasters, such as Chase & Sanborn and Folgers, advertised tea as much as coffee. Only in 1890 did nationalists regularly begin to proclaim coffee "the national beverage" of the United States, arguing that the U.S. had set aside tea definitively and become a "coffee loving country."[49]

For international merchants, the issue had been how much coffee and tea Americans imported, not how much they drank; here coffee towered over tea. The U.S. imported one-third of the world's coffee in the 1880s as annual per capita consumption ballooned from under one pound at independence to nine pounds by 1882. Since the population surged from under 4 million to 50 million during that century, total coffee consumption increased over one hundred fold. Coffee's supremacy over tea would greatly widen as the twentieth century progressed.

If the true divide in the hot beverage war came well after independence, however, the Boston Tea Party disappears as the critical event giving birth to Americans' coffee addiction. What then explains coffee's triumph in the largest coffee-consuming country in the world? The answer is, as Frank Sinatra would sing a half century later, they had an awful lot of coffee in Brazil. But that abundance was not natural or inevitable. Brazilians stepped up coffee production in large measure in response to growing U.S. consumption. Despite the staggering burst of demand in the U.S., its import price in the U.S. during the nineteenth century averaged about one-half of what it had been at Brazil's independence in 1821. By 1906, when Brazil exported almost 90 percent of the world's coffee by volume, the price had fallen to one-third of the 1821 price.[50] Brazilians used their near-monopoly position to vertiginously expand foreign consumption abroad rather than to extort monopoly rents from foreign consumers. Supply-driven demand meant that per capita consumption in the U.S. continued to grow, by over 50 percent between 1870 and 1900, then reaching 13.3 pounds in 1902.[51] The primary reason for coffee's growth was Brazil's ability to increase production without increasing price. The "forest rent" of vast, fertile little-cultivated lands; the sweat of Africans, Afro-Brazilians, and then southern European immigrants; and Brazilian entrepreneurs, all contributed to the historic coffee crops once the countryside was cleared and trees planted.

In 1900 America was the world's greatest coffee market, and coffee the third most important internationally traded commodity. Caribbean trading had created the necessary preconditions to spread and deepen the coffee drinking habit, but the monumental and unprecedented expansion of American coffee drinking in the nineteenth century depended on two additional developments: the drink had to be Americanized, and it had to become a mass beverage.

Coffee's Americanization became blatant in the late nineteenth and early twentieth centuries. Arbuckles Coffee included pictorial histories of Britain's thirteen North American colonies on the back of their coffee brewing instructions. Schnull-Krag & Co. tacitly promoted American coffee by denigrating non-American coffees, damning with faint praise, for example, "fine" but "expensive" Java coffee. Thomas Wood & Co. went further still, graphically demonstrating the seller's support of American expansionism and simultaneous de-exoticization of Puerto Rico, Hawaii, and Manila. According to the Wood advertisements, these sites now fell under the umbrella of Uncle Sam as "his own possessions."[52]

THEY HAVE AN AWFUL LOT OF COFFEE IN BRAZIL

Coffee's development as a Brazilian export was not inevitable and not divinely foreordained simply because "Deus é Brasileiro," God is Brazilian. Rather, by the second half of the nineteenth century, the fortuitous combination of political independence of ex-colonies Brazil and the United States, the disastrous results of Haiti's struggles for freedom, mounting Brazilian coffee production, and swelling consumption at home impelled North Americans to drink more coffee than anyone else in the world.

Coffee was treated differently than sugar and rubber in the nineteenth-century age of empire because its low technological demands meant that an independent former colony, Brazil, could begin producing on an unprecedented scale. Cheap fertile virgin land and abundant and relatively inexpensive slave labor, owing to the proximity of Africa, allowed Brazil to cause world coffee prices to plummet after 1820 and remain low until the last quarter of the century. This trend in turn created supply-induced demand.

Brazilian production not only largely satisfied growing world demand but Brazilians stimulated and transformed the place of coffee on overseas tables. The dependency view of agricultural producers as providers of brute labor power, willingly serving up their produce to the thirsty metropolitan buyers, the masters of the trade, misrepresents the relationship. Brazilians, either native born or immigrants from Africa or Portugal, developed new production techniques, discovered productive **cultivars**, constructed an elaborate transportation network in a geographically unpromising setting, and developed market standards and effective financial instruments. Brazilians were able to out-produce all European colonial growers. Brazil, which produced over half the world's coffee in 1850, accounted for about 80 percent of the subsequent global expansion.[53] By 1906, Brazilians produced almost five times as much as the rest of the world combined.

To give the proponents of dependence theory their due, Brazilians were also successful in the nineteenth century because of British dominance in the form of inexpensive and reliable shipping and insurance, loans, infrastructure investments, and protection of sea routes.[54] So while the tea-drinking British did not export or import much coffee from their own colonies by the mid-nineteenth century, they exported and re-exported a lot of coffee from Brazil. Much of it went to their former North American colonies. Thus the British were partially responsible for North Americans' coffee habit, not because of the stamp tax on tea but because of their role in commerce, finance, and transport of the Brazil-U.S. trade.

The explosion of coffee in the nineteenth century was not brought about by new production methods.[55] Until the last quarter of the century, cultivating, harvesting, and processing continued to be done manually by slave labor, of the sort previously used for sugar, by French coffee planters on the African island of Reunion, and on a greater scale for coffee in Haiti. Indeed, these practices were known at the time as the "West Indian" cultivation system. But the enormity of some Brazilian plantations and industrial-scale picking, which lowered both the cost and the quality of coffee, were new.

Improvements in the late nineteenth-century industry, such as a growing demand for knowledge and industrial capital, were more evident in transportation than in cultivation. While railroads did not dramatically reduce cargo costs, they did help improve the quality of coffee at port. More important, cheaper, more fertile lands became accessible in the interior, and ever larger amounts of the harvest could be brought to market faster, reducing interest charges on working capital. In other words, the railroads, some of which pioneered impressive engineering feats to climb the steep escarpments, allowed Brazilians to take advantage of their country's vastness. They thereby escaped the geographic trap that prevented earlier, smaller producers, for instance Yemen and Martinique, from qualitatively transforming the world market and taking advantage of economies of scale. The tremendous volume of low-priced Brazilian coffee making its way to international ports on railroad tracks expanded and reconfigured the world market. The effect was particularly noticeable in the United States.

Relations between the U.S. and Brazil grew stronger once American merchants and shippers came to dominate the Atlantic slave trade after His Majesty's government outlawed British involvement in 1807. American slavers integrated Brazil and Africa into a U.S.-based triangular

Figure 43.1.   Illustration from *Frank Leslie's Illustrated Newspaper*, April 24, 1875.

trade after Brazilian independence in 1822. A spurt in commercial relations between newly "free" Brazil and the recently "freed" United States was based mostly on the flourishing slave trade. Kenneth Maxwell wrote of this apparent paradox that, "Those who were the strongest supporters of laissez faire when it meant the removal of the regulatory functions of the state [particularly free trade] were also most committed to the slave trade and slavery."[56] This is really not so strange. Southern planters in the U.S. held the same position until the Civil War forced them to relinquish it and their slaves. Brazil had long been the world's leading importer of African slaves, first via the Portuguese, then Dutch, Angolan, Brazilian, and British slavers. American slave traders, forbidden from importing into the United States after 1808, benefited from anti-slavery campaigns that hindered British competition in the chattel trade. The slave trade was an exception to the otherwise warm commercial relations between the U.S. and the UK. Brazilian customs laws awarded British shippers of non-human goods preferential treatment, to the extent that Brazil was considered a central part of the UK's "informal empire" or "a virtual British protectorate."[57] Still, North American merchantmen carried some of the greatest annual slave importations into Brazil until the British navy terminated the Atlantic slave trade in 1850.[58] Until then, ships brought trade goods to Africa, where slaves bound for Brazil filled the holds. In Rio the vessels replaced the Africans with coffee for the U.S. market. Slaves were transmuted into coffee in this trans-Atlantic sleight-of-hand.

The role of the U.S. merchant marine in the Brazil trade, and in the Atlantic in general, declined with the prohibition of the Atlantic slave trade. American investors turned to the home market and developed the West as railroads reached ever further towards the Pacific. But Americans' reorientation from the Atlantic to the western frontier did not thwart their budding romance with coffee. Brazil's coffee exports jumped 75-fold by volume between independence in 1822 and 1899 as Brazilians responded to—and stimulated—new opportunities and as British bottoms took the place of Yankee ships. British moralists who subdued the lucrative transoceanic commerce in humans in the first part of the 1800s were not able to convince their countrymen to forgo profiting from a slave-grown crop, an industry much larger after 1850 than before. Given Britain's new reliance on Indian tea grown under dubious circumstances, the lack of protest in the UK about slave labor in coffee is not surprising. Brazilian coffee exports, three-quarters of which went to the United States, eclipsed sugar. They always constituted over 40 percent of Brazil's exports after 1830, reaching 50 to 70 percent by the 1870s.[59] Thus the growing capitalist economy of the United States enabled the rise of scores of slave baronies in Brazil.

CONCLUSION

National identity through consumption has long been closely related to international trade networks, and coffee was clearly an important commodity in America's economy. But its historical and social development reveals larger cultural connotations that need to be reconsidered. Coffee was a democratic drink in the U.S. insofar as working people had it regularly at meals. But its ties to liberty and equality are tenuous if not disingenuous when we take into account its provenance. The patriotic American drink became widely available because slaves in the Caribbean colonies and then in Brazil sweated in the hot fields. Although coffee contributed to the consolidation of Brazilian independence, it also perpetuated that society's dependence on slavery until it became the last country in the hemisphere to emancipate slaves, in 1888. American purveyors had figuratively ended slavery earlier through the magic of publicity and labeling. They erased coffee's Janus face by recasting the commodity as an all-American consumable; American importers, consumers, and government policy paid little attention to the labor form or U.S. imperialist policies that brought them their morning wake-up call. The average Joe performed his (and her) Americanness daily as consumer but rarely looked beyond the label and the border to appreciate coffee's international drama. By the late nineteenth century, the "literary men about town, and strangers of distinction," wrote one society columnist, "discuss the latest topics of the world and day" over "the fumes of coffee, and a slice of French rolls." The news and food still had international cachet, but coffee had become thoroughly domesticated.[60] The United States' direct contributions to the world of coffee were democratic: the coffee break, the cafeteria, instant coffee. But coffee in America long depended on unfree institutions.

Brazil's role in making the United States the world's coffee capital has been obscured in both countries. The South American giant has received neither credit nor blame for converting Americans to the coffee habit and American roasters to a dominant world position. Although the price of Rio Number 7 and then of Santos Number 4 were the industry standard by the late nineteenth century, coffee packaged in the U.S. rarely bore Brazil's name. In 1877 Brazil's consul general to the United States, Salvador de Mendonça, complained that "it is a generally recognized fact that the classification of Brazilian coffees in this market is done to the detriment of the Brazilian product, which is sold in the spot market according to how it is imported, but changes its denomination when it enters retail where it soon takes on the classification of Java or Mocha."[61] Upon occasion Brazil's role drew more attention, for example during the valorizations (export price fixing) of coffee between 1906 and 1929. In 1908 Senator George Norris protested that "Other monopolies levy their tribute but this monster

[Brazilian valorization coffee] is a daily uninvited guest at every breakfast table in the land."[62] The role of Brazilian coffee was also acknowledged during the world wars when coffee was deemed a national strategic necessity and Frank Sinatra sang his caffeinated samba. But Brazilian growers failed to create a brand for Brazilian coffee or a logo like Colombia's Juan Valdez.

Today, wandering through the coffee aisle of a supermarket, you will see a United Nations of producers: Colombia, Costa Rica, Honduras, Peru, Java, Ethiopia, even Bolivia and New Guinea. But Brazil will be almost invisible, even though it still is by far the world's largest producer of coffee.

It is time that Brazil and the United States took their rightful place in shaping world history. Coffee provides a macro lens for understanding both nations' international connections across the globe and over time as well as coffee's own duplicitous past. Coffee is more than just a drink or a commodity. It is a contested story about origins whose narrative is deeply entwined with its lore and with consumer identities.

NOTES

This is a revised version of a paper presented at the Boston Area Latin American History Workshop and the Harvard Brazil Studies Workshop at Harvard, February 6, 2008. Part of it was previously published as "Culture and Consumption: National Drinks and National Identity in the Atlantic World," in *Food and Globalization: Consumption, Markets and Politics in the Modern World*, ed. F. Trentmann and A. Neutzenadel (New York: Berg, 2008), 109–27.

1. See, for example, E. Hobsbawm, "Introduction: Inventing Traditions" in *The Invention of Tradition*, ed. E. Hobsbawm and T. Ranger (Cambridge: Cambridge University Press, 1983).

2. The United States is still today the world's largest total consumer of coffee, and three of the world's largest global coffee corporations are American: Philip Morris, Smucker's, and Sara Lee, as Starbucks spreads the coffeehouse habit to ever more parts of the world.

3. J. H. St. John de Crèvecoeur, *Letters from an American Farmer*, 1793; D. F. Sarmiento, *Estados Unidos*, 1849–51; A. de Tocqueville, *Democracy in America*, 1840; T. Paine, *The American Crisis*, 1776.

4. B. Mifflin and S. Massey, Ledger, 1760–1763, Historical Society of Pennsylvania, 1 volume, Amb. #9112; A. Adams to J. Adams, July 5, 1775, Adams Family Papers, Massachusetts Historical Society; E. Forman Crane et al. (eds.) *The Diary of Elizabeth Drinker*, 3 vols. (Boston: Northeastern University Press, 1991) 3: 1081, 1081n, and 2016; C. B. Dew, *Bond of Iron: Master and Slave at Buffalo Forge* (New York: Norton, 1994), 114.

5. Marquis de François Jean Chastellux, *Travels in North America*, 2 vols, 1787, 2:52.

6. See the Warshaw Collection and Hills Brothers archives in the Museum of American History at the Smithsonian in Washington, DC, for examples of nineteenth-century trade cards. Also see F. Fulgate, *Arbuckles: The Coffee That Won the West* (El Paso: Texas Western Press, 1994), 117–37.

7. Fulgate, *Arbuckles*, 68; J. Rischbieter, "Globalizing Consumption: Coffee Trade and Consumption in Imperial Germany," delivered at the conference Food and Globalization: Markets, Migration, and Politics in Transnational Perspective, Leipzig, Germany, September 2005. For U.S. ads, see *The Tea and Coffee Journal* and *The Spice Mill*. For the appearance of foreign coffee workers in commercials see M. Seigel, *Uneven Encounters: Making Race and Nation in Brazil and the United States* (Durham, NC: Duke University Press, 2009), 13–66; P. Munoz, "Juan Valdez: The Story of 100% Colombian Coffee," unpublished paper, University of California Irvine (Winter 2006); and M. C. McDonald, "The Real Juan Valdez: Opportunities and Impoverishment in Global Coffee," Harvard Business School Working Paper Series, No. 9-806-041 (November 2005): 1–23.

8. W. T. Sherman, *Memoirs of General W. T. Sherman*, Rpt. 1990, 882. We thank Madeleine Foote for this quote.

9. Oxford English Dictionary Online, "Joe" 5a.; BBC (British Broadcasting Company),online "h2g2" "A Cup of Joe," www.bbc.co.uk/dna/h2g2/A1300410.

10. Smith's iconic status in U.S. history continues as can be seen in D. Hoobler and T. Hoobler, *Captain John Smith: Jamestown and the Birth of the American Dream* (Hoboken, NJ: Wiley, 2006).

11. F. B. Thurber, *Coffee, From Plantation to Cup* (1881), 212. By contrast, tea imports at the time were only one-twelfth a pound per capita.

12. W. Ukers, *All About Coffee*, reprint (Avon, MA: Adams Media, 2012),102–3; W. Ukers, *All About Tea*, vol.1 (New York: The Tea and Coffee Trade Journal Company, 1935), 65. Ukers did not recognize the implicit contradiction in coffee being a "king" and the "American people" having a "sovereign drink."

13. M. Pendergrast, *Uncommon Grounds: The History of Coffee and How It Transformed the World* (New York: Basic Books, 1999), 15; J. Beilenson, *The Book of Coffee* (White Plains, NY: Peter Pauper Press, 1995), 24; G. Dicum and N. Luttinger, *The Coffee Book: Anatomy of an Industry from Crop to the Last Drop* (New York: New Press, 1999), 34.

14. Dicum and Luttinger, *Coffee Book*, 35.

15. L. Kerber first coined the phrase "Republican Motherhood" in *Women of the Republic: Intellect and Ideology in Revolutionary America* (Chapel Hill: Institute of Early American History and Culture by the University of North Carolina Press, 1980).

16. Ukers, *All About Coffee*, 106, 116.

17. J. Adams to A. Adams, July 6, 1774, Adams Family Papers.

18. J. Adams, *Autobiography*, "Travels and Negotiations," 20 (entry dated May 6, 1778).

19. J. Adams to A. Adams, July 6, 1775, and August 11, 1777, Adams Family Papers, and *Adams Family Correspondence*, 2: 295–96.

20. *American State Papers: Documents, Legislative and Executive, of the Congress of the United States*, 38 vols. (Washington, DC, 1832–61). Hereafter *ASPCN* (Commerce and Navigation) or *ASPFR* (Foreign Relations), with volume and page numbers. The above reference is from *ASPCN*, V: 640.

21. *ASPCN*, V: 640–42.

22. U.S. Congress, *Journal of the House of Representatives* (Washington, DC: 1829). 21st Cong, 1st sess., 8 December, 18.

23. These included France, the United Netherlands, and Sweden with whom the U.S. already had treaties of commerce, as well as England, Hamburg and Saxony, Prussia, Denmark, Russia, Austria, Venice, Rome, Naples, Tuscany, Sardinia, Genoa, Spain, Portugal, and the Barbary States of the Porte, Algiers, Tripoli, Tunis and Morocco. Nations listed in T. Jefferson, *Diaries*, entry for Jan. 4, 1784 (part of the online collection of congressional papers at the Library of Congress); M. D. Peterson, "Thomas Jefferson and Commercial Policy, 1783–1793," *William and Mary Quarterly* 3rd ser, 22, no. 4 (October 1965): 590–91.

24. J. Adams to R. Livingston, August 13, 1783, *Revolutionary Diplomatic Correspondence of the United States*, 6 vol, 1889, 6:649–50 (hereafter *RDC*).

25. T. Jefferson to J. Jay, January 27, 1786, in Boyd, *Papers of Thomas Jefferson*, ed. J. P. Boyd, vol. 9 (Princeton, NJ: Princeton University Press, multiple years), 235.

26. T. Jefferson to R. Izard, November 18, 1796, in Boyd, *Papers of Thomas Jefferson*, vol. 10, 541–42.

27. C. Alexandre de Calonne to T. Jefferson, October 22, 1796, Thomas Jefferson Papers [TJP], Series 1, General Correspondence, 1651–1827; T. Jefferson, Observations on Charles Alexandre de Calonne's Letter of October 22, 1786, on Trade between the United States and France (October 22, 1796), TJP, Series 1, General Correspondence, 1651–1827. See also Peterson, "Thomas Jefferson and Commercial Policy," 599; and J. F. Stover, "French-American trade during the Confederation, 1781–1789," *North Carolina Historical Review* 35 (1958): 399–414.

28. *ASPFR*, 1:195.

29. Mayo, "Instructions to the British Ministers," 35.

30. Deane to the Committee of Secret Correspondence, undated, *RDC*, 2:118.

31. Deane to the Committee of Secret Correspondence, undated, *RDC*, 2:118.

32. A. Clauder, *American Commerce as Affected by the Wars of the French Revolution and Napoleon, 1793–1812*, reprint (Clifton, NJ: Kelley, 1972), and W. Coatsworth, "American trade with European colonies in the Caribbean and South America," *William and Mary Quarterly* 3rd ser. 42, no. 2 (April 1967): 243–66.

33. *Pennsylvania Gazette*, June 26, 1789.

34. B. Schoen, "Calculating the price of union: Republican economic nationalism and the origins of southern sectionalism, 1790–1828," *Journal of the Early Republic* 23, no. 2 (Summer 2003): 184.

35. See M. J. Fernando, "Coffee Cultivation in Java, 1830–1917," and R. Kurian, "Labor, Race, and Gender on the Coffee Plantations in Ceylon (Sri Lanka), 1834–1880," both in *The Global Coffee Economy in Africa, Asia, and Latin America 1500–1989*, ed. W. G. Clarence-Smith and S. Topik (Cambridge: Cambridge University Press, 2003), 157–90.

36. A. Hochschild, *Bury the Chains: Prophets and Rebels in the Fight to Free an Empire's Slaves* (Boston: Houghton Mifflin, 2005), 192–96.

37. "U.S. Revenue from Commodity Re-Exports, 1802–1804," *ASPCN*, V: 642.

38. R. Bisset's two-volume history of the slave trade confirms Laborie's account of coffee slaves' isolation. R. Bisset, *The history of the Negro slave trade, in its connection with the commerce and prosperity of the West Indies, and the wealth and power of the British Empire*, 2 vols., 1805, 1:392.

39. R. Burns, *Restrictive Laws on Food and Trade tried by the Test of Christianity: A Lecture Delivered . . . December 6, 1843*, 1843, 8–9.

40. See, for example, R. Paterson, *Remarks on the Depressed State of Cultivation in the West India Colonies*, 1848, 15.

41. *New York Times*, November 10, 1858.

42. M. Rolph-Trouillot, "Motion in the system: Coffee, color, and slavery in eighteenth-century Saint Domingue," *Review* 3 (Winter 1982): 349–54; C. Fick, *The Making of Haiti: The Saint Domingue Revolution from Below* (Knoxville: University of Tennessee Press, 1990), 19.

43. L. Dubois, *Avengers of the New World: The Story of the Haitian Revolution* (Cambridge, MA: Belknap Press of Harvard University Press, 2004), 171.

44. See, for example, Dubois, *Avengers of the New World*; L. Dubois, *A Colony of Citizens* (Omohundro Institute of Early American History and Culture, Williamsburg, Va., by the University of North Carolina Press, 2004); M. R. Trouillot, *Silencing the Past: Power and the Production of History* (Boston: Beacon Press, 1995).

45. Thurber, *Coffee*, 138. L. A. Perez, *Cuba and the United States: Ties of Singular Intimacy* (Athens: University of Georgia Press, 1990), 7–19; J. Opatrny, *U.S. Expansionism and Cuban Annexationism in the 1850s* (Lewiston, NY: Mellen, 1993), 39–40. R. Guerra y Sánchez, *Sugar and Society in the Caribbean: An Economic History of Cuban Agriculture*, trans. M. M. Urquidi (New Haven, CT: Yale University Press, 1964), 47–53.

46. O. V. Reiner, US Consul's 1887 Consular Report in Bureau of American Republics, *Coffee in America: Methods of Production and Facilities for Success, Cultivation*, 1893.

47. L. A. Pérez, *Winds of Change: Hurricanes and the Transformation of Nineteenth-Century Cuba* (Chapel Hill: University of North Carolina Press, 2001), 93, 94.

48. Thurber, *Coffee, from Plantation to Cup*, 205–6. The *Spice Mill* Convention Supplement, November 1911, 989.

49. The *American Grocer* cited in the leading coffee trade journal, *The Spice Mill*, July 1891: 172 and February 1890: 37. We thank Sarah Gingles, who pointed out tea's continuing popularity in her excellent unpublished essay, "Social Beverages: Ale's Condemnation Creates Coffee's Public Glory," University of California Irvine, May 2006.

50. E. Bacha and R. Greenhill, *150 Anos de Café* (Rio de Janeiro: Salamandra Consultoria Editorial, 1992), 335.

51. Calculated from Ukers, *All about Coffee*, 521.

52. Arbuckles Coffee Co., "Illustrated Atlas," Donaldson Bros. Lithographers (1889); Schnull-Krag Coffee Co., "It Is the Best Coffee Ever Sold," Indianapolis, IN (undated); "Washington's Coffee,"

New York Tribune, June 22, 1919. Library of Congress, Serial and Government Publications Division; Thomas Wood & Co., "Uncle Sam's High Grade Roast Coffee" (1880).

53. Calculated from Bacha and Greenhill, *150 Anos de Café*, 307; J. A. Ocampo, *Colombia y la economía mundial 1830–1910* (Mexico City: Siglo Veintiuno Editores, 1984), 303, Brazil, I.G.B.E., *Séries Estatísticas Retrospectivas*, vol. 1 (Rio: IBGE, 1986), 84.

54. P. J. Cain and A. G. Hopkins, *British Imperialism. Innovation and Expansion 1688–1914* (London: Longman, 1993), 298–306; R. Graham, *Britain and the Onset of Modernization in Brazil* (London: Cambridge University Press, 1968); D. C. M. Platt, *Business Imperialism, 1840–1930: An Inquiry Based on British Experience in Latin America* (Oxford: Clarendon, 1977); R. Miller, *Britain and Latin America in the Nineteenth and Twentieth Centuries* (London: Longman, 1993).

55. V. D Wickizer, *Coffee, Teas and Cocoa* (Stanford, CA: Stanford University Press, 1951), 36.

56. K. Maxwell, *Naked Tropics: Essays on Empire and Other Rogues* (New York: Routledge, 2003), 130.

57. Miller, *Britain and Latin America*, 53–54; Cain and Hopkins, *British Imperialism*, 298; P. R. de Almeida, *Formação da diplomacia econômica no Brasil* (São Paulo: Editora SENAC, 2001), 69–70, 368, 369.

58. J. F. Rippy, *Rivalry of the United States and Great Britain over Latin America* (Baltimore: Johns Hopkins University Press, 1928); A. K. Manchester, *British Preeminence in Brazil: Its Rise and Decline* (Chapel Hill: University of North Carolina Press, 1933), 266; L. Bethel, *A Abolição do trafico de escravos no Brasil* (1976), 272, 273.

59. Bacha and Greenhill, *150 anos de café*, 355.

60. *Philadelphia Gazette*, October 18, 1844.

61. Consular letter reproduced in J. A. Mendonça Azevedo, *Visa e Obra de Salvador de Mendonça* (1971), 349.

62. United States *Congressional Record*, 66th Congress, April 25, 1911, 638.

44

The Ecology of Taste

Robusta Coffee and the Limits of the Specialty Revolution

Stuart McCook

The dominant story in coffee over the past generation has been the **specialty coffee** revolution. In the 1980s and 1990s, a new segment of the coffee market emerged (at least in the United States), sometimes called "yuppie coffees." An important subset of specialty coffees were the "**ethical coffees**"—**fair trade**, certified **organic**, **Bird Friendly**, and so forth. These ethical coffees blended consumers' desire for good coffee with their wish to consume in ethical ways.[1] Among other things, the specialty revolution offered the promise of a new model of **sustainable** development for **peasant** coffee producers, in a period of historic low prices.

There is, it seems, an implicit narrative, a story line, in recent popular and academic studies of the coffee industry. Books such as Mark Pendergrast's *Uncommon Grounds* and Gregory Dicum and Nina Luttinger's *The Coffee Book* end their overviews of the global coffee industry with studies of the specialty revolution and ethical coffees.[2] Much recent scholarly literature on coffee and development, similarly, focuses heavily on this sector of the global coffee industry. The implicit narrative in these studies suggests that specialty and ethical coffees might someday become the norm in the global coffee industry. All coffee will be ethical, be sustainable, and taste good.

While all this would be ideal, the broader history of coffee over the twentieth century suggests that it is unlikely. For all the attention that specialty coffees have received, by most estimates they account for about 20 percent of the global coffee market—with ethical coffees constituting an even smaller subset of that. Most of the coffee produced and traded around the world is not specialty coffee. While some mass-market coffee has been influenced by the specialty revolution's emphasis on quality and taste, most of it has not. And, more important, ecological constraints on coffee cultivation mean that most of the world's coffee producers *cannot* emulate the current specialty model. Only a handful of coffee environments, mostly in northern Latin America and eastern Africa, can produce the high-quality arabica beans that are the essential starting point for any specialty coffee. Coffee farms in Brazil, central and western Africa, and Asia continue to produce large quantities of middling and low-quality mass-market coffee. These coffees nonetheless provide a living, such as it may be, for millions of small farmers around the world, and as such deserve attention.

The global coffee market divides **arabica** coffee into three broad categories, roughly from highest to lowest quality: (1) **Colombian milds**; (2) **other milds**; and (3) Brazilian **naturals.**

Botanically, virtually all specialty coffee is arabica coffee (*Coffea arabica*), although not all arabica is specialty coffee. Much of coffee's quality depends on the specific **variety** grown, the ecology of the landscape where it is grown, and the way it is processed. Specialty arabicas are from the first two categories. In the 2009–10 harvest year, Colombian milds and other milds together accounted for just under a third of global production (32.35 percent).[3] In this same period, Brazilian naturals accounted for roughly another third (32.16 percent) of global coffee production. This is the low- to middling-quality arabica coffee found in many grocery store and mass-market blends.

Today, the largest single segment of the global coffee trade belongs to a fourth (and arguably lowest-quality) category—**robusta**. Botanically, robusta belongs to the same genus as arabica coffee, but is a distinct species (*Coffea canephora*, var Robusta). Robustas currently have a larger share of the global coffee industry than do all specialty and ethical coffee combined (35 percent by the latest figures). This is particularly surprising given that robusta coffee was not globally cultivated or traded before the early twentieth century and that most of its growth has happened in the last half-century. The spread of robusta contributed to the resurrection of African and Asian producers as major players in the global coffee economy, after their almost total collapse in the late nineteenth and early twentieth centuries.[4] Robusta's expansion has taken place in the face of several significant challenges. Beyond the issue of taste, significant in itself, simple economics would suggest that robusta would not have been viable. For much of the twentieth century, the global coffee market has been dealing with an oversupply of arabica coffee, suggesting that there would not be much room for even more low-quality coffee. And from the planters' perspective, robusta coffee usually fetched a lower price than did arabica.

Nonetheless, robusta did prove to be economically and ecologically viable. Robusta cultivation and consumption spread in three major waves. The first took place in the Dutch East Indies and Africa between 1910 and 1930, as part of imperial schemes to promote colonial development. A second wave, largely in West Africa, took place in the decades after World War II. The third wave saw the (re)emergence of producers in Africa and Asia and the opening of significant robusta pioneer fronts in the Americas for the first time. In the last half of the twentieth century, Uganda, Indonesia, the Ivory Coast, Brazil, and above all Vietnam have emerged as major players in the global coffee industry, on the strength of their production and export of robusta coffee. Vietnam has now supplanted Colombia as the world's second-largest producer of coffee.

In spite of these trends, robusta has been almost invisible in the scholarly and popular literature on coffee. Why has robusta received so little attention, given its significant place in global coffee production? Part of the answer is that the robusta **commodity chain** is difficult to follow. Robusta has historically been purchased in bulk by large **roasters**. Given robusta's reputation for low or mediocre quality, roasters have not usually highlighted its use in their blends. Most specialty coffee roasters are actively prejudiced *against* robusta coffee, which they see as the antithesis of everything that specialty coffee stands for. This outlook has, in turn, infused much of the academic and popular literature. A commonplace observation, for example, is that the rapid expansion of robusta cultivation in Vietnam during the 1990s triggered the global coffee crisis of the early 2000s.[5] In short, robusta coffee plays the role of the villain in the global story of coffee.

In spite of all this, robusta coffee has succeeded in the marketplace, as a result of colonial, national, and multilateral development schemes over the long twentieth century. The history of robusta thus sheds light on a hidden history of development during that period. The several robusta booms were the products of intertwined biological and political processes, an interplay between landscapes and institutions. In the **producing countries**, growers, often encouraged by national or international institutions, adopted robusta because ecological conditions prevented them from cultivating arabica. Growers and scientists, often supported by empires, states, or multilateral organizations, carefully selected and manipulated the robusta plant and its environments. In the **consuming countries**, robusta found a niche in the market segment primarily driven by *price* rather than by taste. Over the twentieth century, then, robusta production and consumption co-evolved. New robusta fronts emerged in Africa, Asia, and ultimately the Americas. At the same time, new forms of robusta consumption emerged, in roasted and ground blends, and later in instant coffees. In most instances, colonial and national states expanded robusta cultivation to promote some version of "development," usually directed at peasant producers rather than at estates. [6] In short, the "bad" robusta coffee sector is itself the product of several generations of development projects.

THE FIRST WAVE: ROBUSTA, RUST, AND THE ECOLOGICAL REVOLUTION IN THE OLD WORLD COFFEE INDUSTRY, 1900–1940

Before the mid-1800s, arabica was the world's only cultivated coffee. During the nineteenth century, demand for coffee in Europe and North America surged. Planters across the tropics moved to feed this growing demand, and for much of the century the demand for coffee far exceeded the supply. New arabica fronts opened in northern Latin America, in Java and Sumatra, the Philippines, India, Ceylon, Madagascar, and many other places. Many of these coffee landscapes—especially the mountainous highlands of northern Latin America—mimicked the native home of arabica coffee on the hillsides of southwestern Ethiopia. Others, however, did not. Planters pushed arabica into areas that were at the extreme ecological limits for the species: into the humid coastal lowlands of the Indian Ocean Basin and the Pacific or into comparatively dry or cool subtropical parts of Brazil, some of which were susceptible to killing frosts. Arabica coffee grown at lower altitudes often had a poorer **cupping** quality than mountain-grown arabica, but the thirsty markets of the north could still absorb this produce. [7]

Then in the late nineteenth century, an epidemic disease swept through the coffee farms of the Indian Ocean Basin and the Pacific. The **coffee leaf rust** (caused by the fungus *Hemileia vastatrix*) was first detected on the coffee farms of Ceylon in 1869. Within two decades, the epidemic caused losses of more than £1,000,000 on the island; by the mid-1880s the island's coffee industry had almost completely collapsed as planters abandoned coffee for tea. Between 1870 and 1920, the coffee leaf rust spread to virtually all of the Old World's coffee zones. It left "arabica graveyards" scattered throughout the region. The rich coffee zones of southern India, Java, Sumatra, Madagascar, and the Philippines were almost completely wiped out. The epidemic was particularly severe in hot and humid lowlands, which favored the fungus's rapid reproduction and spread. Only a few small enclaves of arabica survived in the highlands of southern India, the highlands of Java and Sumatra, and a handful of other places. In these high and comparatively dry sites, the levels of infection were low enough to allow for the continued production of arabica coffee. Meanwhile, the coffee farms of the Americas remained free of the epidemic, protected by oceans, vigilant inspectors, and a hefty dose of luck. [8]

Not all arabica planters, however, abandoned coffee cultivation. As the coffee leaf rust epidemic spread, Europeans exploring equatorial Africa discovered new species of coffee. Planters hoped that some of these new species might be resistant to the leaf rust and thus a viable substitute for arabica coffee. Most discoveries were not. But in the 1870s, Ceylonese coffee planters adopted one species that looked promising. This was liberian coffee (*C. liberica*) that grew wild in West Africa. Unlike arabica coffee, liberia grew best in the humid lowlands—the very landscapes more seriously devastated by the coffee leaf rust epidemic. The plants had broad, thick leaves, which seemed to be rust-resistant. But coffee from liberia beans tasted different and worse than liquor made from arabica. In any case, after some initially successful crops, liberia coffee also succumbed to the rust epidemic, and planters abandoned it as well.[9]

Although this experiment failed, coffee researchers and planters kept looking for other kinds of coffee that might substitute for arabica. Planters and researchers in the Dutch East Indies imported new varieties and species of wild and domesticated coffee, hoping to find something that might work. Most of the coffees they imported proved to be just as susceptible to the coffee leaf rust as arabica and liberia had. But eventually, Dutch coffee growers imported one species of coffee from central Africa via Brussels that seemed to resist the rust's onslaught. This variety was known commercially as robusta coffee. After much debate, the plant was classified botanically as *C. canephora*, var. robusta. Like liberia, robusta grew wild in the humid lowlands of Africa. Robusta coffee trees were tall and produced many beans with a comparatively high caffeine content. But also like liberia, robusta beans were of indifferent quality.[10]

In the early 1900s, scientists in the Dutch East Indies began a program to systematically select and improve the imported robusta coffees. Their main goal was to create a coffee with a neutral flavor, which could be blended with arabica coffee. By 1910, the Dutch colonial government began a systematic program of propagating robusta coffee across the Dutch East Indies. Robusta coffee was planted as a monoculture and also **intercropped** with other cash crops. In particular, it was used as a **catch crop** for rubber, to provide rubber growers with some temporary income while they waited for the rubber trees to reach maturity. According to coffee expert William Ukers, by 1935 robusta coffee accounted for 94 percent of the coffee lands under cultivation in Java and 93 percent of the coffee acreage in neighboring Sumatra.[11] Robusta cultivation seemed promising, and other growers in the Indian Ocean Basin and the Pacific soon followed suit. Farmers in Malaya (now Malaysia), parts of southern India, and Madagascar adopted robusta on a large scale. Robusta did not, however, replace arabica everywhere. In Ceylon, most coffee growers had switched to tea, and they never looked back. In fact, an ethnic/racial divide appeared to emerge along with the growth of robusta coffee. Arabica coffee was predominantly (although not exclusively) farmed on European-owned estates, while robusta coffee grew primarily on smaller farms run by locals.

Much of the robusta produced in the Dutch East Indies was exported to the vast U.S. market. The American government and the coffee industry were, however, ambivalent about robusta coffee. The USDA had defined "coffee" as being the seeds of *C. arabica* or *C. liberica*. In 1912, the New York Coffee Exchange refused to trade robusta coffee. The adulteration and mislabeling of coffee were rampant throughout the industry. In spite of regulations, the adulteration of arabica coffee remained commonplace in the United States in the 1920s. The botanist Ralph Holt Cheney found that wholesale merchants "in both the producing and consuming countries add small African and Indian beans and considerable quantities of Liberian and Robusta coffees to Arabian coffee."[12] Apparently, some of the robusta produced on the island of Java was marketed in the United States as "Java" coffee, to give buyers the impression that it was the higher-quality arabica coffee for which the island was famous. In 1921, wrote William Ukers, the U.S. Bureau of Chemistry, part of the U.S. Department of Agriculture, ruled that "*Coffea robusta* could not be sold as Java coffee or under any form of labeling which tended either directly or indirectly to create the impression that it was *Coffea Arabica*." Still, that same year scientists at the Bureau of Chemistry also noted that "*Coffea robusta* has obtained great economic significance, and is grown in increasing amounts. While it has . . . not as yet been possible to obtain a strain that would be as desirable in flavor as the old 'standard' *Coffea Arabica* . . . its merits have been established."[13] In 1925, the New York Coffee Exchange began trading robusta coffee once again, and in 1929 the USDA expanded its definition of "coffee" to include robusta.[14]

In spite of robusta's growing role in the U.S. coffee industry, it remained largely invisible to consumers. Besides the clandestine adulteration described above, coffee roasters began to use robusta in blended coffees. During the 1920s, blended coffees became more commonplace in the United States, carefully packaged and sold on the shelves of supermarkets. These blended coffees were generally marketed by brand name, not by the origins of the beans. They often included coffees from several different origins, combined to achieve a specific taste. Cost was also an issue; roasters looking to economize would blend some higher-quality arabicas to add flavor, with lower-quality coffees to add bulk. "Robusta coffees are principally used as a 'price' proposition in the United Sates or as a filler to reduce the costs of other growths of coffee," wrote Ukers. "They are rather neutral in the cup and therefore useful in blending."[15] Coffee roasters had first used low-grade Brazilian arabicas as filler for their roasts, but increasingly they turned to robustas. It is hard to trace exactly how robusta was used, since roasters often kept their recipes for coffee blends a secret. In any case, these blends often changed over time.

After World War I, several European colonies in Africa began producing robusta coffee on a large scale. Unlike the situation in Asia and the Pacific, the coffee groves in large parts of Africa consisted of robusta coffee from the start. European colonial powers had carved up continental Africa starting with the "scramble for Africa" in 1885. The continent's new colonial rulers were anxious to make the colonies pay for themselves, and they promoted the cultivation of tropical crops. In the early twentieth century, European missionaries, governments, and individuals imported arabica coffee to their colonies. Arabica enjoyed limited yet spectacular success in a few places, especially Kenya and Tanganyika. In Kenya, the colonial government restricted arabica coffee cultivation to European settlers. Elsewhere in Africa, two main ecological checks limited arabica cultivation. The first was climate: many early experiments in arabica cultivation failed because the climate was too hot, too humid, or too dry. The second obstacle was diseases and pests. Africa was home to the genus *Coffea* and to all of its pests. In the Great Lakes region, coffee rust fungus spread rapidly from wild and semi-cultivated coffee plants to the cultivated arabica plants. Only a few choice mountain environments, especially along the slopes of Kilimanjaro in Tanganyika and in the highlands of Kenya, could produce arabica coffee.[16]

Uganda emerged as one of the global powerhouses in robusta production. Planters there experimented with both arabica and robusta. Arabica enjoyed limited success in a few areas, but elsewhere could not withstand the onslaught of rust and pests. A government agricultural officer at Kampala began experimenting with robusta in 1915; after World War I, he developed a reliable improved strain of robusta well adapted to Uganda's conditions. With encouragement from the government, African peasants began to adopt robusta cultivation on a large scale. Even some European planters began to cultivate robusta. In 1914 there were only 367 acres under robusta cultivation in Uganda; by 1934, there were 6,946 acres. In the late 1930s, 60 percent of Uganda's coffee lands were under robusta cultivation. Uganda was exporting a greater volume of coffee than Kenya, although Uganda's robustas never achieved the same fame as did Kenya's prized arabicas. Accordingly, the value of Kenyan coffee exports was much greater.[17] Similarly, after 1925 France and Belgium began promoting robusta cultivation in their African colonies, in places where arabica cultivation was not viable. For example, in 1920 the former German colony of Cameroon exported virtually no coffee; by the late 1930s there were 26,000 **hectares** of coffee under cultivation, three-quarters of which was robusta. In the French colony of Ivory Coast, coffee exports expanded from 51 tons in 1925 to 15,605 tons in 1939, almost entirely of robusta coffee.[18] The area under coffee cultivation in the Belgian Congo expanded eightfold between 1925 and 1940, 94 percent of which was robusta.[19] The figures for robusta consumption remain unclear, but at least one statistic suggests that in 1938, robusta coffees (mostly from France's overseas territories) accounted for more than a third of the coffee consumed in France.[20]

THE SECOND WAVE: ROBUSTA BOOM IN AFRICA, 1950–1970

After World War II, robusta cultivation spread into the forests and plains of Africa. This boom far outpaced the relatively modest experimentation with robusta cultivation in the 1920s and 1930s. Arabica coffee had never played a significant role in most of Africa owing to ecological conditions. Meanwhile, global supplies of robusta were falling in the immediate postwar years. Robusta farms in the Dutch East Indies had been devastated by World War II and the wars of independence (1945–49) that led to the formation of Indonesia.

In Africa itself, colonial powers and new nations alike hoped that coffee production would be the engine of economic development. "If you don't want to vegetate in bamboo huts," said Felix Houphouet-Boigny, the future president of Ivory Coast in 1953, "concentrate your efforts on growing good cocoa and coffee. They will fetch a good price and you will become rich."[21] In the Ivory Coast, coffee production, most of it robusta, expanded from 36,000 tons in 1945 to 112,500 tons in 1958. Angola, still a Portuguese colony, expanded coffee production from 44,000 tons in 1948 to 90,000 tons in 1956. Almost 60 percent of Angola's robusta exports were destined for the United States. Robusta production in the Belgian Congo almost tripled, from 16,000 tons to 47,000 tons, between 1948 and 1959.[22] Although the main new pioneer fronts for coffee were in west Africa, the older producers of robusta were also buoyed by the high prices of the 1950s. For example, between 1951 and 1962, Uganda's robusta production expanded from 34,000 tons per year to an average of 120,000 tons per year.[23] Driven largely by robusta cultivation, Africa captured a major share of global coffee production in the 1950s and 1960s. On the eve of World War I, Africa accounted for less than 2 percent of global coffee production; by 1965 it accounted for 23 percent. Three-quarters of this was robusta coffee, accounting for some 17 percent of global coffee production.[24]

A revolution in consumption accompanied the rise of robusta production. In the 1950s and 1960s, consumption of **instant** coffee, of which robusta was a key component, expanded rapidly across Europe and North America. During World War II, the Allied militaries, especially the American, included instant coffee in soldiers' rations, and the troops brought a taste for instant coffee home. Instant coffee accounted for almost 18 percent of the coffee consumed in the United States in 1956; just three years later it accounted for 30 percent.[25] Robustas also continued to be used in standard blends of roasted and ground coffee found on supermarket shelves. In Europe, especially in France and Italy, robusta was used in the ubiquitous **espresso** coffees. Some espresso aficionados argue that a good cup of espresso *requires* some robusta to produce a good **crema**.

Robusta consumption was not evenly distributed across all countries. For example, in 1960 robustas accounted for three-quarters of the coffee consumed in France, half the coffee consumed in the United Kingdom, 40 percent of the coffee consumed in Italy, and 30 percent of the coffee consumed in Belgium and the Netherlands. In the United States, African robusta coffee accounted for roughly 9 percent of coffee consumption. Although this share was small in relative terms, it was large in absolute terms; the United States consumed 4.5 times more robusta than the UK did.[26]

Producers of Brazilian coffee were not happy with the success of African robustas. One French writer noted that robusta's success on the global markets had been "resented by the Brazilians, who were too confident in their 'Santos' and their 'Rio' coffees, judged by them not to be replaceable by the so-called 'African' (robusta) coffees, whose aroma and taste they judged harshly."[27] The high coffee prices during these years, coupled with the climatic conditions under which robusta was cultivated, gave African smallholders little incentive to produce high-quality robusta. In Uganda, for example, the heavy and year-long rainfalls produced a mixed blessing. On the one hand, they helped stimulate the yields of robusta plants. On the other hand, the rains made it difficult to process the harvested beans properly. "Artificial drying is out of the question for the peasant producer," wrote J. W. F. Rowe, "and there is no dry period of any appreciable length." The beans could not be dried on patios in the sunshine for long periods, and the beans produced by the traditional **drying** process had a marked "musty" or "grassy" flavor. Climate, then, contributed to Uganda's production of low-quality arabicas during the 1950s and early 1960s. The comparatively high prices robusta fetched during these years also meant that African farmers had little reason to try to improve their cultivation practices.[28] Many of the robustas shipped to the world's markets, then, were of low quality. This has helped give the bean a bad reputation among some coffee experts. But it also highlights the point that quality is determined by many factors, whose importance varies from time to time and place to place. The poor quality of Ugandan robustas in this period, for example, owed as much to the conditions of climate, labor, and economy as it did to any inherent quality in the bean itself.

In some instances, African and estate producers did produce high-quality robusta coffees. They processed it using **wet processing**, commonly used for arabica. The wet process "suits Uganda with its continuous rainfall better than sun-drying, and avoids any possible mustiness," noted Rowe in 1963, "and there is a definite demand for these washed Robustas from the blending trade because they are more 'neutral' in flavour than standard [sun-dried] Robustas."[29]

Standardization was also a much larger problem for robusta coffee than for arabica. Arabica coffee was self-fertilizing, and cultivated arabica had a narrow genetic base, so the trees (and beans) remained stable from one generation to the next. Robusta coffee, however, was highly variable. Farmers in Africa compounded this natural variability by cultivating many varieties of robusta, both wild and domesticated. The resulting **green coffee**, therefore, had a wide range of tastes.[30] Governments tried to encourage farmers to cultivate only a limited range of carefully selected varieties. The French government established the Institut français du café et cacao (IFCC) in 1950, to try to promote just such standardization. Some African producers developed national institutions and national standards to promote and grade high-quality robusta coffee, such as the Congo's "Office du café robusta" (OCR). This agency promoted **washed** robustas. The OCR's own literature drew a sharp distinction between the Washed Congo Robusta, which had a mild taste, and the Natural Congo Robusta, whose taste was bitter. In fact, low-quality naturals had a taste that was described as "sour," "earthy," or "woody."[31] Only one African producer, Angola, produced robusta primarily on estates. According to one survey, Angola was "considered to produce one of the best robustas on the market with regard to the size of beans and cup quality."[32]

By the late 1950s, the global supply of coffee had begun to catch up with demand, and the prices for all grades of coffee declined once again. In the early 1960s, the world's producers and consumers of coffee entered into a series of trade agreements aimed at stabilizing world coffee prices. These culminated in the **International Coffee Agreement** (ICA), signed in 1962. A major goal of this agreement, signed in the wake of the Cuban Revolution, was to prevent a collapse of global coffee prices, which in turn might lead to rural discontent and revolution. It was at this point that the ICA divided global coffee production into the four categories described earlier: Colombian milds, other milds, Brazilian naturals, and robustas. In creating the category of robustas, the ICA acknowledged that this sector of the industry had become a major part of the global coffee industry,[33] In 1958, a coffee exchange dedicated to robusta futures had opened in London.[34] After the ICA agreement was signed, robusta production stabilized through much of Africa, with many producing countries exploring means of diversifying their agriculture and eliminating marginal coffee cultivation.[35]

In the late 1960s, African robustas briefly faced renewed competition from Brazilian arabicas. Brazilian producers developed a **soluble** arabica, which tasted better than the robustas, and this attracted the attention of some buyers in the U.S. However, this move also put the Brazilian manufacturers of soluble coffee in direct competition with U.S. corporations. Ultimately, the Brazilian initiative foundered, and African robustas retained their niche in the global coffee market. Demand for soluble coffee in the U.S. and other countries increased through the 1970s, so that by 1981 it accounted for 28 percent of the coffee consumed in America. This demand helped boost robusta's share of the global coffee market. During the 1970s, robustas reached about a quarter of global coffee production, a share that remained steady into the 1990s.[36] Other producers, encouraged by the high prices, began to expand robusta production and exports. In the early 1980s, Indonesia regained its prewar position as the world's largest robusta producer and exporter, averaging some 6,000,000 **bags** per year. Not everyone welcomed this resurgence. One coffee roaster in the United States commented that the "EK-1 and 20/25 grades of INDO robustas became almost synonymous with the poor worldwide reputation of the American cup in the 1960s and 1970s."[37]

THE THIRD WAVE: ROBUSTA PIONEER FRONTS IN ASIA AND LATIN AMERICA, SINCE 1970

During the 1980s and 1990s, new robusta pioneer fronts emerged in Asia and—more surprisingly—in the Americas. Robusta cultivation remained a niche activity in much of Latin America, generally in countries that were minor exporters. In the late nineteenth and early twentieth century, coffee growers in Costa Rica experimented with growing liberica and robusta coffees, although both efforts were ultimately abandoned because the coffees were deemed inferior. In the early 1960s, the American coffee expert Frederick Wellman had found "good sized commercial plantings" of robusta in the Dominican Republic and also noted that it could even be found in "restricted field corners in Costa Rica and Nicaragua," and in "rather large fields in Guatemala"—three countries that had historically exported high-quality mild arabicas.[38] But coffee producers in the Americas had historically been reluctant to cultivate robusta on a large scale. In the mid-1950s, Ecuadorean coffee planters had started planting some robusta, mixed in with arabica. Ecuadorean trade associations protested, fearing that the mixed cultivation of arabica and robusta there would "discredit the quality of Ecuadorean coffee."[39] In Brazil, some coffee planters began lobbying to plant robusta, after a major frost and the coffee rust struck the coffee plantations. Planters were especially interested, according to one source, in planting robusta in rust-affected areas in Espírito Santo, Rio de Janeiro, and Minas Gerais and also in areas with "poor soils and warm temperatures." Brazil began cultivating robusta on a large scale during the late 1980s, with a particularly large push between 1985 and 1990, when cultivation expanded from 1.8 million bags to almost 5.3 million bags. The Brazilians actually cultivated a variety of *C. canephora* known as **conilon** (or kouillou in Africa). Roughly 1.5 million bags of this coffee went to Brazil's vast domestic market; the rest was exported.[40]

Robusta coffee also made its way into new parts of Asia. The largest of these pioneer fronts was in Vietnam. Historically, Vietnam had produced little coffee. In the 1980s, Vietnam's coffee industry received development support from its partners in the Soviet Bloc. It exported much of its coffee to Soviet Bloc countries, although France and Singapore were also major markets. This initial expansion was driven primarily by the Vietnamese government through its policies of creating New Economic Zones and developing the Fixed Cultivation and Sedentarization Program. These policies focused on coffee production on large-scale collective farms. After the mid-1980s, however, the government switched to promoting peasant coffee cultivation under its new Economic Renovation Policy, which emphasized market-oriented economic reforms. The collapse of the Soviet Bloc did not halt the expansion of robusta production in Vietnam. It is frequently asserted that the World Bank financed this expansion, although bilateral development initiatives likely played a more important role. Some observers questioned the wisdom of this rapid expansion: "We can ask whether it is a good idea to support the appearance of a new producer," mused one French coffee expert in 1992, "in a zone where this product is not widely consumed and if much of this new Vietnamese production will increase global coffee supplies."[41] Still, rising prices for robusta between the mid-1980s and mid-1990s attracted a flood of migrants to the central highlands of Vietnam. Between 1975 and 1997, the area under coffee cultivation in Vietnam grew from 6,000 hectares to 130,000 hectares. Vietnamese robusta succeeded in the global markets because low domestic prices for land and labor made it comparatively inexpensive. Much of this coffee was, however, of poor quality. As in other robusta-producing areas, buyers did not pay much of a premium for quality beans, so farmers had little incentive to produce them. Still, even the poor-quality Vietnamese beans found a market, and by the early twenty-first century Vietnam was the world's second-largest coffee producer.[42]

ROBUSTA COFFEE, SPECIALTY COFFEE, AND THE COFFEE CRISIS SINCE 1989

The declining quality of coffee in the United States led to a backlash in the 1980s and 1990s. Increasingly, consumers and roasters became interested in *quality* coffees. Dicum and Luttinger note that "the specialty industry tapped into an unfulfilled desire for diversity and quality among affluent coffee drinkers." The spectacular growth of Starbucks coffee was one of the most visible manifestations of the specialty revolution.[43] In the United States, the revolution was founded upon 100-percent arabica coffee. To the advocates of specialty coffee industry, robusta coffee symbolized everything that was wrong with the mainstream coffee industry.

Even mentioning robusta coffee at meetings of the **Specialty Coffee Association of America** could provoke a strong reaction. Donald Schoenholt, a specialty coffee roaster and specialties editor for the *Tea & Coffee Trade Journal*, wrote a tirade against robustas that is worth quoting at length:

> I have discouraged the acceptance of *C. canephora* because . . . to my mind the species is incompatible with the spirit of virtue that our coffee should represent to the world. The gospel according to David Weinstein . . . calls for uncompromisable coffees. *Coffea canephora* is a compromise. No coffee man adds *canephora* to a blend based on the taste qualities it brings to the table. On historical principles, the American trade should abstain from the use of the coffee as an atonement for the *C. canephora* excesses of the last generation. It would be best to scrupulously avoid its use except in the very narrowest drawn circumstances and applications. This is prudent. It is sometimes not unwise to be overly cautious, even to err on the side of caution. We in the United States should understand, though, that "Gourmet" blends containing *C. canephora* are accepted in polite European coffee society. Indeed many Americans prefer blends which include these coffees.[44]

In spite of his disdain for robusta coffees, however, Schoenholt proceeded to write a four-part history of robusta coffee for the *Tea & Coffee Trade Journal.*

While the specialty market gained visibility and popularity through the 1980s and 1990s, conventional coffee, and robusta producers, continued to hold on to their share of the global coffee markets. The emergence of the specialty revolution had helped change the taste of consumers in the United States. Coffee companies, even large roasters, began to feel commercial pressure to use only "100% arabica coffee." On their North American packaging, industrial coffee roasters have also sometimes used creative (but true) descriptions like "100% coffee" or "100% Brazilian beans," which likely hide the fact that the blends contain robusta. In spite of the pressures from the specialty coffee industry, however, robustas still occupied a large share of the instant and blended coffees.

The collapse of the International Coffee Agreement in 1989 meant that the global coffee economy returned to a virtually free market, and through the 1990s it began a new cycle of booms and busts. On the whole, coffee prices declined, and by the late 1990s and early 2000s the global coffee industry had entered a sustained period of overproduction and low prices. Many observers blamed the situation on the rapid expansion of Vietnam's robusta industry. For many coffee producers, arabica and robusta alike, the price of coffee fell so low that they could not even cover their production costs. Nonetheless, the fall in global coffee prices struck robusta producers much harder than arabica producers. "In spite of increased production," wrote Pierre Leblanche in 2005, "market share of Robustas has decreased 10% in volume at 40% in net worth."[45] The price differential between average arabica and robusta prices also increased. Competition between robusta-exporting countries became fierce in the early 1990s. The volume of Indonesia's robusta exports dropped 40 percent between 1989 and 1992; the Ivory Coast's exports dropped by about ten percent. At the same time, Vietnam and Brazil gained market share.[46]

Robusta producers around the world have been developing a range of responses to the coffee crisis. One is to promote domestic consumption. Some robusta-producing countries, including Brazil, Ecuador, India, Indonesia, and Vietnam, have significant domestic markets for robusta. Brazil and Indonesia in particular have domestic consumption of more than 1 million bags. Half of India's robusta production is directed towards the domestic market. Recently, the Mexican government, in conjunction with Nestlé, announced plans to expand robusta coffee production from 150,000 sacks per year to 500,000 sacks per year by 2012 and to increase the processing capacity of Nestlé's soluble coffee plant. This expansion is likely aimed both at the markets of Mexico's NAFTA partners and at Mexican domestic demand.[47]

Since the nineteenth century, observers have noted that many consumers in Africa and Asia actually *prefer* the taste of robusta and liberica coffees to that of arabica. There is also an element of national pride among some robusta producers. Tins of instant coffee produced in the Ivory Coast, for example, clearly proclaim that the coffee is made of robusta from that country. Robusta does not carry the same stigma there as it does in the Americas. Even so, efforts to increase domestic robusta consumption in recent years have met with little success.[48]

Some robusta producers and traders are trying to find a place for their product in the specialty coffee market. Pierre Leblanche, a vocal advocate for "gourmet robustas," was a driving force behind the creation of the World Alliance of Gourmet Robustas (WAGRO) founded in 2002. Leblanche and others argue that robustas are not inherently bad coffees; it is just that most of them are poorly processed using **dry processing.** If properly processed or washed using the same wet process as high-quality arabica coffees, Leblanche and others argue that robustas could find a niche in the specialty coffee market. One common refrain among robusta advocates is that a carefully washed robusta will always taste better than a poorly processed arabica. Leblanche identified small initiatives to produce gourmet robustas in such diverse places as India, Ecuador, Madagascar, Brazil, Uganda, Cameroon, and Guatemala. Some observers present the problem of robusta quality simply as one of know-how. According to a recent issue of *Roast* magazine, "as Robusta producers become more informed about growing and processing procedures, but also about the specialty market, they are likely to begin producing Robustas that meet the specialty industry's quality standards." Leblanche argues that "Robustas have potential if properly washed and marketed. . . . on the consumer side, we must make people aware that Robustas could be good."[49]

It seems unlikely, however, that specialty production will do much to help the robusta industry as a whole navigate the coffee crisis. Even optimists like Leblanche recognize that the robusta industry faces deep structural problems. Political chaos has plagued some of the largest robusta producers, such as the Ivory Coast. The coffee crisis itself makes it difficult for robusta growers to invest in the equipment and labor necessary to improve the quality of their coffee. In Vietnam, for example, many small farmers have responded to the crisis by reducing or abandoning the use of **fertilizers** altogether and by limiting or abandoning irrigation. It is difficult to see how they would be willing or able to invest in any kind of infrastructure to improve their quality without significant assistance.[50] "On the consuming side," notes Leblanche, "[the market for robustas] is still mostly driven by price, not quality. Big volume importers have rushed to take advantage of the very low prices ushered in by the new major origin [Vietnam], and restrict the role of [robustas] to solubles and fillers. They feel no incentive to change this."[51]

Still, some French researchers suggest that there may be a way to develop a differentiated robusta industry, by creating robusta **terroirs** that emphasize origins and qualities, albeit on different terms than arabica coffee is differentiated. "For example," they write, "a terroir producing a coffee with a strong potential for extraction would get the attention of makers of soluble coffee. . . . In this context, the *terroir* or the origin would not necessarily be an attribute of robusta listed on the package with the aim of attracting the . . . consumer. Rather, it could introduce a market segmentation at the level of roasters, without this being visible to the end consumer."[52] Recently some movement in this direction has occurred. The Rainforest Alliance has certified some coffee production in Vietnam, working in conjunction with the coffee exporters Dakman Vietnam and ECOM group, which in turn sell to large roasters like Kraft.[53] While this strategy has had important ecological benefits for the Vietnamese coffee planters in the scheme, it is not yet clear if this will lead to any significant market segmentation. Still, approaches like this seem to offer the most long-term promise for robustas and other mass-market coffees. Rather than trying to emulate the solutions embraced by the specialty and alternative trade coffees, they must look for solutions that reflect the distinct characters of their own market segment.

CONCLUSION: ROBUSTA AND THE ECOLOGY OF DEVELOPMENT

The livelihoods of millions of farmers depend, at least in part, on the production of robusta coffee for the mass market. They have felt the impact of the coffee crisis just as severely, if not more so, than the producers of high-quality arabicas. Some of the producers who live in favored landscapes may be able to improve their situation by planting arabica and adopting more sophisticated processing techniques. But for many, if not most coffee farmers, producing specialty coffee is out of the question. Their landscapes do not allow the cultivation of arabica, or they lack the means to process their coffee adequately. Strong institutional factors, in particular the large industrial coffee roasters, are not primarily interested in quality and will resist attempts to increase the producer prices of coffee. Most cultivators of robustas and naturals, then, will likely continue to produce coffee for the mass market, although they may seek to improve their position within this segment. As this study of robusta has shown, mass-market industrial coffees have become, and are likely to remain, the dominant sector in the global coffee industry. Promoting environmental and social sustainability in this sector of the coffee industry, where neither roasters nor consumers are likely to pay premiums for sustainable production, will require different solutions than in the specialty sector. These solutions will need to recognize and address the social and ecological contexts in which these coffees are produced.

NOTES

1. William Roseberry, "The rise of yuppie coffees and the reimagination of class in the United States," *American Anthropologist* 98, no. 4 (December 1996): 762–55; Robert A. Rice, "Noble goals and challenging terrain: Organic and fair trade coffee movements in the global marketplace," *Journal of Agricultural and Environmental Ethics* 14, no. 1 (2001): 39–66.

2. Nina Luttinger and Gregory Dicum, *The Coffee Book: Anatomy of an Industry from Crop to the Last Drop,* rev. and updated (New York: New Press, 2006); Mark Pendergrast, *Uncommon Grounds: The History of Coffee and How It Transformed Our World* (New York: Basic Books, 1999).

3. Gordon Wrigley, *Coffee* (Harlow, UK: Longman Scientific and Technical, 1988), 565. Coffee statistics taken from the International Coffee Organization website, http://www.ico.org/prices/m1.htm. Of the aggregate total for milds, Colombian milds accounted for 8.94 percent of global coffee production in this period, and "other" milds accounted for 23.41 percent.

4. This essay can be taken as a sequel to William Clarence-Smith's "The Coffee Crisis in Asia, Africa, and the Pacific, 1870–1914," in *The Global Coffee Economy in Africa, Asia, and Latin America, 1500– 1989,* ed. W. Clarence-Smith and S. Topik (Cambridge: Cambridge University Press, 2004), 100–119.

5. The point here is that the relative lack of scholarly and popular attention to robusta coffee is not random but rather the product of historically specific processes. For a pioneering study on the cultural production of ignorance, see L. Schiebinger, "Agnotology and exotic abortifacients: The cultural production of ignorance in the eighteenth-century Atlantic world," *Proceedings of the American Philosophical Society* 149, no. 3 (2005): 316–43.

6. The industry calls instant "soluble coffee," but here I use the term more familiar to consumers. On the interconnection between biological and cultural processes in tropical agriculture, see John Soluri's

Banana Cultures: Agriculture, Consumption, and Environmental Change in Honduras and the United States (Austin: University of Texas Press, 2005).

7. Stuart McCook, "Global rust belt: *Hemileia vastatrix* and the ecological integration of world coffee production since 1850," *Journal of Global History* 1, no. 2 (2006): 177–95.

8. McCook, "Global rust belt," 180–87.

9. Francis Thurber, *Coffee: From Plantation to Cup*, 14th ed. (1887), 107–116; Frederick L. Wellman, *Coffee: Botany, Cultivation, and Utilization* (London: Hill, 1961), 76–79.

10. P. J. S. Cramer, *A Review of Literature of Coffee Research in Indonesia* (Turrialba, Costa Rica: SIC Editorial, 1957), chapters 18–21.

11. W. H. Ukers, *All about Coffee* (New York, The Tea and Coffee Trade Journal Company, 1922), 188–89.

12. Ralph Holt Cheney, *Coffee: A Monograph of the Economic Species of the Genus Coffea L.* (New York: New York University Press, 1925), 130.

13. Ukers, *All about Coffee*, 282, 370.

14. Wrigley, *Coffee*, 57.

15. Ukers, *All about Coffee*, 210.

16. For a recent overview of coffee's main diseases and pests, see J. M. Waller, M. Bigger, and R. J. Hillocks, *Coffee Pests, Diseases, and Their Management* (Wallingford, UK: CABI, 2007).

17. A. E. Haarer, *Modern Coffee Production*, 356–58.

18. On the French policies and incentives to promote Ivorean coffee cultivation in the 1930s, see C. A. Krug and R. A. de Poerck, *World Coffee Survey* (Rome: FAO, 1968), 36.

19. Figures drawn from Rene Coste, *Cafés et Caféiers*, 1989, 408 (Cameroon), 428 (Ivory Coast), 466–67 (Belgian Congo).

20. Coste, *Cafés et Caféiers*, 702.

21. Quotation from Pendergast, *Uncommon Grounds*, 259; John M. Talbot, *Grounds for Agreement: The Political Economy of the Coffee Commodity Chain* (Lanham, MD: Rowman & Littlefield, 2004), 55–56.

22. Coste, *Cafés et Caféiers*, 422, 455, 462, 467.

23. J. W. F. Rowe, *The World's Coffee: A Study of the Economics and Politics of the Coffee Industries of Certain Countries and of the International Problem* (London: H. M. Stationery Off., 1963), 146.

24. Krug and De Poerck, *World Coffee Survey*, 7.

25. Coste, *Cafés et caféiers*, 693–94.

26. Coste, *Cafés et Caféiers*, 398. Statistics for the United States derived from tables CCXXXVIII and CCXXXIX of Coste, *Cafés et caféiers*, 690. Statistics for the United Kingdom derived from tables CCLIX and CCLX of Coste, *Cafés et caféiers*, 712. Statistics for France derived from table CCXLVII Coste, *Cafés et caféiers*, 702.

27. Coste, *Cafés et caféiers*, 387. In short, the Americans had become "clients of Africa" when buying inexpensive coffees (704).

28. Rowe, *The World's Coffee*, 146, 148–49.

29. Rowe, *The World's Coffee*, 159.

30. See Krug and de Poerck, *World Coffee Survey* 43. On the many varieties of robusta cultivated in the Ivory Coast, see Roland Porteres, "Valeur agronomique des caféiers des types kouilou et robusta cultivés en Côte d'Ivoire," *Café, Cacao, Thé* 3, no. 1 (January–April 1959): 3–13.

31. Coste, *Cafés et caféiers*, 474–76, 479.

32. Krug and De Poerck, *World Coffee Survey*, 112.

33. "L'évolution des cours des cafés Robusta," *Café, Cacao, Thé* 7, no. 4 (October–December 1963): 440–44.

34. Wrigley, *Coffee*, 557–59; "Réouverture du marché à terme des cafés de Londres," *Café, Cacao, Thé* 2, no. 2 (May–August 1958): 100.

35. Krug and De Poerck, *World Coffee Survey*, 37.

36. Wrigley, *Coffee*, 512–13; Talbot, *Grounds for Agreement*, 135–61; Guy Delaporte, "Robusta quality for top-of-the-line products," *Tea & Coffee Trade Journal* 163, no. 1 (January 1991): 38. On soluble coffee consumption in the early 1980s, see Wrigley, *Coffee*, 550, table 13.5.

37. Wrigley, *Coffee*, 57; Donald N. Schoenholt, "*Coffea canephora*: The 'R' word," *Tea & Coffee Trade Journal* 164, no. 3 (March 1992): 43.

38. Mario Samper K, "The Historical Construction of Quality and Competitiveness: A Preliminary Discussion of Coffee Commodity Chains," in Clarence-Smith and Topik, *Global Coffee Economy*, 146–47; Wellman, *Coffee*, 84.

39. "Opposition à la culture du caféier Robusta en Equateur," *Café, Cacao, Thé.*

40. "Bilan du plan d'éradication des caféiers au Brésil," *Café, Cacao, Thé* 15, no. 2 (April–June 1971): 149; "Production et commercialization mondiales du Robusta," *Café, Cacao, Thé* 37, no. 2 (April–June 1993): 162.

41. Frédéric Fortunel, *Le café au Viêt Nam: de la colonisation à l'essor d'un grand producteur mundial* (2000), 56, 121–29.

42. "Avenir de la production caféière au Viêt Nam," *Café, Cacao, Thé* 35, no. 1 (January–March 1991): 66. Quotation from "Le café du Vietnam," *Café, Cacao, Thé* 36, no. 2 (April–June 1992): 156–57. Sylvie Doutriaux and Charles Geisler, "Competing for coffee space: Development-induced displacement in the central highlands of Vietnam," *Rural Sociology* 73, no. 4 (2008): 528–54; Dang Thanh Ha and Gerald Shively, "Coffee boom, coffee bust, and smallholder response in Vietnam's central highlands," *Review of Development Economics* 12, no. 2 (2008): 312–26; Gerard Greenfield, "Vietnam and the world coffee crisis: Local coffee riots in a global context," March 1, 2004, http://www.probeinternational.org/coffee/vietnam-and-world-coffee-crisis-local-coffee-riots-global-context.

43. Quoted in Dicum and Luttinger, *The Coffee Book*, 172.

44. Donald N. Schoenholt, "*Coffea canephora*: The 'R' word," *Tea & Coffee Trade Journal* 164, no. 3 (March 1992): 40.

45. Pierre Leblanche, "Gourmet robustas: The quest goes on," *Tea & Coffee Trade Journal* 177, no. 12 (December 2005): 32.

46. "Production et commercialization mondiale du Robusta," *Café, Cacao, Thé* 37, no. 2 (April–June 1993): 162.

47. Mica Rosenberg, "Mexico eyes instant coffee market with robusta push," n.d., http://blogs.reuters.com/mica-rosenberg/2010/04/26/mexico-eyes-instant-coffee-market-with-robusta-push/; Emilio Godoy, "Bitter Taste in Mexican Coffee Farmers' Mouths," *Inter Press Service*, April 26, 2010, http://ipsnews.net/print.asp?idnews=51202.

48. Wellman, *Coffee*, 77; "Production et commercialization mondiale du Robusta," *Café, Cacao, Thé* 37, no. 2 (April–June 1993): 162.

49. Shanna Germain, "Ready for Robustas? What Robustas Have to Offer the Specialty Coffee Industry" *Roast Magazine*, March/April 2006, http://www.roastmagazine.com/backissues/marchapril2006/readyforrobustas.html; Pierre Leblanche, "Gourmet robustas: The awakening of specialty coffees," *Tea & Coffee Trade Journal* 176, no. 12 (December 2004): 26–30; Pierre Leblanche, "Gourmet Robustas: The Quest Goes On," 32–35.

50. Dang Thanh Ha and Gerald Shiveley, "Coffee boom, coffee bust, 312–26.

51. Leblanche, "Gourmet robustas: The quest goes on," 34.

52. Christophe Montagnon, Thierry Leroy, Ronald Onzima, and Magali Dufour, "Porquoi pas les terroirs Robusta?" in *Cafés: terroirs et qualités*, ed. Christophe Montagnon (2003), 145.

53. Rainforest Alliance, "A Healthier Future Is Percolating for Vietnam: More than a Thousand Coffee Farms Have Earned the Rainforest Alliance Certified Seal," n.d., http://www.rainforest-alliance.org/profiles/documents/vietnam_coffee_profile.pdf; "Rainforest Alliance Certifies Coffee in Vietnam: Coffee and Conservation," n.d., http://www.coffeehabitat.com/2010/04/rainforest-alliance-certifies-coffee-in-vietnam.html.

45

The Espresso Menu

An International History

Jonathan Morris

The **specialty coffee** revolution of the last thirty years has been driven by **espresso-based drinks**. Whether it is the pure **espresso** itself—whose devotees are forever discussing how to achieve the "God shot"—or the **cappuccino** and **latte** that coffee shop customers have adopted around the globe, espresso beverages have both fuelled and financed the current wave of interest in coffee. The success of what I have termed the "cappuccino conquests" has been so great that the same espresso beverages are now found in coffee shops from Pakistan to Panama.[1]

This chapter explores the history of the main items on the international coffeehouse menu—first "black," then "white"—to demonstrate the complexity of appropriation and reconfiguration of traditional Italian beverages. Charting shifts in the characteristics of these coffee drinks provides insight into the changing structures of the coffee and café trades, technological innovations within the industry, and the appeal of beverages to different sets of consumers. It reveals many different forms of interactions between espresso-drinking cultures around the globe, with transfers not just from, but also to, Italy, while others involve no Italian mediation at all.

The most fundamental beverage transfers have not crossed international boundaries, but rather the division between domestic and out-of-home coffee beverages. Espressos, cappuccinos, and lattes command premium prices because they cannot be reproduced in the average home: however, over the history of the beverages this barrier has been crossed both ways.

PART ONE: BLACK

Espresso is best understood as the product of a preparation process rather than as a type of coffee or coffee beverage. Espresso coffee is made using pressure to force ("express") water through the coffee. The Italian description of this process relies on the four "M"s: *macchina, macinazione, miscela,* and *mano* (machine, grind, blend, and the hand of the barista). The **barista** selects a suitable blend of coffee beans and grinds these to fineness such that their resistance to the hot water being forced through the **coffee cake** by the machine enables delivery of the beverage within desired parameters of time, volume, and temperature.

In 1998, a group of **organoleptic** analysts set up the Italian National Espresso Institute (INEI). After evaluating the sensory profile of an "Italian espresso" (*espresso italiano*), they defined parameters for its preparation and gained state recognition for a quality certification based upon this standard. Their parameters are specified in table 45.1.

Table 45.1. Italian National Espresso Institute (INEI) Parameters for the Preparation of Italian Espresso

Portion of ground coffee	7 grams ± 0.5
Water pressure	9 bar ± 1
Temperature in brew chamber	88°C ± 2°C
Delivery time	25 seconds ± 5
Volume in cup (with crema)	25 ml ± 2.5
Beverage temperature	67°C ± 3°C
Caffeine	<100 mg

The sensory description highlights that

Espresso Italiano has a hazel-brown to dark-brown foam—characterised by tawny reflexes—with a very fine texture. . . . The nose reveals an intense scent with notes of flowers, fruits, toasted bread and chocolate. Its taste is rounded, substantial and velvet-like. Sour and bitter tastes are well balanced and neither one prevails over the other.[2]

Although INEI's parameters supposedly captured the qualities of "traditional" Italian espresso, none of the beverages described as espresso possessed these characteristics until the 1960s.[3]

"Original" Espresso

Espresso evolved in response to the quickening pace of life toward the end of the nineteenth century. The time required to prepare and brew a pot of coffee, as well as the waste involved in making a single cup, induced café owners to adopt the partial solution of using a one-cup drip filter to produce *caffè express*. Inventors across Europe began experimenting with various forms of pressure brewing in order to reduce the contact time needed between the water and the coffee. Angelo Moriondo, a Turin hotelier, deposited patents in Italy and France for machines to brew coffee using steam pressure in 1884 and 1885, but despite his invitation to visitors to "Come to the Hotel Ligure, we'll make you a coffee in a minute," he never brought these to market.[4]

The Milanese entrepreneur Desiderio Pavoni began producing the Ideale, the first commercial **espresso machine** in 1905, using a patent purchased from the engineer Luigi Bezzera.[5] A vertical boiler generated the steam used to force hot water down a tube and through the cake of ground coffee. This was contained in a **portafilter**, clamped to the machine at the so-called group heads. Whereas Moriondo's machines brewed coffee in bulk for later delivery, the Ideale made a fresh cup "expressly" for the individual customer within an "express" time, by "expressing" the water through the coffee.

The resultant beverage was very different from the traditional espresso described by INEI. The pressure generated was only around 1.5 bars, meaning that no **crema** formed on top of the coffee liquor. And the high temperatures in the groups and the almost inevitable contact with the steam scalded the coffee cake, so the eventual espresso was black in color, smelled burnt, and tasted bitter. It was delivered in around forty-five seconds and served in a significantly larger volume than today. The taste was like a somewhat concentrated filter coffee.

Espresso machines began appearing in the smart cafés, upmarket hotels, cocktail bars, and transport terminals across much of Western Europe during the first half of the twentieth century. As well as Pavoni and Arduino, constructors included non-Italian manufacturers such as the French Reneka.[6] Although the quality issues caused by the use of steam were widely recognized, the apparatus remained much the same until the postwar era.[7]

Crema Caffè, Crème Café, Café Crème

In 1948 Achille Gaggia began manufacturing coffee machines, declaring they produced a new beverage, *crema caffè*. The barista operated a geared, lever spring piston to draw hot water directly from the boiler and drive it through the coffee puck. This method eliminated the steam and generated much higher pressures, ranging from 3 to 12 bars during delivery. Consequently, the essential oils and colloids in the coffee created a mousse on the top of the beverage that we know today as *crema*.

The first semi-automatic machine—relieving operators of the need to supply the manual power for delivery, while retaining control of the brewing process—arrived in 1961. This was the Faema E61, which incorporated an electrical pump that provided a consistent nine bars of pressure, operated by a simple on-off switch.[8] Water was drawn directly from the café's main supply, then pressurized and passed through a heat exchanger in the boiler, before reaching the group head. This allowed "continuous erogation," the delivery of cup after cup without waiting for the boiler to refill and reheat the water. With relatively stable temperatures at the group head, rapid delivery of consistent cups of coffee became possible—a truly "express" service.

The E61 defined the current conception of espresso: it was the first machine capable of realizing the parameters later specified by INEI. By the mid-1970s semi-automatic machines had become standard equipment in Italian coffee bars, and the public reverted to simply ordering a *caffè* (never an espresso).

Crema remained the critical visual clue to the distinctiveness of the new form of espresso, conveying with it connotations of smoothness and luxury.[9] As customers in neighboring European markets preferred larger beverages, operators employed a coarser grind, allowing a greater volume of water to be passed through the group head using the same time and pressure parameters as for espresso. In German-speaking regions this was described as *crème café*, a larger, less intense beverage but, critically, still topped by a mousse of crema. In France it was served as *café crème*, usually finished with steamed milk. Roasters started producing bespoke lighter roasted blends for use as *crème café*.

Ristretto, Single-Origin, Romano, Double, Lungo

Ironically the best coffees at producing a highly visible, thick crema are robustas. Furthermore, because the espresso process intensifies the organoleptic qualities of the beans, high-quality arabicas can produce imbalanced flavors, whereas **commodity coffees**, notably Brazilian naturals, with their low acidity and relatively bland profiles, are well suited for espresso. One reason for the evolution of espresso in Italy was that the process was suited to the poor quality portfolio of coffees that the country imported due to its relative economic weakness.

A critical skill for Italian roasters is to blend their coffees to produce a rounded cup combining substantial body with a balance between sour and bitter tastes. In general, the farther south one travels in Italy, the greater the proportion of robusta in the blend, with a consequent darkening of the roast in an attempt to mitigate the bitterness of robusta beans. This probably accounts for the habit of adding sugar as standard practice, to the point that baristas often spoon it in automatically—and to serving espresso as a *ristretto*, at around 15 ml, thereby reducing the caffeine content.[10] Nonetheless the resultant beverage still packs a notable punch!

INEI maintains that authentic Italian espresso can only be achieved with **blends**. The Institute characterizes the difference between espresso prepared from **single-origin** coffee and that derived from a blend as similar to the contrast between listening to a solo instrument and to a symphony orchestra. To capture the diversity of Italian practice from region to region, any blend is allowed, be the beans arabica or robusta, provided that the sensory outcome satisfies INEI's requirements.[11]

When espresso became a flagship beverage for the U.S. specialty coffee movement, what had evolved as a relatively cheap way of preparing individual cups of coffee using low-quality blends was now presented as the incarnation of the highest expression of coffee itself. This was encouraged by Italian roasters such as Dr. Ernesto Illy, the keynote speaker at the 1992 SCAA conference, who realized that his company's upmarket all-arabica blend was perfectly suited to the specialty community's emphasis on quality.[12]

In recent years, **third wave** artisans from the specialty sector have posed uncomfortable questions about the assumptions behind the parameters for "traditional" Italian espresso, calling for a scientific approach to espresso rooted in measurement and calculation. The specialty movement has begun preparing single-origin coffees as espresso, preferring to highlight their characteristics through intensification, rather than balancing them through blending.[13] The parameters for dosing are also under attack, as the realization took hold that these sprang as much from economics as from a taste profile. Changing the dosage, tamping pressure, and flow time produces very different sensory results; instead of the 14 grams of coffee conventionally used for two shots, today 19–21 grams may be tamped into the basket.[14]

The strict adherence to 9 bars of pressure has similarly been challenged, on the grounds that the figure was merely the standard of the semi-automatic machines. Today's top professional machines allow baristas to vary pre-infusion times, temperature, and pressure during a shot and between shots and, having established the profile that best suits the coffee being served, to use digital technology to record and reproduce a shot. Microchips can not only maintain temperature stability, but can set minor variations in group head temperature that can significantly affect quality in the cup. Perhaps the most devastating observation is that crema may not be the source of espresso's unique flavor, as so often maintained, but may actually impair the taste.

Together, these criticisms present a trenchant challenge to conventional thinking about espresso. The Australian commentator Instaurator has criticized the Italian industry for creating a series of shibboleths about espresso that were "data free observations."[15] Yet it should be remembered that for most of the twentieth century, technology left Italian baristas little choice other than to guesstimate these answers using the evidence of their own senses, while accepting the logic of a market that (unlike specialty) was conditioned, above all, by price.

Such challenges to Italian espresso practices are not reflected in mainstream coffee shops, where the principal problem is an overemphasis on the notion of express service, to the detriment of the coffee itself.[16] Keen to serve coffee quickly, baristas deliver espresso using short run times—not least because in the Anglo-American markets, additional time must be spent on foaming the milk mounted on the vast majority of shots. The result is usually an underextracted espresso that tastes sour and bitter when drunk on its own.[17]

During the first fad for Italian style coffee, in the 1950s, it was common in the U.S. to add a twist of lemon peel—no doubt mimicking the practices of cocktail bars—and to call the resulting beverage an *espresso romano*.[18] This is unknown in Italy where such a combination is normally only used as a purgative, although it is possible lemon was used as a flavor enhancer for coffee on the Amalfi coast—which is where American troops landed during World War II.[19] More likely lemon was added in the U.S. to try and mask the fact that the shots were overextracted in order to generate larger volumes in the cup, usually resulting in dull-tasting beverages. The double-espresso similarly appears to have been developed as a value proposition for foreign markets. It is rarely seen in Italy, where the more usual variation is a **lungo**, a thinner single shot of around 40 ml.

Americano

The most well-known adaptation of espresso to suit foreign tastes is the Americano, a term originally used for cocktail beverages to which soda was added.[20] When the term first came to be applied to coffee is unclear: a journalist observing opera impresarios in Milan in 1931 noted that "Every afternoon between three and four o'clock . . . most of the world's important contracts are agreed upon . . . at one of the cafés over an 'Americano' or a caffè espresso."[21] The context suggests that this "Americano" was an early espresso beverage for foreigners.

Caffè americano was certainly prepared for U.S. servicemen during the Second World War and tourists thereafter as a way of offering them a coffee beverage closer to that they were used to at home. Baristas added hot water onto a shot of espresso, dissipating the crema, and reproducing the body and appearance of a drip-brewed, black coffee.

The Americano played a key role in the transfer of the contemporary specialty coffee shop formula into the UK during the 1990s. Serving purely espresso-based beverages meant that all the coffee drinks offered could be prepared using one machine and a single blend—saving on capital, running costs, and staff training. However, that left the question of what to do when customers requested an "ordinary" black coffee? Answer: prepare an Americano by filling a cappuccino cup with hot water and dropping an espresso shot on top of it. This preserves some sense of the novelty of the beverage in that the crema remains on top, and can be recast as a specialty beverage even though the overall body is closer to drip coffee.

Within the UK market, Americano is the premier black coffee drink consumed out of the home. A survey of the last beverage that customers had consumed in a UK coffee shop in 2011 recorded that 15 percent had ordered an Americano, 4 percent a filter coffee, and just 2 percent an espresso.[22]

Domestic Espresso: Moka, Machines, Pods, and Capsules

The evolution of espresso created a fundamental dichotomy between the styles of coffee consumed in bars and in the home. This helps explain the historically high market share enjoyed by coffee bars in Italy and other Mediterranean countries, where consumers are rewarded for leaving the house. Recently this distinction has begun to erode, leading to a significant transformation in out-of-home coffee culture.

The most common domestic brewer in Italy during the first half of the twentieth century was the *napoletana*, a **flip-over** brewer usually made from tin. The device had two sections separated by a filter. Once the water boiled in the bottom part, the user turned the apparatus over so that the water filtered back down into what was now the lower serving chamber, complete with handle and spout.[23] In the 1930s, Alfonso Bialetti started producing the *moka* pot, made of aluminum, again consisting of two chambers separated by a funnel in which a coffee filter was mounted.[24] Steam pressure built up in the sealed lower chamber once it was placed on the stove top, forcing the remaining hot water up through the funnel into the upper chamber—effectively brewing coffee at 1.5 atmospheres.

The austerity economy imposed by the Fascist regime of the 1930s and by wartime demands held back the development of the domestic coffee market, so it took the economic miracle of the late 1950s to allow the *moka* or *machinetta* (little machine) to replace the *napoletana* in Italian households. Bialetti began promoting his device as a branded product, the Moka Express pot, with which domestic users could supposedly produce "at home, an espresso like that at the bar."[25]

The irony was that while this was probably true in the 1930s, the Gaggia revolution meant it was no longer plausible. One look at coffee prepared with a moka, which lacks any crema, made this clear. Nonetheless, the assertion suited producers like Bialetti and Alessi and roasters like Lavazza, who transformed themselves into national operators by exploiting the growth of the domestic market. Currently around three-quarters of all coffee consumed in the Italian household is prepared with a moka, with household penetration widely estimated at near 100 percent.[26] Yet the continued high proportion of consumption outside the home suggests that Italians understand the contrast between home and bar beverages.

The principal market for espresso machines as domestic appliance has always been found outside Italy. Models such as the Pavoni "Europiccola Professional" of 1974 and the "Baby" Gaggia launched in 1977 traded on the heritage of the two companies, by selling into a luxury market, but were followed by foreign manufacturers such as the German giant Krups and the Portuguese firm Briel, who both started producing entry point machines as part of their range of domestic appliances in the early 1980s.[27]

Such machines use a vibrating pump that can produce high pressure (typically 15 bars) but only with small flows of water. Correctly configured, they can brew a standard espresso shot at around 9 bars, but it is difficult to maintain a stable temperature and pressure to achieve consistent results over a number of shots. The length of time required for the machines to reach their operating temperature and the lack of a direct water supply mean that, far from continuous erogation, substantial time has to pass between shots. Steaming milk adds even more time while the boiler heats up again, usually making domestic espresso brewing anything but "express."

Another difficulty of home operations is controlling flow through the coffee cake. Short of adding a grinder to their setup, domestic users have little option but to use pre-ground blends which, even if sold as espresso, might be better suited for a moka. It is also difficult to dose and tamp this coffee to suit home machines. A potential solution came in the form of the ESE (Easy Serving Espresso) **pod** option, a pre-ground and tamped dose in a paper filter to be placed directly into the portafilter. Pioneered by several roasters and machine manufacturers, notably Illy, the ESE was introduced in the late 1980s as a form of "open-source" standard that any producer could adopt.[28]

Despite its advantages, the ESE system remains a one-size-fits-all approach whose outcomes can be disappointing. Nor does ESE address the long waiting times experienced at home. Its greatest success has been in the out-of-home commercial market, either in nonspecialist outlets such as restaurants whose volume of usage does not merit using fresh coffee or employing trained baristas, or to provide a quick way of serving decaffeinated espresso in coffee bars without separate grinders devoted to decaffeinated beans.

Conversely, **single-portion capsule** machines can deliver both the "express" and "expressly for you" elements of the original espresso proposition to the home or office, as the machines are much quicker to reach operating mode and avoid wasting coffee in producing a single cup. Furthermore, little cleaning and maintenance is required compared with a traditional domestic espresso machine.

Capsule systems had been around for decades, but it was only after consumers became used to espresso beverages in specialty coffee shops in the 1990s that these machines began to experience exponential growth in sales. The Nespresso format was launched as a stand-alone business by Nestle in 1986. Originally built around selling "grand cru" coffees from identified origins on subscription, Nespresso counted 600,000 members in 2000 and had just opened its first boutique. By 2010, the club numbered 10 million, with 215 boutiques worldwide. Total sales of the capsules reached CHF 3.2 billion (US$3.425 billion) as the division maintained an annual growth rate of over 20 percent.[29]

Nespresso's success again raises the issue of increasing divergence between the notions of "espresso" and "Italian espresso." Nespresso's own communications materials are keen to portray the beverages produced by the system as corresponding to the classic Italian recipes. The capsules contain doses of around 5 grams and are delivered into an espresso cup of 40 ml or a lungo of 110 ml. Capsule machines are equipped with a vibrating pump that operates at high pressures (up to 19 bars), and delivers the shots much more quickly than a standard espresso machine.[30] Far from being an Italian espresso, the resulting beverages resemble the thinner-tasting Swiss-French versions of espresso and *café crème*. The fear (from an Italian perspective) is that this will become the standard European conception of espresso.

Italian firms now produce capsule systems for domestic and office use, as well as vending systems that benefit from the latest innovations. These trends have reconfigured the out-of-home market, as the customary stroll to the bar has been replaced by a few steps to the office coffee machine. Italian bars have lost nearly a third of their market share to single-serve machines in the last two decades.[31] Ironically the Italian preference for pure espresso has compounded this problem—capsule systems may be tolerable for shots of espresso, but they have great difficulty reproducing the "white" beverages that dominate most international markets.

PART TWO: WHITE

The key to the evolution of the international espresso beverage menu lies in the addition of a fifth "M," milk. Industry sources claim that Italians take over 80 percent of their coffee as pure espresso, whereas in the Anglo-American coffee shop, over 80 percent of espresso beverages are taken "white." The milk, rather than crema, acts as a visual marker of "authenticity" and quality. In the 1950s, cappuccino was more accessible than espresso to consumers used to drinking white coffee. During the 1980s the foaming of the milk and its pouring as latte art reinforced the American specialty movement's claim that these were artisan, handcrafted beverages., Since the 1990s international coffee shop chains have exploited the opportunity offered by milk to adapt to local preferences, notably by sweetening the beverages.

Macchiato

Italians regard milk as a substance that sits heavily in the stomach and requires digestion: it is a food rather than a beverage. Coffee is considered a digestive, helping to cleanse the stomach rather than fill it. It is therefore natural to take it after the meal or as a way of preparing oneself to eat later. In the 1890s, the leading Italian food writer, Pellegrino Artusi, advised limiting oneself to a cup of black coffee upon awakening. People should eat only a light meal, perhaps of toast and milky coffee, and only after they were convinced that the stomach was empty and ready to receive food, while still leaving time and space to consume the day's main meal at lunchtime.[32] Today, this view translates into a preference for beginning the day with a black coffee brewed in a *moka*, accompanied at most by a dry biscuit, before perhaps taking a cappuccino and croissant an hour or two later in the bar either on the way to or during the first break from work. Coffee might follow lunch or dinner to aid digestion, but Italians never drink a milky beverage after meals that would sit on the stomach. At most, postprandial coffee might be **macchiato**, "marked" with a splash of milk.

Kapuziner, Cappuccino, Caffèlatte, Latte Macchiato

It seems probable that the term **cappuccino** entered the Italian language during the period of Austrian domination over much of Northern Italy, as a derivative of the Austrian *kapuziner*. So named because its color matched that of the robes worn by Capuchin friars, the *kapuziner* bore little resemblance to the beverage we know today. An Englishman caught up in the Viennese popular insurrection of 1848 recorded how:

The coffee-house was my only resource: there was at least some comfort in sipping a *kapuziner*. This word means in English a Cappuchin [sic] monk, but it signifies in Austrian parlance a glass of coffee with milk. The Austrians take their coffee in glasses, like the Russians, but they do not sweeten it with honey as that civilized nation are wont to do.[33]

Travel guides to Austria in the early 1900s confirm that *capuziner* or *kapuziner* was a beverage "with more coffee than milk" in contrast to *melange* for which the reverse was true.[34]

By this time the term *cappuccino* was already in use in Italy. Baedeker's 1904 guide provides an introduction to the coffee menu and café culture:

Cafés are frequented mostly in the late afternoon and evening. The tobacco-smoke is frequently objectionable. *Caffè nero*, or coffee without milk, is usually drunk. *Caffè latte* (served only in the morning) is coffee mixed with milk; *cappuccino*, or small cup, cheaper; or *caffè e latte* i.e. with the milk served separately, may be preferred.[35]

Both cappuccino and caffè **latte** were combinations of coffee and milk that could as easily be prepared at home as in the café, while the difference between the two was the relative proportions of coffee and milk in the cup. In the first edition of his dictionary of new words in Italian in 1905, Alfredo Panzini confirms that the smaller quantity of milk in the cappuccino spawned its name. He defined cappuccino as "Black coffee 'corrected' with milk. A colloquial term probably derived from the similar color to the habit of the capuchin friars."[36]

Panzini suggested that the word cappuccino had a regional origin, linking it to northern Italy during the period of direct Austrian rule that lasted until the 1860s, and in the case of Trieste, the Habsburgs' principal port on the Adriatic, to 1918. There is little demand for cappuccino in those southern regions of Italy that never came under Austrian control, while a cappuccino in Trieste is served much shorter than elsewhere, usually in an espresso cup, perhaps reflecting its likely original serving style in a demitasse.

Analyzing subsequent editions of Panzini's dictionary, it becomes clear that the use of "cappuccino" in relation to coffee preceded that of "espresso." In the 1918 edition, for example, cappuccino is defined as above, but "espresso" is only mentioned to denote fast trains and postal deliveries, perhaps because the first espresso machines claimed to make "instantaneous" coffee. Even in 1931, when Panzini stated that it was commonplace to use "espresso" to describe a coffee made "using a pressure machine or a filter," the fact that he links both forms of preparation placed the emphasis on express service rather than on the coffee itself. His definition of cappuccino remained essentially unchanged: "black coffee mixed with a little milk."[37]

This suggests that it was some time before Italians came to expect that a cappuccino could only be prepared using an espresso from a pressure machine or that the milk to be mounted on it should be foamed, or even heated, prior to serving. Individual barmen probably experimented with using the steam wands attached to the early, vertical machines to warm milk, but these were primarily used for warming the ingredients for the "hot toddies" served in the upmarket cocktail bars, where most machines were installed.[38]

This appears to have changed during the 1930s. In 1933, *Harper's Bazaar* wrote of how Rome's "eyeopener is an express strong coffee diluted with milk and called cappuccino," which it recommended drinking on a café terrace at breakfast while watching the Fascist black shirts go by.[39] By 1938 a slang term *cappuccio* was already being used "somewhat jokily instead of cappuccino, almost as if to recommend to the barista not to give one too little" (*-ino* is an Italian suffix meaning rather small).[40] *Barista* itself was a new term whose origins likely lie in the Fascist insistence on replacing foreign words (in this case *barman*) with Italianate terms. Its inclusion in the definition suggests that cappuccino was by now principally a beverage taken in the bar and made with espresso.

Caffèlatte (one word) made its first appearance in the 1935 edition of Panzini's dictionary, defined simply as "coffee and milk."[41] Mussolini supposedly started the day with caffèlatte, as did many ordinary peasants and workers, for whom caffèlatte was seen as a breakfast in itself, often served combined with some bread in an almost broth-like concoction. This was likely to have been prepared using branded coffee surrogates such as Caffeol, made from **chicory** and chickpeas, which became popular during the 1930s. A 1953 survey found that 42 percent of the population consumed caffèlatte first thing in the morning.[42] However when the same survey attempted to calculate average daily coffee intake, it deliberately excluded caffèlatte from its calculations due to its lack of coffee content. Caffèlatte then was understood to be a domestic beverage that did not necessarily contain coffee, let alone espresso. Indeed, we know that even Mussolini's caffèlatte was no more than warmed milk.[43]

The revolution in espresso preparation in the postwar era also changed the nature of cappuccino, given the new taste profile at the base of the beverage. Into the 1980s, however, a sense persisted that drinking cappuccino was somewhat feminine, and to this day the *latte macchiato* (prepared by dropping an espresso shot into a glass of steamed milk) remains a rare sight in the Italian bar—ordered only by children, convalescents, and those (usually ladies of a certain age) with fragile stomachs.[44] Caffèlatte remains strictly a domestic drink, and if requested in a hotel arrives as a pot of coffee and jug of steamed milk to be mixed to suit one's personal tastes.

INEI devised parameters for certified Italian cappuccino that were approved by parliament in 2007. The guidelines are 100 ml of cold milk expanded to a volume of 125 ml by foaming to a temperature of around 55°C and poured over a certified Italian espresso of 25 ml in a 150–160 ml cup.[45] Note here the overall proportions of the beverage and the relatively low temperature of the milk, meaning that the cappuccino can be drunk straight away. Both of these would have to be adjusted to facilitate the transfer of cappuccino beyond Italy.

The Cappuccino Conquests

Domenico Parisi, a former barber, who opened the Cafe Reggio in New York's Greenwich Village in 1927, invested his savings into importing the first espresso machine into the United States. An article published about the café in 1935 noted that it served "Cappucino [sic] (a marvellous blend of strong coffee, steamed milk and cinnamon)." According to the *New Yorker*, which caught up with Parisi, still using his machine some twenty years later in 1955, "he releases a valve which allows steam to whip milk into a froth and emit an appalling, ripping sound, like a barrage of rockets fired from a dive bomber."[46]

Cappuccino, rather than espresso, was the main feature of the coffee menu. Parisi appears to have prepared it topped with frothed, not just steamed milk, if we assume his technique was essentially the same over the twenty-year period; and he appears responsible for the use of cinnamon as a topping—an innovation widely copied across the U.S. but for which there was no clear precedent in Italy. The benefit was to further sweeten the milky beverages that, Parisi was the first to realize, were more easily adapted to local tastes.

The Gaggia revolution sparked a new interest in espresso machines outside Italy during the 1950s. These were largely distributed through agents, so that it was left to local importers and entrepreneurs—by no means all Italian immigrants—to transfer and adapt espresso culture. In the UK, the first Gaggia machine was installed in the Moka Bar in London's Soho in 1952; by 1960, there were supposedly some 2,000 coffee bars in the country, of which over 500 were in London itself.[47]

This boom was fuelled by cappuccino rather than espresso. The beverage offered many advantages to both caterers and customers. The appearance of the frothed milk on top of the coffee and the theatricality of its preparation, notably the sound of the steam, served to highlight the novelty of the beverage to a public shaking off the austerity of the postwar years. Yet it was also more accessible to British customers who had long been in the habit of adding milk to their hot beverages and were already acquainted with the American milkshake. It was served dusted with cocoa powder, again adding to both the visual appeal and the sweetness of the drink.

Cappuccino's greatest advantage was that it fit closely into the sociocultural expectations of what the British wanted in beverages away from home. Cappuccino took longer than espresso to consume, providing the appearance of greater value for money. The longer time frame also created a social context that could allow conversation to develop, an important consideration to the significant proportion of customers who were teenagers on dates. Serving the cappuccino "hot" extended the time further and also met the expectations of consumers used to beverages prepared with boiling water. These features resulted in one of the iconic images of the period after an Italian client at a Soho coffee bar commented that he could shave in the time it took for his cappuccino to reach a drinkable temperature and was invited back to be photographed doing so!.[48]

Many British cafés developed more ersatz versions of the beverage, simply heating milk with a steam wand and mounting it on top of conventionally brewed or even instant coffee. This was usually described as "frothy" coffee. The Anglo-Italian proprietors who dominated the "working-man's café" sector were as complicit as anyone else in this development.[49] The consequent devaluation of cappuccino was captured in a sketch from "Not the Nine O'clock News," a British TV comedy show of the 1980s, in which an Italianate café proprietor is shown cowering behind a Gaggia and making steaming noises while pouring boiling water onto instant coffee, mixing in ingredients such as cigarette ash and dish detergent, and finally blowing bubbles into his creation through a straw.[50]

That joke contrasts with the fetishization of cappuccino in the Café Nervosa, the fictional Seattle coffeehouse frequented by the Crane brothers in the U.S. television hit *Frasier* a decade or so later. By this juncture, Italian-style coffee beverages had been recruited to do the hard work for the U.S. specialty coffee movement by persuading the public that coffee could be a premium artisan food product, with the foamed milk reinforcing the claim that these were handcrafted beverages. In 1994, gourmet retailers reported that in-store sales of espresso-based beverages were outstripping those of traditional drip brewed coffee.[51]

Caffè Latte

The most successful beverage of the new age, however, was caffè latte. Its popularity was such that by 1991 it accounted for 75 percent of all sales from the coffee carts that brought espresso to the streets of Seattle.[52] It was marketed as an Italian version of the better known French combination of brewed coffee and warmed milk, *café au lait*, but with a more discernible coffee taste as a result of using espresso. That said, its primary attraction was that the steamed milk used in the latte made it taste significantly sweeter than cappuccino.

This was the moment that caffè latte (two words) became codified as an espresso-based beverage served at the coffee cart, bar, or shop as opposed to the Italian *caffèlatte* (one word) that was prepared with a home-brewed moka. At first it was served as, in effect, a latte macchiato, with the espresso shot poured into a transparent glass already containing the steamed milk, but now topped with a small head of foam. This produced a spectacular theatrical effect as the espresso blended into the steamed milk, gradually changing the beverage's color, while leaving a white head on top. This is still highly popular in the German market. A quicker method of preparation for Anglo-American operators, however, was to reverse the process by beginning by delivering an espresso shot into a wide-brimmed cup that could be placed directly under the portafilter and then adding the steamed milk topped with foam. Some theatrical "value added" and sense of artisanship could be produced by training baristas to pour "latte art" onto the beverage.

The difference between cappuccino and caffè latte at this point revolved around the preparation and proportion of the milk used. Steaming milk is simple: the wand is placed around the pitcher and the steam is turned on. The milk is warmed but does not expand. Frothing milk requires the introduction of air alongside the steam by putting the tip of the wand in close to the surface of the milk so that air is sucked in, filling the milk with bubbles. When poured, the steamed milk in the body of the jug will emerge first, followed by the foam from the top. The standard food service definition was that cappuccino consisted of equal proportions of espresso, steamed milk, and frothed milk, so the difference between this and the caffè latte lay simply in the proportions of the two types of milk poured into the cup. This meant, as Nick Jurich argued in his highly influential 1991 guide *Espresso from Bean to Cup*, that "the line between a latte and a cappuccino becomes quite vague."[53]

Some operators have attempted to redifferentiate the two beverages by increasing the frothed proportion of the cappuccino, benchmarking their baristas' success to the height, rather than the quality, of the foam.[54] This has resulted in a shift from the "wet" version of cappuccino, comprising equal portions of steamed and frothed milk, to the "dry" version composed largely, if not entirely of an airy "macrofoam" that comes from intensive frothing. The high end of the specialty industry, however, has increasingly sought to "texture" milk by creating a vortex on the surface that helps to "spin and stretch" the milk and results in the entirety being transformed into a creamy, smooth, microfoam. David Schomer, a specialist in "espresso preparation as a culinary art" who founded Seattle's Espresso Vivace in 1988, argues that because "ultra-fine texture is the only desirable foam consistency for espresso-making," the main distinction between the two beverages is that cappuccino is served in a ratio of 5 parts milk to 1 part espresso in a 6- or 7-ounce cup, whereas latte needs a 12-ounce cup and a 6:1 ratio.[55]

Tall, Grande, Venti, Skinny, Soy, Syrup, Breve

In his 1996 book *Espresso Coffee: Professional Techniques*, Schomer predicted that, "We [Americans] are a health-conscious people, and soon we will reject the drinking of 12–16 ounces of milk a day with our tall latte. . . . I believe that the culture will evolve into custom-ers ordering less milk."[56]

Precisely the reverse has occurred. The 16-ounce cup has become standard, while the 20-ounce "venti" is now firmly entrenched in popular culture. Increasing the volume of the beverage not only created a sense of greater value for money (particularly useful for the takeaway trade) but also increasing the proportion of milk to coffee further sweetened the beverage. Today, the three standard Starbucks' sizes are the tall at 260 ml, the grande, 340 ml, and the venti, 450 ml (compared with INEI's recommended 160 ml).[57] In the U.S., the tall is still brewed with just a single shot of espresso, in contrast to Schomer's recipe, which calls for two. This alters the taste while offering the opportunity to charge customers for an extra shot.

The commodification of caffè latte within the coffee shop format has gone much further. The nature of the milk used in the coffee can be used to present a supposedly healthier propo-sition: Starbucks customers can choose whole milk, 2 percent, nonfat, and soy. Certainly this choice has some impact—according to figures provided by Starbucks in 2004, the 260 calories in a grande latte made with whole milk fell to 210 when prepared with soy and to 160 if made with nonfat milk. Conferring Italianate names on other concoctions helped to camouflage their properties—the "breve," for example, made with "half and half," half milk, half cream, yields 550 calories as a grande latte and a whopping 770 for a venti (around a third of the recommended adult daily caloric intake).[58]

Intriguingly the figures given on the Starbucks website of 2012 are significantly lower, with a whole fat grande latte now listed at 220 calories, while a latte made from 2 percent milk—the default option in the U.S. since 2007—rings in at 190 calories. The much higher foam content of a cappuccino in Starbucks' interpretation of the beverage is captured in the fact that the whole milk grande cappuccino contains only 140 calories, dropping to 80 in the nonfat version.[59]

The latte can also incorporate additional flavorings, usually added through syrups. The first man to spot this potential is widely believed to be "Brandy" Brandenburger, a veteran member of the San Francisco coffee scene. After making various experiments in the legendary North Beach Italian-American coffee house Caffè Trieste, Brandenburger recommended that Torani, a syrup manufacturer, develop a line for use in coffee shops.[60] The most popular flavors are the classics, almond, caramel, and vanilla; but a big advantage of syrups is that they can easily be used to create "new" or "seasonal" beverages such as the Starbucks Gingerbread Latte.

Syrups, alongside milk type, cup size, the extra shot, and the foaming style (dry or wet), provide customers with a set of choices to customize their beverages. The ability of cappuc-cino and caffè latte to accommodate these is a further reason for their centrality within the international coffeehouse menu.

Mocha, Marocchino, Babyccino, Flat White

Although cappuccino and caffè latte are clearly connected to Italy, the origins of other beverages that are rapidly becoming standard items within the coffee shop offer are more obscure. The most well-known is *mocha*, now standardized as latte with chocolate and served in most international coffee shops.

The closest beverages to mocha to be found in the 1960s U.S. coffeehouse manuals were *caffè chocolaccino* ("it is really frothy cappuccino, but is served in a tall cup and topped with whipped cream and a mound of shaved French chocolate") and *caffè Borgia* (in which grated orange peel replaces the chocolate shavings).[61] These coffees were partly designed to satisfy consumer desires for a beverage that could be ordered as a substitute for dessert.

Mocha continued in this role during the specialty era. Jurich castigated all who failed to realize that "cherries, chocolate sprinkles, and whipped cream have no place in cappuccino," but then offered a recipe for caffè mocha in which a shot of espresso was added to chocolate syrup, steamed milk and whipped cream were mounted on top, and then dusted with grated chocolate, powdered cocoa, chocolate chips, adding sugar or vanilla sugar to taste, and with an option of brewing with cloves.[62] In 1993, Kenneth Davids reported that "American caffès [sic] simply add chocolate fountain syrup to a caffè latte and call it a mocha," although he noted that Starbucks termed this a *moccaccino*, a now abandoned term that was consistent with the chain's policy of giving quasi-Italian names to non-Italian concoctions.[63]

The success of the mocha has had repercussions in Italy itself. In the late 1980s, coffee bars began serving the *marocchino*, an espresso dusted with sweet chocolate powder, then topped with textured milk, and re-dusted with chocolate powder, thus giving it a darker appearance than a cappuccino or indeed espresso macchiato.[64] In effect this was an Italianized version of the mocha, enabling the reappearance of the chocolate/coffee combination on the Italian espresso menu. It is sometimes claimed to be a modernization of the *bicerin*, a pre-espresso mixed beverage of chocolate and coffee served at a coffeehouse of the same name founded in Turin in 1763. Less convincingly the name is said to refer to the color of Moroccan leatherbound books; maybe, but the term *marocchino* ("Moroccan") came into vogue as a generic slang term for African immigrants before the beverage surfaced in coffee bars.

Another beverage that has had most impact on the international menu is the *Babyc(c)ino*. This seems to have originated in Australasia in the late 1990s, providing children with a caffeine-free imitation beverage to sip while their mothers enjoyed their lattes.[65] It consists of foamed milk, usually served in an espresso cup, at times with the addition of chocolate sprinkles. It crossed into the UK and found its way onto the menus of the chains, including Costa and Starbucks, and has also subsequently been recorded in Italy and the U.S. (though not on Starbucks' menu).[66]

The Australasian beverage that has had most impact on the international menu is the flat white. It initially took the form of a long black (an Australian version of Americano) to which either cold or warmed milk had been added, prepared for those who did not appreciate the frothy cappuccinos that appeared in Australia from the mid-1950s.[67] The flat white first mutated into a mini-latte, but by the 2000s had developed into a more refined beverage, consisting of a strong double espresso brewed with around 21 grams in the portafilter, served in an 8-ounce cup topped with milk that had been microfoamed into a creamy velvet-like consistency. There was no doming of the milk at the surface (unlike cappuccino), so some latte art could be poured on, typically in a fern-like design resembling the national symbol of New Zealand.[68]

This version of the beverage arrived in London at the end of 2005, when barista owners from New Zealand and Australia opened the Flat White café in Soho. The café's success led to a quasi-chain migration of other antipodean baristas to the British capital, playing a prominent role in the establishment of a high-end independent café culture. The beverage itself showcased all the advances made within the artisan sector: a much stronger espresso than the traditional Italian version, milk-foaming skills necessary to produce the requisite smoothness, and latte art.

The chains responded by adopting and adapting the flat white, with Starbucks UK rolling it out in December 2009 and Costa in January 2010, the latter describing it as "richer than a Latte, creamier than a Cappuccino . . . a true coffee lovers' coffee," despite serving it in a standard 12-ounce cup.[69] The managing director of another Italian-branded chain claimed that what they were launching was actually "the antipodean Flat White with a genuine Italian taste."[70] About 14 percent of UK coffee shop customers now regularly order a flat white, despite paying more for it than for cappuccino or latte.[71]

Of Milk and Machines

While the Italian coffee industry has benefited enormously from the global boom in the consumption of Italian-style coffee beverages, it has had to adjust to this being driven by the milk beverages. Early suppliers of machines to the American specialty operators, such as Kent Bakke of Espresso Specialists in Seattle, had to seek out machines that were best suited to preparing cappuccinos and lattes. Bakke chose to work with La Marzocco, a small artisanal machine manufacturer from Florence, essentially because its dual boiler system, in which one boiler is used purely for steaming, made it much easier to prepare milk beverages than the equipment produced by the bigger, better-known Italian companies.[72] In 1994 Bakke headed an American consortium that took a 90 percent stake in the company and opened a U.S.-based subsidiary, principally to satisfy the demands of his leading client, Starbucks.

In 2000, however, Starbucks turned to the Swiss manufacturer Thermoplan to provide the push-button Verisimo machine. This "super-automatic" device grinds the beans and brews the espresso shots automatically, leaving the barista with responsibility only for frothing the milk and assembling the beverage.[73] Starbucks' change of supplier symbolized a much broader trend. Espresso beverages shifted from specialty beverages to mass-market commodities, demanded as part of the standard menu in most retail outlets. Nonspecialist operators needed equipment that enabled them to deliver the drinks to a consistent recipe without investing in barista training. Non-Italian manufacturers, most notably Swiss firms such as Egro, Franke, Jura, and Schearer, had long been interested in automating the entire process, producing superautomatic bean-to-cup machines that even assemble the beverage on the push of a button. These are highly sophisticated machines, but their essential function is deskilling the barista.

At the same time, the traditional Italian semi-automatic and automatic machines have had to be redesigned, if only to create sufficiently large clearance heights for the outsized cups used abroad under the group heads, while much investment has gone into the refining of the steam wand, creating injection systems that deliver both steam and air into the beverage and automatically heat the milk to a predetermined temperature, thus again reducing the time and technique demanded from the barista.

Home machine manufacturers too, starting with Krups, have developed "frothing sleeves" that fit over the normal steam wand on the machine and supposedly assist in sucking more air into the milk to assist in foaming. Yet the small boiler capacity of most such machines

CONCLUSION

It is now over a century since Pavoni began manufacturing the first commercial pressure brewing machine, introducing the world to the concept of espresso and setting in course the chain of events by which domestic beverages such as cappuccino and caffè latte would come to be redefined as part of the espresso menu. The versions that we currently consume are merely the latest expressions of an ongoing process of international experimentation and exchange. Both Italy and America have played leading roles in these transfers, but increasingly they are responding to, as much as driving, the continuing evolution of global espresso culture.

NOTES

1. The Cappuccino Conquests research project was funded by a grant from the AHRC/ESRC Cultures of Consumption research programme (RES-154-25-0015). See Jonathan Morris, "La globalizzazione dell'espresso italiano," *Memoria e Ricerca* XIV, no. 23 (2006): 27–46; "The Cappuccino Conquests" (pdf), 2007, http://herts.academia.edu/JonathanMorris.

2. Centro Studi e Formazione Assagiatori, "L'Espresso Italiano Certificato," supplement to *L'Assaggio* no. 6, September 1999, 7.

3. Jonathan Morris, "Making Italian espresso, making espresso Italian," *Food and History* 8, no. 2 (2010): 143–68.

4. Franco Capponi, *La Victoria Arduino* (2005) 4–7.

5. Bezzera also continued making machines under his own name. See Elena Locatelli, *La Pavoni 1905–2005* (2005); Franco Capponi, "Espresso coffee machines and their history," in *Nuovo Simonelli and Its Roots,* ed. Maurizio Giuli (2011), 253.

6. "The History of Reneka" (pdf), 2007, http://www.reneka.com/expresso-brand.phtml.

7. On the evolution of espresso machines see Ian Bersten, *Coffee Floats, Tea Sinks* (Roseville, Australia: Helian Books, 1993); Enrico Maltoni, *Espresso Made in Italy* (Collezione Enrico Maltoni, 2001), www.espressomadeinitaly.com.

8. Enrico Maltoni, ed., *Faema Espresso* (Faenza, Italy: Faenza Industrie Grafiche, 2009).

9. Roland Barthes, *Mythologies* (London: Cape, 1972), 37.

10. Carlo Grenci, "The other Italian coffee tradition," *Café Europa* 15 (2003): 3.

11. Luigi Odello, *Espresso Italiano Specialist* (Brescia, Italy: Istituto Nazionale Espresso Italiano, 2003), 72–78.

12. Ernesto Illy, "Espresso Trends," keynote address to SCAA, Seattle, 1992 (audio copy in SCAA library).

13. Kenneth Davids, "Better than ever: Boutique espressos," *Coffee Review,* May 2006, http://www .coffeereview.com/article.cfm?ID=184.

14. See James Hoffman's 2009 video blog and subsequent comments at http://www.jimseven .com/2009/07/06/video-1-crema/.

15. Instaurator, *The Espresso Quest* (Loowedge, Australia: Copacabana Publishing, 2008), 21–28.

16. Paul Meikle-Janney, "Back to Basics," presentation to UK Coffee Leader Summit, London, March 29, 2012.

17. Jim Schulman, "Some Aspects of Espresso Extraction," 2007, available at http://coffeecuppers.com/Espresso.htm.

18. Pan-American Coffee Bureau, *Fun with Coffee* (New York: Pan-American Coffee Bureau, 1956), 7–8.

19. My thanks to Claudia Galetta and her colleagues at Lavazza for this information.

20. Alfredo Panzini, *Supplemento ai dizionari italiani*, 3rd ed. (1918), 37.

21. Myra Davis, "The Song Market," *Manchester Guardian*, February 20, 1931, p. 6.

22. Allegra Strategies, *Project Cafè11 UK* (London: Allegra Strategies, 2011).

23. Adelaide Del Sant, *Coffee Makers* (1995), 31–33.

24. Jeffrey T. Schnapp, "The romance of caffeine and aluminum," *Critical Inquiry* 28, no. 1 (Autumn 2001): 249–69.

25. Schnapp, "Romance," 265.

26. Maurizio Cociancich, *100% Espresso Italiano* (2008), 140.

27. http://www.krups.com/Focus/History; www.briel.pt/the company; accessed April 5, 2012.

28. Corby Kummer, *The Joy of Coffee*, rev. ed. (Boston: Houghton Mifflin, 2003), 110.

29. Maarten Decker, "The Nespresso Story," presentation to Allegra European Coffee Symposium, Berlin, November 24, 2011.

30. "Nespresso: Parla Marco Zancolò direttore generale della filiale italiana," *Comunicaffè* 23 (September 2010).

31. Vincenzo Sandalj, "Mediterranean markets," *Café Europa* 45 (2011): 18.

32. Pellegrino Artusi, *Science in the Kitchen and the Art of Eating Well*, trans. Murtha Baca and Stephen Sartarelli (Toronto: University of Toronto Press, 2003), 560.

33. "Vienna during the siege and after it," *Fraser's Magazine for Town and Country* 39 (1849): 457.

34. *Baedeker's Guide to Austria including Hungary, Transylvania, Dalmatia and Bosnia* (1900), 2; John Murray, *A Handbook for Travellers in South Germany and Austria* (1903), 32.

35. K. Baedeker, *Italy from the Alps to Naples* (1904), xxii.

36. Panzini, *Supplemento ai dizionari italiani*, 3rd ed. (1918), 93; probably a straight reprint from the first edition of 1905.

37. Panzini, *Supplemento*, 6th ed. (1931), 229, 108.

38. The patent for Arduino's original Victoria machine presented in December 1906 described it as an instantaneous warmer for all liquids. Capponi, *La Victoria Arduino*, 15–17.

39. This reference can be seen at Google Books: http://books.google.co.uk/books?sourceid=navclient&ie=UTF-8&rlz=1T4GGHP_en-GBGB461GB461&q=harpers+bazaar+cappuccino+1933.

40. Alfredo Panzini and Bruno Migliorini, *Dizionario moderno delle parole che non si trovano nei dizionari comuni* (1950), 801.

41. Reprinted in Panzini and Migliorini, *Dizionario moderno*, 97.

42. Pierpaolo Luzzatto Fegiz, *Il volto sconosciuto dell'Italia* (1956), 123–31.

43. Carol Helstosky, *Garlic and Oil* (Oxford: Berg, 2004), 99.

44. Interview with Sergio Guarnieri, LaCimbali, Binasco, January 27, 2005.

45. "Cappuccino Italiano Certificato" (pdf), www.espressoitaliano.org.

46. Both articles are on the Caffe Reggio website, http://www.cafereggio.com/press (accessed May 8, 2012).

47. Edward Bramah, *Tea and Coffee* (London: Hutchinson,1972), 67–75.

48. "Guerra e pace a Soho attorno al caffè espresso," *La Voce degli Italiani*, December 1954, 5.

49. Jonathan Morris, "Imprenditoria italiana in Gran Bretagna," *Italia Contemporanea*, 241 (December 2005): 540–52.

50. *The Best of Not the 9 O'Clock News* (DVD), vol. 2 (2004).

51. Gallup, *Study of Awareness and Use of Gourmet and Specialty Coffees* (1994).

52. Himanee Gupta, "Espresso to Go," *Seattle Times*, September 24, 1990, B.1.

53. Nick Jurich, *Espresso from Bean to Cup* (Missing Link Press,1991), 112.

54. Meikle-Janney, "Back to Basics."

278

Jonathan Morris

55. David C. Schomer, *Espresso Coffee: Professional Techniques* (Seattle: Peanut Butter Publ.,1996), 131, 155.

56. Schomer, *Espresso Coffee*, 152.

57. *Starbucks Order Guide*, Point of Sale Literature, UK, 2002.

58. *You, Starbucks and Nutrition*, Point of Sale Literature, USA, 2004.

59. http://www.starbucks.com/menu/catalog/nutrition?drink=all#view_control=nutrition, accessed May 6, 2012.

60. Interview with Sonia Giotta, Caffè Trieste, San Francisco, August 2, 2010.

61. The Coffee Brewing Institution, *Today's Coffeehouse (A Handbook)* (1964), 10.

62. Jurich, *Espresso*, 113.

63. Kenneth Davids, *Espresso: Ultimate Coffee*, 2nd ed (New York: St. Martin's Griffin, 2001, original 1993), 43.

64. Touring Club Italiano, *L'Italia del caffè* (2004), 9.

65. Sue Butler et al., *Australian Phrasebook* (1994), 91.

66. See http://reversecultureshock.com/2010/03/09/the-starbucks-babyccino/, accessed May 6, 2012;

67. Greg Dixon, "Coffee . . . for kids!" *The Brooklyn Paper*, February 15, 2012.

68. "How Cafes Make the 'Flattie,'" *Boughton's Coffee House*, July/August 2009, 6.

69. "Flat White," Costa Coffee Point of Sale Brochure, 2010.

70. Boughton's newsflash, March 16, 2010.

71. My thanks to Anya Marco of Allegra Strategies for her advice on this section.

72. Interview with Kent Bakke, Seattle, January 7, 2005.

73. Howard Schultz with Joanne Gordon, *Onward: How Starbucks Fought for Its Life without Losing Its Soul* (New York: Rodale, 2011), 121–22.

Eli Rosenberg, "The Birth of the Cool," *New Zealand Herald*, July 22, 2008.

46

The Competing Languages of Coffee

Signs, Narratives, and Symbols of American Specialty Coffee

Kenneth Davids

The initiating act of the American specialty coffee movement is generally assumed to be the opening by **Alfred Peet** of his Peet's Coffee & Tea store on Vine Street in Berkeley in 1966. Small, roaster-in-the-back-of-the-store coffee companies surviving from the early part of the twentieth century doubtless helped provide Peet his model, but the dark-stained pine counters and glass-fronted coffee bins of the Vine Street store, the coffee bags on the walls, a sprinkling of antique coffee gear and tribal knick-knacks, all redolent of a kind of fusion of the European and the exotic, proved to be particularly inspiring to a generation of entrepreneurs and provided the American specialty industry's founding imagery.

From its inception, **specialty coffee**'s self-representation was propelled by an assumed moral or aesthetic superiority. In way of justification for this stance, the industry developed a range of metanarratives and symbolic representations that express sometimes overlapping, sometimes conflicting aspirations and appeals.

What follows is a rapid, irreverent run, as I interpret messages about coffee, through these histories and imageries, roughly chronological, but focused as well on their ongoing interdependency and implicit dialogue.

METAHISTORY 1: THE SPECIALTY COFFEE INDUSTRY'S FOUNDING MYTH, AUTHENTICITY REVIVED (OR COFFEE GROWS ON TREES, NOT IN CANS)

The specialty coffee industry arrived to save the consumer from the manipulations of an increasingly hegemonic commodity system that gradually reduced coffee, a living, natural product rooted in diverse histories and cultures, to a bland, brown, heavily processed substance sold in branded cans and bottles. This salvation is achieved through a product fresh-roasted by hand, sold in bulk, and expressing the authentic source of the product by telling us which exotic tropical places it comes from.

*"This salvation is achieved through a product fresh-roasted by hand, sold in bulk . . . "*The appeal to artisan authenticity and product freshness originally was expressed most vividly through

sensory spectacle rather than secondary representation in signs and labels. In Alfred Peet's Vine Street store the antique roaster and its slightly crooked pipe rising to the high ceiling were situated immediately in back of the sales counter in plain view of customers. Even when single stores expanded to modest chains with a centralized roasting facility, the freshly roasted beans still glistened in glass-fronted bins and the smell of roasted coffee permeated the premises.

However, as the specialty industry expanded and consolidated, the freshness spectacle became increasingly marginalized as a means of invoking the authenticity narrative. Today, Starbucks and other large specialty companies roast and package their coffees hundreds or even thousands of miles from where they are ultimately sold, the main difference being the coffee is often whole bean rather than pre-ground, and the packaging is marginally more technically sophisticated than the familiar metal can. The best Starbucks could do with its back-to-our-roots Pike Street Market blend launched in 2008 was print a "Scooped on" date on the bag (that is, scooped out of a five-pound bulk bag, a rather odd reference to the considerably more meaningful "Roasted on" dates that appear on the bags of coffees offered by more traditional specialty companies). Nevertheless, the original freshness spectacle lives on, deployed by a contingent of new, small-scale regional roasting companies started by entrepreneurs who passionately re-embody variations on the original Alfred Peet model.

"Expressing the authentic source of the product by telling us which exotic tropical place it came from." In Alfred Peet's Vine Street store the brown-toned menu listed coffees for sale identified by names both mysterious and exotic: Guatemala Antigua, Kenya AA, Sumatra Mandheling. The "exotic origins" element of the founding metanarrative of specialty coffee has turned out to be particularly productive in generating continued refinements of representation, since it does not require the physical reinforcement of sensory spectacle. It can be conveyed in secondary representations on signs, labels, brochures, and brands. It has contributed to two of the most ubiquitous and conflicting symbol sets of specialty coffee, taken up later in this analysis under the headings Safari in a Cup and Save the World One Cup at a Time.

METAHISTORY 2: COFFEE, THE WINE OF DEMOCRACY

From its inception specialty coffee incorporated a second stream of commerce and myth: The café or coffee house. This element of the specialty coffee industry required a justifying myth of European origins, a myth most thoroughly expressed by William Ukers's encyclopedic book *All About Coffee* (1935) and carried forward by many popularizers:

Before the advent of coffee, Europe was run by morose aristocrats in impractical clothing, sitting around drafty castles wasting their mental energy digesting breakfasts consisting of warm beer, bread, and other weighty, thought-inhibiting substances. Then came coffee and coffeehouses, and Europe was energized. In due course democracy, individualism, modern culture and the specialty coffee industry were born, and castles were turned into museums with attached cafés.

In the 1950s and 1960s neighborhood coffeehouses were opened in American cities by Italian immigrants, initially for a clientele of other Italian immigrants. In many of these neighborhoods the Italians were soon joined by artists and other bourgeois bohemians of miscellaneous heritage. Howard Schultz's great innovation with Starbucks was fusing the Italian-style café (properly, caffè) and the specialty coffee store à la Alfred Peet into a single, Americanized package, accessible and largely free of intimidating insiders slouching at marble-topped tables dressed in the hip uniform of the day. With the café or caffè, the symbolic referencing was not to tropical origins, but rather to European antecedents. The emphasis was on what the roasting machine and espresso machine did to the coffee, not on where the green, unroasted coffee beans came from. Rather than Kenya AA or Guatemala Antigua one chose from either (1) a nameless espresso **blend** or (2) various blends of coffee named with reference to the degree or darkness of the roast rather to the **origin** of the green coffee: French Roast, Italian Roast, Viennese Roast. The iconography of the Wine of Democracy metamyth originally ran to marbletop tables together with either wood engravings of eighteenth-century cafés and coffeehouses or art deco posters from the early days of espresso in Italy, but variations include the thrift store furniture mode of many college caffès together with various Starbucks-inspired postmodern pastiches.

METAHISTORY 3: COFFEE THE OPPRESSOR OF THE TROPICAL POOR AND AGENT OF CAPITALIST ADDICTION

Both the authenticity myth and the wine of democracy history were soon challenged by a third narrative, crystallized in the late 1990s:

Coffee is just another addictive drug that early mercantile capitalists jumped on to supplement sugar and tobacco in the development of global capitalism. Louis XV or Voltaire, Eisenhower or Ginsburg, it doesn't matter, they're all just addicts supporting the exploitation of slave labor and the ruination of nature. Baristas are nothing but parasites with cool tattoos unwittingly collaborating with a system in which slaves have been replaced by free workers whose freedom consists largely of choosing between starving on the land or migrating to a slum and selling Chiclets. The only answer is fair trade certification, which has the added advantage of clearly dividing the coffee-drinking population between those addicts who are virtuous and those irritating, trivial snobs who rationalize their addiction by yammering on about floral notes and crema on their espresso shots.

This metanarrative, invoked in part by Gregory Dicum's and Nina Luttinger's *The Coffee Book* (1999), gained traction in particular around a successful media campaign mounted by TransFair USA (now **Fair Trade USA**) on behalf of fair trade **certification**, a campaign that coincided with a period of extreme low **green coffee** prices that devastated producers (2000 through about 2003). In industry gatherings like the annual conference of the **Specialty Coffee Association of America** (SCAA), implicit and explicit debate intensified between adherents of the previous myths and a (usually) younger generation busy invoking this newest coffee narrative as a basis for promoting (and often commercially exploiting) a variety of third-party certifications attesting to the positive socioeconomic and environmental credentials of the certified green coffees: **organic** (the original coffee certification), fair trade (the favorite), **bird friendly**, plus more comprehensive certifications for **sustainability** like Rainforest Alliance and the still mainly European-centered Utz Kapeh (now called Utz Certified Good Inside).

METAHISTORY 4: SPECIALTY COFFEE AS WIN-WIN SOLUTION, OR QUALITY OF LIFE AND QUALITY OF COFFEE COINCIDE

This metanarrative gradually evolved as a synthesis of specialty coffee's founding focus on artisanry combined with a less institutionalized, more ad hoc approach to social and environmental amelioration. It increasingly has been invoked not only by the latest generation of artisan specialty coffee sellers but by development agencies and their allies who support this vision for its potential to fuel market-oriented solutions to rural poverty driven by specialty products like coffee:

> Coffee snobs will demand a better, more distinctive coffee and will be willing to pay for it, while consumers who have lead palates will be intimidated into paying more for coffees because they too want to be cool. Coffee growers, assisted by air travel, the Internet, and partnerships with roasters greedy to prey on coffee snobs and impressionable consumers, will catch onto the game and together with their roaster partners and abetted by development agencies, will take advantage of snobs and their followers by getting higher prices for their coffee, making more money, and in some cases becoming as rich and famous as wine producers. Meanwhile, while the best cooperatives and farms in the best regions for growing coffee are flourishing, commodity coffee production will be taken over entirely by progressive industrialized farms in Brazil with good child labor practices and reassuring forest reserves. Lower elevation producers elsewhere will convert out of coffee and make lots of money growing cacao for the specialty chocolate industry.

The last two sentences of the preceding are not, of course, part of the narrative as it is advanced by its adherents. The practical weakness of this approach as a comprehensive tool for alleviating coffee-region poverty is the fact that many poor coffee farmers are not located in areas conducive to growing top-quality coffee. Nevertheless, at this writing this narrative is being deployed with persistence, skill, and increasing success by those who are updating Alfred Peet's artisan vision with programs with titles like **relationship coffee** and **direct trade,** programs that personalize coffee producers rather than marketing their coffee under generic origin and grade descriptions. In other words, a certain coffee may be sold as "Colombia Micro-lot Wilmer Delgado" (name of the farmer) rather than "Colombia Supremo" (name of a coffee origin and grade). Proponents of the win-win narrative typically pay farmers impressive premiums for coffee the buyers consider superior in quality and distinction. Extending the premiums paid for the product itself are roaster-supported programs that fund modest community infrastructure projects like improved schools. Development agencies typically deploy both certification strategies and the win-win narrative with its buyer network in their efforts to transform coffee-growing regions dominated by disorganized and demoralized small producers into disciplined producers of fine coffees that command top market prices. Rwanda is currently a successful showcase for such efforts.

PACKAGE IMAGERY AND NARRATIVE APPEALS: FIFTY YEARS OF SELLING THE SPECIALTY IDEA

Now to the symbolic strands of representation that in various ways reference the dominant metanarratives. I omit espresso and its Euro-American oriented set of symbols and allusions. The symbol sets I describe often overlap and are not mutually exclusive. Starbucks, for example, has deployed almost all of them. Again, these strands of representation are presented here in very rough chronological order, but all are currently in play in the American specialty coffee industry.

Good Cuppa Joe 1.0 (Original, Traditional Edition)

Before the onset of the specialty coffee movement, dominant American mythology represented coffee as everyman's luxury, affordable and democratic. Rather than the vicarious coffee safaris to multiple exotic coffee destinations proposed by specialty coffee's founding authenticity myth, traditional coffee imagery focused on the singular "perfect cup." Founders of the specialty coffee movement contended that the perfect cup, an everyday luxury accessible to all, had been degraded by intensifying cost-cutting in the years following World War II and needed to be taken back to its roots and diversified. Nevertheless, the general set of associations around coffee as an inexpensive beverage of comfort and accessibility remains deeply resonant in American culture and appears to be making a comeback, apparently driven by several factors, including the recession beginning in 2008.

Good Cuppa Joe 2.0 (Dark Roast Coffeehouse Edition)

In what can be seen as an extension of the traditional Good Cuppa Joe iconography into specialty coffee, a symbolic cluster of associations around dark roast "strong" coffee, college coffeehouses, and left-leaning populism updated the original Good Cuppa Joe 1.0 for the new world of specialty coffee starting in the 1970s. Today the typical roasting company drawing on this symbolism fuses an often rural-oriented populism with collegiate irreverence in a defiantly local, brown-paper-bag style.

Company names like Rusty Car, Muddy Dog, Industrial Joe's, and Island Joe's emphasize the style's plainness and irreverence. With Good Cuppa Joe 2, coffee was typically roasted dark to emphasize its bitter pungency and intensity, thus its "strength" or "realness." Rhetoric around Fair Trade USA and other third-party certifications made a natural fit with Good Cuppa Joe 2.0's populist tendencies, and starting in the 1990s the fair trade narrative in particular was built into its general communication set.

Safari in a Cup 1.0 (Coffee Adventurer Edition)

Until recently one of the most prevalent representation sets of specialty coffee, this iconography associates romantic images of exotic places with the coffee grown in those places, and it associates the coffee drinker with a tropical adventurer. To some degree, this iconography, usually awash with imagery of volcanoes, giraffes, samba dancers, and the like, constitutes a

Figure 46.1. An example of the irreverent populist imagery and naming prevailing among many smaller independent roasting companies in the 1990s. At the time, these companies tended to fill bags labeled like these with hearty, dark-roasted coffees, the bitter pungency of which signified outsider machismo or "realness." Courtesy of Rusty Car Coffee.

coffee equivalent of the imagery of manor houses and vineyards deployed in the early promotion of wine in America.

However, the coffee-centered Safari in a Cup imagery suggests penetration by the paler-skinned known into the darker-complected unknown rather than a return to a site of superior knowing and prestige implied by imagery associated with European wine-growing regions.

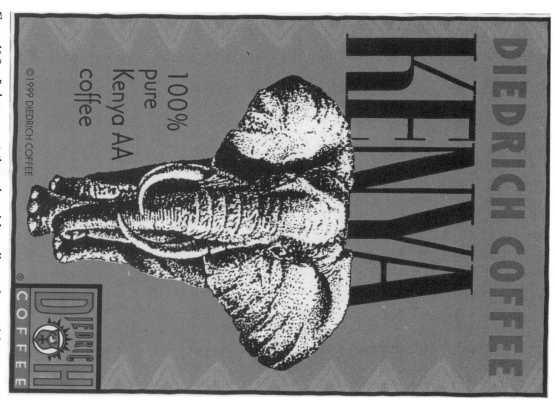

DIEDRICH COFFEE

KENYA

100% pure Kenya AA coffee

©1999 DIEDRICH COFFEE

DIEDRICH COFFEE®

Figure 46.2. Early representations of specialty coffee made use of the names of countries where the coffees originated to signify the new movement's authenticity and sensory diversity. These origin-country "brands" tended to be represented by generic, travel-poster imagery rather than imagery or information specific to the actual coffee in the bag. Here, as it often was, Kenya coffee is represented by an elephant. Common alternatives were Mt. Kilimanjaro or a giraffe. Such imagery suggested specialty coffee offered vicarious adventuring in exotic tropical places, a kind of sensory safari. Courtesy of Green Mountain Coffee.

SAFARI IN A CUP 2.0 (SAVE THE WORLD ONE CUP AT A TIME EDITION)

This symbol set implies helping impoverished subsistence coffee farmers through buying coffee that supports socioeconomic and environmental causes. Although it would appear to starkly oppose the Safari in a Cup symbolism, it also can be seen as simply another side of the same arguably patronizing coin: the North continues to embody knowledge and power, the tropical South passivity. The original romantic Safari in a Cup symbolism can even be seen as less patronizing than the messaging around Save the World One Cup at a Time, given that the Safari in a Cup assigns a vibrant if unself-conscious vitality to the South, something mysterious yet of great value because it is more closely connected to nature and tradition.

However, by the 2010s coffee-oriented development programs became sensitive to such patronizing tendencies and consequently increasingly employed imagery that attempts to foreground the contributions of individual growers and their cultures, presenting them as co-creators of a complex product.

The Wine Analogy 1.0 (Estate Edition)

The estate coffee movement and attendant representations grew up in the early 1980s driven by the persistent drive in specialty coffee to create value through product differentiation. It was a way of breaking free of the old Safari in a Cup generic language of country and grade by personalizing the production of coffee, while simultaneously associating it with the growing prestige of wine. Rather than Costa Rica Strictly Hard Bean, or even Costa Rica Tarrazu, one could buy Hacienda La Minita Tarrazu, a special selection of coffee associated with a specific farm, a **terroir**, a preparation, and even a coffee guru (in this case grower William McAlpin).

Today genuine coffee **estates**, family-owned farms managed by passionate and knowledgeable coffee producers, continue to produce exceptional coffee, often while pursuing impressive social and environmental responsibility. However, these farms market their branded **green coffee** to roasters directly; they typically do not retail their coffee themselves or create image systems to sell it. Their green coffee estate brands and their narratives are subordinated to the roaster's brand, effectively complicating communication and discouraging the most simplistic style of myth making.

The "estate" imagery has hung on in the retail arena, but most often as a **branding** strategy by mid-market coffee sellers. In these cases, entrepreneurs often sell ordinary specialty coffee under a fictional estate name. It is only a small exaggeration to say that in these cases the estate name on the bag may have as much direct relationship to the coffee in the bag as Marie Callender does to her namesake pies.

The Wine Analogy 2.0 (Micro-Lot and Direct Trade Edition)

Starting in the early 2000s the leading edge of specialty coffee began to replace the imagery of coffee estates with communication focused on specific small lots of coffee defined by crop year, botanical variety of coffee tree, and terroir. Accompanying the more specific referencing of the coffee source and the details of its terroir, botany, and production is an emphasis on direct relationships between roaster buyers and producers. Many small roasting companies have built their business around such direct relationships with growers, promoting them under program names like "direct trade," "relationship coffee," and "micro-lot coffee."

Rather than recycling cumbersome wine-world languages, micro-lot and similar communication sets accept and even celebrate the technical limitations of coffee and its time-sensitive fragility. Roasted coffee, unlike wine, cannot be bottled and cellared, and even green coffee ages relatively quickly. By emphasizing the seasonal nature of the product (enjoy it now or it's gone) and the complex synergy of coffee grower and coffee roaster, such programs advance a relatively realistic model of coffee that establishes it on a prestigious cultural track parallel to wine while honoring its tropical origins and the technical peculiarities of its production.

SEASONAL SELECTION

BWAY!
LOT NO. 8
KAYANZA, BURUNDI

SWEET LEMON, BUTTERSCOTCH, FIG, WINE

MILL BWAYI
REGION KAYANZA, BURUNDI
VARIETIES FRENCH MISSION
BOURBON, JACKSON, MIBIRZI
ALTITUDE 1760–1850 M
HARVEST JULY–SEPTEMBER

NET WT. 12 OZ.

COUNTER CULTURE COFFEE

W W W . C O U N T E R C U L T U R E C O F F E E . C O M

Figure 46.3. By the mid-2000s closer relationships between coffee producers and coffee roasters encouraged developments in coffee presentation based on an increasingly sophisticated understanding of the technical issues and processes that create sensory character in coffee, an understanding that in turn promoted the use of more objectively detailed text in coffee labeling and specific coffee information in place of repurposed travel imagery. Images, if they were used at all, tended to be subordinate to text and more specific and less generic than the older imagery of elephants, volcanoes, and so on. Courtesy of Counter Culture Coffee.

Figure 46.4. This label from Green Mountain Coffee Roasters suggests the complexity of communication developing around coffee in the 2010s. Pictured here are three panels of a four-panel sleeve that entirely wraps around the bag. Courtesy of Green Mountain Coffee.

However, the imagery and communication set around The Wine Analogy 2.0 is complex and difficult for consumers to absorb. Injecting a mythic, soundbite version into contemporary consciousness is slow going. Furthermore, the growing success of wine analogy at the top end of the specialty coffee market may do little to help those producers whose farms are located in regions less conducive to the production of fine coffee owing to lower growing altitudes, the prevalence of certain pests or diseases, and similar challenges. Nevertheless, development agencies have chosen to support the direct trade and micro-lot movement in regions where the potential for producing fine coffee is proven and production is dominated by smallholders. They have recognized that its potential for amelioration of poverty in these regions is profound, given the possibility of a lift-all-boats wave of cultural change around coffee that repositions it as a beverage worthy of connoisseurship and high prices, elevating communities of smallholding producers along with it into a position of greater prestige and (hopefully) affluence.

Part IV

THE QUALITIES OF COFFEE

47

Coffee Quality

Geoff Watts

There are a lot of moving parts in the coffee supply chain. Coffee quality is very fragile, very delicate. There's really no end to how much attention and consideration you can give to each of the individual parts of the production process. It really is an endless pursuit; there's not any point where you've figured it out and you can say "all right we've got the formula, we know where to buy coffee, we know how to roast it, let's sit back and watch it work." You're dealing with an agricultural product that is dynamic, that is constantly changing; you're dealing with a pretty complex chemical transformation in the roaster, and then you're dealing with trying to preserve whatever quality is there and make sure that it somehow translates into a great cup when somebody ends up drinking it. If somebody screws it up at that last second, then everything else we've done has been lost. It's something that requires a constant sort of mindfulness.

PROMOTING EXCELLENT COFFEE

There are a lot of ways of going about trying to capture somebody's interest or get them excited about coffee. I've found that if you start in a very simple way and you begin by talking about things that people are already very familiar with, like sweetness, it can begin an exploratory process on the right foot. The idea that coffee can be and should be sweet, and that it doesn't require sugar to make it sweet, is a foreign idea to a lot of people. They're used to, without even thinking about it, reaching for the sugar and putting it in there, and there's a perception of coffee that coffee is by nature a bitter beverage. So that's one place you can start: explaining that it doesn't have to be bitter. There are coffees that are extremely sweet and have a lot of natural sugars so they don't require you to add anything to get a nice, sweet cup.

Then we start to build from there. Once you've got a sweet cup, what are the flavor characteristics that are going to make this Kenyan coffee different than this Colombian coffee? I like using a fruit analogy. So you can ask, "Do you like oranges that are really tart and tangy and have a pleasing citric bite, or do you like oranges that are just really juicy and sweet and don't have any kind of sharpness? Do you prefer lemons, or do you prefer tangerines? Would you rather have a glass of lemonade or pulped mandarins or fresh peaches?" By making these kinds of comparisons, we can start to steer people into different categories of coffees, and they

291

begin to see those relationships, and see that, for example, this Kenyan coffee has a red currant or blackberry taste, or this other coffee has a floral aspect that's interesting. You may be someone who prefers coffees that are more caramel-like and have kind of a stone fruit quality with very soft acids and a brown sugar type of sweetness to them as opposed to this bright citric character. And that takes people into a place where they're now beginning to differentiate between types of coffees from different origins.

Then you introduce them to the reality that there are dozens of variables that impact coffee quality on the production side and that there are entire countries whose economies depend on the production of this stuff to thrive. The fact that there are individual producers who, through their own efforts and activities on the farms, are impacting the way the coffees taste is not common knowledge among coffee drinkers. At that point you can start to talk not just about the difference between a Kenyan and a Colombian coffee but about the differences between these three specific Colombian coffees that were produced by three different farmers, each of whom has their own way of doing things. Then you start to talk about the soil and the impact that very specific environmental growing conditions have, and all of a sudden it becomes this big world. Coffee has moved from being just a hot black liquid with caffeine to something that's got so many different shades of taste so you can approach it with curiosity from a culinary perspective. You've got this big world of agronomy and **terroir** and the influence of biological processes leading to specific tastes in the coffee.

Once people start to peel back the curtain a little bit and see that there is a lot of complexity behind the cup they begin to ask the questions, and that's the start of somebody beginning to transform from a habitual coffee chugger to somebody who is appreciating the drink for all of its intrinsic merit and seeking out coffees of high quality. You can draw on well-known wine terms too. That's a good place to start because people accept the idea that this wine is different than that wine, that there's a large range of qualities and prices. They accept it as a basic truth, and they also acknowledge that there's this whole group of people worldwide that obsesses about the flavor of wine. If you explain that coffee is just like wine—it's a fruit that grows in tropical areas, it requires fermentation, it involves processing to taste the way it does—people make that connection pretty easily. Their perceptions and beliefs about what coffee is are completely transformed. Then it's a matter of digging in further and starting to understand the details. We as a coffee industry look a lot to the wine industry and what they've done over the last few decades. We borrow ideas from them because we can see all of the aspects in which wine and coffee are analogous. People today think about wine a lot differently than they did twenty years ago and we can achieve that in coffee too.

ON ESPRESSO

We accept that coffee is dynamic and that you're not going to have just one consistent, unchanging, and unwavering taste profile. So rather than try to fight a losing battle for consistency in taste, we try to create something that meets a certain level of expectation in terms of quality, and again we focus on the sweetness as one of the things that's critical. Without sweetness all else is lost, so that's the first litmus test. Beyond that we want a certain amount of dimension and character in the cup. We don't want something flat or boring. We want layers of flavor and a substantial mouth-feel and a pleasurable texture on your tongue. We want the sweetness, a dimension of flavor, a finish that's not dry or astringent, and we have a very low threshold for any sort of bitterness. That's the primary target. If we can achieve that, we'll accept a little bit of variability in the type of nuance and the type of flavor as long as it's adhering to these core criteria.

I personally believe that the idea of crema is a little overblown in terms of its relative importance to the quality of an espresso. There are many better indicators. Not to say that crema is not nice, because it does provide a textural element; having no crema is not something I'd aim for. But many people look at crema as the main indicator of whether they've achieved their intended result, and that perspective is very flawed. We should instead focus on the flavor, the sweetness, the balance, the aftertaste, the mouthfeel. Those are the things that define a quality espresso and equate directly to a positive, pleasurable taste experience. You could have a mountain of crema, but if the coffee is flat or leaves an extremely sour or bitter taste in your mouth, can you really say that you find the drink enjoyable?

If you compare drip/filtered coffee with espresso you could perhaps say that drip is like a dog—consistent and predictable—whereas espresso is more like a cat in that it can be somewhat whimsical and moody. Its very preparation is dependent on so many tiny variables that can dramatically alter the profile of the coffee that it will always be somewhat more volatile than drip. In some ways that's what makes it so fascinating. We've got a whole team (the Black Cat Team) that is responsible for daily quality control because we accept that we need to be tinkering with this thing every single day in order to keep it performing the way we want it to.

We're working with this particular group of farmers in Brazil that we've been buying from for many years now. Our buyer for Brazil goes down there several times each year and works with them on trying to define the types of coffees we're looking for and to set up protocols for quality control and lot separation (as opposed to random bulking). Then when harvest time comes, we'll go through the process of getting samples, selecting individual coffees, putting them together in specific combinations, and then having the coffees milled together so that they form a lot. Once they are ready the farmers put the Black Cat logo on there and send them up for us; each lot will become one of the components that we're using for the next couple of months in our espresso blend. After we receive the coffees there is another stage of evaluation and blending where we combine different lots to achieve a specific taste profile that adheres to the established profile for the blend.

The farmers are paid very well to produce this coffee, and they're excited that their coffee is gaining some recognition on the world stage because it's being sold with the name attached and not just in an anonymous way. Farmers love that—to be able to go on a website, or show up in Miami and go to a coffeehouse, and see that their farm is being promoted very specifically, that it's not faceless, that it is not anonymous anymore.

ON POUR-OVER

The art of pour-over is that the people making the coffee are manipulating the extraction using the turbulence that they're creating by maybe holding the pot a little higher or lower. You'll see some people dripping just small drops of water onto the various points in the coffee, and then using a particular pattern when they're pouring or a certain flow rate. They have competitions, extraction competitions essentially, to see who can get the best result out of this little dripper just by manipulating the water. It's amazing.

ON SHIPPING COFFEE

Our green coffee is vacuum packed in a thick foil bag and arrives here in Chicago in essentially the same state that it left Kenya. You'll open this bag and the coffee smells very fresh, has a lot of vibrancy and vitality to it, and it'll cup just about identically to the way it cupped when I was in Kenya back when I bought the coffee. When you send coffee in a traditional jute **bag**, what you receive is invariably a little bit different than what you shipped because the coffee has been through a pretty high impact and somewhat difficult journey from **origin** to where we are now.

Another shipping option are GrainPro® bags. These are jute bags with a liner inside, a bag technology that's been used for other grains for a long time, for things like rice and wheat. The bags have two layers of this synthetic material, and inside, between the two layers, is a small gas barrier. So these bags are not vacuum-*sealed*, but you tie them up and it creates a closed hermetic environment for the coffee and protects it. They've got extremely low permeability, so big molecules can't get in and out. They protect the coffee from moisture damage, and they protect and insulate the coffee from the conditions they go through during shipping. GrainPro bags have the advantage of not creating the environmental impact that vacuum bags do. Vacuum-sealed bags use a lot of extra material. The GrainPro bags are much better because you can actually reuse these bags. We get the bags, and once we dump the coffee out we can store the bags and send them back to origin to use the next season. So you're achieving more or less the same effect in terms of preservation but you're doing it at a much smaller environmental cost.

Compostable bags would be the next step. We've had some success reusing the GrainPro bags, but I think after about three or four uses, they begin to wear out. So we are looking at compostable bags or even just shipping the coffee in larger quantities so we get more coffee per bag and use less material overall.

NOTE

This chapter is excerpted and edited from an interview of Geoff Watts conducted by Robert Thurston at Intelligentsia Coffee's roastery, Chicago, December 2009.

48

Why Does Coffee Taste That Way?

Notes from the Field

Shaun Steiman

As people discover the wide diversity of the coffee taste experience and delve deeper into the world of coffee, they inevitably ask the question, "why does coffee taste this way?" They want to know what happened in the coffee's past that caused it to taste as it does. This is a fair question and one that everybody wants the answer to. But the reality is that nobody knows why coffee tastes the way it tastes. This chapter examines why the taste is such a complex problem and why we don't really have many pieces of the answer. What pieces are known that relate to coffee production will be discussed in the second half.

The question of why coffee tastes as it does is really a subject for scientists. They use a methodology to approach and answer the question that is designed to be fairly objective and reproducible. Thus, their instrumentation and procedures are, whenever possible, designed to be objective, not just precise. The information they generate isn't flawless nor is it guaranteed. In fact, scientists never speak in assurances, only in probabilities; there is always a chance they got something wrong (this is one reason science can seem flawed; the understanding of a topic can, over time, be viewed from very different positions).

Coffee is a complex object, both in its chemical composition and the number of steps it must go through to get to a mug. There are over 1,000 unique volatiles (chemicals in the brew **aroma**)[1] and several hundred are estimated to be in the brew solution.[2] **Green coffee** is not quite as chemically complex, but a few hundred unique compounds in its makeup is a reasonable guess. Having such a large number of chemicals means there are many things to be influenced by external or internal factors. Many of those factors appear in the steps that coffee goes through during growing, **harvesting**, and **processing**, and each one of those steps can usually be divided into several components. Considering all the combinations of steps and chemicals, coffee's journey to the cup has many pathways and many destinations. That's a lot of different things to understand, scientifically.

It is relevant to mention all the chemicals in coffee because they are integral to the sense of taste. While the importance of the human factor (psychology, history, culture, emotions) on the taste experience cannot be understated, ultimately, what produces any physical stimulation is some combination of those chemicals. So understanding what influences the taste of coffee requires both an understanding of the chemistry of coffee and the taste.

Scientists use both of those tools to address the question. They often use chemical markers to show that if something "x" happens to coffee, then chemical marker "y" can be seen to change. However, just because "y" changes, there is no guarantee that the taste changes, too (not everything in coffee matters to our sense of taste). Using taste, then, is the most useful way to figure out what is changing that is important to people. Unfortunately, using coffee taste as a response in the scientific arena is tricky for many reasons, many of them related to the human factor in taste. Consequently, there's considerable desire in the industry to figure out what chemicals make what tastes. This has proven difficult to enumerate. To date, we have almost no knowledge of what, chemically, makes coffee taste like coffee.

Not only is coffee a complex object to study, but the best means to study it (people) aren't all that reliable. Still more reasons play into our poor understanding of coffee quality. Foremost, the current idea and passions of **specialty coffee** quality are relatively new; there has been no longstanding reason for scientists to study it. In the past, scientists focused their attention on different areas of research, mostly unrelated to cup quality, as there was little demand for it. When those areas did involve quality, they rarely addressed the question of what was creating a taste. Even today, few scientists approach the problem as specialty coffee geek does, so most current research is not looking at the problem as specialty coffee geeks want it to.

Even when scientists do ask the "right" questions in the research, they rarely use the correct tools to answer them. Many of the scientists who have added to this small body of research were agronomists and chemists, not sensory scientists. This in and of itself is not necessarily a problem. The real difficulty is that the agronomists and chemists don't have the knowledge to design, execute, and analyze the sensory aspect properly—understandably, as few of them have trained in it. Only a handful of studies use an appropriate sensory experimental design and statistical method to properly answer the questions. What little research is available sometimes must be regarded as highly tentative. To complicate matters, proper sensory experiments are time and labor intensive. The panelists must be trained in sensory perception and all of the quality assessment must be replicated (in addition to the other replications already in place in the experiment). This has led, unintentionally, to shortcuts that weaken the quality of the data.

To complicate matters even further, well-practiced sensory science has limitations to the amount and type of data that can be generated at any single **cupping** session. Often, this information doesn't explain the differences in taste that people may want to know about. In a cupping session, accurate data can only be generated for five to eight terms. For coffee, researchers tend to use the characteristics like **body** and **acidity**. However, changes in those characteristics won't capture important ways the coffee may change, for instance in its "floral" component. Moreover, the conclusion people most want to draw from this research is whether a coffee becomes better or worse from a treatment. This desire, along with measuring the judges' preference, is entirely inappropriate to ask in most experiments because they are not designed to measure or even describe that outcome.

Despite all these challenges, scientists have explored the question of why coffee tastes as it does, and some data have been generated. The results of most experiments are interesting and useful, but they must be interpreted carefully and not just because of some of the problems arising from the topics just discussed. For one thing, it is difficult to isolate every single variable in an agricultural setting to ensure that that variable is the only one being manipulated. To take one example, if you explore the effect of altitude on cup quality, you'll find it very different to control all the differences in soils, rainfall, light exposure, temperature, humidity, and cultural practices while altering the altitude where the coffee is planted. This isn't to say it can't be done, but that to do so requires a great deal of time, expense, and ingenuity.

An extension of this problem is the interaction that can occur amongst variables. It is difficult to account for and understand everything. Will 'Typica' respond the same way to a change in temperature or processing method as 'Caturra'? If trees are harvested in the beginning of a picking season in Honduras, will the data generated be similar to that if it were repeated in Uganda? That one experiment yielded a certain result is no guarantee that, for whatever reason, a similar experiment won't yield a different one.

Another issue in looking at experiments is the importance of a statistical difference versus a practical difference. A researcher, using the mathematics underlying statistics, may make a statement about the change in acidity among plots growing at different elevations. While that difference may exist in the numbers, it may not be a big enough difference that, out in the real world, consumers, or even experts, will notice the difference. After all, a controlled research setting usually isn't quite like reality. These complications don't invalidate the scientific method or data that are presently available. However, it does mean the interpretation of the results should be made with great care.

The following section reviews available research on production factors (through green bean storage) that correlate with, but not necessarily determine, aspects of **organoleptic** quality. It is not a comprehensive review, particularly because of the absence of the plethora of research that is not published in English or is buried in obscure journals. Also, nearly all of the research cited is strictly from peer-reviewed journals; it neglects often valuable data found within conference proceedings and books. Finally, only research that directly measured organoleptic quality is included. Unless otherwise stated, the scientists used *Coffea arabica* in the experiment.

GENETICS

Among the 124 species currently counted in the genus *Coffea* (6 more, as yet unpublished, will be added soon),[3] it is generally accepted that they taste different from each other, though no published data exist. For most people, that difference is only relevant to *Coffea **arabica*** and *Coffea canephora* (**robusta**), the two most important economic species. The difference in taste highlights the importance of genetic makeup to cup quality, and it is frequently discussed in breeding programs.[4] However, varieties within a species, even without interspecific heritage, are known to have different cup qualities.[5] The greatest challenge of this research is that unless the two species or varieties are grown in the exact same location, the environmental impact is difficult to separate from the genetic.

ENVIRONMENT

Plants, no matter what their genetic makeup, do not live in isolation. They, like humans, are subject to the nature vs. nurture conversation. Plants are so highly integrated into their environment that it is difficult to tease apart the influences of various components of "environment." This is especially true for coffee cup quality. Nonetheless, experiments sometimes produce data that demonstrate that the environment is playing a role, even if the experiment wasn't designed to produce specific cup quality responses.[6]

ELEVATION

While it is a tenet of specialty coffee that higher elevations produce better tasting coffees, the available data do not and cannot make such sweeping claims. In fact, in what must have been very surprising results to Guyot et al., they saw no change in cup quality due to elevation for 'Catuaí' or 'Bourbon' varieties.[7] Using composite scores that correspond to grades of quality, Cerqueira et al. also found no correlation between altitude and quality.[8] Bertrand et al., studying 'Caturra,' found that higher elevations produced coffee that was less bitter, was more acidy, and had more intense **aroma**. However, this relationship was not linear, as a middle elevation had higher ratings than some higher elevations.[9] Some increases in acidity and body were found by Avelino et al., though acidity was also influenced by slope exposure.[10] Unfortunately, while the researchers mentioned using 'Caturra' and 'Catuaí,' they did not clarify which cupping data corresponded to which varieties, making drawing any conclusions difficult for the reader.

TEMPERATURE

As mentioned by Bittenbender (this volume), elevation is really a proxy for temperature. Coffee likely doesn't respond to air pressure. However, no research, as far as this author knows, has examined the effects of just temperature or just pressure on cup quality.

LIGHT

The backlash against **sun-grown** coffee spurred research that attempted to explain why growing coffee as part of an agroforestry system was a good idea. That corpus contains a small collection of studies that explore whether light/**shade** has any influence on cup quality. Unfortunately, the conflicting results from the research make it difficult to draw conclusions about light and coffee quality.

Muschler was the first to design an experiment to explore light and quality. He found no effect on 'Caturra' but an increase in body and aroma with 'Catimor 5175.'[11] In the work by Avelino et al., observers found that coffee growing on the east-facing slopes had higher acidity, hypothesizing that the coffee responded to the extra morning light it was receiving.[12] With shade cover and the variety 'Costa Rica 95,' Vaast et al. observed increased acidity, lower body, less bitterness, and, in one year, lower astringency.[13] Contrary to other data, shade was found to decrease fragrance, acidity, body, and sweetness in 'Caturra KMC' by Bosselmann et al.[14] Steiman et al., working with 'Typica' and mostly artificial shade (as opposed to shade trees, like the other researchers), found practically no difference in taste due to shade, though shade did decrease body in one year of the study in one study region.[15] Bote and Struik found no effect of shade on cup quality (variety not given).[16] Measuring the natural solar radiation hitting various farms, Cerqueira et al. found no correlation between incident light and quality.[17]

CULTURE

Once a farm is planted, its location cannot be changed, nor can the genetics of the trees. The coffee does, though, require tending; it must have access to food, water, and light (which can be manipulated with the addition or removal of shade trees). There is a dearth of research exploring the role basic cultural practices may have on coffee quality. This is probably a result of the assumption that a healthy coffee plant is most likely to reach its quality potential than an unhealthy plant. Consequently, agricultural research has often focused on optimizing plant health (and yield), not cup quality.

Muschler postulated that shade does not affect cup quality at all. Rather, shade trees, with their ability to reduce incident light, temperature, and wind, are able to ameliorate less-than-ideal growing conditions, permitting the trees to fulfill their taste potential. Thus, shade, like many other cultural practices, may only indirectly play a role in cup quality.

If the assumption is correct, then suboptimal amounts of water, nutrition, and light will have a relatively negative influence on cup quality. Testing this assumption is extremely difficult. For example, if a researcher could manage to control water input (but if it rains, it rains), it would still be difficult to decide if any response was due to lack of water or lack of nutrition; water is necessary for plants to take up nutrients from the soil.

NUTRITION SOURCE AND SOIL TYPE

A question related to nutritional need is whether the source of nutrients influences cup quality. At the most basic level, this is a question about the use of organic or synthetic **fertilizers**. Plant roots are limited in what they can absorb. In the case of nitrogen, they can only absorb it as part of the molecular ions ammonium (NH_4^+) or nitrate (NO_3^-). Whether those molecules are derived from leaf litter, manure, or a manufactured chemical, the plant cannot tell the difference.

The question then becomes whether there are other molecules that plant roots absorb, depending on whether the amendment is organic or synthetic, that influence the seeds. If the answer is yes, then the source of fertilizer may have a chance of influencing cup quality. If the answer is no, then they probably have no impact. This same reasoning can be applied to considering the effect of soil type on cup quality. If roots are affected by the environment created by different soil types in a way that causes a change in the seeds, then cup quality may be impacted. If any such data exist that explore the influence of roots on cup quality, they are unknown to the author.

Malta et al. experimented with a variety of organic fertilizer sources and compared their influence with that of conventional fertilizer in the first two years of the transition to organic production.[18] They found no differences in cup quality the first year. In the second year, some of the organic treatments showed greater intensities for some characteristics. However, there was no discernible pattern to the increases nor conclusions about why some organic treatments influenced cup quality while others did not.

Looking at soil physical attributes (soil/silt/sand composition), concentrations of some soil nutrients (phosphorus, potassium, zinc, copper, and boron), and soil organic matter content, no correlation was found between any of these and cup quality.[19]

PESTS AND DISEASE

Quantifying the influence of pest and diseases on cup quality has not figured much in the scientific literature. Presumably, investigators assumed in only a few instances that a pest or disease was directly causing a flavor taint. Generally, pests and diseases weaken the plant or inhibit its ability to grow properly, thus serving as indirect causes to a change in cup quality. Most people who pay attention to field-derived **defects** in coffee, such as discolorations and partially eaten seeds (by pests), attest to their negative impact on quality. Franca et al. support this claim, as they were able to correlate grades of Brazilian coffees with defect count. They did not attempt to correlate specific defects to specific organoleptic traits.[20]

Kenny et al., comparing levels of anthracnose (*Colletotrichum* spp.) infestation to cup quality, found no correlation.[21] A more direct quality response seems to come from microorganisms via insects. In specialty coffee, the most well-known case of this is the connection with the potato taste defect, the variegated coffee bug, and a bacterium. The insect bores into the seed causing physical damage as well as leaving behind the bacterium. The bacterium, then, is assumed to cause the defect taste. Although no direct link between the bacterium and the taste defect has been demonstrated, control of the insect typically diminishes the presence of the defect.[22]

HARVESTING

There is perhaps no more common assumption in the coffee industry than the notion that unripe and sometimes overripe coffee **cherries** lead to coffee that tastes different than coffee from ripe cherries. Perhaps this is the explanation as to why so little scientific research has been executed to quantify it. While Montavon et al., studying robusta, declared that ripe cherries produced the best cup quality, they did not attempt to correlate specific tastes with ripeness.[23]

PLANT AGE

Due to the difficulty, if not impossibility, of testing the effect of plant age on cup quality, no research was found on this topic. This research would be particularly difficult to conduct because it would hardly be possible to control for all the other variables that may influence cup quality. Not only variables in production but in processing and quality assessment as well would need to be controlled over many years.

AGROCHEMICALS

Effects of agrochemicals (any chemical used in an agricultural setting) to control pests, diseases, and weeds tend to be discussed in relation to human and environmental health. Only infrequently do those discussions involve an impact on cup quality. No research was found on this topic.

PROCESSING

After coffee is harvested, the layers surrounding the seed must be removed and the seed dried and stored before roasting. While it is well accepted by all members of the coffee industry, including scientists, that processing and storage play a role in cup quality, there is little information published in English on the subject.

Cherry Processing

Fruit removal and drying of the seed can be done in a number of different ways in a number of different orders. Each of these variations is often credited with influencing cup quality. The most commonly used variations are as follows.

Farmers with sufficient access to water commonly remove the outer fruit layer from the cherries and then soak the remaining seeds and layers in water until the **mucilage** is removed (**washed process/wet fermentation**). Alternatively, instead of soaking the seeds in water, the seeds can be left to sit without water (dry fermentation) or a machine can be used to mechanically remove the mucilage immediately after removing the pulp (**demucilation**). Another method is to dry the entire cherry, including the seed, before any layers are removed (**dry processing/natural processing**). A variation of this is to leave the cherry to dry completely on the tree before harvesting (natural process, but cherries are then called **raisins**). Last, the fruit can be removed but the mucilage is kept on the seed during the drying process (**pulped natural/honey processing**).

While comparing wet fermentation to demucilaged coffee, Quintero found almost no difference in cup quality, except for slightly more bitterness in the demucilaged coffee.[24] Gonzales-Rios et al., measuring aroma differences, found that wet fermentation differed from dry fermentation and that wet fermentation differed from demucilaged coffee. The researchers did not attempt direct correlation of process to cup quality and the statistical method used makes interpretation difficult as there appeared to be an interaction with roasting.[25] In a study designed to explore the temperature of drying coffee, Coradi et al. showed that wet fermentation tasted different than natural processed coffee and that coffees dried in the sun or in a dryer set to 40 or 60°C tasted different (quality scores were composites of several characteristics).[26]

Storage

Coffee is dried to 9–12 percent moisture content to stabilize it across time and to reduce the chances for pests and diseases to influence it. If the moisture content is too high and ambient temperature too warm, green beans may have higher concentrations of volatile compounds that are recognized as being smoky, spicy, sweaty, and fruity, but lower concentrations of compounds recognized as grassy and peasy (no statistical analyses were reported on the data).[27] Coffee samples that were wet fermented or natural processed, when stored at 23°C and 60 percent relative humidity, showed no difference in cup quality when stored 180 days.[28] Under good storage conditions, Ribeiro et al. also found no significant difference in cup quality for coffees that were stored in large, hermetically sealed bags.[29] Flushing the bags with CO_2 also made no difference in quality.

Given all the cups of coffee consumed daily, it is surprising that so little information can be found in the scientific literature about why it tastes the way it does. It is worth noting that cup quality information can be accurate even if it hasn't been tested using the scientific method and published in a peer-reviewed article. For example, ripe cherries do produce different tasting coffee than unripe cherries. Informally, that experiment has been done many, many times. It is unlikely that any person would dispute this. Considering the cost and effort required to perform such an experiment in a lab, it is not surprising that hard data on this point either do not exist or are featured in obscure publications.

Shaun Steiman

Moreover, a lot of informal data hasn't been peer reviewed or published. This does not invalidate the information. Many research teams conduct experiments without any intention or need to share that information with others. The data may exist; they just may not be publicly available or known about by others.

There is a long journey ahead for researchers interested in teasing apart the details of coffee's organoleptic quality. Fortunately, there is a small body of information to build upon and a growing population of coffee drinkers interested in knowing more. With the effort and innovation of organizations like the newly created World Coffee Research, an organization designed and dedicated to funding and exploring coffee quality research (among other topics), the body of knowledge on coffee cup quality is about to get a whole lot bigger.

NOTES

1. D. Ryan, R. Shellie, P. Tranchida, A. Casilli, L. Mondello, and P. Marriott, "Analysis of roasted coffee bean volatiles by using comprehensive two-dimensional gas chromatography–time-of-flight mass spectrometry," *Journal of Chromatography A* 1054 (2004): 57–65.

2. I. Flament, *Coffee Flavor Chemistry* (Chichester, UK: Wiley, 2002).

3. A. P. Davis, J. Tosh, N. Ruch, and M. F. Fay, "Growing coffee: *Psilanthus* (Rubiaceae) subsumed on the basis of molecular and morphological data; implications for the size, morphology, distribution and evolutionary history of *Coffea*," *Botanical Journal of the Linnean Society* 167, no. 4 (2011): 357–77.

4. B. Bertrand, B. Guyot, F. Anthony, and P. Lashermes, "Impact of the *Coffea canephora* gene introgression on beverage quality of *C. arabica*," *Theoretical and Applied Genetics* 107 (2003): 387–94; Thierry Leroy, Fabienne Ribeyre, Benoît Bertrand, Pierre Charmetant, Magali Dufour, Christophe Montagnon, Pierre Marraccini, and David Pot, "Genetics of coffee quality," *Brazilian Journal of Plant Physiology* 18, no. 1 (2006): 229–42.

5. Benoît Bertrand, Philippe Vaast, Edgardo Alpizar, Hervé Etienne, Fabrice Davrieux, and Pierre Charmetant, "Comparison of bean biochemical composition and beverage quality of Arabica hybrids involving Sudanese-Ethiopian origins with traditional varieties at various elevations in Central America," *Tree Physiology* 26 (2006): 1239–48; Olika Kitila, Sentayehu Alamerew, Taye Kufa, and Weyessa Garedew, "Organoleptic characterization of some Limu coffee (*Coffea arabica* L.) germplasm at Agaro, Southwestern Ethiopia," *International Journal of Agricultural Research* 6 (2011): 537–49; Abeyot Tessema, Sentayehu Alamerew, Taye Kufa, and Weyessa Garedew, "Variability and association of quality and biochemical attributes in some promising *Coffea arabica* germplasm collections in Southwestern Ethiopia," *International Journal of Plant Breeding and Genetics* 5 (2011): 302–16; C. W. Kathurima, B. M. Gichimu, G. M. Kenji, S. M. Muhoho, and R. Boulanger, "Evaluation of beverage quality and green bean physical characteristics of selected Arabica coffee genotypes in Kenya," *African Journal of Food Science* 3, no. 1 (2009): 365–71; and Marcelo Cláudio Pereira, Sara Maria Chalfoun, Gladyston Rodrigues de Carvalho, and Taciana Villela Savian, "Multivariate analysis of sensory characteristics of coffee grains (*Coffea arabica* L.) in the region of upper Paranaíba," *Acta Scientiarum Agronomy* 32, no. 4 (2010): 635–41.

6. F. Decazy, J. Avelino, B. Guyot, J. Perriot, C. Pineda, and C. Cilas, "Quality of different Honduran coffees in relation to several environments," *Journal of Food Science* 68, no. 7 (2003): 2356–361.

7. B. Guyot, D. Gueule, J. Manez, J. Perriot, J. Giron, and L. Villain, "Influence de l'altitude et de l'ombrage sur la qualité des cafés Arabica," *Plantations, recherche, développement* July–August (1996).

8. Elder S. A. Cerqueira, Daniel M. de Queiroz, Francisco C. de A. Pinto, Nerilson T. Santos, and Sonia M. L. R. do Vale, "Analysis of the variability in productivity and quality of mountain family coffee farms," *Revista Brasileira de Armazenamento* 36, no. 2 (2011): 119–32.

9. Leroy et al., "Genetics of coffee quality," 229–42.

10. Jacques Avelino, Bernardo Barboza, Juan Carlos Araya, Carlos Fonseca, Fabrice Davrieux, Bernard Guyot, and Christian Cilas, "Effects of slope exposure, altitude and yield on coffee quality in two altitude terroirs of Costa Rica, Orosi and Santa María de Dota," *Journal of the Science of Food and Agriculture* 85 (2005): 1869–76.

11. Reinhold Muschler, "Shade improves coffee quality in a sub-optimal coffee-zone of Costa Rica," *Agroforestry Systems* 85 (2001): 131–39.

12. Avelino et al., "Effects of slope exposure, altitude and yield on coffee quality in two altitude terroirs of Costa Rica, Orosi and Santa María de Dota," 1869–1876.

13. Philippe Vaast, Benoit Bertrand, Jean-Jacques Perriot, Bernard Guyot, and Michel Génard, "Fruit thinning and shade improve bean characteristics and beverage quality of coffee (*Coffea arabica* L.) under optimal conditions," *Journal of the Science of Food and Agriculture* 86 (2006): 197–204.

14. Aske Skovmand Bosselmann, Klaus Dons, Thomas Oberthur, Carsten Smith Olsen, Anders Ræbild, and Herman Usma, "The influence of shade trees on coffee quality in small holder coffee agroforestry systems in Southern Colombia," *Agriculture, Ecosystems and Environment* 129 (2009): 253–60.

15. Shawn Steiman, Travis Idol, Harry Bittenbender, and Loren Gautz, "Shade coffee in Hawai'i: Exploring some aspects of quality, growth, yield, and nutrition," *Scientia Horticulturae* 128 (2011): 152–58.

16. Adugna D. Bote and Paul C. Struik, "Effects of shade on growth, production and quality of coffee (*Coffea arabica*) in Ethiopia," *Journal of Horticulture and Forestry* 3, no. 11 (2011): 336–41.

17. Cerqueira et al., "Analysis of the variability in productivity and quality of mountain family coffee farms," 119–32.

18. Marcelo Malta, Rosemary Pereira, Silvio Chagas, and Daniel Ferreira, "Cup quality of traditional crop coffee converted to organic system," *Bragantia* 67, no. 3 (2008): 775–83.

19. Cerqueira et al., "Analysis of the variability in productivity and quality of mountain family coffee farms," 119–32.

20. Adriana Franca, Juliana Mendonc, and Sami Oliveira, "Composition of green and roasted coffees of different cup qualities," *Food Science and Technology* 38 (2005): 709–15.

21. M. K. Kenny, V. J. Galea, P. T. Scott, and T. V. Price, "Investigations on the causes of coffee berry antracnose in Papua New Guinea and its effect on coffee quality," *PNG Coffee Journal* 14, nos. 1 and 2 (2010): 37–46.

22. B. Bouyjou, B. Decazy, and G. Fourny, "Removing the 'potato taste' from Burundian Arabica," *Plantations, recherche, développement* 6 (1999): 113–16.

23. Philippe Montavon, Eliane Duruz, Gilbert Rumo, and Gudrun Pratz, "Evolution of green coffee protein profiles with maturation and relationship to coffee cup quality," *Journal of Agricultural and Food Chemistry* 51 (2003): 2328–334.

24. Gloria Quintero, "Influencia del proceso de beneficio en la calidad del café," *Cenicafé* 50, no. 1 (1999): 78–88.

25. Oscar Gonzalez-Rios, Mirna Suarez-Quiroz, Renaud Boulanger, Michel Barel, Bernard Guyot, Joseph-Pierre Guiraud, and Sabine Schorr-Galindo, "Impact of 'ecological' post-harvest processing on coffee aroma: II. Roasted coffee," *International Journal of Food Microbiology* 103, no. 3 (2005): 339–45.

26. Paulo Coradi, Flávio Borém, Reni Saath, and Elizabeth Marques, "Effect of drying and storage conditions on the quality of natural and washed coffee," *Coffee Science* 2, no. 1 (2007): 38–47.

27. Claudia Scheidig, Michael Czerny, and Peter Schieberle, "Changes in key odorants of raw coffee beans during storage under defined conditions," *Journal of Agricultural and Food Chemistry* 55 (2007): 5768–75.

28. Quintero, "Influencia del proceso de beneficio en la calidad del café," 78–88.

29. Fabiana Carmanini Ribeiro, Flávio Meira Borém, Gerson Silva Giomo, Renato Ribeiro De Lima, Marcelo Ribeiro Malta, and Luisa Pereira Figueiredo, "Storage of green coffee in hermetic packaging injected with CO2," *Journal of Stored Products Research* 47 (2011): 341–48.

49

Coffee Quality and Assessment

Shawn Steiman

Coffee quality means different things to different people. To a farmer, coffee quality may mean the size of the cherries or the resulting seeds. To a consumer, it might be about price or availability. For many people, though, coffee quality relates simply to its taste. A formal but more accurate way of saying "taste of the coffee" is **organoleptic** quality. "Organoleptic" refers to the experience of the senses, particularly the senses of taste and smell (because so much of what we experience as taste is actually smell).

A common term in the coffee industry is "cup quality." Understanding this phrase is no simple task. It involves understanding who might be interested in the coffee, what is important to them, and how they measure what is important. This chapter discusses these various components and offers a framework with which to think about cup quality. It then discusses how that quality is assessed. Many approaches to understanding coffee cup quality are possible, and each contributes valuable insight into the sensory evaluation of coffee.

QUALITY

A discussion of coffee quality must begin with the word "quality." Its most appropriate definition here is "degree of excellence." Quality is the relationship of an item to an accepted standard of excellence. The standard is a construct based on previously defined criteria, such as rarity, size, color, or taste. The measurements of those criteria then serve to assess how well a specific item compares to the standard and, consequently, to determine its quality.

The measurements can be done using objective and/or subjective metrics. Objective metrics are true for everyone. For example, the length of a meter is always the same; it is independent of anyone's perception. If the quality of a building depended on how close it was to four meters in height, anyone could measure its quality by seeing how close its height matched the four-meter standard. On the other hand, subjective metrics depend on the individual and are expressed as how one feels or thinks. A subjective measure might indicate how pleasing that building's height feels to the measurer.

Quality depends upon predefined criteria and different situations or needs may rely on different criteria. In defining a standard for shirts, long sleeves might be most important in some areas, but not in hot, humid zones. People value different criteria depending on their perception of what properties are important. The same object, then, may have several different definitions of quality, dependent entirely upon who is doing the defining.

COFFEE QUALITY CRITERIA

Throughout this book, numerous groups of people have been discussed in relation to coffee. Among them are producers, manufacturers, roasters, baristas, consumers, and trade organizations from many different countries and cultures. Each group has a unique relationship to coffee and each has its own needs, desires, and expectations for coffee. All of these categories of people are entitled to approach and experience coffee however it pleases them, using criteria and a definition of quality that suits them best.

Over time, the coffee industry has accepted some common criteria used in defining coffee quality. Here are some current criteria employed globally to discuss coffee, divided into two groups based on the regularity of their occurrence within any given cup of coffee.

CHARACTERISTICS

These are sensory criteria used to describe or measure any cup of coffee. They are the skeleton upon which the quality evaluation is built.

- *Fragrance and aroma*: The smell of coffee before (fragrance) and after (aroma) brewing.
- *Acidity*: The bright, lively, tingly taste created by acids, commonly tasted as citrus fruits and vinegars.
- *Body*: A tactile experience, not a taste. It describes how viscous or thick the coffee feels in the mouth. Consider milk; skim milk feels much thinner than whole milk. Body is also called "mouthfeel."
- *Flavor*: The essence of the cup, the coffeeness. This is what people think of when they think of the coffee taste experience.
- *Sweetness*: A subtle taste reminiscent of sugar or honey.
- *Aftertaste*: The echo of the taste that remains after the coffee has left the mouth. It is also called **finish**.
- *Balance*: The harmony or discordance the other characteristics have as they interact with each other. For example, if a coffee is very acidic, it may be hard to taste any sweetness.

DESCRIPTORS

Descriptors are tastes and smells that do not occur in every cup of coffee. They tend to be subtle or nuanced and add complexity and uniqueness to any particular cup. They can be considered positive or negative experiences. Some cups have none of them while others have several. There's no limit to descriptive terms for coffee tastes. A few examples are floral, lemony, berry, caramel, chocolate, smoky, nutty, spicy, moldy, sour, and bitter.

MEASURING COFFEE QUALITY

Characteristics and descriptors simply indicate what aspects of coffee are generally present and, therefore, useful to talk about. However, being on the list says nothing about how a characteristic relates to the standard of excellence for a particular group of evaluators, only that those criteria are part of that standard. Knowing what instruments measure those criteria and how they are measured facilitates defining excellence.

No machine can experience a cup of coffee and craft a nuanced statement about its quality; only humans can do that. Thus, people are the only instruments available to evaluate the quality of an extremely complicated drink. While machines can only use objective metrics, humans also use subjective metrics. For example, machines can measure the amount of light present in a room but can't determine if there's enough light to read by (because readers, subjectively, disagree about how much light is necessary).

Human thoughts and feelings interfere with their ability to measure experiences objectively without inserting commentary about how much they *like* those experiences, a phenomenon well known to scientists.[1] Coffee is no exception. When humans measure coffee quality, they often include a subjective component that indicates whether or not they prefer that coffee.

Consequently, coffee quality is often measured on a gradient of "like" to "don't like." Each of the criteria can be measured in this way. Balance can *only* be measured this way as it requires cuppers to decide on its level based on their internal interpretation of it. Two people who taste the same coffee may have different ratings of that coffee's balance if they differ on how much they like the presence of a particular characteristic or descriptor, such as fruitiness.

While humans may never be able to measure coffee completely objectively, they can incorporate much objectivity into their ratings. To do so requires a metric that is human-independent: intensity. Each of the characteristics and descriptors mentioned above, except balance, can be scaled on a gradient of "not present" to "no coffee can have a greater amount than this one has." The upper limit of intensity is arbitrary, as nobody can experience every coffee in the world in order to discover the upper limit for a particular characteristic. However, an upper limit can be approximated by finding an available taste or sensation that users can be taught about and calibrated to. For example, coffees can be compared side by side to see which ones have more intense taste characteristics. If a particular coffee in that lineup is spiked with citric acid, creating an acidity that approaches the upper limit of acid intensity, the other coffees' acidities can be evaluated in terms of how much less intense they are than the spiked coffee. Using this type of metric and with a great deal of training and practice, the amount of subjectivity incorporated into a measurement can be minimized, though never eliminated.

DEFINING COFFEE QUALITY

Using any set of criteria and knowing how each will be measured, a particular standard of excellence can be created to define coffee quality. For example, a coffee with a lot of acidity and some body with a lingering aftertaste could be defined as the standard of excellence. Then, any coffee could be compared with that standard and classified as of high or low quality.

THE ABSOLUTENESS OF GOOD COFFEE?

Some experts in the specialty coffee industry believe that there are inherently, that is, objectively, higher-quality coffees among all those available. The assumption is that anyone tasting these coffees would find them to be of high quality. These coffees tend to have high intensities of the characteristics, complex flavors, and no negative descriptors. Often, though, non-experts do not like those coffees! This preferential divide suggests there is no absolute "good" coffee.

As people begin exploring a product with a large variation of organoleptic experiences, they typically enjoy broad, simple experiences of that product, being quite comfortable with fairly nondescript tastes. They tend to seek out tastes they already expect to find. These tastes might be thought of as generic; coffee should taste like coffee, rather than like blueberries.

When people gain more experience and a deeper understanding of the variety of the product, they tend to enjoy the generic less. Eventually, the most pleasing examples of the product are ones that are the most organoleptically complex and stimulating. Consequently, they begin to develop a narrow definition of what a "good" experience of that product is. This change in perspective may lead them to believe that certain tastes or smells are inherently better than others and that, within the diversity of that product, some characteristics are intrinsically "good," some intrinsically "poor."

If a standard of excellence rests on a definition of quality, no particular coffee is intrinsically better than another. Rather, any particular cup of coffee could be simultaneously of high or low quality. However, it is still important to acknowledge that experts, with their extensive experience and breadth of knowledge, offer valuable insights in defining a standard of excellence. Ultimately, however, it is the coffee drinkers, expert or not, who are the arbiters of the quality they prefer.

ASSESSING COFFEE QUALITY

Assessing coffee quality is about more than drinking and enjoying the beverage. Being critical and analytical about the beverage itself and trying to describe what the coffee tastes like allows drinkers to recognize organoleptic differences among coffees, typically leading to a deeper understanding and, consequently, enjoyment of coffee. Also, proper assessment allows people who are trying to understand a given coffee to talk about it productively because they have common analytical tools and descriptive language.

Consumers benefit from assessing coffee because it adds an extra dimension to their experience. However, assessment mostly benefits industry members who gain from knowing specific details about the coffee. That gain takes several forms. First, assessment is used for quality control. Farmers, coffee traders, roasters, and baristas need to know what they taste to ensure it meets their quality benchmark and is consistent with the standards of their brand. Second, with the information acquired from assessing quality, buyers and sellers of coffee can agree on a fair price.

Coffee quality is assessed using two general methods: **tasting** and **cupping.**

TASTING

Coffee tasting is the simplest form of assessment, as it involves nothing more than sipping brewed coffee and evaluating its characteristics and descriptors. The coffee can be brewed using any method, though it is rare to use a pressure-based method like **espresso**. Because the time and equipment required to brew many different coffees simultaneously are limiting, a small sample of coffees is usually assessed at any one time. Roasters, restaurants, and cafés use tasting to evaluate the guest experience, typically only evaluating a few coffees at one time.

Tasting coffee tends to be informal; the quality, appropriately, is usually measured subjectively (though objective metrics can be used). As most people drink coffee out of a cup for enjoyment, their ability to be objective while tasting is affected by their emotional response to the experience. Memories they associate with coffee can be influential, for example, of cups they had while vacationing in Hawaii.

CUPPING

Cupping is the formal way of assessing coffee quality based on rigidly consistent methodologies. Except for a small number of consumers interested in the experience, it is only used by coffee professionals. Cupping is an old practice, though exactly when and where it appeared is unknown. Nearly all coffee bought and sold in the U.S. prior to 1900 was chosen based on appearance,[2] which lends support to the idea that the importer Clarence Bickford may have invented it in the 1880s[3] or at least introduced it to the United States. The coffee historian William Ukers notes Bickford's role in the San Francisco coffee trade but doesn't mention his cupping coffee, only that he realized the color and size of the seeds say nothing about the taste.[4]

Cupping is a methodology that facilitates greater objectivity in rating coffee. This is an important achievement, as cupping was developed long before the birth of modern sensory science in the 1940s.[5] Cupping methodology likely developed as a way to taste many coffees in a short period of time, although the ability to do so with simple equipment while standardizing how the brews were made had probably also been noticed as nice perks of the process. Analytically, the greatest advantage of cupping over tasting is how much it removes tasters from the emotional experience of drinking coffee and puts them in a situation used solely for evaluation.

No one precise protocol determines cupping. Rather, there is a basic methodology, and individuals and groups practice what they were taught or tweak it to suit their specific needs. The most important factor in cupping is consistency in methodology within and between sessions. Small variations in the methodology, particularly within a single cupping session, can significantly influence the experience of the cup being measured. The highest level of precision can be reached only by limiting as many sources of variation as possible. That is why the **Specialty Coffee Association of America** (SCAA) has defined a standard cupping methodology; the organization hopes it will become the industry standard, minimizing variation within and between cuppings. Below is a description of the general cupping method, which includes the physical act of tasting the coffee and recording the information and the analytical act of measuring quality.

CUPPING EQUIPMENT

1. A deep, rounded spoon. *Used for ingesting the coffee, preferably one made of stainless steel or silver to help dissipate the heat and prevent any chance of the material chemically reacting with the brew.*

2. 3–5 wide-rimmed cups or bowls that hold 150–180 milliliters (5–6 ounces) of water. *Multiple cups of each coffee are steeped to capture any possible variation in the taste or smell, as a single cup of coffee may not be representative of the whole lot.*

3. 8.25 grams (29 ounces) of whole bean coffee dosed for each cup/bowl. *The coffee is weighed as whole bean to promote uniformity and consistency between the multiple cups. If only a single bean causes a defective flavor, it will show up in just one cup. If the coffee were ground first, then weighed out, that single defective bean would be spread across all cups and potentially left undetected. To maximize freshness, the coffee should be ground (medium-coarse) just prior to beginning the cupping.*

4. 150 milliliters (5 ounces) of 90–96°C (195–205°F) water for each cup/bowl. *The amount of water and coffee is not absolute. Any ratio will work as long as it is defined and used consistently. These numbers are based on the SCAA's recommended brew strength of 55 grams/liter (7.3 ounces of coffee/1 gallon) of water.*

5. A cup of water for rinsing the spoon. *To prevent contamination of brews when moving to taste the next cup/bowl, the spoon is rinsed between each bowl. The cup is best filled with the same hot water used to steep the coffee so that any change in the spoon's temperature does not risk affecting the evaluation.*

6. A spittoon. *After tasting the coffee, it is common to spit it out.*

7. A score sheet to record data. *Without recording the data, few cuppers can remember all the details even minutes later, never mind months or years later.*

8. An understanding of the characteristics and descriptors as described above. *These are the specific experiences to be measured.*

9. A clock that measures seconds. *Different cupping steps occur at different times. Having a stopwatch helps keep track of the time.*

10. A cup of water or neutral food (plain bread or crackers) for clearing the palate between samples (optional).

PROCESS

Once everything is prepared and the coffee ground, the cupping can begin. The first step is to sniff the dry grounds and assess the fragrance of each cup. Many cuppers agitate the grounds to assist with this. Add the water and start the timer. Allow the coffee to brew for two to five minutes; the exact time is arbitrary. When the time has been reached, the crust (the floating coffee particles) should be broken with the spoon and the aroma assessed. Some cuppers simply smell the aroma released from the crust while others ritually stir away the crust three times or smell the grounds on the back of the spoon. Note that agitation of the grounds will influence the extraction and change the cup; thus, if done, it must be applied identically to every cup.

Any floating grounds need to be removed, as they impede the comfort of ingesting the coffee. Using one or two spoons, the floating grounds are scraped off without removing much liquid. For convenience, they can be tossed into the spittoon. When moving between cups, the spoons should be rinsed in hot water to avoid contamination. Cuppers who strive for the greatest precision will tap the rinsed spoon on the rinse cup's edge or the table to remove even a drop of water.

Once the coffee has cooled somewhat, it is ready to ingest. The brew is collected in the spoon and slurped vigorously into the mouth. While slurping helps coat the entire mouth at once and, as some cuppers contend, aerates the coffee, the most critical reason to slurp from the spoon is that coffee is not drunk this way; this is an analytical process of assessing quality and it promotes objectivity. Once in the mouth, some cuppers swish the coffee around while others spit it into the spittoon immediately. As the amount of time the coffee is in the mouth and the agitation in the mouth will change how the coffee is perceived, maintaining a consistent practice is important.

When tasting many coffees, spitting out the coffee helps limit the amount of caffeine taken into the body. Spitting also helps improve the precision of the assessment because, again, it is an atypical practice reserved for assessment. Moreover, when coffee (or any food) is swallowed, the mouth and throat are coated with remnants until they are washed with another sip or saliva. If the coating isn't cleared away, residual tastes and smells may contaminate the experience of the next sample as they move through the retronasal passage in the skull to the olfactory bulb in the brain.

It is usually necessary to taste each coffee several times to appreciate its complexity. As the coffee cools, its taste will change; some taste buds interact with temperature, altering the perception of taste of many foods at different temperatures.

As each coffee is tasted and each characteristic and descriptor assessed, the cupper should record experiences on the score sheet using the objective or subjective metrics discussed above, or a combination of the two.

IMPLICATIONS OF OBJECTIVE AND SUBJECTIVE METRICS

Within the limits of a human's ability to be an objective instrument, an objective measuring system is largely descriptive. As a result, the information generated about each coffee can be efficiently transferred between people because there is no subjective encoding to the information. Users' views do not need to be adjusted to one another or to a specific definition of quality; coffees do not need to be measured within the context of other coffees, for example, by cherry **processing** technique, roast level, or growing region. Any coffee can be measured and described objectively, allowing any other drinker to get a good idea of what the coffee tastes like, independent of any historical, cultural, emotional, or personal bias. An objective system precludes any given coffee to be deemed inherently as "good" or "bad"; those are opinions generated by a drinker.

Subjective measuring systems are more difficult to translate between users as no person completely understands another's feelings and experiences. For subjective systems to be effective, cuppers must be close to each other in understanding, rather than to an external standard. The greatest advantage to a subjective measuring scheme is that a number scale can be used for describing quality; characteristics are scored, tallied, and measured against a standard of excellence represented as 100 points. The scale provides a quick and simple way of communicating and comparing coffees' quality—a useful tool for coffee reviewers and competitions—although it requires a thorough understanding of the definition of quality used for it to be effective in discussions with others who do not share the same preferences.[6]

Most of the coffee industry uses a combination of objective and subjective measurements. For example, the characteristic acidity is often measured on its relative intensity and how the cupper feels the level of acidity fits within the context of that particular cup and, often, the coffee's origin (where origin is a proxy for a definition of quality).

RECORDING INFORMATION

There are many ways of recording assessment data. The design of the score sheet depends largely upon how the characteristics are measured and what the user feels is important to remember. While many different sheets exist, the score sheet designed by the SCAA has become common throughout the specialty industry.

Most sheets use a numbering system to quantify the cupper's experience. Lower numbers correspond to low intensities or preferences whereas high numbers correspond to high intensities or preferences. Occasionally, score sheets have an anchored line on which the cupper marks the intensity of the experience where the anchors act as the extreme points on that gradient. Almost all sheets have specific listings for the characteristics. For the descriptors, it is most common to just list their presence as they not only appear irregularly but they tend to be of such low intensity that mentioning their occurrence is enough.

The roast date of the coffee should also be recorded. Coffee can change dramatically within even a few days after roasting. Knowing the time from roasting (freshness) is a valuable piece of information about organoleptic quality.

CONCLUSION

Coffee is a complex organoleptic experience that anyone can simply enjoy. However, assessing quality in a standardized way can add depth to the emotional and intellectual experience of drinking it. Deciding how to assess quality is a joint effort between different stakeholders in the industry as they seek to define the standards of excellence that guide their work. As the specialty coffee industry grows, its members will continue to negotiate the definition of high-quality coffee, incorporating a dynamic approach involving objective and subjective evaluations. Using standardized evaluation methods such as cupping ensures that these measures of quality are reasonably reproducible, while more simple tastings allow consumers and retailers to compare the holistic experience of drinking different coffees. In the long run, it may be appropriate to consider separate or overlapping standards of excellence in coffee quality as the specialty market expands its global presence and addresses the diverse demands of the coffee-drinking world.

NOTES

1. Morten Meilgaard, Gail Civille, and B. Carr, *Sensory Evaluation Techniques* (Boca Raton, FL: CRC Press, 1991), 33–37.

2. William H. Ukers, *All About Coffee* (New York: The Tea and Coffee Trade Journal Company, 1922), 356.

3. Mark Pendergrast, *Uncommon Grounds: The History of Coffee and How It Transformed Our World*, rev. ed. (New York: Basic Books, 2010), 117.

4. Ukers, *All About Coffee*, 487.

5. Herbert Stone and Joel Sidel, *Sensory Evaluation Practices* (Orlando, FL: Academic Press, 1985), 3–6.

6. For a more thorough discussion of measuring systems and the 100 point system used in coffee, see Shawn Steiman and Ken Davids, "The Points Principle," *Roast Magazine*, July/August 2010, 20–34.

50

Distinctive Drinking

Specialty Coffee and Class in the United States

Jonathan D. Baker

This chapter considers the connections between **specialty coffee** and class or social status in the U.S. To understand the link between consumption and status, it is useful to think of specialty coffee as part of the larger category of gourmet food. However, coffee has both gourmet and mainstream forms, a characteristic it shares with many other foods. Further, there is a tension between the more elaborate, high-status forms and manners of consumption, and the more generic, mainstream ways in which it is made and drunk. Coffee has flirted with the gourmet food world for a long time;[1] the current wave of specialty coffee exemplifies many traits that appeal to people who regularly consume gourmet food, the foodies.

Consumption is at least partly public and expressive. People make public statements about themselves and their values through what they consume and how they consume it, and others are able to perceive these expressions to some degree. And, because people are aware of the public aspect of consumption, they can to a certain extent manage how they are perceived by modifying their consumption.[2] Yet eating and drinking do not take place in a neutral field where all tastes and preferences enjoy equal social value: some preferences are associated with higher status than are others. And to a large extent, anyone's basic aesthetic tastes are relatively inflexible and determined early in life through social position, education, and upbringing. To some degree, people can emulate higher-status preferences. The desire by the lower class to do this reflects the social influence of the elite class on what is perceived to be good and valued. In regard to food, and specifically coffee, one means of publicly emulating high-status values is by consciously choosing foods and crafting attitudes toward them. Advertisers can appeal to consumer desires, emotions, and values by associating their products with certain ideals. Examples abound of advertising that links consumption and identity; for coffee, see the following discussion and Davids, this volume, as well as William Roseberry's discussion of imagery used to market coffee.[3] Martha Kaplan shows the way Pacific Island natural imagery, used to market Fiji bottled water, is linked to consumer values regarding nature and health.[4] Raymond Williams provides a more general discussion of the apparently magical manner in which commodities are imbued with life-affirming characteristics via advertising.[5] How does this kind of association take place within the realm of U.S. coffee consumption?

Here the analysis draws on work by sociologists on consumption and social status, an intellectual lineage that largely descends from Pierre Bourdieu's examination several decades ago of the relationship between social class and taste in France.[6] For a discussion of specialty coffee, the key to Bourdieu's work is his argument that the process by which some tastes and preferences become associated with "good taste" is a reflection of the power and influence the dominant class has over social matters. Bourdieu further argues that, for those who are not a part of this dominant class, there are cultural and economic barriers that make it difficult to develop the good taste favored by the elite. Consumption, as a visible and public expression of taste, can therefore serve to distinguish people from each other or to mark inclusion or exclusion in certain social classes or groups. Cultural and economic capital, acquired from birth in and outside the family, is expressed in taste. Good taste, which depends on possessing a high level of cultural capital, effectively excludes those without it from participating in or influencing the dominant social class and its preferences.

Because class-based tastes and preferences are learned early in life, they are difficult to overcome or change. It is more than just a matter of which forms of art or music or which foods are preferred. Taste also encompasses the manner in which people consume things. With respect to food, this includes standards of etiquette as well as notions of how meals should be apportioned, the types and amounts of foods that should be consumed, how they should be prepared, when, where, and with whom they should be eaten, and so on. These larger sets of class-based attitudes and mannerisms shape how individuals approach coffee.

Other sociologists analyze the discourses—the particular usage of words and symbols—surrounding food and foodies in the U.S.[7] The trends seen in specialty coffee can be better understood if they are placed in this wider context of foodie discourse and narratives. Josée Johnston and Shyon Baumann identify authenticity and exoticism as the two key frames through which foodies assess and appreciate what they ingest. These writers see these frames as being supplemented by discourses of democracy and distinction. Because democratic inclusiveness is an important ideal in the U.S., there is a shift away from past forms of overt snobbishness in how things are consumed and a move toward a more open, omnivorous pattern of consumption.[8] Johnston and Baumann describe such consumption as an appreciation of a wide variety of forms within any given genre (for instance, music, literature, food). Because this way of consuming allows a broader view of what is considered good, it fits well with ideals of democracy and inclusiveness. Yet it still functions as a means of displaying refinement and good taste; despite democratic appearances, not everyone will have equal opportunities to develop an omnivorous consumption pattern, and not every form of food (or music, literature, etc.) will be viewed as good by any particular social group.

Sociologists have described omnivorous consumption in many different genres besides food, including music and reading.[9] Display of good taste is marked by eclectic, yet discerning, consumption across a wide range of high and low status forms within these different genres. The discernment that forms the basis of social distinction is not based on preferring the "right" high-status commodities –for example, "highbrow" classical and opera music, French cuisine, and Jamaica Blue Mountain coffee— but rather on the attitude with which these commodities are assessed and selected.[10] This approach to consumption can be expressed through diverse preferences: for example, through preferring a specific local coffee roaster, by knowing of a hole-in-the-wall ramen shop with exceptional fresh-made noodles, and by appreciation of vintage outlaw country music from the 1970s (e.g., Johnny Cash, Merle Haggard). With coffee, appreciation of diversity of origin, roast, and brewing technique reflects the omnivorous approach: there are many good coffees out there, and different roasts and preparations have their merits depending on the properties of the coffee itself and the desired end taste. This conscious development of sophisticated attitudes toward consumption contrasts sharply with the more overt class-based distinctions of high/low culture that Bourdieu analyzed in France.[11]

Johnston and Baumann observe that foodies seek out "authentic" food. Food is perceived to be authentic "when it has geographic specificity," is "simple," has a personal connection, can be linked to a historical tradition, or has "ethnic" connections."[12] Authenticity acts as a standard by which foods can be assessed. And because the characteristics that mark authenticity seem objective (when compared with past distinctions made on the basis of high/low class or culture), they do not directly contradict the norm of democratic inclusiveness. But authenticity itself is a socially constructed attribute of foods, not something inherent in a food's substance or properties. For example, "Italian" cuisine developed only in the late nineteenth century, partly in response to calls from the elite to create a new national culture. It is how the food is perceived in a social context that determines its level of authenticity.[13] Likewise, the value placed on authenticity of this sort is socially constructed to be a positive attribute of a food.

Exoticism, the other dimension identified by Johnston and Baumann, is a feature of the discourse about coffee that has already been acknowledged; see, for example, Roseberry's discussion of coffee and the re-imagination of class in the U.S. The desire to consume the exotic Other—meaning here some group that has been identified as distinctly different from the observer's people—and the use of exotic imagery and themes to make food compelling to consumers strike an uncomfortable balance between romanticizing colonial exploration and plantation agriculture and expressing a more culturally sensitive and politically aware interest in social and cultural difference.[14] Ultimately, this line of analysis traces back to the work of Edward Said, who examined Western culture and its connection to the exotic Other.[15] Stereotypes about cultural difference are widely deployed in Western life, in marketing, the media, entertainment, and so on. Coffee advertising featuring exotic places and cultures is part of this much larger way that Westerners think about other places and cultures.

Johnston and Baumann identify two dimensions of exoticism: social distance and normbreaking. For both aspects, the assumed context for comparison is well-off, white, cosmopolitan Americans. Social distance can be marked by geographic or cultural distance and is primarily a function of accessibility and rarity. Those goods that are less easily available are more exotic. Likewise, foods that break norms, for example, foods made from animals or animal parts not frequently eaten in mainstream American cuisine, are considered more exotic. While both these dimensions play a role in how coffee is perceived **(kopi luwak** is an example of norm-breaking), social distance, marked as well by geographic distance and rarity, is the most prevalent.

Some of the features that make specialty coffee attractive to foodies are relatively obvious: geographic specificity, which contributes both authenticity and exoticism; personal connections to specific regions, farms, and farmers; relatively small-scale production, reflecting "simple" (e.g., handpicked, not mechanized), personal aspects while also contributing to rarity; and historical and ethnic traditions, somewhat problematically connected to the colonial past but also balanced by more modern concern about farmer well-being. These themes, in various forms, have long been a staple of the U.S. specialty coffee market.

Coffee authenticity is linked to exotic peoples and locales but through direct and hopefully beneficial connections to specific farmers and co-ops: **fair trade certification**, micro-lot production, **single origin**, **relationship coffees**, and so on.[16] These factors all serve to mark specialty coffees as authentic and exotic in various ways, which make them appealing to foodies because they can be employed as indicators of cultural capital and good taste.

The methods of evaluating specialty coffee currently in vogue also allow for this not overtly exclusionary form of social distinction. These techniques allow for social boundaries and statuses to be enforced without directly challenging the democratic inclusiveness favored in the U.S. One of these methods of assessing coffee, **cupping**, appears to be gaining popularity beyond just coffee professionals. Coffee bars increasingly offer cupping nights to consumers as a way of exposing them to a diversity of coffees while also helping them cultivate the techniques needed to distinguish the coffees from each other. These cuppings are analogous to wine tastings.

Mastery of cupping techniques requires a relatively high degree of social and economic capital. To be skilled at tasting the nuances and differences in specialty coffees requires access to a wide diversity of coffees to sample. It likely also requires training and socialization—we typically learn to cup coffee from experts. To be able to cup properly, using the vocabulary and techniques of the specialty coffee industry, requires several things: a drinker needs to be socialized, via education and experience, to conceive of coffee as a substance worthy of evaluation akin to ranking other high status foods, especially wine; there must be physical and economic access to a sufficient variety of coffees to taste; and a drinker must learn to discern the differences and must develop the language to describe them. To become good at distinguishing the nuances of coffee tastes also requires practice over time. The would-be cupper must have access to all these resources for a period of time, rather than just once, to master the technique.

Despite the fact that anyone with normally functioning senses of taste and smell is physically able to learn to do this, relatively few have the time and money to do so. The seemingly objective nature of cupping techniques—anyone can do it!—masks the role they play in distinguishing those with expert or good taste from those without it. The social and economic barriers restricting access to specialty coffees allow them to continue to play a role in social class distinction. The most obvious barrier is cost: though many Americans drink coffee, relatively few can afford specialty coffee prices. Fewer still will see the price as justified. And of those who do try high-end specialty coffee, few will have the food-tasting experience (or, in Bourdieu's terms, the embodied class-based tastes and abilities) to be able to ascertain the relatively subtle differences in specialty coffee tastes.

Yet most advocates of specialty coffee generally do not see it this way. In fact, much like the foodies Johnston and Baumann interviewed, the dominant theme I have encountered, both in popular articles on specialty coffee and among people I have interviewed, is one of populist inclusion. The focus is on the quality of the coffee and on introducing people to it because the brew is exciting and tastes good. There is of course a promotional aspect to emphasizing quality, as specialty coffee advocates are also often involved in selling it. But rather than positioning specialty coffee as an elite product, the retail industry concentrates on technique, expertise, and quality by means of technology and precision, more objective criteria not necessarily associated with class judgments.

Coffee is a beverage that straddles multiple class identities. In some contexts, it is a daily accompaniment to meals—as in diner coffee or something made in a Mr. Coffee pot. Those brews are anything but elite. Rather, they are more working class and democratic, consumed by people at the lower end of the socioeconomic structure to help fuel their productivity and keep them going longer (an attribute that led anthropologist Sydney Mintz to refer to coffee, along with tea and sugar, as "proletarian hunger killers"[17]). In this context, there is less concern with origins of coffee or nuances in flavor. Coffee should just taste like coffee; it should be "strong." This manner of consuming coffee still dominates in America, alongside the relatively

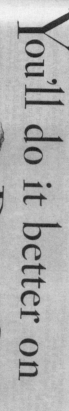

Figure 50.1. An ad by John Lagatta in *The American Magazine*, May 1933.

newer, more specialized segments of the coffee market. And populist imagery, focusing on coffee's affordability, accessibility, and comforting properties continue to be a part of how it is advertised. The persistence of the view that coffee is a democratic, non-elite, working-class beverage is also used by savvy advertisers as a means of product differentiation and further market segmentation.

In the ostensibly democratic U.S., tension has appeared between consuming coffee in a manner that marks high cultural capital and status and consuming it in a more common manner. Different images of coffee compete in marketing (elite, exotic, authentic, specialized vs. common, comforting, accessible worker fuel), and I have found them in my own research. At this point, it is difficult to pinpoint the degree to which American coffee consumers sense these differences, and more ethnographic research is needed to clarify matters. At any rate, coffee marketers already play up these different attitudes to further define and target different segments of the coffee market. On the one hand, aspects of authenticity and exoticism are drawn out of the highest echelons of the specialty coffee world into the more popular realms of specialty coffee, such as Starbucks. On the other hand, new means of separating the highest status coffee and its consumption from the rest continue to evolve. A pattern is developing: elements that used to define the most elite patterns of consumption are popularized, while new exclusionary aspects emerge to maintain the boundary between elite and common.

Reaction against exclusionary and elitist elements of coffee appears in advertising campaigns that specifically make fun of these aspects. Backlash against perceived snobbery has been used as a means of marketing—see, for example, Dunkin' Donuts' 2006 coining of the term "Fritalian" to describe the language of drink sizes and names at coffee establishments such as Starbucks: "Is it French, or is it Italian? Maybe Fritalian?"[18] Both Dunkin' Donuts and Mc-Donald's now sell versions of coffee drinks formerly associated with high status (for example, cappuccinos), a sign that these beverages have moved even further into mass consumption. In a 2008 commercial, upon learning that McDonald's now sells cappuccinos, one character says, "That's awesome! I can shave this thing [a goatee] off my face." The other character notes that they no longer have to call movies "films" and that they can now sit around watching and talking about football.[19] The ironic aspect of these anti-elitist marketing campaigns is that they represent appeals carefully tailored to segments of the U.S. coffee market, and the coffee products sold are more expensive than black coffee. They are specializations cloaked in the guise of being less specialized. This trend is seen in grocery store sales of coffee, too. Bags of Dunkin' Donuts coffee (typically marketed as not elite) sell for the same price as Starbucks (often associated with higher status, despite actually being somewhat mainstream). So, while these coffee products may in part reflect a reaction against elitist aspects of coffee, there is an effort underway to get more American coffee drinkers to buy more expensive coffee products, while using populist, democratic, anti-elitist themes to promote this trend.

These are some of the ways coffee and its consumption are connected to ideas of class and status in the U.S. Coffee straddles class lines and has a diverse history with both populist and exclusionary dimensions. In some contexts, appreciation of the most elite aspects of specialty coffee can function as a means of social distinction, marking refinement and good taste. Yet, there appears to be reaction against the exclusivity and snobbishness of specialty coffee, even while this resistance appears to be functioning primarily as a means of further defining and segmenting the U.S. coffee market. The push and pull between these different images of coffee will likely continue to appear in various guises throughout the American, if not the global, coffee market and will continue to be incorporated into our narratives about status and class.

NOTES

1. William Roseberry, "The rise of yuppie coffees and the reimagination of class in the United States," *American Anthropologist* 98, no. 4 (1996): 762–75.

2. Pierre Bourdieu, *Distinction: A Social Critique of the Judgment of Taste* (1984); Gary Alan Fine, *Kitchens: The Culture of Restaurant Work*, trans. Richard Nice (Cambridge, MA: Harvard University Press, 1996); and Josée Johnston and Shyon Baumann, *Foodies: Democracy and Distinction in the Gourmet Foodscape* (New York: Routledge, 2010).

3. Roseberry, "Rise of yuppie coffees."

4. Martha Kaplan, "Fijian Water in Fiji and New York: Local politics and a global commodity," *Cultural Anthropology* 22, no. 4 (2007): 685–706.

5. Raymond Williams, "Advertising: The magic system," in *Problems in Materialism and Culture: Selected Essays* (London: Verso, 1980), 170–95.

6. Bourdieu, *Distinction*.

7. Johnston and Baumann, *Foodies*.

8. Richard Peterson and Roger Kern, "Changing highbrow taste: From snob to omnivore," *American Sociological Review* 61, no. 5 (1996): 900–907.

9. Peterson and Kern, "Changing highbrow taste"; Jane Zavisca, "The status of cultural omnivorism: A case study of reading in Russia," *Social Forces* 84, no. 2 (2005): 1233–55.

10. Johnston and Baumann, *Foodies*.

11. Bourdieu, *Distinction*.

12. Johnston and Baumann, *Foodies*.

13. Research on the socially constructed nature of the authenticity of national cuisines is very rich. For example, on whether an authentic American cuisine exists: Sydney Mintz, "Eating American," in *Tasting Food, Tasting Freedom: Excursions into Eating, Power, and the Past* (Boston: Beacon Press, 1996), 106–24; on efforts to "reauthenticate" regional food traditions in the UK: Craig Wight, "Reengineering 'Authenticity': Tourism Encounters with Cuisine in Rural Great Britain," in *Food for Thought: Essays on Eating and Culture*, ed. L. C. Rubin (Jefferson, NC: McFarland, 2008), 153–65; on the role of cookbooks in defining authentic Indian national cuisine: Arjun Appadurai, "How to make a national cuisine: Cookbooks in contemporary India," *Comparative Studies in Society and History* 30, no. 1 (1988): 3–24. For a more general discussion of the taste of authenticity and culinary travel, see Lisa Heldke, "But is it authentic? Culinary travel and the search for the 'genuine article,'" in *The Taste Culture Reader: Experiencing Food and Drink*, ed. Carolyn Korsmeyer (Oxford: Berg, 2005), 385–94.

14. Roseberry, "Rise of yuppie coffees"; Johnston and Baumann, *Foodies*, 100–107.

15. Edward Said, *Orientalism* (New York: Vintage, 1978).

16. For example, see M. Doane, "Relationship coffees: Structure and agency in the fair trade system," in *Fair Trade and Social Justice: Global Ethnographies*, ed. S. Lyon and M. Moberg (New York: New York University Press, 2010), 229–57.

17. Sydney Mintz, "Time, sugar, and sweetness," *Marxist Perspectives* 2 (1979): 56–73.

18. Dunkin' Donuts (2006), "Perhaps Fritalian" (commercial), http://www.youtube.com/watch?v=2y_GwKzxck, accessed March 25, 2012.

19. McDonald's, "Now Selling Cappuccinos," (commercial), 2008, http://www.youtube.com/watch?v=Cg87E1tjTOE, accessed March 25, 2012.

51

Brewing

Dissolving the Puzzle

Andrew Hetzel

Add hot water to ground coffee, filter out the wet grounds, and drink the remaining liquid. Brewing coffee is simple, right? Well . . . yes, technically the *task* of brewing coffee is easy, but consistently achieving good flavor from brewing requires some knowledge of the underlying science at work. What happens when water meets coffee makes all the difference for those who purposefully control flavor in the cup. Everybody else is simply going through the motions and hoping to get it right.

WHAT IS COFFEE BREWING?

Brewing coffee is about creating a beverage that we enjoy. It is pretty easy to know what we like and don't like, but unfortunately we don't know what chemicals in the beverage create our perception of the taste. What we do know is that manipulating how coffee is brewed changes our perception of it.

Even though we can taste every cup of brewed coffee to know whether or not we got it right, it is cumbersome and often too late to use only taste as a tool for measuring success. To aid us in understanding brewing and how to become more consistent with it, we have discovered a few metrics (objectively measurable responses) that can help guide us towards understanding whether we've likely brewed the coffee in a way that we will like or not: extraction yield and brew strength. These metrics, though imperfect proxies for taste, are quick, useful tools in exploring coffee brewing.

Coffee brewing uses water to extract chemical compounds found in roasted coffee. As water comes into contact with coffee grounds, it dissolves some of those chemicals, most of which eventually pass into the cup. Once those chemicals are in the water and away from the coffee grounds, they are called solutes. The **Specialty Coffee Association of America** (SCAA) advises an extraction yield of 18–22 percent, meaning this percentage of coffee should be dissolved out of the original coffee mass to optimize the flavor of a brewed cup. The range is slightly wider for espresso due to its smaller liquid volume. Interestingly, the vast majority of each batch of roasted coffee is never meant to be consumed and is destined to become used coffee grounds—sad to envision, but the waste is necessary to attain good flavor in the cup.

319

Extraction yield merely describes how much coffee should be extracted. It doesn't describe *what* should be extracted. There are usually several ways to attain the desired extraction yield, any of which will produce an acceptable, yet different, cup of coffee.

More than 1,500 distinct chemical compounds can be extracted, some of which create the complex **flavor** and **aroma** that we know as coffee. Those coffee solubles include lightweight, fast-dissolving compounds like the citric acid that gives Kenyan coffee its lemony flavor, mid-range dissolving compounds like sugars that make good coffees naturally sweet, and some heavy, slower-dissolving bitter compounds that are necessary to add complexity and balance.

Lipids (oils) are also present in brewed coffee. Lipids in the coffee beans liquefy at normal extraction temperatures, and while they never completely dissolve in the water, they do make it into the cup, contributing along with soluble bean fiber to the texture/viscosity of coffee, perceived as thickness or **mouthfeel.** Slightly bitter caffeine, coffee's most famous soluble, dissolves easily in coffee, as it is equally soluble in both water and oil—which is the reason for its rapid permeation of the stomach lining, permitting direct entry into the bloodstream, similar to absorption of alcohol.

Take out too few soluble elements during an extraction (<18 percent) and the results are an underextracted cup of coffee that is sour and weak; take too many (>22 percent) and the cup will be overextracted, burnt, and bitter tasting. Ideally, all of the right compounds should be extracted and combined in one harmoniously balanced beverage—which is the challenge of brewing good coffee.

BREWING PARAMETERS

Many different brewing methods can create such a harmonious beverage. Each method manipulates a set of parameters that influence the extraction, therefore determining how many solubles are dissolved to become liquid coffee and how many stay behind as used coffee grounds. These parameters all work in concert to produce a desirable beverage. When they are adjusted individually, they tend to throw a harmonious beverage out of alignment, potentially missing the ideal extraction yield. Thus, different **brewing methods** tend to tweak multiple parameters to achieve the harmony.

GRIND PARTICLE SIZE AND SHAPE

The purpose of grinding coffee is to increase and control the surface area that will come into contact with water. The exponential increase in surface area created by breaking the coffee into smaller particles (grounds) speeds up the rate of dissolution. Larger coffee particles have less total surface area available for contact and subsequently have a slower process. Bigger particles have the opposite effect on the rate at which water flows through coffee grounds, since smaller pieces leave smaller gaps through which water may travel.

The goal in grinding is to obtain particle uniformity, since large and small particles combined in the same brewer extract at different rates, leading to unpredictable results. Substantial emphasis should be placed on the reduction of extremely small particles, "fines," that break off from coffee beans during the grinding process and almost always fully dissolve, with bitter consequences.

WATER TEMPERATURE

Because heat increases molecular activity, water temperature strongly influences how much of a substance dissolves and the rate of dissolution. Essentially, raising the temperature speeds up the movement of molecules and therefore increases the opportunities for water molecules to come into contact with coffee grounds. For purposes of illustration, pour sugar in glasses of increasingly hot water; the sugar dissolves more quickly in each successively warmer glass. Lower temperatures have the opposite effect.

Cold water, when a short contact time is used, dissolves only the quickly soluble elements in coffee, most notably sour-tasting acids, but leaves others behind. Some compounds are not greatly impacted by increases or decreases in temperature. Repeat the same experiment with table salt and you will notice little difference in dissolution time from cup to cup.

WATER PRESSURE

High-pressure systems increase the solubility of gases into any solution, allowing more gas to be squeezed into the liquid. In **espresso**, volatile compounds created by **roasting** are captured by the pressurized water stream. When the pressure is released, the gas leaves the solution (just like opening a can of soda). In espresso, the gas gets trapped by lipids and becomes part of the **crema**.

The more important effect of the high pressure is to increase the efficiency of extraction. To some degree, this works like increasing the temperature: water comes into contact with the coffee more often. However, the bigger effect is probably from the sheer force of movement from the water. Imagine a person standing in a narrow hallway. If other people meander through the hall, that lone person may or may not get bumped and pushed down the hall. If those other people burst through the hallway as one large mass, that lone person is more likely to be dragged along with the group. With espresso, the lone person is the coffee solute and the rush of people is the high-pressure water.

AGITATION

For extraction to occur, water molecules must come into contact with coffee grounds. The more frequently the molecules bump into the coffee, the quicker the extraction. So, as with increasing the temperature, agitation during brewing will increase the extraction rate. Agitation occurs naturally in **filter brewing methods** because the percolation of water due to gravity, through the coffee bed, counts as movement. In other methods and sometimes in conjunction with filter brewing, manual agitation in the form of stirring speeds up the extraction.

WATER-TO-COFFEE RATIO

The term "strong" is overused by marketers to describe the flavor of coffee, almost always incorrectly, typically referring to roast degree, bitterness, caffeine content, or, more sadly, a high **defect** count that creates wildly imbalanced and unpleasant sensations in the cup. The only true measure of brew strength is soluble concentration, the percentage of dissolved coffee solids in the water, also known as total dissolved solids (TDS).

The SCAA recommended strength of brewed coffee lies in the range of 1.0–1.5 percent TDS, which can be produced from a coffee to water ratio of about 1:18 by weight. Historically, that value was originally set at between 1.15 and 1.35 percent, but in recent years it has drifted closer to 1.5 percent and, in some cases, beyond, as consumer preferences gradually trend toward lighter roasted coffees brewed to higher concentrations.

The reason for the shift, I believe, is that darker roasted coffees exhibit dry distillate flavors (spicy, smoky, resinous) that are perceived as being far more intense than delicate enzymatic flavors (floral, citrus, berry) more often found in lighter roasted ones; so light roasted coffees tend to be brewed at higher concentrations than their dark roasted cousins in order to achieve the same perceived brew strength. This phenomenon accounts for the notion that light roasts contain more caffeine, which in reality is not greatly affected by roast degree at all.

CONTACT TIME

The ideal time for water to stay in contact with coffee for a proper extraction depends largely on the particle size, water temperature, and pressure variables mentioned above, with one additional condition: water quality. In general, the longer coffee and water are in contact, the greater amount of material will be extracted from the coffee.

A mantra of the specialty coffee community, "coffee is 98.5 percent water," is worth repeating (we discussed the other 1.5 percent above). Small variations in mineral content, alkalinity, and chemical additives like chlorine dramatically change the coffee extraction. While chlorine and other compounds negatively impact cup quality, the mineral content determines water's bonding capacity with coffee solubles and can subsequently trump all other extraction variables. Brewing water must contain some amount of dissolved mineral solids like magnesium and calcium to extract what seems to be a good balance of coffee solids.

The SCAA guideline for water quality is to use water at or near neutral pH, containing 75–250 ppm total dissolved solids and 20–85 mg/liter calcium hardness with little or no other elements and compounds like chlorine, sulfur, or silicates.

FILTER TYPE

Filter type influences coffee brewing in two ways: it can affect the rate of brewing and influences what ultimately passes through the cup. Filters vary in their porosity and material composition. The most common types of filters are made from paper, cloth, and metal.

Heavy paper, cloth, and metal filters with very small holes slow down the rate of brewing, which can translate to an increase in extraction yield. Paper and cloth filters also trap some of the chemicals extracted from the beans, most notably some oils. Consequently, the actual composition of a cup of coffee will be different depending on whether a paper or cloth filter is used rather than a metal one.

IN APPLICATION

Every brewing technology applies the variables above to obtain a beverage the user enjoys. Each technique tries to balance water of a certain temperature and quality that is put into contact with a specific ratio of coffee grounds that have been ground to a certain particle size at a given pressure for a specific amount of time.

As a baseline in the United States, **drip brewing** applies approximately 1 liter (about 34 ounces) of clean water, heated to 92–95°C or 198–203°F, to 55 grams or 1.94 ounces of coffee, ground to ~750–1,000 μm particle size using gravity (1 atmosphere, or ATM) slowed by a filter for approximately three minutes.

In espresso, coffee is ground smaller to increase surface area, the mass of coffee to water is increased significantly, pressure is increased to 8–10 ATM, and contact time is reduced to 20–30 seconds. The dissolved solids are close to 5 percent. In the end, it is the taste of the beverage that matters, not achieving a one-size-fits-all brew strength.

In cold-brewed coffee, the particle size is increased dramatically and water temperature is lowered to room temperature, but the contact time increased to as much as twenty-four hours to allow even extraction. By contrast, the **Turkish brewing** or Arabic style of coffee preparation pushes extraction yields beyond the edge of commonly accepted specialty coffee standards by using an extraordinarily fine coffee grind, boiling water, but no filter in the extraction. This is another case where the metrics don't apply; they are trumped by user preference.

Whether preparing cold brew coffee, filter coffee, pressed coffee, or espresso, the core process of extraction remains the same. It is a matter of extracting chemicals from coffee grounds while manipulating a few basic parameters. Innovation in the use of these parameters will continue to increase the types of coffee beverages available as well as variations on ones we currently enjoy. Quite recently, **espresso machines** have been designed to permit the adjustment of the water pressure and temperature to the demand of their operators during the brew cycle or as a prerecorded profile. Experimentation will certainly continue to introduce new catalysts and to manipulate factors that are today accepted as constants in order to improve extraction quality.

Which method of brewing makes the best cup of coffee? All of them can make a good cup; the best may be different for any roasted coffee and any drinker, but the preparer needs to apply knowledge of the brewing process to coax out the best qualities in each.

52

Roasting

Developing Flavor in the Bean

Colin Smith

After it has been processed from **cherry** to **green bean**, coffee still resembles a green, hard stone, lacking any discernible taste or **aroma**. It is the work of a skilled **roaster** to develop a flavor in the coffee that makes it desirable to drink. Every **origin** has different flavor characteristics, and careful roasting will bring out these flavors. Subsequently the aroma of the coffee pervades the roastery. Many have said that they prefer the smell of roasting coffee to the actual taste in the cup! Such comments are typical of people who have not experienced coffees correctly roasted to bring out the differentiation of taste present in origins and blends.

Beans, when roasted in the traditional manner at anywhere from 190–250°C (374–482°F) for 10–15 minutes, change color to shades of brown (the roast temperature is chosen by the roaster who is influenced by practical and cultural circumstances). The chemical processes that occur during roasting are diverse and usually affect each other as they develop. For example, **Maillard reactions** occur when sugars and amino acids combine, resulting in complex molecules that are largely responsible for the brown color of coffee. Pyrolysis, a generic term for the decomposition of substances with heat, generates many products not found in green coffee. The myriad of reactions is responsible for oils, acids, polysaccharides, volatile compounds, and many more substances.

The roasting process first evaporates most of the water content in the coffee (usually 9–13 percent before roasting), which contributes to a total reduction in weight of some 15–20 percent. The increased pressure from the water vapor violently breaks the cells, the coffee audibly "cracks," and the bean expands. At this point, the coffee has a light brown color. Further roasting will cause a second crack, this time from carbon dioxide breaking through cells. As roasting progresses, the brown color darkens (it is usually stopped well before it blackens) and oils start to exude, first from the ends of the beans, then all over the surface.

During roasting, coffee beans expand, increasing their volume by about 60 percent as they lose their water content, while at the same time, any **silverskin** still on the beans flakes off as chaff. Larger machines have attachments to suck out the chaff, which can be used as compost, or can be burnt off in the roaster or in an **afterburner**.

The challenge for the roaster—here I mean the operator of the machine—is to extract the maximum flavor from each lot of beans. Certain coffees, due to their chemical makeup, are better roasted to certain colors. For example, the high acid content in Kenya coffee becomes quite bitter if the coffee is overroasted, whereas Sumatran coffee, which has a low **acidity** and a full body, develops a more pleasant flavor when roasted longer. Darker roasting produces more bitterness in the flavor. This can have an advantage in respect to cultural tastes. Some countries or regions like their coffee very bitter, perhaps while using an **espresso machine,** so that the roast and the preparation should enhance this characteristic. Light roasted coffees, on the other hand, will taste more acidic than they would at a darker roast. Certain origins—those of Central America, for example—will perform well as a lighter roast as the acidity factor balances other **flavor** components within the bean.

Coffee roast level terms are relative to the color, so in the UK we have light, medium, and dark roasts and then a range of terms in between such as full medium, continental, and light continental, which in the U.S. is full city roast. The trend at the moment is to roast darker, at least in many UK coffeehouse chains. The **roasting** entry in the glossary lists old-style U.S. terms for darkness.

In **specialty coffee,** lighter roasts have come to predominate. The roaster's responsibility is now phrased as revealing the character of the beans. While lighter roasts are trendy in specialty coffee, roasting too light, underroasting, produces a thin, grassy flavor. Coffee assessment is usually undertaken when the bean is just past this stage but still fairly light. The bean is cooked through and all the potential details of the coffee are apparent.

The traditional method of roasting is to judge the end of the roast by the coffee color against a sample color (sometimes a previous batch of the same beans, thus when a previous batch is used it is important to renew it regularly as the coffee fades with age). The color can also be checked and regulated with the use of a spectrometer (a.k.a. spectrophotometer), a necessity for quality control of batch roasts. However, this must be done after the roast is complete, not during the roasting process.

When the desired color is reached and the roasting is complete, the coffee is emptied onto a cooling tray where cold air is drawn through the coffee. Large batches may use misted water in the roasting drum to cool the coffee first before dumping it (called water quenching). This will reduce the coffee temperature to room temperature and stop the roasting almost instantaneously. All of the water is evaporated from the beans before they leave the roasting drum.

ROASTING MACHINES

Coffee was originally "roasted" using frying pans, Arabian style. The beans would be cooked over open fires and tossed to try to gain uniformity of doneness, though this happened infrequently. This method is still used during the traditional Ethiopian coffee ceremony. Into the early twentieth century, Western housewives, and some home aficionados to this day, also roasted green beans in their ovens (this also includes lovers of very smoky kitchens!). Later, the open pans were covered and paddles inserted to agitate the beans to prevent burning. Drum roasting developed in the nineteenth century with an external heat source, originally wood or coal but latterly gas fired. External heat application was the norm, but later gas burners were fitted inside the drum to give direct heat to the coffee beans. A new development is to heat the air externally and pass it through the rotating drum. This gives a more uniform roast and stops the beans coming in direct contact with the heat source.

The next development was the fluid bed coffee roaster, in which air is heated and pumped at high temperatures through the bed of coffee, in a small chamber, creating a cyclone effect among the beans. This method can roast coffee very quickly, 60 kilograms in five minutes, if so desired. The coffee is then moved to another chamber for cooling with cold air. For large quantities, managed under computer control, this is an efficient way of continuous roasting.

In small roasting operations, the bags of unroasted coffee are piled against the wall or on shelves. In a large roasting operation, coffee is stored in large silos, each containing a different origin. On request, coffees are dispatched, with computer control, straight into the roaster. This system can also control blend proportions of the green bean. The blend will be roasted as a unit before automatic equipment moves the roasted coffee from the roaster to the packing department. In some smaller specialty roasters, the components are roasted separately and blended later. This enables blends with two or more colors of roast to be blended for specific flavors.

Many roasters, especially on the specialty side, roast and offer coffees from single locations and, if possible, from single farms. Nearly all roasters also offer blends of coffees. These blends can be composed of coffees from different origins, farms, cherry processes, or roast levels. They are blended to create specific flavor profiles, to cater to specific brewing methods, or to offer products at a certain price.

All methods of roasting can be adapted to profile roasting. Profile roasting occurs when the amount of heat used during roasting is manipulated throughout the roast. This will lead to different events (like the bean cracking) occurring at different times as well as different end roasting times. In smaller roasting operations, the variation of heat can be done manually. In larger operations, sensors within the roaster can take measures and, with the aid of computer programming, adjust the heat input during the process to achieve the desired roasted color.

In many countries, the smoke and smell created by commercial coffee roasting is regulated by law. Large machines will have built in afterburning systems that eliminate particulate emissions and dispel any waste still in the roaster before it enters the atmosphere. To prevent fires and ensure the quality of the roast, these devices must be kept clean. Often, a roasting plant will have a cleaning system for the green beans before roasting begins, to extract foreign bodies. Some plants, however, clean the coffee after roasting. Magnets and de-stoners can be used to assure the removal of all unwanted materials.

Roasting machines are produced in various sizes to suit the capacities required, from 2.5 kilograms upward. Very small machines, which handle around 125 grams at a time, are produced to roast samples of coffees, to test them for flavor, and determine the roast color required for optimum flavor.

KEEPING COFFEE FRESH

Roasted coffee exposed to air will lose some flavor through oxidation. Carbon dioxide, along with many other volatile compounds, is released from the beans directly after roasting. Some of these volatiles contribute to the coffee's flavor. The loss occurs more readily when the coffee is ground, as its surface area has increased, providing more sites for oxygen to "attack" and more sites for volatiles to leave. Packaging has therefore been developed to help retain the gases and hold the flavor in the bean.

Vacuum packaging creates a fairly stable environment within the sealed bag as it prevents fresh oxygen from affecting the coffee. Thus, on opening, the coffee should taste really fresh, but the introduction of air causes quick deterioration of the remaining contents. Flushing the packaging with inert gases, for example nitrogen, will keep the coffee in an oxygen-free environment for some time. The offending gases are expelled during the packing process to be replaced by the inert gas. The majority of retail bags that are sold also contain a one-way valve. This allows gasses, generated by the roasted coffee, to exit the bag while preventing oxygen from entering.

These methods aim to preserve the coffee's flavors for up to a year. It is still recommended that the coffee should be consumed as soon as possible after roasting to achieve the best flavors. This applies even more so after opening the pack, at which point oxygen is available to react with the coffee. Locally roasted coffee will exceed all imported options for freshness and taste.

HOW SHOULD I BUY MY COFFEE?

Always consider how you make your coffee. Coffee tastes fresher in the cup if you use a burr **grinder** and prepare each cup from whole beans.

The coffee should be ground according to the way you make it. Coffee-making methods are dealt with elsewhere in the book in the sections on espresso, "Brewing," and "How to Make a Great Cup of Coffee," but each technique is capable of producing a fine cup if used properly. Commercially, coffee is ground in large roller mills. Two or three pairs of rollers, at progressively smaller settings, assure uniformity of grind. These machines are usually water cooled to stop excess heat from affecting the coffee. On a smaller scale, in both shops where coffee is ground to order and in homes that take extra care with brewing, corrugated plate (burr) grinders are used. Small domestic burr grinders are efficient, but the use of a spinning blade is quite common in small electric grinders. These machines are not very accurate for defining specific grinds.

Once opened, the coffee rapidly loses freshness. The coffee should be sequestered from air as well as possible. If it came in a bag, the pack can be rolled down and fastened closed. Putting the coffee in an airtight container will work well, too. Buying small quantities of coffee, as required, from a local roaster or a trustworthy Internet purveyor will help ensure a fresh coffee experience.

FINAL THOUGHTS

The preparation of coffee from the time the tree flowers to liquor in the cup usually takes more than a year. Much of the taste depends on how the coffee is roasted and prepared. A year's work can be ruined quickly, sometimes within seconds, if roasting isn't done well.

A good roaster will be able to offer the right coffee for the customer. Unfortunately, these days, price rules, and **commercial coffees** (those roasted by large operations) are not always as good as they can be. **Blends** are often developed according to the price of the coffee, not the taste. You don't have to pay a lot of money to get a really good coffee, although as in all things, you get what you pay for.

Talk to your roaster to learn about the coffees and the flavors and try different origins and blends to find out what you really like. Many people ask me, "what is the best coffee?" The range is huge; the answer lies with the beholder.

53

Roasting Culture

Connie Blumhardt and Jim Fadden

Every year hundreds of coffee **roasters** set their daily production quotas, green coffee orders, and equipment maintenance schedules aside for a long weekend to gather with other like-minded professionals to impart the very information that gives them an advantage in their commercial pursuits. Others gather in smaller, regional groups across the country, giving up their weekends, volunteering to share knowledge in the simple pursuit of roasting better coffee.

These gatherings exemplify a unique culture that has evolved around the profession of roasting **specialty coffee.** This is a culture of sharing, competition, and education, not with the goal of winning professional accolades or an improved bottom line, but to advance the understanding of how the science of coffee roasting yields the art of a perfect beverage. Put another way, bragging rights around the bonfire after winning a roasting competition come in a distant second to seeing the look on their peers' faces when the winning roast is sampled, when their peers recognize the perfect match of coffee to roast level that brings out the unique qualities inherent in each coffee based on its **origin, variety, processing,** and other variables.

There is no playbook to describe the typical background of a successful coffee roaster. Some approach roasting as a second career, some as an evolution from roasting at home, and some from having worked many years in the coffee business as **baristas.** Although there is no typical career path for becoming a roaster, there are common personality traits of those that do turn roasting into a profession. Perhaps the words "passionate geek" best describe the collective personalities of this group. They are passionate not just about the final quality of their product, but about the proper sourcing of their product, how their product is prepared, how it is labeled and marketed, even how to evaluate their own work. The excitement and dedication that is brought to coffee roasting is similar to a master brewer or vintner and has much in common with artists and musicians. Like conductors unifying the individual sounds within a symphony, roasters aim for an aesthetic that melds the story of the coffee, the taste of the coffee, and the look of the coffee together to create not just a taste, but an experience. In fact, many roasters have an artistic background.

The best coffee roasters exhibit the qualities of the best stereotypically geeky engineers and designers. Like a designer, a coffee roaster has the responsibility to create a product for a specific purpose, for example, a blend of a sweet Sumatran coffee with a less acidic Costa Rican coffee to achieve a particular flavor profile that complements a specific dessert

Figure 53.1. Roasting at Intelligentsia Coffee, Chicago, 2010. The machine is a heavily refurbished Gothot, built originally in the 1930s. Photo by Robert Thurston.

in a restaurant. Like an engineer, they also have the responsibility to efficiently source and repeatedly manufacture a consistent product. In fact, many coffee roasters also come from a technical background.

An obsessive focus on the improvement of the methods of roasting coffee is intrinsic in the culture of the coffee roaster. Roasting coffee involves physics and chemistry to understand and manipulate variables that transform the hard, dense, green, and relatively tasteless bean into a light, airy, brown, consumable product. It requires hands-on adjustments of the machinery and a commitment to record keeping and data analysis. These are the topics that dominate conversations between roasters, whether at professional gatherings, on public message boards, or in private conversations and they are discussed passionately. The relative merits of theory and practice are often openly discussed without regard to business competition but rather with the focus on raising the bar for all, driving forward improvements in quality.

The evolution of today's unique culture in specialty coffee is largely a function of the history of the industry in the twentieth century, of the nature of the job, and of the process required to become skilled in the field.

The middle of the twentieth century saw the rise of convenience as the prime goal in all areas of American life. Be it the invention and marketing of time-saving devices like the dishwasher, the microwave, and the electric can opener or the invention and marketing of time-saving consumables and services, like the quickie mart, TV dinners, and drive-through restaurants, consumers were taught that convenience trumped quality. Coffee was not immune to these trends and the rise of nationally commercialized, roasted and ground supermarket coffee resulted in the fall of most craft, local, specialty coffee companies. Most, but not all. A few companies and the roasters that they employed kept the thin thread of specialty coffee intact during these years. Alfred Peet of Peet's Coffee, Ted Lingle of Lingle

Bros. Coffee, Paul Katzeff of Thanksgiving Coffee on the West Coast, and Don Shoenholt, of Gillies Coffee on the East Coast are a few of the individuals that were able to continue with thriving businesses based on the small lot production of specialty coffee. To succeed, these individuals had to rely on their own passion and dedication to their craft and on any help and advice they could glean from each other. A spirit of cooperation developed out of the necessity to survive against the supermarket giants. Techniques, processes, and sources of green coffee had to be shared, or risk being lost to history. These influential leaders, through their openness and their passion, set the foundation of the spirit of cooperation that continues to be a hallmark of the roasting culture today. They also had the vision to understand that this knowledge had to continue to be developed and disseminated, leading to their founding of the **Specialty Coffee Association of America** (SCAA).

The coffee roaster, by nature of the job, has one foot in the world of the modern consumer and one in the world of the developing world of the coffee farmer. The way of life for a coffee roaster requires that the needs of both worlds are well understood and balanced. As a group, specialty coffee businesses must source their raw materials (**green coffee beans**) in a manner that ensures there will be a supply of quality crops well into the future. This extends beyond the pure economics of balancing the price paid for green coffee beans with the price consumers are willing to pay for the finished product. Roasters carry their culture of education and passion for quality back to the farmers who cultivate the beans. Many well-traveled roasters join together to establish cupping labs or give processing advice (gathered from their travels around the world) to teach farmers to identify both the traits that make high-quality (and higher-priced) coffee and the **defects** that render coffee unusable in the specialty market. For example, the revival of coffee cultivation in Rwanda owes much to the spirit of cooperation between roasters and farmers. Following the terrible genocide of the 1990s, the Rwandan coffee farms and markets were in shambles. With the great loss of lives also came the loss of agricultural tradition and knowledge. A country with all of the key physical attributes to grow great coffee—the proper soil, elevation, and ideal climate—had no knowledge of the qualities that constitute specialty coffee and how to grow and process the beans to meet those exacting qualities. Through working closely with government and academic aid agencies, roasters cooperatively engaged with the Rwandan farmers and processors to improve the quality and, consequently, the sales volume and price of a key component in the Rwandan economic model. The roasters benefited from a new, exceptional flavor profile that became popular with consumers, allowing the roasters to command a higher market value as well. This would not be possible if it weren't for the culture of cooperation and the desire to enhance the understanding of coffee among the roaster community.

The obsession of the roasting community for increasing their understanding of coffee and the desire to communicate to others this understanding owes itself in large part to the process by which one becomes a coffee roaster. Coffee roasting is an experience-based skill. It is not something that can be mastered through book study; all the senses must be trained and engaged. Beyond the obvious mastery of the palate, coffee is produced through use of sight to identify the proper roast level, through the use of hearing to interpret the story told by the cracking of the beans as they near completion, and certainly by the use of the scent in both identifying the different stages of the roasting process and in sampling the finished product. Coffee roasting is learned through apprenticeship, through the tutelage of a more experienced roaster, through hands-on experience (trial and error), and through the roaster community at large. As shown earlier, today's coffee roasters stand on the shoulders of those that kept the flame burning during the **commercial coffee** years. The traits of those roasters, mainly their openness, cooperation, appreciation of the craft, and pursuit of quality, attracted people with the same qualities to become coffee roasters. Building on the model of the SCAA, a variety of guilds, regional groups, conferences, and educational resources have been developed to augment the traditional mentor-apprentice model.

The identity of the coffee roasting community is dynamic. There are numerous changes in the business of coffee that will challenge today's version of the roaster's culture. How will the increasing use of automation in the roasting process affect the community? Will increasing competition for the specialty coffee segment lead to a more closed culture, one that is less willing to cooperate? Will traditionally underrepresented subcultures of coffee roasters, for example women roasters, raise the bar for the next generation? How these questions play out will undoubtedly impact the next generation of coffee roasters. But if the next generation is drawn by the same core characteristics of quality, passion, and curiosity, then the culture and identity of the specialty coffee roaster will remain intact.

54

Barista Culture

Sarah Allen

When Danish barista Fritz Storm breezed into the opening cocktail reception of the **Specialty Coffee Association of America**'s annual conference in Boston in 2003, there was an air about him—something special. A handful of young people looked up, recognition registering in their expressions, and they hustled after him, catching up to Storm as he sipped from a glass of wine. "You're Fritz Storm, right? You're the World Barista Champion?"

Nearby, crowds turned toward the commotion—*World what?* they wondered. The concept, in 2003, of a barista being a champion of anything was completely foreign to 95 percent of those gathered in Boston for this, the world's largest gathering of specialty coffee professionals.

Just across the ocean in Scandinavia, however, while it wasn't exactly commonplace, the professional **barista** was a known commodity. Norway, Sweden, Finland, and Storm's home country of Denmark were known in the early 2000s as breeding grounds for the best and brightest coffee craftspeople. While the word *barista* is Italian in origin, it was in Scandinavia that specialty coffee artisans were breaking ground for an international industry. It would take less than a decade for the concept to sweep the world.

The original and, to this day, most well-respected barista competition is the **World Barista Championship** (WBC), of which Fritz was the second titleholder. Developed by Norwegians Alf Kramer and Tone Liavaag, the WBC was intended to provide specialty coffee with a serious stage upon which coffee excellence could be brought to the public. While most coffee lovers are familiar with the concept of the barista as the serviceperson from whom they buy daily lattes, few—especially in 2003—understood the complexity of the work, including many of the baristas themselves.

The growth of the WBC was undeniably aided by the introduction of two other establishments designed to reach the masses of undereducated coffee professionals, who up until this point had very few options for professional development: the Barista Guild of America, which was formed in late 2002, and the trade publication *Barista Magazine*, which launched in 2005.

While the Specialty Coffee Association of America (SCAA) along with sister associations in Europe, Japan, and other parts of the world were by their very nature charged with the education of this specific industry, those organizations have, until recently, focused the bulk of their efforts on the professional development of the people recognized as leaders and future principals of the industry: coffee roasting companies primarily. In the first few years of 2000,

Figure 54.1. Pete Licata of the Honolulu Coffee Company winning the United States Barista Championship in 2011. Photo by Ralph Gaston.

baristas were still considered temporary blips on the specialty coffee radar—kids who worked with coffee as a college job, who weren't going to stick around to develop a career in the industry. So why provide them with costly training seminars and materials?

Those early organizers of the WBC—which bore the necessary national barista competitions to generate champions to perform at the international level—along with the Barista Guild of America (BGA) and *Barista Magazine*, however, recognized something profound in this young community of baristas: potential. And truly, the mere existence of a guild, a structured competition, and a targeted journal lent confidence to this young faction of coffee obsessives, who thought to themselves, *if all these people and organizations are providing us with professional resources, perhaps we can truly become professionals.*

Over the next five years, this confidence only grew: baristas outside of Scandinavia were beginning to identify themselves as craftspeople, to dedicate their time and money to growing their passion, and to set their sights on careers as professional baristas. This occurred particularly in the United States, and the mindset grew fast. By 2008, a mutual respect could be observed between the leading baristas from both sides of the Atlantic. When questioned about their line of work, countless people were starting the answer with "I'm a barista," adding almost as an afterthought, "oh, and I also own my own café." Pockets of the U.S. were identified as the leading areas for barista excellence, among them Chicago, San Francisco, Milwaukee, Austin, and most of all, Portland, Oregon. And many readers might be wondering at this point, *What about Seattle? Isn't that where this all started?* True, the green mermaid's hometown changed specialty coffee forever when it debuted in the early 1990s. In fact, every independent, artisan café owes a debt of gratitude to Starbucks for introducing the **espresso** lexicon to the American public; before Starbucks, only a handful of people knew what a latte was, and virtually no one ordered one by name. But Starbucks was, as they say in the coffee industry, **second wave** coffee culture. People knew that coffee that was better than the freeze-dried stuff their parents drank was available; it was out there for the taking. But they not only were clueless about the story behind the coffee, they didn't care to learn it.

Café owners who define the present-day **third wave** took a cue from Starbucks by designing specialized café menus and firmly planting the barista in front of the clientele as the important point-person in the transaction of coffee buying. But third wavers went a step further—make that many steps further. Pulitzer Prize–winning food critic Jonathan Gold of the *LA Weekly* says it like this: "The first wave of America coffee culture was probably the nineteenth-century surge that put Folgers on every table, and the second wave was the proliferation, starting in the 1960s at Peets and moving smartly through the Starbucks grande decaf latte, of espresso drinks and regionally labeled coffee. We are now in the third wave of coffee connoisseurship, where beans are sourced from farms instead of countries, roasting is about bringing out rather than incinerating the unique characteristics of each bean, and the flavor is hard and true."[1]

Further, the third wave defines the barista as a studied educator. Rather than the button-pusher service people they were in the second wave, baristas at quality cafés are expected to complete rigorous, sometimes months-long training on not only coffee and espresso preparation, but coffee history, in-depth discussions of particular farms and regions, extensive **cuppings**, and palate development.

A great example of third wave coffee at work is the Stumptown Annex, located in Portland. Stumptown has long been considered one of the most persnickety, quality-driven coffee roasting and café companies in the world. Its baristas not only train initially and repeatedly, but they are offered superb health care and dental benefits in addition to excellent salaries. Stumptown pours its resources into its people not only because, as owner Duane Sorenson says, "it's just the right thing to do," but also because such benefits and treatment build loyalty; more than 50 percent of Stumptown's baristas have been with the company for more than five years.

Sorenson opened the Stumptown Annex in 2005, just two doors down from one of its most popular cafés. The Annex, as it's referred to, isn't a café, however—it's more of a tasting room in the same vein as tasting rooms one would find at top wineries. The small space contains between ten and twenty glass jars of whole coffee beans at any time, showcasing the best of the best of what Stumptown currently has on offer. Educated baristas are eager to talk about coffee flavors and nuances, discuss geographical details about specific coffee farms, and guide customers through cupping sessions. Free public cuppings are offered twice a day, every day of the week.

The thinking behind the uber-educated barista is simple: engage the customer in the experience of coffee, and he or she becomes empowered; therefore the customer himself becomes an ambassador for the specialty coffee craft. The theory goes hand in hand with the slow food movement: if people are engaged in and connected to their consumables, they'll be loyal to them.

Of course, the average café rarely has the resources to provide this level of education to its staff of baristas. But a motivated barista can still build his or her resume, while developing passion for coffee, through a multitude of other channels.

The Specialty Coffee Association of America (SCAA) offers classes in education and training to any barista worldwide who signs up for one of the organization's classes. Workshops are taught in various locations, around the United States primarily, and sometimes in conjunction with a trade show or coffee-related event. The only downside to the SCAA's classes and workshops is that they often come with hefty price tags, though some discounts are available.

There are still many other options for the enthusiastic barista to further his or her education—and do it without spending big bucks. Independent trade shows, for example Coffee Fest, which takes place three times a year in different parts of the United States, offer great classes and workshops, a full trade show floor with a bent toward the independent café owner, and fun events such as a latte art competition, all for less than $50 for a weekend.

The SCAA-run Barista Guild of America debuted a wonderful retreat concept in 2011 called Camp Pull-A-Shot, where around 150 baristas gathered in a woodsy camp setting in Southern California for three days of nonstop barista education and activities. The no-frills camp was plenty comfortable for the baristas, who were pleased with the low cost (around $550 for room, board, and all educational classes) that the BGA could offer for such rustic accommodations. The success was so great that a second West Coast Camp took place a year later, and the BGA is now working on an East Coast Camp, to take place in the summer of 2012.

Still more resources exist for baristas, and there are plenty that baristas can study from the comfort of their own home, such as the online social network Barista Exchange, which is essentially Facebook for coffee people. All are welcome to set up an account for free, cruise forums on coffee trends, and ask for advice from the more than 10,000 registered users.

There's a reason camaraderie comes so easily when a group of coffee people come together: baristas often share personality traits such as a curiosity for mechanics, a social nature, and the kind of character that becomes passionate. The barista community can be likened to musicians: there is a common ground they have right away, they tend to be artistic and intelligent, and they like to socialize and have fun.

Another commonality is that they often make a low wage. While there has been maturation of the concept of the barista as a professional in the United States in years past, most coffee professionals still make a fairly low wage (except in some pockets of the country like Portland, San Francisco, and New York). While employers understand the need to take care of their baristas by paying them enough money that the baristas take their jobs seriously as well as stick around for several years to make the investment into training time worth it, independent café owners have a hard enough time paying themselves a livable wage. It's the nature of coffee, just like any other facet of the service industry.

Barista competitions and the proliferation of educated baristas who can share the amazing story of coffee with customers are leading the way in bringing the professional barista the esteem he or she deserves. But while the growth of the barista community and the barista as a craftsperson has grown enormously in the last decade, really, it's only the beginning.

NOTE

1. Jonathan Gold, "La Mill: The Latest Buzz," http://www.laweekly.com/2008-03-13/eat-drink/the-latest-buzz, accessed August 22, 2013.

55

Brewing Culture

Alf Kramer

If you promise not to tell the geeks, brewing is both fairly simple, regardless of method, and universal. With the use of water, you extract some soluble substances from the bean, around 1.5 percent in the final solution, the **liquor**. Then you get coffee and drink it. Easy as that. Now, if you want a fine coffee, the process becomes more difficult. If you want superb coffee, some science has to be introduced into brewing. Some will claim that at this level, the task is more advanced than rocket science, but that may be going too far. Any number of myths, fairy tales, and beliefs clutter the picture. But luckily for those who believe in science, quality brewing is measurable. It has been for a while, but now it is even easy. That said, one thing is not measurable, human coffee taste preferences. These most certainly change from time to time, place to place, from fashion to fashion, or what we might call culture to culture. That's what this article is all about.

HOW IT ALL STARTED

Some of the oldest cultures of extraction from the coffee tree may date back 2,000 years. Are those ancient techniques actually still around today? No; they concerned extraction from the leaves of the coffee tree, not the fruit or the seeds. In western Ethiopia, on the border with Sudan, tribes still collect leaves from the wild coffee trees. People ferment the leaves, dry them, and infuse them the way we use the leaves of *Camellia sinensis*, the original tea bush. They sweeten the brew with honey, add some spices, and drink it. Whether we should call it coffee or tea is optional. Let us say it tastes different than just about any of today's coffee liquor. In recent years, a coffee leaf beverage has actually been recycled in El Salvador and presented as "breaking news." Time flies.

THE IDEA OF BREWING

Brewing concerns the extraction from the roasted bean. And while brewing tea in its present form is some 5,000 years old, brewing coffee in its present form is more like 500 years old, depending on who writes the history. The original Ethiopian coffee ceremony is in principle the same as brewing tea, but with finely ground beans. The Ottoman Turks really set the ball rolling. A quick look back in history shows that there were advanced coffeehouses not only in the Ottoman capital of Istanbul but also in other parts of the Ottoman empire including North Africa, the Balkans, and Greece, where the Turks were uninvited guests for some 400 years. They left a lot behind wherever they went, including coffee-brewing culture, that is still very much alive and kicking.

INDIGENOUS COFFEE CULTURE

The Turks' **brewing method** was, and is based on the *cezve*, or in Greek the *ibrik* or *brikki*. This is by far the most dominant brewing culture in the areas known as the old Ottoman empire. In the home it still dominates, in the rural coffeehouses it is equally important, but in the more urban areas **espresso** culture is gaining a foothold. No statistics are available, but there are good reasons to believe that until very recently, more coffee was brewed around the world using a cezve/ibrik than an **espresso machine**. There are after all more than 150 million coffee consumers in Turkey and Egypt alone, and there are 5 million coffee-drinking Turks in various European countries.

EARLY BREWING

The cezve/ibrik method is really the mother of all brewing cultures. In order to speed up the extraction process, the surface area of the coffee is enlarged through grinding. The grind is very fine, although there are huge cultural differences in roasting colors; then water is added and heated to a boil. That may be repeated with or without sugar, depending on the culture. The principles are the same more or less in the Ethiopian coffee brewing ceremony.

The concept caught on. More and more people enjoyed the beverage. The advantages with this brewing culture were obvious. The equipment was minimal and inexpensive, heating was simple. **Turkish** coffee—or "Greek," "Mediterranean," and so on, depending on where it was served—became both fashionable and an affordable luxury. The disadvantages were several: volumes in the cezve were limited; the very fine coffee grounds could blend with the beverage in an unpleasant way, even though most of the grounds sank to the bottom of the cezve/ibrik; and the procedure was time consuming. For a few hundred years, brewing principles remained the same, and nothing new really happened. Then came three major developments and inventions.

BREWING IN A COFFEE KETTLE

Volumes were increased by introducing a large cezve, or rather a kettle, as seen over the campfire and on stoves in thousands of homes throughout the world. Now called the steeping method, this technique was dominant in most of the world until well after the World War II. Under this brewing heading we must include the **percolator**, which re-extracted the coffee again and again. It became the same kiss of death to fine coffee culture that tomato ketchup became to fine gastronomy. But volume certainly increased. This kind of coffee is still around, but mainly as a part of hiking in the wilderness.

FILTER BREWING

A second invention was even more successful. In the early twentieth century, Madame Melitta Benz came up with the idea to put the grounds in a **filter**, thus keeping them out of the extracted coffee. Her idea prevented, to some extent, overextraction, and a particle-free coffee was certainly more pleasant to drink. It proved an extremely good idea; today roughly 70–80 percent of coffee worldwide now passes through a filter, not through the original fabric but through paper or metal.

AT LAST, ITALIAN BREWING CULTURE

One disadvantage to the old techniques was that they were time consuming. In earlier times that was not really an issue. We had time, and, as in the Japanese tea ceremony, the process was often as important as the end result. But then came the industrial revolution with its demands for efficiency and the development of machines that, by adding pressure, could speed up brewing time to an express rate (see "The Espresso Menu"). By the 1950s a new brewing culture had arisen, 500 years after the original idea of brewing coffee beans by extraction. Let us call it a native Italian coffee culture that gradually is conquering the world.

With the exception of **soluble**, there have been no other major innovations in brewing cultures. Recent developments are really variations of the above, or recycling or reinventions of half-forgotten brewing ideas, like the Chemex.

Painting with a broad brush and without hard evidence, we may make the educated guess that filter coffee amounts for some 70–80 percent of all coffee drunk, espresso 5–10 percent, soluble around 10 percent, *cezve/ibrik* 5 percent plus, and other means, like extracts, syrups, **pods**, and so forth about 5 percent. Of course, vast differences exist from country to country. Italy altogether, in and out of home, comes in at about 90 percent espresso, Norway 1 percent. The UK drinks 70 percent soluble, others no more than 5 to 10 percent.

MEASURABLE QUALITY

While brewing methods slowly improved, the idea of measuring quality made a huge leap forward from the 1950s onwards. At that time the Pan American Coffee Bureau in New York made studies that lifted brewing quality to science by introducing measurable results for extraction related to brew strength.

The Bureau realized that brew strength can only be measured by the relation between water and coffee in the extracted solution. The amount of soluble solids extracted is another variable. Combining the two parameters allows measurement of the ideal extraction in a brew within the given brew strength. This is based on the theory that the ideal extraction is between 18 and 22 percent and that this extraction arrives at a combination of particle size in the grind, brewing time, and water temperature, regardless of coffee quality.

By measuring the weight of the ground coffee before and after extraction, the exact extraction rate can be concluded. A hydrometer can also be used, just as in measuring alcohol strength in wine. The same parameters of time and temperature can then be used to assess the quality of filter brewers. This is all time consuming, but with recent development of electronic **refractometers**, the horizon is broadened and measuring made easy.

The Pan American Coffee Bureau unfortunately closed in the early 1970s, but the technology, the literature, and the equipment were transferred to Norwegian coffee-brewing companies and adapted there. The trade wholeheartedly adapted it all. At the time, per capita consumption in the U.S. and in Norway were the same, some six kilos per year. But when the Norwegian trade adapted the Pan American system, per capita consumption nearly doubled.

With a few exceptions, this scientific brewing culture was elsewhere ignored or forgotten. It was replaced by the ideology that if you use **commodity coffee** you can get more out of each bean and save money. Consequently the total market did not increase with growing wealth and population. Many variables influence the total market in coffee, but as 80 percent of consumption was filter, coffee brew strength would necessarily have a major influence.

The dreadful ideology of more from the beans and the business concept of saving money at home were based on the fact that a great number of consumers did not taste the difference between bitter, overextracted, and strong coffee; they could not sense the ratio between water and coffee. It therefore became tempting to roast darker, grind finer, and overextract in the brewing process. The brew became measurably more bitter, but consumers could mask this taste by adding sugar and milk. That said, both sugar and milk are, deserved or undeserved, getting negative reputations in the specialty market, and an increasing number of consumers are trying to avoid them.

The market is thus mainly divided between the industrial and the specialty coffee lines. If the brew is overextracted, all coffees basically taste the same, so why bother with a quality coffee? Or the other way around: if you buy a quality coffee, you need proper brewing or the extra money is wasted.

For the specialty coffee community, it is vitally important that coffee is brewed properly. The market segment of quality coffee is small, and it can only expand through quality brewing. The parameters for quality brewing became known in the 1950s. They were practiced with huge success in Norway for four decades, contributing to a stable market for all coffees.

WHAT NEXT?

A lot of differences in coffee have appeared since the 1950s. Coffee beans and their **processing methods**, **roasting**, brewing technology, and above all, consumer habits and preferences have changed. There is a polarization of qualities in the marketplace. The **Speciality Coffee Association of Europe** has therefore launched a long-term scientific program to look deeper into the parameters for coffee quality as seen by consumers. The SCAE has in mind not consumers in general but those who drink fine specialty coffees. What exactly their taste preferences are depend on time, place, habits, and perception of quality. In short, preferences depend on coffee culture. The first findings of these studies will be presented in the near future; more will follow in time to come. Worldwide brewing cultures and preferences are a complex science. Whether it is universal remains to be seen.

COFFEE AND HEALTH

56

The Long Debate over Coffee and Health

Robert W. Thurston

In his chapter in this volume, Lawrence Jones discusses recent scientific findings on coffee and health. This section provides a brief treatment of the periodic public debate about the drink's effect on the mind and the body. Since its initial appearance in England, coffee has been the subject of grand claims for its health benefits and vigorous counterthrusts alleging that it causes substantial harm. These exchanges form another chapter in the social history of the beverage.

Just like traveling to a foreign country, the expectations anyone has about a food or a drink often go far to condition the experience of trying it. We have all heard stories, for example, of the guy who claimed to be really drunk on beer, only to find out that he had been drinking a non-alcoholic brew. Sweet substances appeal immediately to people who have never had them before. But for most other food or beverages, a process of education, formal or informal, has to be under way to make any item appealing. This is especially so for liquids that are either not sweet, like beer, or whose natural sweetness may not be evident, for example mediocre coffee. As the anthropologist Sidney Mintz wrote, "What constitutes 'good food,' like what constitutes good weather, a good spouse, or a fulfilling life, is a social, not a biological, matter. Good food, as [the French anthropologist Claude] Levi-Strauss suggested long ago, must be good to think about before it becomes good to eat."[1] The expectation that coffee would be good to drink, or at least good for the body, appeared early in the story of coffee in the Western world.

DEBATING COFFEE AND HEALTH

The first known coffee advertisement in the West, a broadside posted on London walls and poles, dates from 1652. It emphasized the health benefits, not the taste or pleasure, that the drink supposedly conferred. All spelling and emphases are in the original for this and other documents mentioned below. The 1652 broadside announced that coffee "closes the Orifice of the Stomack, and fortifies the heat within." Coffee is "very good to help digestion . . . [it] quickens the *Spirits*, and makes the Heart *Lightsome*. It is good against sore Eys. . . . It suppresseth Fumes exceedingly, and therefore good against the *Head-ach*. . . . It will prevent *Drowsiness*, and make one fit for busines." In a final promotional touch, the ad claimed that, "*It is observed that in Turkey, where this is generally drunk, that they are not trobled with the*

343

Stone, Gout, Dropsie, or Scurvey, and that their Skins are exceeding cleer and white."[2] Although the Turks were Christian Europe's grave enemy at this point, they were considered a fierce and worthy opponent, not the "Sick Man" that perplexed the continent in later years. Thus their favorite drink was something that commanded respect in 1652.

The first known newspaper ad, in London in 1657, follows the same lines in regard to coffee and health, but without reference to the Turks. To the points made in the earlier broadside, this announcement adds the notion that coffee is useful in warding off gout and the "King's Evil," scrofula, a disfiguring skin disease.[3]

But a counterattack soon arose, claiming that coffee undid men who drank it. The infamous and oft-quoted "Women's Petition against Coffee" of 1674, with the author given as Well-Willer, blasted coffee as

that drying, enfeebling liquor. . . . [coffee has led to] *Decay of that true Old English Vigor*; our *Gallants* being every way so *Frenchified*, that they are become meer Cock-sparrows, fluttering things that come on *Sa sa*, with a world of Fury, but are not able to stand to it, and in the very first Charge fall down *flat* before us. Never did Men wear *greater Breeches*, or carry *less* in them of any *Mettle* whatsoever. . . . Excessive use of that Newfangled, Abominable, Heathenish Liquor called COFFEE, which Riffling Nature of her Choicest *Treasures*, and Drying up the Radical *Moisture*, has so *Eunucht* our Husbands, and *Crippled* our more kind *Gallants*, that they are become as *Impotent* as *Age*, and as unfruitful as those *Desarts* whence that unhappy *Berry* is said to be brought. [Coffee induces men] to run a *Whoring* after such distructive variety of *Foraign* liquors, to trifle away their *time*, scald their Chops, and spend their Money, all for a little *base, black, thick, nasty, bitter, stinking, nauseous* Puddle-water. . . .

[Men] run the hazard of being *Cuckol'd by Dildo's*. . . . *We Humbly Pray* [that] Drinking COFFEE may on severe penalties be forbidden to all Persons under the Age of *Threescore*; and that instead thereof, *Lusty happy Beer, Cock-Ale, Cordial Canaries, Restoring Malago's, and Back-recruiting Chochole* be Recommended to General Use.[4]

The Petition makes for good reading. But it would be unwise to take it too seriously, or as a general statement of what women thought of coffee. First, we have no idea who actually wrote it, or even if women had any role in its composition. Second, it is not addressed to any particular authority, but "To the Right Honorable the Keepers of the Liberties of *Venus*; The Worshipful Court of *Female-Assistants, &c.*" Third, if women wrote it, they may have been protesting their exclusion from early English coffeehouses more than registering their loathing for the drink itself. Fourth, the pamphlet is as much a nationalistic tract as anything else; the disparaging references to the French demonstrate that point. Fifth, the Petition was only one of many pamphlets scorning, or appearing to scorn, the use of coffee, other drinks, and tobacco in the same period.[5] Finally, the Petition was of no avail against the rising tide of coffee in England. Both the number of coffeehouses and the consumption of the brew in the country continued to increase into the eighteenth century. Later tea displaced coffee in Britain; but that is another story.

Somewhat more serious in the debate about coffee and health were attacks from the French side of the channel. There, too, the question may have been largely about national tastes and identity: "We note with horror," wrote a doctor from Marseilles in 1679, "that this beverage . . . has tended almost completely to disaccustom people from the enjoyment of wine." Another physician asserted several years later that coffee "dried up the cerebrospinal fluid and the convolutions . . . the upshot being general exhaustion, paralysis, and impotence."[6]

On the other hand, another Marseilles figure, the apothecary Philippe Sylvester Dufour, published an enthusiastic work on coffee in 1671, *De l'usage du caphé, du thé, et du chocolate* (On the usage of coffee, tea, and chocolate).[7] This book "was generally regarded as propaganda for the beverage; and indeed, it proved an excellent advertisement, being translated into English in 1685."[8] The translation was entitled *The Manner of Making of Coffee, Tea, and Chocolate as it is used In most parts of Europe, Asia, Africa, and America. With their Vertues.*[9] In that same year, Dufour published *Traitez nouveaux & curieux du café, du thé et du chocolate: ouvrage également nécessaire aux médecins, & à tous ceux qui aiment leur santé* (literally A new and curious treatment of coffee, tea, and chocolate: a work equally necessary for doctors and all who love their health).[10] This book quickly appeared in German, Dutch, and Latin; an English version came out within months of the French original as *Treatise new and interesting on coffee, tea, and chocolate: a work equally necessary to doctors and to all those who like their health.*[11] Dufour now made extensive claims for coffee, as well as tea and chocolate—then known only as a beverage—as "three of the Drugs whereof Heaven has shewed itself liberal to Men. These have required so great a vogue or credit, and so particular an esteem through all Europe by the signal effects which they are daily found to produce in an infinite number of People, who make use thereof with good success that I have thought it a thing of great importance to communicate to the publique some Discourses and Treatises made on this Subject."[12]

The wide acceptance of the *Treatise* overrode most objections to coffee. Especially in France, where Dufour's countrymen discovered in the eighteenth century that they could make large profits by importing beans from the colony of St. Domingue (now Haiti), criticisms of coffee subsided.

Yet doubts about the drink and health continued. It was not until 1819 that the German Friedlieb Runge isolated the most active ingredient in coffee. For lack of a better name, he called it caffeine. It was already clear that something in coffee quickened the pulse—blood pressure had not yet been discovered—and had, as the first ad suggested in 1652, a certain "drying" effect. That is, drinking coffee increased the rate of urination. Beyond those points, little could be said with certainty about coffee's effect on the body for some time to come.

Lack of precise knowledge did not deter new critics. By the late nineteenth century, a fresh battleground opened over coffee, this time in America. In the great age of advertising, hype, and concern about emotional disorders, an assault on coffee and the touting of substitute beverages supposedly much better for health was probably inevitable. Now the critics focused on coffee's purported effect on "nerves." The most fashionable ailment of the period was the newly coined "neurasthenia," a syndrome that rendered middle- and upper-class Americans unable to do much more than lie in bed and worry.

In a broad but unscientific campaign to improve Americans' minds and bodies, the new competing drinks were grain beverages. The first acclaimed inventor of a grain brew was Dr. John Harvey Kellogg, the breakfast cereal king and creator of quack diets and cures for nervous diseases. In the 1890s he assigned much of the blame for those problems and many others on coffee and argued that "Tea and coffee are baneful drugs and their sale and use ought to be prohibited by law."[13] Instead he served "Caramel Coffee," a grain product.

But a stay at Kellogg's Michigan sanatorium failed to soothe the nerves of C. W. Post, the second cereal mogul of the period. Striking out on his own, Post more or less copied Kellogg's drink with one of his own, the much more successful **Postum**. An ad of 1907 instructed readers on "How to Lie Awake—DRINK COFFEE. Then after a while you can have a round with Nervous Prostration. Plain old Common Sense suggests leave off the irritating, delusive drug and use POSTUM."[14] In the next year, another Postum ad featured a testimonial from a young man "Nearly wrecked by coffee."[15]

Meanwhile, in 1883 Harvey M. Wiley, M.D., became the U.S. Department of Agriculture's first chief chemist. He soon began to campaign for a pure food and drug act, modeled after a British law of 1875. Congress finally passed the Pure Food and Drug Act, largely written by

Wiley, in 1906.[16] Unfortunately, he also became an anti-coffee crusader. In 1910 he maintained in a speech that "coffee drunkenness is a commoner failing than the whiskey habit . . . This country is full of tea and coffee drunkards. The most common drug in this country is caffeine."[17]

Needless to say, the coffee industry fought back hard, albeit in a confused manner at first. Some roasters claimed that they had eliminated the harmful ingredients in coffee, for example the "tannin-bearing chaff."[18] The *Tea and Coffee Trade Journal*, established in 1901 as American industry's voice for both beverages, mounted a more concerted campaign of pro-coffee advertising and information. After its founding in 1911, the National Coffee Roasters Association, now the National Coffee Association of USA, promoted two "national coffee weeks," one in 1914 and another in 1915, wherein an excellent foundation was laid for the big joint coffee-trade propaganda that followed."[19] In 1920 the Association published a series of pamphlets for doctors, explaining none too subtly that coffee was not harmful in reasonable amounts. Between the coffee men, the force of habit, and the tremendous boost that World War I gave to the consumption of coffee, at least by American soldiers overseas, the puddle water won.[20]

Another wave of attacks on coffee appeared in the 1920s and 1930s, warning against irritation or even violence among couples allegedly caused by "stale" coffee, as Chase and Sanborn claimed. Postum comic-strip-style ads in the 1930s featured an evil ghost, Mr. Coffee Nerves, who tried to keep nervous insomniacs on coffee, only to be chased away by the grain drink.[21] Sanka—a word drawn from the French "sans caffeine"—continued to target regular coffee as the cause of anxiety and sleeplessness into the 1970s. Kraft Foods, which had acquired Postum, discontinued the drink in 2007 but plans to reoffer it starting in June 2012. Other grain beverages are available. A few rearguard actions damning coffee are still going on,[22] but they appear to have little or no impact on the public.

A report published in the prestigious *New England Journal of Medicine*, too late for Lawrence Jones to discuss in his article, describes the effects of coffee among more than 400,000 Americans tracked from 1995 to 2008. The investigators adjusted for tobacco use, which muddied many previous surveys. The results show that coffee drinking is "inversely associated with most major causes of death in both men and women, including heart disease, respiratory disease, stroke, injuries and accidents, diabetes, and infections."[23] That is, people who drink coffee are significantly less likely to suffer from those problems. These findings match other recent conclusions. Presumably coffee users have fewer accidents and injuries because they are on average more alert.

Even though coffee drinkers eat more red meat, exercise less, and use more alcohol than nondrinkers do, the coffee crowd lives longer. Men who drank four or five cups a day through 2008 registered 88 percent of the mortality of non-users. For women, drinking four or five cups reduced mortality to 84 percent of the nondrinkers' figure. No difference appeared between those who drank decaf and those who drank regular coffee. People who never smoked or who had stopped at the time the survey began, but did drink coffee, had the lowest mortality rate of all.[24] Since a cup of coffee contains more than 1,000 chemical compounds, something besides caffeine is at work. Scientists don't know which compounds help, but clearly coffee benefits most people.

New uses for coffee, for instance as a key ingredient in soap, have appeared in recent years. There is still more good news, if only for brunettes. Instead of paying extra for potions to color their hair between visits to the beautician, they "should rinse with 2 cups of cool black coffee over damp hair in the shower; leave on for 10 minutes, then shampoo." This keeps highlights from fading until the pros can take over again.[25]

Harvey Wiley was correct in saying that caffeine was the country's favorite drug, and that is still true today, as it is around the world. But now it seems clear, for most people who use coffee moderately, that the beverage is much more beneficial than harmful. Drink it down or pour it on: coffee is good for you either way.

NOTES

1. Sidney W. Mintz, *Sweetness and Power: The Place of Sugar in Modern History* (New York: Viking, 1985), 8.

2. In William H. Ukers, *All about Coffee*, 2nd ed. (Mansfield Center, CT: Martino, 2006 [originally published 1935]), 50.

3. Ukers, *All about Coffee*, 470.

4. A Well-Willer, *To the Right Honorable the Keepers of the Liberties of Venus; The Worshipful Court of Female-Assistants, &c. The Humble Petition and Address of several Thousands of Buxome Good-Women, Languishing in Extremity of Want*, 1674, available in the collection Early English Books on Line.

5. Ukers, *All about Coffee*, 65–68.

6. Mark Pendergrast, *Uncommon Grounds: The History of Coffee and How It Transformed Our World* (New York: Basic Books, 1999), 8–9.

7. I have not yet been able to locate this work; it is mentioned on WorldCat under its title as published in Lyon by J. Girin et B. Rivière, 1671. By 1685 an English version of this book was published; see note 16.

8. Ukers, *All about Coffee*, 471.

9. Philippe Sylvestre Dufour, *The Manner of Making of Coffee, Tea, and Chocolate as it is used in most parts of Europe, Asia, Africa, and America. With their Vertues*, 1685.

10. Philippe Sylvestre Dufour, Antonio Colmenero de Ledesma, and Bartolomeo Marradon, *Traitez nouveaux & curieux du café, du thé et du chocolate: ouvrage également nécessaire aux médecins, & à tous ceux qui aiment leur santé*, 1685.

11. *Treatise new and interesting on coffee, tea, and chocolate: a work equally necessary to doctors and to all those who like their health*, 1685.

12. *Treatise new and interesting on coffee, tea, and chocolate*, 4–5.

13. Pendergrast, *Uncommon Grounds*, 97.

14. The image can be found at http://www.amazon.com/Postum-Cereal-Coffee-Breakfast-ADVERTISING/dp/B005DGXIR8, accessed February 5, 2012.

15. http://www.periodpaper.com/index.php/subject-advertising-art/food-soda/coffee/1908-vintage-print-ad-postum-drink-coffee-substitute, accessed February 4, 2012.

16. http://www.fda.gov/AboutFDA/WhatWeDo/History/CentennialofFDA/HarveyW.Wiley/default.htm, accessed February 5, 2012.

17. Quoted in Pendergrast, *Uncommon Grounds*, 108.

18. Ukers, *All about Coffee*, 473.

19. Ukers, *All about Coffee*, 473–77; quote on 477.

20. Examples are in Ukers, *All about Coffee*, 474.

21. Examples can be found at http://mattauber.blogspot.com/2010/08/mr-coffee-nerves.html, accessed February 7, 2012.

22. See T. R. Reid, "Caffeine," *National Geographic*, January 2005.

23. Neal D. Freedman, Yikyung Par, Christian C. Abnet, Albert R. Hollenbeck, and Rashmi Sinha, "Association of coffee drinking with total and cause-specific mortality," *The New England Journal of Medicine* 366, no. 20 (May 17, 2012): 1897.

24. Freedman et al., "Association of coffee drinking," 1894, 1897.

25. Bobbi Brown in *Health* (January–February 2012): 28.

57

Caffeine

How Much Is in Your Cup, and How Much Is Bad for You?

Robert W. Thurston

Investigators disagree on the amount of caffeine in an "average" cup or espresso shot. That is partly because it's impossible to say what an average portion is, partly because different varieties of beans contain different amounts of caffeine and partly because the way coffee is made affects the amount of caffeine it contains.

The amount of caffeine in coffee beans may vary from harvest to harvest or tree to tree, perhaps even from the berries at the bottom of a tree to those at the top. Brewing time and methods can result in different levels of caffeine from the same beans. Meanwhile, U.S. federal regulations state that for any coffee to be labeled decaffeinated, 97 percent of the caffeine has to be removed. But that says nothing about how much caffeine actually remains in the drink! In short, there is no way to tell how much caffeine is in your drink without testing it. Table 57.1 lists estimates for coffee, tea, Red Bull, and one stay-awake pill.

Table 57.1.   Estimates of Caffeine in Beverages

National Geographic

Brewed coffee, 12-oz. cup	200 mg
Espresso, 1-oz. shot	40 mg
Brewed tea, 8-oz. cup	50 mg
Red Bull, 8.3-oz. can	80 mg

Dicum and Luttinger

Drip arabica coffee (8 oz.)	95 mg
Drip robusta coffee (8 oz.)	130 mg
Espresso, from arabica (1.5–2.0 oz.)	95 mg
NoDoz	100 mg

***Harvard Health Letter*, January 2012**

8-oz. short cup of Starbucks bold coffee	180 mg
8-oz. cup of Lipton green tea	35 mg
8.4 oz. can of Red Bull	80 mg

Mayo Clinic, "Nutrition and Healthy Eating," October 2011

"Generic brewed coffee," 8 oz.	95–200 mg

Sources: T. R. Reid, "Caffeine," *National Geographic* 207, no. 1 (January 2005); Gregory Dicum and Nina Luttinger, *The Coffee Book: Anatomy of an Industry from Crop to the Last Drop* (1999), 117.

348

A study at the University of Florida College of Medicine tested ten coffee samples of decaffeinated coffee from different shops; the drinks contained a range of 0 caffeine to 13.9 mg per 16-ounce serving. The researchers also tested Starbucks **espresso** and brewed coffee from one store; these samples registered between 3.0 and 15.8 mg/shot of espresso and 12.0–13.4 mg/16-oz. serving of the brewed coffee.[1] A Mayo Clinic report found that "eight ounces of generic, brewed decaffeinated coffee" can contain from 2 to 12 mg of caffeine, while one ounce of "espresso, restaurant-style, decaffeinated" can have from 0 to 15 mg.[2] At the upper level of these numbers, caffeine intake can be a problem for people with high blood pressure or various other medical conditions and of course for anyone who is simply intolerant to caffeine. Since the chemical is also found in chocolate, many over-the-counter medications, and some foods, anyone who reacts to caffeine should be careful about drinking "decaf." The Mayo Clinic recommends no more than 200–300 mg per day for "most healthy adults."[3]

Caffeine in dried, powdered form is a highly powerful, toxic substance that has medical uses. Whether caffeine or any other drug put into the body helps or hurts typically depends on the dosage. Aspirin in huge quantities can kill you. The *Harvard Health Letter* states boldly that, "The lethal dose of caffeine is about 10 grams, which is equivalent to the amount of caffeine in 100 cups of coffee."[4] But the fatal amount depends on body weight and other factors, including gender, and the statement does not address the issue of how much caffeine is in any given cup. "In short," writes Bernadine Healy, M.D., "it all depends on how your body handles the stuff."[5]

Let's assume, however, that it would take 100 cups of coffee drunk in the span of a few hours to kill you. But "only small amounts [of caffeine] are around eight to 10 hours later" in your system, once you stop ingesting coffee, says the *Harvard Health Letter*. In all likelihood your body would rebel at the quantity of liquid necessary to take in 10 grams of caffeine by drinking buckets of coffee; you would vomit or gag and be unable to drink more. Do not try this at home.

If you can't carry a gas chromatograph around to test the amount of caffeine in a beverage, what can you do? Test strips are now available (we are not recommending any particular brand, nor can we vouch for the accuracy of any on-the-spot testing) that supposedly indicate within seconds of being dipped into a spoonful of liquid how much caffeine is in the drink. Maybe the best advice is the obvious: if you have a problem with caffeine, be careful.

NOTES

1. R. R. McCusker, B. Fuehrlein, B. A. Goldberger, M. S. Gold, and E. J. Cone, "Caffeine Content of Decaffeinated Coffee," *Journal of Analytical Toxicology* 30, no. 8 (October 2006): 611–13.

2. http://www.mayoclinic.com/health/caffeine/AN0121, accessed January 29, 2012.

3. http://www.mayoclinic.com/health/caffeine/NU00600, accessed January 29, 2012.

4. "What Is It about Coffee," *Harvard Health Letter*, January 2012, 4.

5. Bernadine Healy, "On Health," *U.S. News and World Report*, March 20, 2006.

58

Recent Research on Coffee and Health

Lawrence W. Jones

As a roaster-retailer and a practicing physician, I am increasingly asked by the public for my opinion regarding coffee and health. The world specialty market is preoccupied with health issues surrounding coffee, and I am sure that other roaster-retailers and practicing physicians also frequently receive queries. Besides concerns about coffee's direct impact on the brain and body, people are interested in decaffeination and the possibility of reducing gastric irritation. This review outlines the current state of research and views on coffee and health.

Health and wellness have become increasingly serious matters for consumers. One best-selling author advises, "Eat non-processed food . . . not too much . . . mostly plants."[1] With those principles in mind, what could be better than coffee, a natural beverage? As awareness grows that coffee in moderation is part of a healthy lifestyle, health concerns are affecting the world coffee market.

From the earliest known coffee advertisements forward, coffee's effect on health has been the object of considerable speculation. Only in the past several decades has our scientific knowledge of the beverage developed substantially. Biochemical and behavioral scientific investigations of caffeine undertaken in the latter half of the twentieth century helped to define coffee's influence on health. Earl W. Sutherland studied adenosine triphosphate (ATP) and cyclic adenine monophosphate (cAMP). He demonstrated that hormones like adrenaline activate specific receptors on cell walls that send signals to the cell interior by increasing production of cAMP. He further showed that caffeine inhibits the breakdown of this cAMP stimulus.[2] For this work, Sutherland won the Nobel Prize in physiology and medicine in 1971.

Three developments thereafter were responsible for changing how we look at coffee and health. Despite limitations of food-frequency questionnaires, most of this discussion is the result of large Western European databases.[3] The populations are stable, the data collection is comprehensive, and the analysis is thoughtful.

Modern advances in cell biology have provided laboratory confirmation of data-based epidemiologic studies. High-performance liquid chromatography is used to identify the molecular composition of complex solutions such as coffee.[4] Mass spectroscopy is employed to define the chemical structure of each molecule of interest.

Recent biomedical discoveries have come from our ability to selectively "knock out" genes coding for specific molecules one gene at a time. Hence, every human disease including neurodegenerative and metabolic disorders has a corresponding mouse model. Coffee-related health issues are no exception.

Four agents in coffee may affect health: caffeine, the diterpenes (cafestol and kahweol), chlorogenic acids, and niacin. Here is how these compounds work.

1. Caffeine in the brain acts by a variety of chemical and electrical mechanisms. It is a central nervous system stimulant. It is a potent source of the energy mediator nitric oxide through cyclic guanosine monophosphate (cGMP) accumulation and sugar production through glycogen breakdown.[5] Outside the brain, caffeine is also a selective smooth muscle relaxant, notably in peripheral and cavernosal vessels and in the bronchial tree.[6]

Caffeine results in improved physical and cognitive performance during and after exercise.[7] In the liver, acute caffeine administration impairs glucose tolerance, but increases insulin sensitivity and promotes energy metabolism. Administered chronically, coffee improves glucose tolerance.

Decaffeination typically leaves about 3 percent caffeine behind. Less than 10 percent of coffee sold is decaffeinated. Nevertheless, most diet surveys separate the two and fail to identify significant health differences.

Caffeine increases urinary output by actively inhibiting sodium reabsorption. Renal concentration of urine decreases as water follows sodium.[8]

2. The diterpenes alter lipid enzymes, contributing to increases in cholesterol and low density lipoproteins.[9] They are absent in coffee brewed with paper **filter** techniques. The adverse effect on cholesterol of coffee brewed by other methods is marginal, yet sufficient to contribute to an increasing demand for paper filtration brewing in preference to boiled or steam extraction techniques.

3. Chlorogenic acid and cinnamic acid are polyphenol antioxidants. Dietary polyphenols are a group of chemical substances found in plants, characterized by the presence of more than one phenol unit or building block per molecule. They are generally divided into hydrolysable tannins and phenylpropanoids, such as caffeic acid. As a group of natural antioxidants, plant polyphenols are thought to protect against cardiovascular disease and cancer. Although this class is of intense interest to the lay public, there are few reports validating its clinical relevance.[10]

4. In conventional coffee usage, one micronutrient, niacin, may modify lipids and thus contribute to the control of atherosclerosis. The other micronutrients, magnesium, potassium, and vitamin E, are only present in 0.1 to 5 percent of recommended daily requirements. Therefore, coffee's potential contribution is negligible.

Thanks to modern research techniques, a revolution is taking place with how we regard coffee in relation to the pathology and epidemiology of specific health issues. Coffee drinkers are at less risk for neurodegenerative disease such as the dementias and Parkinson's disease. This may be due to a neuroprotective influence of caffeine that prevents leakage of toxic serum protein into neural tissue. Coffee protects against disruptions of the blood-brain barrier in animal models of Alzheimer's disease as well as Parkinson's disease.[11] Indeed, there is strong evidence that caffeine and coffee may be therapeutic against Alzheimer's disease by reducing deposits of toxic beta amyloid polypeptides (proteins).[12] It has been proposed that other neurodegenerative disorders such as posttraumatic brain injury, HIV-1 dementia, stroke, and multiple sclerosis may be similarly amenable to pharmacologic stabilization of the blood-brain barrier.[13]

Coffee drinkers are at three to five times less risk than non-coffee drinkers for Parkinson's disease. Dopamine-like drugs are used to treat Parkinson's disease. Caffeine promotes dopamine action in the brain stem by competing with dopamine's antagonist, adenosine A2, a caffeine look-alike molecule.[14] Adenosine A2 antagonists such as caffeine may palliate Parkinson's disease.[15]

Mild to severe headaches, including migraine, can be lessened by coffee. Caffeine is effective in the treatment of the acute migraine attack.[16] Its mechanism of action may be to counteract genetically related dopamine hypersensitivity. It may also act by preempting the more severe postvasoconstriction vasodilatation that causes the headache. Recent work suggests that migraine may be associated with transmembrane sodium pump alterations.[17] This mechanism of action can be modulated by caffeine. However, the potential for caffeine's role in migraine treatment has not yet been studied.

Depression and depression-related suicide risk in the U.S. is 50 percent less in moderate coffee drinkers than in non-coffee drinkers.[18]

One study on strokes demonstrated less cerebral arterial occlusion in coffee drinkers. Also, there has been nothing to suggest an association between coffee, hypertension, and cerebral hemorrhage.[19]

Adenosine controls the sleep-wake cycle. Sleeplessness due to caffeine is mediated by its effect on adenosine A1 and A2 receptors.[20] The speed of caffeine breakdown may also contribute to sleeplessness. Variability in the enzymatic breakdown of coffee may account for caffeine's variable effect on sleep induction and arousal.[21]

In Holland, a study of 17,000 Dutch men and women found 50 percent less risk of type II diabetes in heavy coffee drinkers compared with light or non-coffee drinkers. Similar studies have been reported from Finland, Sweden, and the United States.[22]

Liver injury, cirrhosis, and liver cancer may all be alleviated by coffee. In patients with liver disease, certain liver enzymes are lower in coffee drinkers. Likewise, the risk of cirrhosis and cirrhosis-related death is lower. Finally, in one study, patients with hepatitis B or C who had isolated reports of paroxysmal atrial tachycardia, there is no association between coffee consumption and ventricular fibrillation or sudden cardiac death.[26] at least one cup of coffee per day lowered the risk of liver cancer by 48 percent.[23]

Palpitation is an awareness of perceived heart rhythm irregularities and can be caused by excess caffeine. Palpitations are seldom associated with organic cardiac disease.[24] However, significant arrhythmias such as atrial fibrillation and flutter have not been found to be associated with caffeine.[25]

The odds of a heart attack are significantly lower in people who consumed up to three cups of coffee daily than in those who did not drink coffee. No relation between coffee intake and cardiac arrest in patients with established coronary heart disease has been found. Despite isolated reports of paroxysmal atrial tachycardia, there is no association between coffee consumption and ventricular fibrillation or sudden cardiac death.[26]

In patients susceptible to osteoporosis, the risk can be minimized by calcium and vitamin D supplementation and coffee consumption limited to three cups of coffee or less per day.[27]

With regard to gout, serum uric acid, the marker for gout, is lower in coffee drinkers including drinkers of decaffeinated coffee. Uric acid is not lower in tea drinkers. Perhaps chlorogenic acid, absent in tea, is responsible for controlling gout through its antioxidant properties.[28]

Suggestions that coffee may increase the risk for cancer have not been validated.[29] On the contrary, recently, a prestigious journal reported a study that uncovered a significantly lower incidence of high-risk prostate cancer among coffee-drinking men.[30]

Lay literature often supports restrictions on coffee for individuals complaining of urinary frequency. Coffee's effect on causing urinary frequency may be due to its diuretic action. Coffee's diuretic effect occurs at the level of the proximal tubules of the renal nephron. Coffee may also irritate the urinary bladder mucosa. However, there is nothing to suggest a relationship between coffee and chronic interstitial cystitis.[31]

In regard to kidney stones, caffeine modestly increases urinary calcium as well as oxalate. Despite these effects, controlled studies have failed to substantiate any differences in stone incidence as a function of coffee intake.[32] It may be that the lack of a significant difference is due to caffeine's diuretic effect, thus reducing stone formation by solute dilution.

Coffee may alter sexual behavior. Male rats treated with caffeine prior to copulation demonstrated significantly decreased latency and increased rate of coitus.[33] Caffeinated female rats showed an increase both in sexual motivation and locomotor activity.[34] Fertility rate probabilities in women may be obscured by alcohol, tobacco, and drug use. Nevertheless, for women desiring pregnancy, few studies support coffee limitation below three cups per day. Spontaneous abortion is likewise not associated with coffee intake below three cups per day. Coffee does not cause preterm delivery or birth defects. Caffeine is present in the mother's milk of coffee drinkers; however, the American Academy of Pediatrics categorizes caffeine as a maternal medication that is usually compatible with breastfeeding when consumption is below three cups per day.[35]

In children, any drink containing more than 3 milligrams of caffeine/kilogram may cause nervousness in children.[36] This finding prompted Canadians to limit caffeine intake for children to 2.5 milligrams/kilogram per day—that is, approximately a half cup for a six year old.

Low acid coffees are hitting the markets as a coffee source that provides symptom relief for those with dyspepsia, diarrhea, bloating, pain, and irregular defecation. Coffee increases gastrointestinal motility but lifestyle studies suggest that dyspepsia is the consequence of food intolerance rather than the cause.[37]

Does **organic** coffee affect health? To our knowledge, no toxic levels of herbicides or pesticides survive the **roasting** process. One German study tested pesticide residues in raw and roasted coffee and their degradation during the roasting process.[38] The residues were reported to be reduced to insignificant amounts during the roasting process.

The relationship of coffee consumption to mortality has recently received new attention. Regular coffee consumption is not associated with an increased mortality rate in either men or women. Indeed, the major study on this question suggests the possibility of a modest benefit on all-cause and cardiovascular mortality.[39]

In summary, coffee consumption contributes to the control of type 2 diabetes mellitus (metabolic syndrome), Parkinson's disease, liver disease, perhaps depression, suicide risk, dementia, and migraine. Moderate coffee intake, below 300 milligrams per day, or 3 milligrams/kilogram in children, will not increase the risk for stroke, arrhythmia, hypertension, cardiovascular disease, cancer, infection, complications of pregnancy, calcium imbalance, bone disease, or kidney stones. Finally, coffee may be associated with a variety of adverse but relatively inconsequential side effects such as sleeplessness, heart palpitations, and urinary frequency.

Quality over quantity is an emerging market consideration for heavy coffee drinkers. From the roaster-retailer's standpoint, these changes in public opinion are increasing the demand for specialty coffee. Specifically, they are focusing the public's attention on brewing techniques, caffeine content, and quality. The public should regard coffee in moderation as generally beneficial and, with minor qualifications, seldom harmful.

NOTES

1. Michael Pollan, *In Defense of Food: An Eater's Manifesto* (New York: Penguin Books, 2008), 244.

2. R. W. Butcher and E. W. Sutherland, "Adenosine 3,'5'-phosphate in biological materials," *Journal of Biological Chemistry* 237, no. 4 (1961): 1244–50.

3. J. V. Higdon and B. Frei, "Coffee and health: A review of recent human research," *Critical Reviews in Food Science and Nutrition* 46 (2006): 101–23.

4. M. A. Ramírez-Coronel, N. Marnet, V. S. K. Kolli, et al., "Characterization and estimation of proanthocyanidins and other phenolics in coffee pulp (Coffee Arabica) by Thiolysis-High-Performance Liquid Chromatography," *Journal of Agricultural and Food Chemistry* 52 (2004): 1344–49.

5. Z. Huang, Y. Urade, and O. Hayaishi, "The role of adenosine in the regulation of sleep," *Current Topics in Medicinal Chemistry* 11 (2011): 1047–57.

6. J. D. Corbin and S. H. Francis, "Molecular biology and pharmacology of PDE-5-inhibitor therapy for erectile dysfunction," *Journal of Andrology* 24, no. 6 (2003): 38–40.

7. E. Hogervost, S. Bandelow, J. Schmitt, et al., "Caffeine improves physical and cognitive performance during exhaustive exercise," *Medicine and Science in Sports and Exercise* 40, no. 10 (2010): 1841–51.

8. D. G. Shirley, S. J. Walter, and F. H. Noormohamed, "Natriuretic effect of caffeine: Assessment of segmental sodium reabsorption in humans," *Clinical Science* 103 (2002): 461–66.

9. A. De Roos, R. Van Tol, L. M. Urgert, et al., "Consumption of French-press coffee raises cholesteryl estertransfer protein activity levels before LDL cholesterol in normolipidaemic subjects," *Journal of Internal Medicine* 248 (2000): 211–16; S. H. Jee, J. He, L. J. Appel, et al., "Coffee consumption and serum lipids: a meta-analysis of randomized controlled clinical trials," *American Journal of Epidemiology* 153, no. 4 (2001): 353–62.

10. I. C. Arts and P. C. Hollman, "Polyphenols and disease risk in epidemiologic studies," *American Journal of Clinical Nutrition* 81, no. 1 (2005): 317S–25S. K. M. Wilson, J. L. Kasperzyk, J. R. Rider, et al., "Coffee consumption and prostate cancer risk and progression in the health professionals follow-up study," *Journal of the National Cancer Institute* 103, no. 11 (2011).

11. X. Chen, O. Ghribi, and J. D. Geiger, "Caffeine protects against disruptions of the blood-brain barrier in animal models of Alzheimer's and Parkinson's diseases," *Journal of Alzheimer's Disease [JAD]* 20 (2010): 127–41.

12. G. W. Arendash and C. Cao, "Caffeine and coffee as therapeutics against Alzheimer's disease," *JAD* 20 (2010): S117–26.

13. Chen et al., "Caffeine protects against disruptions."

14. G. W. Ross, R. D. Abbott, H. Petrovich, et al., "Association of coffee and caffeine intake with the risk of Parkinson disease," *Journal of the American Medical Association [JAMA]* 283, no. 20 (2000): 2674–79; K. Saaksjarvi, P. Knekt, H. Rissanen, et al., "Prospective study of coffee consumption and risk of Parkinson's disease," *European Journal of Clinical Nutrition* 26 (2008): 908–15.

15. Chen et al., "Caffeine protects against disruptions," 127–41.

16. P. Dusitanond and W. B. Young, "Neuroleptics and migraine," *Central Nervous System Agents in Medicinal Chemistry* 9, no. 1 (2009): 63–70.

17. M. G. Harrington, A. N. Fonteh, X. Arakaki, et al., "Capillary endothelial Na(+), K(+), ATPase transporter homeostasis and a new theory for migraine pathophysiology," *Headache* 50 (2010): 459–78.

18. I. Kawachi, W. C. Willett, G. A. Colditz, et al., "A prospective study of coffee drinking and suicide in women," *Archives of Internal Medicine* 156, no. 5 (1996): 521–25.

19. S. C. Larsson, J. Virtamo, and A. Wolk, "Coffee consumption and risk of stroke in women," *Stroke* 42, no. 4 (2011): 908–12.

20. Z. Huang, Y. Urade, and O. Hayaishi, "The role of adenosine in the regulation of sleep," *Current Topics in Medicinal Chemistry* 11 (2011): 1047–57.

21. M. R. Youngberg, I. O. Karpov, A. Begley, et al., "Clinical and physiological correlates of caffeine and caffeine metabolites in primary insomnia," *Journal of Clinical Sleep Medicine* 7, no. 2 (2011): 196–203.

22. R. M. Van Dam and F. B. Hu, "Coffee consumption and risk of type 2 diabetes, a systematic review," *JAMA* 204, no. 1 (2005): 97–104.

23. T. Shimazu, Y. Tsubono, S. Kuriyama, et al., "Coffee consumption and the risk of primary liver cancer: pooled analysis of two prospective studies in Japan," *International Journal of Cancer* 116 (2005): 150–54.

24. R. Mayou, D. Sprigings, J. Birkhead, et al., "Characteristics of patients presenting to a cardiac clinic with palpitation," *Quarterly Journal of Medicine* 96 (2003): 115–23.

25. L. Frost and P. Vestergaard, "Caffeine and risk of atrial fibrillation or flutter: The Danish diet, cancer, and health study," *American Journal of Clinical Nutrition [AJCN]* 81 (2005): 578–82.

26. J. A. Greenberg, C. C. Dunbar, R. Schnoll, et al., "Caffeinated beverage intake and the risk of heart disease mortality in the elderly, a prospective analysis," *AJCN* 85 (2007): 392–98.

27. J. V. Higdon and B. Frei, "Coffee and health: A review of recent human research," *Critical Reviews in Food Science and Nutrition* 46 (2006) 101–23.

28. H. K. Choi and G. Curhan, "Coffee, tea, and caffeine consumption and serum uric acid level: the third national health and nutrition examination survey," *Arthritis and Rheumatism* 57, no. 5 (2007): 816–21.

29. International Agency for Research on Cancer [IARC], *Coffee, tea, mate, methylxanthines and methylglyoxal*, Monographs on the Evaluation of Carcinogenic Risks to Humans, 51 (1991): 41–197. IARC, *Caffeine*, Monographs on the Evaluation of Carcinogenic Risks to Humans, 51 (1991): 291–390.

30. K. M. Wilson, J. L. Kasperzyk, J. R. Rider, et al., "Coffee consumption and prostate cancer risk and progression in the health professionals follow-up study," *Journal of the National Cancer Institute* 103, no. 11 (2011): 1–9.

31. G. Tettamanti, D. Altman, N. L. Pedersen, et al., "Effects of coffee and tea consumption on urinary incontinence in female twins," *BJOG International Journal of Obstetrics and Gynecology* 118, no. 7 (2011): 806–13.

32. G. C. Curhan, W. C. Willett, E. B. Rimm, et al., "Prospective study of beverage use and the risk of kidney stones," *American Journal of Epidemiology* 143, no. 3 (1998): 240–47. G. C. Curhan, W. C. Willett, F. E. Speizer, et al., "Beverage use and risk for kidney stones in women," *Annals of Internal Medicine* 128 (1998): 534–40.

33. P. G. Zimbardo and H. Barry III, "Effects of caffeine and chlorpromazine on the sexual behavior of male rats," *Science* 127 (1958): 84–85.

34. F. A. Guarraci and A. Benson, "'Coffee, tea *and* me': Moderate doses of caffeine affect sexual behavior in female rats," *Pharmacology, Biochemistry and Behavior* 82 (2005): 522–30.

35. American Academy of Pediatrics, "The transfer of drugs and other chemicals into human milk," *Pediatrics* 108, no. 3 (2001): 776–89.

36. P. Nawrot, S. Jordan, J. Eastwood, et al., "Effects of caffeine on human health," *Food Additives and Contaminants* 20, no. 1 (2003): 1–30.

37. R. Lind, S. Olafsson, I. Hjelland, et al., "Lifestyle of patients with self reported food hypersensitivity differ little from controls," *Gastroenterology Nursing* 31, no. 6 (2008): 401–10.

38. M. Cetinkaya, J. von Duszeln, W. Thiemann, et al., "Organochlorine pesticide residues in raw and roasted coffee and their degradation during the roasting process," *Zeitschrift fuer Lebensmittel-Untersuchung und -Forschung A* 179, no. 1 (July 1984): 5–8.

39. E. Lopez-Garcia, R. M. van Dam, T. Y. Li, et al., "The relationship of coffee consumption with mortality," *Annals of Internal Medicine* 148, no. 12 (2008): 904–14.

Part V

THE FUTURE OF COFFEE

59

Coffee Research in Kenya

Current Status and Future Perspectives

Elijah K. Gichuru

Kenya predominantly produces **arabica** coffee (*Coffea arabica* L.), which was introduced into the country around 1900 by French missionaries. Since then, it has been a crop of major importance in the country's economy. Formal coffee research in Kenya started with the appointment of a coffee entomologist in 1908 by the colonial government. In 1963, the government passed the responsibility of managing the research to coffee growers through the Coffee Research Foundation (CRF), which was incorporated as a company limited by guarantee. It is managed at the policy level by stakeholder representatives plus representatives from relevant government ministries and national agricultural research institutions. Its headquarters are in the central part of the country but with subcenters in other coffee growing areas. The themes of coffee research expanded with time, and the Foundation is currently mandated to investigate all issues along the coffee **value chain** and to recommend ways to promote the production of high-quality coffees that meet consumer needs.

Currently, CRF is organized into seven technical research sections: Plant Pathology; Chemistry, comprising crop nutrition, processing and quality units; Crop Physiology; Plant Breeding; Entomology; Agronomy; and Agricultural Economics, as well as two information dissemination sections, Research Liaison and Advisory, and Kenya Coffee College.

CRF is a farmers' organization funded mainly through a levy on green coffee sales within the country, an arrangement that has helped to develop a unique relationship between the institution and stakeholders along the coffee value chain. In addition, more funds are obtained from income-generating activities, government of Kenya grants, externally funded collaborative projects, research grants from development partners, and collaborative activities with the private sector. The Foundation has consequently developed strong collaborative linkages with national, regional, and international partners.

ACHIEVEMENTS

Over the years, CRF has generated remarkable research outputs that have contributed to the growth and development of the coffee industry. These include selection of arabica coffee **varieties** with high yields and quality, development of disease-resistant coffee varieties, disease and pest management programs, soil fertility management recommendations suitable for different areas, and coffee **processing** technologies. These technologies are disseminated to stakeholders through advisory and training activities supported by services such as soil fertility analysis, production of planting materials, and quality control checks for production inputs and coffee product. CRF also provides technical backstopping to regulatory, policy development, and marketing organizations of the government. In carrying out its core services, CRF is a beacon benchmarked with similar national and international institutions with which collaboration has been developed. In fact, the Foundation is an international hub for research and development in coffee.

CHALLENGES

Challenges facing CRF in its operations are characteristic of agricultural research globally. One of the main issues is adequacy and sustainability of funding. For continued and enhanced research, CRF needs to develop and sustain capacity in terms of skills, instrumentation, and infrastructure that respond to new technologies and demands. This creates vibrant dynamics in the economics of financing research for development. Although rapid changes in technology would imply high depreciation of equipment due to obsolescence, increased efficiency and high-value results make the investments suggested by research pay off. Such benefits should then attract further funding for research and development. Research managers and policy makers therefore need to emphasize their successes and develop strategies leading to sustainable financing of research organizations.

The main source of funding for CRF is a 2 percent levy on green coffee sales within Kenya. This amount is barely adequate to support research, especially when total revenues are low due to low production, low prices, or both. Furthermore, emerging marketing systems and new legislation could negatively impact the collection of the levies. CRF constantly faces the challenge of enhancing both the amount and sustainability of its funding.

Private sector players, including farmers' organizations, civil society groups, companies, and individuals, can contribute to funding the institution. However, currently their contribution is low due to several factors, such as inadequate opportunity to derive direct economic benefits from the generation of knowledge and technology by the public sector. This problem can be addressed by strengthening intellectual property rights, which in turn would promote private investment in agricultural research. It should be noted that the system of funding the Foundation is one whereby the coffee sector funds coffee research; the long-term existence of this mechanism is testimony to the fact that the financiers derive benefits.

Researchers hope that in the future, CRF will be increasingly geared towards the generation of knowledge and technology while partnering with the private sector to improve and commercialize technology. This will encourage more investment by the private sector in research as a step upstream while private farmers benefit downstream. Such efforts could be in the form of contract research, competitive grants, and consultancies. Other internal revenue generation activities can also be enhanced and diversified to include, among other points, contract research, consultancies, charging for services, enhanced commercial agricultural production, hospitality, and agrotourism.

Another challenge is institutional research capacity. As is the case with many research institutions, CRF does not by itself possess adequate technological, infrastructural, and skills capacity to meet all its needs. This gap is aggravated by rapid changes especially in technologies such as analytical instrumentation, computer science, and molecular techniques. The Foundation has invested considerable sums in modern equipment, laboratories, and staff training to address issues such as DNA technology, tissue culture, soils and leaf nutrient analysis, pesticide residues analysis, biochemical analysis, and coffee quality assessment. To complement its capacity, CRF has developed partnerships with other research and training institutions around the world. These connections build on the now widely accepted reality that partnership and sharing of resources improves efficiency and outputs compared with isolated individual work.

CURRENT AND FUTURE RESEARCH AREAS

Agricultural development is increasingly concerned with diversification, improving product quality and safety, capturing markets, mixing on-farm and off-farm incomes, adding value, entering market niches, and balancing agricultural and ecological interests. Dynamics arising from processes such as liberalization of markets and national economies, globalization and regionalization of markets, advances in science and technology, and evolving ideas on the roles of the public and private sectors pose constantly evolving challenges. These issues create the need for more complex research programming, on which CRF is focused and will continue to be responsive to emerging needs.

In particular, CRF is currently addressing the effects of climatic change on the entire coffee value chain, emerging markets fragmentation, the socioeconomic patterns of production, customer concerns such as health and safety, environment protection, involvement of youth, gender balance, and diversification of coffee products. Information technology and access to computers have also helped the CRF in Kenya by disseminating timely information, especially to stakeholders located at a distance from the research station.

Even as global coffee consumption increases, various constraints have reduced production. Past efforts to boost yields have focused on these constraints either through research or policy development. In addition to breeding for the traditional agronomic traits of yields, quality, and tolerance to biotic and abiotic stresses, future coffee breeding programs will address emerging producer and consumer issues including parameters of climatic changes, soil fertility and salinity status, the biochemical composition of coffee, and suitability for alternative coffee processing technologies is also a priority. CRF will endeavor to obtain basic solutions that improve agricultural practices, especially in pest management, uniform flowering due to artificial induction of stress, genetic control, or even application of hormones. Incorporated into these concerns will be sensitivity to water conservation and pollution. **Agroforestry** and **intercropping** are becoming more common, and future production systems need to be compatible with these systems. Some effects of climatic changes have socioeconomic attributes related to coffee production levels or patterns. Coffee research programs in Kenya have initiated studies to address, among other issues, uniformity of cropping, water harvesting and conservation, the influence of climate on coffee physiology, biochemical composition, and sensory attributes. Development of suitable alternative coffee processing technologies is also a priority. CRF will endeavor to obtain basic solutions that improve agricultural practices, especially in pest management, uniform flowering due to artificial induction of stress, genetic control, or even application of hormones.

Socioeconomic analysis will not be limited to monetary factors alone. Evolving consumer preferences, lifestyles, and market fragmentation will be analyzed to provide information about potential markets. In this respect coffee may not only be marketed as a beverage but may expand into other market sectors such as cosmetics, landscaping, and potted ornamentals. The viability of coffee farming will also be aligned to emerging farming enterprises such that complementarity is maximized. Tied to some of these farming systems is **certification** of coffee and its implication in socioeconomics. It is important to note the intricacies that emerging issues such as agroforestry and certification will have as a dimension of the carbon credits market, which is potentially a large source of funds for development. It will also be important for research to address gender, youth, and sociocultural aspects of coffee farming and consumption in support of holistic policy development and practices.

CRF has been a premier institute of coffee research and has achieved the following, among other marks of progress:

- Selection of high yielding, quality Arabica coffee varieties such as K7, SL28, SL 34
- Development and production of disease-resistant arabica coffee **cultivars** Ruiru 11 and Batian
- Development of good agricultural and manufacturing practices (GAP and GMP) along the value chain
- Establishment of a credible and responsive field advisory and training system
- Mainstreaming socioeconomic issues in the research programs
- Networking and collaboration with international organizations

To ensure greater performance and service delivery, CRF will pursue benchmarking and accreditation of its laboratories, which will enhance support to the coffee industry. The Foundation also strives to decentralize farmer-oriented laboratory services such as soil, leaf, and agrochemical formulation analysis and coffee quality assessment. We will incorporate modern information delivery technologies for dissemination. The Foundation will also enhance partnerships with private and public agencies at both the international and national levels.

Coffee in Kenya, like the crop almost anywhere around the world, faces daunting challenges. But the Coffee Research Foundation expects to stay abreast of or ahead of problems in the industry. We will continue our critical efforts to improve cultivation, processing, marketing, and the lives of everyone who works with coffee.

60

Genetically Modified (Transgenic) Coffee

Robert W. Thurston

A number of European governments, among them France and Germany, have expressed opposition to genetically modified (GM) foods, in particular to corn (maize). This resistance to GM is based on grassroots discussions that reveal broad dislike of any GM crops. The American corporation Monsanto has been denied permission to experiment with an altered form of corn in France.[1] At the same time, consumers in the U.S., and the farm animals they raise, eat enormous quantities of GM corn. American law does not require GM foods to be labeled as such, so that in the U.S. few people are aware that their food often began life in laboratory experiments. On the other hand, it is hard to imagine that many Americans would care to know. Different cultures produce, once again, different attitudes toward food.

Those people who fear and dislike genetically modified food and drink products naturally oppose GM or "transgenic" coffee. But farmers desperate to reduce losses from pests and diseases, as well as to lower costs for treatments designed to defeat those problems, are deeply interested in engineered strains of the plant. Moreover, if **arabica** coffee trees can be developed that are more resistant than natural **varieties** to drought, frost, global warming, poor soils, and **wind** damage, the range and productivity of high-quality coffee can expand. Could good coffee be grown in the Mexican desert or the Amazon jungle? These questions, and in fact any and all issues related to GM, are sometimes answered ideologically or on the basis of hopes for a particular crop or region.

Work on genetically modified coffee began only in 1993. More recently, researchers in various countries have announced several intriguing but largely undeveloped results. Here the goal is to present recent research and offer some ideas about where GM coffee is going—because like it or not, it is going somewhere.

The University of Hawaii received a patent in 1999 for procedures involving the coffee genome.[2] The patent describes how biotechnologists have "switched off" the natural ripening processes of coffee cherries. The purpose of this delayed ripening is to bring about uniform ripening with the result that all coffee cherries would develop to become green and hard but no further ripening would occur. Final ripening could then only be triggered after berries were exposed to a sprayed application of ethylene, a naturally occurring plant hormone. Harvesting would then be easier, and yields higher but there is, as yet, no indication that the quality of coffee produced in this way would be retained.[3]

363

As early as 2000, field trials of coffee, altered in the French Agricultural Center for International Development, were underway. The tests occurred in French Guiana, specifically chosen because no coffee is grown there commercially, thus reducing the chances of accidental cross-fertilization with existing, natural varieties. Then in 2004, someone cut down the experimental plants, all but ruining the trials. Nonetheless, French scientists state that they gathered enough data to confirm that, "Seventy percent of our GM trees were totally resistant to the coffee leaf miner."[4]

In 2003, the Hawaii Agriculture Research Center reported on work that transferred "new germplasm and selected genotypes" to arabica plants; the resulting hybrid was much more resistant to attacks on the roots by nematodes than were natural plants.[5] According to a recent report circulating on the web, the state's Integrated Coffee Technology, Inc., located on Oahu, started field trials of transgenic coffee engineered to ripen simultaneously after ethylene spraying.[6] However, the company has gone out of business, and nothing came of their efforts.

Researchers at Japan's Nara Institute of Science and Technology reported in 2003 that they had developed transgenic coffee seeds. These work on an "RNA silencing technique," meaning that the introduced genes take the place that caffeine would occupy in normal molecular structures. The caffeine content in the new trees is reportedly 70 percent lower than in "conventional seeds in the natural plants." Yet at the same time, the research team said that it would take another four or five years before actual results from coffee plants could be measured,[7] presumably in field trials. The research was conducted on arabica beans, but the Nara scientists predicted have as much as twice the caffeine content of arabica beans, but the Nara scientists predicted success for arabica as well.[8]

In any event, the amount of caffeine in "natural plants" varies, so there is no absolute standard against which transgenic coffee could be measured. Perhaps unfortunately, high caffeine levels in "selected" arabica plants from Ethiopia and Kenya demonstrate increased resistance to both **coffee berry borer** disease and **coffee leaf rust**.[9]

The Colombian research center for coffee, CENICAFE, is working on coffee that would contain inhibitors for digestion in the coffee berry borer, or *broca*.[10] If the borer can't eat inside coffee berries, it will certainly decline and perhaps even disappear as a pest. What a colossal break that would be for farmers!

A combined Brazilian/Colombian group of scientists has carried out more work on coffee designed to thwart the berry borer. This time, the researchers took genes from common bean plants and inserted them into arabica coffee DNA. The results are promising; the new bean genes inhibit up to 88 percent of the enzyme activity in the coffee berries that is necessary for broca's survival.[11]

Peter Baker of CABI believes that GM coffee varieties will probably be "high-yielding dwarf varieties requiring high inputs to perform well." Smallholders who cannot afford to replace existing plants, which may in any event require more application of sprays and other treatments than conventional coffee, may be overwhelmed by large corporations who have the capital to make fundamental changes. But that scenario is likelier to occur in robusta production rather than in arabica fields, where the emphasis will continue to be on quality.[12]

Thus GM coffee presents a tangled web of interests and hopes. Will coffee cherry without caffeine grow beautifully on the trees, both robusta and arabica? Could GM reduce dependence on 'synthetic herbicides and pesticides, thus benefiting the earth and greatly reducing farmers' costs? Could it expand the range and productivity of arabica, and might that in turn save the species—or lead to so much production that prices would again crash? Will big farmers reap most of the gains and wipe out the little guys? Today about all that can be said for certain, in a tale that unfolds almost daily, is that GM is likely to become a major factor in the coffee industry.

NOTES

1. http://earthfirstnews.wordpress.com, January 26, 2012, citing Gordon Davis in *The Scottish Farmer*, accessed April 16, 2012.

2. Ezzeddine Boutrif, chairperson (Food Quality and Standards Service, United Nations Food and Agricultural Organization), Seminar on Genetically Modified Coffee, International Coffee Organization, 2005, http://dev.ico.org/event_pdfs/gm/presentations/Ezzedine%20Boutrif.pdf.

3. "GM coffee: Brewing up a storm?" *New Agriculturalist on line*, http://www.new-ag.info/01-4/focuson4.html, accessed April 16, 2012. No author or date is given, but Peter Baker (see his "Coffee as a Global System" above) of CABI is listed as the person to contact for further information.

4. Andy Coghlan, *New Scientist* 186, no. 2501 (May 28, 2005): 44.

5. Powerpoint show by Chifumi Nagai, "Coffee Breeding Update with New Tools," HCA Conference 2003, at http://www.hawaiicoffeeassoc.org/03pdf/HCA03-CNfinal.pdf.

6. Erica Strauss, "Genetically modified coffee confrontation brewing in Hawaii," June 2009, http://www.pccnaturalmarkets.com/sc/0906/sc0906-coffee-gm-hawaii.html, accessed April 16, 2012.

7. *Asia Pacific Biotech News*, July 7, 2003.

8. Shinjiro Ogita, Hirotaka Uefuji, Yube Yamaguchi, Nozomu Koizumi, and Hiroshi Sano, *Nature* 423, no. 6942 (June 19, 2003): 823.

9. Vinod Kumar and G. A. Ravishankar, "Current trends in producing low levels of caffeine in coffee berry and processed coffee powder," *Food Reviews International* 25 (2009): 175–97, 176.

10. Diana Molina, Humberto Zamora, and Alejandro Blanco-Labra, *Phytochemistry* 71, no. 8/9 (June 2010): 923–29.

11. Aulus Barbosa, Érika V. S. Albuquerque, Maria C. M. Silva, Djair S. L. Souza, Osmundo B. Oliveira-Neto, Arnubio Valencia, Thales L. Rocha, and Maria F. Grossi-de-Sa, "α-Amylase inhibitor-1 gene from *Phaseolus vulgaris* expressed in *Coffea arabica* plants inhibits α-amylases from the coffee berry borer pest," *BMC Biotechnology* 10 no. 44 (2010), http://www.biomedcentral.com/1472-6750/10/44.

12. "GM coffee: Brewing up a storm?"

61

Mechanization

Robert W. Thurston

In the coffee industry, mechanization generally refers to the use of machinery in harvesting, as opposed to picking coffee cherry by hand. Machines for **processing** coffee fruit, for example pulpers (which would be better called depulpers, as they are in Spanish) have been used for many decades around the world. At first pulpers were hand-operated; today even relatively small farms can often afford one that runs on gasoline, natural gas, or electricity.

Harvesting mechanically is another story. Essentially, two types of machines can harvest coffee. One is a tool resembling a grass trimmer in size, weight, and configuration, except that the working end is a scissors-like assembly. These machines usually run on gasoline. An operator first spreads a cloth around the bottom of a coffee tree, then positions the machine where a branch emerges from the tree trunk. Pushing a button makes the blades, which are deliberately dull, close around the branch. The operator pulls the whole device toward himself, stripping all the coffee fruit from the branch, along with lots of leaves and twigs. All this falls onto the cloth. Once a tree, or several at a time, have been stripped of fruit—giving this technique the name of strip harvesting—the cloth is pulled away and its contents dumped into a large container. Strip harvesting can also be done by hand; pickers just wrap their hands, hopefully in strong gloves, around a branch and pull all the fruit off. But the mechanical stripper does that faster and with less physical effort.

If pickers are working by hand or with a small blade stripper, and any breeze is blowing, they may flip the contents of the cloth into the air, so that the wind carries leaves away. Pickers may also have small, round, handheld screens, again used to flip the harvested matter into the air. People also pull out the more obvious twigs. Pickers are usually paid by the weight of what they bring in, but there are penalties for too much debris with the **cherry**.

At this point the coffee fruit and anything else on the cloths is collected and conveyed, by machine, human beings, or burros, to a central point. There it is dumped by hand or machine onto a screen that captures most extraneous material but allows the fruit to fall through. In **wet processing**, the leaves and twigs must be removed before depulping; in **dry processing** this should occur before the cherry is spread on a patio to dry. Sometimes stones and an occasional bullet make it all the way through processing at origin, and from there in bags of coffee to roasters in consuming countries—hence the need for mechanical destoners in roasteries.

Back on the farm, the second, much larger and more expensive kind of mechanical harvester is a self-propelled machine that straddles coffee trees as it rolls forward. Tall but still hulking, these harvesters are built in an upside-down U shape and have nylon or fiberglass wands that vibrate in the central cavity. The driver has to climb a ladder to reach the cab at the top of the machine; from there she controls the speed of the vehicle and the operation of the wands. As the machine crawls over the tops of coffee trees, it covers them completely, while the wands knock the fruit off. All the cherries, along with lots of leaves and twigs, are collected in a pan at the bottom of the harvester. From there they are either sent on a conveyer to a bin at the back of the machine, in a self-contained unit, or the beans are pushed up and through a pipe over to a separate truck or trailer pulled by a tractor. The tractor driver stays on the side of the trees being harvested, between that row and the next one over. Whatever the catcher vehicle, it has to keep pace with the harvester. All mechanical pickers move at a leisurely pace, only a few miles an hour.

This way of harvesting gathers much more waste, in the form of unripe and overripe cherries, leaves, and branches, than the handheld machines do. Of course, the capital needed to acquire a self-propelled harvester and a truck is considerable; a large harvester can easily cost $100,000. Finally, such machines can only operate on ground that is at most gently rolling. **Shade** trees would get in the way of the big harvesters, so they are used on **technified** or **sun-grown** coffee. On the muddy, 45° slopes of Nicaragua or Kenya, where human pickers must sometimes tie themselves to trees to keep from rolling down the hill, such machines don't work.

Nor are the big harvesters an option for small family farms. Like any large piece of agricultural machinery in use from Manitoba to Queensland and the Brazilian Cerrado, the rolling harvesters are most effective on contiguous, open land. Any time they spend moving from one field to another is wasted. So while in theory co-ops could buy wand machines, getting them from one farm to another would seriously reduce their utility. Small farmers will therefore largely continue to depend on their own and their families' labor.

When the mechanical harvesters, either handheld or self-propelled, produce waste in picking, extensive sorting systems separate usable fruit from unripe berries and debris. After the nonfruit debris is excluded, the beans are separated by their different stages of ripeness. Using water channels to move and divide the cherries, dense ones (underripe and ripe) fall, while lighter cherries (overripes) float and are channeled away. The underripes and ripes are then sent to a pulper where the ripes are depulped and the underripes pass through unchanged. Then, using a rotating slotted cylinder, the seeds from the ripe cherries fall through the slots while the underripes and pulp are moved away. The overripes (sometimes called **raisins**) are essentially **naturals** that are dried on a deck or, occasionally, in a mechanical dryer. In our heavily capitalized scenario, pulped seeds are either sent to fermentation tanks to remove the **mucilage** or to a demucilager to mechanically remove the mucilage before **drying**. The underripes are sent to be dried right away.

After the coffee has dried and the outer layers (pulp/fruit, mucilage, and **parchment**) have been removed, the green beans may go through a number of sorting stages, depending on how automated the operation is. First, they may be separated by bean size. The coffee will be placed on motorized shaking beds with screens set at a slight angle, perhaps 30°. As many as eight screens, with holes of different sizes that get smaller towards the bottom, can be set up, including screens to separate out **peaberries**. These machines accomplish two tasks: First, they allow beans of certain sizes to fall through the holes. The smallest fall to the bottom of the apparatus, while bigger beans fall to the screen whose holes are too small for them to pass through. Wherever they land, each screen establishes a more or less uniform sized lot of beans that will be shaken and moved by gravity to one side and thence into separate containers. At the same time, any remaining extraneous material such as leaves and branches will be borne to the side of the top screen and removed.

After sorting by size, the beans may be taken to a density (also called gravity) table. These devices are slightly inclined in both the direction of flow, down and forward, and perpendicular to flow. The surface vibrates and has perforations that permit air to be forced upwards through the surface. When uniformly sized green beans pass over the table, the vibration and tilt cause them to separate according to small changes, as little as 1 percent, in density. The tables remove many **defects** that come either from the field, for instance, from insects, or from machinery during pulping.

Finally, in some well-financed operations, the coffee is separated by color. This occurs in plastic tubes perhaps one foot (about 300 centimeters) in diameter and several stories high, mated with color sensors. Beans are conveyed to the top of the tubes and then allowed to fall through them. The sensors recognize off-color beans and shoot out puffs of air to expel them from the main channel. Since roasting coffee properly depends to a fair extent on the evenness of bean size, these **sorting** techniques affect quality in the cup.

Another way that machines have replaced workers in coffee processing also involves drying. Large Brazilian farms, for example, have huge drying patios, where the coffee is constantly spread out and respread for several days; this can be done by one person driving a small vehicle with a rake attached to the back. I have seen two types of these machines: one was clearly built for this purpose, while the other was a converted motorcycle that pulled a rake behind it. On the other hand, I have seen perhaps fifty people at a time raking drying fruit on patios in Nicaragua.

Mechanical dryers for pulped cherry or for naturals are also fairly common today on bigger farms. Partially dried fruit is fed into the dryers, which sometimes look like big clothes dryers, sometimes like large metal chutes, that can be as much as 90 feet (27.4 meters) tall. One way or another, for example by blowing warm air into chutes, the dryers move the beans about and slowly heat them, just enough to dry them out. This process is much quicker than patio drying, and the machines don't care whether the sun is out or not.

Productivity per worker soars with mechanical sorting and harvesting. Patrick Installe, managing director of the coffee trading company Efico, told interviewers from Oxfam in 2002:

> To give you an idea of the difference, in some areas of Guatemala, it could take over 1,000 people working [picking] one day each to fill the equivalent of one container of 275 bags, each bag weighing 69 kilograms. In the Brazilian cerrado, you need five people and a mechanical harvester for two or three days to fill a container. One drives, and the others pick. How can Central American family farms compete against that?[1]

Actually, my own observations in Brazil's Sao Paulo state indicate that mechanical harvesting equipment can require only two workers, one to drive the harvester and one to drive the truck. With the completely self-contained harvesters that convey coffee into a container at the back of the machine, one person does all the work.

Capitalized production, with a correspondingly low number of employees, is vividly demonstrated at Kauai Coffee Company. Their orchard occupies 3,400 acres (about 1376 **hectares**) of land on the island of Kauai in Hawaii. The firm brags in a 1999 film that, on its fully mechanized estate, it employs 57 workers in harvest season, while a farm of equal size elsewhere but not mechanized might need 3,000 pickers. Kauai Coffee harvests twenty-four

Figure 61.1. A mechanical harvester at work; the cherries are shot into the bed of a truck to the right. Brazil, 2010. Photo by Robert Thurston.

hours a day, seven days a week in peak season, bringing in between one-half and three-quarters of a million pounds of cherry every day. Bob Rose, mechanical equipment and harvesting manager at the time the film was made, put the company's goal for harvesting in these terms: "maximize the amount of ripe coffee collected with a minimum amount of employees."[2]

At Kauai Coffee, every part of managing the orchard, harvesting, and processing is mechanized. Machines with large spinning blades march through the fields to prune the sides and tops of the trees. The whole estate is supplied with drip tubing for irrigation—2,000 miles (3,320 kilometers) of it in 1999. Coffee cherry is moved from mechanical harvesters to dump trucks by wheel loaders. All sorting is done by machines, and the beans are dried in the kind of columns mentioned above. The color sorters, the slowest pieces of equipment on the farm, can handle about 300 pounds of coffee per hour. The sorters look at every single bean from two sides and blow out discolored ones.[3]

Since 1999, the changes in the company's production appear to have been in quantity, not in the basics of the operation. Now there are 2,500 miles of irrigation tubing. Herbicide use has been cut by 75 percent "through our cultivation practices" (presumably this means in the past few years). The average daily amount of coffee cherry processed is now given as 650,000 pounds. Each year the company produces over half of all coffee grown in the United States.[4]

To return to Patrick Installe's question about how small farmers can compete with large, mechanized operations like Kauai Coffee, the answer has to be quality. Mechanical harvesters and pruners do not discriminate between useless fruit and cherry at the peak of ripeness. Handpicking and **pruning** are still considered by many to be the best ways of ensuring that only quality beans reach the market, although some mechanically harvested farms are earning high marks from specialty coffee drinkers. Yet hand-harvesting, too, has another cost: pickers must usually make three or more passes through the trees to catch berries that, naturally, fail to ripen simultaneously.

Arnoldo Leiva, then president of the Costa Rican Specialty Coffee Association, said in 2008 that small machines, more or less the size of a roto tiller, are under development in his country. The need for a portable, reliable, inexpensive machine that can traverse the slopes of many coffee-producing lands, without doing too much damage to the trees, is growing. For some years, Costa Rican farmers have relied on migrant labor from Nicaragua to harvest their crops, but the laws regulating immigration into Costa Rica for any purpose are becoming tighter. Hawaiian farmers have imported Mexican workers. But, as levels of education and urbanization rise in poorer countries like Nicaragua,[6] the supply of people willing to work extremely hard for a few months of each year, then somehow get by the rest of the time, will decline.

Meanwhile, the overall quality of Brazilian coffee, for example, continues to improve. Yet, given the growing global demand for the finest arabicas, there will surely be a niche for the best handpicked and hand-sorted coffees for a long time to come. But for anything of lower quality that comes from a nonmechanized farm, the future may not be bright.

NOTES

1. Quoted in Charis Gresser and Sophia Tickell, *Mugged: Poverty in Your Coffee Cup* (Oxford: Oxfam, 2002), 18.

2. Kauai Coffee Company, *Kauai Coffee: From Tree to Cup* (video), 1999.

3. Kauai Coffee Company, *Kauai Coffee*.

4. http://www.kauaicoffee.com, accessed March 31, 2012.

5. Interview with Arnoldo Leiva, San Jose, Costa Rica, May 27, 2008.

6. At the moment, Nicaragua is not making great progress in education, despite the Sandinista government's commitment to it. Teachers' salaries are abysmally low, and only 45 percent of elementary school pupils go on to secondary school. Their dropout rates are high, even for the developing world. See *The Christian Science Monitor*, March 26, 2012. Yet at some point the general improvement in Latin American economies over the past ten to fifteen years will also reach Nicaragua, making the supply of people desperate to find any kind of work shrink.

62

A Life in Coffee

Ted Lingle

Editor's Note (SS): Ted Lingle is one of the most respected and admired elders of the specialty coffee industry. He was actively supporting specialty coffee before the term even existed. A founding member of the Specialty Coffee Association of America, he has been active in the organization since its inception. Perhaps he is best known for writing the Coffee Cuppers' Handbook, a guidebook for cupping that has probably influenced more cuppers than anything else. His likely final contribution to specialty coffee, quality standards for robusta coffees, will be another large part of his legacy. The following chapter is a brief autobiography by Mr. Lingle, featuring his relationship to the specialty coffee industry.

I was very fortunate in beginning my coffee career in the 1970s, as it was a period of transition for the coffee roasting industry in the United States. Many small and medium **roasters** were either selling out or closing their doors, as the multinational and big regional roasters were intensifying the price competition in the industry and consolidating the market. Lingle Bros. Coffee, Inc., a small Southern California roasting business started by my grandfather and his two brothers in 1920, was among this group of struggling roasting operations. On my third day of work after joining my father at Lingle Bros., I will never forget visiting with a longtime customer who had announced he was switching to another roaster the week before. During the "lost customer interview," he told me that "the owner wanted to switch to using raw butter, and I needed to save money somewhere in order to keep my food costs down. So I switched in order to save 3 cents a pound." At that moment in time, I knew the coffee industry needed a major transformation if it was going to survive and prosper. If coffee values were only determined by price, not quality, the consumer would lose in the process and migrate to other beverages.

During the early 1970s a small group of roasters joined together to form a national sales and purchasing group. Known as DINE-MOR FOODS, it was comprised of a number of firms and individuals just like me. They were from second and third generations of sons now in closely held family roasting businesses that served small regional markets. The driving force in pulling this group together was Bill Smith of Royal Cup Coffee in Birmingham. It was a great experience for me because of the integrity and openness of the individuals in the group. Besides being great coffee men, they ran very successful operations. These coffee friends opened their plants, their coffee-buying strategies, and even their financial statements, and through them I was able to see and understand the changes I needed to bring to Lingle Bros. to make it a stronger company. Lingle Bros. was a DINE-MOR member for over decade and I was able to meet and get to know a large number of terrific coffee people all over the United States.

Selling coffee to restaurants in the Southern California area had some daunting challenges, low prices being but one of them. But it also had its rewards; one was getting to know Marvin Saul, the owner of Junior's Deli in Los Angeles. Marvin was not only a great "foodie," but also a tremendous and unafraid marketer. If he liked something personally, he would introduce it in Junior's, immediately. My favorite memory is Marv calling me up, saying his doctor had put him on decaffeinated coffee and wanting to know if Lingle Bros. had any decaf.

I was out to see him the next day with a decaffeinated Colombian coffee we carried for our specialty coffee and office coffee service customers. He instantly liked it, and the next day he was serving it in his restaurant. By the end of the week he had sold out and not only wanted more coffee but also the supporting items: orange-handled coffeepots and colored coasters to help the waitresses distinguish the decaf drinkers from the regular drinkers. We eventually caught up with Marv's needs to make fresh brew decaf a regular item at Junior's. Within six months, fresh brew decaf was a regular item with all of our food service customers, and through a DINE-MOR connected customer, Far West Services, it was on everyone's menu nationwide. Goodbye Sanka, the leading instant decaf coffee of the era.

In addition to selling to restaurants, Lingle Bros. also created products for and sold to the office coffee service (OCS) industry. One of our customers, Don Stoulil, was the brother of an employee, George Stoulil. And like many of the great customer relationships I've had through my twenty-year career at Lingle Bros., Don and I became close personal friends. He is and remains a true testament to the American dream of building a business from scratch and, through hard work, turning it into a major success. And there are many success stories like this in the OCS industry. In fact, the OCS industry was actually the springboard that launched my coffee career, so that it became my avocation and my vocation.

The turning point came during a sales call on one of my other favorite OCS customers, Don Donegan of Major Domo Coffee Services in Los Angeles. Don was on the board of the National Office Coffee Service Association (NCSA) and asked me if I thought the NCSA members needed to spend $1,200 a session for a training program currently being offered by Michael Sivetz, one of the great coffee technicians in the industry. My answer to Don was that for what the OCS industry needed to know, I didn't think their money would be well spent hiring Mike. So with his great Irish charm, Don asked me what I thought NCSA should do. I told Don I would think about that and get back to him. A few days later, I was back in his office with a proposal for a day-long class called the "Coffee Blending Game." Don loved the idea and within sixty days I was giving the class for the first time in Los Angeles. The next month I gave the second class in San Francisco, and by the end of the year I had given the class four more times across the country. It was a great success, and it remains one of my favorite classes to teach nonroasters because it is highly interactive.

The following year, I was asked to join the board of NCSA, and I was now standing on the springboard. NCSA, at the time (1978), was the most vibrant and active trade association in the United States. It enjoyed the leadership of three dynamic individuals: Don Donegan, Tom Williams, and John Conti. It was the NCSA board who decided they wanted to begin a coffee promotion campaign to help build market share for the OCS industry. With coaching from me, they sent a proposal to the **International Coffee Organization** similar to one crafted by Alf Kramer for Norway, which the ICO had approved the year earlier. It was a modest proposal, a $100,000 program based on matching funds from the ICO and NCSA. It got the ICO's attention, and their executive director, Alexander Beltrao, sent his friend and confidant in the United States, Sam Stavisky, to a meeting with the board of the NCSA. We earned his trust, and the promotion program went forward.

As the relationship with the ICO continued to develop, NCSA created two more promotion programs. At this point, Beltrao organized a joint meeting with key members of his ICO staff and the NCSA Board. The ICO wanted more promotional activity in the United States and NCSA wanted a bigger program. Accompanying Beltrao from the ICO were Barry Davies, the promotion fund officer, and his assistant Marsha Powell. Two big projects were started as the result of this meeting; number one was the launch of the Coffee Development Group (CDG), initially the Office Coffee Development Group (OCDG), and number two was the beginning of the effort to form an association within the specialty coffee industry.

The Coffee Development Group (CDG) concept came from Arman Duplaise, an OCS operator in the Baltimore area. It was based on his experience with Burger King in which field representatives carried out a series of consumer-focused marketing campaigns on a national level. In the CDG concept, field reps would work in the areas of office coffee service, vending, specialty coffee, and food service. The annual budget for this program exceeded $2,000,000 per year over a ten-year period and resulted in a quantum leap in changing the perception of coffee in the minds of U.S. consumers. I still like to remind my friends at the ICO that this was the best use of the Promotion Fund they ever made.

By default, I became one of the principal coffee trainers of the CDG staff. By design, the CDG staff were selected based on their "youth and inexperience" in the coffee field. We wanted to tap into the generation that appeared to be "leaving coffee" at the time. Two of the great hires at the time were Stuart Adelson and Susie Newman (now Susie Newman Spindler). In the year following their start with CDG, I spent a great deal of time working with these two people, who struggled through an uneven start at CDG headquarters in its quest to find the right executive director. For reasons still unclear to me, they embraced coffee with a dedication and passion that I had never seen before. Susie was an intuitive marketer, and her guidance in all of CDG's programs brought depth and finesse to the consumer outreach. Stuart, who had a food service background through his experience at Universal Studios, brought real-world strategies into the theoretical discussions of coffee promotions.

Together they helped design and execute three of CDG's most successful campaigns. First was a program for the vending industry that helped change the consumer perception that vending machines brewed bad-tasting coffee. Second was the college campus program that put over 200 "coffee cafés" on major college campuses across the country. These cafés trained a generation of young consumers for more than a decade in the 1980s on the wonders of **espresso-based drinks;** in turn, that created a ready and waiting market for Starbucks to fill when the company emerged nationally in the 1990s. And third, and in my opinion CDG's finest accomplishment, was the discovery, creation, and launch of iced cappuccino through a promotion carried out during the 1984 Summer Olympic Games in Los Angeles. It was a "shot heard 'round the world," as some form of iced cappuccino is now included on the menu board of every coffee café in the world. Both Susie and Stuart remain part of the coffee industry, with Susie going on to form the Alliance for Coffee Excellence (ACE) and Stuart becoming the corporate counsel for SCAA.

The second major development to come out of the ICO-NCSA collaboration at the end of the 1970s was the formation of the **Specialty Coffee Association of America.** It started with a question from Barry Davies of the ICO Promotion Fund Office. He asked me if there was any organized group representing the fledgling specialty coffee stores in the United States. I responded that there was no specialty coffee association at this time. He said that was too bad, as the ICO Promotion Fund could not give money to individuals or individual companies. I told him I would check with my friends in the specialty industry to see if there was sufficient interest to form one. Based on Barry's encouragement, I drafted a rough outline and charter for the Specialty Coffee Advisory Board, an association created to do coffee promotions, and sent it out to the people I knew were operating specialty coffee bean stores. Included on this list was Marvin Golden in Boston, who was active in both the office coffee service and specialty coffee segments of the industry. Marvin in turn sent it out to his friends on the East Coast, including Donald Schoenholt of Gilles Coffee in New York, whom I had never met.

About a month after the draft of the specialty coffee association charter went out, I got a call from Schoenholt, who spent the first thirty minutes of the call explaining to me why this was a bad idea and would not work and then spent the next fifteen minutes telling me what to do to get it started. The result was a series of meetings over a two-year period, mostly in conjunction with the Fancy Food Show, in which a group of people volunteered to serve on a steering committee to rewrite the charter for the Specialty Coffee Association of America (SCAA). Ten of us met at the Hotel Louise in San Francisco and hammered out a charter in 1982. We sent out the final version of the charter to everyone in the specialty coffee sector we knew and asked them to send me a check for $100 in dues if they wished to become charter members. At the end of 1983, we had thirty-three charter members and $3,300 in a bank account opened with my social security number, as we had yet to form a corporation.

For the next five years, SCAA grew slowly; that it grew at all was mainly due to the efforts of Dan Cox of Vermont's Green Mountain Coffee Roasters, who virtually ran the association from his desk drawer. SCAA had two sources of revenue in the beginning, membership dues and sales from the *Coffee Cuppers' Handbook*, which I wrote and gave to SCAA in 1984. By 1987, SCAA had about 225 members, too large a group for Dan to handle by himself, so SCAA's board made the decision to hire a management firm to take over. SCAA, with the help and underwriting of CDG, began organizing a conference in 1989, with the first one held in New Orleans in 1989. We had about 100 attendees and 25 tabletop exhibits. It was a close-knit and intimate meeting, but it was the precursor of bigger things to follow.

As CDG was winding down in 1990, so was my career at Lingle Bros. It was obvious to both my brother Jim and me that when my dad retired from the company, he and I would not be compatible business partners to co-manage a small family business. So I left the family business and after a brief sabbatical, I began to look around for a new job. At the same time, SCAA's board began looking for a full-time person to take over operational control from the management firm. I went for my "job interview" at SCAA's third annual conference in Orlando in April 1991. Essentially the board said if you can find an appropriate place from which to run the association, we will give it a shot. In June of 1991, we moved SCAA's headquarters to the Greater Los Angeles World Trade Center in Long Beach, opening a new chapter in SCAA's development.

The next fifteen years is best described as a "rocket ride," with SCAA experiencing record growth in both membership and conference attendance. When we finally leveled out in 2003, we had over 3,000 members and our conference attendance in Seattle exceeded 10,000 people. I attribute SCAA's success to four factors. First, we were part of a new and growing market segment, specialty coffee cafés. Second, we were doing the right things in focusing our efforts on standards, education, and ethics. Third, we were blessed with outstanding board members.

Figure 62.1. The SCAA "Event" and Trade Show are held every year in April. This is the 2012 edition. The specialty industry of America and of many other countries gathers to trade information, hear lectures, attend workshops and training sessions, look at new equipment, and just talk and make contacts. One of the nicest things about the show is that race and ethnicity seem to disappear; the subject is coffee. Photo by Robert Thurston.

And fourth, we had a superb meeting planner, Jeanne Sleeper, who did an unbelievable job in making the conference a huge success in each and every year she was the show manager.

During this period of unprecedented growth, under the leadership of Phil Jones of Barnie's Coffee in Florida, SCAA created the International Relations Committee, giving the specialty coffee movement an international character while assisting in the formation of a number of specialty coffee associations worldwide, including Europe and Japan. Under the goading, prodding, and guidance from Paul Katzeff, SCAA stepped into a leadership role in the area of **sustainable** coffee agriculture. At the urging of Mohamed Moledina, SCAA opened the Specialty Coffee Institute, which later became the **Coffee Quality Institute**. With the assistance of Ellen Jordan Reidy and Karalynn McDermott, SCAA developed an incredibly rich and diverse educational curriculum. Under the guidance and direction of Don Holly, SCAA's administrative director, who later joined Green Mountain Coffee, SCAA launched the **World Barista Championship** in partnership with the **Specialty Coffee Association of Europe**. With assistance from Linda Smithers of Susan's Coffee in Ohio, Becky McKinnon of Timothy's Coffee in Toronto, JoAnne Show of the Coffee Beanery in Michigan, and Mary Petitt of the Colombian Coffee Federation in New York, SCAA formulated strategic plans that guided SCAA through its dynamic period of growth.

By 2004, I was burning out as SCAA's executive director and began working with the board to find my replacement. The search was complicated by the discovery that SCAA's new administrative director had embezzled funds from SCAA; the transition became even more difficult when SCAA's board hired someone to replace me who did not work out. But by 2007, I had matriculated to become the executive director of the Coffee Quality Institute. CQI gave me the opportunity to initiate coffee **cupping** training programs on an international level, culminating in a program to set standards for robusta coffees in order to reframe the industry and consumer views on what this species of coffee could and should be. CQI's board is now in the process of finding my replacement, which hopefully will happen in 2012. Then I can keep a promise to myself, and more important to my wife, Gale, that it is time for me to leave the "fast lane" of coffee.

As I wind down my career, I cannot thank my wife enough for keeping the home fires burning while I was out championing my coffee causes. And I also need to thank my brother Jim for tending the store at Lingle Bros. that helped fund, indirectly, many of my coffee campaigns.

My advice to anyone interested in making that great journey in changing coffee from an avocation to a vocation is simply, "Take only memories; keep only friends; and give back all you can—it's a mistake not to."

63

How to Make a Great Cup of Coffee

Robert W. Thurston with Shawn Steiman and Jonathan Morris

There are more ways to make a cup of coffee than you can shake a stick at. Here we will briefly discuss only two ways of preparing brewed coffee and will offer a few comments on espresso.

Although a wide range of electric coffeemakers has long been available, and the **Specialty Coffee Association of America** has begun to recommend some of them, we will stick with the simplest, manual methods of making brewed coffee. **Espresso** is a world unto itself, one which has evolved extremely rapidly in the past few years. To make good espresso, a machine is necessary; below we will mention several of the features to look for in a home **espresso machine**.

To make any kind of potable coffee, some basic factors must be in place, namely good beans, proper water, and a mechanism for extracting solids from the beans. Coffee in your cup is mostly water; only about 1.25 to 1.45 percent of any cup is composed of solids extracted from ground coffee as water passes through it.

Start with good **beans**: it's impossible to make a good cup of coffee from poor quality beans. Ideally, the beans will be **specialty coffee**, roasted no more than a week before using. Grind the beans just before making each cup or pot. Using coffee that is already ground, whether from a bag or from a can, will simply not produce tasty results. Store beans in a container that is as light- and airtight as possible. Keeping unused beans in the original bag, folded down to the level of the beans and crimped or held in a rubber band, then placed in a dark cupboard, is a handy way of storing them. Most coffee industry people we know don't recommend keeping beans in the freezer or refrigerator, since they may pick up moisture every time they are taken out of there. But there are some pros who do store beans this way and say the results are fine.

Get a good **grinder**, which means a burr grinder. In these machines, the coffee beans fall between two metal burrs, which are disks with low ridges or with grooves cut into them. The beans are literally ground, not chopped. Many people have small electric machines that are called grinders, but which actually rely on a blade that spins around in a top chamber and cuts or chops the beans into small pieces. The major problem with these devices is that they produce an uneven grind, which makes the coffee brew uneven and unpredictable. Choppers may have to run so long to get the desired fineness that they will heat the coffee. While there seems to be no evidence that extra heat at this point affects the taste in the cup, we say why take a chance? If roasting the coffee has been done properly, all the heating of the beans necessary has already occurred.

Use good water: not "hard" water that contains much iron, calcium, or magnesium but "soft water," which does not have more than tiny traces of these elements and is free of chlorine. In some areas of the Western world, water straight from the tap is okay for making coffee and tea. But generally, even clean drinking water should be filtered—and the filters changed regularly—to remove undesirable chemicals. Water passed through a reverse osmosis system is preferable. On the other hand, don't use distilled water for brewed coffee. Different explanations have been offered as to why some "hard" content in the water is necessary for proper extraction of flavor from the beans. At any rate, the simple fact remains that distilled water won't do the trick.

The SCAA recommends the use of 55 grams of coffee per liter of water, or 1.925 ounces by weight of the coffee per 34 liquid ounces of water. As a very rough rule of thumb, use about 10.6 grams—slightly over a third of an ounce—of coffee, or about 2 tablespoons, per 6 ounces of water. That is a ratio by weight of about 18:1 water to coffee (though this ratio is somewhat a question of personal taste). In the specialty industry, ratios of as low as 15:1 have become common. A kitchen scale, handy for many other purposes as well, makes it easy to measure the coffee and the water. One serving would therefore be about 15 grams of coffee, 225 of water. Another, easier but less precise way to reach a reasonably effective ratio is to use two tablespoons of coffee per six ounces of water.

An all-glass water boiler or a stainless steel kettle, preferably with a long, goose-necked spout that allows pouring the water with precision, is a great addition to the process. Kettles that automatically maintain a desired temperature are now available. The water should be between 195 and 205°F, or 92–96°C; that means just off the boil.

BREWED COFFEE MADE IN A CAFETIÈRE/FRENCH (PISTON, PLUNGER) PRESS

Many coffee lovers prefer the **French press**, invented in France and often called by its proper French name, cafetière. There are no paper filters involved, the press can be washed easily, and the coffee retains all of its flavor. For these devices, the coffee should be ground fairly coarsely; follow the instructions on your grinder for the proper setting. The ground coffee should feel a bit on the chunky side. Experimentation is the way to discover the right grind at home.

Ground coffee is dumped into the cylinder of the press and hot water is poured in. Insert the plunger/piston at the top of the cylinder. Wait four or five minutes, push down the piston to trap the grounds, pour and enjoy. What could be simpler?

BREWED COFFEE USING A FILTER

The other simple brewing method we'll discuss is commonly known as the **pour-over** or manual method. All that is required is a cone-shaped funnel for holding the coffee and the **filter.**

Most upscale coffee bars use paper filters. Yes, they are made from trees, but they can be composted with used grounds inside. The grounds, incidentally, make an excellent soil amendment for many plants. Which paper filters to use, brown or white? Try a taste test with each; keep in mind that today's white filters are not bleached using nasty chemicals but with oxygen. Many experts prefer white, as it definitely does not affect the taste of the coffee. Some industry figures and good home brewers like metal filters; be sure to wash these carefully after each use, so that they don't retain flavors from the last batch of coffee made or from all that has gone before. Many coffee professionals are fond of paper-filtered **liquor** because it produces a "clean cup" and has no fine coffee particles, the results most likely to be free of **flavors** or influences other than those revealed from the beans themselves. After all, the goal should be to experience the natural qualities of the coffee.

If you like paper filters, keeping in mind the happy thought about their beneficial effect on cholesterol mentioned above by Dr. Jones, place one that is the proper size into the kind of cone funnel you are using and put the cone onto a cup or carafe. Bring the water to a boil, with a little extra for the next step, depending on the size of the filter. Now wet the filter—without any coffee in it yet—and allow the hot water to flow into the cup or carafe. Dump the water out. The point is twofold: to rinse the filter and remove any taste it might have, and to heat the filter and the cup. Grind the beans just before using them; the grind setting will depend largely on the brew method but also on the amount of coffee you are making. Since the point of making filtered, or any kind of coffee, is to get the proper extraction from the grounds, the time that it takes the water to pass through the grounds is important. Given equal amounts of water and coffee, the more finely ground the beans are, the longer it will take the water to go through. The greater the quantity of coffee used, the longer the water will take. Therefore a small amount of coffee should be ground more finely than a large amount. Coffee can be overextracted if the grind is too fine or the quantity of coffee too much for the amount of water used, resulting in a bitter brew that smothers delicate flavors. Coffee can also be underextracted if the grind is too coarse or too much water is used for the amount of ground coffee, producing a weak, thin liquor. Here, too, experiments are in order.

Whatever the quantity and grind used, put the ground coffee into the wet filter; give it a shake to settle the coffee and to make sure it is more or less level. Now pour on just enough water to wet all the grounds. Note that some baristas find that this process of infusing the grounds slightly dampens the highlights of some coffees; everyone is experimenting, it seems. If you do wet the grounds, wait twenty or so seconds to allow various gases to escape, then pour on the rest of the water, not too fast. For best results, stir the coffee once, gently, as it goes down through the grounds. Don't put the carafe on a burner at this point or later. If you want to keep the coffee hot for a while, make it directly into a thermal vessel. However you catch the brewed coffee, it should be cool enough to drink right away. Starting with water at 195°F and following the directions just given, the cup temperature should be about 175°F.

Most electric coffeemakers work on the principles just described. However, with a few exceptions, these machines don't reach or at least don't maintain the proper temperature for brewing. And their water lines and other parts can be next to impossible to keep really clean.

Old sayings along the line of "coffee should be hot as hell, black as night, and sweet as love" might be amusing on a tee-shirt or potholder, but they don't point the way to optimal flavor. In really hot coffee, as in very close to the boiling point, the heat will override many subtle characteristics. Black is fine, and the natural sweetness in excellent beans is great. Our house rules for anyone drinking a cup we've prepared is to take a sip of unadulterated coffee first. Then our guests can put anything they like into it, from sugar to fake cream to rum and whiskey. But we hope everyone will come to enjoy coffee, just coffee, because of its own complexity and flavor.

Another experiment to try: make a cup of coffee and drink it slowly, even over the course of several hours. See what different flavors emerge as the coffee cools to room temperature.

ESPRESSO

In the past few years, espresso has become more and more complex. New **blends** and **single-origin** beans that are great for espresso appear almost daily. The industry has moved away from using only dark roast beans, which tended to produce a standard flavor, to beans roasted across a spectrum from fairly light to moderately dark.

The central factors involved in making good espresso are pressure and time of extraction. Pressure is provided by the machine or stovetop device. Extraction time depends above all on grind; that is, extraction is controlled largely by the fineness of the grind. Therefore you must have a grinder capable of producing grains of coffee that are like very fine sand and that are even in size. Extraction also depends on the amount of coffee put into the basket of the machine's coffee holder, the **portafilter**, and on the operation of the machine. Any good barista or home coffee brewer must practice to get the right grind and quantity of coffee for a particular machine. In fact, good coffee bars will "dial in" the espresso several times a day by adjusting the grind, amount of coffee in the portafilter, and, if possible with the machine in use, extraction time.

Again, as with brewed coffee, the goal is to achieve a certain percentage of solids in the liquor. But of course the extraction system is different in the two methods: brewed coffee

Figure 63.1. A few pieces of basic equipment for making brewed coffee at home. A glass water kettle is good for large servings, but the stainless steel goose-neck kettle provides more accuracy in the pour. The scale is almost essential; it allows the preparer to be consistent in making coffee. Stiff brushes are useful for keeping a grinder and other equipment clean. Filter cones obviously come in different sizes; some are now designed to agitate the water as it passes through the ground coffee. Photo by Robert Thurston.

depends on gravity, or in the French press on simple infusion of the grounds; for espresso, you must have a device capable of forcing the water through the ground coffee at relatively high pressure. A pressure of 15 bars, or roughly fifteen times atmospheric pressure, is necessary for a home machine, which produces only a few cups at a time. Commercial machines in continuous use typically operate at 9 bars. Most tabletop "espresso" pots should better be called by the Italian term *moka*; they do not produce enough pressure to make true espresso. If that is to your taste, no one should argue with you.

But a serious espresso machine that reaches 15 bars of pressure at home, 9–12 bars in a coffee shop, does a much better job of bringing out the depth and finish of a good "shot." Hundreds of fine machines are available; at the top end are ones that allow the home or professional barista to preinfuse the grounds—again, to allow a little water into them for a few moments—and to regulate the pressure as the shot is pulled. The barista may, for example, keep the pressure at 9 bars for the first part of the shot, then raise it to 12 bars, then ease up for the remaining time. The whole shot should last 25–30 seconds in a commercial operation, probably less at home. Equipment capable of such finesse, including machines that can program shot profiles, costs thousands of dollars. But excellent espresso can be made by machines that cost far less.

We will not delve here into issues of tamping the grounds into the portafilter; of adjusting the grind according to air temperature, humidity, and barometric pressure; or of many other steps that baristas can take to pull superb shots. Then there is the realm of steaming milk, getting the proportions of a cappuccino or latte just right, and even developing latte art skills. All well and good, but we want to emphasize that any good **espresso-based drink** must start with good espresso liquor.

Espresso alone is so complex that it can be a road to heaven or to madness. Talk about machines to your friendly local barista. Go online to compare machines, looking carefully at their features. With a little investment of time, including really learning how to use the machine you buy, and hopefully not too large a financial outlay, you will impress your friends.

Final words: There is no limit to the number of coffee-making devices you can buy and the money you can spend on them. But it is possible to make excellent coffee at home with simple equipment.

Acknowledgments

Besides, of course, the contributors to this volume, we owe many deep debts to others in the coffee industry.

Robert Thurston: Thanks for all your help and generosity to:

Brazil: Edgard Bressoni, Christian Wolthers

Colombia: Jaime Raul Duque Londono, Oscar Jaramillo Garcia, Pedro Segovia

Costa Rica: Ermie Carman and Linda Moyher, Arnoldo Leiva

Ethiopia: Kedir Kemal, Ato Million, Meskerme Tessema

Germany: Mohammed Taha

Italy: Dr. Isabella Amaduzzi, Dr. Alessandra Cagliari, Enrico Maltoni, Paolo Milani, Roberto Turrin

Kenya: Kennedy Gitonga, J. K. Kinoti, Samuel Mburu, Peter Orwiti, Michael Otieno, Solomon Waweru

Nicaragua: Father James E. Flynn, Denis Gutierrez, Mausi Kühl

Switzerland: Dr. Monika Imboden, Cornelia Luchsinger, Paolo Stirnimann

United States: Bob Arceneaux, Katie Barrow, Anna Clark, Pan Demetrekakes, Judith Ganes-Chase, Tracy Ging, David Griswold, Bill Mares, Sidney Mintz, Stephen Morrissey, Jenny Roberts, Kelly Stewart, Brett Struwe, Quentin Wodon

I also thank the History Department and other divisions of Miami University, Oxford, Ohio, for granting me funds and time to pursue the research and writing of my sections of this book.

Jonathan Morris: I've been helped by so many people in the industry over the years that there is no space to list them all here. For specific help with the pieces in this particular volume I'd like to thank:

Costa Rica: Gonazlo Hernandez Solis

Germany: Jens Burg, Barbara Debroeven, Stefan Graack, Margrit Schulte-Beerbuehl

Italy: Isabella Amaduzzi, Elena Cedrola, Maurizio Giuli, Angela Hysi, Enrico Maltoni, Carlo Odello, Luigi Odello

Mexico: Rachel Laudan

383

Switzerland: Manuela Flamer, Roman Rossfeld

United Kingdom: Claudia Baldoli, Laura Dalgleish, Claudia Galetta, Barry Kither, Anya Marco, Charles Praeger, Michael Segal, Jeffrey Young

United States: Kent Bakke, Mark Prince, David Schomer

And finally I'd like to acknowledge the support of the University of Hertfordshire in granting me sabbatical leave and awarding me a travel grant to pursue my research.

Shawn Steiman: As with anything I've ever written, my work always becomes better with the assistance and generosity of others. I especially thank my wife, Julia Wieting, for her time and brilliant editing skills. I'm also grateful for the friendship and expertise of:

United Kingdom: Dr. Peter Baker

United States: Dr. Skip Bittenbender, Dr. Mel Jackson, Ric Rhinehart, Miles Small, Spencer Turer

Glossary

acidity: A sensation in the mouth when tasting coffee. Acidity is a bright, lively, sparkling feeling, most often associated with citrus fruits and vinegars. In coffee, acidity is typically considered desirable. If too intense, it may seem sour, like a lemon, rather than merely acidy, like an orange. Acidity is a basic characteristic of coffee quality and is almost always described in quality assessments. Note that in the context of coffee tasting, acidity does not refer to pH balance.

aeropress brewing: A brewing system using a column that sits on top of a cup or carafe. Water and ground coffee are allowed to sit in an upper chamber for a few minutes, then the water is pressed through the grounds into the cup.

afterburner: A device attached to a roasting machine that burns away particulates coming from the roaster and chaff from roasting beans, thus reducing emissions to a minimum. Afterburners can cost $14,000 and more, even for a small roaster.

aftertaste: The echo of flavor that remains once coffee leaves the mouth. The intensity of that echo or its pleasantness is the aftertaste. It can also be called the finish. Aftertaste is a basic characteristic of coffee quality.

agroforestry system: An agricultural system involving the production of coffee beneath a species-diverse canopy of shade trees. *See also* **shade/shade-grown.**

Agtron numbers: A measure of roast level by color. An Agtron is a spectrometer, a machine designed to measure light intensity. Agtron machines measure the reflectance of light from whole bean or ground coffee and translate it into a number on a scale of 0 to 100. Higher numbers represent more reflectance and, hence, lighter coffees.

altitude: The geographical altitude at which coffee is grown, thought to influence its cup quality; higher-grown coffees are generally considered better tasting by the specialty coffee industry. Higher altitude coffees are widely perceived as more acidy and more complex. The scientific literature both supports and disagrees with this idea. Air pressure and ambient temperature decrease as altitude increases, but temperature is thought to have more influence on cup quality. Consequently, altitude is only a proxy for temperature and latitude, which highly influences ambient temperature, and which must also be considered when predicting potential cup quality.

arabica: Common name of the species *Coffea arabica.* It is one of 124 known and published species in the genus. Considered to be the most pleasant tasting of the *Coffea* species, arabica makes up about 70 percent of world coffee production.

aroma: The smell of brewed coffee. It has no specific smell-type other than "coffeeness." As green coffee ages or roasted coffee stales, the intensity of aroma tends to decrease. Aroma is a basic characteristic of coffee quality and is almost always measured in quality assessments.

bags: The packaging for coffee beans, traditionally a jute sac containing 60 kilograms, or 134 pounds, of coffee beans. *See also* **packaging.**

balance: All of the individual characteristics of a cup of coffee that interact to create a united taste for the cup. Balance describes how they fit together in relation to one another. It is a subjective description of the coffee based on the drinker's sense of how everything interacts in the cup.

barista: The person operating the coffee brewing equipment, principally the espresso machine, in a coffee shop. Although Italian in origin, the word only became established in that language in the 1930s, when the Fascist administration attempted to suppress foreign words such as "barman." But "barista" became firmly established as both a standard term and a specialized profession only with the rise of international espresso culture.

Barista Guild of America: An official trade group, founded in 2003, of the SCAA. Its purpose is to train and certify baristas while celebrating the barista profession. It offers classes at official SCAA events like the annual exposition and also operates Camp-Pull-A-Shot, annual training retreats held on both coasts of the U.S.

biennial bearing: The two-year production cycle in coffee where one year a tree produces a lot of coffee and in the next year much less. It results from coffee's phenology: the branches that will produce the next year's crop are unable to grow very much because they are competing for nutrients with the current maturing berries. Biennial bearing can be mitigated with pruning and shade.

Big Four (sometimes Big Five): The largest international coffee companies, which market largely commodity (or commercial) coffee. With their headquarters country and their leading brands, they are now: Nestle (Nescafé, Nespresso, Taster's Choice), Switzerland; Smucker's (Folgers), U.S.; Sara Lee (Douwe Egberts, Senseo, and others), U.S.; Kraft Foods (Maxwell House, Sanka), U.S.; and, in some counts, Tchibo (Tchibo, Piacetto), Germany. Together these companies control 50–60 percent of global coffee sales. The composition of the Big Four has changed in recent years, as Procter & Gamble and Phillip Morris (now Altria) have left the coffee business.

biodynamic agriculture: Farming according to the principles of Rudolph Steiner, known for Waldorf schools, but based on earlier, traditional practices of following the cycles of the moon for such work as pruning. Biodynamic farms are managed according to moon phases and position of the stars. Organic vessels, for instance a cow horn packed with manure, are buried in the earth or left to dry out on the soil's surface. The idea is to draw cosmic and terrestrial forces into the packed material and thence into the soil.

bird-friendly: Coffee farms that have a considerable amount of overstory trees, which are attractive to migratory birds. Bird-friendly coffee is a trademark of the Smithsonian Institution, which promotes this certification as a way of encouraging farmers to plant more shade trees, in turn attracting not only more birds to the land but also spiders, bats, and other creatures that are a pleasure to observe and also help control coffee pests.

blends: Beans that are mixed from various origins or varieties, with the goal either of balancing characteristics in the cup or keeping the cost of the coffee low.

body: The level of viscosity or thickness in coffee. Two common drinks with noticeable body are milk and red wine. Skim milk has little body; whole milk has a lot. Red wine has more body than white does. Not well understood chemically, coffee's body is likely derived from dissolved cell wall bits and oils that made it into the cup. Body is another basic characteristic of coffee quality.

branding: The presentation of a product by a specific company, usually with a label and a logo. Branding contrasts with generic coffee, marketed without indication of who put it into salable form. Brands offered by coffee companies began to appear in the U.S. after about 1862. The idea behind branding was to cement an association in the consumer's mind between a product and a company: ads urged coffee drinkers to demand Hills Brothers, Folgers, and so on.

Brazilian naturals: *See* **naturals.**

brewing methods: The way in which water is used to extract flavor from the ground beans, resulting in coffee liquor. *See* the individual methods: **aeropress, clever, Clover, dial in, drip, espresso, filter, flip** (Neapolitano), **French press, percolator, Turkish/Mediterranean, vacuum. broca** (Spanish). *See* **coffee berry borer.**

C coffee: The coffee that serves as the basis of the C price.

C price (C market, Coffee C): The "C" price refers to a number in dollars per 100 pounds of arabica coffee on the New York ICE commodity exchange. Officially called the Coffee "C"®, the C price is usually cited in dollars per pound, for example $2.46. How the C price is derived is a complex process; *see* chapter 15, "The 'Price' of Coffee."

caffeine: A purine derivative xanthine with methyl groups attached at positions 1, 3, and 7. Its stimulating properties are the reason many people drink coffee in the first place. Caffeine, which long had a fairly bad reputation in the public mind for causing health problems, has lately been found to have various health benefits, if consumed moderately in coffee (three to four cups a day of brewed coffee).

caffè latte: A single or double shot of espresso topped with large quantity of steamed milk and a small head of foamed milk on top in which latte art can be created. *See* the discussion of the many variations of the beverage in terms of *size* and coffee to milk proportions in chapter 45, "The Espresso Menu."

California red worms: Widely used in Latin America, worms that digest coffee fruit skins and pulp and, in a matter of weeks, produce useful compost. One of the most effective means of reducing pollution and waste from the harvest and of recycling material on the farms.

cappuccino: A single or double shot of espresso, topped with equal parts of steamed and foamed milk—increasingly served "dry," that is, with a greater proportion of foam which has often been heavily aerated (macro-foamed). Often topped with a dusting of cocoa powder or cinnamon.

capsules: A single portion of ground coffee sealed into a small disk, usually aluminum, that can be used to brew a single cup of coffee in an appropriate machine. Nestle originated this technology for use in its Nespresso machines; *see* chapter 45, "The Espresso Menu." Keurig is the market leader in the United States, but Starbucks recently launched its own capsules and machines for using them. *See also* **pods.**

catch crop: A crop, usually a fast-growing one, that can be used to provide some income while waiting for another crop (such as tree crops like rubber or cacao) to reach economic maturity.

certification: Programs designed to provide a good price to farmers for their coffee, to protect and improve the environment, or to improve working and living conditions for farmers and their hired labor. *See* chapter 20, "Coffee Certification Programs."

chemical composition of the beverage: The complex chemical makeup of coffee. No complete description of the composition currently exists. Many factors influence the composition of any given cup. Among them are the genetics, the environment the tree grew in, the processing method, storage conditions, roasting, freshness, and brewing. A cup of coffee likely has at least 300 different compounds in the liquid brew. Over 1,000 compounds have been detected in the aroma.

cherry: The ripe coffee fruit (or berry). Generally used in the singular, it is called "cherry" because some varieties have a deep red color when at their peak, ready to be picked, and because the size of coffee cherry is often close to that of cherries. Certain varieties produce yellow, pink, or orange ripe berries, which are still called cherry. In Spanish, coffee fruits are called "grapes" (*uvas*).

chicory: *Cichorium intybus,* a small, herbaceous, perennial plant. In many parts of the world, its root is used as a coffee substitute. Chicory became associated with France when it was widely used to compensate for the loss of access to coffee supplies following the Haitian revolution and the British blockade of Napoleonic Europe in the late 1790s. In the United States, it became a common coffee substitute or additive during the Civil War, when the South had little access to coffee due to the Northern blockade. Coffee with chicory remains popular in the southern United States, particularly in New Orleans.

Clever brewing: A brewing system using a device that allows coffee to infuse in a self-contained plastic cone, then to be released into a carafe.

climate change: The incremental rise of global temperatures. Climate change poses a serious problem for the coffee industry. As average temperatures rise, many current locations for growing coffee will be too hot to continue quality coffee production. New land, at higher elevations, is scarce, less fertile, and not easy to farm. Whether more land at low to moderate elevations but high latitudes will become available for coffee has not been determined. The warmer temperatures also facilitate the spread of some coffee pests, particularly the coffee berry borer.

Clover brewing: A brewing system using a machine that can be adjusted in many different ways, for example brew temperature and extraction time, according to the coffee used in it. Starbucks purchased the right to manufacture and use the Clover in 2008.

coffee bean: The seed of the coffee plant, encased within the coffee fruit.

coffee berry borer: *Hypothenemus hampei*. This pest originated first in Angola but now exists in nearly every coffee-producing country in the world. It is considered the most disastrous coffee pest as it is very difficult to control and, so far, impossible to eliminate. The female insect bores through a coffee cherry and into the seed, where she lays eggs. Once they hatch, the newborn insects mate and the pregnant females leave to begin the cycle anew.

coffee cherry: *See* **cherry.**

coffee fruit: The fruit of the coffee plant. The coffee fruit is covered first with a skin. Below that is mucilage or pulp. Next is parchment, and finally there is a thin layer called silverskin that envelopes the beans (seeds). *See* figure 2.1 for an illustration of the parts of the fruit.

coffeehouses (bars, cafés): A business whose principal source of revenue comes from selling coffee beverages for consumption on the premises. The first coffeehouses appeared in Arabia during the fifteenth century, reaching Cairo in the 1500s and Istanbul, the capital of the Ottoman empire, in 1554. The first European coffeehouses appeared in England in the 1650s, with the first American coffeehouse opening in Boston in 1670. In continental Europe the café, combining alcohol, food, and coffee service, developed into the dominant coffee retailing institution. In the twentieth century the espresso bar evolved, with customers drinking their beverages while standing at the counter, while the branded coffee shop has become the primary location for coffee consumption in the twenty-first century, featuring a comfortable furnished environment and the provision of facilities that encourage customers to treat the coffee shop as providing a "twenty-minute experience," which is paid for in the price of a premium coffee. *See* chapter 42, "Coffeehouse Formats through the Centuries."

coffee leaf rust: A fungal disease (*Hemileia vastatrix*) considered one of coffee's worst pests. The fungus appears as rust-colored spots on leaves, causing them to function less efficiently and, in many cases, killing them and the whole tree. It is considered the most severe coffee leaf disease. Arabica is much more susceptible than robusta to rust. Robusta's superior resistance is one major reason for breeding programs that aim to incorporate robusta lineage into arabica varieties.

coffee plant: A member of the botanical family *Rubiaceae* and the genus *Coffea.* The two commercially important species are *Coffea arabica* (arabica) and *Coffea canephora* (robusta). It is an evergreen tree with glossy leaves that form as pairs along the branch. The flowers are white and pleasantly aromatic.

Coffee Quality Institute (CQI): A nonprofit organization affiliated with the Specialty Coffee Association of America (SCAA). It works internationally to improve the quality of coffee and the lives of the people who produce it through training, building institutional capacity, and operating quality standard systems. CQI provides training and technical assistance to coffee producers and operates both the Q and R programs (for arabica and robusta coffee, respectively), which certify cuppers to grade coffees using a standardized system of evaluation.

coffee taster's wheel: A wheel, usually presented as a poster, that lists both defective and positive flavors in coffee. Examples of negative ones are horsey; hidey; woody; of positive ones, floral, citrus, malt-like.

Coffee "C" price: *See* **C price.**

The wheel gives terms for defects produced in growing, processing, and handling coffee, while the pleasant descriptors refer to flavors and scents revealed during proper roasting.

Colombian milds: Wet-processed Colombian coffee that serves as the standard level of quality for Coffee C.

commercial coffee: Coffee that is not specialty. Usually sold in grocery or big box stores already ground in cans or plastic tubs, such coffee is a blend of low-quality arabica and often robusta. Still the world's most widely consumed kind of coffee. *See also* **Big Four.**

commodity chain: All the people and stages in handling a commodity from the ground to retail sales.

commodity coffee: Non-specialty coffee. For coffee, the major markets for selling commodity coffee are, for arabica, Intercontinental Exchange (ICE, New York), which determines the "C" price, and for robusta, the London International Financial Futures and Options Exchange (LIFFE).

condiments: In coffee shops, milk, cream, sugar, and artificial substitutes for them.

conilon: Brazilian robusta.

consuming countries: Those countries that grow little or no coffee but consume imported coffee. A country may be both a producer and a consumer; examples are Brazil, Ethiopia, Kenya, Colombia, India, and Vietnam.

conventional coffee: Coffee that is not certified, for example, non-organic.

crema: The layer of foam typically found on the top of an espresso coffee (from the Italian word for cream). Under high pressure, the water used in the espresso brewing becomes supersaturated with carbon dioxide and other volatile gases. As the liquor leaves the portafilter, the gases begin to disperse and move out of the water. These gases are then trapped by a mixture of water and non-water soluble compounds, likely mostly oils. These trapped gasses create microbubbles that determine the sensory characteristics of the crema. Although a layer of crema indicates that the coffee has been brewed under high pressure, it offers no guarantee of cup quality in itself. Indeed there is now a school that holds that espresso tastes best after the crema has been removed. *See* chapter 47, "Coffee Quality," and chapter 45, "The Espresso Menu."

crème café **(French):** Taken from the term *caffè crema* (Italian), an espresso beverage served above all in France and Germany. *Crème café* is larger and less intense than Italian espresso but still topped by a mousse of crema.

cultivar (or variety): Within a species, types different enough in some way to warrant classification as a subcategory (for example, 'Fuji' and 'Red Delicious' apples or poodles and golden retriever dogs). These differences tend to manifest themselves physically, which is how farmers and breeders tend to identify and select different cultivars. In coffee, differences in cultivars can be related to plant height, fruit color, or cup quality, for example. There are many cultivars of *C. arabica*, and new ones are being actively created by breeders.

Cup of Excellence: A competition measuring coffee quality. The Cup of Excellence (CoE) competitions began in 1999 as a price discovery system based on cup quality. Coffees within a country are submitted to the competition and judged by local cuppers. A group of international experts conducts the final round of judging. After the experts score the coffees, they are sold at an online auction.

cupping: Cupping is the formal method for evaluating coffee cup quality. Coffee is brewed in cups or bowls, ingested using spoons, and often expectorated. An array of quality traits, like body and acidity, are assessed and recorded. *See also* **Q-grader cuppers.**

decaffeination: The process of removing caffeine from unroasted coffee. To be classified as decaffeinated coffee, at least 97 percent of the caffeine needs to be removed. There are three main methods. The chemical method treats green beans with a solvent; common ones are water, ethyl acetate, supercritical carbon dioxide, and methylene chloride. The solvent removes the caffeine and some other compounds. The caffeine is separated from the extract and the other compounds are returned to the coffee. The Swiss water process works without the use of chemicals. The caffeine is removed by soaking the beans in hot water for an extended period of time. This water is then channeled through a series of charcoal filters to remove the caffeine, before the water is returned to the beans. Although this may sound like a "purer" approach, critics claim that it removes more of the flavor than the other methods. A recently developed alternative uses CO_2 to remove caffeine.

defects: Problems in the beans that can result in unpleasant tastes. Defects may result from pest infestation, overripeness, overfermentation in processing, diseases, and other problems in cultivation, processing, or storage. Broken beans are also considered defects, as their multiple surfaces are inviting to mold.

Demeter: Named after the Greek goddess of fertility, an organization based in Philomath, Oregon, that certifies coffee grown according to biodynamic principles. *See also* **biodynamic agriculture.**

demucilation: A form of washed processing in which the mucilage is mechanically removed from the seed. The seeds are then moved directly to drying or soaked in water.

density: A physical property of an object that is defined as its mass per its volume. Green coffee can be graded according to density using a density table. Denser coffees are considered to be of higher quality.

depulping: The action of removing the outer layer of fruit, the pulp, from the coffee cherry. This is the common term in languages other than English, which for some reason uses "pulping" instead.

dial in/to brewing: The process, in making espresso, of adjusting the grind, the amount of coffee in the portafilter, and the extraction time.

direct trade: A system of buying and importing coffee that links importer/roasters directly with farmers. *See* chapter 21, "Direct Trade in Coffee."

drip brewing: A brewing system using any machine or hand device that uses gravity to pass water through ground coffee.

drying: The process in which, before coffee is shipped and roasted, it is dried down to a certain level of moisture (humidity). This can occur using the sun on specially made drying decks, the ground, tarpaulins, or elevated (African) screens. Alternatively, mechanical dryers can be used to reduce the seed's moisture content to 9–12 percent.

dry processing: *See* **natural processing.**

ejido system: In Spanish-speaking Latin America, a system of land tenure in which all land is held in common, for example by a village, but plots are farmed individually. Many nineteenth- and early-twentieth-century non-indigenous commentators found this system objectionable, as in their eyes it encouraged "native" people to stay at home and not work on large commercial farms.

energy drinks: Heavily caffeinated beverages. These drinks are designed to be alternatives to beverages that naturally contain caffeine; they are essentially stay-awake products. The best known of these is Red Bull, invented in Thailand in the 1970s and marketed internationally from 1984 on. As sold in the West, Red Bull contains about 80 milligrams of caffeine per 8.3-ounce can.

espresso: Coffee brewed under high pressure. The coffee is finely ground and tamped (i.e., pressed) into a filter basket. The basket sits in a portafilter that is clamped on to the espresso machine at the so-called group head. The bottom of the portafilter contains two spouts through which the coffee flows into two cups positioned underneath. Sawing off the bottom of the portafilter (making it a "naked" portafilter) is sometimes done to produce a more theatrical effect. Hot water is forced through the coffee cake, usually under around 9 bars of pressure, to produce a shot of around 25–30 milliliters. Adjusting the grind of the coffee will alter the length of the delivery time (usually 25–30 seconds), which in turn affects the extent of extraction and taste of the coffee in the cup. Espresso brewed under high pressures will be topped by an emulsion known as **crema.** Espresso is closely associated with Italy, where most machine manufacturers are still based. For an extended discussion of the history of espresso, *see* chapter 45, "The Espresso Menu."

espresso-based drinks: Beverages in which espresso provides the coffee component. Although originating in Italy, many of these take different forms elsewhere in the world. *See* **cappuccino, caffè latte, lungo, macchiato,** and **ristretto,** and chapter 45, "The Espresso Menu."

espresso beans: Beans used to prepare espresso coffee (as espresso refers to a process rather than an origin). In Italy espresso is nearly always produced using a blend of beans, traditionally combining arabica and robusta beans, although the proportions vary dramatically. Many specialty blends are 100 percent arabica or even single-origin.

espresso brewing: Coffee made under pressure. The term *espresso* first appeared in Italy in the early twentieth century, although the machines of that era brewed at much lower pressures than today. A manually operated piston to power the water through the ground coffee cake appeared in 1948, resulting in the *crema* (Italian for cream) on top of the coffee shot. During the 1960s, new machines switched to electric pumps, operating at around 9 bars of pressure, which remains the norm today. *See also* the main entry **espresso.**

espresso coffee: Coffee used for espresso, often dark roasted in deference to the supposed Italian tradition. This probably stems from the fact that the blends often feature substantial quantities of robusta beans whose bitterness in the cup can be somewhat counteracted by caramelizing through dark roasting. However, many northern Italian blends, which tend to be higher in arabica content, are light roast.

espresso machines: Machines intended to brew espresso. They are usually divided into "traditional" semi-automatic machines in which the barista controls most of the brewing parameters, "automatics" in which these are regulated by the machine itself, "supra-automatics" that include the grinding process, and "bean to cup" machines that also prepare and mount milk onto the beverages. The espresso machine has evolved substantively over the years. The first so-called espresso machines, such as the original Pavoni Ideale of 1905, relied on steam to generate pressure and brewed at little more than one and half atmospheres. Achille Gaggia's manually operated piston, developed in 1948, revolutionized espresso by introducing high-pressure brewing and its accompanying crema. This system was later superseded by the use of electric pumps in the first semi-automatic machines such as the Faema E61. *See* chapter 45, "The Espresso Menu."

estates: Large coffee farms using hired labor. Estate coffee is truly single-origin and is likely to be marketed as such.

extraction: The process of drawing or forcing water through ground coffee to produce liquor. Proper extraction time for the device used to make a coffee beverage is critical to its quality.

fair trade: A system of coffee contracts that provides a guaranteed minimum price for green beans, regardless of movement in global markets. The American oversight and labeling organization is Fair Trade USA, having changed its name from TransFair USA. For more on Fair Trade and other ethical certifications, *see* chapter 20, "Coffee Certification Programs," and chapter 22, "Fair Trade." *See also* **Fair Trade USA.**

Fairtrade International: A fair trade organization based in Bonn, Germany, that provides certification and labeling for fair trade practices.

Fair Trade USA: The American organization that provides ethical certification for coffee. *See also* **fair trade.**

farm gate price: The price actually paid to the farmer for coffee. Since coffee passes through many hands before it is made into a beverage, the price rises as it passes in turn from a buyer to an exporter, an importer, a roaster, and a retail establishment.

fermentation: One of the initial stages in dealing with harvested coffee. After picking, the cherry is generally either pulped (wet processing) or left in the skin (dry processing). In the first case, the mucilage is removed by microorganisms present in the fruit and by immersion in water. In dry processing, the microorganisms carry out mucilage degradation by themselves. Both processes bring down the level of acidity—here the word does refer to the pH scale—to below 5 or even below 4.

fertilizer: Any substance added to a living system that is intended to provide nutrients. In agriculture, fertilizers can be derived from organic sources (typically compost from decomposed plant matter, manure, or animal parts) or produced in factories. Organic and synthetic fertilizers may be the same in the chemical composition of the nutrients they are promising to provide; *see* chapter 5, "What Does 'Organic' Mean?"

filter brewing: A brewing system using material, usually in a cone or another holder (dripper), that holds ground coffee in drip systems. It can be made of metal, paper, cloth, sometimes even an old sock in Costa Rica.

finish: *See* aftertaste.

first wave: A presumed stage of development of the coffee trade in which coffee was mass produced with little regard for quality. In the Western world, this phase lasted roughly from the mid-1600s into the 1970s and 1980s. Trish Skeie Rothgeb coined the phrase in 2002, but coffee professionals and historians disagree about the periodization of coffee in the Western world. The only phrase widely used to designate a period of coffee-making is third wave. *See also* **second wave; third wave.**

flavor: The paradigmatic taste of a beverage, in this case the essential coffee flavor. Cuppers add a point value for flavor to the scores they have assigned to any coffee for its other characteristics in the cup, for example, finish.

flip (Neapolitano) brewing: A small metal stovetop device from Italy. An upper compartment is a basket for ground coffee; a lower compartment holds water. When the water boils, the whole device is flipped upside down. The hot water falls through the grounds in the basket and back into the container that first held the water.

FOB: *See* **free on board.**

Folgers: One of the **Big Four** brands. Recently sold by Procter and Gamble to another Ohio corporation, Smucker's, Folgers remains one of America's most popular commodity coffees. Jim Folger began the company with several partners in the California gold fields in the 1850s. Riding the crest of mass advertising and communications, Folgers became a national brand in the next forty years. In 1963 Procter and Gamble bought the company, helping it to become America's top seller into the early 1980s.

Food Safety Modernization Act: A U.S. law adopted in 2011 that gives the Food and Drug Administration the ability to issue mandatory recalls of processed foods suspected of being contaminated.

fragrance: The smell of freshly ground, unbrewed coffee. It has no specific smell-type other than coffee-ness. As green coffee ages or roasted coffee stales, the intensity of fragrance tends to decrease. Fragrance is another basic characteristic of coffee quality.

free on board: A designation for any commodity or product, manufactured or otherwise, that is on a ship and ready for departure from a port. That is, all taxes, duties, charges for labor, perhaps even bribes, have been paid. The FOB price is quite different from the farm gate price.

French press brewing: A brewing system invented in the early nineteenth century in France using a piston press or *cafetière*. A cylinder, usually of glass, is held in a frame that keeps the bottom of the device above the level of a table or counter. Fairly coarsely ground coffee is poured into the bottom of the press, followed by water just off the boil. Then a piston or plunger is inserted in the top of the cylinder. After four minutes or so, the piston handle is pressed down. Attached to the bottom of the handle is a close mesh screen, which traps virtually all of the grounds at the bottom of the cylinder. The coffee liquor can then be poured into a cup.

futures: A system of buying and selling many commodities, especially raw materials and agricultural products. Contracts are made, usually between a large buyer and a commodities dealer, that specify a certain amount and quality of coffee to be acquired for a set price on a certain date. *See* chapter 15, "The 'Price' of Coffee."

grading: A quality measure typically made at origin by an authorized government agency. Different governments use different criteria for grading coffee. The criteria can include coffee species, elevation at which the coffee was grown, bean size, cup quality, and defect count.

green: *See* **green coffee/bean; green movement; green taste.**

green coffee/bean: The processed, dried form of coffee that must first be roasted before it becomes a palatable product. Green coffee is the coffee of commerce; it is above all in this form that coffee is exported from producing countries. In Spanish, coffee at this stage is called *oro*, gold.

green movement: An effort to preserve and improve the environment through the use of recycling, composting, and self-sufficiency in energy and soil amendments. The coffee industry in general, and specialty coffee in particular, has put considerable emphasis on going green; after all, the environment must be carefully tended in order to grow coffee on a sustainable basis. Western cafés are increasingly using biodegradable cups, for instance, or giving customers discounts for bringing their own mugs.

green taste: A grassy taste in coffee, often from insufficient drying time.

grinders, types of: Machines used to grind coffee. There are two main types. (1) The blade machine (which should really be called a chopper) uses a whirling metal blade to chop and bash coffee beans into smaller particles. It is the cheapest type of coffee grinder, and it produces non-uniform sized and shaped particles. (2) Burr grinders use metal or occasionally ceramic ridged plates to pulverize beans, resulting in more or less uniformly sized grains of coffee. Such machines are more expensive than blade grinders but provide more control over fineness and evenness.

hardness: A descriptive term (largely used in Latin America) related to the altitude at which coffee is grown. Hardness can be noted as "hard bean" or "strictly hard bean" and is related to quality in the cup. Coffee berries grown at higher altitudes take longer to mature and are often considered to be of higher quality than those from lower elevations, though many consider the key element to be temperature rather than altitude. *See* chapter 3, "Digging Deeper," and chapter 48, "Why Does Coffee Taste That Way?"

harvesting: The removal of the cherries from the coffee trees. With hand harvesting, the coffee cherries are removed from the trees without tools of any kind. Selective picking aims to gather only ripe cherries, whereas strip picking is more indiscriminate; all cherries are stripped from the tree regardless of ripeness. Mechanical harvesting uses machines to assist in harvesting coffee. Small mechanical harvesters are handheld and either gently vibrate a branch, shaking the coffee from the tree, or have scissors-like jaws at the end that close around a branch. The operator then draws the machine toward himself, stripping all berries, ripe or not, from the branch. Large mechanical harvesters require a driver. These machines, equipped with fiberglass rods, shake and beat the tree branches, causing the cherries to fall into a capturing bin.

hectare: A common measure of land area, 100 meters on a side, about 2.5 acres. Abbreviated "ha."

honey processing: *See* **pulped natural processing.**

horeca: The hotel-restaurant-café market for coffee, as opposed to home consumption.

hotel-restaurant-café: *See* **horeca.**

hulling (or milling): The process of removing parchment from the beans. Hullers operate by rubbing the beans against each other or by gently beating them with strings or rods. Machines must be calibrated for the size of the beans put into them. Hulling too deeply or at too high a temperature will damage the beans and their taste in the cup; hulling too lightly will not remove enough parchment, which may cause problems in roasting.

humidity: *See* **moisture.**

industrial food: Food produced for a mass market; the term implies that the produce is not organic, probably not sustainable, and probably not especially tasty.

insecticides: Chemicals used to kill or control insect pests in an agricultural setting. Insecticides can be derived from natural products, like plants, or synthetically created in a factory.

instant: Also called soluble, a coffee that requires only the addition of boiling water to make a cup. Invented in 1906 in Guatemala by a Belgian by the quaint name of George Washington.

intercropping: An agricultural design in which at least two crops share the same field. It is often designed by farmers to increase their potential sources of income. By diversifying the ecological conditions, intercropping may also provide habitat for a variety of fauna.

International Coffee Agreement (ICA): An agreement first signed in 1962 to set export quotas for the major coffee-growing countries. The pact was renewed three times before collapsing in 1989. A new ICA was signed in 1994 and revised in 2001 and 2007, but these agreements do not specify export quotas. *See* chapter 19, "The Global Trade in Coffee."

International Coffee Organization (ICO): The organization created in 1963 to oversee the first International Coffee Agreement. Reorganized in 1989 as a recordkeeping and advisory group, with producing and consuming member countries. *See* chapter 19, "The Global Trade in Coffee."

International Women's Coffee Alliance: An organization founded in 2003 by six American women (now with chapters around the world) with the goal of improving the lives of women in coffee through financial support, special purchasing mechanisms, and technical advice. *See* chapter 12, "How a Country Girl from Arkansas Became an Importer Leading Other Women in Coffee."

kopi luwak: From the Indonesian word for coffee and the name of the local species of civet cat, a coffee that has been partly processed in the body of the cat. One of the few animals that eat coffee cherries, the Indonesian civet cat digests the soft part of the fruit and excretes the beans. The price for this product, considered by most in the industry to taste awful, can be $300 a pound roasted, or more than $40 a cup in a high-class establishment.

Kraft Foods: An independent company selling Maxwell House until 1988, when it merged with Philip Morris. Subsequently spun out of Philip Morris as an independent corporation again in 2007, Kraft also owns Kenco, one of the UK's leading coffee brands. *See also* **Big Four.**

latte: *See* **caffè latte.**

leaf rust: *See* **coffee leaf rust.**

liquor: The industry term for basic brewed coffee with nothing added.

lungo: A "long" espresso, delivered to a greater volume in the cup. In Italy around 40 milliliters—which, of course, can be the standard size of an espresso elsewhere.

macchiato: An espresso "marked" with milk—hot or cold, steamed or foamed in Italy, nearly always foamed in the Anglo-American markets.

Maillard reactions: A class of chemical reactions that occur in coffee during the roasting process. They are characterized by the reaction of amino acids with sugars. In coffee, these reactions generate the compounds that are largely responsible for the brown color as well as some of the antioxidant properties.

marketing: Setting and carrying out a strategy to sell any product. Much of the cost differential between the farm gate or FOB price of coffee and its eventual sale price in a cup is due to the expense of marketing in consuming countries.

Max Havelaar: A novel, whose full title in English is *Max Havelaar, or The Coffee Auctions of the Dutch Trading Company,* by Multatuli. This was a pseudonym of Eduard Douwes Dekker, who had worked in Java in the Dutch civil service—that is, the colonial administration. The book first appeared in Dutch in 1859; it remains a classic of Netherlands literature. It exposed colonial practices that forced Indonesians to deliver great quantities of food to their own nobles and to the Dutch, often reducing peasants in a highly fertile land to starvation. Max Havelaar was adopted as the label for products sold under the auspices of the first Fair Trade organization, created in 1988 and based in the Netherlands.

Mediterranean coffee: *See* **Turkish/Mediterranean brewing.**

milds: A term usually used to describe high-grown Colombian coffee. These beans became the standard around which the C price has been constructed for many years.

milling: *See* **hulling.**

moisture (or humidity): The moisture content of the beans, determined at the final stage of processing for coffee on the farm when the beans are dried. The goal is to achieve 9–12 percent moisture content. This level renders the seeds fairly stable and unattractive to many pests and diseases. In wet processing, the beans are dried after pulping and fermentation. In dry processing, the cherry dries as it is spread out on a patio or on drying racks. Humidity is also often checked again before coffee is roasted, as a way of helping to determine the optimal roast profile.

mouthfeel: *See* **body.**

mucilage: The sticky, sugary component of a coffee cherry. Mucilage is the thickest layer of the coffee fruit; it is on top of the parchment. *See also* **coffee bean.**

National Coffee Association: A trade group founded in 1911, partly to combat the negative image that coffee was receiving in ads for grain beverages like Postum. Now the major trade association in the U.S. for all kinds of coffee, commodity and specialty. Publishes various reports including an annual one on coffee drinking trends in America.

natural (or dry) processing: A method of drying the coffee cherry after harvesting. In natural processing, the cherries are sent directly to a drying area, without removing any parts of the fruit.

naturals (or Brazilian naturals): Beans that are dry processed on patios until they have reached a desired level of fermentation and humidity.

Neapolitano brewing: *See* **flip brewing.**

Nestle's: *See* **Big Four.**

NGOs: Non-governmental organizations. In the coffee industry, many of these operate to improve farmers' health and environmental conditions, the status of women, food security, school programs, and much more.

organic: In regard to agriculture, any compound or material found in nature, as opposed to inorganic compounds or substances, which are produced in a laboratory or factory. For example, bird excrement, guano, which contains nitrates and used to be the world's choice for commercial fertilizer, is organic. But if chemists make some of the same compounds that are in guano—which is done on a huge scale around the world—and offer them as fertilizer, the product must be called inorganic or synthetic. There is no evidence that plants that take up nutrients from soil or sprays distinguish between organic and synthetic chemicals having the same molecular structure. The U.S. Department of Agriculture, which certifies organic produce for America, bars "most conventional pesticides" in organic crops and animal products. But farmers may apply some synthetic substances to fields and plants and still retain organic certification. *See also* **organic farming** and chapter 5, "What Does 'Organic' Mean?"

organic farming: Farming that is entirely organic or, in the U.S., nearly so. Certified organic farms use only organic materials throughout production. For example, an organic cheese maker in Vermont must use organic fodder for the cows.

organoleptic: A term that describes perceptions of the human senses, particularly the senses of taste and smell. In coffee, it typically refers to the drinker's taste experience of the beverage, as in "organoleptic quality."

origin: The site where a particular coffee is grown, typically referring to a specific country, region, or even farm. "Going to origin" means traveling to actual coffee farms. Such trips are organized regularly by groups like the Roasters Guild of America. In recent years, many less professionally oriented trips to origin have been organized, for students, bird watchers, or tourists.

oro: *See* **green coffee.**

other milds: Beans that are similar to Colombian milds. Colombian milds, always arabica, are the standard for Coffee C. Other similar beans, especially from Latin America, are considered in calculating the C price at any given moment.

overstory: The tallest level of trees in a forest or on a shaded coffee farm.

packaging: The material for shipping green coffee or selling roasted coffee. The standard bag for shipping green coffee has traditionally been made of jute. In recent years, vacuum sealing has been popular for the highest grades of coffee. Bags with several layers of material and an inert gas between them have also come into use. Whole bean or ground coffee is sold in metal cans, plastic tubs, or sealed bags. The latter usually have one-way valves that allow gasses produced during roasting to escape, while keeping oxygen from entering the bag. In recent years, compostable bags for retail sales have appeared in specialty coffee, as have steel cans that customers may return to a shop or recycle. *See also* chapter 47, "Coffee Quality," and **bags.**

parchment: The hull of the coffee fruit, called *pergamino* in Spanish.

peaberry: A bean that develops as a single, rounded entity in the fruit instead of two separate beans with flat facing sides. Peaberries are usually the result of a common mutation, but may also develop because one embryonic seed was somehow not fertilized. About 5 percent of all coffee is peaberry. While some drinkers find that peaberry is naturally sweeter, most cuppers do not note this difference. If peaberry has a smoother taste than the usual beans of the same variety, that may be due to the uniform size of the bean, which facilitates proper roasting.

peasant: A small farmer who is forced by law, custom, or taxes to give away much of his crops, either to an institution or individual. Peasants may contribute little to the ultimate price of an agricultural product, especially one—for example, coffee—that must be shipped overseas to consumers and that must undergo further processing before it can be sold at retail.

Peet, Alfred: A Dutch immigrant to the U.S. (1920–2007) who opened a small roastery and coffee shop in Berkeley, California, in 1966. Many of the first American enthusiasts for specialty coffee were introduced to it by Peet.

percolator brewing: A brewing method using an appliance with a chamber for water, into which a tube with a basket at the top is inserted. Ground coffee, fairly coarse, goes into the basket. The apparatus is set on a burner. When the water boils, it moves up the tube and spills over the ground coffee. This process continues until all the water in the bottom chamber has turned into coffee liquor. The percolator was a staple item in American kitchens into the 1970s and even later.

pesticides: A generic term for chemicals that are used to kill or control pests in an agricultural setting. The pests can be microorganisms, weeds, or insects. Pesticides can be derived from natural products, like plants, or synthetically created in a factory.

phenology: The timing of recurring biological events, for instance bird migration or the flowering of coffee plants.

pods: Ground coffee sealed in permeable paper, ready to insert in certain coffee makers.

point of sale (POS): A system that allows recording and tracking of all sales through a computer. Handheld POS devices or ones that work with pads are now common, allowing retailers to accept credit cards or account numbers away from a store or warehouse.

portafilter: A detachable component of espresso machines that holds the basket containing the coffee, usually with two spouts underneath. A "naked" portafilter has no spouts at the bottom, allowing coffee to flow straight through into the cup.

POS: *See* **point of sale.**

pour-over: A system for making brewed coffee that involves putting ground coffee into a filter, which in turn fits into a cone (dripper) of glass, plastic, or ceramic. Hot water is poured onto the grounds, at first just a little to wet them and allow certain gasses to escape, then the rest of the (carefully measured) water.

Postum: A grain-based beverage invented by C. W. Post, of ready-to-eat cereal fame, in the 1890s. Long touted as better for health than drinks with caffeine, Postum ceased to be manufactured in 2007 but resumed production in 2012.

price of coffee: *See* **C price** and chapter 15, "The 'Price' of Coffee."

processing: The steps involved in coffee production after harvesting the fruit but before roasting. Processing involves removing the outer layers of the cherry and then drying and storing the coffee bean. *See also* **drying, pulped natural processing, washed processing,** and **wet processing.**

producing countries: Those countries in which coffee grows. As coffee is a tropical crop, only countries with tropical and sometimes subtropical climates can produce it in appreciable amounts.

productivity: Output per unit of input. Agricultural productivity depends on human or machine labor, quality of the soil, variety of coffee grown, capital inputs, and technical advice and assistance.

pruning: The process of carefully cutting back coffee trees. Coffee trees must be pruned to remain productive. Both the height (1.5–2 meters) and girth of trees need to be kept manageable, so that hand pickers or machines can access the cherries relatively easily. Carefully planned pruning also helps reduce biennial bearing on a farm. Many different pruning strategies exist. One approach is to conduct a first or main pruning to shape the tree, maintain its desired size, remove any small shoots or "suckers" growing out of the main trunk, and cut away dead branches. This first stage is usually done with large pruning shears or, on mechanized farms, by machines with whirling blades set vertically or horizontally. A secondary round of pruning is often called "handling." This involves "opening up the tree" by cutting away excess branches. The purpose is to induce the tree to put more of its energy into producing fruit and less into producing branches. After several years of production, a span that can vary widely by variety, place, and general conditions, a tree may be "stumped." In Hawaii, trees may be stumped as often as every three or four years. The entire tree is cut down except for a stump perhaps 100 centimeters high, but sometimes much lower; from the remaining part a new trunk, stems, and branches will emerge.

pulped natural (or honey) processing: A drying method in which, after the coffee cherries are harvested, they are depulped, then sent directly to drying, leaving the mucilage on the seed.

Q-grader cuppers: Individuals who have been licensed by the Coffee Quality Institute to evaluate coffees according to the Q-system. The Q-system is based upon the SCAA coffee grading and assessment protocols. To become a Q-grader, aspirants must take courses and pass a battery of tests on sensory acuity and ability to cup coffee. The Coffee Quality Institute reported that in 2011 there were nearly 2,000 Q-graders working in more than forty countries.

Quaker bean: Defective beans that show up in roasted coffee as pale colored beans. They were immature when harvested or suffered from stress while on the tree. In a brewed cup, they produce bitterness and have diminished intensity of most characteristics.

raisins: Coffee cherries that dry on the tree before being harvested. They are most often associated with mechanically harvested operations. Even though the raisins remain attached to the tree, they are no longer physiologically connected to the tree. Consequently, they may overferment or the skin may acquire molds, either of which may detract from the cup quality. While high-quality liquor is difficult to attain from raisins, it is not impossible.

refractometer: An instrument that measures the refraction, or bending, of light caused by a substance. In coffee, refractometers are used to measure the total dissolved solids in liquor. Brewed coffee is put into the refractometer, which generates a pulse of light. The light is bent through the liquid at an angle proportional to the amount of material dissolved in the brew. Using a predefined calibration curve, the proportion of solid material can be calculated.

relationship coffee: Coffee that is purchased directly from a producer by a roaster in a consuming country. *See also* **direct trade.**

ristretto: A "short" shot of espresso, one that is smaller in volume and more concentrated than a regular shot. A ristretto may be about .75 ounce, or around 15–20 milliliters in Italy where it is particularly popular in the south of the country, possibly because of the greater proportion of robusta used in blends there. The drink can be made on an espresso machine equipped with a lever by literally pulling the shot for less time; it can also be made by grinding the coffee more finely than for a regular espresso or by tamping extra coffee into a one-serving portafilter basket.

roasters: The machines that cook green coffee beans, and also the people who operate those machines. Roasters (machines) range in size from small tabletop models about the size of a home blender to gigants that fill large rooms. Capacity per roast likewise ranges from 150 grams up to 100 kilos or more. Drum roasters have an internal, rotating chamber into which green beans are poured. These machines work by convection—heated air in the drum helps cook the coffee—and by conduction—heat transferred to the bean by direct contact with the hot surface of the drum. Fluid bed roasters, sometimes called air roasters, use hot air pushed through tall columns, into which green beans are poured. The air flow keeps the beans moving, which prevents them from burning—unless, of course, the roast is allowed to go on for a long time. Sample roasters are small machines used by professionals to test small batches of coffee, in order to decide which coffees to buy in larger lots.

Roasters Guild of America: Founded in 2000, an official trade group of the SCAA. Its purpose is to train and certify roasters while celebrating the roasting profession. While it offers classes at official SCAA events like the annual exposition, it also operates an annual retreat that has begun alternating sites between the coasts of the U.S.

roasting: The process of heating the harvested and dried coffee beans prior to brewing. Here are some of the phrases traditionally used to describe the level of roast. From lightest to darkest, they include light cinnamon (very light brown), cinnamon (light brown), New England (moderate light brown), American or light (medium light brown), city, or medium (medium brown), full city (medium dark brown); oily drops produced from sugars in the beans may appear on their surface), light French, or espresso (moderate dark brown; oil lightly coats the beans), French (dark brown; shiny with oil, the beans have begun to burn), Italian or dark French (really dark brown and shiny with oil; burnt tones dominate in the cup), and Spanish (oil everywhere; the beans are seriously burnt). Although some companies still use these terms, they have tended to give way to simpler descriptions. Note that, outside of certain chains, "bold" is not considered a useful adjective for degree of roast. *See also* chapter 52, "Roasting," and chapter 53, "Roasting Culture."

roast profile: The time and temperature curve of a roast. Beans at room temperature are dumped ("charged") into the drum, or column in an air roaster, and heated to the desired color in a certain period of time, usually 12–16 minutes. An infinite variety of ways to get to any final color and temperature of the beans exists; for instance, the operator could take the temperature in the roaster machine up very fast for a while and then finish the roast in a long, slow temperature climb. Or the temperature could be made to climb slowly and finish in a sharp climb. Different roast profiles can produce quite different flavors in the beans, even if they are brought to the same final color and temperature. In theory, an optimal profile exists not only for every variety but for every lot of beans. Many roasters (operators) take hours to experiment with sample roasts to determine the best profile for a given coffee.

robusta: *Coffea canephora*, one of two commercially important species of the genus *Coffea*. While it grows better under more stressful conditions than arabica coffee, it is generally considered to be of lower cup quality. Recently, some farmers have begun to work to improve robusta quality to produce a specialty robusta coffee.

roya **(Spanish):** Rust. Commonly used in Latin America to refer to **coffee leaf rust.**

rust: *See* **coffee leaf rust.**

Sara Lee: *See* **Big Four.**

SCAA: *See* **Specialty Coffee Association of America.**

SCAE: *See* **Speciality Coffee Association of Europe.**

second wave: A time period roughly estimated as extending from the early 1970s into the early 1990s. The second wave was dominated by businesses that intended to offer better coffee than the bottomless cup of American homes and offices but whose efforts resulted in the branded coffee shop model epitomized by Starbucks. Coined by Trish Skeie Rothgeb in 2002. *See also* **first wave, third wave.**

seed: *See* **coffee bean.**

shade/shade-grown: A coffee agricultural system in which the coffee is grown underneath larger trees that provide shade for the coffee. Shaded coffee systems can have several benefits for the farmer and the environment, although they are not ideal for every coffee farming scenario. Shade-grown is often associated with bird-friendly and sustainable coffees.

silverskin: A thin layer of the coffee fruit between the parchment and the coffee bean (seed). *See* figure 2.1 for an illustration of the parts of the fruit.

single-estate: Coffee whose beans come from one known estate, with an emphasis on the quality and taste specific to that origin, in contrast to coffee that is a blend of beans from different origins.

single-origin: Beans from a single farm, estate, or region, and which are supposed to be uniform in size and characteristics.

single-serving/portion: Coffee packaged in a pod, capsule, or the like that is intended to brew just one serving at a time.

single variety: Roasted coffee product that is composed of a single variety, for example 'Typica' or 'Yellow Bourbon.'

slave labor: Slaves used to pick the largest share of the world's coffee. Slavery was finally abolished in Cuba in 1884 and in Brazil in 1888. Other forms of unfree labor, only a small step above slavery in regard to the degree of freedom that peasants had, characterized Dutch practice in Indonesia into the twentieth century and was also customary in various Latin American countries, for example Guatemala, until the 1950s or later. In systems of unfree labor that were not outright slavery, peasants or members of indigenous communities were required to work on coffee farms; failure to do so could result in severe fines and punishments.

social life: The social interaction that can develop around any product. Harley-Davidson motorcycles, for instance, are at the center of an extensive American culture of bikers. Coffee as a beverage has a long history of promoting social interaction either in the home or in cafes.

social responsibility: The notion that the members and companies in the coffee industry in the wealthier parts of the world should assist farmers, hired labor, and the environment in the poorer producing countries. Such efforts could be in the form of increased, "ethical" payments for coffee; donor projects for schools, clean water, and so on; and technical assistance.

soluble: *See* **instant.**

solubles: The compounds of the coffee bean that are extracted during brewing.

sorting: The process of removing unwanted materials from the seeds after harvesting and of separating poorer quality seeds from more valuable ones. After the parchment has been removed from the coffee seed, the seed can be sorted to remove defects and unwanted material such as twigs. The seeds can be sorted by *size*, density, and color. Various machines, color sorters (*see* chapter 61, "Mechanization"), can do this task. In countries with a vast, poor labor supply, for example Ethiopia, much sorting is done by hand, usually by women.

Speciality Coffee Association of Europe (SCAE): A trade organization in Europe for specialty coffee. Founded in 1998, its goals are similar to those of the SCAA. It sponsors many events and championships and publishes the newsletter *Café Europa.*

specialty coffee: Good to outstanding coffee whose origin is known, which is treated carefully from farm to cup, and which has depth, character, and subtlety in the liquor. Erna Knutsen, a highly respected importer, is credited with coining this term in 1974. *See* chapter 17, "What Is Specialty Coffee?"

Specialty Coffee Association of America (SCAA): A trade organization dedicated to the specialty coffee industry. The SCAA sponsors an annual symposia of presentations on successes and challenges in specialty coffee, a trade show, and courses throughout the year for cuppers, baristas, and roasters.

Starbucks: The largest chain of coffee cafés in the U.S. Founded in 1971 in Seattle by three men inspired by Alfred Peet, the company remained small until Howard Schultz purchased it from the original owners in 1987. Schultz has repeatedly said that he drew his inspiration for coffeehouse design and service from a trip to Italy, although the Italian style of making and serving coffee is in fact quite different from most American practices (*see* chapter 42, "Coffeehouse Formats through the Centuries"). Schultz built Starbucks into an international giant that now has more than 15,000 stores in 50 countries. Much further expansion is planned, especially in India and China. Starbucks is simultaneously envied, loathed, and loved by the independents in specialty coffee. On the one hand, they appreciate that the Mermaid introduced many Americans and others to the idea that coffee could be better than swill. On the other hand, independents sometimes regard Starbucks as a huge bully that grabs the best locations and makes mediocre coffee or milk drinks with some coffee in them.

stinker bean: Defective coffee beans that produce an unpleasant, sour, fermented taste in coffee. One stinker bean is potent enough to negatively influence an entire pot of coffee. Stinkers are thought to result from overfermented beans or cherries that weren't processed soon enough after harvesting.

strictly hard bean: A quality term conveying beans of a certain baseline hardness, often grown at higher altitudes, usually about 4,500 feet above sea level. The hardness of the beans correlates, in the view of some specialists, to a denser flavor. *See also* **hardness.**

strip harvesting: The process of pulling all coffee berries, ripe or not, from a branch of a tree in a single motion, either by hand or using portable handheld machines.

sugar: A popular addition to coffee, largely for two reasons. First, the coffee served in English coffeehouses in the seventeenth and eighteenth centuries was a terrible brew, as it was made in large iron kettles that hung constantly over open fires. Sugar helped to make such stuff palatable. The second reason that sugar became associated in Britain with coffee, as well as with tea, is that British plantations in the Caribbean, and later elsewhere, began to produce a copious amount of sugar in the seventeenth century. Its cheapness and caloric value, even if the calories were "empty" (providing energy but no nutritional benefit), made it popular in Britain and America.

sun drying: Allowing coffee cherry in the skin to dry on patios to a desired level of acidity and humidity. *See also* **dry processing** and **natural processing.**

sun-grown: A coffee agricultural system in which coffee is the only crop or plant grown in the field. It is typically used to refer to coffee farming without any trees growing over and shading the coffee.

sustainable: An approach to farming that values the long-term health of the land and environment. Much discussion has taken place in an effort to define "sustainable." A simple approach to the word is that in sustainable agriculture, nothing valuable is removed from the soil without providing an equal replacement. Nutrients taken from the soil by plants are replaced; the soil does not degrade. Therefore the agriculture can continue indefinitely. Sustainability considers the environment, the people, and the economy. Sustainable agriculture is frequently equated with organic farming; however, little evidence supports the contention that conventional agriculture or a system balanced with conventional and organic practices can't be sustainable. Sustainability is often discussed in the coffee industry in regard to every stage, from farming to cafés.

tasting: An informal method for evaluating coffee cup quality. For most people, tasting is equivalent to simply brewing and enjoying coffee. When tasting is used to evaluate cup quality, the coffees are often brewed using common home brewing devices.

Tchibo: *See* **Big Four.**

technified: *See* **sun-grown.**

terroir: A French term, literally soil or ground, referring to the soil and atmosphere of agriculture land. In the global coffee industry, this term refers to farms in a philosophical sense, as locales where the farmer has a particular love for the land and its produce. More specifically, terroir is used to describe the influence of the place (soil, climate, husbandry, and so forth) on the product's quality.

third place: A term coined by Roy Oldenburg to indicate a happy site of sociability where people go to relax (the first place is home, and the second is work). *See also* chapter 42, "Coffeehouse Formats through the Centuries."

third wave: A phrase coined in 2002 by Trish Skeie Rothgeb of Wrecking Ball Roasters to describe the coffee renaissance she had witnessed in Norway. It has been adopted by many members of the specialty coffee community as an almost symbolic descriptor for an approach to coffee. These roasters and baristas emphasize their artisanal focus, a willingness to question established notions, and a preference for "scientific" methods of appraising beans and liquor, in the quest to deliver the highest quality coffee. Volume or profits are less important. For Rothgeb, "the Third Wave is a reaction to those who want to automate and homogenize Specialty Coffee." *See also* **first wave, second wave.**

traceability: The ability to document the origin of a particular batch of coffee as well as the hands that it passed through (roaster, importer, etc.) before reaching the consumer.

trade magazines: Magazines that cater to the interests of those in the coffee business. *Tea and Coffee Trade Journal* is the leading magazine with a global focus, while other major U.S. publications are *Barista, Coffee Talk, Fresh Cup, Roast,* and *Specialty Coffee Retailer.* In Europe, key publications include *Café Europa,* the journal of the SCAE, and the daily e-newsletters *Comunicaffè* (Italian) and *Communicaffé International* (English).

TransFair USA: *See* **Fair Trade USA.**

trophic: Pertaining to nutrition and to nutritive processes. It can also refer to the position of a food in the food chain.

Turkish or Mediterranean brewing: A method in which the coffee is ground very finely, like powder, and is poured into any small device that can be put directly on a burner. The common words for such devices are *cezik* or *ibrik,* and they typically have a long handle to keep the user from being burned. Water is added to the device, and spices such as cardamom may also be used. The mixture is then brought to a boil several times and poured into small cups.

understory: Trees growing beneath the overstory. Coffee originated as an understory tree in the highlands of what is today Ethiopia.

unfree labor: *See* **slavery and coffee.**

vacuum brewing: A brewing system using a device with two chambers, in which water is heated in a lower chamber, creating steam which pushes most of the water up a tube into an upper chamber, where it infuses with ground coffee. When the apparatus is removed from heat, a vacuum in the lower chamber is created as the remaining steam in the lower compartment condenses, thereby sucking the coffee liquor down into it. A filter separates the two chambers, keeping the coffee grounds in the upper chamber. Vacuum coffee makers can be inexpensive hand-operated products, but machines that operate on the same principles can cost as much as $20,000.

value chain: The value added to a product at each point in its processing, shipping, wholesale distribution, and retail sales.

varietal: An adjective that originally referred to a wine composed of a single cultivar/variety of wine. Recently, however, "varietal" has been adopted by the coffee and other industries (including now wine) as a noun referencing a particular breed of plant, usually as a synonym to "cultivar" or "variety," as in 'Bourbon' varietal.

variety: *See* **cultivar.**

virtuosi: English gentlemen of the seventeenth century with a fascination for the rare, novel, surprising, and outstanding in all spheres of life. Possessed of an intellectual curiosity that at times led them into quasi-scientific inquiry, they were also avid travelers or at least readers of travel literature who embraced exotic commodities such as coffee. They seized the chance to discuss their enthusiasms in the coffeehouses that first appeared in England in the 1650s. *See* chapter 42, "Coffeehouse Formats through the Centuries."

washed: Coffee beans that have been processed using washed processing.

washed processing: The process, after harvesting the coffee fruit and squeezing the seeds from the pulp, of removing the remaining mucilage from around the seeds. The mucilage is eliminated by one of three methods: (1) The coffee is immersed in water and soaked until the mucilage is degraded (wet fermentation). (2) The coffee is not covered in water but is left to sit until the mucilage has degraded (dry fermentation, but also called "pulped naturals"). (3) Immediately after depulping, the mucilage is removed mechanically (demuciliation). In each case, the seeds are usually given a final rinse/wash to clean off any adhering material.

wet processing; *See* **washed processing.**

wind: A highly important factor in coffee agriculture. Too little wind, and the leaves do not dry out, especially on their undersides, after a rain. The dampness encourages mold and especially leaf rust, which can destroy the crop of an entire tree, or many trees. Too much wind, and leaves and flowers are blown off the tree; no flowers, no fruit.

World Barista Championship: An international, annual competition where baristas compete, on behalf of their country, for the title of best in the world. In fifteen minutes, competitors must prepare three sets of beverages—an espresso, a cappuccino, and a signature beverage (which must contain a shot of espresso)—for a panel of four sensory judges. The barista is also graded on technical ability by other judges. The WBC evolved out of the Nordic barista championships and is jointly owned by the SCAA and SCAE. In 2011, baristas from fifty-three countries participated in the competition.

Index

About the Editors and Contributors

Entries have been supplied by the contributors. If they supplied an e-mail address, it is given at the end of the entry.

Abbreviations: SCAA = Specialty Coffee Association of America; SCAE = Speciality Coffee Association of Europe

Robert W. Thurston, senior editor. BA, Northwestern University, MA and PhD in modern Russian history, University of Michigan. Currently Phillip R. Shriver Professor of History, Miami University, Oxford, Ohio. Author of books on twentieth-century Russian history, the European witch hunts, and lynching around the world and of various articles on coffee in trade journals and encyclopedias. Managing Director, Oxford Coffee Company. thurstrw@gmail.com.

Jonathan Morris, European coeditor. PhD, modern Italian history, Cambridge University. Research Professor in modern European history at the University of Hertfordshire, UK. Author of books and articles on modern Italian history. Director of the Cappuccino Conquests research project tracing the transnational history of Italian-style coffee, which resulted in articles in both the English and Italian academic and trade press. Jonathan is currently completing *Coffee: A Global History*. j.2.morris@herts.ac.uk.

Shawn Steiman, scientific coeditor. BS, biology, Oberlin College. MS and PhD, tropical plant and soil sciences, University of Hawai'i. His research has explored coffee science in horticulture, biochemistry, and sensory evaluation. Author of articles on coffee in academic journals, trade magazines, newsletters, and newspapers, as well as *The Hawai'i Coffee Book: A Gourmet's Guide from Kona to Kaua'i*. Owner of Coffea Consulting, which works with members of the coffee industry, from farmers to consumers. Shawn is also a Q-grader. steiman@coffeaconsulting.com.

Sarah Allen. Masters, journalism, University of Oregon. Editor of *Barista Magazine*, the international journal for café owners and baristas, since 2005. In providing *Barista*'s savvy readership with relevant training and business articles, Sarah consults café owners around the globe to determine the most advantageous strategies for success in the coffeehouse environment. She

411

has written specifically for the coffee industry for ten years and has lectured around the world. sarah@baristamagazine.com.

Jonathan D. Baker. PhD, medical anthropology, University of Hawai'i at Manoa. Lecturer and adjunct professor in the Department of Anthropology at UH Manoa. His research focuses on nutrition, diet, and health and explores the overlap of food and medicine. He is currently studying biological and social aspects of food tasters and tasting. pnethyst@gmail.com.

Peter S. Baker. PhD. More than thirty years' experience in research, training, and consultancy in science for development with particular experience in coffee, including sustainable coffee production, farmer participatory approaches, biodiversity, coffee quality, climate change, and smallholder farmer issues. He has worked as researcher, project developer, manager, and team leader of international coffee projects, including four years with the Colombian Federación Nacional de Cafeteros. For six years he was head of a CAB International research station in the Caribbean, then spent six more years researching coffee in southern Mexico. Author of more than seventy research articles, reviews, and monographs. p.baker@cabi.org.

Jonathan Wesley Bell. A consultant and contributing writer to *STiR Tea & Coffee Industry Bi-Monthly*, he has published over 250 articles on coffee.

Clare Benfield. MBA, University of Stirling, where she also studied publishing. Editor of the UK trade magazines *Café Culture* and *Pizza Pasta & Italian Food*, for nearly ten years. Earlier she worked in marketing communications roles. clare@jandmgroup.co.uk.

H. C. "Skip" Bittenbender. MS and PhD, horticulture, Michigan State University. Coordinator of the University of Hawai'i's College of Tropical Agriculture and Human Resources research and extension (outreach) activities for coffee, cacao, and kava. With V. E. Smith, coauthor of *Growing Coffee in Hawaii*, a revision of the coffee series by B. Goto and E. Fukunaga. Skip's research on coffee variety evaluation with Cathy Cavaletto and on mechanized pruning with Loren Gautz contributed to the rapid expansion of Hawaii's coffee industry in the 1990s. hcbitt@hawaii.edu.

Connie Blumhardt. Founder and publisher of the award-winning *Roast Magazine*. Connie has spent twenty years in magazine publishing and has worked in the coffee industry since 1997, serving the roasting community daily by bringing education to thousands of roasters through the magazine. In her spare time she can be found drinking lots of coffee and chasing around her twin daughters. connie@roastmagazine.com.

Willem Boot. Willem is the founder of Boot Coffee, a consulting company that works with coffee producers, roasters, and NGOs on quality improvement and strategic marketing programs. It also offers training on the art and science of coffee.

Carlos H. J. Brando. Director and partner at P&A International Marketing, a coffee consulting, marketing, and trading company. P&A exports Pinhalense coffee machinery and consults for the industry around the globe on technology, quality, marketing, coffee consumption, and strategy. Carlos has coordinated coffee projects in over fifty countries and is a frequent speaker at coffee events. He is a member of the boards of UTZ Certified, Coffee Quality Institute (CQI), Ipanema Coffees, and the Santos (Brazil) Coffee Museum.

August Burns. MPH, CM, PA. August is an expert in women's health who has worked in more than a dozen countries. She is coauthor of *Where Women Have No Doctor*, a health guide for women in low-resource settings, translated into more than thirty languages.

Luis Alberto Cuéllar. BA, economics, Grancolombia and El Rosario Universities, Bogota, Colombia; MA, International Labor Organization University, Turin, Italy. His career developed as follows: manager of a coffee cooperative in Quindio, Colombia; coffee cooperative adviser for the National Federation of Coffee Growers of Colombia; international professional in cooperatives and rural development for the Inter American Institute for Agricultural Cooperation; program director and country representative for Colombia for ACDI/VOCA, responsible for specialty coffee programs in five Colombian departments; and currently senior technical adviser for ACDI/VOCA's Agribusiness/Specialty Crops Portfolio.

Olga Cuellar. BA, social psychology, Pontificia Universidad Javeriana. MA, Latin American studies, University of Arizona. Born into a Colombian family immersed in both specialty coffee and international development. Her MA thesis examined the empowerment of women coffee growers in Colombia. Olga spent two years researching rural development programs with agricultural cooperatives and rural communities in Colombia, Brazil, and Paraguay. She is also a licensed Q-grader. Currently she works for Sustainable Harvest as a development manager for Latin America.

Kenneth Davids. Ken has published three books on coffee, including *Coffee: A Guide to Buying, Brewing & Enjoying*, in six editions, including a Japanese translation. He coproduced, hosted, and scripted *The Passionate Harvest*, an award-winning documentary film on coffee production. His coffee reviews appear regularly in *Coffee Review* (http://www.coffeereview.com) and in *Roast Magazine*. He has presented workshops and seminars at coffee meetings on six continents. Last but not least, he is professor of critical studies, California College of the Arts, San Francisco.

Jim Fadden. Jim is a mechanical engineer and frequent contributor to *Roast Magazine*.

Elijah K. Gichuru. Graduate, Plant Science Department, University of Nairobi. Plant pathologist. He has worked for Kenya's Coffee Research Foundation since 1994. In 2010 he became deputy director. He has conducted research work in laboratories in Portugal and France related to molecular diversity of coffee pathogens and identifying molecular markers (DNA and biochemical) for disease resistance in coffee. Author of more than twenty journal papers and articles in conference collections as well as chapters to two books. He currently researches the mechanisms of plant pathogen interactions and plant resistance.

Jeremy Haggar. PhD in agroecology. A tropical agroecologist with over twenty years' experience working in Central America and Mexico on sustainable production systems. Between 2000 and 2010 he ran regional projects building capacity in the coffee sector of Central America as program leader for Tree Crops in Agroforestry at the Tropical Agricultural Research and Higher Education Centre (CATIE), Nicaragua. Currently head of the Department of Agriculture, Health and Environment in the Natural Resources Institute at the University of Greenwich in the UK. j.p.haggar@gre.ac.uk.

Andrew Hetzel. Founder of the specialty coffee consulting firm CafeMakers. Hetzel provides consulting and training services for a diverse range of coffee agriculture and roasting clientele in North America and rapidly emerging consumer markets of Russia, India, Asia, and the Middle East. ahetzel@cafemakers.com.

George Howell. Owner of Terroir Coffee, Acton, Massachusetts. Founder of the "light roast" movement in America, an originator of the Cup of Excellence program in various countries, George is widely recognized as one of the most knowledgeable and opinionated people in the specialty coffee industry. His company's web site is http://www.terroircoffee.com/.

Juliana Jaramillo. PhD, entomology/biological control, Universitaet Hannover. Visiting scientist at University of Hannover / International Centre of Insect Physiology and Ecology. Her research on insects and coffee is based in Kenya.

Phyllis Johnson. Phyllis is the cofounder of BD Imports, which imports green coffee (unroasted) from sustainable sources in coffee-producing countries and markets to roaster retailers and roaster wholesalers located in the United States, Canada, Japan, and Taiwan.

Lawrence W. Jones. M.D., director, Prostate Research Program, Huntington Medical Research Institute, Pasadena, California. Larry is both a practicing physician and a roaster-retailer. He has been a surgeon and a scientist for forty years and has been involved with his family as roaster-retailers for twenty years. He has presented to conferences on coffee and on medical topics.

Alf Kramer. Alf has been in the industry since 1980, first as leader of the Norwegian Coffee Information Centre, later as leader of the ICO-owned Nordic coffee Centre. He founded the Speciality Coffee Association of Norway in 1990 and then proposed a similar association for Europe. He served as SCAE's first interim president, then president. He is an active author and speaker around the world. Among many awards he has received is the European Lifetime Achievement Award in Coffee in 2011.

Ted Lingle. BS, science, United States Military Academy, MBA, Woodbury University. Vice President of Marketing for Lingle Bros. Coffee, Inc., for twenty years. A member of the National Coffee Association's Out-of-Home Market Committee from 1974 to 1990. He served on the Board of Directors of the National Coffee Service Association and was elected an honorary member in 1990. He was a founding co-chair of the SCAA. Appointed executive director of the SCAA in 1991, he held that position until 2006, when he became executive director of the Coffee Quality Institute. Author of *Coffee Cuppers' Handbook* and *Coffee Brewing Handbook*. Awarded medals for contributions to the coffee industry by the Federation of Coffee Growers of Colombia, the National Association of Coffee Growers of Guatemala, and the Eastern Africa Fine Coffee Association.

Stuart McCook. PhD, history, Princeton University. Associate professor of history at the University of Guelph, Canada. He researches the environmental history of tropical crops, especially the relations between commodities, societies, and landscapes in the tropics. He has written on the environmental history of sugar and cacao. He is currently writing a global history of coffee rust (*Hemileia vastatrix*), as well as on other aspects of coffee's environmental history. stuart.mccook@uoguelph.ca.

Michelle Craig McDonald. MA, liberal arts, St. John's College. PhD, history, University of Michigan. Associate professor of history at Richard Stockton College. Author, most recently, of *Public Drinking in the Early Modern World: Voices from the Tavern, 1500–1800*, with David Hancock. Presently working on a history of United States investment in the Caribbean coffee industry.

Sunalini Menon. Sunalini has more than thirty years of experience in the coffee industry both within India and internationally and is directly associated with quality and quality-related aspects of domestic and international coffee. She worked in the Quality Control department of the Indian Coffee Board from 1972 to 1995, ultimately becoming the director of Quality Control. In 1997, she established her own company, Coffeelab Limited, in Bangalore, India, the first organization of its kind in the Indian private sector. It provides comprehensive quality related services for the Indian coffee industry. One of Asia's finest coffee cuppers, she regularly travels to coffee origins to conduct cupping workshops and speaks to coffee entrepreneurs and enthusiasts on nuances in the cup. coffeelab@vsnl.com.

Jati Misnawi. PhD, food chemistry and biotechnology, University of Jamber. Researcher, Indonesian Coffee and Cocoa Research Institute.

Joan Obra. Joan is the latest generation to join Rusty's Hawaiian, the coffee farm, mill, and roastery founded by her late father in Ka'u, Hawai'i. When it comes to coffee processing, Joan has one of the best teachers: her mother, Lorie Obra. Rusty's Hawaiian was the grand champion of the Hawaii Coffee Association's 2010 and 2011 statewide cupping competitions, as well as a winner of the 2012 Roasters Guild Coffees of the Year competition. joan@rustyshawaiian.com.

Price Peterson. PhD, neurochemistry, University of Pennsylvania. Owner, with his family, of Hacienda La Esmeralda, Boquete, Panama. One of the world's most respected coffee farmers and innovators. With his son Daniel, developer of the variety 'Gesha' as a highly sought-after coffee. The farm web site is http://haciendaesmeralda.com/.

Rick Peyser. Director of Social Advocacy and Supply Chain Community Outreach for Green Mountain Coffee Roasters, where he has worked for twenty-four years. He is a past president of the SCAA, served six years on the Fair Trade Labeling Organizations International (FLO) Board, and currently serves on the board of directors for Coffee Kids, Food4Farmers, and Fundacion Ixil. Rick.Peyser@gmcr.com.

Sergii Reminny. Sergii was the first Ukrainian National Coordinator for the SCAE, 2005–2010. He is the owner of the company IONIA il caffe (Ukraine). He is a blogger and author about coffee, drawing on the expertise gained by visiting more than fifty countries of the world.

Paul Rice. BA, Yale University. MBA, UC Berkeley. President and CEO of Fair Trade USA, a non-profit organization and the leading third-party certifier of Fair Trade products in the United States. Before opening the doors of Fair Trade USA in 1998, Paul worked for eleven years as a rural development specialist in Nicaragua, where he founded the country's first fair trade, organic coffee export cooperative.

Robert Rice. PhD, UC Berkeley. Robert has been at the Smithsonian Migratory Bird Center (SMBC) since 1995, working within the Smithsonian Conservation Biology Institute on landscape change and managed lands, with a specific focus on agroforestry systems in the tropics. In recent years he has also coordinated the SMBC's "Bird Friendly" coffee program, a shade coffee certification using science-based criteria from ornithological fieldwork.

Carlos Saenz. Carlos Saenz is a small coffee farmer in Genova Costa Cuca, Quetzaltenango. His family has run their coffee farm, Finca Las Brisas, for four generations.

Vincenzo Sandalj. He was president of the Sandalj Trading Company, one of the leading specialty green coffee importers in Italy. He coauthored the book *Coffee: A Celebration of Diversity* and was a past president of the SCAE. He passed away in July 2013. www.sandalj.com.

Colin Smith. Colin is the managing director of Smith's Coffee Company, UK, and a founding member and past president of the SCAE. colin@smiths-coffee.demon.co.uk.

Steven Topik, PhD, history, University of Texas. Professor of history, UC Irvine. Author of several books on the history of Brazil. Coauthor of *The Second Conquest of Latin America: Coffee, Henequen, and Oil during the Export Boom, 1850–1930.* Coeditor and contributor to *The World That Trade Created* and to *The Global Coffee Economy in Asia, Africa and Latin America, 1500–1989.* Currently working on a history of coffee on four continents.

Tatsushi Ueshima. Tatsushi Ueshima was appointed representative president of UCC Ueshima Coffee Co., Ltd., in 1980. This led to his current post as representative-chairman, appointed in 2009. He has served as chairman of various coffee industry groups representing Japan: All-Japan Coffee Association, All-Japan Coffee Fair Trade Council, Association of Regular Coffee Industry for Household Use, and the Specialty Coffee Association of Japan. Awarded the "Cordon of the Rising Sun" from the Japanese government for contributions to the Japanese coffee industry. He has also been awarded medals from coffee-producing countries such as Brazil, Colombia, and Jamaica.

Camilla C. Valeur. Graduate, Roskilde University, MBA, Copenhagen Business School and University of Rome. Currently project manager at the Danish Federation of Small and Medium-Sized Enterprises (DFSME). Camilla formerly worked as head of secretariat at The Danish Network for Coffee, Tea and Cocoa and as market access expert at Oxfam Italia. She has worked with coffee farmers, buyers, and end-consumers with special attention to sustainable coffee trends. She has over ten years of experience with sustainable business development in Asia, Africa, and Latin America. caceva@hotmail.com.

Geoff Watts. Vice president of coffee, Intelligentsia Coffee and Tea, Inc. Geoff has spent the last seventeen years pursuing better coffee as Intelligentsia's chief buyer. He has served as an official judge in more than thirty international coffee competitions. As a pioneer of the direct trade approach and consultant for several development organizations, he has spent more than half of his time over the last decade working closely with coffee growers in East Africa and Central/South America to improve quality and build systems for ensuring traceability and transparency in the supply chain.

Britta Zietemann. Deputy managing director of the German Coffee Association, Hamburg. Britta has worked in coffee for nearly five years now, after studying media and English and working in PR. In 2007, she joined the German Coffee Association (*Deutscher Kaffeeverband*) with responsibility for communications, information, and events. She is coauthor, with Holger Preibisch and others, of *Faszination Kaffee,* the only recent comprehensive German reference book about coffee.